CRISIS OF SOCIALISM—
Notes in Defence of a Commitment–Vol. 3

THE WORLD AFTER THE COLLAPSE OF THE SOVIET UNION

CRISIS OF SOCIALISM—
Notes in Defence of a Commitment–Vol. 3

THE WORLD AFTER THE COLLAPSE OF THE SOVIET UNION

Randhir Singh

THE WORLD AFTER THE COLLAPSE OF THE SOVIET UNION
Randhir Singh

First Published, 2011

ISBN 978-93-5002-118-7 (Hb)

Published by
AAKAR BOOKS
28 E Pocket IV, Mayur Vihar Phase I, Delhi 110 091
Phone : 011 2279 5505 Telefax : 011 2279 5641
info@aakarbooks.com; www.aakarbooks.com

Printed at
Mudrak, 30A, Patparganj, Delhi-92

Contents

Publisher's Note

Professor Randhir Singh's *Crisis of Socialism—Notes in Defence of a Commitment* (Royal size xiii+1087 pages) was originally published by Ajanta Books International in 2006. A response to the collapse of the Soviet Union's 'actually existing socialism' and dealing with the basic issues of the why and how of this collapse, its implications and where it leaves the question of socialism in our time, the book has been hailed as a pioneering work—'one of the most important, if not *the* most important book we have ever read', 'a key to all that is going on in our world today', 'if there were a required reading list for the U.S. left, this should be on it', and so on—and there has been a persistent demand for its argument to be available in a form easier to handle and access. Therefore, with the consent of the author and in consultation with him, we at Aakar Books have decided to publish it as a thematically reorganised 6-volume edition : Volume I (chapters 2 and 3, titled **Of Marxism and Socialism** — available in the author's **Marxism, Socialism, Indian Politics—A View from the Left**, published by us); Volume II (Prologue chapters 1, 4, 5, 6, 7, 8, 9, 11, 12, 13 and Epilogue, titled **What Was Built and What Failed in the Soviet Union**); Volume III (chapters 10, 14, 15, 16, 17, titled **The World after the Collapse of the Soviet Union**); Volume IV (chapters 18 and 19, titled **The Right Lesson and the Wrong Conclusion**); Volume V (chapter 20, titled **Contemporary Ecological Crisis—A Marxist View**); Volume VI (chapter 21 and 22, titled **Struggle for Socialism—Some Issues**).

—K.K. Saxena

In Lieu of a Biodata*

There is a certain inevitability about it. Sooner or later someone was bound to ask me, again, for my biodata.

A 'biodata', now, has been a source of perennial embarrassment for me. For I simply don't have any—I have no credentials at all so far as scholarship in the academy goes. I have only a life to speak of, lived somewhat differently, and on a generous interpretation, maybe a little more meaningfully too. Here, very sketchily, then, is some of the more public part of the story, for whatever it is worth.

Childhood, they say, is important, always and in many ways. For me it was a rather unhappy childhood, very bleak and altogether lonely. I literally lived and survived on books, which partly explains my lifelong love for and involvement with them. This childhood, possibly, also left me with a certain sensitivity for the reality of suffering in the human condition of our time.

Over this childhood loomed large the heroic figure of Bhagat Singh. A morning is still vividly etched on my mind, the morning after he and his comrades were hanged. I was detained, briefly, while passing in front of the Lahore Central Jail on my way to the Borstal primary school in the neighbourhood. The army and the police, a surging sea of humanity, tears in each eye and the

---

* An 'autobiographical note' written in response to a request for biodata for a felicitation volume (1988).

proud faces, portraits, of the martyrs everywhere—and the defiant unending cry of '*Inquilab zindabad*'.... That morning was born a dream which, I believe, in some form or the other, has always stayed with me. Years later I was to spend a few months, among the happiest in my life, in the 'Terrorist Ward' of this very prison with some of the surviving comrades of Bhagat Singh—Kishori Lal and others—who had in the meantime joined the Communist Party.

Thus I grew up. And in due course, on the eve of the Second World War, I again came to Lahore, this time for my studies at a college there. My father, a remarkable man in his own mixed sort of way—a brilliant physician and surgeon, profoundly religious and puritanical, with a rather deadly combination of Gandhi and Lenin in his head—sensing the turbulence inside me, his only son, had advised: 'Do anything out there but don't join some illegal organisation'. Predictably, this was the first thing I did on reaching Lahore. Even as I was searching for it, the Communist Party found me. When my father admonished me that I had shown scant regard for the family, I wrote back: 'I have found my real family'. The Communist Party meant this and very much more in those days, to many of us at least. Besides, there was a certain pride in being a Communist. I still remember from those times two lines from the poet C. Day Lewis. A question and an answer, they went something like this:

> Why do we on seeing a Red feel small?
> For he is future walking to meet us—

Fifty years later, badly buffeted, some of this pride yet remains. Incidentally, this is also how I came to Marxism—beginning with whatever Marxism was then available with the Comintern and permitted or possible in our country under the British rule.

Followed years of hectic activity in the students' movement and in the underground with the Communist Party, including entire vacations spent with workers in factories away from Lahore or with peasants in their villages.

We were good students, among the best in the University. I duly qualified for admission to the Medical College. But it was clear that the demands of ever-increasing political work would be impossible to reconcile with those of a study in medicine. I decided to shift to a 'soft' discipline. I was advised that Political Science was, possibly, the easiest subject to get your master's degree in. That, perhaps, is one reason why I could never take it seriously. Later I was to discover that it is also, possibly, the poorest among the social sciences. And if I may suggest, one important reason for its poverty as a social scientific enterprise is its near-universal ignorance of or hostility towards Marxism as social science; though, in recent years, it has not been averse to recognising Marxism as 'political thought'.

Be that as it may, in a couple of years even the pursuit of Political Science had to be given up for full-time work with the Communist Party—on the party wage of, I think, rupees twenty or twenty-five per month. For most of the next five years and more, till after the Partition, I moved around the villages and towns of Punjab, organising people and persuading them to move through their struggle for freedom towards a social revolution in this country, which I believe still needs to be made.

Soon enough I landed in prison, charged with opposition to 'the war effort' of the British Government in India. (Incidentally, it was 'the people's war' period!) Released, after nearly a year's imprisonment, I was for some time put under the usual restrictions on movement, meetings, etc. I filled up the time with a stint on the editorial staff of the Party's Punjabi weekly, *Jang-i-Azadi*. I also started work on a biography of the still active legendary revolutionary, Baba Gurmukh Singh, a fragment of which was later published as *Ghadar Heroes: A Forgotten Story of the Punjab Revolutionaries of 1914-1915* (1945). My professor at the University—he was none other than Dr. J.N. Khosla—who was rather fond of me, insisted that I use this opportunity to at least finish my studies. The Party gave me the required leave for a couple of months, and my professor provided me with the necessary certificate of attendance at classes—which partly overlapped the period I was in prison! I duly took the examination—and was soon back in the villages. (The degree, a first-class-first, was to come in very handy later in my life, at Delhi.)

Came the great popular struggles, the near-revolutionary upsurge of the mid-1940s, the haggling and compromising presided over by Imperialism, the consequent riots, the Partition, and more riots—and Indian independence. A faith had been kept *and* betrayed. Those were glorious yet ignominy-laden years, the years at once of victory and defeat for the Indian people. More specifically, it was the final success, however ambiguous, of a Gandhi and bourgeois-led politics, and a definitive failure, only temporary we thought, of our Communist politics, which included that last adventurist flourish with B.T.R. as well as the heroic struggle in Telengana. One lived, shared and fought through it all—and survived. Some of this experience, intensely personal as well as political and collective, found expression in a small collection of poems in Punjabi—*Rahan Di Dhoor* (1950). In one of these, I recorded:

> A caravan has reached the destination,
> And yet lost its way—

I never wrote poetry again—don't ask me why. Only very recently I have learnt that early in 1951 itself, a distinguished critic had, in a review, hailed my book as a truly significant piece of work. A contemporary scholar even considers it to be the best poetry of that period, though, as he told me, he had difficulty in locating its author!

It would appear that, as in scholarship, so in poetry, and may be in much else besides, I am a genuine 'might have been'.

I came to Delhi sometime after the Partition, having lived with death the previous few months and on the way. Uprooted, a refugee, everything around me, including my politics in a shambles, I sought a new foothold in life—only temporarily, I had then thought, mistakenly. I started teaching at what was then known as Camp College, an institution set up by the Punjab University at Delhi for refugee students and teachers. Even as I began to enjoy my new vocation, the Party, passing through a series of crises, both internal and external, finally opted for 'peaceful', 'parliamentary' ways. And so it came to pass, with other tangible and not-so-tangible factors contributing, that, over a period of time—during which I still edited from Delhi its theoretical monthly in Punjabi, *Sada Jug* (till removed, charged with 'individualism' and 'intellectual arrogance' for refusing to publish a BTR criticism of Mao Tse-tung), and translated *Communist Manifesto* and some more Marx into Punjabi—I just opted out of the Party. [Later, soon after its formation, I was to spend a few years in the Communist Party (Marxist)]. For me the comforting rationalisation was that in our society, after 'revolution-making', teaching perhaps holds the maximum possibilities for a non-alienated life. Here, if you want, but only if you *want,* earning your living can be at the same time living your life. So teaching it was to be for me for the rest of my life. Soon I moved from Camp College to Delhi College, where I was to teach for nearly two decades; then, after a brief stint at Jawaharlal Nehru University, in 1972 I joined Delhi University, rather late in life, as Professor of Political Theory.

Thus it is that having spent some of the best years of my life elsewhere, away from the academy, and the rest only teaching, scholarship has simply passed me by. Hence, as I said in the beginning, 'biodata' has been a perennial embarrassment —for I never managed to acquire one as a scholar. I have no research degrees and no publications except some odd entirely casual exercises, including the book, *Reason, Revolution and Political Theory,* which was an ad hoc response to a provocation in the classroom when my students wanted me to explain and defend an observation I had made. I have had no string of scholars working 'under' me, no fellowships, no research projects, no study or other academic leaves, no 'seminaring', national or international, nothing—not even a visit abroad that has come to certify any sort of achievement or standing as a scholar these days!

Recently, the Indian Council of Social Science Research, perhaps wanting to be helpful, more than once extended me invitations involving 'a foreign visit' each time. Having somehow missed or evaded every such opportunity or activity in the past, I thought, I would make a virtue of it—and declined. Besides, it seemed a bit too late in life for me to now get started on this. Perhaps I also wanted to make certain that there is at least one professor in this country who has not been abroad!

Incidentally, the Council have also very generously offered me a National Fellowship which I have accepted. So I may yet end up as a scholar, though, I am not too sure. For the subject on which I have chosen to write a brief monograph is rather away from what have been my major concerns as a teacher—Western Political Thought, Contemporary Political Theory, Marxism. My subject is so obviously *political*, not 'scholarly'; I seek an understanding of Indian politics which may, it is hoped, help towards 'a more effective people's intervention in what is happening in our country'. What is more, contrary to the current fashions in the world of Marxian scholarship, where 'orthodoxy' is almost a dirty word, and a comfortable and comforting 'post-Marxism' is abroad, I visualise my work as an exercise in Marxist orthodoxy!

If I have, most of the time, done none of the things that scholars are normally supposed to do, I have been, most of the time, busy with what they are normally supposed to keep away from. Which is as well, for life has been such fun this way. I have thus functioned, in the profession and in the university, more as a militant on the Left—even when revising the syllabi in Political Science whenever or wherever I got the opportunity to do so, or putting in a rather noisy plea on behalf of Political Theory in general and Marxism in particular on the campuses of Indian universities. As a militant, the aim was always *hegemony* and not factional or mere economic or organisational gains.

Over the years, teaching and related work apart, I have, along with many others of course, spent a great deal of time helping build up the teachers' movement, fighting for democratic rights and reforms in the university (with the vice-chancellors and against them), carrying on socialist education among workers, students and teachers, including school-teachers, running Marx Clubs and putting together Socialist Groups (one such effort, incidentally, went into the making of the Communist Party (Marxist) on Delhi University campus), writing and publishing pamphlets and bulletins, editing and producing, distributing or circulating journals like *Enquiry*, *Socialist Digest*, *The Marxist Review*, *Monthly Review*, *Science and Society* and *New Left Review*, campaigning on issues like Vietnam and Czechoslovakia, collecting signatures for Iranian students and others, mobilising and marching for all sorts of popular causes, associating with almost any radical initiative on the campus and every revolutionary venture off it, an association which on occasions, quite understandably, even ended in a love–hate relationship, —and so on. That is how it has been for the most part over nearly forty long years.

But if scholarship has passed me by, I have not done too badly as a teacher. At least that is what my students, colleagues, and many others tell me. And I am inclined to believe them; maybe because I very much want to. I have taught in the departments of History, Political Science, and occasionally Philosophy. Students have come to my classes from other disciplines and other universities, from Economics and Sociology, Law and Literature, Mathematics, even Chemistry and Physics. (Perhaps Commerce and Business Management alone have been missing!) And they have given me abundantly of their love and affection, and thoughtful appreciation. This has been compensation enough for whatever I may have missed out on not being a scholar. It was compensation enough especially during periods of bitter conflict and controversy which, inevitably, have been a persistent feature of my long career as a teacher. It is the students who first spoke of 'a legend in Delhi University'. And it is, above all, to them that I trace the real source of an observation Bertell Ollman has made, though it is also expressive of his own characteristic generosity. After his recent visit to Delhi and Jawaharlal Nehru Universities, he writes: 'If I wasn't already over 50, I would probably say something like: when I grow up I want to be a Professor like Randhir Singh.' Yes, teaching has been compensation enough.

At one of the farewell meetings at Delhi University, they questioned me on the subject of my teaching. I responded that, given the 'functional rationality' governing the organised structures of teaching and research, so that scholarly writing is increasingly addressed not to problems or publics but to peers and to prestige and preferment in the needlessly bureaucratised academic professions, and given the growing, and often mindless, specialisation in the social sciences (including Political

Science) which is resulting in a situation where fewer and fewer people are hearing more and more about less and less—given all this, a certain lack of conventional academic scholarship can even be an advantage in that it may help one see the social reality as a whole, see the wood and not just the trees, and thus address, as teacher or scholar (or activist), the real problems of society.

Incidentally, I also told them, my students and colleagues, that, for one speaking up for Marxism, my knowledge of Economics is shockingly poor and that I have always regretted it. But this lack, perhaps, has made me that much more sensitive to the humanist, philosophical, and above all political dimensions of Marxism. Of course, I added that 'politics as revolution' is central to Marxism, at least to Marxism as Karl Marx practised it. 'Marx was before all else a revolutionist', as Engels put it.

These are, however, somewhat peripheral considerations. I had gone on to suggest that its strictly academic aspects apart, my teaching could be viewed as a form of 'robinhooding' which, even as it functions within the system, yet seeks to stretch it to its limits. Of course, this 'robinhooding', this functioning as a radical or a Marxist inside the classroom, has its problems and its risks too. The most important problem is that it needs to have a certain quality about it which, above all, demands a genuine and acknowledged familiarity with the mainstream scholarship in the concerned field or discipline, one's reservations about it notwithstanding. Lacking this, it can easily degenerate into vulgar propaganda or empty moral rhetoric. As a student coming from the discipline of English literature, in a complementary reference, once said: 'One needs to have that rare combination of idealism and intelligence.' As for the risks, the most important ones concern the security of job and the denial of promotion. I must admit that I have been rather lucky in this regard. It is true that whenever interviewed, the selection committees invariably turned me down. Yet appointments came, by invitation, including the professorship in 1972, when, incidentally, seeing everyone making a beeline for Jawaharlal Nehru University, I chose instead to opt for the University of Delhi.

'Robinhooding' has its minor risks also. For me it has meant another continuous struggle from the day I started teaching. At the very outset they asked for an undertaking 'not to teach subversion'. Later, they stopped you, again and again, from teaching, or teaching a particular course. For long years, they would let me teach only Plato and not Marx—so that you learn to teach Marx via Plato, which is not only possible but is in some ways far more effective also, for obvious reasons. They can organise harassment and humiliation for you in diverse ways, with the lumpen elements in the academic community thrown in.... One has struggled against all this and *them* all along, and with a reasonable measure of success. My only regret is for the students and teachers who, now and then, had to suffer for their association with me.

There are problems and there are risks. And for better credibility here one must learn to say 'no' to at least some of the innumerable benefits, the cooptive attractions the system has to offer even to a radical teacher, though this 'no' is only of symbolic value. But the most important thing is to be aware of the limitations, even ambiguities, inherent in the very nature of 'robinhooding' as an academic exercise. And for this reason one needs to be very modest about what one is doing or achieving here.

What is more, in so far as it is an exercise *within* the system, it is always in danger of itself becoming a form of cooption into it. In fact, the more you succeed in what you are doing, the more you are also, in an important sense, lending legitimacy to the system as a whole. Such is the dialectics implicit in this mode or style of teaching. That is why its quality is of decisive importance. Even so, how effective it is in its own modest manner, and how it contributes to any qualitative departures in the system, will be determined by other, larger social forces at work in the historical process in this country. We can only recognise and try to help these in whatever way we can.

I will only add that what goes on within the discipline of Political Science or its classrooms, or, for that matter, within the universities and the social science institutes of this country, is only of marginal relevance to the problems and prospects of the Indian people's struggle for a better future. But this is where we work—teachers, students, scholars, all others. And it is axiomatic, for most of us, that we make our efforts where we work, or we shall make no effort at all.

Preface to the Original Edition

This is a book which ought to have been published more than a decade back when its argument was first delivered as a series of lectures in memory of my friend and political associate Professor Moin Shakir at Marathwada University, Aurangabad, in February 1991. The writing naturally bears its mark but the delay has taken nothing away from the validity or relevance of my argument.

I had spoken from detailed notes and was supposed to produce a written version of these lectures. Associated with the communist movement for more than half a century, and mindful of Moin Shakir's concerns, I proceeded to write them down as a militant's response to what had happened in the Soviet Union, addressed to fellow militants in the movement and radicals at large. Part of what I wrote was published from time to time in the following years. The opening section was published in 1992 itself – in *Economic and Political Weekly* – entitled 'Crisis of Socialism – Notes in Defence of a Commitment'. This piece of writing, conveying something of my 'journey through communism' since 1939, was much noticed and appreciated at home and abroad and was reproduced and translated in many places, including an Urdu journal in Pakistan. Victor G. Kiernan, the distinguished historian, called it a 'splendid article'. Paul Sweezy and Harry Magdoff were equally appreciative. Sweezy noticed its appeal for readers of *Monthly Review* – 'many of whom (perhaps too many!) have been through similar experiences in their own lives' – and wrote to me: 'I read the piece with great interest and found it both eloquent and moving. Different as our experiences have been during the last half century, there is still much we have in common in reacting to the collapse of the revolutionary experiment in which and for which we had such high hopes'. This article soon came to be viewed as a document of the times. I have included it here as a *Prologue* to the book.

I had begun writing this draft but could not, or did not, complete it for reasons as diverse as my diffidence or lack of discipline when it comes to writing things down, more pressing or welcome academic engagements or political work, bouts of personal ill-health and, not the least, the hassles and harassments of ordinary middle class existence in the corrupt, communalised and mafiaised polity that much of India is today. The most important reason, however, was my awareness that scholars far more competent than me were writing on the subject, making it unnecessary for me to carry out the essentially secondary exercise of putting on paper what I had said at Aurangabad. And I was not wrong. We have since, for example, lstvan Meszaros' magisterial *Beyond Capital – Towards a Theory of Transition,* which has been rightly assessed as 'the definitive Marxian synthesis for the present moment, the phase of what Meszaros calls capital's *structural crisis*'. I have myself found it most useful for my argument in several places while completing these notes.

I however kept speaking on the subject or its sub-themes, discussing them with radical groups, at universities and other formal and informal gatherings; and pressure kept mounting, as much from the old-generation friends of socialism as from the new crop of young activists, that I put down my argument, such as it is, in writing. A National Fellowship at the Institute of Advanced Study, Shimla, finally persuaded me to take the plunge. But for this fellowship I would have made no progress at all with the completion of these notes. But the unexplained termination of this fellowship proved equally disruptive and delayed the completion of even this first draft by a few years. The writing is therefore obviously flawed in many ways. It bears the mark of being written, or completed, in bits, over a long period of time. That its sub-themes were the subject of separate treatment or lectures at different times or places has also contributed to uneven writing and to repetition in parts of the book. The format of Notes, with its need to provide the context of and complete the specific point being made has also added to the problem of repetition. I had expected my student and friend Arvind N. Das to take care of all this, edit and put this draft in proper shape for publication. But his premature death ruled this out. I thought of doing the needful myself, but somehow this has not been possible. In the meantime, the publication of some parts in the weekly *Mainstream* had created a constituency for what I have to say. The desirability of a better organised, more rigorously argued, and linguistically felicitous book notwithstanding, there was a growing demand that these notes be published, as they are – in their present rough form, even without references or footnotes – without any further delay. S. Balwant at the Ajanta Books International having agreed to do so, I, for myself, can only seek reader's indulgence, ask her or him to bear with the many inadequacies of this publication. What is important or really matters is its basic argument.

Occasional use of my earlier writings, particularly *Reason, Revolution and Political Theory* apart, these notes are based on my necessarily limited reading, rather what I remembered of it. I have borrowed freely from other scholars, taken their analyses as my own, used their arguments, at times in their own words, and not hesitated to quote them at length for the simple reason that they had expressed the idea or the argument better than I could have done. My debts are far too many to be acknowledged. Those familiar with the literature will easily recognise them. For me it is enough to rationalise it all by saying that these are scholars who are, so to speak, more or less on my side of the barricades.

There is one debt, however, which I would still like to explicitly acknowledge – to *Monthly Review*. It is the journal I have felt most comfortable with, intellectually and politically, over the past 50 odd years, and my debt here is writ large over several important parts of this book. For Marxist theory and sustained revolutionary commitment, there has been indeed nothing else like *Monthly Review*. Its authentic Marxist analysis of developments across the globe, easily accessible yet sophisticated in the best sense of the word, its unwavering commitment to the cause of socialism and principled support to revolutionary struggles everywhere, have educated, encouraged and inspired socialists and radicals throughout the world. Paul Sweezy and Harry Magdoff have been a constant source of enlightenment and inspiration. For me personally, Paul Sweezy was and remains a model of what a Marxist intellectual should be in our times. In recent years I have much benefited from the wide-ranging work of Ellen Meiksins Wood and John Bellamy Foster's writings in the field of ecology.

The original impulse for this writing lay in my long-time interest in understanding why and how things had gone wrong with socialism in the Soviet Union. As the crisis in Soviet society deepened in the 1980s, the subject became a matter of still more serious concern. Sometime before 'the earthquake of 1989', in my Preface to Bertell Ollman's Indian publication, *Marxism: A Uncommon Introduction*, referring to Macpherson's view that 'the utility of Marxism as a means of understanding the world is increasing over time', I had added: '"the world" includes.... not only the advanced capitalist countries or India and the so-called Third World, but the world of "actually existing socialism" also, with its troublous past, continuing problems and the truly historical predicament today'. The predicament soon ended in the ignominious collapse of Soviet socialism and then of the Soviet Union itself. But no viable Marxist explanation of what had happened was forthcoming from within the country's communist movement – a situation that still persists; even the later, more informed or updated 'official' efforts are a string of eclectic propositions: 'serious mistakes'; 'wrong notions of the role of the Party and the state'; 'the failure to effect timely changes in the economy and its management'; the failure to 'deepen socialist democracy'; 'the erosion of ideological consciousness'; etc. In this situation, as the enemies' explanation – 'socialism has failed', 'Marxism is dead', etc. – held sway, there was a demand on me to share my understanding of what had happened. The opportunity to put my ideas together for the purpose came in the form of the invitation to deliver the Moin Shakir Memorial Lectures at the Marathwada University. As originally written or rather loosely expanded or updated in many places, these lectures – my 1991 response to the inter-related set of issues involved in the collapse of the Soviet Union – constitute the core of these notes, now being published as a book.

This response is obviously not an academic exercise, a work of scholarship or historical research, and it makes no claims, absolutely none, to originality. As the sub-title indicates, my response has a strong personal dimension to it. But this does not make it merely a declaration of faith. On the contrary, what is presented here is a serious argument in behalf of the continuing validity and relevance of socialism as a historically necessary, superior-to-capitalism, social order, and the need for the common people everywhere to struggle for it. Even as each chapter stands by itself, different chapters well hold together in support of this argument. The text apart, evidence in support of my argument is there, scattered all around us, only if we are willing to see; a little reason and ability to interconnect is all that is needed.

Not an academic exercise, these are notes of a militant in the movement, 'a small "C" communist', to borrow that most helpful self-description from E.P. Thompson. And the argument is addressed to fellow militants in what is left of the communist movement, to 'social democrats' who still remain socialist, to the new crop of radicals, in the social movements or outside them, struggling to find their bearings in a world now almost universally dominated by capitalism, and to all those on the Left who share my concern with the present and future of socialism. Even others may find it of interest for their present and future too is now involved in the present and future of socialism in a way that was never the case before. If anything, these notes are an exercise in theory, a plea to parties and activists on the Left for a return to the basics. Theory, it may be added, does not directly yield a political programme which is the task of political parties or activists on the ground. But it serves to provide a basic understanding of things, a perspective or sense of direction, most necessary for the success of any popular struggle. A struggling people will not get very far without some substantial knowledge of the structures they need to overthrow for their emancipation and a sense of direction in their struggle.

[The format of Notes has enabled me to deal with a wide range of issues in this regard, many of them raised with me by the concerned activists or friends on the Left. (The chapter on Marxism, for example, in its overall thrust and detail, is very much a response to an express request from two such friends, most eminent in the fields of literature and people's theatre in Punjab). The way the original lectures were planned and delivered, there is little direct reference to India, but relevance to India is more than implicit in the argument throughout these Notes. The language (English), I know, is a handicap in reaching out to a larger readership, especially at the level of activists on the ground. I hope translation will help out as has already happened with some already published parts of these Notes.]

I have already regretted the repetition that marks these Notes and offered an explanation, not justification, for it; though even a justification is not to be entirely ruled out. Gunter Grass has said: 'In politics you have to repeat and repeat, like a parrot, ideas you know to be correct and proven as such, which is exhausting – you constantly hear the echo of your own voice, and end up sounding like a parrot even to yourself. But this is evidently part of the job, if one is to find any listeners at all in a world so full of different voices', or, I may add, when the noisy voice of those currently dominant in society seeks to drown all other voices and wants us to forget what was said earlier and has been proved to be true, or forbids what needs to be said or repeated anew today.

If my experience with the sophisticates of the academy or bourgeois ideology, or plain anti-socialist propagandists, is any guide, 'crudeness and simplification' is a charge sure to be brought against my argument. I will not here argue or complain over it, but borrow from Marcuse to suggest that, at times, crudeness and simplification also help to make the truth of an idea more visible. And truth of the socialist idea is my main concern in these Notes.

During the heady, rebel days in the late sixties, students of Paris used to ask of everyone who would address them to first tell them: 'where do you speak from?' For every speaker, and for that matter every writer, inescapably speaks or writes from a particular philosophical-political standpoint and owes it to his audience or readers to publicly state it. It is only fair to acknowledge that I have written from the standpoint of Marxism, rather Marxism as I understand it. For I have no pretensions to scholarship in Marxism. I picked up some on the way and have found it useful not only in my politics or profession as a teacher but in living my life as well. This last is not just a formal statement. Knowing Marx does make a difference to what sense you make of life, how you understand, live and act in the world. 'Indeed, I must confess that Karl Marx made a man of me', is how George Bernard Shaw once put it. Marx, therefore, is important to me and, I believe, he is important to all of us, today more so than ever before, if for no other reason than this: the world we are living in is a capitalist world, more capitalist than ever before after the Soviet collapse, and Marx more than any other human being, then or now, devoted his life to explaining the reality of this world and his achievement here remains unrivalled. In one sense, this is what this book is about.

I know that the way I have been speaking or writing about Marx, about capitalism, socialism, and such other things, in recent years, not a few have thought of me as someone woefully out of sync with our post-modern, neo-liberal or globalised times, a 'dinosaur', as it were, from another age. Many will think the same of this book and will be similarly dismissive about its argument. This is nothing to be surprised at or complain about, only something that even the best among us have to endure. Paul Sweezy and Harry Magdoff had the distinction of being referred to as 'paleolithic sectarian survivals' in the aftermath of the Soviet collapse because they continued to argue and speak up for socialism. Recently we have had the example of the Nobel Laureate Gunter Grass and the world famous sociologist Pierre Bourdieu. Holding that neoliberalism is 'simply a return to the methods of nineteenth-century Manchester liberalism', 'a strange revolution that restores the past but presents itself as progressive, transforming regression itself into a form of progress', they have said: 'It does this so well that those who oppose it are made to appear regressive themselves. This is something we have both endured: we are readily treated as old-fashioned, "has-beens", "throwbacks"... "dinosaurs".' Grass and Bourdieu have nevertheless insisted that one must continue to speak up.

So have Paul Sweezy and Harry Magdoff, all along. Some years back, apropos post-Soviet capitalist triumphalism, they had written: 'Capitalism's victory settles nothing. In its global form, it encompasses ever more people and intensifies their exploitation and oppression. History shows that there have been alternatives in the past, and reason tells us that there will be others in the future.... It is of the greatest importance to keep the radical tradition alive and vigorous, ready to undergrid and give direction to the revolutionary struggles that lie ahead'. This is how I too had conceived this writing in 1991. Since then, the euphoria over 'capitalism's victory' long over, the struggles that lay ahead are already on the agenda of the peoples everywhere. This is where I locate whatever relevance this book has.

I would like to thank the Institute for Development and Communication, Chandigarh and its Director Dr. Pramod Kumar, for providing the facilities to complete and put together the manuscript of this book and getting the book itself into shape for the printer and publisher at Delhi. I can never be too thankful to Ashwini Kumar for the hard work he personally put into all this. I am grateful to my wife, Mohinder Kaur, for bearing with me as I struggled with this writing in Delhi, Shimla and Chandigarh. Not exactly thanks but something more is due to Priyaleen, Shimareet, Meenakshi Gopinath and Bertell Ollman who, each in her or his own way, sustained me in writing these Notes. The responsibility for the argument, of course, remains mine.

Randhir Singh

March 2004

1

Of the Third World

I

The collapse of the Soviet Union has seen the revival of an argument within Marxism, and even outside it, concerning the impossibility of socialism in one country, least of all a backward one. Adopting a strictly determinist standpoint, the argument primarily takes into consideration the objective circumstances of Russia's economic underdevelopment in the second decade of the 20th century and concludes that no other outcome except failure was possible in the Soviet Union since the conditions which Marxism was deemed to have considered necessary when foreseeing socialist revolutions and consequent socialist transitions were missing. It has even been suggested that the Soviet failure to realise the promise of socialism, far from being a failure of socialism or a repudiation of Marxism, establishes Marxism's status as a science, it is in fact a vindication of Marxian social science. It was simply impossible to build socialism in Russia. In justification, appeal is made to Marx himself.

There is no denying that, especially in early Marx, there is an argument for such an impossibility, no coherent theory surely, but significant statements that lend support to this view (some of which, incidentally, we have already duly taken note of). His extrapolation of the historical tendencies inherent in capitalism and own revolutionary optimism led Marx to postulate the growth of 'a world market' giving rise to a world (really Europe-wide) revolution and only that as providing an adequate material basis for building a communist society. For example, this is how Marx put it in the *Grundrisse*: 'The world market... forms the presupposition of the whole as well as its substratum. Crises are then the general intimation which points beyond the presupposition, and the urge which drives towards the adoption of a new historic form.' It is the world which is seen as constituting the totality within which all the contradictions of capitalism come into play, a world revolution matures and occurs and the 'drive' towards 'a new historic form', communism, comes to be realised. Again, in the *German Ideology:* 'Empirically, communism is only possible as the act of the dominant peoples "all at once" and simultaneously, which presupposes the universal development of productive forces and the world intercourse bound up with them.' Without the full, 'universal' development of human productive powers, a revolution in one part of the world could only give rise to communism 'as a local phenomenon' which would serve only to generalize want and thereby 'the struggle for necessities. would begin again, and all the old filthy business would necessarily be restored'. Communism, it was suggested, 'can only have "world historical" existence.' A local communism was bound to be mired in the struggle for necessities and what is more, doomed to be 'abolished' with the development of the productive forces and of 'the world intercourse bound up with them.'

Marx's argument here is cited as a prediction, indeed a judgement in advance on what has now happened in the Soviet Union and thus as a vindication of 'the science of Karl Marx'.

It may be immediately stated that such argumentation not only ignores Marx's life and work (including his theory) as a whole, or the changed situation resulting from the 'trick' that history has played with Marx's main (but not the only) perspective on socialist revolution, but also betrays a complete disregard of Engels' injunction, all the more relevant in the changed situation, that to be *Marxist* is not to 'pick quotations from Marx' but to 'think as Marx would have thought in their place'. The argument misses out on the real task, namely, concrete Marxist analysis of the Soviet experiment in socialism which was certainly not predetermined to fail the way it did, an analysis of what, how and why went wrong? how socialism could be better and more successfully attempted there, not to achieve (immediately and in 'one country') all that Marx had envisioned but to build it as genuine in itself, and as a genuine transition towards the post-capitalist communist society of the future visualised by classical Marxism. There is the *apriori* assumption that industry and modern technology as developed in capitalism alone represent prerequisites for socialism, that socialism can only be achieved in one way: through capitalism and industrialisation of the capitalist type as complete and pre-existing accomplishments. The question is not posed whether it is possible, or even necessary, to create a different technical foundation or a different conception of production which would really have the function of satisfying human needs and would constitute a more adequate basis for the creation of a new socialist civilisation, that it may become historically necessary for a country or society to do so, to simultaneously develop both productive forces and relations of production on a new, different from capitalism, socialist basis. (For Marx, there was no objective logic of 'the necessary stages of development' in history. He indeed foresaw *other* possibilities, including a post-revolution socialist transition in Russia on the basis of traditional rural communes). In other words, what we have here is an essentially academic exercise in economistic or scientistic Marxism which clouds the issues involved and in the name of 'impossibility of socialism in one country' evades or undermines the *real* struggle for socialism in our time.

II

Such thinking was a feature of early Marxism. Engels himself took for granted throughout his career the need for a socialist revolution to be coextensive with the advanced capitalist world as a whole. But throughout there were indications of a different kind and of other possibilities as well, especially with Marx (some of which we have noticed earlier), though Marx never entirely abandoned his optimistic perspective of an European revolution. And throughout, the all important underlying assumption was that socialism can be successfully built only on a material base provided by the productive achievements of capitalism. Quit understandably, therefore, following upon the Bolshevik seizure of power, the legitimacy of the October revolution and even more of Lenin's socialist enterprise was questioned, especially by those who took an evolutionist, scientistic or strictly structuralistic view of Marxism. It was even argued that the Bolshevik enterprise was foredoomed to fail, above all because of the Russian backwardness.

Thus, for example, at the very outset Kautsky and the Mensheviks had insisted that Russia in 1917 was only ripe for a bourgeois and not a socialist revolution. Others on the Right of the international socialist movement echoed this insistence and were downright sceptical of the Bolshevik effort, though, it seems less for reasons of Marxist theory and far more because of their own reformist predilections. Thus the social democratic leader Otto Bauer, having tamely surrendered the revolution in Austria, now joined in pronouncing that the Russian enterprise was doomed to failure 'by the very low level of development of the productive forces.' From within the revolutionary tradition of classical Marxism, Rosa Luxemburg who both admired and criticised the Bolsheviks from the Left, simply asserted: 'the socialist order of society can only be achieved internationally.' And over the years a section of the Trotskyite tradition within Marxism continued to insist that only an international revolution can create the conditions for a socialist transition anywhere. Revolutions which seek a 'national solution' will inevitably founder and degenerate into some form of 'state-capitalism' or 'bureaucratic socialism.'

III

Lenin took notice of such criticism – that it had been wrong and contrary to Marxism to carry through a socialist revolution in a backward country like Russia – and answered it effectively in his *Our Revolution* (January 1923). It is not necessary for me to go over this issue again or to reproduce Lenin's answer except to suggest that it echoes Marx's own life long distaste for such critics to whom, as Shanin has put it, 'the punch-line of Marxist analysis was the adoration or elaboration of irresistible laws of history, used as the license to do nothing'. Pointing out that 'they are complete strangers to the idea that while the development of world history as a whole follows general laws it is by no mean precluded but on the contrary presumed that certain periods of development may display peculiarities in either the form, or the sequence of this development,' Lenin underlined the 'scientific' passivity underlying the argument of his critics and asked: 'But what about a people that found itself in a revolutionary situation such as that created during the first imperialist war? Might it not, influenced by the hopelessness of its situation, fling itself into a struggle that would offer it at least some chance of securing conditions for the further development of civilisation that were somewhat unusual?' Again: 'What if the situation..... gave rise to circumstances that put Russia and her development in a position which enabled us to achieve precisely that combination of a "peasant war" with the working class movement suggested in 1856 by no less a Marxist than Marx himself as a possible prospect for Prussia?' And finally: 'It would be a fatal mistake to declare that since there is a discrepancy between the economic forces and our political strength it follows that we should not have seized power. Such an argument can be advanced only by a man in muffler'. As to what followed the October revolution, we have a already discussed Lenin's heroic effort to meet the challenge posed by the survival of European revolution only in Russia, his perspective on the construction of socialism in his backward country. Lenin refused to abandon the revolution and took the only possible position for a revolutionary Marxist: 'Struggle, and struggle alone will decide..... how far we shall advance.'

IV

The struggle, especially after Lenin's departure, as we now well know, did not prove adequate enough and the Soviet collapse has, quite naturally, witnessed a vigorous revival of reformist or scientistic criticism of the October Revolution and the consequent experiment in socialism. In the erstwhile

Soviet Union itself, we have scholars, including former Marxists, who are, after years of silence or servility, or both, even arguing that Russia would have been better off without the Revolution and the socialism which followed. Elsewhere 'orthodoxy' is invoked and Marx is again selectively quoted to insist that 'socialism only becomes possible when capitalism has exhausted its capacity for development of the forces of production – when it is a fetter on the future development of society's productive capacity.' We are warned that 'attempts at revolutionary ruptures with capitalism in backward, non-industrialised countries would ultimately fail to accomplish their positive objectives', and only produce, as in Russia, 'a hybrid', indeed 'a parody of socialism'. 'Not a refutation of Marxism', the demise of communist regimes, we are told, 'is a refutation of Leninist voluntarism' that sought 'to build socialism on inadequate material foundations'. Any number of scholarly critics have further advised us 'to draw the proper lesson' from the Soviet experience and not attempt anything so 'unviable' again; there is no socialism 'unless and until there is a more or less simultaneous movement in the same direction in at least a number of developed capitalist states of the world'. And so on.

The theoretical poverty, historical irrelevance and rank opportunism of most such argumentation need not detain us here. But the argument has also found a more credible and theoretically serious expression in contemporary radical literature and it has focussed on an issue of vital relevance for the ongoing and future struggle for socialism in a manner that demands to be specifically taken note of.

Possibly most significant and certainly typical here, differences among them notwithstanding, is the argument persistently elaborated and presented by the contemporary school of world-system theorists, as part of their general theory concerning global capitalism. In a neo-Marxist respecification of Marx's accumulation model of capitalism, this theory sees capitalism as a world system in which the core/periphery hierarchy is a necessary, regularly reproduced, institutionally structured system of inequality among 'developed' (core), and 'less developed' (peripheral) countries. (Semi-peripheral countries are those displaying combinations of core and peripheral forms of capitalism). Imperialism, thus, is better visualised, not as a stage of capitalism but as a necessary and permanent feature of the capitalist world system. It is this larger world system that develops, not national societies; 'national development' so-called is really upward mobility in the core/ periphery hierarchy. In this perspective, socialist revolutions of our times did not seize state power in the core, but rather in semi-peripheral and peripheral countries of the world system, and thus were never in a position to transform the basic logic of capitalism. The post-revolutionary states failed to institutionalise a self-reproducing socialist mode of production because of the strong threats and inducements emanating from the larger capitalist world system. They only ended up using socialist ideology to mobilise an industrialisation seeking to catch up with core capitalism. The global threat encouraged militarism, authoritarianism, and even a certain 'defensive' imperialism, and the existence of a dynamic and competitive capitalist world market encouraged corruption, consumerism, political opportunism by the new class of political and economic power-holders, party bosses, technocrats and bureaucrats who could bolster their own positions by ideological and repressive devices on the one hand and by mediating the importation of sophisticated technology from the core on the other.

Thus a reincorporation of these 'socialist' states in the global capitalist economy, their crisis and ultimate collapse into capitalism, was inevitable. In fact, in a strictly world-system theory's perspective, these states were *never* really outside of the capitalist world economy, and their economic and political development, even when building 'socialism in one country', is better understood as a response to the threats and inducements of the larger, global capitalist environment. This development was quite successful in terms of standard measures of economic progress as decreed by capitalism, but a complete failure as an effort to build an alternative, socialist, mode of production, or a socialist society as envisioned by classical Marxism.

An extremely rigid, structuralist interpretation of Marxism leads world-system theory to regard the world capitalist system as a rigidly integrated global social formation with an almost absolute dominance in the world economy. And an important conclusion follows: this precludes the possibility that individual nation states can separate themselves from the powerfully hegemonic, all-encompassing capitalist world system. It is simply not possible for a single country to break away for a socialist transition in one country, least of all in a backward peripheral or semi-peripheral country. Even if a country does initially succeed in breaking away, it will be soon compelled to make compromises which will inevitably lead to its incorporation or reincorporation into the world capitalist system. Thus, as with an earlier and continuing Trotskyite tradition, unless a simultaneous international socialist revolution occurs, or by some historical process at least most of the world goes socialist, no country can really hope to make its transition to socialism.

V

World system theory as such is not my concern here, nor its view of socialism built in the Soviet Union, except to say that the theory is mistaken in entirely overlooking the *systemic* character of the conflict between the West and the East in the post-1917 period; the capitalist West's more than seventy years long struggle to destroy the erstwhile Soviet Union did express, in however partial and distorted manner, the conflict between capitalism and socialism. It only needs to be noticed that the theory's real strength lies in its central focus on the global political economy and its rejection of the developmentalist model, with the West as ideal type, of modernisation theory, the view that by judicious policy choices, including structural adjustment programmes of IMF and World Bank, underdeveloped countries too can one day achieve the end-state, that is catch up and be like the advanced capitalist West – a view, really an illusion, nurtured and propagated by the ruling classes and their academic and other representatives in the third world countries, including India. This apart, the world-system theory's perspective on the future of socialism is seriously flawed.

There is no denying that the world system theory's is a powerful and persuasive argument. There is a great deal in this argument with which most Marxists would agree. It states with exceptional clarity and much needed emphasis the inimical context of the dominant world capitalist system within which revolution occurs and the emerging revolutionary state, in one or more countries, seeking transition to socialism, has to operate. It draws attention to a host of extremely important problems, short and long term, which the intricately integrated nature of global capitalism poses for such a socialist enterprise – problems involving all sorts of structural constraints and dependencies which would obstruct and may even finally undermine the proposed socialist transition. The world-system theory's perspective does indeed encourage us to examine global level constraints (and opportunities) and to allocate our political energies and economic resources in ways that will be most productive when these structural constraints are taken into account. All this is important and necessary knowledge for revolutionaries anywhere in the world, at the core or in the periphery of the world capitalist system. But, conceding all this, does it necessarily follow that attempt to make socialist revolution or to build socialism at the local or national level is altogether futile, it is bound to fail?

The crucial question is what does the world-system theory's perspective imply for revolutionary strategy anywhere, particularly in the dependent, underdeveloped countries in the periphery or semi-periphery of the global capitalist system? What guidance in theory and practice it provides the revolutionaries in these countries where revolutions have occurred in the past and where, if past is any precedent, they are likely to occur in future regardless of the current collapse of 'actually existing socialism' or the fate of the socialist movement in the advanced capitalist world?

The world-system theory's analysis of the actually existing capitalism has not only highlighted, as never before, the decisively important fact that in its worldwide expansion, capitalism has given rise to a regularly reproduced centres/ peripheries polarisation; it has also made it abundantly clear that it is impossible to overcome this polarisation within the framework of capitalism itself. But this analysis offers no help or guidance about how to break out of this framework, to transform it and to go on to build the alternative system which, in however short or long term a perspective, can only be socialism. Its one-sided emphasis on the structural importance of global relations, which it criticises so well, in political practice only leads to do nothingism, while we wait for socialism to emerge at the world level. The historical fact that needs to be recognised is that no world state exists corresponding to world capitalism. While global capitalism is a reality and a dominant international capital is emerging at an incredible rate, no super-national state is visible on the horizon against which the needed counter-hegemonic alliances could be structured, that is a state which could be the site of the struggle for political power, for a socialist revolution that overthrows capitalism and clears the path for a socialist reconstruction of society. The emergence of socialism, as a democratic collective rationality at the world level is not only likely to be a slow process, it is going to take a different, tortuous path via local or national state systems. 'International proletarian socialist revolution' is alright and most welcome. But if the historical experience of more than a century since the Paris Commune is any guide, surely such an expectation is essentially utopian. The fact that cannot be ignored is that the world revolutionary process has turned out to be extremely uneven and has moved from country to country.

VI

No doubt the dominant framework of Marx's thinking and his revolutionary expectations were based on *his* understanding of the historical tendencies of development of capitalism in Europe at the time. But as we have already seen there is more to Marx's theory of socialist revolution than this. Apart from the general consideration that Marx is self-admittedly always open to correction, his argument here or elsewhere should always be assessed in its specific context and in the context of his life and work as a whole. And a distinguishing feature of his life and work is that even as he sought authentic understanding of historical processes of his time, it was, as noticed earlier, always accompanied by a truly remarkable boldness in thinking of and pursuing revolutionary possibilities in every part of the capitalist world, including, especially in his later years, those in its backward, underdeveloped parts. With him a socialist revolution and transition to socialism has to be attempted from the real world situation that has come to exist actually, historically.

And here, within his global perspective, Marx's politics recognised the historically given reality of 'the nation' (or the nation state which is where most of us still live, and are likely to go on living), making for a certain common identity, Benedict Anderson's 'imagined community', which is not the less real for being imagined. Of course 'nationalism' poses its own problems for revolutionary politics and Marx indeed spoke of 'opium of patriotic feelings', but even of the much hoped for European revolution, he was realist enough to point out that the proletariat, the driving social force of this revolution, has to be itself 'national, though not in the bourgeois sense'. It was as a class, or a class alliance, that the Third Estate in the French Estates General of 1789, had decided to declare itself 'the nation' as against the minority of the feudal ruling class, thus creating the very concept of the political 'nation'. Marx now envisaged such a transformation for the proletariat. As he put it in the *Communist Manifesto*: 'Since the proletariat must first of all acquire political supremacy, must raise itself to be the leading class of the nation ('to be the national class' is how the original German edition has it), must constitute itself *the* nation, it is, so far, itself national, though not in the bourgeois sense of the word'. Again; 'Though not in substance, yet in form, the struggle of the proletariat with the bourgeoisie is at first a national struggle. The proletariat of each country must, of course, first of all settle matters with its own bourgeoisie.' And yet again, in the *Critique of the Gotha Programme*: 'It is perfectly self-evident that in order to be at all capable of struggle the working class must organise itself *as a class* at home and that the domestic sphere must be the immediate arena for its struggle'.

It is thus the national or local state system, and not the

world-system of capitalism, which is 'first of all' the site of 'settling matters with the bourgeoisie', of social revolution that alone opens the path for a socialist transformation. This is where the crucial issues of 'acquiring political supremacy', breaking away from capitalism and transition to socialism are raised and have to be resolved. And every such effort, each revolution is the product or culmination of its own specific circumstances, it comes with its own features and historical baggage and of necessity compelled to itself work through its problems, its compromises, adjustments and detours. An essentially uneven, mixed-up historical process, there is no neatness, set models or 'pure' phenomena here. As Lenin said: 'Whoever expects a 'pure' social revolution will never live to see it. Such a person pays lip-service to revolution without understanding what revolution is'. The world-system's theory, its claims to Marxism notwithstanding, has little relevance to this real world situation of revolutionary process, the situation revolutionaries confront in any particular country in making a revolution or attempting the transition to socialism. Remarkably successful in establishing the essentially predatory character of global capitalism and therefore well justified in postulating the need for a 'world revolution' against it, the theory simply ignores or bypasses the crucial issue of the struggle to get there. However valuable otherwise, it yet remains an interpretation of the world. It has no answer to the question: 'what is to be done' to change it? Here its wisdom only adds upto this: only when the world is socialist can the world be socialist!

The issue here is of crucial importance for the struggle for socialism which goes on despite the Soviet collapse, and for the same reasons that first gave rise to it. Certainly, after the disintegration of the Soviet-led internationalism of the world communist movement, however problematic or even spurious it may have been, and especially in light of the 'globalisation' tendencies of contemporary capitalism, there is the need for a renewed internationalism, particularly in terms of strategic and organisational coordination and cohesion of parties, unions and social movements on a regional and world basis. Such coordination of struggles and strategies is useful and necessary, and any effort to establish viable supranational basis for resisting the neo-liberal agenda being imposed on the world is most welcome. Given the continuing crisis of global capitalist economy, the inability of late capitalism to resolve its inherent problems at home (recurring recession, unemployment, etc.) and mass poverty abroad – poverty amidst evermore glaring contrasts of poverty and affluence – or to reconcile the imperatives of ever expanding accumulation with the need of ecological preservation, there are real possibilities here for a genuine socialist internationalism. But this internationalism certainly must not be advanced at the expense of deriding or giving up on the struggles that remain so necessary and inevitable at the level of the nation state, and indeed, at local or subnational levels. In fact national or state units remain, for a foreseeable future, the sites of socialist renewal and struggle. Also it must not be forgotten that capitalism, no matter how globalizing its reach today, it still relies on nation states more than any other structures for its preservation and further expansion, for securing the conditions for the reproduction of global capital accumulation. The multi- or transnational corporations continue to be locally or nationally entrenched and their power and place in the world is ultimately traceable to the political support and military might of the home country. As we shall see later, the hoopla about retreat of the nation state notwithstanding, this state is central to the ongoing globalisation, to the spread and domination of global capitalism, at both the centre and the periphery, and thus remains the decisive arena of struggle against it. To ignore or give up the struggle for socialism at the national level in the name of world revolution, to postulate a global socialism to match or fight a global capitalism is to indulge in an ineffectual romanticism.

The state system, thus, remains, for our times, the primary arena of revolutionary struggle for socialism. It only needs to be added, without any underestimation of the prospects of socialist renewal in the advanced capitalist West or the erstwhile 'socialist world', that it is the countries of the third world which are likely to be the storm centres of such struggle, keeping socialism still on the agenda for the future of humankind. For the simple reason that they have no other choice, the common people there have no future otherwise. For the same reasons as in the past, the world revolutionary process is more likely to proceed through the backward, 'less developed' or 'developing' countries of the periphery and semi-periphery of the world capitalist system.

VII

In his dominant way of thinking Marx analysed the capitalist mode of production as it came up in Western Europe, and even as he visualised a rapid worldwide universalising mission for it, he focussed on the fundamental class struggle between the proletariat and the bourgeoisie in the advanced capitalist countries. Recognising the proletariat as the worst victims of the irrationality and exploitation of capitalism, as they indeed then were, and optimistic about their 'winning the theoretic awareness of their loss', Marx postulated 'workers' revolutions', which would open up, on the basis of advanced productive forces, a successful transition to socialism/communism, the higher form of society he visualised as a transcending successor to the capitalist social order. But the further development of capitalism (which, incidentally also witnessed the rise of reformism in the socialist movement) falsified these assumptions and history took a different course. This however was not entirely unanticipated by Marx.

At the very outset, in the *Communist Manifesto*, this is how Marx characterised the ever expanding capitalist world market:

> the need for a constantly expanding market for its products chases the bourgeoisie over the whole surface of the globe. It must nestle everywhere, settle everywhere, establish connections everywhere. The bourgeoisie has through its exploitation of the world-market given a cosmopolitan character to production and consumption in every country. The bourgeoisie by the rapid improvement of all instruments of production, by the immensely facilitated means of communication, draws all, even the most barbarian, nations into civilisation. It compels all nations, on pain of extinction, to adopt the bourgeois mode of production...

But even as Marx underlined this globalising nature of

capitalism, he saw it making 'nations of peasants (dependent) on nations of bourgeois, the East on the West'; and the *Manifesto* unambiguously suggested that the capitalist world market cannot rescue these backward (peasant) nations from their misery. Later he wrote of the devastation, the misery and suffering British rule caused in India, and noticed, in *Capital,* the emergence of a new, an international division of labour suited to the requirements of the chief centres of modern industry, which 'converts one part of the globe into a chiefly agricultural field of production for supplying the other part' etc. etc. The point to notice here is that as part of this other understanding of capitalist development, its uneven, unequal or combined character, which he never lived long enough to develop, he had all along postulated another theory of revolution, this time in the underdeveloped parts of the capitalist world.

This we have discussed earlier in some detail. The important fact is that, as a result of the unequal development in capitalist expansion, for causes that are neither local nor conjunctural but systemic and structural to capitalism as a world system, socialist revolutions or revolutionary movements of our time have appeared most often not at the centre but at the periphery of world capitalism – in Russia, China, Cuba, Indo-China, or in the name of socialism, in Asia, Africa, and Latin America. For this is indeed where the worst victims of global capitalism's irrationality and exploitation are to be found, and therefore from where the challenge to capitalism emanated. The collapse of Soviet Union does not end or modify the structural logic of global capitalism as manifested in poverty, underdevelopment, deindustrialisation and exploitation in Asia, Africa, and Latin America. It has only made global capitalism all the more powerful and given a new edge to its predatory logic. Any social system built on inequality in the command of human and natural resources works in many ways to reproduce itself and to increase the extent of the in-built inequality. So does capitalism. But as a market governed system capitalism carries this process to the extremes. The law of accumulation of capital inexorably produces, reproduces, and enhances inequality –

wealth at one end and poverty at the other, not only within countries but on a world scale. And this is precisely what *globalisation* – another of the currently fashionable, reality-obscuring buzz words – does. It has only sharpened the global capitalism's contradiction between its developed centre and exploited periphery. But this, if past is any guide, also makes this periphery, the third world of the worst victims of contemporary capitalism, the site of revolts, of new countrywise challenges to the global capitalist order.

VIII

Globalisation so-called is a subject I shall be specifically returning to later in these notes. In the immediate context it needs to be recognised that it is no sudden new condition or phenomenon it is often made out to be. On the contrary, it is a process that has been going on for a long time, in fact ever since capitalism came into the world as a viable form of society four or five centuries ago. Capitalism was indeed born in the process of creating a world market through its centuries long spread by conquest and exploitation of Asia, Africa and Latin America and economic penetration and plunder everywhere. Thus born, capitalism in its innermost essence is an expanding system both internally and externally, its different units constantly compete among themselves for control of the weaker including remaining non-capitalist areas. The classic analysis of emergence, evolution and expansion of capitalism is of course Marx's *Capital*. And he showed that the logic of the always expansive and often explosive capital accumulation necessarily generates inequality in society, wealth and affluence at one end, poverty and deprivation at the other. In other words, capitalism can not and does not make for universal success and prosperity. It can only universalise its contradictions, its polarisation between rich and poor, exploiters and exploited. In fact, insofar as it is successful, its successes are also its failures. The more successful it is on its own terms, that is, the more it maximises profit and so called growth, the more it devours its own human and natural resources. In doing so, one may add, capitalism also makes for new opportunities for that unfashionable thing called class struggle.

The general law of capitalist accumulation, as Marx called it, which governs the dynamic of capitalism, and generates increasing wealth and affluence at one pole of society and growing poverty and degradation at the opposite pole, does so not only within nations but, as a global or world system, among nations as well, leading necessarily to the polarisation of the world into centre and periphery nations, nations rich and poor. This double process of polarisation is immanent in capitalism, its permanent and basic feature, a product of the structural logic of actually existing capitalism. This predatory logic has been, now and then, somewhat curbed, but never irreversibly, within the countries of advanced capitalism –a curbing made possible by the successful struggles of the working classes and an expanding capitalism which could accommodate the success of these struggles, and facilitated by the threat of socialism, through Soviet existence or otherwise, which exercised its own *civilising* influence on metropolitan capitalism. But the accumulation process has operated all the more effectively and ruthlessly on the world scale, all the time shaping and reshaping the peripheral economies in line with the needs of capitalism at the centre and thus all the time widening the overall gap between the countries of the centre and those of the periphery or semi-periphery in the third world. By its very nature global capitalism tends to perpetuate and deepen this structural inequality and disparity, regardless of the intentions of individual capitalists or state managers. This is a characteristic of capitalism in all its stages of development that was explicitly noticed by Marx and further theorised by Lenin and later Marxists. Throughout it has been in the interest of the first world of advanced capitalist countries to have colonies or semi-colonial areas as preserves to make profit in whatever way it could be made. Contemporary 'globalisation' is no exception. In relation to the third world, it is imperialism all over again, albeit in a new shape or form, when, the logic of capitalism now become more or less universal, imperialism achieves its ends not so much by the old forms of military expansion or political control – not that these have become unimportant – but primarily by unleashing and manipulating the exploitative and destructive impulses of the capitalist market. As against the conventional liberal wisdom, it has to be clearly understood that the increasing disparity observed at the periphery of the system, the all too visible underdevelopment and its consequences, is not a vestige of a pre-capitalist past (the fashionable neo-Weberian thesis), but the inevitable product of their capitalist present, not a condition of inadequate capitalist development (the developmentalist thesis) but in reality an inevitable outcome of the accumulation process of the global capitalist system to which countries of the periphery, that is the third world, belong as much as those of the first world.

The post-Second World War period, a period of rapid and generally sustained capitalist expansion also saw new world-wide awareness of the deep rooted disparities between the rich countries and those of the third world, an awareness which in the West was certainly compelled by the attraction the alternative Soviet model of development exerted in the post-colonial third world. But despite all the noise made about bridging the gap between the North and the South, the promises based on the supposedly scientific discoveries of a new discipline called 'development economics', UN resolutions and foreign aid programmes, all the talk about the New International Economic Order etc. etc., the gap between the rich and poor countries kept widening. As Harry Magdoff has put it: 'Despite the striking transformations in the world capitalist system since the end of the Second World War, two major distinguishing features of the third world did not change: in general, and in a fundamental sense, the chains of dependency binding the periphery to the centre remain, (and) the gap between the periphery and the centre, as throughout the history of capitalism, keeps on widening'. It is important to recognise in this connection that this North-South gap and the conflict resulting from it, which is one of the basic contradictions of actually existing capitalism, has never been the product of East-West, that is, US-USSR conflict or its projection outside Europe, though a reciprocal interaction was always there and the support of USSR for certain third world nationalist forces helped sustain this impression. The North-South conflict is anterior and primordial, it has defined, for five centuries, capitalism as a polarising world system, bringing only misery and suffering to the peoples of the third world, and for this very reason intolerable to the vast majority of people on this planet, earth.

IX

'Globalisation', today's watchword was thus a reality yesterday too – a capitalist world economy characterised by centre-periphery relations of domination and exploitation –though this reality was somewhat distorted and obscured by the post-war retreat of the all too visible colonial empires. But, part of an ongoing process with a five centuries old history, the current splurge of globalisation, as with all such phenomena, has its historical specificity which in its own way reinforces the subordination of the periphery to the more self-driven productive accumulation pattern of the centre: it is simultaneously propelled by a new accumulation crisis of capitalism and a renewed ascendancy of right-wing politics the world over.

The economic context of today's globalisation has been the current recession of capitalism beginning in the 1970s, marked by the interrelated processes of retarded growth, ever increasing monopolisation and transnationalisation of the economy and the financialisation of the accumulation process, with all their contradictions. There is a swelling flow of profits but a reduced demand for additional investment in increasingly controlled markets and thus a shift away from capitalism's productive moorings accompanied inevitably by exceedingly high levels of unemployment in the advanced capitalist world as a whole. There is the growing tendency for profits, unable to find profitable outlets in real capital formation, to be diverted into purely financial, and mostly speculative channels. An increasingly intense double process of faltering real investment and burgeoning financialisation has been on, the ongoing technological, especially information revolution facilitating literally worldwide fluidity of highly volatile finance capital ('hot money' economists call it), with all its contagious uncertainties and exploitative-cum-explosive consequences. Central to the current economic recession has been a slowing down of capital accumulation and with it of economic growth which under capitalism is powered by capital accumulation. This crisis within capitalism as a profit-driven system, a crisis made all the more intractable by growing class conflict, has underlined the insufficiencies of the limited globalisation of the earlier period associated with the welfare state. Therefore even as the welfare state is dismantled (and with it disappear the remaining illusions of Keynesianism), a new overseas expansion, an absolute breaching of the national barriers, becomes more urgent than ever before. It is this compulsion, and not the much too abstractly treated 'technological changes' or 'world market imperatives' which underlies the current thrust of global capitalism, its need, even as it 'restructures' economy at home for intensified exploitation of working classes, to prise open the third world economies for penetration not only of metropolitan goods and capital, but even more importantly of metropolitan finance with all its speculative proclivities. From the other end, economic instability or breakdowns in the countries of the third world, often facing a crisis if not a failure of their projects of national development, together with the collapse of economies of Eastern Europe and Soviet Union, have made for both a need and an opportunity for global capitalism to intervene in order to protect and secure its world-wide old and new imperial interests.

The political context of this new globalising thrust of capitalism was provided, along with a general failure of social-democratic Left in the advanced capitalist countries, by a world-wide retreat of radicalism, and more particularly defeats of the revolutionary left in Latin-America, Africa and Asia during this period, notably the destruction of the guerrilla campaigns in Latin America followed by the rise of military dictatorships, exhaustion of socialist hopes in Ethiopia, Mozambique and Angola in repression and civil wars and, buttressing the earlier destruction of Indonesian communism, the consolidation of the capitalist turn in China in the late 1970s and 1980s. This collapse or destruction of the Left in the third world which was, as is now well-documented, actively engineered, supported or abetted by the capitalist powers led by the United States, simply 'disorganised' any real opposition to global capitalism. To cap it all came the collapse in Eastern Europe and the disintegration of Soviet Union leading to a capitalist triumphalism where 'the market' comes to be so celebrated as to question and run down all forms of real or perceived intervention against it, not only traditional socialism but even Keynesianism, any kind of welfarism by conventional social democracy, third world nationalism, the statist dirigisme developmental model, everything. The new agenda must reflect the all-encompassing sovereignty of 'the market': rapid and comprehensive liberalisation of trade, capital flows and foreign direct investment, the cutting down of state budgets and subsidies or social welfare, privatisation of public sectors and security for now more than ever sacred private property rights of both local and foreign investors, and, of course, a starkly diminished role of the state so far as economy is concerned. Given its historically specific economic and political context the ongoing globalisation has, in recent years, literally acquired the form of a worldwide offensive of global capitalism, carried out with its economic instrumentalities of foreign investment, money-lending and international trade, organised institutional structures like the World Bank and the International Monetary Fund, the World Trade Organisation, etc., and buttressed by the neo-liberal ideology with its reductionist remedy for all ills – the market.

X

Globalisation, in its current neo-liberal version, has presented itself as a benign process that brings multiple benefits to those who participate in it, all inhabitants of capitalist countries, at the centre as well as the periphery. Academic experts, public officials and the mass media alike have gone to town interpreting it as something fundamentally different from what we have known, indeed as a new era in human affairs where national economies, functioning as units of a world market, undergo, and share in the advantages of, a mutually beneficent integration and recomposition. But this is only so much bourgeois ideology purveying the conventional wisdom of capitalism. The process of globalisation has indeed produced much that is new in the world's economy and politics but it has *not* changed the basic ways capitalism operates. And unequal access to natural resources, control over international financial institutions, scientific and technological monopolies, extra-economic mechanisms of political and military coercion, together with the cultural domination of lifestyles that the powerful reach of modern media ensures, have only served to intensify exploitation and increase in every dimension the polarisation between the rich and poor countries produced by the structural logic of capitalism. That some third world countries have managed to make at times – often only for a time – notable progress with their industrialisation and trade, or that third world elites have conspicuously benefited from globalisation, does not alter this basic fact, the overall gap between core and periphery nations has kept widening. Within the globalised capitalist world, the poor, polarised third world as a whole remains what it has been throughout the history of capitalism, the locus for capital accumulation and profit-making by giant corporations and financial institutions of the advanced capitalist nations. And it must so remain. With four-fifths of the world's population as a vital reserve army of labour and indispensable natural resources, the periphery must be preserved – it is not marginal as many economists believe, the two Gulf Wars are a good recent illustration –and subordinated to the expansion of capital however polarising this may be – to the extent that even as this permits a certain peripheral industrialisation in one part, it makes for the 'fourth-worldisation' of another, as, for example, in parts of Africa, creating nations like Haiti which were formerly integrated into the capitalist system but have been since marginalised, even abandoned, by the resulting exhaustion of their natural resources. This 'fourth world' is sometimes spoken of as something new but we know of areas destroyed by capitalism in its earlier forms. Such destruction in fact has been a constant feature of capitalist expansion.

XI

The current globalisation has been pre-eminently propelled by global capital's macro-economic 'structural adjustment programme' (SAP), a powerful instrument of economic restructuring which bears a direct relationship to the above-mentioned process of global impoverishment; it further deepens the centre-periphery polarisation. The development of the periphery has in fact been the history of a never-ending 'adjustment' to the demands and constraints of the dominant global capitalism. The centres 'restructure' themselves and the peripheries are 'adjusted' to these restructurings. And International Monetary Fund and World Bank have been the two most important institutions involved in sponsoring the current programmes of 'economic stabilisation' and 'structural adjustment' in the third world. This is what Harry Magdoff has to say on the significance of these transnational institutions' rise to world dominance in recent years:

> I don't think that there has been a significant change in the role of the IMF and the World Bank. From their inception at the time the Second World War was winding down to this day, their main function has not varied. Their job has been, and continues to be, the strengthening and enlargement of the imperialist network of trade and investment. There have been three key components to this strategy. The first was to reconstruct and stabilize the international financial system which had been wrecked by the Great Depression and the war. The second was to tie the colonial, and subsequently decolonized, nations firmly to the economies of the great powers, and thereby widen investment opportunities and enlarge markets in the periphery. The third was to sabotage the efforts of those nations that wanted to break out of the imperialist network by shifting to policies of self-reliance and/or developing close relations with non-capitalist countries.
>
> The increasing level of activity of these agencies in recent years reflects not a new role but the spread of a general crisis in the last quarter century. As the so-called golden years of the 1950s and 1960s turned into a long-run stagnation, these agencies intervened more often because breakdowns in the periphery threatened the stability of financial institutions and markets of the leading capitalist powers. In addition, these agencies have become more

> brazen and open in imposing conditions for granting loans. Before 1972 these conditions were by and large kept secret as long as possible. They became overt when the axe fell on the masses, who were expected to pay directly and indirectly the debt service charges to international banks. The more recent openness in disclosing the conditions imposed by the IMF and the World Bank no doubt reflects the increasing hegemony of bourgeois ideology, according to which the removal of subsidies that give some protection to the poor, so-called free markets and free international trade, privatisation, and unrestricted foreign investment are supposed to be principal ways to obtain economic recovery and growth.
>
> Increasing intervention by the IMF and the World Bank? Yes, but it is intervention for the sake of capital and its financial markets. Why put the finger on the servants instead of the masters? There has been no significant change in the thrust by the imperial powers to control and influence the periphery. What is new is the inability of capital to creep out of the morass of a long-lasting stagnation, accompanied by increasing fragility of financial institutions. In such times, the squeeze on the weaker nations is bound to get tougher.

The Fund-Bank sponsored SAP has been, with a few variations to account for the inescapable local conditions, offering almost identical answers to problems in diverse places – be it Russia and other countries of ex-Soviet Union, the transition economies of East Europe, the Sub-Saharan Africa and the poor countries of Latin America, East and South-East Asia, including India, and so on The formulas being advanced are the same everywhere: a rolling back of the state from the economic arena so that private enterprise and free markets can get on with the job of 'growth' (really profit making) unencumbered by any controls or regulations, disinvest-ment or wholesale privatisation of public sector enterprises, free and friendly entry for foreign capital, liberalisation of international trade with elimination of tariff and other barriers, drastic cutting of government expenditure on social services and subsidies for mass consumption and, above all, dependence on loans from international financial institutions and reliance on export-led growth even at the cost of domestic needs, etc. etc. – the essence of it all being a development governed by external imperatives, those flowing from the world capitalist market. The outcome, naturally, has been more or less the same everywhere: stagflation and recession, crisis and virtual collapse of domestic economy and of course an ultimate fall into the debt trap. All this is accompanied by rising unemployment, a drastic fall in basic consumption, deterioration of education, health and social welfare, aggravating the sufferings of the poor millions in the periphery of global capitalism who indeed bear the brunt of the Fund-Bank sponsored 'structural adjustment', all the more so when it comes imposed in its draconian form known as 'shock therapy'.

This should be no cause for surprise. After all, International Monetary Fund and World Bank are not in the business of philanthropy, or in the development and growth business either as they claim or are claimed to be. They are in the business of lending and making money on it for, or otherwise securing the interests of, their global masters. Surely it is not their business to help develop new rivals to them in the ever shrinking world market. As instruments of global capitalism, they are committed, through 'conditionalities' they impose, to promote the interests of major capitalist powers who, especially the United States, have clout in them and exercise it to enforce neoclassical policies of stabilisation and structural adjustment in the borrowing countries. The IMF is now widely, and very rightly, perceived as a 'gendarme of international rentier interests', and together the Fund-Bank duo has been well described as 'watchdogs of global capitalism'. It is not at all surprising that Fund-Bank sponsored structural adjustment has been a systemic mechanism which cannot but distort economies, reproduce unequal development and perpetuate capitalism's ancient polarisations within and across countries on a global scale.

That this is indeed the case is now widely recognised. United Nations Human Development Report (1996), for example, identified five types of distortions or 'imbalances' that can come to afflict the process of economic growth anywhere: jobless growth (growth without new employment), ruthless growth (inequalising growth with rich becoming richer and poor not any better off), voiceless growth (rapid growth under an authoritarian regime, where economic prosperity is not accompanied by political freedom), rootless growth (where material prosperity is achieved at the cost of cultural, social and ethnic identity), and, finally, futureless growth (growth which is environment-unfriendly, where the present generation squanders resources needed by future generations) – these distortions or imbalances are today a more or less conspicuous feature of the economic development in Fund-Bank loan or aid recipient countries of the third world, accompanied by the reality of a world further divided into two unequal worlds, each unequal within itself with growing inequalities of its own. Systemic inequality engendered by a turn to free market apart, even as the rolling back of the state from economic sphere (deregulation, privatisation etc.) has directly benefited the dominant classes within and the foreign investors, its retreat from the social sphere (cutting of state welfare expenditure and consumption subsidies, etc.) has only added to the misery and suffering of the common people living in the periphery and semi-periphery of global capitalism. Speaking of the 'fiscal stabilisation' and 'structural adjustment' programmes of the IMF and World Bank, Human Development Report has wryly quipped: 'they often balanced budgets by unbalancing people's lives'.

XII

Capital is now globally mobile, more so than ever before, the amount of Foreign Direct Investment involved varying from country to country, depending as it does on the local economic and still more political climate, and producing for the investors maximum and needfully resilient profits. With rising labour costs and the shift to higher value-added products at home, multinational corporations have moved an increasing part of their production elsewhere. Products now produced in countries abroad by their foreign affiliates are then sold there as well as exported across the globe including to the home countries of the multinationals. The important point is that, even when entering into partnership with local capital, rarely do these multinational corporations relinquish control over either advanced technology or their production-sales chains, thus ensuring a steady stream of profits for stockholders back home. But far more important than such foreign investment is the fact that what has become generally mobile across countries is not so much productive capital as short-term finance in the form of foreign currency deposits, portfolio investment, etc., which are essentially indistinguishable from 'hot money' (a most important aspect of today's 'actually existing capitalism') which moves around from country to country in search of quick profits, especially in the form of speculative gains. In other words what has really happened in world capitalism is not so much a tendency towards globalisation of production as a tendency towards globalisation of finance. And this form of capital does not generate economic growth in the recipient country. The foreign creditors are not interested in undertaking any productive venture, speculation in the market is their preferred interest; though the 'hot money' inflow can be and has been as well used for stimulating imports of consumption goods for the local elite. Needless to add, the inevitably sudden outflow of such capital plunges the recipient country into a new financial crisis. The imperative to generate the requisite surplus for financing the outflow compels a drastic squeeze on the living standards of the poor, sharp cutbacks in whatever productive investment was occurring and the transfer of national assets to foreign creditors 'for a song', as has indeed happened in recent years in Mexico and elsewhere. Lenin had pointed out that finance capital is associated with swindling, bribery and corruption – what European 'professors' of his time condescendingly called 'the American ethics'. The third world is today witness to a wholesale resurgence of this 'ethics of the market', the emergence of an entire new breed of buccaneers in business or sharks on the stock exchanges, international racketeers, fixers, upstart middlemen, often with non-resident origins or links or linked to smuggling and arms trade, parasitic intermediaries – all without any real production base and all of them in pursuit of their 'holy grail' in a 'free' and 'open' economy.

It is advocated that 'free trade' is the very *basis* of economic development and that all attempts to regulate trade are therefore responsible for slowing down growth and perpetuating underdevelopment. Bourgeois ideologue Thomas Friedman has even contended that the anti-globalisation protesters 'by inhibiting global trade expansion are choking the only route out of poverty for the world's poor'. There could not be a more phoney argument. As Arthur MacEwan, has pointed out: 'there is no substance to the neo-liberal claim that "free trade" has been the foundation, historically and in the current era, of successful economic growth.' It is a historical fact that England did not become a vigorous advocate of free trade until it had a marked advantage as the leader of the industrial revolution and found the tariff walls standing in the way of its road to global hegemony in industry, finance, and empire-building. From the other end, the rising rival empire builders and industrialisers – Germany, the United States, and Japan – thumbed their noses at the ideology of free trade. They built high tariff walls to protect their infant industries. Today's enormous pressure by the rich nations to impose free trade on the poor has a clear aim, consistent with history: to increase the wealth of the rich and impose chains on those countries that hope to develop and protect their own industries and thus find the way for economic independence from the imperial powers. That the ruling classes or elites of the poor third world countries are, by and large, succumbing to the pressure of the rich nations does not alter the fact that the effect, in practice, of 'trade liberalisation', as it is called, will be to re-institute the colonial pattern of international division of labour.

The neo-liberal dispensation ordains 'free trade' to supplement capital's freedom to flow, in or out, across state frontiers, though labour's freedom to do so, to so migrate, is no part of this dispensation. The overall interests of capitalist centres would not countenance this. The same reason explains why in this age of 'globalisation' and 'free markets', so much importance is being given to monopolising trade and transit routes. While constant and relentless pressure is brought to bear by World Bank and the World Trade Organisation regime (with its trade related aspects of International Property Rights, etc.) on the third world countries to open up their economies more and more, latter's access to the American and European markets faces all kinds of obstacles including those arising from matters unrelated to trade, for example, the so-called 'social clauses' Legitimate concerns such as environmental protection, human rights, labour standards, the protection of children from exploitation, health and safety norms, etc. are sought to be misused as protectionist measures by the advanced capitalist countries. The rules of the game being fashioned and implemented by the WTO regime are and continue to remain loaded against the countries of the third world.

In an earlier era of imperialism (before the First World War), when trade was an important feature of the economy and free trade a proclaimed principle – 'Jesus Christ is free trade. Free trade is Jesus Christ', John Cobden had pronounced in the middle of 19th century – it was even then not such an era of trade liberalisation as it has been often made out to be. Even at its victorian high noon, economic liberalism was never *that* free as its protagonists then claimed. On the contrary trade policy in the developed centres was a picture of 'islands of liberalism surrounded by a sea of protectionism', while the periphery was characterised by 'an ocean of liberalism with islands of protection'. This openness in the periphery – free access to products of the colonial powers – was a most important aspect of colonial rule. Since then, as monopolisation and transnationalisation of capital has grown apace, genuinely free or competitive 'market forces' is a dogma long dead in global capitalism. And as in the past, so now, in the new type of 'imperialism' that is globalisation, 'free trade' is turning out to be a selective mixture of liberalisation and protectionism designed to expand the power and profits of transnational corporations.

XIII

Capitalism's 'global treadmill' as it has been called, is indeed so designed that the poor countries of the world often end up help financing the rich ones – a recent study has found the Third World a 'net *exporter* of hard currency to the developed countries, on average 30 billion dollars per year' during the period from

1982 to 1990. Indebtedness via Fund-Bank loans and grants with their conditionalities has only facilitated this capital transfer from the poor South to the rich North.

During the 80s and 90s of the last century the Third World debtors were calculated to have remitted to their creditors in the wealthy nations an average of almost 12.5 billion dollars per month in payments on debt alone. In one specific case, Africa from 1990-93, 57 per cent of gross bilateral loans and grants were reported to have been diverted to debt services which often went straight back into the coffers of rich creditors. 'Every man, women and child in Sub-Saharan Africa now owes $400 to rich creditors,' the report said. 'That is less than one week's wages for many people in Britain, but more than many Africans earn in a whole year.' These loans and grants have certainly benefited – apart from Fund-Bank bureaucrats and 'many heads of government, especially those who rule without the support of their populace, (who) have relied on the Bank to supply the cash they could not otherwise obtain' as one commentator has put it – a whole army of contractors and consultants, besides the multinational corporations and international banks whose activities have primarily helped the richest citizens of the rich countries. But in the Third World, whatever needs of 'the economy' or the locally dominant rich they may have served, they have served no needs of the poor. Instead, as the ghastly effects of debt-trapping – which have surfaced in many third world countries 1980's onward – have demonstrated the poor have paid dearly for these financial tie-ups between ruling classes at home and abroad and, unless a major reversal of policy at home takes place, their descendants will continue to pay dearly in future. As Harry Magdoff has summed up: 'With debt as with foreign investment by the multinationals, while the foreign funds might be used for developing productive resources, the net result, in the short as in the long run, is (1) a transfer of economic surplus from the underdeveloped countries to the centres of capital, and (2) an entrenchment of dependent ties from the weaker to the stronger nations'. Herein indeed lies the real importance of the foreign debt of the Third World: it gives the First World a means or an instrument by which it can circumscribe the economy, and even politics, of the indebted Third World and dictate 'structural adjustments' which make any pro-people industrialisation or economic development impossible. The instrument is ideal for it secures this objective in ways that apparently have nothing to do with it. The objective is obscured; what is visible is the debt of the Third World countries and their inability to pay it, not the determination of the First World to perpetuate the peripheral or semi-peripheral character of development in these Third World countries.

XIV

The overall outcome of the 'globalised' economic growth in the Third World is now well documented, not the least in Reports coming from the United Nations itself: the benefits have mainly flowed to a small number of countries at the top and to the rich of the world, they have simply failed to trickle down. Thus, as some recent reports have it (and figures here always admit of a certain give and take), 89 countries and a quarter of the world's population, overwhelmingly in the third world, are now worse off economically than they were ten or more years ago. A small group of billionaires – 358 of them – control assets greater than the combined income of countries with 45 per cent of the world's people. Between 1960 and 1991 the share of the richest 20 per cent rose from 70 per cent of global income to 85 per cent, while that of the poorest 20 per cent declined from 2.3 to 1.4 per cent. The income gap between the richest and poorest of the world's population escalated from a ratio of 30 to 1 in 1960 to 74 to 1 in 1997. More than three-fourths of the world's people live in the so called 'developing countries' but they enjoy only 16 per cent of the world's income while the richest 20 per cent have 85 per cent of global income. The number of poor on this globe continues to grow relentlessly. A third of the global population of around 6 billion lives below the poverty line. Over a billion people are hungry every day. Pointing out that 'as the social effects of adjustment processes become more obvious it can also be seen that the heaviest burden is falling on the children', UNICEF has reported that 12 million children under the age of five die every year from preventable illnesses including malnutrition. That is 33,000 children dying everyday, overwhelmingly large number of them in the Third World. A more recent (1997) United Nations report on 'world social situation', has yet again confirmed that poverty and deprivation is on the rise in Asia, especially South Asia (which includes India), Africa and Latin America. According to the data and definitions presented in this report, the number of people below the poverty line rose from 480 million to 550 million in South Asia, from 180 million to 219 million in Sub-Saharan Africa, and from 91 million to 110 million in Latin America, between 1987 and 1991. Currently more than 1.3 billion people live on below one dollar a day. UNDP administrator, James Gustave Speth, in his preface to one such report has concluded: 'The world has become more economically polarised, both between countries and within countries (and) if present trends continue, economic disparities between industrial and developing nations will move from inequitable to inhuman'. World Bank and IMF themselves have been finding it difficult to gloss over the evidence of deepening poverty and inequality in different countries as a result of their prescriptions of 'economic reforms'. Several of World Bank's own reports apart, its ex-chief economist, Joseph Stiglitz, has recently told us how Fund-Bank policies – policies, in effect, tailored to benefit financial conglomerates in the West – have aggravated the situation in many places (Southeast Asia, Russia, Brazil, Argentina, etc.), and no less a person than Michel Camdessus, former chief of the International Monetary Fund has described as 'morally outrageous' the gap between the rich and the poor today.

XV

There is no doubt that polarisation characteristic of global capitalism has today given rise to wide and ever widening gap between the living standards of the core capitalist countries and those of the dependent or underdeveloped countries of the periphery or semi periphery. Long range study of global economic patterns by Giovanni Arrighi and others have shown the extraordinary rigidity of this unequal relationship. Despite the post-war decolonisation and after more than thirty years of developmental efforts of all kinds, this overall hierarchy of wealth remains, the gaps that separate the incomes of the South from those of the North are today wider than ever before. It would suffice to notice here what the Canadian economist Michel Chossudovski has to say on this. Describing the 1980s as 'the decade of global impoverishment', Chossudovski has written:

> The disparities in income and life-styles between the 'rich' and the 'poor' have reached unprecedented proportions: an average middle class family in a Paris suburb has an income more than one hundred times higher than a rural household in south-east Asia; a Filipino peasant has to work for two years to earn what a New York lawyer earns in an hour. The amount spent by Americans (30 billion dollars a year) on Pepsi and Coca Cola at fast food outlets and super-markets across the United States is nearly twice the gross national product of Bangladesh... The per capita income of a middle class household in an industrialised western country (17,470 dollars) is approximately 100 times higher than the per capita income of an average rural household in south-east Asia.

Even as he explores 'the nature of this unfolding world economic system, on what structure of global poverty and income inequality is it based?' and points out that 'by the turn of the century, world population will be six billion of which five billion will be living in poor countries'. Chossudovski adds:

> While the rich countries with some 15 per cent of the world population – including the rich oil producers of the Persian Gulf – control close to 80 per cent of total world income, some 56 per cent of the world population constituting the group of 'low income countries' (including India and China) and a population of nearly three billion receive 5.4 per cent of world income, less than the GDP of France and its overseas territories.

This system of global inequality reinforces not only overpopulation (since poverty spurs population growth) but also rapacious economic development associated with the destruction of tropical rain forests in the Third World. Summing up the work of several scholars pointing to the new dimensions that world inequality has now reached, James Petras and

Chronis Polychroniou have written:

> At the same time, the principle of profit maximisation, which nowadays goes completely unchecked under the pretext of operating in a 'global market', threatens the world with an ecological disaster. The tropical forests, already eliminated by more than 40 per cent, are disappearing 'at a rate of 30,000 to 37,000 sq miles every year'...as multinational timber companies are having a field day under free trade, free market legislation.
>
> Indeed, the ecological effects of globalisation are strikingly catastrophic. Under the fiscal pressures imposed by capital movements, the third world state in particular sells off more and more of its public resources – forests, mining regions, natural reserves, maritime resources. In this context, the greater the external integration, the greater the exploitation of domestic resources to fuel overseas expansion. External linkages between third world capitalists and the multinationals require vast amounts of capital and, in a dependent capitalist setting, cheap labour and pillage of the natural resources are the only means available for the necessary accumulation of capital. For the economic elite, the price of 'integration' into the world economy is expensive and the quickest road is via unlimited exploitation of non-renewable resources. This is the lesson of Brazil, Chile, Mexico, Guyana, Nigeria and so many other third world nations.

XVI

The evidence, now available in UN reports and studies by concerned scholars makes it abundantly clear that the 'structural adjustment'-governed and 'market'-driven policies pursued in the third world countries have not helped them overcome their poverty and underdevelopment. Instead they have left an overwhelming majority of their citizens worse off. Large parts of Africa, exposed to more than two decades of so-called 'economic reforms' are today disintegrating before our eyes, still trapped in the colonial-age international division of labour and populated by swelling masses of pauperised and marginalised people. Globalisation in Latin America has been equally 'a very destructive and painful process', as a scholar, Arthur MacEwan, has put it, especially for the peasantry who now face a prospect of precarious survival at ever deeper levels of pauperisation and misery. Neo-liberal economic policies have forced many to become part of a genuine rural proletariat, working on plantations and other large estates. Others have migrated to the cities and into the slums and joined the informal sector of the economy. 'Free trade' only accentuates this break up of peasantries, just as the rest of 'reforms' (involving austerity programmes, cuts in social spending and consumption subsides, lowering of wages and rising unemployment, etc.) continue to further depress the living conditions of the working people in the industrial and urban sectors. 'Reforms' have worked no differently in Africa or Asia. Of India, among the more developed countries in the third world, surveying 6 years of its open and active pursuit of the new economic policies, a discerning critic had written: 'Two Indias are emerging: a desperately poor two-thirds backwater, and a not-so-poor but unbalanced and sleazy one-third. Urban-rural disparities have increased too. Ill-managed cities are imploding under the impact of rural migrants unable to subsist on land. They are super-polluted cesspools of anomie, crime, social unrest and deep resentment.' Since then the situation in India, as elsewhere, has only worsened. Globalisation of poverty is emerging as *the* distinctive feature of capitalism's new international economic order.

Recently we have had the warning that unless the countries of the South woke up, 'those managing the international economic system will continue to pay inadequate attention to the concerns of three-fourths of humanity living in the developing world'. It came from no less a person than the economist who, as India's finance minister definitively pushed India into 'globalisation', opening up its economy to the Fund-Bank and the multinationals. May be it was a momentary lapse into lucidity – for he even spoke up for 'the vision of a people-centred self-reliant development' – induced by the occasion, a meeting at the South Centre in Geneva where he had once penned his *South Report*, for – may be as part of his new found political career – he still finds it necessary to press for 'reforms' at home; though the possibility cannot be ruled out of political career in whatever kind of democratic politics

India still has forcing some, genuine or spurious, 'rethink' – for democracy and neo-liberal policies simply do not go together in the third world. Be that as it may, there is no discounting the harsh truth implicit in the economist's rather mildly worded warning. For the now abundantly documented fact is that the Fund-Bank sponsored, big stick liberalisation policies are, more than anything else, the instruments for the mass impoverishment of the third world, and this now includes quite a bit of East Europe and the whole of Yeltsin's and now Putin's Russia that on their own now stand reduced to be a part of the third world.

That economic growth or progress of a kind has occurred in many of the third world countries is not to be denied; growth rates and certain macro-economic statistics can be cited in its favour. But such growth or progress has primarily benefited foreign investors and multinationals and the domestic elites, including 'the national bourgeoisie' and a class of the new rich and affluent middle classes. For the bulk of population, it has only meant further impoverishment which finds its worst victims in women and children, an absolute deterioration in living conditions even as 'the new poor' appear alongside the old ones and all of them bear the grim consequences of the debt-trap into which the ruling classes have led their countries. That this is indeed the case was endorsed by the International People's Tribunal to Judge the G7 in their Tokyo verdict of 1993. As one report summed it up: 'According to the Tribunal, the general consequences of SAPs have been: a sharp increase in unemployment, a fall in the remuneration of work, an increase in food dependency, a grave deterioration of the environment, a deterioration in healthcare systems, a fall in admissions to educational institutions, a decline in the productive capacity of many nations, the sabotage of democratic systems and the continued growth of external debt.' An important explicitly stated conclusion was that the policies instituted by international institutions in obedience to strategies adopted by the G7 are the cause of the brutal and massive impoverishment of popular majorities, particularly in the South and East. In a sharper comment, recognising globalisation as world capitalism's offensive against the third world, leader of Brazil's Workers' Party, Luis Ignacio da Silva (Lula) – whatever be his later compromises with this situation – has said (at the Havana Debt Conference in 1985):

> Without being radical or overly bold, I will tell you that the Third World War has already started – a silent war, not for that reason any the less sinister. This war is tearing down Brazil, Latin America and practically all the Third World. Instead of soldiers dying, there are children; instead of millions of wounded there are millions of unemployed; instead of destruction of bridges there is the tearing down of factories, schools, hospitals and entire economies.... It is a war by the US against the Latin American continent and the Third World. It is a war over the foreign debt, one which has as its main weapon, interest, a weapon more deadly than the atom bomb, more shattering than a laser beam....

(That come to power as President of Brazil, Lula has, to the dismay and disillusionment of his people and many in his party, deserted this understanding is a common experience with social democratic leadership of even professedly socialist parties).

Decades of austerity, deregulation and structural adjustment in Latin America has swelled the ranks of the rural and urban poor and squeezed the livelihood of most employees and small producers, and with the US-backed ruling classes embracing neo-liberal economics, set the scene for a social rebellion in the continent's backlands and in the *barrios* where the impoverished people struggle to make ends meet. This is how Argentina's communist leader, Luis Zamora has recently put it:

> Neo-liberalism and globalisation is nothing more than imperialism in a sweet-smelling fancy dress. It is this killer force that has pushed us into the ground. Over 60 per cent of our people are living below the poverty line and there's no sign that we have reached the bottom of the trough. Our country is ruled not by a bunch of Mafiosi but by a Mafia state buttressed by the US.... We simply cannot continue in the old ways, which means that the diseased political scum that has misruled us for decades must be discarded. It goes without saying that in this blueprint of ours the IMF and the World Bank and their masters will have no place.

In his speech at the opening session of the Group of 77 (G77)

South Summit in April 2000 in Havana, Cuba, Fidel Castro thus noticed 'the mucky social results of this neoliberal race to catastrophe': 'in over one hundred countries, the per capita income is lower than fifteen years ago; at the moment, 1.6 billion people are faring worse than at the beginning of the 1980s; over 820 million people are undernourished and 790 million of them live in the third world; it is estimated that 507 million people living in the South today will not live to see their fortieth birthday; in the third-world countries represented here, two out of every five children suffer from growth retardation and one out of every three is underweight; thirty thousand who could be saved are dying every day; two million girls are forced into prostitution; 130 million children do not have access to elementary education; and 250 million minors under fifteen are bound to work for a living; the world economic order works for 20 per cent of the population but it leaves out, demeans, and degrades the remaining 80 per cent.'

He also pointed out: 'If Cuba has successfully carried out education, healthcare, culture, science, sports, and other programs, which nobody in the world would question – despite four decades of economic blockade – and revalued its currency seven times in the last five years in relation to the US dollar, it has been thanks to its privileged position as a non-member of the International Monetary Fund (IMF).'

Castro posed the issue facing humankind today and warned of the catastrophic future that globalisation portends:

> Never before did humankind have such formidable scientific and technological potential, such extraordinary capacity to produce riches and well-being but never before were disparity and inequity so profound in the world.
>
> Technological wonders that have been shrinking the planet in terms of communications and distances coexist today with the increasingly wider gap separating wealth and poverty, development and underdevelopment.
>
> Globalisation is an objective reality underlining the fact that we are all passengers on the same vessel, that is, this planet where we all live. But, passengers on this vessel are travelling in very different conditions.

> Trifling minorities are travelling in luxurious cabins furnished with Internet, cell phones, and access to global communication networks. They enjoy a nutritious, abundant, and balanced diet as well as clean water supplies. They have access to sophisticated medical care and to culture.
>
> Overwhelming and herded majorities are travelling in conditions that resemble the terrible slave trade from Africa to America in our colonial past. That is, 85 percent of the passengers on this ship are crowded together in its dirty hold, suffering hunger, diseases and helplessness.
>
> Obviously, this vessel is carrying too much injustice to remain afloat and it pursues such an irrational and senseless route that it cannot call on a safe port. This vessel seems destined to clash with an iceberg. If that happened, we would all sink with it.

Samir Amin has written:

> It is commonly believed that Marxism in general and Maoism in particular belong to the past. This is certainly nonsense. On the contrary, it is the neo-liberal reactionary utopia which constitutes the dominant fashion today that has no future. It does not provide any answer to the social problems with which the vast majority of peoples are confronted everywhere, in the South as well as in the former East and even the West. In fact, the liberal recipe and all the so-called structural adjustment policies are generating only growing mass poverty, unemployment, marginalisation and dislocation of whole societies. It does not even create a 'sound ground' for relaunching a new wave of capitalist expansion. It generates only chaos: social, economic and political; and cannot therefore last....

XVII

The 'structural adjustment' or 'economic reform' of course began with and continues professing different, benevolent aims, promising stabilisation and growth of third world economies including eradication of poverty in countries willing to so adjust or reform. The evident failure of the Fund-Bank sponsored programme to deliver on its promises is explained away as 'the price we have to pay for a period of transition' that will eventually lead to a new, allegedly healthier and more dynamic economy from which all will benefit. Often, amidst a chorus of 'irreversibility of reforms' among the ruling circles on both sides, the failure so far is attributed to the ill effects of slow or inadequate integration into global economy and more of such reforming integration is recommended, which however has the same disastrous consequences as before – mounting unemployment, inflation, degraded environment and the debt-trap. One witness to it all is Latin America where the debt-crises of early eighties led to Fund-Bank successfully pushing for yet more 'reforms' and now the same eighties are being described as the 'lost decade'! Faced with the rather dismal outcome of its efforts, World Bank has, in recent years, gone in for 'self-criticism', shedding tears over the plight of 'the poor' and, in tandem with that interesting phenomenon of recent decades, 'summit-led humanitarianism', spoken of humanising its programmes, of giving adjustment a 'human face'. Tony Blair has even been advocating 'globalisation with a conscience' or 'compassionate globalisation'. This is a tacit acknowledgement that the earlier 'liberalisation' or 'reforms' or 'globalisation' have been indeed inhuman, without 'conscience' or 'compassion', that is, iniquitous and harsh on the poor. But then 'the poor' were never on the agenda of policies carried out earlier, before the eighties, and even now it is hard to see this 'human face' anywhere, least of all in the African and Latin American countries which have received multiple-doses of 'adjustment'.

The harsh fact is that there is no such thing as 'liberalisation with a human face'. By definition the poor are the residual in its market processes since they simply lack purchasing power or financial muscle; 'marketisation' only marginalises them still more. 'Free market' is by definition free of morality, equity, justice or concern for the poor, market-commanded growth naturally tends to flood up and not trickle down, which even in the best of circumstances means, as Galbraith's 'less than-elegant metaphor' put it: 'if you feed the horse enough oats, some will pass through to the road, for the sparrows'. Humanism in the prevailing economic order, based on cut-throat competition for control of the market, would ensure no return in terms of profit. 'Free market' simply cannot be on friendly terms with any genuine notion of human development. One may add, not friendly to the poor or any *humane* development, free market is more than friendly to drug-trafficking, arms and flesh trades, gambling and speculation, and similar other profit-yielding enterprises – all of which today stand well and truly globalised.

XVIII

Amply documented in the literature on the subject, the failure – in terms of the publicly professed aims – of structural adjustment programmes is tacitly acknowledged by the IMF and World Bank themselves whose own evaluative studies over the past decades 'cannot say with certainty whether programmes have "worked" or not.' In taking note of this, we may here as well notice a similarly admitted important aspect of the politics involved in the 'working' of these economic programmes – a subject to which I will return for a slightly detailed comment later in these notes.

Viewed as a failure or otherwise, the outcome of 'structural adjustment' clearly establishes its character as a form of economic repression, which has inevitably given rise to a parallel political repression to support it, of course with the collusion of the third world elites. The social unrest and political instability flowing from this programme, including the popular resistance often evoked by it, has led to a strengthening of the internal repressive apparatuses in the concerned states. Despite the neo-liberal rhetoric about 'democracy' and 'free market' going together, the implementation of the 'economic reforms' has invariably required the firm backing of the military and of the authoritarian state. It is only a seeming paradox that a liberalised market-oriented economy needs its obverse in politics, an autocratic regime, to sustain it. This in fact confronts the existing democracy in the third world, which is already falling short of addressing fundamental social problems within or challenging the relations of dependence and subjugation to global capitalism without, with an insoluble problem. Its surrender to the demands of the 'structural adjustment programme' in opting for a market based industrial take-off will compel it to give up even more on any substantial social reforms and thus lose whatever legitimacy it still has. Popular resistance will only drive the political system into one or the other form of authoritarianism. A stable democracy accompanying a 'structural adjustment' governed capitalist path of economic development will turn out to be an illusion in the third world countries. The World Bank has itself admitted that authoritarianism often has been 'a useful, if regrettable, expedient for effective policy-making' in pursuit of its programme, while democracies have been 'unable so far to make a rapid progress'.

We have already noticed the true nature of this 'progress.' It has meant surrender to world unification through the market on the part of the countries of the periphery which transforms them into open economic territories and their 'national economies' into reserves of cheap labour and natural resources, establishing a new form of 'market colonialism' which subordinates peoples and governments to itself through the impersonal interplay as well as deliberate manipulation of market forces. The structural adjustment programme applied in over 70 countries simultaneously has already exacted devastatingly high economic, social and cultural costs from the peoples there, particularly from the urban and rural poor, the vast masses in the third world, the outsiders to the market. This official economic medicine has really been itself a disease, all the more ravaging for the moral and cultural sickness that inevitably comes with it. That it is best administered through authoritarian means is therefore no cause for surprise.

XIX

Apropos the just mentioned politics of structural adjustment, let me digress a little to discuss a theme in the mythology of globalisation which has interpreted it as 'retreat of the state'. It is in many ways on old theme, which acquired new dimensions in the Reagan-Thatcher era as the two went about dismantling the welfare state at home. The structural adjustment programme in the third world too set out demanding that the state cut down its social welfare spending and consumption subsidies etc., to balance budgets and stabilise the economy. The theme gathered momentum with the collapse of the so-called 'statist socialism' of the Soviet Union, and charged with a certain triumphalism, the discourse of economic liberalisation, the supporting theory of globalisation, has rather aggressively, and successfully, insisted that state withdraw from ownership as well as control of operations in the economy, which is best left to private enterprise and the market. Equally if not more significant in this connection is the argument of international finance capital – as represented by the IMF, the World Bank, the WTO, etc. – that the concept of 'nation state' is now *passe*, the world is at last truly 'global', and the third world states should open up to an all barriers-free flow of metropolitan goods and capital. The state in the periphery and semi-periphery is sought to be ideologically delegitimised to not only facilitate this process but also undermine its capacity to defend national interests against the onslaught of global capitalism – though, rhetoric over 'global village' notwithstanding, no country at the centre is willing to give up its own status as a nation state to be able to defend its own economic interests, primarily the interests of its still nation-based multinationals. Again, as it is, facing a crisis of their own post-colonial development, a crisis now made worse by the impact of globalisation, third world nations, or 'nations-in-the-making', are facing the prospect of being 'nations-in-the-unmaking', torn within by all sorts of disruptive developments, often around genuine grievances, just as they are also being unravelled by the legitimate and not so legitimate demands of other or alternative identities which in turn is giving rise to movements for alternative life styles, traditional ways of managing things (environment etc.) and a certain kind of localism that looks askance at the centre – all of which has been, quite expectedly, taken positive note of by theorists of 'civil society' in their criticism of the state. Of particular interest here is that the World Bank too has not been unwilling to nod its post-modernist approval of such developments. This may not seem very consistent with its policies that seek to globalise the power of the market, that is the power of a handful of transnational corporations. But an ideologically delegitimised and enfeebled state or power at the centre, incapable of standing up to or challenging the controllers of global governance, is surely not unwelcome to this foremost financial institution of the globalisers. The supposed 'retreat of the state' has also been seen, in some Left or progressive circles, as a welcome trend towards 'internationalism' or the much hoped for 'one world'.

Developments such as these do lend substance of one sort or the other to the argument in favour of 'retreat of the state'. But to accept it would be most misleading, for, as we shall be arguing, whatever be the extent or nature of its retreat, the state remains central to the economy and politics of our globalised world. Briefly put, and looked at from opposite ends, the state is central not only to world capital's ability to push through globalisation but even more to peoples' ability in the third world to effectively resist it and secure conditions for an autonomous economic development in their own interest.

XX

In the 'state versus market' part of the ideology of globalisation, 'the state' is supposed to have retreated before 'the market' and the latter is then treated almost as a mythical identity. Now, to speak of 'the market' or 'market forces', 'power', 'imperatives' or 'demands' of the market, is certainly meaningful in making sense of what happens. But the use of such language must not involve an anthropomorphism which obscures the objective reality of things. Strictly speaking, the market 'enforces' or 'demands' nothing. Only specific people (based in class like corporate executives) or organised in economic institutions (like directors of the IMF and the World Bank) demand (and enforce) – in the name of the market – economic policies favourable to their interests. The 'market' is a symbol or code word for capitalists, and the 'world market' for capitalists linked to multinational corporations and banks. This apart, the basic questions relating to the behaviour or functioning of the market – for example, how open or closed an economy will be in relation to the market – are essentially political questions which are ultimately resolved by state policy, that is, by political decision makers. That is how the globalisation of production and exchange is not the outcome of any 'world market imperatives'; a particular decision emanating from a set of classes (big capitalists, exporters, financiers, etc.) it is yet a product of state policies linked to international economic institutions. Again, it is mistaken to think that these inter- or supra-national agencies directly reflecting the interests of world capital – like the International Monetary Fund or the Group of Seven – have supplanted territorial state sovereignty, directly imposing the concrete terms of national economic interventions. Far from constituting themselves independently as new sources of autonomous political and economic power to which states are forced to submit, these agencies reflect state-sponsored processes of globalisation. I may add that like market or supra-national agencies, 'technology' too is not an autonomous social force at work in globalisation, as it is sometimes made out to be. The new computer-driven technologies do make for better information flows, increase the velocity of transfers and movements of capital, provide the communication networks that ease plant relocations, etc. etc., but it is the rates of profit which determine how and where these technologies will be utilised and this utilisation is, ultimately, a matter of socio-political decisions; the new technologies only facilitate and provide resources for such decision-making by class or classes currently dominant in the economy and the state. As Nicos Poulantzas has pointed out, the internationalisation of capital 'neither suppresses nor by-passes nation state, either in the direction of a peaceful integration of capital "above" the state level (since every process of internationalisation is effected under the dominance of the capital of a definite country), or in the direction of their extinction by the American super-state'. On the contrary, national states provide the necessary mechanisms and 'take charge of the interest of the dominant imperialist capital in its development within the "national" social formation'. Arguing the point with his characteristic lucidity and forcefulness, Harry Magdoff has stressed: 'it is important to keep in mind that almost all the multinationals are in fact national organisations operating on a global scale. We are in no way denying that capitalism is, and has from its very beginning been, a world system, or that this system has been further integrated by the multinationals. But just as it is essential to understand, and analyze, capitalism as a world system, it is equally necessary to recognize that each capitalist firm relates to the world system through, and must eventually rely on, the nation state.' Multinationals may operate across national boundaries but this does not mean that they are not based in a nation. It is the nation state on which they depend for protection and promotion of their interests both at home and abroad. 'The term "multinational"', Meszaros has suggested, 'is frequently used as a complete misnomer, hiding the real issue of domination of the local economies – in tune with the innermost determinations and antagonisms of the global capital system – by the capitalist enterprises of a more powerful nation. As a rule the dominant capitalist nations enforce their interests with all means at their disposal, peacefully for as long as they can, but resorting to war if there is no other way of doing so.... The representatives of the most powerful sections of capital understand that they are not in a position to dispense with the protection afforded to their vital interests by their national states.'

This is how the modern state, at the centres of global capitalism, has been throughout active in helping capitalism along, creating conditions conducive for its development and, when necessary, through direct intervention in the economy. Therefore it has also been throughout an imperial state, promoting (through economic policies, military alliances and wars) capitalist expansion abroad, intervening to retain old and secure new regions for imperialist exploitation, and, in recent years, brokering 'transitions' from colonies to political independence that guaranteed access and opportunities to its multinationals in the post-colonial states. In still more recent years the state has played a most important role in formulating and executing the strategies of globalisation, allocating economic resources to 'global actors' (that is, its multinationals), bailing out elite losers and reinforcing the policing of victims and opponents of globalisation. The multinationals and their state backed exploitation at home and abroad is thus not a new phenomenon in the history of capitalism. But a certain shift in the situation has certainly occurred. Earlier, often still national firms in terms of who owned their capital, for their deployment and activity abroad they needed and sought the active, positive support of their government. Today, as multi- or transnationals, they have become powerful enough to not only develop their own strategies of overseas expansion but, in pursuit of their private interests, subordinate the state policies to these strategies. At home the imperative is a more effective extraction of domestic resources to finance overseas expansion, and abroad the securing of more effective conditions for the reproduction of global capital accumulation. An important aspect of the former imperative, especially in a situation of economic stagnation, is the dismantling of the welfare state, which had in a way meant subordinating 'the market' to serve social interests, at least to a limited degree and in the short run. Here a very real retreat of the state has indeed occurred but accompanied by, as it were, a compensating advance for it as a coercive state (breaking the power of the trade unions, etc). Abroad the state has played the principal role in opening the world economy through the creation of supposedly international economic institutions such as the World Bank, International Monetary Fund, World Trade Organisation, etc. Controlled by the appointees of the respective states, and backed by their political and military power, their function – especially with the globalising thrust and the intensive 'adjustments' of the 1980s – has been to break down all barriers, displace national markets and local producers and undermine popular social legislation in order to facilitate the entry of multinationals and help secure the primacy of domestic export elites producing for the markets of the countries at the centre. That United States has led in all this and its officials and spokespersons have publicly acknowledged these international economic institutions as 'long standing furtherers of American influence' which 'support our values and policy goals', 'our foreign policy objectives', and 'provide a powerful way for us to leverage our resources', underlines not only the importance of state in the process of globalisation, but, more specifically, also United States' long standing role of what Issac Deutscher described as 'world's gendarme of counter revolution', seeking to preserve the 'free world' as a freely exploitable area in which not only American corporations but global capitalism as well can do business on their own terms.

Arguing that globalisation emanates from no imperatives of either 'a world market' or 'new technologies', but is rather the result of the superior politico-military organisation of social classes linked to 'global markets', James Petras and Chronis Polychronion have written:

> In a word, the imperial state played a fundamental role in the economic reconstruction of the major corporate dominated economies, provided a military-political shell for its expansion, intervened to preserve and deepen its presence while it financed at the same time 'international' lending agencies that were established for the sole purpose of opening new markets and creating new investment sites. Far from being anti-statist, multinational capital demands an 'activist state', but one that dismantles the welfare state in favour of globalisation. Under the impetus of export/multinational capital, the imperial state subsidises and finances global expansion while facilitating internal exploitation to accumulate capital for export.

It hardly makes any sense to speak of a retreat of the state at the centres of global capitalism.

XXI

That the imperial state has been more than active in the periphery, backing up particular multinationals and global capitalism as a whole, with all its economic, political and, when and wherever necessary, military might is too well known to need any elaboration. But the third world state itself has been no less active in the interests of the globlising multinationals and the collaborating local elites, a 'conditionalities'-laden dialectical relation obtaining between the state's role in the domestic economy and its integration into the world market on the one hand, and the state ceasing to be an active agent of control in the economy to become a facilitator in the process of globalisation on the other.

Disturbed by the consequences of its early policies – when, obsessed with trimming the fiscal deficits of countries which approached them for 'structural assistance', IMF and WB had compelled them to restructure and cut down expenditure on social welfare, leaving little if any scope for public transfers for health and education or alleviation of poverty and unemployment – in a significant reversal of its policy position, the World Bank has been asking the state to be active with 'social safety net' and 'investing in people'. And why not? One might ask. After all the citizenry needs to be reasonably healthy and educated enough for extraction of surplus value and piling up of profits. World Bank's concern, however, has been different. It is the long-term social unrest and conflicts in society generated by structural adjustment which have been and continue to be more worrisome for the powers that be, especially when the much-touted 'social safety net' has turned out to be only a euphemism used for maintaining the facade of the welfare state – whatever of it there has been in the third world – while it continues to be dismantled. Still more alarming have been the economic crises and financial breakdowns among countries undergoing 'adjustment', and the new phenomenon of the 'failed states', as they are called. Naturally enough, the World Bank's thoughts have of late turned to the question of 'governance', the need for 'good governance' in the 'interests of society'. A departure from neo-liberal orthodoxy, it is however a far cry from a similar departure earlier, the philosophy of the Keynesian state, when the Great Depression had led to state intervention against depredations of the market which threatened capitalism itself. The purpose now is stability to secure better implementation of the policies of liberalisation and globalisation. Terms like democracy, responsive government, transparency, social protection for the vulnerable, concern for environment and human rights, etc. – in any case unavoidable these days – now abound in its literature, but what is really sought by the World Bank is a 'politics-free' techno-economic state with a decisive role for bureaucracy whose decision-making is supposed to be impersonal and governed only by considerations of expertise. Needless to say, if this state does materialise, which is least likely, as facilitator of globalisation it will need to be as active and effective as any other. Only with its 'politics-free' pretensions and throwing of a mantle of technocratic legitimacy over the adjustment measures, it will also serve to shift attention away from the other more substantial shift in class power and privilege which the typical adjustment programme invariably involves. Such shift, however, has been difficult, if not impossible to conceal, and this also explains why in the real world, structural adjustment has generally found its best desirable political counterpart in the authoritarian state. This is how Barton Biggs (Director of Global Strategy, Morgan Stanley), speaking about South Korea, has put it:

> It's very helpful to have a dictatorship in the bootstrap stage of an emerging market and an emerging economy. Dictators make the tough decisions and demand the sacrifices that have to be made to turn a poor country into a wealthy one...

Fund-Bank's heightened concern with governance is understandable. Given the lender-borrower nexus involved, the due has a legitimate stake in the capacity of its borrower governments to pay and, in order to do so, to effectively implement (or 'govern') the projects and programmes assisted by it. But this concern does not mean any abandonment of their earlier belief. This is clear from the way bad management or governance of society is defined, namely, the refusal by the old state to take the intrinsic wisdom of the market as the beginning and end for all action, for that is where the 'interests of society' ultimately lie. Good governance is precisely a reversal of this folly or sin which ensures that market-serving technocratic imperatives prevail. In other words, rhetoric apart, Bank's view of good governance has little to do with popular participation in politics and policies, with democratic governance, which can only be a hindrance to the smooth introduction and execution of structural adjustment; given democracy, people would be simply unwilling, and will refuse, to pay the price of adjustment. It is not surprising that, as suggested above, adjusting countries have invariably experienced atrophy of their democratic institutions and growth of authoritarianism. The World Bank has itself reported that, though it is regrettable, adjustment has worked more effectively under authoritarian auspices. If some of the more committed ideologues have favoured deceit and camouflage to manipulate people and push adjustment through – 'Losses and benefits to various constituents should not be made clear. The higher the potential political and economic costs of adjustment, the greater the premium on obfuscation', as one of them has urged – others have suggested 'deliberately provoking a crisis' or conceiving a 'pseudo crisis' to smoothen the authoritarian path to adjustment.

So much for the neo-liberal discourse on 'retreat of the state'. The state at the centre and in the periphery, that is in the third world, remains on essential element in the ongoing globalisation, elaborating and executing 'structural adjustment' that facilitates it, benefiting the rich and powerful in both places while shifting at the same time the burdens and costs of it all on to the shoulders of the common people everywhere. Insofar as the state has indeed retreated from its welfare functions, this, together with the resistance that adjustment provokes from the people, has necessarily enhanced its role as the most formidable instrument of coercion in society.

It only needs to be added that this centrality of the state to the economy and politics of our globalised world, also makes it, everywhere, the most important site of struggle against globalisation.

That the state is the most important site of struggle against globalisation has an aspect to it in the third world that needs to be specifically underlined. 'Anti-statism' has been a distinctive, almost defining feature of the neo-liberal project. For its purposes in the third world, it has aimed directly at discrediting and dismantling the state. But to discredit the state is to discredit the one agency best capable of organising and articulating people's collective aspirations and of developing effective resistance to neo-liberal depredations. Hence the overriding reason for peoples in the third world needing the state for their own purposes. That the third world bourgeoisie or ruling elites in control of the state have failed to deliver so far as common people's interests are concerned and far from providing leadership in the struggle against its intrusions have now opted for collaboration with global capitalism, takes nothing away from the decisive importance of the state, the nation state, in third world people's struggle against neo-liberal policies, the new imperialism that is globalisation, and for securing autonomous economic development that serves their interests. Of course this implies not phoney 'empowerment' being dished out by ruling establishments, but real people's power in the state, it has to be *their* state. Fashionable academic talk of 'failure of the Third World state', must not be allowed to obscure this fact. It has not been a failure of state *per se*. William Graf has rightly observed:

> 'The' real state in the Third World thus remains the major, and perhaps only, framework within which the important social and political issues can be dealt with in the context of a world system permanently stacked against peripheral societies and economies, while the theoretical state is probably the only conceptual framework capable of developing a counter-hegemonic project sufficiently comprehensive to challenge neo-liberal globalisation. Without the state, therefore, there can be no large-scale, long-term emancipatory project for the South. After all, 'insofar as there is any effective democracy at all in relation to the power of capitalists and bureaucrats, it is still embedded in political structures which are national or subnational in scope'.
>
> Only the state can offer a feasible *agency* capable of aggregating the multifarious counter-hegemonic forces in the peripheral state. Only state-economic power in the South has any prospects of standing up to, negotiating with or countering the pervasive economic power of international capital... only the state... can forge collective emancipatory projects directed against the hegemonic powers. And certainly any strategy for democratic or radical change, in a globalized world of states, must start from the state.
>
> Without a real state, and a real state theory, then, the South would appear to have no way forward, out, or back. The question that needs to be posed, therefore, is not: state or market? but: what kind of state, and whose state?

XXII

Marxism, fully sensitive to the complexity of social reality, does not postulate any absolute determinism or unilinearity in historical processes; *the law-like tendencies* in capitalism summed up in the law of accumulation of capital as discovered and defined by Karl Marx, are indicative of dominant, but not exclusive, lines of causation in the functioning of capitalism, its historical spread and domination in the world. Therefore the generalised assessment of global capitalism, its centre-periphery dialectic as delineated above, does not mean that it applies to every third world country the same way. For obvious reasons there is extraordinary diversity here, through no country is fully exempt from this dialectic. Indeed there can be and there is, as part of global capitalist development, a significant degree of substantial industrialisation in several countries of the semi-periphery. Though no full industrialisation has been possible, that is, the achievement of advanced industrial development status comparable to and successfully competitive over time with that achieved by advanced capitalist countries which, as argued above, indeed remains impossible to achieve for a post colonial third world country. It has been customary, till very recently at least, to counter this argument by citing the experience of the countries of East Asia (South Korea, Taiwan, Hong Kong and Singapore, the four 'tigers' as they were called), especially that of South Korea, where remarkable levels of sustained economic growth along capitalist lines were seen to have been achieved in the post-Second World War period.

This experience was interpreted not only as a refutation of the theory of polarisation inherent in worldwide capitalist expansion (which however must not be confused with vulgar versions of 'dependency' theory) but also as the inspiration and the romance of the emerging future for Asia (where Japan and China were other exemplars). These countries were indeed worshipped, in Fredrick Clairmonte's words, 'as quasi-divinities and public relations icons by the World Bank, the IMF, the state department and the propagandists of what subsequently would be labelled by the trite buzzword of globalisation'. They were the archetypes for all to applaud, and models for emulation by countries of the third world, which needed to follow in the footsteps of the four 'tigers', with their export oriented strategies, to overcome their economic backwardness. The engine of growth and escape from debt trap was to be found in a major expansion of export of manufactured goods. The 'catching up' with the advanced industrial west was not only possible, but possible of achievement only through active integration into the world market. Usually, South Korea was picked up as the ideal model for escape from underdevelopment. Also cited in this connection was South-East Asian experience (Malaysia, Thailand, Indonesia).

Before we proceed with our argument, it needs to be pointed out that the much-noticed rapid economic development of the countries of East Asia (or for that matter South-East Asia) represented no triumph of free market policies as has been often claimed by Fund-Bank's neo-liberal globalisers as they have gone about advising governments in the third world to 'similarly' privatise, liberalise and globalise. The policies pursued in fact constituted, if anything, a rejection of 'free market'. It was a state-driven command capitalism which suborned the market, central to whose success was an authoritarian state's intervention in the economy which, among other things, provided effective and energetic, virtually 'planned', support to industrialisation, disciplined the corporations it helped come up and regularly subsidised, protected the markets at home and abroad, and controlled or suppressed the workers even as its investment in social sector (education, health, etc.) made for more effective extraction of surplus value from them. 'Free market' can indeed take little credit for the post-war economic development of the so-called 'Asian tigers', particularly the much-cited South Korea.

The intelligent and aggressive state intervention apart, these countries were the beneficiaries of an exceptional set of geo-political conjunctures, economic circumstances, even ironies of history. Hong Kong and Singapore, as small city states, with their specificities of history and structure were exceptionally exceptional. But beyond the locally or nationally specific social structures and 'cultural' factors which are relevant for economic development anywhere, there were more or less shared important 'exceptional' factors here, relevant particularly to the so-called South Korean 'miracle' as also to Taiwan's economic development. Located in a region where after 1945, advanced capitalism, led by the United States, had to perforce make huge political-military investment to contain 'communism', these countries could extract the maximum mileage from the geo-politics of the Cold War era. The special relationship their ruling classes came to enjoy with the US imperialists meant not only benefits in military-related aid to sustain them as bulwarks against communism, but also a strong American interest in presenting them as successful examples of capitalism to counter the attractions of communism. For that purpose, development funds flowed to them on an unprecedented scale, technology was obtained at low or no cost, markets were thrown wide open for their products in the metropolitan countries. (South Korea alone received more aid from USA than the whole of Europe during the Marshall Plan). They were left free to pursue their own independent, rigidly state-interventionist policies (including a certain level of national planning and development of a public sector) and embark on, in Bruce Cummings words, 'remarkably similar import-substitution programs' in which key industries were 'protected by and nurtured behind a wall of tariffs, overvalued exchange rates, and other obstacles to foreign entry' – policies or programmes which were opposed in other third world countries. Its Cold War interests persuaded the US to tolerate or condone such violations of free market canon and its security umbrella, while releasing them from the heavy defence expenditure (which burdened the economies of other post-colonial societies), made resources available for investment in social sector which in its own way is facilitative of all kind of economic growth, including the capitalist. Thoroughgoing US imposed land reforms, even as they weakened or forestalled peasant insurgency, broke up the old feudal estates, clearing the ground for an effective capitalist development. Particularly noticeable is the fact of these countries' loose or minimal ties to the imperialist centres, latter's networks of direct foreign investment and trade, during the early period of most rapid growth. Transnationals were virtually absent from the scene till about the mid-1960s. Japanese investments, confiscated at the end of the war, don't reappear till then and North American companies were busy taking over the more familiar markets of Latin America (in Brazil, Mexico, etc.). South Korea and Taiwan were too small and poor and without any history as markets for the US, and successful communist take overs in North Korea and China now made them even less attractive as investment sites. This early period of withdrawal, 'delinking' as it were, from the international market was indeed critical to the construction of an industrial base in both countries, paving the way to their export-led growth. (Even later, some leeway for this was provided by the offsetting pressures of the two powers in the Pacific, the United States and Japan). The Korean war in a way, and more importantly the Vietnam war, with its massive military procurement orders or contracts too helped as did the authoritarian political regimes which ensured repression and subordination of the working masses and imposed ideological conformity in the name of 'national development' and 'unity' against communism. All this was indeed exceptional in the East Asian experience. It is obvious that 'exceptionalism' of this experience is not likely to be repeated elsewhere in the third world.

The 'success story' of economic development in countries of East Asia, particularly South Korea, was literally advertised as the romance of capitalism in the third world. This development, of course,.had its determining features as a capitalist development: for example, the cheap and ruthlessly exploited and over-worked labour force, with its low wages, little security and long working hours (in South Korea it was an average of 54 hours a week, the longest in any country surveyed by the ILO, accompanied by the world's highest rate of industrial accidents) – the harshness of these working conditions well secured by more or less authoritarian regimes through despotic control of the production process at the enterprise and state levels and a systematic prevention and, when necessary, brutal destruction of independent working class organisations. As capitalism the fact stood out that the benefits of development simply failed to trickle down to the people – the sizzling growth rates were accompanied by a worsening distribution of incomes and wealth, an ever widening gap between the haves and the have-nots, which only exemplified a former Brazilian president's inadvertent admission of the structural logic of capitalism, when reporting in Washington on the situation back home, in his 'developing' country, he had said: 'The economy is doing fine, the people are not'! But important in the context of our immediate argument is the fact that, despite 'miracles' seen in their economic development, the countries concerned not only remained remote from becoming new centres within global capitalism but also markedly weak in relation to the regional groupings of more advanced capitalism (centred in America, Europe and Japan) competing in the world market. For all its achievements, theirs was a rather fragile development which remained threatened, like capitalist development elsewhere in the third world, by the dismantling that World Bank advises and demands and by the comprador class ambitions of the local ruling classes. In the end, the fragility of their development turned out to be much too fragile to withstand or survive the crisis that global capitalism soon brought along with it. As we now know, the denouement that awaited these countries was entirely different from what the ideologues of capitalism had boastfully promised or forecast.

In the meantime however the success of 'the new developmental model' for the third world was crowned in mid-nineties with South Korea's membership of the Organisation for Economic Cooperation and Development, the exclusive club of high income, industrialised countries; it was a transition from the third world to the first, well supported and commended by the IMF and the World Bank. For ideologues of capitalism and contemporary liberalisation, this transition provided the much needed proof of the claim that any developing country could prosper, and finally arrive, so long as it adhered faithfully to market-oriented policies. But the nemesis was not long in coming. It came, following the crash in South-East Asia, in early 1998.

As suggested earlier, during this period, under the benign-cum-coercive aegis of the IMF and World Bank, East Asia was also being increasingly imbricated into the world market via the transnationalisation of capital, which had already witnessed pace of its growth and concentration speeding up during the past few decades. The situation was now obviously very different from the early post war years, even 60s and 70s. Accelerated globalisation in the midst of stagnation that had set in during late seventies, stimulated the industrial powers to seek even closer ties with the third world countries, suborning their economies to the requirements of transnational capital and corporations in the ever sharpening search for a higher rung in the hierarchical ladder of global capitalism. The 'Asian tigers' (along with Japan, another beneficiary of 'exceptionalism' noticed earlier), whose own markets were protected but who had penetrated the markets of Europe and the US, were fast changing from Cold War military allies to serious economic rivals. Their markets had to be and were now prised open for foreign trade and investment as demanded by the IMF-WB's ongoing liberalisation programmes. With the end of the cold war, and therefore of its compulsions, the US itself began tightening the screws on its former allies in East Asia. Soon enough the accumulating contradictions of bureaucratic-state capitalist development, the inherent limits of export-led growth in shrinking global markets and volatility of the global finance capital, whose strength, given the freedom of liberalisation, can play havoc with local or national economies, all this burst into a financial and economic crisis of unpresented proportions in Asia. Across the region a wave of stock market crashes, plant closings, mass layoffs, government cuts, and currency depreciations wrought havoc on the lives of millions. Massive capitalist investment and accumulation collided with the logic of production for profit. East Asia was now in the grips of, in the words of *Communist Manifesto*, 'an epidemic that, in all earlier epochs, would have seemed an absurdity' – the epidemic of overproduction. And skidding fast, the authoritative model of high-speed export-oriented industrialisation simply passed from the scene, leaving behind a massive trail of unemployment, pollution and devastated environment together with equally massive corruption in the state and economy. The 'economic miracle' itself came to be transliterated into crony capitalism. There was no longer any 'Asian model' for the third world to emulate or for that matter to break down.

It was indeed no surprise to find that rapid growth with the help of foreign capital had ended up in its equally rapid disintegration, or that globalisation, far from sustaining any 'miracles' in the third world, only makes for their destruction. We are aware of 'the lost eighties' in Latin America and the disastrous collapse of 'the great success story of the reform process' that was Mexico. So it was now with 'the economic disaster that has overtaken Asia', as the economist Paul Krugman put it. In a rather technocratic interpretation, Radelet and Sachs acknowledged it as 'the sharpest financial crisis to hit the developing world since the 1982 debt crisis'. But the crisis is surely more than merely financial. This is how Clairmonte summed up this denouement of the East Asian experience:

> They were baptized – by whom we know not – as predators: tigers and dragons. The origin of these asinine epithets does not matter now; and, in fact, never did. The loathsome carnivorous appellations nonetheless stuck. With the onset of what indubitably is one of capitalism's most shattering economic, social and political crises of the post-war world, it is daily becoming more ominous that the erstwhile 'tigers' are losing their fangs; their claws are blunted; and their howls have turned into a whine. Already the reverberations of their agonies, not to speak of their spreading ecological apocalypse, itselfthe emanatio of corporate greed, are felt beyond the region.

The Asian crisis prompted what has been described as 'the largest financial bailout in history' – the great Asian bailout by the IMF. Claiming, almost as a conditioned reflex, that the crisis was caused by *insufficient* liberalisation, the IMF, through its 'conditionalities', pressed the crisis-ridden countries hard to further open up their markets to western capital and business, abolish trade monopolies, bring down the trade barriers to facilitate entry of foreign products, raise the ceilings on foreign ownership for easier foreign investment in domestic assets, cut down government expenditure and legislate new labour laws making it easier for firms to carry out mass retrenchment, and so on. In the meantime, taking advantage of this 'conditionalities'-governed bailout, the foreign companies launched an offensive of their own, using the crisis to weaken the strategic position of local capital by buying up assets on the cheap and gaining market access at a time when local firms were particularly vulnerable. The backstage managers of globalisation indeed found it difficult to temper their philistine enthusiasm. The Netherlands's minister of economic affairs was not alone in stating that now was the time to take over business enterprises and banks in South-East Asia at bargain prices. Said Mark Mobius, a leading US mutual fund manager: 'We view the situation with delight. This has given us the opportunity to buy cheap stock.' George Baeder, vice president in the San Francisco office of A.T. Kearney, an international consulting firm, gleefully echoed: 'I think we're on the verge of huge and significant changes that will have tremendous benefits for US companies that are aggressively and intelligently pursuing these opportunities.' The crisis in East and South-East Asia was indeed good times for what has come to be known as 'vulture capitalism'. Needless to add, this crisis, in its precipitation and outcome, only emphasised the neo-colonial character of the globalisation process and did so more strongly than was previously the case.

The so-called 'Asian model' was the success story of capitalism in the third world. The World Bank had hailed it as *'The Asian Miracle'* which had demonstrated the ability of capitalism to promote third world development. Throughout ruling circles it was touted as proof that open markets and the free flow of capital would be the salvation of humankind, reinforcing the ideology which has become so familiar in the years following the collapse of the Soviet Union, that 'there is no alternative' (TINA) to capitalism. Its crisis and collapse came as a shock not only to governments and business leaders but also to bourgeois ideologists and development economists. This crisis or collapse, however, was not about corruption, crony capitalism, or overly regulated markets as such or similar facile explanations of the business press or establishment economists have it. Historical specificities apart it was a crisis of capitalism *per se*, its causes lay deep in capitalism's essential dynamics and contradictions which came into full play once, following the Soviet collapse, the political imperative to maintain the East Asian economies or showcases disappeared. The crisis in fact revealed just how explosive capitalism's contradictions, which have dogged it throughout its history, can be. We were here once again face to face with the classic problem of capitalist over accumulation and excess capacity that has regularly plagued capitalism and plagues globalising capital today. The economy indeed boomed, but once the boom reached its limits, the results were predictable: excess capacity and serious problems of profitability. That this crisis of capitalism came in association with globalised finance, understandably hit the third world with particular severity, as it has done before and afterwards – for example in Mexico and Argentina. Sweezy and Magdoff have commented:

> The periodic surge of capital investment to the point where capacity far exceeds effective demand is an innate characteristic of capitalism. It is in fact at the heart of the system's recurrent economic crises and is especially threatening in a period of stagnation, such as that which began in the 1970s. The impact of glutted markets is particularly severe in countries on the periphery of the imperialist network. This is so not only because so much of their economic performance depends on exports to the rich countries, but also because the expansion of their productive capacity is typically funded by direct investment of multinational corporations or loans from foreign banks. Payment of profits on investment and debt service has to be made in dollars, yen, marks or other strong international currencies which are obtained by a surplus of exports over imports. If the market for exports shrinks or fails to expand in line with growing capacity, the peripheral country has only one recourse after exhausting its reserve of foreign currencies. And that is to increase its foreign debt or attract more investment from abroad. If this way out works for a while, it can only lead to more trouble in the longer run, as debt service obligations and payment of profits to foreign capital keep on increasing. Debt peonage is usually the final outcome.

The 'exceptionalism' in East Asia, thus, was not so exceptional after all. And even if it comes to be repeated elsewhere in the third world which is not likely, one can be rightly sceptical of such, similarly 'successful', capitalist development ending up differently in today's globalised world. In other words, as a generalisation about the structural logic of capitalism as a global system, its centre-periphery dialectic, the classical Marxist view still holds true and is likely to continue holding true in future. In any case, whatever be the future of such or similar 'exceptionalism', given the overwhelming dominance of global capitalism, its financial, technological, cultural and military mechanisms of new polarisation underway, the newly industrialising or industrialised countries in the third world are not semi-peripheral nations on the way to becoming new centres, but the true periphery of tomorrow. In light of our overall historical experience the generalisation holds that global capitalism, even as it permits, even needs for its intensified imperialist exploitation, a certain degree of capitalist development in the periphery, it denies individual third world countries the space for an autonomous, endogenous and self-generating national development process geared towards the satisfaction of internal demand in accordance with freely chosen economic and social development objectives.

For this they will need to fight global capitalism to make a space for themselves and build their economies on a different, alternative basis which, defined in strategic terms, can only be socialism.

XXIII

In the context of contemporary globalisation, two facts particularly need to be recognised. In the first place the world capitalist system is not to be considered a neutral or ambiguous, or even remotely a benevolent factor in the world which, giving it the buzz-name 'globalisation', its ideologues are making it out to be. Capitalism today is so pervasive and powerful as to have become invisible, and is all the more powerful for this invisibility, leading, even among many on the Left, to a failure to see it or a refusal to name it properly. Invisible as globalisation, it masquerades, without a proper name – it is 'liberalisation', 'structural adjustment', 'new economic policy', 'economic reform', 'reform process', 'industrialisation', even 'democracy', anything but 'capitalism'. But globalisation has its proper name, capitalism, and in the third world it is the continued reality of imperialism. It is customary in polite academic and political circles these days to deny the existence of imperialism. The concept itself is often dismissed with scorn as 'unscientific' in the West or as 'outdated' by the ruling classes in the third world. Professors, journalists and government officials use euphemisms or weave fancy theories to disguise what is going on. That some third world countries manage, with whatever ultimate outcome or denouement, to advance beyond the typical third world lot, or that forms of exploitation in Africa, Latin America or Asia have diversified beyond simple extraction of minerals and agricultural produce, does not mean the end of imperialism. The major segments of third world countries (as indeed their counterparts in industrial capitalist and erstwhile 'socialist' countries) continue to experience the aggressive encroachments of imperialism under the aegis of policies of 'free market economics' and 'liberalisation' that globalisation stands for. That globalisation has found it increasingly necessary to speak in the language of 'integration' – it helps create the illusion of inclusion or sharing in a worldwide economic development – does not alter the fact that it is imperialism in a new form, that globalisation is really a code word – an obscuring or misleading one at that – for a system in which the logic of capitalism has become more or less universalised and where imperialism achieves its ends not so much by the older 'extra-economic' and military ways but by unleashing and manipulating the exploitative and destructive impulses of the capitalist market. Globalisation is thus the reality of imperialism whose intervention, economic, political, cultural or military, in the affairs of the third world has always been essentially negative. It has never brought with it economic prosperity, or for that matter democracy, to the peoples of Asia, Africa or Latin America. Today as in the past or in the future, the thoroughly integrated global capitalist system, dominated by the double-dialectic of centre-periphery and development-under-development, often backed by its armies, can only bring to these peoples further servitude, the exploitation of their labour, the expropriation of their riches and the denial of their rights. Given its structural logic, the model of productive growth and consumption of the West, even if deemed desirable – and this is surely questionable – cannot be extended as such to the rest of the world. Countries of the periphery or semi-periphery of global capitalism can never hope to reach the levels of its dominant centre. They can only be the sites of misery and inequality, social desperation and hopelessness of peoples impoverished by the interplay of global market forces backed by the economic and armed might of the dominant centre.

The other fact that needs to be particularly recognized is that today this dominant centre, itself in deep crisis in the capitalist heartlands, in an effort to cope with the inherent problems of late capitalism, is opting for a harsher selection in its attitude to the countries of the periphery and semi-periphery (which now includes the former 'socialist' countries). In doing so, it seeks to co-opt a certain fringe of countries and classes, and hasten the marginalisation of the rest, almost the whole African continent and huge masses of people in Asia and Latin America, all the while tackling the ensuing conflicts, opposition or resistance, by means of an armed-to-the-teeth international police, the global gendarme that America has become today. The economic order produced by the world market and presided over by the North is turning out to be a grand disorder needing to be capped with a military order that ensures effective repression of recalcitrant states or popular revolts in the South, selectively permitting festering situations and suppressing those become threatening to capitalism, and secures unquestioned domination for global capitalism. All these trends have been apparent in the Gulf Wars, the war on Afghanistan, the strangling of Nicaragua and similar plans for Cuba, and the conversion of NATO into a rapid-deployment force on behalf of global capitalism led by the United States. We are becoming familiar with the affluent capitalist West's supercilious reference to the rest of the world as 'residual countries' oftentimes fit only to provide markets for arms and obsolete technologies and sites for still profitable but polluting industries!

Herein lies the real or ultimate meaning of contemporary globalisation. In a clever if not cynical political manoeuvre, it has borrowed its terminology from the language and politics of the radical 1960s, but what has been conducted as 'liberalisation', 'structural adjustment' or 'economic reforms', etc., is essentially a class struggle under another name which has everywhere organised a drastic shift in class power to the benefit of the rich and the privileged. In the third world, as argued above, it is only a new form of imperialism, with consequences that imperialism always had in the third world. As 'structural adjustment' or 'economic reform' are universalised so is peripheralisation of the peoples in the third world. Alongside, its 'global interdependence or unification' has involved a worldwide cultural penetration of global capitalism. Imperialism or global capitalism has always sought to buttress its economic and political domination with ideological, and equally with its cultural domination. This is how during the last 3 or 4 decades, it has forged a new mould of global culture, shaping and turning it variously in accordance with the requirements of the late capitalist market. Western economics, capitalist production and technological advances have so combined that cultural life has been homogenised through uniformities and standardisations or regimentations which now determine fashion, musical tastes (for example, pop culture), food consumption (for example, fast foods), leisure activities and numerous other material and non material spheres of life. What is on is an attempt to steal and standardise the imagination of the world, a massive corruption of consciousness and culture in behalf of capitalism which at times is nothing less than 'culturecide' by capitalism. It is this new-fangled global culture – which in its American version, with its overriding consumerist thrust, has earned the name of 'McDonaldisation' – that is invariably accompanying the process of globalisation, finding eager adherents or converts among the elites of the third world (as well as the politically powerful and economically affluent sections of the former 'socialist' countries), who, dazzled by the high lifestyles and high-tech culture of the West, the fads and fashions of upper class western consumerism, see the accumulation of computers, automobiles and gadgets of all kinds as the purpose of life and elevate quantity and style of personal possessions over the quality of life for society as a whole. This for them is the criterion for development and progress. What is indeed underway is a cultural assault which threatens erosion, corruption and 'McDonaldisation' of local life and cultures, even as it successfully co-opts the local elites and reaches out to the middle class and petty bourgeoisie of the third world countries, thus extending the social base for globalisation in both urban and rural sectors, by integrating 10, 15 or even 20 per cent of the country's population into the socio-political and cultural system of global capitalism.

This cooption, the emerging divergence of values, attitudes, culture and lifestyles between the elites and the common people – a cultural 'secession of the successful', counterpart of what is happening in the economic sphere – does not exhaust the phenomenon underway. Culture penetration is not just an extension but integral part of globalisation as imperialist domination. Imperialism has never been merely an economic-military system of control and exploitation. Cultural domination, an effort to penetrate and dominate the cultural life of the popular classes in order to reorder the values, behaviour, institutions and identity of the oppressed peoples to conform with the interests of the imperial classes, was always an integral part of it. So it is now with globalisation as a new, latest form of imperialism. Besides, there are now direct material benefits to be had, as never before. Recognising American economic and cultural domination in the on-going globalisation, James Petras has written:

> US cultural imperialism has two goals – one economic and the other political – to capture markets for its cultural commodities and to establish hegemony by shaping popular consciousness. The export of entertainment commodities is one of the most important sources of capital accumulation and global profits displacing manufacturing exports. In the political sphere, cultural imperialism plays a major role in dissociating people from their cultural roots and traditions of solidarity, replacing them with media created 'needs', which change with every publicity campaign. The political effect is to alienate people from traditional class and community bonds, atomising and separating individuals from each other.

It may be mentioned that religious fundamentalism (especially Islamic or Hindu) so rampant today, is significant, partly at least for its opposition to 'consumerism of the west' or 'the American way of life', the imperialist cultural domination it is resourceless to understand or overcome. But it has acquired this significance primarily because the traditional Left alternatives, in particular the great revolutionary traditions of Marxism and communism seem to have become, for the time being at least, unavailable.

XXIV

It was material and moral devastation wrought by capitalism in Western Europe during the eighteenth and nineteenth centuries – extreme polarisation of society into rich and poor, wealth, privilege and power on the one hand and poverty, suffering and helplessness on the other, traditional social relations torn apart, masses of people uprooted from their homes and now subject to the tyranny of impersonal market forces, forces beyond their understanding or control, an old world destroyed, a new world in chaos, etc. etc. – that gave birth to socialism as an ideal and to the struggle for socialism in our times. With the further development of capitalism as a global, imperialist system, which in its own way helped undermine the struggle for socialism in the West, a similar devastation, on a far more enormous scale became the lot of the vast majority of humankind living in the periphery of the global capitalist system, giving birth to socialism there and eventually to the socialist revolutions of the twentieth century. Capitalism's new lease on life in the centre was largely won at the cost of the impoverishment of the masses in the periphery, who have had and can have no chance to pillage and live off other peoples as the West had done and continues to do. Their impoverishment has continued, and within the global capitalist system it is irreversible. The masses of the third world are truly what Frantz Fanon called the 'wretched of the earth'. For them there is no salvation within the capitalist system. What they need is not 'adjusting' to its market, its law of accumulation, but opposing and breaking away from it in a strategy of *disconnection* from global capitalism.

Capitalism, a necessarily global system, is also necessarily polarising and destructive in the third world. The development that can meet the basic human needs of the people of the third world is thus impossible within its framework. The economic growth and development under capitalist auspices, undertaken by the dictatorial or democratic bourgeois regimes during the post-colonial period, have simply failed to deliver so far as the common people are concerned. The failure of capitalism, nationally or internationally, to solve any of the most urgent and appalling problems of vast and growing populations all over the third world is today perfectly evident. Economic crisis, even deaccumulation, and wretched poverty are the most salient traits of market economies in peripheral societies. It is this characteristic outcome of capitalism on a global scale which creates a situation which makes it necessary to consider alternative development outside capital's bounds, outside the imperialist arrangements of the world capitalist economy. It is this indeed which brings on to history's agenda revolution by peoples of periphery and semi periphery. For it is but inevitable that the people who are its principal or worst victims, those living at the periphery of the system, will revolt against it. It is in the third world, more than anywhere else, that, as Marx once put it '(the) circumstances cry out: Things cannot remain that way, they must become different and we ourselves, we human beings, must make them different'.

Of course imperialist capitalism carries within itself not only this explosive contradiction between imperialism and the third world but also very significant internal class and inter-imperialist contradictions. All these classically defined major contradictions of contemporary capitalism exist and interact, each capable of becoming more or less important politically at particular historical conjunctures. But in the current historical situation, above all for the reason mentioned above, the chances of a breakthrough against capitalism, of revolution occurring, 'peacefully' or otherwise – which however is not a real issue – are greater in the third world than in the developed capitalist countries. As in the past the contradictions within and between the developed countries, especially the former are extremely important in weakening imperialism's capacity to control third world revolutionary movements. But it is the contradiction between imperialism and the third world which is likely to be more important in the near future. The current character of global capitalism and the increasing misery that results from the economics of structural adjustment and recolonisation continue to create revolutionary situations first and foremost in the third world, making it the site where the whole set of contradictions which late capitalism cannot cope with or absorb, explode in another revolutionary wave which in its spread will weaken the capitalist centre, and open the route to revolution at the centre itself.

However powerful global capitalism may appear to be and however bleak their prospects at present, the historical experience of 20th century gives us every reason to believe that the objective conditions of mass misery and inequality will continue to give rise to revolutionary struggles in the third world. These will have each its own specific expression, characteristics and pace of development, but they will be standing up against actually existing capitalist development that has become unbearable. As the eminent economist Joan Robinson once wrote: 'It is not easy to see how the Third World can mount the attack on mass poverty and unemployment while preserving private property in the means of production and respecting the rules of the free-market economy'. Of necessity these struggles will have a strong anti-capitalist dynamic that would strive to go outside capitalism and seek a systemic alternative. Provided with requisite political consciousness, levels of organisation, mass support and tactical sophistication, this alternative can only be socialist. The question of future of socialism is thus not settled by the fate that has overtaken 'actually existing socialism' in the Soviet Union and elsewhere. It certainly remains very much open in the third world. I will only add that this socialism in the third world is not a ready made model, but nor is it a prospect for a remote future. It is here and now, to be viewed as breaking away from capitalism in a transition to a socialist society, however long this transition may take. The revolutionary struggles in the third world have to be geared to this end.

XXV

Global polarisation has been the historical force behind past revolutions in the periphery of world capitalism and in the very nature of things they were unmistakably socialist in intent.

Given a true understanding of the real situation, their continuing experience with global capitalism, the struggles of the people of the third world against it, now or in the future, to be really meaningful for the vast masses cannot but have a socialist content or direction. But there is a specific, post-colonial aspect to this historical experience which deserves attention in that it further confirms our argument for the necessary socialist orientation of people's ongoing and future struggles in the backward or 'developing' countries of the third world.

In a certain evolutionist, stageist or determinist interpretation of the historical processes of modern time – which has been a persistent tendency within conventional Marxism – there is the schema, taken from European experience, concerning development of society from feudalism via a bourgeois revolution to capitalism and then via a proletarian revolution from capitalism to socialism. A bourgeois democratic revolution is postulated, led by the bourgeoisie in alliance with workers and peasants and then later, a proletarian revolution to overthrow capitalism. In the colonial countries, it envisioned the opposing forces as an imperialism allied with the feudalists and a bourgeoisie leading the struggle for national independence and then carrying out bourgeois democratic reforms and opening up society for a new struggle for a proletarian socialist revolution, etc. etc. It is this overall perspective that underlies the simplistic but quite influential later notion of a backward society needing to 'catch up' with the advanced capitalist societies before being able to effectively carry out the desired transition to socialism. As we have already noticed, Marx himself never entertained such mechanistic understanding about bourgeois or proletarian revolutions. His writings on the revolutions of 1848, and later on the possible futures for backward Russia, and particularly his sharp strictures on the role of the bourgeoisie in the German Revolution and its implications for 'bourgeois' or bourgeois-led revolutions of the future, make this abundantly clear. It is on this, Marx's dialectical understanding of history and revolutionary processes, that Lenin based himself and in defiance of the conventional schema made his socialist revolution in backward Russia, which however soon stood isolated, above all, because of the dominant evolutionist or stageist Marxism of the Second International which literally surrendered the revolution elsewhere in Europe. Later, in a still more backward China, after its disastrous experience with the above-mentioned schema, when Chiang Kai Shek freely massacred communists in the streets of Shanghai in 1927, Mao, following in the footsteps of Marx and Lenin, formulated and successfully practised a new revolutionary conception which relegated the national bourgeoisie to a mere followership role and recognised that serious reforms, whether of a bourgeois democratic or socialist nature could be possible only after seizure of power by the workers and peasants. As against the teachings of Marx and the successful practice of Lenin and Mao, the conventional schema, whose one version or the other still continues to find adherents among certain Marxists, has been a total failure. Its expectations have never been realised anywhere. The history of post-colonial states the world over bears eloquent witness to that, vindicating Marx who had, in his analysis of the failed German revolution of 1848, already said that henceforth the bourgeoisie could not be relied upon to make success of even a bourgeois democratic revolution. Even this 'revolution', in other words, has to be realised as part of people's struggle for socialism in the third world.

XXVI

Post-war decolonisation, significantly facilitated by the presence, prestige and politics of the erstwhile Soviet Union, won for countries of what precisely in this period came to described as 'the third world', their independence. For many it was the culmination of a long struggle whose essential meaning lay in trying to break out of the global system that was imperialism, an integration into the world market that meant polarisation of wealth and poverty at the two poles of imperial centre and colonial periphery – and in case of Africa, through Europe-America linked triangular trans-Atlantic trade of the 18th and 19th centuries, quite literally even slavery for the colonial subjects. Independence however brought only political freedom to these countries which left the old social, economic and political structures, and links with foreign capital, largely intact, transferring political power not to people but local ruling classes, in most (populous, largest, the relatively more developed) countries to the national bourgeoisie. In control of state power the new rulers in each post-colonial country went on to set up a project of 'national development' or reconstruction, generally visualised as a more or less planned, state-supported, autonomous or self reliant economic development to bring the long denied people the economic benefits of political freedom. The Soviet example was there, its existence and aid made for a certain manoeuvrability of action for the new rulers in a world dominated by capitalist powers, just as the rhetoric of anti-imperialism, at times even socialism, helped them gain legitimacy among the people. Aware of the attractions of the Soviet 'socialist' example in the third world, the imperialists themselves responded with their own promises based on the supposedly scientific discoveries of a new discipline called 'development economics'. They came in with their own bilateral aid and joined with their less fortunate third world 'partners' to push through the United Nations resolutions and programmes looking to the elimination of evils inherited from an unenlightened past; in the new terminology at the United Nations and in economic literature these were now 'developing' countries – a kinder and more comforting word than 'poor' or 'backward' or 'underdeveloped'.

The major thrust of this post-colonial 'national development' was on economic growth and the assumption was that, percolating downwards, higher growth would ultimately eradicate poverty and accompanying evils in these countries. Eventually this growth indeed occurred – even significant enough to be so noticed in some cases – but without in any way 'catching up' with the advanced west; linked with and under pressure from global capitalism, it never achieved an industrial status comparable to and competitive with the advanced industrial countries. The spectacular growth rates – which ended up in stagnation and even collapse of the economy sometimes – only served to illustrate a Brazilian president's already noticed luminous statement in Washington: 'The economy is doing fine, the people are not'. It was invariably an unequal and uneven development with incalculable human and ecological costs, and the gains of development simply failed to reach the people, 'to trickle down' as they were supposed to – which 'trickle down', even at the best of times is, to repeat Galbraith's metaphor, 'feeding the horses with oats so that some of it passes to the road for the sparrows'. The post-colonial state itself was soon a case of 'state as private property' and any kind of power in the state a means of 'rapid private accumulation'. Failing to serve as the instrument of equity and distributive justice that it was hoped to be, the post-colonial state continued to be an instrument of repression, even brutal and fascist repression of the people. Far from being a part of any solution, the state itself became a part of almost every problem. At the end of these fifty odd years, the post-colonial 'national project', when not faring still worse, has almost invariably ended up as a more or less developed third-worldist capitalism, a class divided and exploitative society suffering, as Marx once put it in another context, 'not only from the development of capitalist production but also from the incompleteness of that development. Alongside of modern evils, a whole series of inherited evils oppress us, arising from the passive survival of antiquated modes of production with their inevitable train of social and political anachronisms. We suffer not only from the living but from the dead'. As one or other form of belated capitalism, 'national development' everywhere has carried th mark of its essential secondary character. And Marx had written: 'as is well known, *secondary* diseases are more difficult to cure, and, at the same time, ravage the body more than original ones'.

To sum up this post-colonial experience in the third world: national independence was won, political power was transferred, whatever 'bourgeois revolution' was possible indeed occurred, but the peripheral or semi-peripheral capitalism resulting from this bourgeois revolution has never permitted acceptable responses to the problems that motivated the popular revolts in the periphery. It has only exposed the utter inadequacy and fragility of the national bourgeois project – 'nation-building' as it has often been called – undertaken by the hegemonic bourgeoisie now in control of state power. Political power did change hands, capitalist development has taken place, certain sections of the population have indeed benefited, but, notwithstanding all this and more, the social order has *essentially* remained as it was, with the same socio-economic structure, its privileges, inequalities and exploitation, with mass deprivation at one end and great luxury and conspicuous consumption on the other, and of course increasing political repression of the people. Even when democracy has characterised the political system – a hard-won gain of popular struggle – it has served not to empower people to pursue their interests but far more to *contain* popular pressure and drive it into safe channels. India, among the most developed of the capitalist states in the third world, ruled by its own bourgeoisie for the past fifty years and more, is as good an example of the failure of the post-colonial national project in the third world as any other. In the process what has also got underlined is the failure of the conventional evolutionist or stageist schema, its utterly negative explanatory or prescriptive value regarding the historical processes in the third world, particularly in the post-colonial period.

The turmoil we are witnessing in the third world today is really the failure of its post-independent national development, vindicating the Marxist view that the imperialist domination of the global system denies space to peripheral or semi-peripheral third world countries to grow into new centres in the world economy. This 'national development' has simply failed to deliver on its promises of either self reliant economic growth or welfare to the people, and as a capitalist development, made it abundantly clear that while the rich will thrive there is no salvation for the poor in the third world under national bourgeois auspices, in any *national capitalism*. That this failure is at the root of the serious troubles currently faced by most countries in the third world, is generally recognised. But what needs to be clearly understood is that these troubles, which are indeed serious, are neither merely local nor just conjunctural. They are systemic and structural in nature, troubles of capitalism within and of the world system to which the advanced or developed West or North belongs as much as the backward or developing East or South, and whose structural logic has meant that, notwithstanding a new worldwide concern for the deeply rooted disparities which exist between the two, the gap between them has kept widening throughout these fifty odd years, clearly establishing that while the local elites will thrive, there is no salvation for the poor in a *globalised capitalism* either. Beyond vindicating Marxism, the failure of national development in fact leaves the peoples in the third world compelled to once again confront and answer, on pain of a renewed peripheralisation, the most important question of their history, essentially the question that Lenin and his Bolsheviks confronted in 1917, rendered all the more urgent by Russia getting sucked back into global capitalism: what do the people of a third world country do in a situation of global domination of capitalism?

XXVII

The concept 'third world' as distinct from the first world of advanced capitalism and the second world of erstwhile 'actually existing socialism', and from the fourth world of countries in the periphery, exploited and ruined, and now abandoned by global capitalism, always admits of valid if somewhat loose usage. That is how we have used it and will continue to use it to refer to more or less backward or underdeveloped countries in the periphery or semi-periphery of global capitalism in Asia, Africa and Latin America. The concept also had a certain substantive meaning in the immediate aftermath of the collapse of old-style imperialism after the Second World War, as referring to countries sharing a colonial past and an immediate present of freedom from it. But whatever its validity once or usefulness even now, the theoretical status of the concept is ambiguous. Not only because, as has been well said, 'there is only one world', but more importantly because the concept conceals more than what it reveals of the reality it refers to. Barring an odd example like Cuba or the early efforts of the countries that sought to move in the direction of socialism, nationalism as an emancipatory project for the common people has floundered in the decolonised third world. Earlier hopes have been belied and the fifty odd post-colonial years have seen the clear crystallisation of the ruling and ruled classes in these countries, giving rise to exploitative divisions within and conflict of interests among them abroad. The capitalist path of development has created first world enclaves in the third world whose elite sections have achieved or aspire to achieve levels of prosperity of their counterparts in the western world. In other words, North-South divide is no longer a simple one between countries of the rich North and poor South, but has come to be reproduced within the third world. Their own diversities and conflicts apart, it is now virtually impossible for the countries of the 'third world' to come together as a homogeneous group or to confront the North collectively because of the existence of the internal elites having political economic and psychological links to the transnational interests and hopeful of sharing the spoils with them. The much-noticed manoeuvrability of the third world countries in the past was *really* that of their elites in pursuit of their interests.

A rather visible expression of this manoeuvrability, the so-called 'non-aligned movement' (NAM) was no genuine movement, because there really was no such thing as 'a third world'. The term itself soon lost whatever meaning the shared experience of colonial exploitation and hopefulness of early years of freedom had once provided it. A substantive or positive rationale was lacking and conferences and resolution-passing do not constitute a 'movement' in any meaningful sense of the term. This was of course useful in adding a certain pressure to the decolonisation process and coordinating formal resistance of a declaratory kind to such things as apartheid and racism as also for securing diplomatic advantage in intra-NAM disputes. But NAM's substantive rationale was really a negative one, provided by the Cold War, the east-west rivalry in international politics. This rivalry created political and economic space that ruling elites in the third world could benefit from. Among other means, NAM was an important platform for these elites to manoeuvre between the two blocs for aid and largesse in return for suitable political or diplomatic positions. This had a distinct ideological gain too for it made for an easy merger of class interests with pretensions to national self-respect. This manoeuvring could easily be presented as the assertion of the principle of national independence, even anti-imperialism, even as the ruling elites engaged themselves in bartering away their economic and political independence to imperialism. With the Soviet defeat in the Cold War and ending of bloc rivalry, these material and ideological advantages have simply disappeared. The ruling elites have lost the manoeuvrability that contention between two superpowers once provided them, leaving them all the more vulnerable to the pressures and demands of the dominant global capitalism. The promised new world order is an altogether one-sided affair and they are faced with unprecedented pressure to adjust to the 'new realities'. For the third world countries the Cold War was always about imperialism's attack on their right to pursue a different non-capitalist road to development. They were subjected to constant economic and political pressure and, where necessary, economic embargoes, even terrorist wars waged by western-backed surrogates, that undermined or destroyed their national economies and productive bases, all in order to force them to opt for a dependent capitalist path or to seek economic and ideological compromises on terms favourable to capitalism. Now, with the Soviet Union gone, the United States has even more room to intervene without fear of any superpower confrontation. The end of the big power confrontation does not change anything in the imperialist offensive. It only means the loss of an important ally in the struggle to resist it. In fact their class interests making them incapable of even thinking of any other option, the ruling elites are succumbing and opting for what is turning out to be junior partnership within the global capitalist system. Giving in to the dictates of the IMF and WB, these elites are finally and openly 'seceding' from their peoples. While some are more guarded and go in for tough bargaining with imperialism on this or that issue, others jump at the first opportunity to act as 'globalised compradors'. The hope or pretensions of 'self-reliant growth' or 'independent national development' abandoned, the third world countries are ceding the process of accumulation and economic development to transnational and associated 'national' bourgeoisies.

Such being the overall situation on the ground, the concept of 'third world' can be quite misleading in suggesting a homogeneity or togetherness, a commonality of interests of the concerned countries which simply may not be always there objectively. They certainly have a common past of subordination-exploitation under imperialism, but the possibility of different futures – of subordination to or of breaking away from global capitalism, a future of peripheralisation or socialism – is suggestive of sharp differentiation between them. Again, their present, after independence, is not merely one of varied levels of economic development and therefore divergence of 'national' interests involved, but also one of ever-sharpening internal class divisions, above all the emergence of what the Latin-Americans have come to describe as 'anti-nation within the nation' with strong subaltern or comprador proclivities and varying degrees of subservience to the hegemonic influence of the US, which together have shattered the concept of the third world and ended the common front strategies and anti-imperialist connotations of the early Bandung era (self reliant economic development, maximum national autonomy, independent foreign policy, etc.). That is why and how the non-alignment movement has lost whatever *raison d'etre* it ever had and crumbled, South-South cooperation fails to materialise and South versus North ends up only as so much empty, often platitudinous rhetoric, all the more so in a post-cold war world dominated by the US-led global capitalism and without any strong countervailing economic or military power. The concept of 'third world' must not be allowed to obscure the fact that in the foreseeable future the countries of the third world which choose to confront imperialism will have to do so alone and in opposition to their own 'anti-nation within the nation'.

XVIII

Insofar as it is still legitimate to speak of 'the third world', it is only in recognition of its continuing relation of 'subordination-exploitation' to imperialism of global capitalism. And here the collapse of Soviet Union and the accompanying crisis of socialism has been a real disaster for countries of the third world. As we have already noticed on more than one occasion, it is not merely that many of them have been deprived of the military, economic and technical aid they received from the Soviet Union and East European regimes. Far more important, it constitutes a major setback to the global struggle against imperialism and neo-colonialism. Interest in a world revolution had long given way to nationalist concerns in the Soviet Union and the notion, underlying the America-led Cold War, that Soviet Union constituted a major military threat to the West, indeed to the whole world because of its insatiable craving for world domination, was always a myth – perhaps the greatest myth of the 20th century. But the very presence of the Soviet Union in the world, a constant reminder of the promise that was the October Revolution, had its terrors for the global capitalist system. Hence the reality of 'capitalist encirclement' and 'counter revolution' throughout its seventy odd years of existence, and hence also the long Soviet struggle for survival. Compulsions of Soviet history and ideological legitimacy well facilitating it, Soviet aid and support to countries in the third world, as to radical or anti-systemic causes abroad was an important part of its tactics in this struggle with global capitalism, especially the opposing super power. Insofar as this inevitably involved opposition to American purposes in the third world, this was also a token of the fact that the Soviet Union could be reckoned on as a limited counter to the United States on the world scene, and might be counted on to extend help to revolutionary regimes and movements of national liberation. This aid or support was hardly costless in terms of the political and ideological courses into which such regimes and movements were often channelled, but at the same time it was often a critical lifeline for them. Soviet aid, lest people forget, made possible resistance in Korea, Vietnam, Cuba, parts of Africa and even Nicaragua for a decade. Soviet Union did present a permanent challenge to the United States, insofar as its potential intervention, or that of other communist regimes, might weaken American pressure against regimes and movements of which the United States disapproved. The prospect of not standing alone against the massive military, political, economic and ideological power of a hostile capitalist world was an important condition of struggle against imperialist oppression and exploitation in the third world.

The moral, economic and logistical support extended by Soviet Union and allied communist regimes did not merely help the developing third world countries in their efforts to withstand western pressures mounted on them on such issues as tariffs, terms of trade, transfer of technology, international debt burdens or economic development in general, their opposition to the imperialist bloc, the contention between super powers, provided them with space to manoeuvre in pursuit of their interests. If the fear that had haunted all conservative forces ever since 1917 - that communism might yet turn into an attractive alternative to capitalism - was always an element in the political chemistry that produced reform and redistribution in the advanced capitalist countries themselves, it was no less effective in producing capitalist aid to the third world. Apart from Cuba, the Soviet Union did not invest heavily or even otherwise had much economic or political influence in Latin America. Even so right wing politicians there openly admit that the very existence of the Soviet Union enabled them to win some concessions from the government in Washington. With the Soviet defeat in the Cold War and subsequent disintegration, there is no political compulsion and little incentive for the western capitalist powers to show any special consideration to the countries of Asia, Africa, or Latin America. Latter's ability to manoeuvre for it has disappeared and it is nowhere more evident than in the virtual collapse of the Non-Alignment Movement, that peculiar product of the Cold War in the third world.

There should be no misplaced nostalgia for the era of Soviet intervention in Afghanistan, support for murderous regimes like Menghitsu's Ethiopia, and extensive participation in the international arms trade. But unprincipled and unsocialist as the old Soviet policy was, its effect was to create a space where poor nations might attempt to organize their affairs at some distance from the domination of multinational capitalism, a space which has now largely vanished. For the oppressed in the third world, the passing away of the Soviet Union is not so much of a model – mistakenly held and now generally discarded – as of an ally and a support. And with it has gone, despite grave distortions in the ex-Soviet Union itself, a legacy of cultural autonomy which the commonsense of Marxism, in its most diverse forms, deposited in the world, much more widely and deeply than is generally recognised.

Of course, as I have argued elsewhere, the collapse of the Soviet Union is not without its positive side insofar as the Soviet policies were in many ways an obstacle to the development of the revolutionary process in the third world. Other aspects including the precedence given to pursuit of 'national interests' apart, the Soviet policy had been for long, to put it mildly, most ambiguous in its opposition to imperialism, from the 'peaceful coexistence' era of Khrushchev to Gorbachev's 'new thinking', not to mention Comintern's opposition to national liberation struggles in Allied colonies during the Second World War. And its policies quite often provided political support and ideological legitimacy to the emergent ruling classes in the post-colonial third world, directly as well as through its control over the official communist parties. Now some of these political-ideological handicaps will be no more. There is no Soviet Union any more to mislead the socialist formations in the third world or subordinate them to its foreign policy requirements in the name of a spurious internationalism. Henceforth they are on their own, very much free to find answers to the problems confronting them in a world of almost unchecked capitalist domination. Nor can the post-colonial rulers in the third world countries, such as India, any longer put up the facade of anti-imperialism and deceive the people as they once could, thanks to their close economic, political and diplomatic relations with the Soviet Union and Left's obsession with the centrality of the contradictions between 'capitalist' and 'socialist' worlds. Furthermore, as these ruling classes, having lost their ability to manoeuvre between the blocs, succumb to global capitalism and 'secede' from their people, this will clarify as nothing else could, the real issues of economy and politics in the third world countries. Class issues will stand out clearly, opening up spaces for more open class struggles. A class-based people's politics will not only become more necessary but also more possible.

However, these advantages notwithstanding, the overriding fact is that the collapse in the East has left the third world, so to speak, without any place of refuge. The third world finds itself completely isolated, with no second world that it could in any manner ally itself with – the latter itself has been for the most part reduced to a third world status. To the extent there are still remnants of the second world, most of them have abandoned any solidarity with the third world and are happy to join with the first world against it. The capitalism of the 1950s and 1960s was, as we have seen, in its own way concerned with the development of third world countries, above all, to forestall the attractions of socialism and the rise of alternative political movements. But now that there is no fear of alternatives, capitalism can be as unbridled and rapacious as it chooses to be. As it was, it never had any interest in seeing the third world industrialise; it was not willing to accept anything of the sort, wanted no new rivals to emerge in the dog-eat-dog world market. On the contrary, all steps in this direction were systematically blocked. Notwithstanding the fact that a few small countries did somehow succeed in developing through industrialisation, the overall tendency has been for stagnation or decline in the third world economies that developed from the fifties through the seventies, and even the successful ones are no longer the 'tigers' they were. Now, itself in deep crisis, capitalism is more rapacious than ever before, imposing on the third world countries a model of development which not only erodes the strengths, capabilities and skills they had built up over previous decades and makes for more effective transfer of resources from the periphery to the metropolis, but also ensures their under-or-dependent development by tying them in a certain kind of subaltern integration to the power of finance capital, to the trading policies imposed by dominant states, and above all to the type of technological development and consumption which multinational capital, and the market regulated by it, impose 'with a coercive power greater than that of any gunboat in the past.'

That this only perpetuates the centre-periphery polarisation, which has been endemic to capitalism in course of its worldwide expansion and is impossible to overcome within the framework of capitalism, we have noticed before. But what also needs to be specifically recognised about imperialism of the period of late capitalism is that its core-periphery or prosperity-poverty dualism is a growing polarisation not just between but through and across countries. The international polarisation inherent in capitalist expansion has in turn brought about a manifold internal polarisation in the countries of the third world. Income disparities between nations come to be superimposed on and sustained by extremely wide income disparities between social-income groups within nations of the third world. The integration of their economic structures into global capitalism (subsidiaries, joint ventures, junior partnerships, trade relations, etc.) reshapes the class structure within each of these nations and polarises it still more. The third world comes to have its 'first world enclaves', a class of the very rich in the third world who indeed become an integral part of the first world, standing distinct from and confronting the class below, the vast majority of their own countrymen. It is once again wealth and affluence at one end and poverty and immiseration at the other. The luxurious prosperity of the few at the top is accompanied by the marginalisation of the vast masses below, so much so that the essential reserve army of capitalism is now to be found at the periphery of the system. It has been calculated that in most third world countries, approximately 60 per cent of national income is concentrated in the upper 20 per cent of the population. In many low and middle income 'developing' countries, 70 per cent of rural households have a per capita income which is between 10 and 20 per cent of the national average. What was once referred to as the 'two-thirds society' (one-third prospering, one-third coping, one-third abandoned) of a single nation, for example, Britain or the US, becomes more and more the characterisation of the global system as a whole, except that the proportions are reversed with one-third increasingly incorporated into the world market and two-thirds expelled from its 'benefits' and abandoned; the majority in the third world pays the price for the admission of its rich into the first world.

This increasing concentration of income and wealth, in the advanced capitalist countries and the third world, has naturally led to the dynamic growth of the luxury goods economy, (which, incidentally, also serves to provide a temporary 'breathing-space' to a global economy beset with endemic recession). The global productive system is increasingly geared, rather misdirected, towards servicing the rich, supplying an overall limited market, that is, the consumer markets in developed countries and small pockets of luxury consumption in the so-called 'developing' countries – though such 'first-world enclaves' in the third world can be sometime relatively quite large, as in India. A duality of consumption on a world scale has emerged where the third world elites too share in its luxury consumption and thus are both protagonists and beneficiaries of this process.

This internal polarisation has generated strong tendencies towards subaltern integration of the ruling classes of the third world countries, even of their more progressive sections, into the global capitalist system, tendencies which have been reinforced by an offensive from the capitalist camp when, after an initial period of post-war prosperity, the world economy slid into crisis in the mid 1970s and the third world countries were faced with harsher demands of the transnationalisation process, which sought to turn their state machineries into simple transmission belts for the global economy and erect, over the grave of the aborted bourgeois-national project, a subaltern comprador state. There has been opposition and resistance but only with marginal success. In places this resistance has expressed itself in such phenomena as cultural nationalism, nationalist adventurism or religious fundamentalism (as, for example, in the Arab world), some of them well feeding into the emerging concepts of 'irrational regimes', 'rogue state', 'clash of civilisations', etc. in the literature of imperialism. But by and large the third world ruling classes, especially after the Soviet collapse, have responded with a strong tendency of their own to succumb to the demands of global capitalism.

The collapse of Soviet Union, a gain for the ruling classes everywhere, has also been, in its own way, a gain for the ruling elites in the third world in that 'socialism' is now, as it were, a dirty, defeated word, especially with the middle classes and intelligentsia, even its once radical sections (though, one must add, not with the common people), and right wing politics of diverse hues has attained a certain ascendancy for the time being. But, as we have noticed earlier, they have lost a great deal too and not only in terms of economic or trade relations with the Soviet bloc countries. The Soviet Union had long lost interest in world revolution and ceased to be any kind of revolutionary threat, but so long as it survived as a world power, even as it provided check of sorts to specific instances of imperialist politico-military expansion in the third world – with greater success in Africa and Asia than in Latin-America – its existence as a pole of global opposition to Western dominance enlarged the space in which third world ruling elites, especially the 'bourgeois nationalist' segments among them, could feel and act with greater self-confidence and independence than otherwise. They were able to engage in a balancing act between the United States and the Soviet Union to exact advantages from the rivalry of the two 'super powers', manoeuvre between them, with some success at least, to pursue their countries' national interests as they perceived them, and thereby also enhance their own 'national-patriotic' character and, duly certified by the Soviet Union, keep up the facade of anti-imperialism with the people. More than any economic or material loss, the dissolution of the Soviet bloc has meant the elimination of this space and loss of the manoeuvrability that went with it, which has left them weakened and more vulnerable to the pressures and demands of the dominant global capitalism. The globalisation underway throughout this period, with the expanded reproduction of even the better industrialised third world countries increasingly tied to the reproduction process of foreign capital, had already much undermined whatever resistance the ruling elites of the third world were ever capable of. With the Soviet collapse, and pressure mounting, they have increasingly accepted the hegemonic role of the West and adapted their economic and social policies to it, that is, given in to global capitalism, opted for the IMF guided Latin American route to subalternism. Given their class interests, the price for not doing so is beyond their capacity and their will. Even in India which, with its large size, vast human and material resources, a strong and diversified industrial base, a large skilled workforce and industrial, technological and managerial manpower, had the capacity and the opportunity to sustain a significant degree of economic autonomy, Nehru-style nationalist ideology has been worn away by comprador ambitions, and notwithstanding fears or complaints about the incoming multinationals – their 'cow boy' or 'one-way approach', 'merely one-night stands', or 'British Raj (back) in the guise of multinationals', etc. – or hiccups over 'level playing field' and 'nationalist' noise of 'swadeshi' and 'cultural nationalism', the ruling elites have, with the overall backing of India's big business, and through their main political parties, finally succumbed.

This is how the evolving pattern of the relationship between metropolitan bourgeois fractions and third world bourgeois fractions is increasingly coming to range from direct subordination to varying degrees of partnership and 'collaboration'. It needs to be noted that notions of neo-colonialism or semi-colonialism, born of an earlier old-style globalisation, simply do no justice to the new and radically different complexity of this emerging situation in the capitalist world. The significant point is that the ruling classes in the post-colonial states, the national bourgeoisie or the corresponding ruling elites of the third world who had once co-opted national liberation to their own advantage, have already become or are rapidly becoming compradors, under the laws of evolution of the world capitalist system. They are therefore incapable of mediating the new worldwide phenomena to the advantage of their own countries. It is simply impermissible to overrate the anti-imperialist urges of the under-developed bourgeoisie. On the contrary, the growing compradorisation of the privileged classes, the ruling elites of the third world, is the decisive fact to be recognised today. They benefit from the global capitalist expansion, its international polarisation, even if as junior partners. Even as they are in control of the state power in their countries, they are the transmitters of the dependency interconnections or subalternism in the third world, making its people the worst victims of global capitalism. It is erroneous to think that they are in anyway confused or uncertain about the class significance of the ongoing globalisation, either helpless in standing up against it – 'there is no alternative' – or expecting only diffuse and distant gains. On the contrary, the practical unanimity among its advocates and 'a species of aggressiveness' that has come to characterise their proceedings betokens their recognition of globalisation and its 'reform process' as a class issue – whoever does not believe in or questions 'the reforms' deserves to be cast out, ridiculed, denied space in the media. Globalisation is not just a 'development strategy' to facilitate economic progress in the third world, it is a class interests-dictated struggle that local ruling classes or national bourgeoisies in the third world, facing a crisis or collapse of their projects of 'national development', have opted for; it is their strategic option for the future, which has all the elements of a class war against their own peoples. Harvard economist Robert Reich, a liberal, has written of 'secession of the successful', a phrase that is vividly expressive of the structural logic of all capitalism. Globalisation as a strategy, the 'dualism' inexorably involved in the current integration into the capitalist world market, means that 'the successful' of the third world have decided to 'secede' from their not 'successful' peoples. And this is not a 'secession' only in strictly economic terms, it is equally visible in the dramatically changed values and concerns, and consumerism, of the seceding elites, in their changed lifestyles so obviously imitative of those in the affluent west or their images seen on the ubiquitous TV and the coloured supplements of print media, all of which contrasts so sharply with the drab lives of their poor countrymen and their daily concern for sheer physical survival; in other words, it is a 'secession of the mind' and of 'culture' as well. And herein lies the essence of the current impasse in the third world, where instead of the currently fashionable 'a little more or little less of globalisation', the need is for people to come up with a counter strategic option of their own.

XXIX

The third world countries are today indeed in an objective impasse, trapped as it were by capitalist globalisation, the failure of national bourgeois projects and compradorisation of the local ruling classes, and a general exhaustion of the momentum of national liberation movements. The post-colonial bourgeoisie or ruling elites have simply failed to deliver on the promises made and the hopes roused on the morrow of national independence. The impasse was inherent in the way decolonisation occurred and the class or classes it put in power in most countries of the third world, but it was not even visualised as a possibility as, with 'development' or 'non-capitalist path of development' as the new buzzwords, these countries went on to realise the limited potentialities of their 'national development'. These potentialities were not inconsiderable in some cases, and the Soviet Union continued to provide not only inspiration but ideological, military and economic support – primarily for pre-emptive or defensive reasons – for a seemingly possible state-supported alternative road to economic and social development. Even so the overall character and limits of this third world developmentalism were shaped by the needs of global capitalism's accumulation process in a situation overdetermined by the cold war and growing competition between Soviet-style socialism and capitalism. In its ultimate outcome, whatever development occurred only produced, at best, third wordlist capitalisms and helped reproduce the unequal division of labour between the centre and periphery. This post-war national development, under essentially bourgeois auspices, has now virtually collapsed in a peripheral accumulation impasse, debt crisis and intensified economic retrenchment under IMF-World Bank 'adjustment' policies. This collapse, the failure of post-war capitalist developmentalism in the third world has an obvious implication for the future of these countries. The double dialectic of centre-periphery and development-underdevelopment and the accompanying polarisation between and through and across countries, characteristic of capitalism as a world system, leads inexorably to the conclusion that the day of the 'bourgeois revolution' or any strictly national variant of it, is past and that now only proletarian-peasant revolution, with the strategic goal of socialism, can bring genuine liberation to the peoples of the third world. Only, this revolution cannot and must not be viewed in traditional terms, it has to be rethought in the light of the constraints of general development and in terms of the radically different social reality and possibilities of our time. The collapse in the Soviet Union is an important historical experience; without too much distortion, it could even be interpreted as the failure of socialism reduced to just another variant of economic developmentalism. But rethinking about socialist revolution (in the Soviet Union itself and elsewhere in the world) had become imperative even without it. Needless to add, this rethinking, even as it has its international dimension, has to necessarily relate itself to the specific situation in each country, in the third world as anywhere else.

XXX

The current impasse in the third world is manifest in its social unrest and political instability, conflicts, confrontations and upheavals of all kinds. Underlying it all is an undeniable pressure for change. The people are however confused and indecisive, generally unable to respond to the situation in any adequate or constructive manner. Given the inadequacies and deficiencies of social consciousness, this pressure, potentially radicalising, often finds actual expression in all sort of reactionary developments – racism, national chauvinism and Xenophobia, obscurantist traditionalism, religious revivalism and fundamentalism, etc., which rapidly drift into a variety of internecine conflicts, even international wars. This is not to deny that a phenomenon like religious fundamentalism, for example, its overall reactionary nature notwithstanding, may at times have a certain legitimacy for its popular anti-consumerist, even anti-imperialist thrust, a conscious reaction to the economic, especially moral-cultural fallout of globalisation. But even in the exceptional situations where it has triumphed politically, as in some so-called Islamic countries, religious fundamentalism has soon found its positive claims literally wither away.

However effective a force for protest and challenge or solace in troubled times, it has nowhere been able to translate its vision into a coherent or credible economic and political programme and has invariably failed to deliver on its promise of either providing an alternative model of economic development, different from and superior to that of 'the west' it denounces, or improving people's quality of life. Even at its best, it remains more an expression of people's problems than the means to their solution. There is no future for the peoples of the third world here, in religious fundamentalisms, or anti-diluvian nationalisms, traditionalisms or revivalisms, religious or any other. Arising on a real social material basis, all such ideological phenomena are really symptoms of the crisis and never even a remotely adequate response to its challenges. They do not constitute any kind of revolutionary threat or genuine alternative to the established social order, and often end up serving the petty diversionary needs of politics of the ruling classes – *la politique politicienne* (politician's politics) Malraux had called it – which feeds on such reactionary drifts and the conflicts they engender and often becomes quite deadly for the common people. When on the defensive, or facing a crisis, the ruling classes even deliberately turn the peoples energies in these directions, allowing or encouraging low intensity conflicts but suppressing them when necessary. All this may well be the hard school of experience (of being involved in wrong battles) that people have to go through before they find their way to fight right battles of their own.

But the social reality of the third world is not exhausted by these negative phenomena. It holds the promise of other possibilities too. The same structural conditions of poverty and underdevelopment, the overall objective situation of the people of the third world, which gave birth to more or less successful revolutionary struggles of the past, continues to do so in the present too. If the collapse of the degenerated 'actually existing socialism' has produced a political and ideological assault from the right, the complete and obvious failure of capitalism in the third world continues to offer the conditions for a rallying of the forces of the left, of revolutionary thought and action in

Asia, Africa and Latin America. Revolutionary struggles therefore, far from being a matter of the past will still be a part of the future of these countries, regardless of the collapse in Soviet Union. The peoples of the third world have a future only with such struggles.

These revolutionary struggles, facing a 'challenge of historic proportions', will of course each have a different historically specific form in different third world countries. But to be able to face it effectively, and provide a genuine alternative to people, they will all share a common 'historic vision', which can only be socialism. These struggles, as they are already coming up, confront not only world capitalism, its 'globalisation' and 'adjustment' programmes, but their own bourgeoisies or ruling classes seeking a capitalist development open to the world system, which is only another form of oppression for the people. The people need to escape from the vicious circle of the global market, and their adversaries are the ruling elites of their own country as much as the globally dominant capitalist classes, of which these elites are now but a part or expression. Their strategic orientation therefore has to be the reversal of the current tendencies, the outright rejection of bourgeois subalternism, the substitution of popular control, national or regional, for the bourgeois vision of exclusive control by the market. They have to make a choice between the accumulation of 'national' and individual wealth and the search for the welfare of the people, which demands the subordination of external relations to the needs or constraints of a pro-people internal development, not adjusting the internal development to external imperatives, the global expansion of capitalism. If the privileged position of the centre in the global polarization has postponed the question of the eventual socialist transformation in the developed capitalist societies, it demands in the underdeveloped periphery an objective envisaging of a 'different development' from the one that would result from its integration into the world capitalist system, a 'doing of something new' as against the old 'catching up at any price'. And this 'different' or 'new' development can only be a revolutionary project, both democratic and socialist. Revolutionary, because liberalism and reformism remain inadequate for the purpose; and democratic and socialist, not only because one can't really *be* one without the other, but also because of the kind of systemic opposition it seeks to overcome. As the Workers Party of Brazil has put it in its basic document, this project – an anti-capitalist socio-economic transformation – is 'the political expression of all those exploited by the capitalistic system', and: 'Our basic commitment to democracy also makes us anti-capitalist, in the same way that our choice of anti-capitalism unequivocally determines our struggle for democracy'. It cannot be a bourgeois or a national or a national-popular project in the strict sense of the terms.

As we have already noticed, such a socialist project, a breaking away from capitalism will, for a long time to come, take place within the framework of a national state. The needed reversal of the ongoing liberalisation has to necessarily begin at the national level, within the existing class structure, and the nation-state remains the most viable site or terrain of struggle to win political power without which no such reversal or breaking away from capitalism is possible. The revolutionary regime may also legitimately claim to speak for the country or nation as a whole – and in *that* sense *all* the people – against the discredited or 'seceding' post-colonial bourgeois regimes. But for all this, the project or struggle involved will not be national in its essential character. With the national independence won, the language of national liberation movements has steadily lost its relevance and the movements themselves their radical momentum, and the new rulers, gone comprador, have abandoned the once cherished ideals of 'self reliance' as notions which are old, 'autarkic', out of tune with the times. The 'romance of the national bourgeoisie' is indeed long over. The processes of globalisation underway are shifting the balance of class power still further away from the popular classes and towards the locally dominant elites. They bring new economic and political windfall gains to the local upper classes and inflict equally new economic and social damage upon ordinary people. Notwithstanding efforts to mitigate hardships of the poor – via an assortment of poverty alleviation or basic needs programmes, public distribution systems, employment-guarantee or food for work schemes, etc. – globalisation is daily further sharpening the existing dualism in society. As a consequence the social base for 'nationally'-based revolutionary projects can now less than ever count on the support of any politically significant 'nationalist' segment of the ruling classes or sections allied with them. In fact any popular democratic struggle seeking empowerment of the people for the alternative path of pro-people autonomous development, will come into conflict with the classes now wielding political power in the post-colonial state and necessarily become the locus of an objective class, and not national, conflict. For this reason any such struggle can no longer be viewed in simple nationalist terms or do without the *strategic* goal of socialism.

XXXI

The post-colonial national project may have collapsed and, in terms of their objective interests, the paths of the ruling elites and the people may have diverged as never before, *nationalism* yet remains a very strong sentiment among the people in the post-colonial third world. Many of those on the Left who would otherwise agree with the above argument, may yet prefer to see the ongoing or coming struggles in the third world as national struggles, a continuation, as it were, of the earlier national struggle for freedom, which have no doubt failed to deliver but pursued better may do so in future. Specificities of conditions in different countries apart, this persistence of nationalist thinking on the left about politics in the third world, its present and future prospects, is partly explained by the fact that liberation movements in the third world came up as national movements and their anti-imperialist character had great revolutionary potential which, incidentally, Lenin was among the first to recognise when he saw these national liberation movements as allies of the world socialist revolution. Socialist movements in the third world often arose as a part of these liberation struggles and at times it is their socialist leadership which led them in a successful overthrow of the old colonial order. It is therefore not difficult to understand that, however mistakenly, the lone fact of decolonisation came to be seen, for the third world, as the kernel of the revolutionary process, while the class projects of the post-colonial regimes seemed to matter less and less. Next logical step, not difficult to take, was to see nationalism itself not only as the determinate answer to colonialism and imperialism, but also the ideology to inspire and lead future progress in the post-colonial third world countries. Soviet Union made its own contribution to ideological confusion and political disorientation here by the way it interpreted the opportunities opened up by its aid to many non-revolutionary, but nonetheless non comprador national-developmentalist regimes in the third world. In a parody of Marxism, it came up with the concept of a 'non-capitalist road' to development in a third world country on its way to socialism; it was an essentially bourgeois vision which dignified state-capitalist development and legitimised attempts by leftists to cooperate with the nationalist and developmentalist factions of the third world bourgeoisie in the name of Marxism. One result, which in turn facilitated all this, was the internalisation of a *nationalist*, as against a *Marxist*, perspective by many, rather most sections of the left in the third world, including its communist parties, often with disastrous consequences.

Be that as it may, many on the Left continue to speak of the ongoing and coming struggles in the third world in nationalist terms – the language is replete with phrases like 'independent' or 'autonomous national development', 'popular, national and democratic' development, 'national economic reconstruction', 'national compact', 'the national banner', 'anti-imperialist nationalism in a world dominated by imperialism', etc., and above all, the increasingly fashionable 'national popular' – a concept which originated with Gramsci as part of his perspective for a socialist revolution in Italy involving an alliance between the working class and the peasantry, but now more associated with Samir Amin's perspective on peoples' (and not class-specific or socialist) revolutions of the periphery: third world peoples' 'national protection and self assertion' against capitalist development which they find intolerable. It seem to me that such conceptualisation tends to ignore or obscure the facts that nations in the third world are today internally more or less sharply class-divided societies, that imperialism now comes into the third world by the grace of, through the opportunities provided by, or at the invitation of the post-colonial ruling classes, that 'nationalism', regardless of its other aspects or potentialities, is today a potent ideological weapon in the hands of these ruling classes to obscure social reality, mobilise people behind *their* politics and thus defend or promote their own class interests. This, I think, allows of a brief additional comment.

'Nation', notwithstanding immense amount of scholarship expended on the subject, remains 'an ambiguous identity', and equally ambiguous remains the associated phenomenon of 'nationalism'. However, it is not what nationalist ideologues tend to believe, even if they are not always explicit about it: some kind of supra-historical force, a Hegelian absolute, as it were, at work in history, free of, or in any case superior to, all class or historical limitations, moving inevitably to a pre-destined end, the pride and glory of a self-realised nationhood in a nation state. On the contrary, we do know that it is particular objective conditions or historical developments (economic, political, cultural and still other) which combine to constitute and shape such or similar subjective identities as meaningful in society, making them terms for individual self-definition or identification, and diffusing them across population sufficiently to turn them into objective social components of society which react back to themselves affect social conditions or historical developments – the subjective identities coming to play an objective role, for better or worse, in social and historical processes. For the purpose of my immediate argument, we need to recognise only this indisputable fact: a most powerful social, political and ideological force of our times, nationalism is yet a historical phenomenon, with class and society-specific character, potentialities and limitations, and uses, and thus capable of manifesting itself in a variety of forms, including as a liberationist force or ideology it has been in the anti-imperialist liberation struggles of the third world. But we also know of imperialism itself, that is, imperialist ruling classes finding nationalism useful not only to consolidate their rule at home but also to defend and justify their aggression and domination abroad. We have in our time also witnessed nationalism of German, Japanese and Italian varieties which so obviously sacrificed people to the 'nation'. In fact, with the ruling classes, in the normal pursuit of their interests or when faced with situations of crisis in the polity, nationalism has often taken all sorts of anti-people statist, racist, or imperialist forms, providing ideological support or cover to the emergence of reactionary authoritarian regimes. Nationalism therefore is not *ipso facto* a radical or progressive phenomenon. It was radical or progressive, even revolutionary – depending upon class leadership and programme – in the liberation struggles of the third world because it sought to resolve the basic structural contradictions of colonial society, congealed in imperialism, whose resolution, *against* imperialism, alone could clear the path for people's continuing struggle for a better life. But now that what has been built, or got built, post-independence are class-divided, unjust and iniquitous societies and basic structural contradictions are class contradictions *within*, whose resolution, *against* the local ruling classes or elites, alone clears the path for a pro-people economic and social development, nationalism not only does not recognise and cannot resolve these contradictions, but may well help obscure them in the interest of the new ruling classes or elites. 'An ambiguous identity', even 'an imagined community' as a scholar has called it, 'nation' (or nationalism born of it) is nevertheless real enough to inspire or persuade individuals to die for it or in its name. But this 'abstraction' is also capable of serving as an ideological device to deny or disguise, to disaggregate and delegitimise, at least depoliticise, other daily experienced identities and solidarities in society, most importantly its basic class identities and solidarities. Not only that. In a society torn with extremes of socio-economic inequality and conflicting class interests, to postulate 'common national interests', a 'national good' shared by all citizens is surely a most tenuously abstract and deceptive notion. Nationalism, therefore, can well serve to obscure or conceal the essential character of social reality in a post-colonial society, its class divisions, exploitations and oppressions, its 'two nations' and 'internal colonialism', the entire morass of crooked dealings, profit gorging and deceptions, plunder of national resources and indifference to popular welfare, to say nothing of the tragedies the ruling class politics inflicts on the people in the name of nationalism, 'national unity and integrity' etc. Nationalism can be used to cover up, or provide alibis for the historic default of the post-colonial ruling classes and help them divert people from their own, more basic concerns, and mobilise them behind ruling class politics. In other words, nationalism can easily get reduced to a legitimising ideology for the post-colonial ruling classes, used by them to defend and promote their interests and safeguard their economic and political domination in society – dissent can be silenced as 'unpatriotic', and all challenge from below dubbed 'anti-national'. It only needs to be added that this has indeed happened again and again in the third world. The Right, here as elsewhere, in power or out of it, has always claimed and monopolised nationalism as its own and manipulated it well for their purposes. Paralleling their use elsewhere in the capitalist world, 'nation', 'nationalism', 'national interest', 'national unity', 'patriotism', etc. have been a part of the rhetoric of right-wing politics in the post colonial third world.

A questioning of what is third world Left's essentially ahistorical nationalist perspective on third world politics is important because, blurring the distinction between bourgeois and socialist politics, nationalism has disarmed the Left ideologically and disoriented it theoretically, depriving it of the 'independent political position', which Marx always emphasised and Lenin repeatedly endorsed as absolutely necessary in practicing revolutionary politics. It was not for nothing that Marx had spoken of 'opium of patriotic feelings' or Lenin wrote of bourgeoisie's 'striving to fortify nationalism', which the ruling classes find useful for their purposes, especially in troubled times. The overall consequence of internalisation of a nationalist perspective on the Left is that it has been by and large content with operating on the terrain of bourgeois politics, responding to the issues it presents, accepting the choices it officers, and succumbing to the corruption of consciousness all this involves, in the process not only getting marginalised again and again but also losing its character, the revolutionary commitment and élan that defines it as Left.

Possibly the most serious theoretical disorientation has been to see socialism itself as an adjunct of national aspirations. Put simply, Left argument or critique has been that it is not through capitalism but through socialism that 'national development' can be realised, and the current crisis is viewed – when the Left is willing to view it in these and not conventional nationalist terms – as evidence of capitalism's failure to do so. This obviously leaves socialism very much an utopian affair. In a Marxist perspective socialism is born of the irrationality and contradictions of capitalism; it is not just another 'version' of a good society, in the third world or anywhere else. Therefore the need is to analyse the irrationality and contradictions of capitalism – in this case, of peripheral or semi-peripheral, 'third-worldist' capitalism as a part of global capitalism, its historically specific form in each country – which generate the conditions and forces for socialist politics. A nationalist perspective which does not recognise or obscures this need, which is unwilling or unable to concretely analyse the contradictions of these historically specific forms of capitalism, to locate in each case its main or worst victims, who, having gained the requisite revolutionary consciousness – 'won the theoretical awareness of their loss' as Marx put it – shall be the driving social force of a socialism-oriented struggle, and to develop appropriate programme, politics and organisation for this purpose, such a perspective cannot provide for socialism as a historically viable project to struggle for. It only reduces socialism to 'a vision'...

To put the argument more positively, the struggle for socialism in the third world, in more precise historical and theoretical terms, for *a society in transition to socialism*, is a process of class struggle in the proper Marxist sense which eschews its narrow economistic or reductionist interpretations. No doubt a great deal of tactical resilience is necessary in relating this class struggle, theoretically and practically, to the obviously important issue of nationalism. But even if this struggle is viewed as a *national* struggle – 'national-popular' or any other variant – it cannot but be fighting the 'anti-nation within the nation', or 'rescuing the nation' from its ruling classes, or, as Marx would put it, the people 'constituting itself *the* nation'. In other words, people's struggle for a better life now cannot ignore or bypass the question of fighting the locally dominant and exploiting classes in possession of state power in society. It is not a collective struggle of *all* the people, for a *common* good, as *substantially* the national struggle for freedom was. It is above all a struggle for political power, to win it from own ruling classes and for purposes entirely opposite theirs. That is how the national task, recovering the country for its people, remains a class task of the people, of people acting as 'nation class' if you like, to borrow a description from the Guinean Marxist revolutionary, Cabral. At the very least, genuine nationalists must understand that their country's future is tied to the future of socialism in their country.

XXXII

The failure of socialism in the Soviet Union is an important historical experience. But this only calls for an indispensable self-critical attitude towards it and not an abandonment of socialism. This failure in a way also reflects a certain success and continuing strength of capitalism. But this is not to say that nothing could have been done differently. It may be that the conditions that once enabled some third world countries to choose a socialist strategy and break away from capitalism no longer exist. But then those that forced them to do so are stronger than ever. The current situation of socialism in the third world may be bleak, the obstacles indeed too many and enormous. But the choice for these countries is no longer socialist development or capitalist development. It is socialist independence (or independence with an advance towards socialism) or capitalist peripheralisation. It is this which makes socialism the only possible alternative in the third world countries. This is not a plea for voluntarism. This choice, seemingly impossible, is yet grounded in a historically objective situation, where the possibility of a decent, humane existence for all is real enough and achievable, the possibility of climbing up into the first world or escaping ultimate peripheralisation nil. This is one reason – and there are other reasons too as we shall see – why, despite the Soviet collapse and the crisis of socialism elsewhere, the struggle for socialism in the third world will go on. I will only add that while using the resources of every emancipatory tradition within and without, this struggle must necessarily link itself to the multi-hued socialist tradition, above all the tradition of revolutionary Marxism, and recover for itself the heroic legacy of the world communist movement.

XXXIII

The struggle for socialist transformation in the third world will take diverse forms, adapting the revolutionary process to the specific politico-economic and social context of individual countries, basing itself on a self-critical cold analysis of the objective situation in each case. The enemies this struggle faces are the repressive ruling forces in what is, in however qualified a manner, an unipolar politico-economic world order. These are the ruling classes at home and a dominant imperialism abroad, led by the United States, increasingly the gendarme of the world counter-revolution. But this imperialism remains beset with recurrent economic crises within and because of inter-imperialist rivalries, despite the current American domination, a profound crisis of leadership abroad. What is more, the very undeterred domination of global capitalism will reveal its essential class-exploitative character all the more clearly. With the Soviet Union gone – whose existence, its positive role apart, introduced so many ambiguities into the situation and fed into that most disorienting 'black hole effect' of 'anti-communism' we have noticed earlier – the class realities will stand clarified everywhere, confirming and deepening the revolutionary sentiment, and class struggles will explode as never before, not the least in the third world where the worst victims of capitalist exploitation and oppression will now more freely confront their increasingly compradorised ruling classes. There are those who believe, as for example Tariq Ali and his ilk do, 'the game is up' for the Left, for 'four or five decades'. But the oppressed and exploited majority of humankind cannot wait fifty years. They have to fight back or go under now. The repressive ruling forces everywhere are indeed going to be most ruthless. But history has its surprises and revolutions by the oppressed are among the most surprising of these surprises of history. The revolutionary process will go on.

Apropos this revolutionary process, I would like to make two immediately relevant and closely inter-related points concerning the theory and agency of this process in the third world. In the first place, as Lenin had emphasised: 'without revolutionary theory there can be no revolutionary movement'. I have argued earlier how Marxism retains its validity, all the more with the renewed global domination of capitalism, as *the* theory of struggle for human emancipation in our time. Marxism is even more pre-eminently valid as the theory of emancipatory struggles in the third world where live the worst victims of global capitalism, the huge mass of the poor and oppressed who have, as *Communist Manifesto* put it, nothing to lose but their chains but have a world to win.

True, Marxism, as a totally new body of ideas for understanding and changing the world grew out of the proletarian experience in the west, expressive, above all, of the revolutionary interests of the proletariat; and it remained very much a western-centred movement in the period between Marx's death and the Russian Revolution, a fact which reflected the economic and even more the political realities of the time. But Marx and Engels were not proletarians, and having once come into being, Marxism is in no sense the exclusive property of the proletariat or a western phenomenon. Like science and knowledge generally, it is a part f the hertage of humankind, and certainly available for appropriation by non-proletarians whose interests are, quintessentially, the same as those of the proletariat everywhere, especially by the real successors of the proletariat of Marx's time, Fanon's 'wretched of the earth' – the mass of peasants, the rural and urban poor, the unemployed and slum-dwellers who make up the vast majority of the population of the third world today. No wonder that after the October Revolution, as Lenin alone among the great Marxist thinkers of that generation sensed, Marxism increasingly overflowed its European boundaries and reached out to Asia,

Latin America and Africa, to become the revolutionary outlook of the most exploited workers and peasants on a world scale. And so it remains, despite the Soviet collapse, the key to their emancipation.

Along with theory, a central question for any strategy of socialist revolution is the question of agency, through which theory becomes a material force for revolution. In other words, who are the actors who will most vigorously and effectively resist capitalism and construct socialism? I have touched upon this subject earlier and shall have more to say on it towards the end of these notes. Here a brief reference of a specific nature will suffice.

Classical Marxism, as we have seen, located these actors in the industrial proletariat, at the time the worst victims of capitalism, who, winning 'the theoretical awareness of their loss', in an alliance with the mass of peasantry and revolutionary intelligentsia – who even as they feel the oppressions of capitalism have, as Marx put it, 'raised themselves to the level of comprehending theoretically the historical movement as a whole' – shall be the social driving force of a socialist revolution. This political position, its emphasis on the role of the industrial proletariat – which is so obviously historically conditioned – is yet no argument for this proletariat as an 'all exclusive' agency of socialist revolution it has been often interpreted to be. Defended or criticised as a dogma, that was never any part of revolutionary Marxism. To recognise this one has only to explore the obvious implications of Marx's analysis of the failures of 1848 and the prospects of a future revolution in Europe, his comments on the Paris Commune, his highly suggestive insights into the possibility of socialist revolution in backward countries, even of a transition to socialism in Russia without passing though any capitalist 'stage', etc. etc. – matters referred to elsewhere in these notes. In the *Communist Manifesto* itself, where the proletarian emphasis is most explicit, Marx wrote of 'a portion of the bourgeoisie.... and in particular, a portion of bourgeois ideologists (going) over to the proletariat', of 'the lower middle class, the small manufacturer, the shopkeeper, the artisan, the peasant' deserting 'their own stand point to place themselves at that of the proletariat', etc. – the detail is not important but all this is more than merely suggestive of the inbuilt resilience in Marx's political position.

A shift away from any dogmatism in the matter is clearly there in Lenin's theory and practice, his understanding of history as a confluence of class and popular struggles arising out of 'exploitation' (of workers) and 'oppression' (of peoples), his view of national liberation movements as potential allies of the world socialist revolution, his regular use of a category like '*oppressed peoples* of the world', and more specifically, his later writings such as 'Advanced Asia, Backward Europe', etc. The shift is bolder in Mao's differentiation between the leading force (the proletariat), and the main force (the peasantry) and his ever present emphasis on the role of 'the people' or 'the masses' in the revolutionary process. Cabral in Guinea even spoke of a 'nation class' in his argument for a successful revolution in the third world. Castro was to put it all rather bluntly: 'who will make the revolution? The people with or without the Communist parties...'; the rhetorical reference to 'communist parties' is not to be literally interpreted, it is more a pointer to the *real* issue, whether the leadership involved is *indeed*, and not merely in name or by self-definition, 'communist' – correct revolutionary political leadership has been always a central concern for Castro, as for all Marxist revolutionaries. Apart from all this, Marx's socialism was never a narrowly conceived class project, of or for a class only, it was visualised as 'a movement of the immense majority in the interest of immense majority' (*Communist Manifesto*), or as Kautsky, one of the more dogmatic of the traditional Marxists put it: 'Socialism as such is not our goal which is rather the abolition of every kind of exploitation or oppression'. This obviously implies a rather generous view of the agency of socialist revolution.

A recognition of the resilience of revolutionary Marxism in this regard, most important for forging the requisite class alliances, is however no denial of Marx's argument for locating the basic class forces of a socialist revolution. In line with the original Marxist argument, these forces or agents of socialism are today most heavily concentrated in the third world. It is here that, conditioning and sustaining all other oppressions, the capitalist world system is most oppressive, finding its worst victims in the peripheral workers and peasants, making them necessarily the largest 'material' force for a successful socialist revolution. It is they who have the most to win and the least to lose, and who, therefore, given the requisite organisation and revolutionary consciousness, – 'the theoretical awareness of their loss' in Marx's words – along with their allies, will move towards a socialist revolution. In view of its relatively weak numerical presence, the dominant role of the proletariat here is primarily ideological and political, providing the movement with essentially revolutionary attitudes and values and programmatic direction – on the assumption, of course, that it is now itself 'a class-for-itself', that is a revolutionary class.

To postulate a socialist or socialism-oriented revolution in the third world is no voluntarism and to postulate its agency the way it is suggested above is no substitutionism either. Only, the question of political-theoretical leadership of the revolution becomes particularly important in a situation without a majority or significant presence of working class with revolutionary socialist aims. Workers and peasants in the third world will only become a force for socialism if they meet with a political leadership that knows socialist theory and can present it to the people. Equipped with revolutionary socialist theory this leadership, including associated intellectuals, as noticed earlier, has the key task of instilling, as it were, 'a working class consciousness in a society without a working class', as Cabral once put it. The ordinary people, the poor workers and peasants who make up the principal 'material' force of the revolution, may be anti-imperialists but, without revolutionary ideology and leadership, they are not likely to become socialist revolutionaries.

The historical experience of major revolutions of the past in the semi-periphery and periphery of global capitalism, that is, in countries without a working class majority, despite their wide divergence – and none of them is to be taken as offering a rigid model – is quite suggestive. The agent of change was a conscious movement headed by a disciplined political party drawn from various oppressed classes and strata and guided by a clear Marxist understanding of capitalism in its local and global manifestations. And while the composition of the movement and the party naturally varied from one country and region to another (with the proletariat, peasantry, petty bourgeoisie, intelligentsia, students, etc. represented differently according to the history and degree of development of each society), the quality of political leadership was in each case of decisive importance. It does not need to be emphasised that as in the past, so it has to be in the future. The political leadership must be not only theoretically well-equipped, but also needs to be seasoned in struggle, closely integrated with the masses, have a good sense of history and a clear understanding of what must and can be done to achieve liberation from the shackles of capitalist and imperialist exploitation.

XXXIV

To speak of socialism in relation to the peripheral of semi-peripheral countries of the third world, even as it conveys a basic argument, does not mean there is a model of socialism available for them to implement and they can just go ahead and implement it. What lies immediately ahead of their peoples is, instead a long and difficult struggle for power in the state that can open the road to such a social transformation. No revolution in the past occurred according to a predetermined scheme, and revolutions of the future, more or less peaceful or violent, will be as full of surprises. Born in opposition to the cruellest manifestations of capitalism, these revolutions in the third world, necessarily, will also be anti-capitalist. However it is illusory to imagine that, given their poverty and underdevelopment, these countries can immediately afterwards go on to build an alternative socialist society.

Like making a revolution, building socialism too is a matter of both motivation and the opportunity that objective class situation and material conditions provide. The motivation will indeed be there in these countries, but the low level of productive forces will make it harder, though not entirely impossible, to establish socialist institutions. It is simply harder to share power and wealth when there is very little to share. It can, therefore, be legitimately argued that the relatively more developed countries of the semi-periphery provide better opportunity in terms of proletarian leadership of the necessary class alliances and material resources to not only make revolution but also build and protect socialist institutions, when political conditions for their emergence arise. In that sense the countries of the semi-periphery may well be a better terrain today for challenging capitalism and building socialism than the countries of either the centre or the periphery – they may indeed be the weakest link in the capitalist-imperialist world system. Even so, the necessary anti-capitalist revolution does not leave the third world countries in a position to build socialism straightaway – socialism as it has been visualised in the classical tradition. This is obviously impossible. Yet, as we have seen, they have no other choice – the common people in these countries have simply no future in capitalism, national or globalised.

Socialism of the early Marxian era degenerated into social democracy in the west. The Bolsheviks broke away from it, but their heroic effort, despite its early promise, too degenerated, this time into the grievously deformed 'Soviet socialism' which has recently collapsed into history. And now, the countries of the third world are called upon to continue the struggle, 'to do something new', as Lenin and his Bolsheviks once did, or rather tried to. Insofar as poverty, exploitation, oppression are not merely facts but relationships inherent in the class structures of peripheral or dependent capitalism – the poor are what they are because they are oppressed and exploited by other classes – this 'something' can only be the abolition of these relationships. Hence the choice:' socialism or peripheralisation'. This is not to posit socialism as achievable today or tomorrow, or even the day-after for that matter, but to posit it as people's strategic option as against the ruling classes' strategic option of globalisation, wherein socialism is the principle governing people's class-based politics, which links together their immediate, ongoing and emerging struggles in an ultimate project of revolutionary transformation of society, the goal of a long transitional process whose specifics and speed will depend upon the objective material conditions and the nature and balance of the class forces involved at each stage of the struggle for it. What is immediately posited is a socialism-oriented autonomous development. In other words, not prepared to build, the peoples of the third world must yet seek to build socialism, but this building must be viewed as both a beginning and a *transition* to socialism (or even a transition to this transition, if you like). More specifically, in as much as the fact of underdevelopment compels a transitional mixed economy, this is a situation in which forces or tendencies of socialism and capitalism will combine and conflict. In a society moving towards socialism, private property and the capitalist market, relations of production based on exploitation in a minority but far-from-negligible private sector, will for a long time continue to exist alongside a public sector which, genuinely and not merely juridically socialised, will have been freed from it. The private sector will of course, as a part of socialist planning, be subject to stringent regulation, and exploitation will thereby be tempered, but it will not have been abolished. The elements of both capitalism and socialism associated in an undeniably conflictual relationship will thus continue to exist, involving a compromises-laden struggle between the two, their underlying assumptions, reflecting the conflicting interests of classes and the masses. The important point here is that the essential instability of such a balance between the classes and the masses must be, from the very beginning, in a steady democratic process, resolved in favour of the masses, that is, in favour of socialism; the socialist aspect must be manifest in everyday economic policies and political practices and every actual or potential distortion – be it a social practice or a mode of governing – confronted in the light of its historical association with capitalism on the one hand and the principles or demands of socialism on the other. In this sense a socialist transition, or a socialism-oriented autonomous development, has to be from the very outset *socialist*, an assertion of people's revolutionary that is *socialist* self-reliance against global capitalist domination. It may be added, only such a perspective or practice can win people's support and participation and inspire them to struggle and make sacrifices.

XXXV

That there is no fore-ordained model or blueprint of socialism or socialist transition, certainly none suitable for all countries and all times, does not mean absence of general principles that flow from the Marxist tradition, the experience gained in national liberation and social revolutionary struggles and the efforts at socialist construction so far. For this reason critical understanding of Marxist tradition and revolutionary struggles of the past, and an equally critical analysis of and drawing of lessons from the past experiments in socialism, even when they have failed, is more than an intellectual game; it is an urgent and practical necessity for socialists everywhere, including those in the third world, seeking a proper perspective on possible socialist transition in their countries. I have sketched a few considerations on the subject earlier, in the concluding part of the previous chapter. Here I would only like to repeat the central issue involved, *the* principle which should govern a socialist transition *anywhere*: it must put *politics in command*. This principle acquires an exceptional importance in the third world countries where less than adequate economic conditions naturally tend to encourage economistic practices, *economism* as it has been called in socialist theory. (Even otherwise the inadequacy of objective or economic conditions here underlines the need for more than adequate subjective or political practice.) It should, however, be clearly understood that it is not merely a question of state's intervention in or control of economy. It presupposes a transformation of the nature of state or political power itself, in the countries of the periphery as elsewhere. The classical Marxist view of third world movements against imperialism always held that real social change involved winning indigenous *people's control* over the forces of production which mere political independence would not secure and may even result in the continuation of imperialism as neo-colonialism. Political independence was therefore not seen as the end of the liberation struggle but only a phase within it, which opens the way to people reclaiming its history by gaining control over their own productive resources or technologies. For this to happen people must secure *real*, and not some phoney, power in the state. Otherwise the economy simply cannot be reorganised or restructured, disciplined so to speak, to serve *their* interests. It continues to serve other interests, the class interests of those whom economy and politics, each in its own ways, empowers. More than a hundred years of political independence in Central and South America and the more recent post-war experience of Asian and African countries, has made this abundantly clear. Hence the question of political power, the people's power in the state, the struggle for 'political supremacy' or 'state power' of the exploited and oppressed remains central to a socialist transition. Without people in effective control of state power, 'politics in command' is a meaningless phrase.

However with people in power, their 'political supremacy' in society, a socialism-oriented state of revolutionary democracy, 'politics in command' remains the vital principle of a socialist transition. As noticed earlier, by its very nature as a system governed by the profit-imperatives of the market, it is 'primacy of economics' that lies at the heart of capitalism. With socialism, a negation of capitalism, with its explicit primary commitment to human welfare, 'primacy of politics' is the key principle, it is politics, not the market, which must govern the economic processes, including what, how, how fast the productive forces themselves have to be developed. This is true of a socialist transition in a third world country too. Any economistic emphasis or priority in development, a concern with 'catching up' with the advanced capitalist societies and therefore with maximizing the rate of economic growth as the overriding goal, apart from its false 'stageist' version of revolutionary transformations, will lead, and has in the past led, away from social and moral commitments of socialism, producing even class inequalities and regional differences. The need here is to recover, build upon (and where necessary go beyond) the classical tradition of Marxism, which saw socialism as providing a superior and advanced form of freedom and self determination to the people, including in the economy, rather than as a more productive form of economic system. In general, and more particularly in the third world with its strong economistic pressures, the very notion of development, for it to be socialist, has to be shorn of its excessive productivism. It must be infused with and subserve the authentic socialist values, old as well as new, including those concerning ecology and environment. This has to be the decisive thrust regardless of the concessions necessarily made in any transitional economic development to privately-owned production or the market.

'Politics in command' means posing such questions as: growth? but which growth? for what purpose? for whose sake, whose benefit or profit? for what kind of society and within which environment? These are questions which are central to any search for a real alternative to capitalism, vital for the very survival of socialist movement today. They are all the more vital to pose in the third world suffering the worst ravages of capitalism. We must ask: is our goal meeting 'the needs of the economy', its 'anonymous masters' as they have been called – 'abstractions such as financial markets, interest rates, exchange rates, commodity prices, indexes and statistical artefacts of all kinds' – or satisfaction of the needs of the people, allowing citizens the possibility of living as human beings? Is the starting point of our economic exercises to be calculation of deficits in order to cut them at the cost of the people or a determination of resources needed to satisfy people's needs in order to find or raise them? And our language? Do we practice the obscurantism of GDP, fiscal and revenue deficits, balance of payments, growth rates etc., etc. or speak more humanely in terms of such things as food and clean drinking water, health care and sanitation, housing and education, etc. so that economy becomes a transparent and accountable means of integrating these basic human needs of the people with a planned use of domestic resources, an use which also takes care of questions of equality, social justice including gender justice, employment, ecologically sustainable development, etc.?

To argue along with Harry Magdoff, there are always constraints to economic growth, presenting different, often difficult policy choices. The question to be asked of economic development, even more emphatically in the third world, is: what kind and for what purpose? Are social needs the guide here or the market and its profit-making? Put more simply: is it to get the maximum welfare of *all* the people, with priority for the needs of the poorest sections and the most backward regions and for the protection of environment? Or is to satisfy the market-induced, ecologically unsustainable consumerist hunger of the privileged part of the population seeking to maintain or attain the 'high' living standards of the west? Obviously, what is also involved is the view one takes of 'living standards'. For they are not only a matter of quantity that only creates and aggravates inequalities in society, but also quality that makes for a better 'truly rich human life' that Marx wrote of. They need not involve the consumerist accumulation of material goods for private use and may be better ensured by collective satisfaction of needs and by other kinds of goods compatible with the realisation of socialist goals. Obviously, again, the two kinds of economic development – socialist or capitalist – would have a decisive influence on the infrastructure to be built, the choice of technology, nature and location of industries, etc. The former would find it possible to develop productive forces consonant with social, cooperative relations of production as also to respond to the ecological imperatives; 'with politics in command', people would be free to consider the need to slow down or limit growth for the sake of quality of life and to have a habitat in which humans can breathe and stay healthy. The latter, with its limitless expansion for the sake of ever higher material standards of living, will not only need another kind of infrastructure, technology, industrialisation but will also be destructive of environment and inevitably result in the replication of the worst features of class society.

XXXVI

It is obvious that any third world country wishing to turn to socialism in the midst of a capitalist world would be subject to extremely hostile pressure from that world, to direct or indirect intervention by imperialist powers. Only if it can provide early on a minimum of welfare for every one and is genuinely democratic and responsive to people and thus enjoy their willing support can a socialism-oriented regime hope to cope with the imperialist offensive, inspire and mobilise the strongest opposition to it from within, and survive. But such political and military confrontation with imperialism apart, a socialist project in the third world faces what in many ways is a far more serious threat over time flowing from the inherent polarising logic of global capitalism, a threat which has become all the more potent in the current phase of globalisation in a largely unipolar world. It is this indeed which gives oppositional movements or revolutions in the third world their essential anti-capitalist and ultimately socialist, character. But what needs to be even more clearly understood is that the success of any such movement or revolution, any kind of socialist transition in the third world demands effective breaking away from global capitalism. In other words, it demands saying a firm 'no' to and opting out of globalisation.

In his brief but highly perceptive summing up of lessons to be learnt from the failed socialist experiment in Russia, drawing our attention to this particular issue, Harry Magdoff has written:

> a society wishing to turn to socialism – or those who by some other means want to overcome the obstacles created by colonialism and neo-colonialism –in the midst of a capitalist world must work towards opting out of the international network of capitalist trade and finance. How soon it can do so and how far it can go in that direction depends on many practical considerations. By no means is this a question of autarky. But the fundamental principle should be clear: the more an economy (socialist or not) is part of that network, the more it becomes dependent on it, the more its domestic economy must adapt to the world price system, the requirements of international finance (including the discipline imposed by the International Monetary Fund), and the capitalist business cycle. The net result is that the constraints of the world market become a dominant influence in a socialist society (or in alternate social formations that seek to control their own destiny). Planned economies that enter the international trade and financial network with both feet find that they increasingly lose control over their own destiny. Before long planning loses its effectiveness. It becomes the tail that tries to wag the dog.

The essential thrust of this argument is all the more relevant for a third world country now opting for a socialism-oriented autonomous development; to be at all viable, this development must work towards delinking from global capitalism.

The third world is today noisy with the refrain that 'there is no alternative' to globalisation, that the 'economic reforms' are 'irreversible' and that the world must adjust to the so-called rationality and efficiency requirements of 'the economy', which is quintessentially a capitalist market economy. But more than an argument of immediate economic opportunism or political defeatism or impotence, this is an expression of 'ideological poverty' of the colonised mind in the third world arising from its long subjection to imperialist rule. It is not to be denied that even as the economy is handed over to the tender or cruel mercies of 'the market', there may yet be some amelioration with 'trickle down' and social safety nets, with social welfare handed over to government and non-governmental or voluntary agencies. But the historical experience makes it abundantly clear that no effective long term answer to basic problems of poverty and underdevelopment in the third world is possible without breaking away from the structural logic of global capitalism and moving forward in a socialist direction. As the classical Marxist view has long held, only a qualitative break with the capitalist world market could allow post-colonial countries to establish preconditions for a pro-people socio-economic development. Not that a country so breaking away should eschew all economic relations with the capitalist world, but it is a time-honoured tenet of socialist thought that a country with a weak economy that wants to maintain its independence and the possibility of charting its own course in terms of the needs and priorities of its people, needs to protect itself against being overwhelmed economically or otherwise by stronger countries. As can be seen, globalisation underway has already compelled the 'integrated' 'under developed' and 'developing' third world countries to compete in an unequal world , resort to competitive devaluations, and allow transfer of real incomes essentially to the developed market economies; and in the process, also compelled them to adopt and adjust their institutions and policies, even cultures, to the needs and preferences of the stronger partners in the globalised markets of capitalism. As to the rosy future still being promised by the globalisers at home and abroad we have this typically fierce comment from Brecht: 'Those who have eaten their fill speak to the hungry of the wonderful times to come.' The hungry of the third world have to say 'no' to globalisation.

To say 'no' to globalisation however is not to argue, as already clarified, for any kind of 'autarky' in economic development. Essentially, it is a question of control over what a country produces and what is buys and sells aboard, the terms on which it does business with foreigners and engages in international exchange. More precisely, it is to pose the issue of this development being governed by *external* imperatives, those issuing from the requirements of the world capitalist market (export-led growth, etc.) and the associated consumerism of the rich, or primarily by *internal* imperatives, those flowing from an assessment of own resources and the needs of the people. The essential meaning of 'politics in command' we have argued for lies precisely in this concern with pro-people, systemically anti-capitalist nature and direction of economic development. Otherwise questioning or saying 'no' to globalisation, or 'delinking', may well get reduced to an argument for one or the other kind of *national* capitalist development which has already failed to deliver in the third world so far as people's interests are concerned.

'Politics in command', that is, building a socialist society – democratic and humane, ecologically respectful even if economically less prosperous – really involves making a fundamental and principled choice, namely, divorcing the criteria of rationality in economic-social life from those that govern the market-based system of capitalism. 'Delinking' is making a similar choice in relation to global capitalism. No autarky, it is yet reversing the process of peripheral 'adjustment' to global capitalism, that is subordinating external relations to the logic of socialism-directed internal development. Instead of countries' adjusting their internal agendas to the world expansion of capitalism, to the imperatives of global capitalism, it is the imperatives of internal socialist development which must have the primacy.

XXXVII

The post war decolonisation notwithstanding, global capitalism has been all along opposed to any attempts on the part of the third world countries to break away through conscious design – which necessarily means conscious state intervention – from the pattern of international division of labour inherited from the days of colonialism or semi-colonialism. Today's globalisation, through its international institutions like World Bank, IMF, WTO etc. openly seeks to continue this pattern in one form or another. According to the conventional wisdom being daily dished out, the salvation for the third world countries lies in free trade and export-led industrialisation, when it is common knowledge that there are virtually no historical experiences demonstrating that free trade has been the path to long term economic growth even among the so-called developed countries; the late comers among them relied most heavily on government regulation and control of international commerce. The export orientation of a third world economy in fact only further *ties* it to the global economy where international trade has been indeed one of the main mechanism for perpetuating the gap between the core and periphery which has been the distinguishing feature of global capitalism throughout its history. So it is now with the globalisation process underway. It has resulted in ever greater dominance of foreign trade by the giant multinationals, with forms ranging from the crudest type of exploitation to the 'normal' operations of the free market's invisible hand. These multinationals have massive reserves of material, technical, financial and cultural resources which they can and do use to penetrate and dominate any economy open to their intervention and manipulation. And backed as they are by powerful and experienced imperialist governments, they are bound to win out in the end against any wreak player who tries to go head-to-head with them in today's fiercely competitive (not merely interdependent) world market. The situation will be all the more disadvantageous for the weak player when this competition intensifies and the government-imposed barriers spread in times of general economic slowdown, as is already happening. The multinationals, backed by their governments, have immense capacity, on the basis of financial and commercial rules they can impose, to restrict or narrow the trade channels for their rivals, and they are already doing so despite all the tall talk over free trade and the extravagant promises of WTO etc. Cold War exigencies indeed made the west keep its markets open to potential allies, but these considerations do not operate now with the same force. Besides, economic slowdown and high unemployment in the west are compelling a bigger than ever retreat into protectionism, which includes non-tariff barriers and spurious anti-dumping measures. Even otherwise, it has been calculated that if the third world as a whole were to successfully export at, say the same rate as for example 'successful' South Korea once did, it would need more than double the present day world market for its manufactures. Where indeed would be the markets for such an enormous leap in export activities simultaneously in large number of third world countries. The prospect, instead, is one of greater, indeed cut-throat competition between these countries, not only in manufacturing but, for the some reason, in primary production too. There should be no illusions therefore of export-led growth opening the windows of opportunity for the third world in the process of globalisation. It will, together with import liberalisation that globalisation demands, certainly help satisfy the consumerist hunger of the ruling elites, but for the people it will only be a part of the process of their peripheralisation, leaving them with no other option except to 'delink'. But here the questions of economics again turn into those of politics, of people acquiring political power to be able to do so and chart out a path of economic development in accordance with their own interests.

XXXVIII

Any attempt at 'delinking' is likely to exact a heavy price in many ways, including an unavoidable trade-off between the requirements of productivity and those of minimising the polarising impact of global capitalism's enormous economic power. But once 'productivism' is abandoned and human welfare has the priority, this need not be a deterrent to adopting the strategy that 'delinking' involves. The details of economic policies in pursuit of this strategy will obviously vary from country to country. Here only a few broadly suggestive observations can be made which link up with what has been said before and are important enough to bear repetition.

This strategy postulates a revolutionary state, representative of a popular front of workers and peasants, undertaking at the very outset comprehensive programme of eradication of mass poverty, universal primary education, health care, housing, and provision of basic necessities for all. Initiating steps towards redistribution of incomes and development of backward areas will be a priority for state's active intervention in the economy which even as it covers such areas as foreign relations, production and social distribution, research and training, and the like, will need to secure an effective transitional combination of planning and market forces without letting the market or its values take over. Agrarian revolution benefiting the rural proletariat and small farmers, thereby improving the productive capacity in the rural areas, and laying the basis of cooperative effort and voluntary collectivisation of agriculture should be high on its agenda of economic reconstruction, as should be the transformation of the informal sector into a popularly managed transitional economy. A building up or restructuring of industry is obviously necessary. But it can neither be one based on 'international competitiveness'(that is promoting exports through low costs of local labour) nor on 'import substitution' (promoting production for the consumption of the privileged local classes). Not that all effort in these directions is ruled out; some of it may even be necessary. Only priorities, for years to come, lie elsewhere. Important thing is to develop and organise productive forces in a manner that helps the rural sector leap forward, carries industrialisation to the countryside and in general ensures a pattern of growth which, refusing the wasteful production to satisfy elite consumerism, immediately benefits the popular masses, satisfying their basic needs, needs created and satisfiable by the redistribution of income. It should be obvious that the overall development of a third world country today cannot support the first world consumption levels of its elites. What is needed is a diversification and development of internal markets for domestic goods and services governed by the overall principle that, beyond a certain necessary priority charges of an unequal nature, private needs and wants should be satisfied (and this goes for their increasing satisfaction) only at a level at which they can be satisfied for all, and beyond this all increase in the production of consumer goods should be for collective consumption.

Such a socialism oriented pro-people endogenous development process will draw on own strengths and domestic resources and capacities, including those of the hardworking poor who yet remain the most creative and productive force in society. It will give the common people, overwhelming mass of workers and peasants, a positive stake in the economy and mobilise them for building a better society as well as for the inevitable struggle against global imperialism and its local allies or partners – an awakened and aroused people are indeed the best defence even against armed aggression. Needless to add, such popular mobilisation and struggle will be all the time necessary to carry through the strategic option that socialism-oriented delinking involves.

Economic and technological backwardness is often pressed as an argument to counter the plea for such autonomous economic development. (Getting access to the most modern technology is another usual argument for the need to actively participate in world trade). This calls for two very brief observations. In the first place it is useful to recognise that if, despite economic backwardness, the priority is given to the needs of the poorest and most deprived sections of the people, there is much that can be done at the outset even in absence of growth of productive forces. The redistribution of wealth and the use of idle or under utilised human and material resources, their more productive deployment, can bring quick improvement in health, education and general living conditions of large masses of people. Early years of post-revolutionary societies in the Soviet Union and elsewhere provide ample evidence of this achievement which could be the basis for further development along socialist lines.

In the second place once we overcome the fetishism of science and technology – which attributes to them properties or power they do not possess, and at times even expects them to do the job of a social revolution which they simply cannot – and, as with economic development so with technology, ask the basic question: 'technology for what purpose?', the argument for getting access to the most modern western technology via globalisation – even if that was certain which it most certainly is not – loses much of its force. If the purpose in to satisfy the consumment hunger of the privileged part of the population and therefore supply it with the most modern gadgets, designs, and goodies of the west, then rushing into globalisation is indeed understandable. But if the purpose or priority is to meet the needs of all the people for decent food, clothing and shelter, clean water, proper sanitation and health protection, education and cultural opportunities and the like, then devoting scarce resources to the most modern technology will be only wasteful because there is little in the latest technology of the west that would make a significant contribution. In fact what is most useful and relevant in technology, western or otherwise, for improving the way of life of the masses is widely known. Most of this technology is already available at home and what else is needed is obtainable in the normal course of managed trade.

XXXIX

Socialism-oriented autonomous development in the third world is indeed an uncharted territory. But the failure of the world's first experiment in socialism notwithstanding, there is much in its experience to help guide this attempt and be hopeful about it: for example, in the still unparalleled achievements of the early years of the post-revolutionary societies in Russia and elsewhere despite their economic backwardness, in Cuba's heroic on-going struggle to build socialism and save the gains of its revolution, in Lenin's socialist project during the few years that he survived the October Revolution, in the experience of the 'Mao years' in China, and so on. The need is to assess this experience and assimilate its lessons in a revolutionary perspective. The uncharted territory can still be entered with confidence.

As I have argued earlier, our disappointment with the failure of the socialist experiments in the Soviet Union and elsewhere must not be allowed to obscure recognition of their remarkable socio-economic achievements. Particularly significant are the achievements of their early years which all the more effectively establish that if priority is given to the needs of the common people, there is much that can be done at the outset, even in the absence of growth of productive forces, that initial poverty is no bar to enhancing the welfare and capabilities of the vast masses of ordinary citizens, especially the most oppressed and needy among them. Aided by the revolutionary momentum of early years, and what is important, beginning with these years, the erstwhile socialist regimes were eminently successful in addressing some of the key problems of inherited capitalist under-development: eradication of absolute poverty, minimum provision of employment, health care, education, leisure, cultural goods, mass transport, etc. One has only to contrast it with the condition of the masses in other backward societies dominated by the capitalist mode of production, or even with the life-situation of the poor in the advanced capitalist world. They were able to qualitatively enhance the socio-economic condition of the common people in relation to the upper strata of society. Underlying this achievement was a basic fact which G. Arrighi has thus underlined: 'Socialist regimes were able to carry out an egalitarian internal redistribution of resources which compares favourably with the economic record of OECD and third world countries in this respect.'

The aforementioned undeniable achievements of the erstwhile socialist regimes can well be seen as the result of their delinking from the global capitalist system, partly a choice born of the socialist commitment of the leadership which for the period put 'politics in command', and partly an imposition of hostile capitalist encirclement. The early revolutionary era also witnessed flowering of revolutionary idealism, extraordinary popular mobilisation, cultural resurgence on a wide front and significant advance in the development of socialist morality and consciousness among the workers and peasants. But the achievements of these early social and human revolutions and the accompanying mass awakening was not made the basis for a transition forward to genuine socialism in the post-revolutionary regimes. Instead there were serious backslides in the years to follow. 'Politics in command' was given up, and for reasons some of which we have explored earlier, led by the Soviet Union, 'economism' came to command their socio-economic development. Competing with or confronting capitalism on the latters' favourite terrain, they finally lost out, one after another. Only Cuba, with its younger revolution, where socialism was not entirely the promise of consumer prosperity but rather of a richer shared collective life for all, where the ties between the people and leadership remained strong and a certain democratic participation of a socialist kind was practiced, is struggling to confront the current crisis by revolutionary rather than bourgeois means; there is the critique of technocracy, economism and corruption, emphasis on consciousness and collectivity, renewed interest in the ideological legacy of Che Guevara and a campaign of self-rectification and revolutionary repoliticisation – in other words, though badly buffeted, politics remains in command. Whether Cuba survives or succumbs to the onslaught of global capitalism led by the United States, its social and human achievements, as those of other post-revolutionary regimes, remain a testimony to the potential of socialism for the countries of the third world.

I will take a slightly more detailed look, later in these notes, at Cuba's socialist experience, its struggle for survival, and defence of revolution's gains which, as Castro recently pointed out, Cuba has been successful in defending 'thanks to its privileged position as a *non-member* of International Monetary Fund.' We have earlier noticed Marx's very suggestive class and policy-wise perspectives on the future of the Paris Commune and transition to socialism in peasantist Russia, as also how, during the few years that he survived the October Revolution, Lenin himself visualised transition to socialism in backward and beleaguered Soviet Union. But particularly noteworthy in this regard is the experience of what may be described as the strictly

Maoist period of post-revolutionary China. This too we shall look at in some detail later. But the positive thrust or achievement of this period with 'politics in command' may still be briefly noticed here for the lessons this period holds for socialist transition in a backward third world country.

As elsewhere, in China too Soviet Union had been for long seen as a model of socialist construction. But after an initial pursuit of Soviet-assisted planned development along conventional lines, in the late 50s, under the leadership of Mao, China moved away from the Soviet developmental model to chart out a different path for itself, though the ideological break between the two countries did not surface until 1960s. There were the usual early gains of the revolution, consequent upon the liberation from imperialism and the ending of feudal bondage. Basing himself on these, Mao mobilised the newly released energies of the Chinese peasants and workers, their spirit of frugality, sacrifice and hard work, their courage, dedication and selflessness, and above all their will to work for the common good, to take a different from Soviet road to socialism, to roll forward the 'thousand year great task' as they called or visualised it in Mao days.

Central to Mao's departure from the Soviet developmental model – which, he argued, 'distrusted' the peasant and 'squeezed the peasants very hard' – was his different approach to the peasantry. The agricultural cooperatives came up and then the People's Communes, largely through internal peasant upsurges, but led and helped along by Maoist leadership which ensured that care was exercised to both restrict and accommodate the 'rich peasant' (and even the ex-landlord) so that the waste in assets was kept to the minimum. The Great Leap Forward, despite its many flaws and failure in achievement, had this valid and highly suggestive governing principle: by letting the Communes accumulate capital to start 'back yard' industries, it kept part of the savings of the Communes for rural industrial development. At the same time it was an important part of Maoist strategy to maintain a proper balance between town and country, to accumulate capital (without 'squeezing' the peasant) for general industrial development and to take care of the interests of working classes and the urban population.

It was indeed a case of backward China trying to pull itself up by its bootstraps. And however we qualify it, China was succeeding. Collective agriculture worked and the country became essentially self-sufficient in agricultural production. Cooperation promoted capital accumulation and diversity of productive activities in the rural areas, and provided the social and economic basis for mobilising scores of millions of peasants during the slack season each year for capital construction projects – the dams, the irrigation systems, the drainage networks, the hill terraces, the reclaimed wetlands, the manmade river-bank lands, the windbreaks, the dune-stabilisation measures, etc. – and thus build the infrastructure for a more prosperous agriculture. Industry, low- tech or high, developed satisfactorily, in terms of both rapidity and geographical distribution. An outstanding achievement of this period of collective effort was the creation of widely scattered industrial bases throughout the countryside, bringing both small and large scale modern production to hitherto undeveloped regions, using the regional resources and talents to their full capacity with the aim of making every region 'self- reliant'. It seemed as if the Chinese were fulfilling Engels' admonition (in *Anti-Duhring*) to take industry away from the great cities; one result was a significant decline in urban population's overall share in the total. Village-based industrialisation not only ensured the success of 'leave the land but don't leave the village' policy, it also helped towards narrowing the gap between urban and rural life in all spheres.

Mao's was not a one-sided 'peasant vision' it is sometimes made out to be. Its boldness, as in the Chinese revolution earlier, so now in socialist reconstruction, only reflected the revolutionary genius of Mao Tse-tung. Arguing that Mao's strategy with regard to the vast rural population of China was 'not utopian, not voluntarist, not dogma but a realisable future for the peasantry of China so long as they adhered to and did not abandon the socialist road,' William Hinton has written:

> And what would the peasantry have to gain by successively enlarging the scope of collective action as they created the conditions for sustaining larger units? Scale, productive power, capital accumulation, mechanisation, diversification, specialisation, the remaking of nature, and the remoulding of society , especially in respect to social well-being, maternal and child health care, medical services, support for the sick, the infirm and the aged, and education at every level for people of all ages. In the long run it would mean the reduction and final elimination of the three differences, the difference between peasant and worker, between town and country and between mental and manual labour. In the short run it would mean the full mobilisation of all the human and physical resources of every community for all-round local development.

Carrying through Mao's strategy of development was by no means easy. A vast and historically unprecedented institutional innovation was required and there were severe setbacks. On the whole, it worked while it lasted. But it did not last long. Throughout it was the object of bitter inner-party struggles. It was opposed and obstructed by the influential section within the Communist Party leadership. And it was ultimately reversed. Mao's last desperate effort to salvage his strategy through the Cultural Revolution failed. (Incidentally, among the many challenges posed by the Cultural Revolution an important one was to the division between manual labour and intellectual labour prevailing in the Chinese factories where, it was reported, 'thousands of innovations' suggested by workers had been 'blocked by technicians who viewed them as inconsistent with the scientific and technical concepts they had been taught'). With the post-Mao leadership, it was again, as in the Soviet Union, 'economics in command' and, using the social-material base provided by the gains of the Mao period, this leadership set on the road to capitalism. That, however, is another story. In the context of our immediate argument, the crucial fact to note is that the Chinese experience in the period 1956-1965 has shown that the Soviet model, far from being an embcdiment of the 'laws of socialism' it claimed to be, was merely one possible path to economic development and one which was in contradiction with the more basic requirements of a genuine socialist transition, and that another path more consistent with it is possible, even for a backward, under-developed country of the third world.

Writing of the Maoist departure from the Soviet model of development, this is how Paul Sweezy puts it:

> A different course had to be adopted. And it was here that Maoist ideas, based on long years in governing the border regions and conducting the wars against the Kuomintang and the Japanese, came into their own as policy guides for the whole country. Priorities were re-ordered. Industry was to be geared to the needs of agricultureand developed not only in the cities but also and especially in the countryside, employing surplus rural labour and beginning the process of introducing the peasantry to modern technology. The absolute priority accorded to heavy industry in the Soviet model was abandoned, with the development of heavy industry also being integrated into a strategy which put agriculture (and the 80 per cent of the people dependent on it) at the top of the nation's concerns. This meant that the 'capital' needed to develop the Chinese economy was to come not from any pre-existing source of surplus – as both bourgeois economic theory and the Soviet orthodoxy of the period believed essential –but from a general increase in the productivity (agricultural and industrial alike) of the Chinese labour force. In this way the imposition of a special burden on any particular section of the population could be avoided and the whole issue of primitive socialist accumulation rendered irrelevant and meaningless. And politically this would permit the maintenance and even strengthening of the worker-peasant alliance, which in turn would make the build up of a specially repressive state apparatus as unnecessary as it would be irrational...
>
> (The Chinese experience) has shown that a low level of the development of the productive forces is not an insuperable obstacle to the socialist transformation of social relations and does not necessarily entail a process of 'primitive accumulation' and the aggravation of inequalities; that it is self-defeating to try to build the material bases of socialism first , while putting off until later the task of developing compatible social relations; that the socialist transformation of the superstructure must accompany the development of the productive forces, and that this transformation effectively conditions the socialist character of economic development.

The Chinese experience of the Maoistperiod, in Bettelheim's words, 'proves that a low level of development of the productive forces is no obstacle to a socialist transformation of social relations.' The countries of the third world do not have to choose between the capitalist and Soviet roads to economic development. There is another, a more socialist road they can travel, and even build socialism, provided politics is in command and political leadership is correct. This remains a momentous contribution of the Mao period.

(This apart, in view of post-Mao China's turn away from socialism, Mao's analysis of this degeneration which he foresa, and his struggle against it also remain an abiding guide-cum-inspiration for socialist transitions of the future anywhere, including the third world.)

XXXX

Finally, a few gneral observations:

To argue for a socialist transition is not to underestimate the obstacles that the amalgam of old habits, traditions, encrusted beliefs and prejudices presents to any effort at radical, socialist transformation of society. 'The weight of all the dead traditions', Marx had called it. While the consideration here is relevant to all countries including economically advanced ones, backwardness, obviously, of course in its own way, enhances this dead weight. We have on an earlier occasion noticed the sharp distinction Antonio Gramsci had once drawn between 'the East' where, he said, the state was everything and society was 'gelatinous' and 'the West' where a multitude of 'earthworks' and 'trenches' crisscrossed civil society. But a certain usefulness of this distinction notwithstanding, as Magdoff has pointed out, 'no society is really gelatinous – all societies are full of earthworks and trenches and fortifications of many kinds; and this is as true for "under developed" societies as for other ones.' In a socialist transition, as we take account of the specific conditions in each country - historical and cultural inheritance, level of economic development, natural endowment and human resources, etc. – we also need to take note of the specificities of its 'earthworks and trenches and fortifications' as obstructions to social transformation. But specificities apart this poses a serious programmatic and practical problem everywhere: to go fast against habit, tradition, history, fears and prejudices, the established order of things in general, is to narrow your base of support, to go slow is to lose momentum, discourage activists, comfort your enemies. This problem can only be resolved in practice but this practice to be revolutionary, must always retain its vision of socialism. Socialism, again, is building a *new* society after millennia of class-divided exploitative society. It is therefore a long process, not a matter of a decade or two. Even so, you do not build it out of nothing, the new has yet to be built on the basis of the old, with the materials or instruments it makes available. Hence the still more basic problem which Rosa Luxemburg, speaking of political choices involved in this revolutionary enterprise, in part, thus posed: 'We are trying to build a future with the instruments of the past, the instruments of the society we are trying to overcome. To use the past, however, reinforces the past, and while it may help gain support, it also reshapes the movement, alienating those with revolutionary concerns and pushing out such concerns as "utopian", as not yet on the agenda of history.' That is how the creative impulse of the revolution is dissipated, retreats are not recognised as retreats, converted into virtues they end up as the abandonment of the basic concern, socialism itself. This is indeed a real danger. On the other hand, to base politics on the future aspirations alone, to leap without a sufficient base of preparation, is to lose support and court defeat. It fosters a rash and arrogant 'voluntarism' that can easily degenerate into coercion to gain support, lamentations about the 'backwardness' of the people, distrust of democracy and a centralised commandism. Even good decisions, it should be remembered, become retrograde if imposed from above. Both kinds of errors have been, often in an alternating sequence, important in revolutionary history and proved disastrous to the people and the cause of socialism. But, to quote Richard Levins, 'at present the first kind, the compromise with the past, is dominant in European and Asian socialism.'

Lastly, a concern for the future, which is integral to the

socialist vision, does not mean that socialist revolutions are imminent in the third world or elsewhere. On the contrary, the exhaustion of the revolutionary wave of the twentieth century is the overwhelming fact to be reckoned with. This failure of socialism, for which socialists, of whatever hue, are themselves most responsible, is also an involuntary tribute to late capitalism's flexibility and productivity. But late capitalism, a capitalism living beyond its historical time, has also brought us face to face with Marxism's once prophetic poser: 'socialism or barbarism.' And this barbarism of capitalism will be most manifest in the third world. Life for the people there is in fact already tending to be ever more nasty, poor, brutish and short, compelling them, beyond the current confusion or despair, to seek an alternative to capitalism and its globalisation.

Wise men of course tell us 'there is no alternative', that socialism is 'a future that has failed'. Many on the Left too have gone 'realist'; they no longer speak of socialism, of things 'impossible' as they describe them. And they may all well turn out to be right – the history of humankind is a history of tragedies too. But common people, unable to afford such passivity, may yet continue to entertain other ideas.

'Realism' may yet come to be recognised as a cover for abandonment of principles, and the people may yet choose to respond the way those rebel students of Paris admonished way back in 1968: 'Be realist, attempt the impossible'. Late capitalism's contradictions, at home and even more in the peripheries, are indeed so basic and destructive that it is simply inconceivable that the overwhelming mass of its victims will not continue to search and struggle for an alternative, a more just and humane social order. They will, not the least in the third world countries. A long haul, more slow, arduous and painful than the pioneers visualised, the struggle for socialism will go on.

2

Russia—Collapse and After

The crisis of 'actually existing socialism' was no surprise but the suddenness with which it collapsed in Eastern Europe in 1989 or the Soviet Union a year or so later, was indeed astounding. It was the painful defeat of a historical experience that had begun with the October Revolution – an experience which both materially and in terms of ideas often served as a model and almost always as a reference point for broad movements of social liberation seeking an alternative to or escape from depredations of global capitalism. It was in fact so much of a reference point for the entire history of our times that its end has prompted scholars to speak of 'the short twentieth century' (1914-1990), and one of them, the Japanese-American Francis Fukuyama, to announce, with whatever qualifications, the end of history itself. The obvious provincialism of such an announcement apart, there is a great deal of truth in the idea that an important chapter of recent history had indeed come to a close and another chapter into the future was opening – a future immediately defined by a renewed global domination of capitalism. As part of an exploration of its deeper trends and long-term prospects, I have already discussed the hard options this future presents to countries of the third world. Let me supplement that discussion with a quick look at the post-collapse situation of the countries that once constituted the second world (of socialism), particularly Russia, China and Cuba, and the seemingly triumphant first world of capitalism.

The disintegration of the Soviet Union and its elimination from the world scene as the 'other superpower' is obviously a most important feature of the new world that has opened before us. A momentous event in many ways, the fact to be noticed in the immediate context is Russia's decisive retreat from socialism and a turn to capitalism. The people, here as elsewhere in East Europe, may well have initially set out in pursuit of democracy, even a return to the project of reforming socialism or building a 'socialism with a human face' as they put it, but via all sorts of half-formulated plans and hopes and a destination described as 'not this socialism', all of them have moved towards a more or less rapid restoration of capitalism and integration into capitalist world economy, with market as the tutelary deity of the new social order. Like travelling the road to socialism, this road to capitalism, is once again an uncharted territory for them, though, unlike Russia in 1917, Eastern Europe in 1945 had, unfortunately, the deformed Soviet socialist model to copy and emulate.

This is not to imply that the process of transition to capitalism will take the same course in all the former territories of 'actually existing socialism', or that it will be plain sailing in any of them, or even that its successful outcome is in any way guaranteed. There are significant differences between individual countries, and history has its own way of springing surprises. Such historically produced particularities and possibilities, however, do not concern us here. The immediately obvious fact to be recognised is that with the collapse of their old world, people in Russia, as elsewhere, have been hustled or persuaded into believing that capitalism is the only answer to their needs, and they have all chosen to move, for the present at least, in a capitalist direction. For this very reason the immediately important question is not whether the future is capitalism but rather what kind of capitalism is in store for the people of these countries and therefore also what possibilities, if not necessity, this capitalism is likely to generate for yet another, this time a genuine and effective, transition to socialism.

There is no doubt that in addition to reasons specific to each country, the most important common factor behind the setback to socialism and the consequent turn towards capitalism was the kind of socialism that had come to be built in the Soviet Union and Eastern Europe. Over the years socialism (and Marxism) had been identified with the Stalinist bureaucratic system. That had been the only point of agreement between propagandists of the East and their Western antagonists – that these states were socialist, that their leaders were implementing Marxist socialist politics. Given such a unanimous and formidable consensus, socialism in Eastern Europe, and the USSR, came under an even stronger anathema than it did in the capitalist democratic West. Most obnoxious was its denial of democratic freedoms, its authoritarian and repressive, and in this respect almost prison-like character. And if you have been kept in prison for a long time, your first objective is to get out. Other considerations, such as escaping into what? or changing the system, take a back seat as it were. In this situation attractions of democracy and consumerism of the capitalist society next door proved decisive. A turn to the West, especially its capitalism or market economy appeared as an obvious and easy alternative to the system that was being abandoned.

II

Most remarkable about Russia's turn to capitalism was the utter naiveté of most of its proponents and ideologues, a naiveté shared by political leaders and large sections of the population who believed or followed them. Once ignorant of what socialism was really about, they now faithfully parroted the slogans of western neo-conservatism and were thus equally illiterate about capitalism, about its history, its actual existence in the West and as a global system.

These ideologues of capitalism or equally enamoured political leaders were simply blind to the fact that capitalism in the West, with its capitalist class and proletariat, its complex material infrastructure as well as market morality or ethos, were the product of centuries of development, that its key economic concepts were elaborated and the prescriptions applied in conditions entirely different from those now confronting Russia and Eastern Europe, that market economy is not a simple set of rules, a ready-made prescription, which has only to be applied, to produce instant and miraculous results. The idea of 'market economy', like that of 'socialism' once, had acquired almost a religious character so that while pure market had never existed and free-trade had been anything but free in the West, the Russian ruling elite and a wide section of the public were simply overwhelmed by their ideological mystique and even as America and Europe had began to move away from strictly monetarist policies of recent years, in Russia they saw the road to salvation in a literal pursuit of these much-soiled ideas. The dissenting voices were few and lacked credibility; even when they could be discerned in the current cacophony they went unheeded.

The illusions about 'the west' and 'the market economy' swamping all other considerations, the Russian elite failed to see that no 'highway' of European (let alone world) civilisation existed which they could reach by copying the existing models, or that as so-late-comers to capitalism, the goal of becoming a developed capitalist state in the western mould was objectively impossible for them. In the midst of a surfeit of demagogic promises and propagandist myths, they, together with the Russian people, had no awareness of the terrible costs paid by the common people in the capitalist transitions of the past in the West and elsewhere, and naively believed that such a transition could be implemented without generating mass unemployment and impoverishment, gross inequalities of income and without surrendering the Soviet-era gains in social, economic and cultural spheres. They proposed the creation of a labour market and simultaneously argued for private ownership for every one without seeing the contradiction, for who could then be hired to work for the private property owners? On a 'free market' high, they did not know that market is not just the place packed with consumer goodies but also an extremely harsh place where the predatory logic of capitalism works itself out at the cost of human and natural resources. They were simply unaware that free market postulates vast inequalities in the distribution of income, assets and opportunities, that it invokes the sovereignty of the individual but regularly sacrifices him at the alter of profit-making, that its social contract, known as *laissez-faire,* inevitably makes for a society of winners and losers where the winners simply move away and on, trampling over others and leaving them behind – 'secession of the successful', the Harvard economist Robert Reich has called it. There was no awareness at all that free market' arrived in the not too distant past in tandem with the Darwinian principle of 'survival of the fittest'. Given the widely shared illusion that market and democracy go together, there was no recognition either among Russian rulers and intelligentsia that free market first came with, and inherently makes for, authoritarian political rule, that it is against the opposition of capitalist ruling classes that the people have fought for and won democracy, that the marriage of capitalism and democracy has always been an uneasy one and that whenever the crunch came and the choice had to be made, the marriage was dissolved by the ruling classes in favour of capitalism, that is, freedom of the market. It was characteristic of the initial euphoria over 'market' and 'democracy' among the so-called 'radical' ideologists and people around them that their attacks on the *nomenklatura,* which were intended as an indictment of 'privilege' and 'stifling authoritarianism' under 'actually existing socialism', missed the significance of the fact that it was precisely this *nomenklatura* which was, before their very eyes, going into the making of the bourgeoisie of the incipient market society, where not only will its past privileges be nothing in comparison with the social inequalities under 'actually existing capitalism', but its rule may turn out to be another, and possibly worse, form of authoritarianism.

More than much else, the incredible naiveté of the Russian rulers and ideologues was expressed in their enthusiastic espousal of primitive versions of Milton Friedman's 'free market' economics, already discredited in its home countries, and their moronic faith in global capitalism. The transnational financial institutions of the North, like International Monetary Fund and World Bank, were approached as if they were benevolent entities out only to help other countries in economic distress and not coldly calculating capitalist concerns always on the lookout to grab new sources of wealth for some segments of the western capitalist economies, concerns which were now interested not in creating rival capitalist societies in Russia or Eastern Europe but turning them into a new colonial area, the 'Latin-Americanisation' of yesterday's 'socialist second world'. There was no understanding or analysis of how the IMF and World Bank policy packages actually work and an amazing ignorance of the experience with such policy packages in other countries in Latin America, Africa and Asia. There could be nothing more naive than the belief that the gulf in levels of development and wealth between countries can be bridged with the help of a few salutary *laissez-faire* prescriptions. If that were indeed possible, poor and backward countries would have ceased to exist long ago. Whereas the fact is that the overwhelming majority of countries living under capitalism are underdeveloped, their economies poor and their populations living in conditions of poverty. What is more, over the past two decades, despite prescriptions of the IMF and promises of a New International Economic Order, indeed scrupulous observation of these prescriptions and all the rules of bourgeois society, they have become even poorer. And there is the evidence that their underdevelopment and poverty is structurally linked with the development and affluence of the advanced countries of the global capitalist system. Perhaps the most naive of the Russian illusions was a vague notion that in a market economy everyone can get rich quickly – with emphasis on the 'quick' part of it. An observer of the scene aptly commented: 'The prescriptions of the Russian liberal ideologists bring to mind the famous book "One Hundred Ways to Get Rich". As a rule, neither the readers nor the authors of such books have become millionaires. If these individuals are so clever, one must ask, why have they not made their own fortunes?'

III

The naiveté and the accompanying illusions. hopes and desires were however soon shattered and the capitalist dream turned sour for the common people in Russia, as it had a couple of years earlier in East Europe. In its very first flush the people discovered that capitalism is a package of more than consumer goodies on the shelves to be had for the asking. These were indeed now available for the few at the top, but as part of the arrival of the free-market system, the country was flooded with all the diseases of a late capitalism, the 'enormous and blindingly visible explosion of every imaginable human vice', as Vaclav Havel, 'the philosopher-president' of what was still Czechoslovakia, lamented. The first wave of capitalism brought with it, along with the latest colour T.V. and video-sets, a culture of drugs and sex, pornography, blue films and massage parlours, beauty contests and gambling casinos, smuggling and black marketing, a culture of white-collar and weapon-related crimes, of hooliganism, private violence and the gun. The society was now open and with it went the new hazards, among them the nightclubs open till early mornings. As Prague and Moscow grew into twin capitals of Europe's sex industry and trade, a nightclub owner in Paris gloated: 'Some of our best girls come from Poland, Yugoslavia, Hungary, Russia and the other eastern countries and they will do anything, take on any kind of sexual perversion for money.' The spread of prostitution in the cities of Russia and concubinage to foreign carpet-baggers provoked a saddened observer to comment that 'the eventual humiliation of an ex-superpower is (being) played out on the bodies of its women'. Everything barbaric and socially retrograde in capitalism was reproduced, the sense of community gave way to general anomie and disorientation. With the threshold between good and evil lost, the people were out for themselves, reducing Russia literally to a society where 'anything goes'.

In the initial chaos of Russia's capitalist transition white crime spread like an epidemic in its economy and society. The old 'communist system' had spawned its own kind of crime, but the new versions were bolder and more sinister. As reported, Russia came to be plagued with 'crime, corruption and ethnic strife' spread over its '11 time zones, 31 autonomous provinces, and 132 nationalities'. Prominent among the 'entrepreneurs' of the emerging free market economy were the mafias – a socio-economic phenomenon which referred to three principal kinds of related activity: the creation and maintenance of shortages by monopoly structures, the illicit transfer of state resources and funds into private hands, and growing gangster control over economic activity and transactions, all involving the collusion of administrators of the still existing state sector with the 'shadow' economy, which was itself often indistinguishable from the legitimate private sector, at times existing even under the deceptive name of 'cooperatives'. This parasitic growth was a direct consequence of the mindless policies of price 'liberalisation' and privatisation, along with the destruction of ordered exchange between productive enterprises. The mafias first came into limelight in the wake of Gorbachev's perestroika which was dubbed in common parlance as 'the golden age of the mafias'. Now with the economic chaos and active pursuit of free market economy, mafias of various types and dimensions, with political support and participation of the people in power at various levels upto the very top, sprung up across the length and breadth of the ex-Soviet Union and gradually took over the key positions in economy and society. (Power in the localities now often belonged to the chiefs of the 'mafioses'). *Newsweek,* the American magazine, had a long write-up owards the end of 1992 on 'The New Chicago on the Neva' referring in particular to St. Petersburg (till recently Leningrad). Quoting a Russian ministry of the Interior source, it wrote of 3,000 gangs extorting millions of dollars, operating rackets like prostitution, trading in drugs and arms, and exporting billions of dollars of raw materials. Other reports spoke of 5,000 organised crime gangs (up from 785 in 1990), active in different parts of the country, engaged in regular gang warfare and contract killings and accumulating wealth for themselves. In 1993 alone more than 22,000 crimes involving use of weapons and 293 cases of hostage-taking were reported, and in the same year, there were 25000 murders in Russia, many of them by contract killers who could earn up to 15 million roubles for each murder they committed. Crime, murder, people missing, shoot-outs between gangster groups had become a routine affair in Russia's large cities, including the capital Moscow. In 1993 more than 11000 serious crimes were committed against foreigners, every fourth in the capital, compelling international organisations to declare Russia a zone of special danger for business and tourism. Practically all commercial organisations – not only shops, cafes, restaurants but almost all private enterprises and banks – paid money to gangs to stay in business. According to a report prepared for President Yeltsin in January 1994, 70-80 per cent of private businesses were paying protection money. These mafias ran entire networks in the economy (including the agent, importer, wholesaler and retailer) either entirely by themselves or in league with traders and brokers mushrooming all over the country, cornering private trade in virtually all commodities, pilfering on a large-scale goods produced or distributed by the state, grabbing the supply of cheap state sector goods against commission, importing foreign goods worth millions of dollars, often with money borrowed in a dubious way from state banks, etc. etc. Alongside most Russian business – Mikhail Yegorov, a deputy, estimated that 40,000 enterprises were now controlled by criminals – the mafias controlled the private banks too (which were often really money laundrettes of which Moscow alone was said to have more than all of Western Europe). Money laundering itself was leading to the flow out of Russia of funds amounting to hundreds of billions of dollars. It was estimated that more than 1 billion dollars was being deposited in western banks on behalf of criminals every month.

Possible, of course, with the collusion and participation of those in control of state power, capitalist transition's immediate outcome in Russia was a massive criminalisation of its economy and society. As R. James Woolsey, the then CIA boss, who found Russia looking a lot like Germany after World War I – a lost empire, 'shrunken and bitter military and security institutions, inflation-wracked elderly citizens, deep resentment over a supposed Western stab in the back, virulent anti-semitism and shaky democratic institutions' – reported it in Washington: 'Russia is not yet in the final stages of strangulation by organised crime, but I believe its condition is much further along than most public commentary suggest.' Unlike in other countries, where organised crime usually operates on the periphery of the economy – dealings in drugs, prostitution, weapons, etc., – in

Russia it was already a part of the mainstream, if not the mainstream itself.

Incidentally, such was the wealth and political clout of the Russian mafias that, having grabbed much of Russian economy, they were now reported to be trying to strike roots in the United States, compelling the New York F.B.I. boss to warn: 'They are dangerous and we want to prevent them from getting established like the Italian mafia before them'. The warning surely sounds somewhat old fashioned in this age of capitalist globalisation. Today crime is not merely interlinked with business and politics, it is itself a big business in the free market societies. And all big business is going global these days. There is no reason why the Russian mafia should not join in. There was poetic justice too in the Russian mafia thus seeking freedom of the United States. It was as if through this export, the mafia produced by the 'freedom' which American exertions brought it, Russia was repaying some part of its debt to the United States!

IV

We have already noticed that the old centrally planned economic system had broken down during the later phase of Gorbachev's perestroika. Now, what followed as capitalist transition was a three-fold devastation of Russia, involving plunder of its material and human assets, ravaging of its people and an ideological blitz on its culture and consciousness – a devastation that set a pattern of development which has continued and which, unless a major reversion of policies takes place, portends a rather bleak future for post-Soviet Russia.

With the mafias ascendant in the economy, a truly venal set of politicians in power, often in control of the state sector as well, and all sorts of native and foreign speculators and adventurers in business joining them, the first few years of transition to capitalism in Russia witnessed what could well be described as one of the greatest acts of wanton economic destruction in history – a veritable pillage of Russian economy in all sorts of legal, semi-legal and illegal ways. The Fund-Bank advised or imposed 'Shock Therapy' under Yeltsin more than facilitated this pillage and destruction. Liberalisation or 'freeing' of prices not only sent them soaring skywards, it redistributed wealth from the common people to the country's monopoly producers and importers of foreign goods. Liberalisation and 'freeing of labour markets' resulted in a mindless closing-down of enterprises and surging unemployment. Liberalisation or 'freeing' of trade led to export, much of it illegal or plain smuggling out of Russia's rich natural resources, a haemorrhage of Russian raw materials and food staples into the world market where they were sold at a fraction of their world market price to western merchants in exchange for the flooding of the internal market with high priced consumer goods and luxury imports from the west. Making for vast private fortunes, this not only irrevocably ruptured the closed cycle of the national economy but bode ill for its future development. The most obvious of the on-going plundering was the privatisation programmes which, as Yury Luzkhov, Mayor of Moscow and one of Yeltsin's staunchest supporters at the time openly admitted, was a 'deception of the people' that 'sells off state property for practically nothing' to a privileged few who, according to Anatoly Chubais, the privatisation boss, almost naturally came from the criminals of the 'second economy', the fly-by-night operators who often resold and collected their profits. This was in fact the preferred option of Yeltsin and his advisers, both Russian and foreign. (As if to encourage such criminals or mafiosi, the rule that buyers must disclose their sources of income was duly rescinded). While those with administrative power, money and connections, and 'skills' to adapt to market economics, made their kill in the 'free market' and piled up huge fortunes, to the majority of the Russian people it was 'selling off the country for a song', legalisation of the process of expropriation of what they understood to be the national heritage. Moshe Lewin has observed:

> under cover of a counter-ideology ignorant of the realities of the previous system, the country's riches were sold off at the knock down prices in pursuit of a miracle cure known as free market. Supported by Western advisers and extolled by the West's most influential governments and economic institutions, privatisation amounted to highway robbery of epic proportions. Specialists are still struggling to come to terms with the figures involved.

Helping this 'highway robbery' along, under cover of 'economic reform', was the US-led aid programme driven not by a wish to reconstruct but to destroy. According to economist Jeffery Sachs (who, as the leading American architect of reform was in excellent position to know), the core purpose was to finish off the state socialist system and conclude the Cold War agenda. The impact of it all was truly destructive for the Russian economy. As De Groote, an IMF Director for 20 years, summed it up, Yeltsin's shock therapy 'blindly destroyed Russia's social infrastructure, industrial production and scientific technical production...the precipitous rise in crime is a particularly cancerous consequence of the rapid and uncontrolled liquidation of Soviet economic structures and social safety nets.'

A most significant aspect of this destruction or pillage was what took place in the area of research and development base of the Russian economy – potentially one of the stronger legacies of the old regime. The foreign multinationals rushed in to acquire, through 'joint ventures' or otherwise, the services of entire local research laboratories, and the growing economic difficulties not only led to brain drain of qualified scientists and technologists or diverted highly skilled workers into other activities for survival, there was a large scale exploitative appropriation of human capital with Russian scientists working (in subcontracting relations) at 50-100 dollars a month for western hi-tech firms. A special concern of the west was to establish its control over the defence complex and above all to utilise its priceless technologies. Y. Primakov as the former head of the foreign intelligence, reported to the country's leadership at the end of 1994: 'Now our defence scholars who previously worked for the interests of their own country are working for the NATO.'

The capitalist transition, as it began in Russia, not only involved a massive plunder of its natural and human resources, it was disastrous for its economy as a whole. In the first year of 'economic reform', industrial output collapsed by 26 per cent. Between 1992 and 1995, Russia's GDP fell 42 per cent and industrial production fell 46 per cent – far worse than the contraction of the US economy during the Great Depression.

In agriculture, privatising 'reforms' simply failed to work, leading to a plummeting of agricultural production and a rising need for food imports. Economic decline in Russia reached levels unmatched in the peace-time history of the 20th century and there was no end to this decline.

It needs to be added that the plunder of Russia's wealth resulted in a massive outflow of real resources, which, like the looting of state property, criminalisation of economic activity, money-laundering etc., was bolstered by the so-called 'economic reform'. There was a flight of capital which dwarfed the loans negotiated by the Yeltsin regime with the IMF, and only added to the Russian indebtedness. Rather than being aided by the West, there was a net outflow of capital from Russia. As a vice-President of the World Bank, Thalwitz, noted in early 1994: 'Overall... there's little doubt that the capital outflow far exceeds cash disbursements that governments and multilateral agencies like the World Bank have made to Russia.' He wrote: 'The assertion that Russia is giving aid to G7, and not the G7 aid to Russia is, therefore, ... an objective statement of fact. The assistance given by Russia to G7 is a minimum $20 billion a year – $15 billion a year in capital transfers and at least $ 5 billion in cheap energy and metal exports. The receipts in terms of aid to Russia is approximately $2 billion.'

Within the country, the ill-gotten wealth, the plunder and the illegal earnings from the 'broad grey areas of capitalism and economic crime in Russia', concentrated in a few hands, was being mostly blown in luxury consumption of the *nouveau riche* at home or routinely salted away in banks abroad in Switzerland and elsewhere against the day flight from Russia may become necessary. The American magazine *Newsweek* quoted a Central Bank official as saying wealthy Russians held as much as $25 billion, a sum far out-weighing all western aid to Russia in 1992, in bank accounts abroad. (This together with the profligate spending habits of the rich only added to the on-going wastage of resources, impoverishing the country still further, as did the disengagement of material and human resources from production as a result of IMF and World Bank prescriptions.)

V

Russia's 'nascent capitalism' had its beneficiaries. A thin stratum at the top, they were the mafia bosses, domestic and foreign carpet baggers, the few multinationals who had come in for the kill and, of course, the men in power in politics and the state sector of the economy, including the so-called 'Red managers' – all of them making hay while the new sun of market economy shone and conning the casual foreign visitor into believing that the capitalist transition was indeed well underway. High living of the corrupt at the top was already a Brezhnev-era feature of life in the Soviet Union. The new economic dispensation had spawned a high-living strata of super-rich wallowing in luxury beyond the dream of any in the Brezhnev coterie. The streets of down town Moscow were lined with stores and kiosks selling products and services almost unheard of in the bad old days – everything from pineapple to scotch whisky to Rolls Royce cars; the Mercedes Benz alone was reported to be selling more of its top-of-the-lines cars in Russia than in all of Europe combined. Dozens of posh night clubs, casinos and luxury shops had sprung up in Moscow and St. Petersburg and there was a growing Russian presence at the French Riviera and other luxury spots of the western world. Just beyond the Moscow city limits, whole communities of palatial new dachas were springing up, juxtaposed against nearby collective farm villages, like structures transplanted from another universe. The rich were enjoying their new wealth with an exuberance and flamboyance that was least ruffled by any awareness of the general poverty around them. For, while small numbers of former skilled workers and professionals had managed to find more or less decent niches in the emerging market economy, the vast majority of Russians, trapped in sinking state enterprises, collapsing agriculture and vanishing social security system had inexorably lost ground.

VI

Following upon the heady hopes of 1989-90, the Fund-Bank prescribed capitalist transition – 'merciless manipulation of crude capitalism' Gunter Grass had called it – had already led to an economic depression in East Europe which, in terms of its depth and disastrous consequences, was seen as unmatched even by the Great Depression of 1929-33, and had played havoc with the lives of the people. To quote one World Bank study, which can hardly be accused of exaggerating, 'the social costs of transition are higher than expected. Predictions did indicate that some unemployment would emerge. But nobody expected the massive decline (ranging from 10 to 40 per cent between 1987 and 1993) of measured GDP in the transition economies, which dwarfed in its proportion the output and income loss of the United States and Germany during the Great Depression.' UNICEF reported an East European health crisis which 'has no historical precedents', accompanied by an unprecedented rise in criminality and delinquency, an alarming decrease in life expectancy and a drop in the number of children attending primary school. 'As far as health is concerned, this is the most serious crisis Europe has known, with the exclusion of the two world wars', said UNICEF's director James P. Grant. 'The vale of tears' is how the British economist Richard Portes, himself one of the transition advisers, saw its consequences in East Europe. From the other end, the situation was well-expressed in a new Hungarian saying: 'Do you know what is the worst thing about Communism?' 'No, what?' 'What comes after it'.

It was no different now in Russia. The pattern of economic decline, from the earlier slow growth or stagnation to catastrophic negative growth was reported with the same, if not worse, consequences. The economy in its free fall was accompanied by a collapse of health and educational programmes, and a steep fall in living standards of the people which inevitably backlashed in further depressing productive activity in industry and agriculture. In its pursuit of a market economy, Russia seemed to have come close to exchanging 'a poorly working economic system for none at all' as Galbraith put it, and in the process much of the former productive and cultural resources were laid to waste. Towards the end of 1993, the novelist Alexander Solzhenitsyn, for all his anti-communism, wrote in the *New York Times*: 'The current nascent capitalism, fraught with unproductive, savage and repulsive forms of behaviour, the plunder of the nation's wealth, the likes of which the west has not known... (has resulted in a) nostalgia for the "equality of poverty" of the past'.

VII

For the mass of Russian people the first fruits of the attempt to restore capitalism were only sour. The plunge towards what was thought the capitalist miracle had turned out to be no miracle; rather there had come a period of grave economic deprivation and hardship for the people, a quite direct and tangible deterioration in their living conditions. Unemployment emerged as a growing problem, almost of a permanent nature for many, in a society previously unaccustomed to it, much of it also hidden in part-time work, unpaid holidays at enterprises in trouble, etc. This unemployment had important regional and structural dimensions, as of age and ethnic background, but it is women who were the hardest hit – in sharp contrast with the policies of the Soviet era, when women had come to be over 50 per cent of the work force. Women were the first to be laid off, not unoften to make jobs available for men. The then minister of labour Melikyan cynically argued that 'it is inconceivable that women should work if men do not have jobs.' Many were being forced back into the home because state subsidised child care had been cut and others had their wages reduced to an abysmally low 40 per cent of men's wages. Another section badly hit were the professionals – school teachers, doctors, university level instructors and professors, scientists, etc., whose salaries had dipped lower than that of many an unskilled worker in some branches of industry, construction for instance, or of bus drivers, door keepers and waiters in posh restaurants, and so on. While a few had made it to the ruling elite, and some had gone into business or left for better-paid private jobs, others, facing unemployment sought survival in all sorts of unrelated low-paid occupations. Adding to people's woes was the surge of inflation accompanying free pricing which besides wiping out or depreciating household savings and pensions, eroded real earnings of the people and impoverished the still employed wage workers, from unskilled blue collar workers to previously well-paid professionals. As a result, in 1992-93, about four out of every ten people living in Russia were reported to be no longer earning enough to buy even basic food necessities, and another 40 per cent were having to spend almost 90 per cent of their income on food to survive. With the dramatic increase in the levels of critical poverty, 'the poor' and 'the very poor' had emerged as a new feature of Russian society. The absolute and relative increase in inequalities only underlined the increasing loss or deprivation of the Russian people.

The loss or deprivation was, and was experienced to be, all the more ravaging because the free market policies had meant the dismantling of the entire system of social security which the previous regime had provided and which the people had come to take for granted. People were of course tired of standing in long lines, but they were accustomed to being able to purchase the necessities they required at affordable prices. Income disparities among the people did exist, but these were relatively slight and carried virtually no meaning. Indeed, money incomes did not carry the same meaning as they do in market economies, and they made up only a small part of workers' means of subsistence. Much of what the average Soviet citizen consumed was delivered through the mechanism of non-monetized 'social wage', which included free health care, free education, subsidised food, rent, child care, transportation and a host of other heavily subsidised goods and communal services. The Soviet citizens did not know what a medical bill was! No doubt, the average standard of living under the old regime was never high and the goods produced and provided often wanting in quality. Administratively rationed, there were chronic shortages for the majority as well a ladder of access that ensured the higher a person's social rank the better quality goods or services he received, with the *nomenklatura* even living as a ruling class. But whatever the ideological or political repression, almost nobody went hungry and there were no gross inequalities among the people. Everybody was employed, basic human needs were easily satisfied, the essential social services were free and available. Now the guaranteed employment, welfare provision and price stability had disappeared and with them the universally acknowledged achievements of the Soviet system in health care, education, culture and the arts. Hospitals, schools and kindergartens, theatres and museums had been driven into bankruptcy and gone were the days of summer camps for children, of low priced theatre and ballet tickets, discs and tapes of classical music or classics of world literature. As Nadia Surdlova, a school teacher in far away Irkutsk in eastern Siberia later bitterly commented: 'No, we cannot say that we were rich. But neither were we poor. I was raised as a Young Pioneer and that organisation has been abolished. My family and I travelled in the summer to the Crimea and it was paid for by our trade union. That too has vanished. There was no country in the world, I believe, that had access to such cultural facilities for all as our people. Where are those prized achievements now? We never had beggars in Siberia before. We have them in great numbers...Whatever the mistakes of the Soviet Union may have been and they were many, it was paradise compared to the purgatory in which we've been dumped...'

The human costs of 'free market' transition in Russia were, and remain, a high one. Popular impoverishment meant malnutrition and dietary deficiencies on a mass scale which in turn accentuated the link between poor diet and disease. The newspapers reported an explosive return of diseases such as cholera, typhoid, diptheria, unknown since the 1920s, and a sharp increase in the incidence of other life-threatening diseases in different parts of the country. The medical system having decayed, for large sections of the population who could not afford to replace the disappearing state-provided service with a privately purchased one, the loss was permanent, (as it was in the sphere of education and elsewhere). The declining quality of life – the sudden impoverishment of the people, poorer health facilities and the attendant socio-psychological stresses – expressed itself in rising adult, infant and maternal mortality and the death rate exceeding the birth rate. The children were indeed becoming a luxury that many families could now ill-afford. Speaking of this 'shrinkage of population' as a demographic 'katastroika' – cf. Gorbachev's catastrophic perestroika – scholars pointed out that it was 'impossible to find any peacetime parallel for a catastrophe of this magnitude anywhere in the modern world.'

Associated with this frightening indicator of the destitution and distress spreading across Russia was the rise of stress-related illnesses and mental disorders, increases in alcoholism and crimes, especially crimes against women, and an overall disorientation making for an abnormal increase of murder, and still worse, suicide rates, with macabre reports of fathers committing suicide because they could not provide their children with food and shelter and the poverty-stricken bereaved families renting coffins, which had to be returned the day after the burial. Russians were seen to be losing their will to live and even hard-core right-wingers began to talk of mitigating the 'impact of market forces'.

Apropos this 'impact', let me conclude with sharing the following write-up by the eminent economist, Rehman Sobhan:

> Recently on CNN I watched a small item on Mongolia. It showed children abandoned by their parents for reasons of poverty, living in the sewers of Ulan Bator. It appears that in the golden age of the market economy, 25 per cent of the families of Mongolia have fallen below the poverty line which stands at a handsome US $ 10 per month. As with most such encounters with the market reform process children bore the brunt of the degeneration into poverty of their families. These same children now huddling in the streets and sewers during a Mongolian winter had in the bad old days of Communist rule in Mongolia enjoyed guaranteed health care, basic nutrition, primary education and other basic necessities of life, including a roof over their head in a warm home, as a matter of right. Their parents had guaranteed jobs, a secure and predictable future. They however did not have shops full of imported luxury goods or fleets of luxury cars on the streets available to those who can buy them in the free market. Nor were their hotels full of the much sought after foreign middlemen and consultants who are now ubiquitous in Ulan Bator in searchof a quick killing at the expense of Outer Mongolia.
>
> Are Mongolians better off under market economics? Are its citizens better fed, housed, clothed than they were in the bad old days? Obviously UNICEF does not think so. In a recently published report, *Central and Eastern Europe in Transition: Public Policy and Social Conditions*, UNICEF reports on the decline in

public services in the formerly socialist countries of Europe. The report presents some horrifying statistics about the declining standards of living of the 'beneficiaries' of market reforms. The report indicates that in 1992, 53.6 per cent of Bulgarian households lived in poverty. In Hungary, poverty levels in 1991 were 21.3 per cent compared to the pre-reform level in 1989 of 10.1 per cent. In the Czech Republic, poverty increased from 5.7 per cent in 1989 to 18.2 per cent in 1992. In Poland poverty increased from 21.8 per cent in 1989 to 41.4 per cent (57.6 per cent of children live in poverty). In Romania poverty inceased from 27.3 per cent in 1989 to 51.1 per cent in 1992 (70.1 per cent of children live in poverty). In Russia households in poverty increased from 5 per cent in 1989 to 43.8 per cent in 1992. (This assumes a poverty line of 75 roubles. If this poverty line is raised to 118 roubles the households living in poverty rise to 77.1 per cent.) In Ukraine poverty was 35.7 per cent in 1992 (assuming a Rb 118 poverty line). This is a small increase over 1989. In Slovakia poverty increased from 8.5 per cent in 1989 to 30.2 per cent in 1992 (41.3 per cent of children lived in poverty). Thus as in Mongolia all of formerly Socialist Europe has faced a rapid and visible increase in poverty following the move towards the market.

As a consequence of this deterioration in the conditions of life in formerly Socialist Europe, UNICEF reports that between 1989 and 1993 the crude death rate increased by 17 per cent in Romania, 12 per cent in Bulgaria, and by an incredible 32 per cent in Russia where the report states that yearly deaths in 1993 exceeded that of 1989 by 5,47,000 units. To further quote UNICEF on the crisis in formerly Socialist Europe, 'the spread of poverty, birth contraction, escalation of death rates, decline in school enrolments and an unstoppable crime wave have reached truly alarming proportions'. The homeless street children seen in Ulan Bator are now also common in Moscow and many other cities of eastern Europe. This is the by-product of rising levels of unemployment, liberalisation of the housing market and the cuts in social services due to budgetary austerity imposed under the IMF's various stabilisation programmes.

The crisis of living standards posed by economic reforms is of course not unique to post-socialist Europe. Eastern Europe has been the hardest hit because a system, put in place over many years, which guaranteed the basic needs of its citizens in the form of full employment, education up to secondary level, basic health, nutrition, cheap but hardly luxurious housing, cheap transport, was dismantled in rapid order under the *diktat* of the IMF and World Bank who were driven by the compulsion of the dominant western countries to exorcise as rapidly as possible the spectre of Bolshevism which was seen to have been haunting Europe for these many years. The exorcists from the Bank and Fund have done a rather good job of it because they have managed to transform some of the former Communist *apparatchiks* into dollar millionaires by creating opportunities for them to maximise profits as blackmarketeers, currency racketeers, drug dealers, pimps and common or garden criminals, in the name of promoting market economics. This same class can now live in luxurious apartments, drive Mercedes, live on imported luxuries, holiday in Spain and drive past the huddled masses sleeping on the snow-covered pavements of Moscow to an evening at a night club where their bill would support five Russian families for a year.....

VIII

The plunder of Russia's natural and human resources and the ravaging of its people was accompanied by a massive ideological-cultural offensive in behalf of the turn to capitalism. As the Russian newspaper *Pravda* saw it: 'Western economic expansion in Russia is actually an aggression which is being conducted in a "civilised" form using the methods of psychological war and neo-colonialist exploitation. One of the principal means of this expansion is through the liberal market ideology' – so that old norms and values had given way to a moral situation where 'the robber and the thief become the most respectable persons, traitors are turned into heroes and Russophobes and Westerners become the models of the nation.' As part of this offensive, this 'ideological engineering', to make sure of this reconquest of Russia for capitalism, there was a mass penetration of all Russian cultural and media institutions by American 'research' institutes and think tanks (such as the Rand Corporation and the Carnegie Foundation). This is how an account by a foreign observer had it:

> ...in their cultural politics, Russian neoliberals have resorted to the massive importation of Western cultural production as an instrument of 'reforming the people's consciousness.' The population has been subjected to an aggressive acculturation and

> indoctrination in the values of consumerism and a neoconservative ideology patterned after Thatcherism and Reaganism. Imported are not just soap operas, Derrida, the sex shops, the postmodernism, but the very principle of the structuralisation of cultural space into mass and 'high' cultures, and the commodification of cultural production and consumption in art, education, recreation, and personal relations. While the overall effectiveness of this ideological violence may take some time to evaluate, its destructive impact, especially on the young generation, is obvious. According to recent polls taken among female high school students in Moscow, 'hard-currency' prostitution is considered one of the most prestigious occupations. The money/commodity indoctrination is complemented by a new emphasis on the cult of the family, the media-promoted notions of politics as 'dirty business', and the 'end-of-ideology' slogan. All are intended to facilitate the radical split between the private and the public that is characteristic of late capitalist societies, and above all to impede political organisation from below.
>
> A new intellectual culture is also being created through the mechanism of importation, as the political class and the neoliberal sectors of the Russian intelligentsia, that control the media and education, have entered a period of servile apprenticeship to the centres of intellectual power in the West.

As this 'servile apprenticeship' progressed over the next few years, we had, from within Russia, the anguished protest of the sociologist Nikita Pokrovsky which deserves to be noticed in some detail. Witnessing the accelerating speed of collapse in morals and values around him and Russia's growing thraldom to America, he wrote of 'the gathering strength of one particular new Russian ideology':

> This ideology can be explained simply with the aid of an old slogan: 'Enrich yourself!' – with all the means available, instantly, without fear and reproach. It is a goal, a principle and also moral value. It is an indulgence, too, in case there are any leftovers from pangs of conscience. But everybody is doing this, are even proud of it and not ashamed to boast about it. From now on, to live modestly is considered indecent and shameful. Really, 'if you are clever, why are you poor?'
>
> At present we are not dominated by any values except mass intoxication with commerce. All inhibitions, of any sort, have been

discarded. The question is not about business as such but about the philosophy and morals of new Russia in totality. I emphasise, 'in totality'.

What is going on can be summarised this way: he who is not engaged in business, does not enrich himself, is not interested in all this 'buying-selling', should not be considered a significant person at all. He is not regarded as such by anybody, neither by his own family, nor his friends, nor his neighbours, nor by the state itself. A person who is out of business is a useless person, perhaps not a person at all. This kind of spirit is gaining hold very rapidly and establishing a sort of total dictatorship over minds, though it is profoundly alien to Russia. A non-commercial personality is not respectable any more, it is driven underground, reduced to poverty, left in a state of contemplation of its own degeneration, in short, in complete social non-existence....

Apropos 'new heroes of our time' and 'politically correct thinking':

> TV and radio programmes, newspapers, are overflowing with eulogies addressed to these primitive businessmen. Now they are our navigation lights and moral examples. It is not important what kind of businessman – semi-literate, with an obvious criminal past and visible mafia connections in the present, he lays down the law without fail all over the country like a new prophet, a guru of the Russian ideology. He is not satisfied with increasing his capital, no, he has already started philosophising. Don't you know what is the most popular thesis in our country now? It is a highly interesting one! 'The more rich people are there in Russia, the better the life of the whole society'. That is the way. And these words were pronounced as an absolute truth....
>
> New models of the politically correct thinking – especially aloud and in public – have appeared. The superior virtue now is an ability not to ask questions about something serious. Just nonsense, please. Which of the actors make love to which actress, who and where they had a vacation, who has saved up how much money – these are jolly, smart themes for all possible cases. But what about the substance? What is going on around us? If you raise such questions, you are immediately given a hard and icy look and left alone on your own as a clumsy oaf, an uneducated person, lacking social graces...
>
> One style is in which the positivist bursts with indignation, why one cannot understand the quite obvious and elementary

> things which are clear to every normal person. The emphasis is always on 'normal'. It is claimed, all 'normal' people should act and think 'this way'. And if someone thinks differently then he is going beyond all possible limits.

Again:

> We now do not have such a notion as culture. We have only 'show-business', 'casino', 'cruises', 'gatherings of variety stars', 'presentations'. The latter notion and the social phenomena connected with it are the most typical ones...As far as the genuine valuable culture is concerned, they just look 'through' it. Science schools and institutions are perishing ('it serves them right, as if they were scientists!'), universities are becoming degraded to an indecent level ('we will send our children to study in America'), we have no more *belles-lettres* as such ('as for me, I like thrillers more'), no valuable cinematography ('I say! I have a four-head video system at home, I can watch *Basic Instinct*'). And everything in the same vein. So here they are, the 'new' patrons of art. I stress it again – not all of them, but the majority.
>
> In the new 'small villages' one can see only giant brick palaces – private residencies. Nearby, kindergartens are languishing in misery. Children's summer camps are closing one after another. 'Not a sound, my friend, O, not a word' is heard from behind the windows of these mausoleum-like residencies. Simultaneously – endless, boring, vicious, semi-literate and inarticulate philosophising on the worldwide mission of Russian business goes on..
>
> There is no limit to it. Full Stop. In truth, there is one small, niggling thing. It is that the rest of the society, those who do not constitute the notorious 10 per cent upper crust, is kneeling lower and lower. Part of it adores new idols out of inner feebleness, a part cries with the pain of humiliation, and the rest are absorbed in reminiscences of the past. But nobody looks into the future. You cannot do that when on your knees!....
>
> As for thraldom to America, the pain and humiliation of *their* ideological injection: There is a great dose of conscious didactism in this injection: 'You did not want to do things our way; you thought you would leave us behind while developing in your own special way; you made us build bomb-shelters and tremble with fear; so now you dance!' And we dance...

The onset of capitalist transition in Russia was a material and moral devastation that destroyed civil society, disrupted the previous socio-economic structures and accustomed patterns of life, and distorted fundamental social relations, leaving the people with 'a many-layered feeling of moral and spiritual injury, a loss of one's bearings, one's sense of self and society, bewilderment and frustration at the gaping divisions among one's own people, uncertainty about even the physical dimensions of one's country, let alone its values, and a growing fear of still greater insults and privations to come', as Peter Reddaway, the author of *Uncensored Russia* has put it. Atomised in every aspect of their existence, the people found themselves pushed into the harsh world of 'free-market' – an 'elbow society' as a new saying had it, where one wants to push ahead at the expense of others. Humiliated citizens of what only the other day was 'the other super power', they were assailed by new despairs and a palpable sense of lost dignity and self-respect. As one woman textile worker said: 'they have taken away from us our dignity, and one cannot live without it'. All sense of community feeling, of reliance on each other lost, a veritable anomie descended upon the Russian people. Remaining at as tantalising a distance as ever from consumerist cosmopolitanism they had looked forward to, now full of 'anger, hatred, self-disgust and aggressiveness' and facing an identity crisis, they sought refuge in consolations of religiosity, inward-looking identitarianism, or the intoxicating and intolerant morbidities of inflamed nationalism, ethnic strife, xenophobia, anti-semitism and centuries old vendettas, and a neo-fascism finding new scapegoats – 'the internal threat to white Christian civilisation posed by brown-skinned Caucasians and Asians', the new refugees from the South. Confused and disoriented, with no faith in themselves and bereft of any vision of the future, they were only too vulnerable to the demagogy of the likes of Yeltsin and Zhirinovsky.

IX

The transition to 'free market' was virtually a free fall into an abyss. Within a couple of years of the so-called 'market reform', life in Russia was meaner, dirtier, poorer and more crime ridden than ever. As the citizens of Russia, including a major part of the intelligentsia struggled to survive in the new environment, destitution was pushing an increasing number to the lowest levels of civilised existence. The bread lines were now longer and more miserable than any in the Soviet period. For the first time since the Bolshevik Revolution a thoroughly dispossessed and literally homeless population appeared on the Russian scene, 'the very poor' of Russia who could be readily observed in train stations, underpasses and derelict buildings of any of its large cities, including Moscow, their numbers swollen by the influx of Russian-speaking refugees from ethnic wars in the South. Beggars, bagladies and little children roamed the city streets, along with the prostitutes and alcoholics, and a disastrous five to seven-year drop in longevity was reported over the first three years of transition to a free market economy. The gulf between the neo-rich, those with position, power and property, and the neo-poor, a majority of the population, was daily widening and with the scarcities dominating the economy, the black market was the only genuine 'free market' where speculating businessman and criminal gangs muscled in with the power of their guns and goons and political connections, while the newly impoverished and unemployed had the pleasure of watching from a distance these new millionaires walk into stores, now devoid of long lines, and pick up whatever they wanted!

More than one scholar, noticing the destruction of national assets and household wealth, rising unemployment and underemployment and the threat of far worse rises in the offing, falling real wages of the working classes and impoverishment of the peasantry, spreading poverty and destitution together with the corrosion of social security arrangements, growing informal sector and mafia domination of the economy, pointed to a third worldised future for the post-Soviet Russia. The promised quick 'transition to free market', the 'impending take-off' never occurred. (The promised 'democracy', as we shall see, fared no better.) Russia's hope of joining the first world vanished within a few years of market economy. Talk of emulating the economies and politics of Sweden or Austria was replaced by gloomy perusal of the statistics of Mexico or Bolivia, or the only too recent doings of the Chilean Pinochet.

X

The driving force behind the so-called 'economic reforms' in Russia was, and remains, the pressure of the now extraordinarily powerful international capitalist establishment – the leading Western powers and the international financial community – for whom Russia, as Eastern Europe a little earlier, offered a tantalising prize, and whose members, bankers, businessmen, ministers and presidents, descended upon it like vultures, quickly translating liberty and democracy into freedom to plunder and despoil a whole economy. Leading this pressure were international financial institutions like the International Monetary Fund and World Bank, whose market-oriented conditionalities governed the macro-economic stabilisation measures, including 'shock therapy', which had already been tried in Poland and elsewhere in Eastern Europe. The German minister of finance Theo Wagel said that 'Russian leaders must make it clear that economic reforms would continue or lose international financial aid'. Desperate for such aid the Russian leadership under Yeltsin was even otherwise only too willing to oblige. As the multinational capital moved in for the kill, 'shock therapy' produced naked markets – markets opened up to the west by convertibility and privatisation but denied the forms of public subsidy, protection and regulation available in every western capitalist state. 'Russia has undergone fundamental changes and appears to be on the right track...' is how the neo-liberal scholar Aslund saw it, but Sachs, a key figure behind the 'stabilisation' programmes in Poland and Russia, was compelled to recognise the disastrous consequences: 'Russia is in a deep state of crisis that could send the country into a spiral of self-reinforcing destructive behaviours: criminality, regional separatism, tax evasion, and the flight from the currency.'

'Shock therapy' it was said, was all shock and no therapy and when its results were yet described as 'encouraging' by the IMF bosses, the Poles had responded with their proverb: 'the operation was successful but the patient died'. Now the focus was on Russia and once again 'a magical concept of the market' was the essential policy instrument for its capitalist economic transformation. It was really a case of pushing market economy down the throat of a surprised population, or, as a description of the time had it, a 'Harvard experiment... using the Russian people as guinea pigs', supervised by 'zealous young professors' in Moscow subscribing to 'the free market cargo cult purveyed by publications like the *Economist* and the *Financial Times*'. As the IMF and the WB went about this task, Yeltsin's government faithfully followed the recommendations made by them towards turning Russia into a market-based private capitalist economy. There may have been a naive faith in the western experts' pledge to turn Russia into a modern industrial power capable of competing in the world market. But it was more a matter of narrow class interests, and whatever may have been the illusions concerning their role, Yeltsin and his associates or cronies were, at best, playing the part of colonising representatives of western capitalist interests. No wonder All-Russian Officers' Assembly in Moscow (February, 1993) described the Yeltsin government as an 'occupation regime'. More critical and perceptive Russians even suggested: 'We lost the cold war and are now paying the reparations'.

Western capitalism, using its formidable machinery of economic coercion through international financial institutions, pressurised Russia to sell off its historic productive assets, to accelerate the pace of privatisation and marketisation, to cut down subsidies and raise prices more stiffly, to dismantle what they described as 'grossly dysfunctional' social security system and scrap its welfare commitments – that is, end the economic life-support system of institutions of civil society in such areas as health and higher education, arts and culture and shift to private, market-based provision in such matters – to privatise and disperse the research institutes, to, in general, disengage human and material resources from domestic production and reorient the national economy towards the high income western market regardless of its consequences for industrial production and employment at home.

The much promised foreign investment did not arrive as anticipated. Given the economic and political risks involved, foreign capital was cautions, preferring to enter 'through the back door' with small investments, often as joint ventures with the emerging *nouveau riches* of the Russian economy (say, in the consumer or mining and extractive sectors), or to purchase domestic enterprises at very low cost largely to secure control over cheap labour (of highly qualified workers) and factory space. There was marked preference for the immediately profitable areas such as commerce (and not material production) or for production focussing on luxury items for a few rather than mass consumption goods for all. It is this sort of economic activity which, along with the mafiosi enterprise, determined the overall character of the emerging 'entrepreneurship' in Russia.

Western aid from USA as also Japan and other countries was even more of a myth than foreign productive investment. Even so, much of whatever came was reported to have ended up in Swiss bank accounts. It had, along with the worsening balance of payment situation, only accumulated foreign debt and the debt servicing obligation, which in economist Sarafanov's apt phrase, was like a 'slow acting bomb' that will explode with much greater intensity sometime in the future. In fact both foreign aid and investment were more active in facilitating the plundering of Russia by western capitalism, in taking over or destroying whatever was left from the days of the Soviet Union, and thus incapacitating Russia economically for a long time to come. It is not without reason that even a collaborator like Viktor Chernomyrdin, a Prime Minister at the time, accusing the United States of fighting a silent economic war against Russia, complained: 'Those who rule the world markets are not at all interested in letting Russia gain an entry. They want Russia to finally collapse'.

That such a war was on and such was its aim is clear from the way the IMF and western capital in general early focussed on the key sector of the petroleum industry – Russia is one of the largest petroleum producers in the world – in their efforts to open up the Russian economy to western exploitation or sought the stopping of state subsidies particularly to the high-tech and aerospace industries, knowing full well that this will cripple the one area of the Russian economy that could conceivably compete with big western capital. (Entire cities in the Urals and Siberia belonging to the military-industrial complex were dependent on the State credits and procurements). Petroleum and high-tech industries are of course highly lucrative business. If big petroleum corporations sought a grip over Russian petroleum industry, Western high-tech firms (Lockheed Missile and Space Corporation, Boeing and Rockwell International among others) even more avidly eyed the aerospace and aircraft industries, where they could now purchase the services of top Russian scientists in fibre optics, computer design, satellite technology, nuclear physics (to name but a few) for an average wage below 100 dollars a month, at least 50 times less than in the west. Through 'joint ventures' entire research laboratories or institutes in Physics, mechanical engineering, space research etc. were taken over for use of their talent, scientific know-how and production facilities or for dispersal and even closing down if need be. Macro-economic policy advocated or imposed by IMF and other institutions of the international financial community supported the interests of these global enterprises because, apart from ensuring profits for them, it weakened the Russian economy and blocked Russia, as a capitalist power in its own right, from competing on the world market.

It needs to be remembered that the old Soviet Union educated and employed about one fourth of the world's engineers, scientists, physicists and others at the technological frontiers of human progress – scientists and engineers alone counted more than 1.5 million. Many of these were reduced to poverty, forced to leave their fields and work elsewhere merely in order to physically survive. It was literally a case of a quarter of world's scientific and technological capacity withering away or dying. Indeed, one of the most pernicious consequences of the economic disarray over the early post-collapse years, caused by the dismantling of the old system and the transition to 'market economy', was a growing paralysis of the Russian science. Scientific laboratories and institutes, when not taken over by foreign capital, went bankrupt or were dispersed and just about limping along, and there was a virtual stampede for emigration, the west buying out Soviet science, scientists and scientific know-how wholesale and dirt cheap. If it is recognised that in the modern world, the scientific establishment, particularly the Research and Development set-up, lies at the heart of the economy, all this constituted an irreparable loss for any future effort at national reconstruction. Chances of such reconstruction were becoming even slimmer because the 'brain drain' which nearly destroyed Soviet fundamental science was increasingly accompanied by a 'brawn drain', that is, selective emigration abroad of skilled manpower.

In its Fund-Bank imposed transition to 'free market economy', or capitalism which is its proper name, what swept through Russia was no Schumpeterian 'gale of creative destruction', releasing long-stymied inventiveness and enterprise and heralding a bright new capitalist future for the country. It was, in Alec Nove's words, 'destruction with nothing creative taking place', a perverse restructuring of economy whose immediate consequence was the emergence of a mafiosi-capitalism in Russia, clearing the way, at best, for a relatively more stable comprador capitalism of the third world variety; though, given its inherent contradictions, its stable existence seemed almost impossible to sustain.

XI

With the collapse of the Union government in the aftermath of the failed putsch of August 1991, the various economic programmes of the Gorbachev era (Aganbegayan, Shatalin, Abalkin, etc.) for a 'planned' transition towards market economy were shelved. It is doubtful if any 'planned' or even normally painful transition to capitalism was ever a real option in the former Soviet Union. But with the break-up of central political power, the final collapse of the system of planning and state enterprises, and the entry of 'shock therapy' advising IMF and WB, it was no longer even a theoreticl possibility. What Russia, under Yeltsin, now witnessed was a spontaneous process of privatisation, better described as 'wild privatisation' – defended as an 'unfortunate necessity' by the new rulers – in which the former apparatchiks, ex-high party officials, enterprise managers, top level administrators and operators from the 'shadow economy' saw the public assets as if they were no one's property and seized them, often illegally, for their private use. It was a new kind of highwayrobbery, a theft of state property by those who controlled it, an asset-stripping exercise in which those with power either became owners of what were till then public assets or sold it off to others for peanuts and pocketed the black money profits. A process of 'primitive accumulation' characterised by 'grab whatever you can', its most active participants were the ruling *nomenklatura* and the emerging mafias, with the foreign capitalists joining them in this plunder of the Soviet economy. Already, as the old economic system was crumbling during the last phase of the perestroika, and marketisation and privatisation was on, the *nomenklatura*, former communist bureaucrats, controlling most of the state enterprises had come to run their companies like private fiefdoms, setting their own prices, cutting deals with mafias to get supplies and to sell goods, or to create artificial shortages in the market to drive up prices. Now, appropriating the funds of the banned Communist Party and using their positions of power, they seized the new opportunities and embarked on a spree of personal embourgeoisment. Gone entirely commercial, linked no longer to the communist party but to the new industrial concerns and commercial banks, as well as the mafias, this new *nomenklatura* was a corporate elite of a new kind. Dominating the economy, it was a bandit bureaucracy or 'bandocracy' as the Marxist economist Alexander Buzgalin called them.

Notwithstanding the neo-liberal ideologues' insistence on 'the epochal nature' of the transition in East Europe and Russia, possibly, the most significant aspect of this transition was the way in which so much of the old order and its personnel proved able to shift their power base to find niches in the supposedly new order. In the midst of the changes in 1989, the reforming Hungarian sociologist Hankiss had noted that 'a section of the elite in power recognised that it could easily, and without losing anything, transform its authority ... into a political and economic power capable of functioning in a new system'. About the same time, the first Czechoslovak minister of privatisation, putting it more bluntly had said: 'The winners will be the same people who won under the old system.. the directors of the former state companies along with illegal currency dealers and other operators.' He had however added that in the interest of 'reform', 'we have to be blind to this injustice'. 'This injustice' was now most obvious in Russia. Russia's new men in money and power too emerged from two sections of the former Soviet society: the party *nomenklatura* and the black market. The first held – and now continued to hold – political and administrative power, the other had practical financial and marketing skills. Though they were official enemies in the past, clandestine dealings between them were common. Economic reforms had now brought them into the open, hand in hand, along with the mafia which was now an independently significant part of the black market or the 'second economy'.

Mikhail Serdyuk of Russian Interior Ministry's economic department reported, in June 1993, that much of the country's most valuable property was simply disappearing from the public privatisation process. 'The temptation to become overnight the owner of huge material resources is great,' said Serdyuk. 'The appetites of corrupt authorities and economic managers who are involved in privatisation are increasing day by day.' According to Konstantin Borovoi, the self-made millionaire who headed the Russian Party of Economic Freedom, overwhelming majority of the new rich in Russia were not entrepreneurs but corrupt officials who had grown fat on bribes from businessmen. The upshot of it all was an 'apparatchik capitalism', as it came to be called, giving birth to one important variant of Russia's new 'biznesman', an offshoot of the communist *nomenklatura* of the Brezhnev period.

Associated in this process of property formation, a socially cruel and piratical asset accumulation, were open or underground speculators, 'lumpen capitalists' from the 'second economy' (which flourished even under the old regime), and the 'affairists' of the private sector, all of them always close to the official bureaucracy or economic administration. These were entrepreneurs on the margin of legality when not well beyond it. But independently or overlapping these, the most significant other stream providing Russia's new 'biznesmen' were the mafia bosses, whose influence, as we have noticed earlier, had become extensive and crucial in society, particularly in the field of economic activity.

Now that most economic enterprise in Russia had come to be based on the principle of 'quick money', and the practice of this principle best facilitated by corruption and criminal violence, accumulation of wealth by the mafias was only another, though particularly barbaric, form of 'primitive accumulation of capital'. And as the privileges and power previously granted to the state and party elites, far from being abrogated, were now significantly enlarged and passed on to those with private accumulation of wealth, the mafia came to hold real power in society, including its economy and politics. So overwhelming was the mafia presence in the economy that while scholars spoke of capitalist-cum-mafiosi, most people did not distinguish between the two. The journal *Financial Times* was frank enough to write and accept that 'initially much of the new business class will be hardly distinguishable from spies and mafiosi'. Given the mafiosi influence, collaboration, even fusion with the *nomenklatura*, others, more perceptively, wrote of a 'mafia nomenklatura' dominating Russia's emergent 'free market economy'. What best described this economy was the more widely accepted term, *mafiosi-capitalism.*

'Market reform' in Russia, its 'wild west' marketisation and privatisation and the accelerated processes of primary accumulation of capital generated by them, had led to the development of a 'mafiosi capitalism' in Russia – a kind of savage (*dikii*) capitalism – presided over by a 'mafia bourgeoisie' which had little in common with any kind of democracy, legality, egalitarianism or humanism that the naive ideologues of capitalism in Russia had dreamt of. Even when admitted to be 'unfortunate', the powers that be defended this denouement as 'necessary'. The ideologues and defenders, including some from among the new rich of Russia like Borovoi, even quoted Marx on western capitalism's origins in 'primitive accumulation' – a period of outright plunder and exploitation that amassed and concentrated capital, thus making further stages of capitalist development possible – assuming, of course, that further steps along the road to a 'normal and civilised' western-style capitalism were bound to follow. The well-known Russia-born American economist, Vasily Leontieff helpfully suggested that today's 'mafia' is tomorrow's class of 'civilised' capitalists. The crucial question however remained: what kind of 'normal and civilised' capitalism plundered and despoiled Russia could hope for, with the ruling class it had inherited from the old regime, and as a latecomer to capitalism in a world dominated by the advanced capitalism of North America, Western Europe and Japan.

XII

We have noticed the beginnings of the capitalist transition in Russia in some detail, not only because of its intrinsic interest or lessons, but even more because implicit in it are the problems besetting its future, putting a question mark on its ability to hold and grow in the 'normal' way.

Russia simply does not have the normally necessary social force to lead this transition, that is, a capitalist class capable of building a successful capitalist economy. It is not merely that you cannot produce an entrepreneurial bourgeoisie overnight, or that such bourgeoisie needs several generations in the most favourable conditions to come into existence and several more generations to become civilised, or that private enterprise has never and nowhere arisen on the basis of the privatisation of centralised state monopolies, or that 'primitive accumulation' proper was a prelude to industrial society in the west and thus irrelevant to Russia where extensive industrialisation of Russia discouraged the growth of an entrepreneurial industrial bourgeoisie. It is simply that out of the wreckage of the old system, and under the continuing impact of 'market reforms', the new social strata that had emerged were, in economist Tatiana Koryagina's words, 'horribly distorted, completely incomparable with social classes as understood in classical western theory'. As a consequence, she wrote, 'we do not have a rational, thrifty, productive bourgeoisie in the 19th century western sense...The Russian new rich are a marriage of convenience between the most vigorous sections of the old *nomenklatura* and former black market structures. Their idea of doing business is to get rich quickly through easy speculation. There is virtually no productive investment occurring in this country.' These 'new rich' of Russia were, and remain, too busy amassing super profits from non-productive activities and then squandering them on luxury consumption or stashing them in banks abroad, to think of anything else, least of all Russia's development as a 'normal' capitalist economy.

The West had early recognised and accepted that the core of the new domestic capitalist class will be formed of those who had managed to accumulate money-capital under the old disintegrating Soviet regime – currency speculators, black-marketeers, the emergent mafiosi, as well as the corrupt members of state administration especially in the import-export sectors. Such people had shown the entrepreneurial spirit – albeit of a criminal kind. Lord Howe, appointed adviser to the Ukrainian government in 1991, was quite frank on this point. He urged the need for the development of what he called 'bandit capitalism' in Ukraine and drew a favourable parallel with the great robber barons of American capitalism in the nineteenth century. The policy was faithfully reflected in the pages of the *Economist* which, urging that these businessmen 'whose methods of operation hover uneasily between those of Al Capone and those of the early American robber barons ... need to be encouraged to go legitimate', argued for a faster deregulation and liberalisation of the economy for the purpose. This is indeed how it soon turned out to be. But solution enough for the west or its plans for Russia, this bandit or mafia capitalism, held and does not hold any promise of a 'normal and civilised' capitalist development in Russia. In other words, the new bourgeoisie in Russia, recruited from 'the only genuine sources' available, the *nomenklatura* and mafias, its rather strong entrepreneurial and proprietary instincts notwithstanding, has neither the skills nor the foresight (or even the interest) to be a class that Russia is looking for, one capable of building a normally successful capitalist economy in the country.

Resources for the purpose too is a problem. The new

bourgeoisie, despite its accumulated wealth, does not have them and the much promised and hoped for foreign investment has been not only 'dramatically short' of what is needed to rebuild Russian economy as a successful capitalism – assuming that such is indeed the intention – it has been, playing safe in a situation of political uncertainty, attracted primarily to the consumer sector (MacDonald and Coke etc.), or to the immediately profitable mining and extractive sections. (This, however, does not exhaust the question of foreign investment. There is the disconcerting possibility that, especially if the present comprador regime continues or manages to stabilise itself, any thoroughgoing privatisation of the means of production will put the Russian enterprises into the hands or control of those who have the resources and the clout to take over, those who are the possessors of the great bulk of the world's capital; namely, Europe, America and Japan. Such a transfer would follow the pattern of previous international movements of capital, in which Europe, America and Japan have supplied hard currency and expertise to would be capitalisms, which in exchange have made available their only assets – cheap labour and raw materials. In other words, it would firmly entrench multinational capital in the country, interested in exploiting it and not developing a rival capitalism). Russia also does not have a working class of the kind an emerging capitalist economy requires, a desperately poor, beaten down, malleable people ready to do anything in order to survive; despite all that went wrong with it under 'Soviet socialism', the Russian working class will not be easily available for the purpose. Just as market reforms' decollectivisation is finding it difficult to transform the collective farmer again into the peasantry of a capitalist society, its denationalisation or privatisation will not easily yield a peaceable and pliant proletariat to exploit – they have had jobs and social security under the old regime and their collective farms and industrial plants were structurally associated with the provision of social services which included vacation homes, places of culture, housing, polyclinics, sanatoria, kindergartens, and so on. The question of bourgeoisie and proletariat apart, not only does the much needed social peace and political stability remain elusive, all the more so because of pauperisation of the middle class, constructing a proper supportive infrastructure of capitalism – property rights legislation, banking and commercial laws, essential regulatory agencies, communication networks, the diverse basic institutions of the capital market (like the stock exchanges, specialised banking, financial and consulting services), etc. – in a society which had none of it earlier and is now much too lawless and mafia-ridden, continues to pose its own intractable problems. And, one may add, a 'consumerist itch' is no ideological substitute for 'puritan ethics' or 'possessive individualism' of the kind that underpinned the development of capitalism in the west. Compounding the problems of a capitalism now seeking a place under the sun of global market is the fact that there are no foreign markets for most of what a Russian capitalism would produce – these are already glutted with better quality and probably cheaper goods from Japan, Korea, Brazil, China, etc. Russia would indeed be competing for opportunities with those parts of the developing world that have established significant footholds in the global markets including those in certain parts of the advanced world. And this advanced world, as Russia along with Eastern Europe has already discovered, remains quite protective about its markets at home and abroad. Liberal rhetoric apart, western countries have been most reluctant to allow market access to others.

Making the situation more problematic, and worse in many ways, is the reality of the world capitalist system itself being – subject of course to cyclical and regional variations – in a long term crisis since the 1970s. A global capitalism carrying the built-up burden of its own problems is hardly a propitious external economic environment for the capitalist transition in Russia. Along with the questionable assumptions that the new capitalist structures could easily be transported and implanted into Russia, that it was the market elements that were the key components of the west's relatively better performance, the Russian hopefuls had also assumed that the west was doing well enough to be not only a model to be emulated, it was also resourceful enough to relieve their miseries and, providing capital, markets and, of course, advice, help them build a successful and prosperous capitalism of their own. This was and remains a most questionable assumption. The west was and is simply unable, because ill-equipped, to fulfil the promises of bourgeois prosperity held out to Soviet or, for that matter, East European peoples. Even the leader and the only superpower of the west remains too capital-poor, indebted and bankrupt to be able to even think of another Marshall Plan. In other words, if it is bad enough today to see the west as a model to be emulated, it is even worse to expect a stagnant and crisis-ridden western capitalism to use its scarce funds to help build a successful capitalism in Russia, a potential rival in the global markets. It speaks volumes for the desperation as well as the essentially comprador character of the Russian ruling elite that they continue to entertain hopes in this regard. There is an old Chinese proverb that says – 'Don't tie your boat to the tail of capitalist dog just as it is about to go over the waterfalls'. Though, one must add, Chinese themselves haven't paid much heed to this Maoist wisdom.

XIII

As the foregoing argument clearly suggests, whatever be the immediate and not so immediate problems confronting Russia's capitalist transition, there is the basic, long run problem besetting Russia's entry into the global market, where presidents and prime ministers of even leading industrial nations have been regularly travelling to capitals of 'the developing countries' in search of export markets. Is their room, indeed, and if so of what sort, for Russian capitalism in today's global capitalist economy? In other words, the obviously late arrival of Russian capitalism on the scene has its own problems. All the major capitalist states achieved economic predominance in an era when their ruling classes could exploit their own citizens and colonial peoples mercilessly without serious competition from powerful rivals – not exactly the situation for Russia today. Russian economist Belotserkovskii has even argued that the international economic system is no longer capable of sustaining the emergence of a successful large capitalist country. This may or may not be so, and one can point to the late entrants of an earlier era such as Germany in the late nineteenth century, Japan in the twentieth century, and for some time at least South Korea in the post-Second World War period. But apart from the fact that the international economic system was relatively more open for them or there were exceptional historical circumstances not available to Russia, the important point is that they succeeded against initially superior competitors only by means of a heavily state-guided economy. State guidance, including barriers to free trade and foreign investment is what enabled each of them to overcome its initially weak competitive position and avoid being trapped in the unfavourable position of producer of primary products and/or low-wage manufactured goods. This is what gives a certain centrality to the character of the ruling class in Russia and therefore to the role of the Russian state in the ongoing transition to capitalism. It is certainly possible to postulate in theory a strong Russian state emulating the experience of these other late entrants; it could initially maintain a high degree of planning, public ownership, and control over foreign trade and investment, gradually introduce competition and market forces into the economy, take advantage of the highly educated and skilled population and the technologically more advanced sectors to modernise the industry, preparing it over a decade or two to enter the world market in a better competitive position – and then in a well-planned manner move away from planning, public ownership and state controls and go in for privatisation and a full-fledged market economy. In other words the state could help create what can be described as 'national capitalism', a national capitalist economy owned and controlled by a Russian entrepreneurial class and supported as in other major capitalist nations by the economic and political policies of the state.

But this possibility remains only of theoretical interest. Apart from the fact that the entire weight of Western pressure has been geared to preventing such an outcome, what has happened in Russia in the last few years, especially the origins and nature of the 'new bourgeoisie' and of those now wielding political power, makes it most unlikely that the present Russian state will play this kind of strong and decisive role in rebuilding Russia's economy. From the very beginning this bourgeoisie and the state has had what can only be described as a 'comprador' character. As in many third world countries, the emergent Russian bourgeoisie have so far sought to prosper largely through legal or illegal commercial activity and through their subordinate relationship to foreign capital. And the new Russian state has all along acted on the advice of foreign experts and favoured the adoption of the structural adjustment programmes prescribed by the international financial institutions of global capitalism (IMF, WB, EBRD, etc.), which not only further the interests of the new property owning class in Russia but also lead the way to the take-over of the most profitable state enterprises by foreign capital. In many ways it is these institutions, and not the Russian bourgeoisie or the state, who are playing a decisive role in the capitalist restructuring of the Russian economy. Debt conditionality and political pressures from the advanced capitalist countries only reinforce the comprador nature of this restructuring. Part of this process has been global capitalism propping up with advice and aid pliant rulers like Yeltsin against the more nationally inclined political opponents. Nationalism has no doubt acquired a certain pre-eminence in Russian (including Putin's) politics in recent years, but it has been more as an ideological device to win popular support or buttress an authoritarian regime than any kind of basis for new, alternative politics. Also, it is not that nationalism necessarily rules out comprador behaviour or that class interests cease to have their priority with nationalist or 'nationally inclined' ruling class. This is apart from the fact that capitalism, of whatever kind, is today no option for people struggling for a better life – in Russia or anywhere else in the world.

The full consequences of a rapid integration of the Soviet economy into the world market are incalculable. But given the comprador character of the present Russian state and the ruling elite, with macro economic policy under IMF guidance shaping Russia's relationship to the global economy, the prospects are rather bleak. This policy tends to support the free and unregulated export of primary goods including oil, strategic metals, and food staples and other raw materials while consumer goods including luxury cars, durables and processed food are freely imported for a small privileged market. There is no protection of domestic industry, no measures to rehabilitate the industrial sector or to transform domestic raw materials. Foreign capital investment is eagerly awaited. But when it comes it would not only amount to a 'drop in the bucket' if measured against the needs of serious restructuring along capitalist lines, it would be interested not in such restructuring but quick profits; it would almost certainly gravitate towards the service sector, communications and other secondary activities just as it has in the third world. Insofar as it goes into production it will be to use the country as a cheap labour manufactory for the benefit of foreign capitalists, apart from its use as a source of raw materials and a site for their polluting industries. The liberalistion of foreign trade and exposure to the full blast of international competition may in fact set into motion a devastating de-industrialisation which few indigenous enterprises will be able to survive, even the more technologically advanced industries, since very few of them can currently compete with the world leaders in their fields. The outcome would be to turn Russia into a producer of primary products and supplier of cheap labour for exploitation by foreign and local capitalists. Far from developing the forces of production in Russia, the country would be pushed backwards to a more backward stage. The pattern of trade and economic development will very much come to resemble what is happening in the countries of the third world, which have long realised that the old market is not kind to late starters, who are usually pushed towards the lower end of the international division of labour. In short, if the current neoliberal recapitalistion policies continue to be pursued, Russia would soon slide into the ranks of the underdeveloped countries rather than climb into the ranks of the first world. It would be not westernisation but third worldisation or Latin-Americanisation of Russian economy and society.

This outcome dovetails neatly with international capital's intention to insert Russia into the world economy in a manner consistent with continued western hegemony. The West is primarily interested in having Russia remain a semiperiphery to which it can sell industrial goods and food in exchange for raw materials and whose cheap labour is available for intensified exploitation by foreign capital in sectors of the economy it finds profitable to invest. Even if the West were differently inclined, that is, willing to help Russia build a successful modern industrial economy – an entirely hypothetical proposition which the naive in Russia yet swallowed – it does not have or cannot mobilise the resources on the scale necessary for the purpose. It simply lacks the capacity to respond with adequate capital and technology to develop modern capitalism in Russia, especially when the potential investors may hope for better profit-making opportunities in the weaker peripheral countries of the European common market (Greece, Spain, Portugal, Ireland, etc.) which besides having lower labour costs are also more stable politically and better integrated into the financial and servicing structures of advanced capitalism. Then there are the still weaker and more vulnerable countries of the third world competing for influx of foreign capital.

XIV

Implicit in our discussion of Russia's transition to capitalism is the fact that in the final analysis, more than anything else, it is a matter of politics commanding this transition, that is, the policies flowing from the so-called 'economic reforms'. Given the currently comprador character of the Russian state and ruling elite, this in effect means the politics, the political-ideological motivations governing the policies of the capitalist west towards post-Soviet Russia. We may therefore, repetition notwithstanding, well take another, slightly more focussed look at this politics to better understand not only the reversal of all gains of Russia's socialist past or the 'reform' policies which otherwise are evidently failures in any sane economic terms but also what this politics portends for Russia's future.

As part of its historic achievement, Soviet rule had transformed backward Russia into a major industrial power with a strong scientific-technological base to its economy. High levels of education and human skill were achieved, its highly educated population especially well trained in mathematics and sciences. Basic human needs were satisfied and essential physical infrastructure was constructed. Certain state-owned enterprises – even civilian ones – had accumulated technical know-how and skills roughly comparable to those of capitalist firms operating at the world technological frontier. The latter day 'stagnation' was not significantly worse than similar developments in the west and Gorbachev's *perestroika,* while it indeed disrupted Russia's economy, had not destroyed its substantial industrial, scientific-technological and human assets. These Soviet-era assets surely provided a promising structural foundation for Russia's recovery and transformation into a self-generating economy. There was the experience of post-war economic rebuilding of many countries in Europe and elsewhere (where, incidentally, effective state intervention was a decisive factor). Policies consistent with the existing social and personal values, using economy's potential as well as other elements from the past, including its system of social protection, could aim at something like the modern mixed economies of France, Italy, Japan, etc. Russia could be helped to take something like the Chinese road to market economy and capitalist development. The West however did not and does not have any such aims. It had no interest to shore up the Russian economy, much less help it to grow into a modern capitalist system. Of course an all swamping neo-liberal rhetoric was always there, often as free market or *laissezfaire* paradigms dating from the 18th century, text-book models of the neo-liberal fantasy world, highly mythologised interpretations of capitalism's 'free market' past, or Anglo-American folk tales of economic development. But the naïvete of it all notwithstanding, this neo-liberalism had all along well-served as an useful ideological cover for pursuit of more mundane class interests of global capitalism; particularly for its policies which were governed by two entirely different but interlacing objectives. In the first place, socialism remained an enemy to be feared and for this reasons all vestiges of socialism in Russia must be destroyed. Immediately, given the still volatile and unpredictable nature of politics in Russia, the West was far from being convinced that the ghost of socialism had been finally laid to rest in Russia (or for that matter elsewhere in the former 'socialist' world). Collectivist institutions and ethos still remained to be finally uprooted and destroyed; not even a democratic form of collectivism, no 'market socialism' or social democracy, no *third way* could be allowed as an option. Hence the root and branch destruction of the old regime, its social and political remnants, including its chief economic and industrial achievements, was a strategic priority of western capitalist powers. Under their advice and pressure, Yeltsin's initial policy measures were all aimed at doing away with whatever 'socialist' economy Russia still had, abolishing overnight all policy instruments of central planning and state control including regulation of prices, of state ownership and state subsidy to sectors and regions and state control over distribution and supplies, of state-guaranteed security of employment and minimum wages, and so on. With a view to make the path of 'reforms' irreversible, Yeltsin pushed ahead with wholesale decentralisation, free market prices and privatisation as the sheet anchor of his politico-economic policies. Hence also the 'shock therapies', the effort to impose a 'wild west' *laissezfaire* and monetarist model of capitalism and turn the area free-fire zone for a new species of booty capitalism such that the very guts of the old socio-economic structures were knocked out. It was the fear of a return to the old system, which represented the threat of socialism to the West, that led to an exaggerated emphasis on the speed of reforms, in the process also ensuring that no time was allowed to the opposition to realise what was happening and organise resistance.

The market reform in Russia early took the form of dissolving the Union, old institutions and industrial capacity, and disrupting the previous patterns of production, consumption, trade and investment rather than transforming each of these or developing adequate alternatives; the end results were more manifest in the demolished old institutions and mechanisms than in the development of the institutions of a market economy. It was an entirely destructive process, one which simply failed to set the foundations of any kind of either short-run or long-run viable positive growth. As we shall see, even democracy was seen as expendable, and a strong authoritarian regime was welcomed, and commended, to tame and subdue the Russian bear and force the destruction through, even as western capitalism continued taking over the country's talent, science and technology, buying out the human capital, acquiring the intellectual property rights, stripping the assets, closing down factories or turning them into spare part makers, deskilling the workers and so on. Soon far too many in Russian cities were making far more money working as receptionists, doormen and taxi drivers at international hotels and offices than did the teachers, doctors, academics, scientists, and industrial workers, even as unemployment grew and the prostitutes and beggars roamed the streets... While no normal market economy emerged, the Russian transition led to a criminalised economy where criminals established new institutions which were rewarding to their masters but dysfunctional for any kind of sustained economic renewal, which however was not unwelcome to the western policy makers. Stanislav Govorukhin's best selling *The Great Criminal Revolution* is well symbolic of this post-Soviet reality of Russia, of the destruction wrought by the West sponsored or imposed 'market reforms'. Ideological-political concerns governing its policies in Russia, the West's objective, regardless of costs, was to so defeat and devastate the old Soviet system that restoration of capitalism becomes irreversible. The supremacy of capitalist economy had to be established even if most of Russian economy was to be ruined, the labour force unemployed, the population pushed into penury and the establishment of a market economy itself rendered more difficult.

The other major western objective in Russia was to prevent its development as any kind of economic or political power in the world. The policy of the West since the disintegration of the Soviet Union was to put Russia in such a state that it never recovers as a world power. It does not matter whether it is a socialist, Czarist or for that matter a capitalist Russia. Cold War was a war without physical destruction. What was now on was the use of instruments of macro-economic policy to physically dismantle and destroy the economy of a defeated nation. The 'reforms' did not even remotely aim at building a successful market capitalism or western style social democracy in Russia (as claimed by the western policy makers), but at neutralising a former enemy and forestalling its future development even as a capitalist power. Profit motive, it must be remembered, is the fountainhead of all capitalist enterprise, and profit is generated through competition in the market. With the economy in recession, potential markets saturated and overproduction characterising global capitalism, the last thing the West wanted was competition from Russia, least of all by building it up as a rival capitalist power. Hence a reform process which dismantled Russia's industrial base, allowed first-rate firms to go bankrupt and world-scale research and development laboratories to deteriorate or disappear altogether, making for a peacetime economic damage and destruction unparalleled in history. The Fund-Bank sponsored or imposed 'structural adjustment' was predicated on a massive demobilisation of domestic resources and transformation of Russia into an energy-raw materials producing colony integrated into the world market system. An important aspect of this policy was the phasing out of the Russian military-industrial complex including its civilian arm. The various 'conversion programmes', negotiated with NATO and western defence ministries, aimed at physically demobilising Russia's productive capabilities in the military, avionics and high-tech areas while facilitating the take-over and control by western capital of Russia's knowledge base (intellectual property rights) and human capital, including her scientists, engineers and research institutes. Where necessary, military hardware and industrial assets were 'transformed' into scrap metal to be sold on the world commodity market and the proceeds used in meeting Russia's debt-servicing obligations or funding the reform process that further undermined its capacity for any kind of positive economic growth and development.

To make Russia's transition to capitalism irreversible, or prevent its development as a potential rival in the world market or as a world power, did not however exhaust western capitalism's concerns with regard to the present and future of the ongoing economic transition in Russia. There were other concerns too of which at least one needs to be immediately noticed, especially as it well dovetails with the above-mentioned ideological-political concerns. This is how J. Petras and Steve Vieux have put it:

> ...the decision leading to the destruction of productive assets in Russia may reflect western despair over the quality of leadership available to guide the transition in Russia and the potentially explosive consequences of nationalists or socialists coming to power with the military and industrial resources of the old Soviet Union intact. There is no bourgeoisie in Russia. Yeltsin and company are largely ex-communists and bureaucrats. They are being expected to establish a capitalist economy which they have never lived under or governed. The prospects are not bright when one combines considerations such as these with the sheer dangers of the situation: the size of the country and its arsenals, its revolutionary history, the size of the working class and the novelty of the transition. From this view point perhaps it is better to pull the plug on the available military and industrial resources, lowering Russia's capacity of resistance to western impositions and at the same time reducing the possible consequences of the arrival in power of an anti-western regime.

XV

In the final analysis, the destruction done, what western capitalism wanted, as mentioned above, was to exploit Russia's productive capacity, its cheap but skilled labour and material resources and, one might add, weak ecological restraints, to pile up profits for itself, as also to take over its markets – not only the millions who live there but those served by it throughout the former Soviet bloc and the Third World. It desired to reduce Russia to a dependent, second rate capitalist power, a source of raw materials and market for obsolete technologies and consumer goods, primarily a service economy (including tourism industry catering to foreigners) with the local 'businessmen', rather the 'nomenklatura-mafia bourgeoisie' of Russia, acting as the main allies, agents, and business subordinates of western capital, much in the manner of parasitical third world elites. Pressures generated by global capitalism's ongoing recession and stagnation in world trade only reinforced western capitalism's interest in transforming Russia along these lines to complement their 'advanced industrial economies'.

Such 'third worldisation' or 'Latin Americanisation' of Russia was indeed the purpose and outcome of the IMF-Yeltsin programme of economic reforms. This programme, a carbon copy of the structural adjustment programme imposed on debtor countries in Latin America and sub-Saharan Africa, (and now sought to be imposed on India) precluded from the outset a transition towards any kind of 'national capitalism,' a possibility, albeit theoretical, we briefly mentioned earlier. While narrowly promoting the interests of Russia's merchants and business tycoons, it was, through a deliberate manipulation of market forces, destructive of Russian industrial potential. It was simultaneously a programme of compradorisation of the Russian economy, duly propping up, with western economic aid and political support, pliant Yeltsin regime in the domestic power struggle in Russia. As against the 'capitalist heaven' promised by the new rulers and the neo-liberal ideologues, perceptive Russian scholars began speculating about 'other possible fates' for the Russian people. 'You need only look around the contemporary world to realise other possible fates exist for us,' said the economist Tatiana Koryagina. 'We are developing a distinctly Latin American social profile. Our new rich class lack any sense of social responsibility or even elementary patriotism. They sell raw products to the world market, and purchase back from it most of what they consume. They keep their money in foreign banks, spend much of their own time aboard, and do not invest productively in Russia. The economic cycle, involving much of the country's basic wealth, hardly touches the population at all. At the same time, a majority of Russians are being impoverished, stripped of such economic and social rights as they previously enjoyed, and left to find their way in a new world that offers them few opportunities. It's perfectly possible for a country to exist for decades in a chronic state of under-development, endemic corruption and political crisis. Present trends would suggest this is Russia's future.' Apropos western capitalism's policy in Russia, this is how Michel Chossudovsky, quoting from Russian economists, described the situation: 'In Russia we are living in a post-war situation... but there is no post-war reconstruction; "Communism" and the "Evil Empire" have been defeated, yet the cold war although officially over, has not quite reached its climax; the heart of the Russian economy is the military-industrial complex and the G-7 wants to break our high tech industries; the objective of the IMF economic programme is to weaken us and prevent the development of a rival capitalist power. For the west, the enemy is not "socialism" but capitalism.'

The only capitalism the West was willing to permit Russia was of the third world variety, which meant not only a reversion to the conditions of Russia before 1914, backward and subaltern, but also the addition of its resources, land and people to the area of third world exploitable territories. And it included, as is necessarily the case with peripheral capitalisms, a process of subordinate incorporation within the economic, cultural and military-strategic networks of the international capitalist system. Such 'third-worldisation' of the Soviet Union, as of Eastern Europe, was a integral part of the ongoing restructuring of the global capitalist system, though the latter was only of minor importance to it. While there was growing opposition to this restructuring, from the left as well as right at home, in Russia, thanks to Yeltsin and the rest, it had already gone well beyond the ambitions of the most avid proponents of market reforms within the old regime, and, equally, byond the wildest dreams of the most ardent advocates of 'rollback' without, in the west. Scholars had speculated that given the range of human and natural resources and the historical specificities in the belt of nations stretching from Poland through Eastern Europe to the former Soviet Union, the collapse of 'Stalinist socialism' could have a spectrum of outcomes, permitting some of them even to join the (capitalist) First World or become another Southern Europe. It was however soon clear that not only was the transition to capitalism not going to be a bed of roses, they were not likely to be offered the choice between social-democratic Sweden or liberal capitalist United States or even Thatcherite

Britain. Rather than integration on an equal footing, most of them were already being assimilated largely, albeit selectively, as peripheral pools of cheap labour and NATO outposts. The prospects were no less bleak for Russia. It faced being relegated to the (also capitalist) Third World, its rank closer to that of Mexico or Bolivia, a new addition to the whole range of non-European countries that North America and Western Europe treat only as objects of plunder, destruction, surveillance and policing. The fabled free market was already taking on characteristics of Latin America in the former 'socialist' Soviet Union. The opening of the capitalist option certainly announced a new order of the day for Russia. But it was going to be semi-colonial peripheralisation of its economy and society, which, one might add, the depoliticised popular classes were, at the moment, ill-prepared to resist and reject.

This is how Russia set out on the road to capitalism.

XVI

Undeterred by the horrific initial impact or outcome of 'market reforms', the rulers in Russia have continued to pursue the path of capitalist restoration. For the simple reason that this is where the comprador class interests of the new rulers lie. If these interests had led to the orgy of criminal asset-stripping within, with disastrous consequences for the economy and the Russian people, their comprador character has also determined the indiscriminate opening up of the country to foreign capital and avoidable dependence on Fund-Bank credits and therapies. And the 'market reform' has continued. Governments, that is ministers and prime ministers of Yeltsin, have come and gone at irregular intervals and one of the latter, Victor Chernomyrdin, even confessed that 'the period of market romanticism is over'. There have been pleas for a shift from 'shock without therapy' policies to more pragmatic marketisation. More recently a Putin has taken over from Yeltsin. But however modified the old policies have been continued with, almost as an open conspiracy between the IMF, its major stakeholders and the Russian mafia of private businessmen, corrupt officials and politicians. And the outcome has only reinforced the central conclusion emerging from Russia's development so far, namely, the greater the cmmitment to market reforms, the greater the magnitude of economic decline, and worse its consequences for the Russian people.

As restoration to capitalism, Russia is experiencing what can best be described as a process of underdevelopment. The country's economy has been shrinking steadily over these years. Today it is less than half of what it was in 1990, smaller than that of the Netherlands and on par with a country like Spain. Its total banking capital was less than that of Finland. Its imports-exports amount to a mere 0.5 per cent of world trade. A massive disaccumulation of capital has taken place, through large scale disinvestment and otherwise, the situation made worse by a colossal capital outflow – primarily through debt burden and capital flight – which by the most conservative estimate, twice exceeds the size of inflow of foreign investments into Russia. The shrunken size of Russia's economy can be glimpsed in the comparative figures of world GDP where, according to a recent calculation from UN data, Russian share is only 1.1 per cent (below that of West Asia and North Africa) as against the European Union's 29.3 per cent and the United States' 25.2 per cent. The decline in the Russian economy is steeper than that of the United States during the Great Depression (1929-1933).

The decline of economy has a most important aspect, beyond a simple fall in industrial output, in the continuing deindustrialistion of Russia. While Russia's few profitable economic sectors, including industrial assets have been handed over to a small clutch of well-connected tycoons, a plunder well facilitated and partnered by unaccountable foreign capital, hundreds of enterprises still in the state sector remain mired in debt, saddled with outdated technology and cut off from their traditional Soviet-era markets. According to one recent estimate, 40 per cent of Russian industries are effectively bankrupt, surviving on a trickle of state subsidies, by barter transactions with other insolvent firms and by deferring the wages (and pensions) of their employees. An overall primitivisation of the economy has occurred where reversion to a less industrialised economy is accompanied by the enormously increased importance of the subsistence sector in agriculture. With industry and agriculture in ruins, the country survives chiefly on imports of food and consumer goods which it is able to pay for through export of its vast natural resources. These natural resources have even otherwise acquired a new importance in Russia's foreign trade where fuel, raw materials and semi-finished products together have come to account for over 80 per cent of Russia's exports. In other words, low value added primary products are booming ever larger in both the national economy and foreign trade accounts of Russia. Far from joining the 'civilised market economy' of the west promised by its ideologues, the ex-Soviet Union has ceased to compete with the advanced capitalist countries and is now competing with the less developed third world countries. Reversion to a less industrialised economy, dependence on a few specialised primary goods exports, high polarisation of society into rich and poor – production, trade and consumption-wise, Russia continues to acquire the profile of a third world country.

Even as this third worldisation of Russia continues, a decisive blow to the liberal dreams was given by the May-August 1998 financial crisis, the combined effect of the IMF prescribed policies of liberalisation, privatisation and fiscal stabilisation within Russia and the effect of a world economic crisis that first struck South Asia and soon engulfed Russia too. Well and truly globalised, Russia's so-called 'emerging economy' simply could not escape being submerged in the whirlpools of world capitalism's most staggering financial slide since the Great Depression. The immediate cause, of course, was the inability of the state to service its debts. The 'time bomb' we noticed earlier, finally exploded, leaving the Russian economy in ruins. *The Financial Times* ran the front page caption on the morning after the crash and the ensuing bank panic: 'Moscovites' faith in capitalism is crushed'. Not only Moscovites however. Foreign investors too lost faith and fled the country, and their return became rather problematic. As the American banker and industrialist, Thomas Wainwright put it: 'Assuming that foreign investors return, where will they put their money? For what markets will they be producing? The international market is in the dumps; foreign competitors will beat back Russian manufacturers by every conceivable protectionist measure.' *The Financial Times* of August 28 (1998) wrote: 'Russia's credit rating is below Indonesia's. Its economy is smaller than Switzerland's. And its stock market is worth less than the UK water industry. It is a low base from which to build.' The unprecedented crisis left quite a few bourgeois analysts worrying that there may be soon no Russian economy left on which to practice their beloved 'free market'!

Russia's economic disaster in fact runs far deeper than its financial crisis. The neo-liberal ideologues and the free marketeers in Russia still speak of Russia as an 'emerging economy'. But their explanations for the current disaster – 'result of the past Communist regime', 'the inevitable phase of transition', the result of '*not enough* capitalism' or 'inaction by the Centre', etc. – if taken seriously are only a case of exploiting people's credulity. Still hopeful, Anatoly Chubais, amongst other things the former minister of privatisation, says: 'We must recognise that we did not fully understand the scale of the process which we had undertaken. We thought there would be a very difficult three years, five years, eight years. Now, unfortunately, it is clear that reform will take decades... It is now clear that Russia does not need billions or tens of billions but hundreds of billions of dollars.' These hoped-for billions notwithstanding, the Russian economist Shmelev has argued that in the present circumstances there are no good scenarios, and the only choice is between bad, very bad, and catastrophic scenarios. Of the scenario that is now on, this is what the far more perceptive Frederic Claremonte wrote towards the end of 1998: 'According to the official Russian Centre of the Standard of Living, 79 mn Russians (53 per cent) live in poverty – and the numbers are escalating; 2 per cent of top income earners gobble up 57 per cent of the nation's assets; its foreign debts stands at $ 180 bn; its domestic debt at $ 161 bn; the super-rich and the transnational corporations, like mega-parasites, illicitly siphoned abroad (capital flight) around $ 180 bn, a number that does not comprise the bleeding of corporate transfer pricing;

the crumbling of scientific and technological infrastructure; the sedulous introduction of unpaid wage slavery savaging millions of workers; an IMF inspired policy directive engineered to slash inflationary pressures; wage arrears, 11 per cent of GDP in January 1997, rocketed to 27 per cent by end September 1998; farm output bedevilled by the worst harvest since 1945 with food imports accounting for 75 per cent of aggregate consumption; the rouble survives as the vestige of a neo-colonial currency; as "a store of value", a prime attribute of national sovereignty, it is redundant since the imperial greenback, or "dollarisation", extends its primacy into the most trivial economic transactions; the upshot of "the flight from cash" and demonetisation has engendered on a scale comparable to the Russian Civil War (1918-21) the proliferation of barter trade; male life expectancy has tumbled to 58, the level of the Sahel..... An appalling inventory that by no means exhausts the enormity of Yeltsin's crimes, perpetrated with such impunity. Crimes executed in the name of "human rights", the "open society" and "the rule of law".

XVII

As Russia's capitalist restoration has progressed, so has the criminalisation of its economy. The former Soviet Union had its share of corruption and crime even if it was mostly invisible. But its magnitude and intensity now threaten to make organised crime a most important part of the historical specificity of the restored Russian capitalism. As a commentator has it: 'Propagandists of the Thatcherite variety that peddle their garbage are correct in one respect. There has been a resounding "success" of the Russian economic reforms and that is the criminalisation of the national economy.' We have earlier noticed the plunder that was the initial privatisation in Russia, carried out essentially outside the law (except for some loose underpinning by Yeltsin's decrees) to become a major factor in the criminalisation of the country's economy. The plunder has continued so that even the original architect of Russia's 'shock therapy' programme, Harvard economist Jeffrey Sachs is compelled to decry the so-called 'second stage of privatisation' as 'a remarkable plunder of state assets' – worth 'literally tens of billions of dollars' – and call for its 'reversal'; 'a kind of bandit reform' political scientist Andrei Kolganov has called it 'in which those with political power have divided up the country's wealth among themselves and their friends' – 'friends' have included not only large beneficiaries like Victor Chernomyrdin, a former party apparatchik and latter-day 'red director' become prime minister, but also foreign carpet-baggers via bogus Russian companies. Along with 'mafiosi capitalism', 'Robber capitalism' is now another widely used description of Russia's emerging 'market economy'. Says the multi-billionaire American financier and international investor, George Soros: 'I call it a "robber capitalism" because the easiest way to accumulate capital was to rob the assets of the crumbling state. After the elections of 1996 the system of "robber capitalism" has been firmly established and a new oligarchy has emerged.' Other western observers have used the term 'bandit capitalism' and *Time* magazine reports a deepening of the impression in the west 'that Yeltsin's Russia is in danger of becoming what US researchers recently called a "criminal-syndicalist state" controlled by an alliance of corrupt politicians, businessmen and crime bosses.'

This 'alliance', a small gang of racketeering 'capitalists', who came up as political backers of Yeltsin and beneficiaries of his rule, and now owning big banks, nation-wide media networks (newspapers and television) and vast national resources have come to be described by themselves and by others, as 'the Oligarchs', even 'the invulnerables'. Seldom in the history of contemporary capitalism have such a tiny number of rapaciously concentrated financial parasites, wedded to political power, risen so glaringly in so short a time. A ganging together of seven leading bankers (Boris Berezovsky, Vladimir Polonin etc.), the handful of oil magnates (Victor Chernomyrdin etc.) and the politico-financial mafia (Yuri Luzkhov, mayor of Moscow etc.), controlling the bulk of wealth in Russia, and further organised as 'clans' – loose-knit groupings or competing corporate structures of industrial, trading and financial interests, each with a clique of politicians at its head, a mass media outlet under its control, support of corrupt elements of the federal and municipal authorities, and armed formations (state or private) at their disposal – it is this oligarchy which runs the country's economy and, according to an independent analyst Andrei Piontkowsky, 'has sucked the country dry'. The oligarchy has its roots deep in the now criminalised economy into the making of which, as noticed earlier, have gone the wheeler dealers of the Soviet era 'grey economy'. Says K.S. Karol: 'Many of them were intelligent men and, in their own way, they were brave. They defied the laws of a totalitarian regime by organising a whole parallel trade system with the help of corrupt officials and, of course, the criminal under-world. It is not surprising that, when the free market came into being, they should have abandoned their favourite activity (commerce) and gone into banking and business. In Yeltsin's Russia, no one asks anyone about how they made their fortunes. Indeed, such questions are regarded as "totalitarian". There was therefore no legal obstacle to prevent "the bosses who lay down the law for thieves" – *vory v zakonie*, as they say in Russian – from transforming themselves overnight into respectable bankers and businessmen. According to official statistics, twenty-two per cent of these parvenus have done lengthy vocational courses in prison, and twenty-five per cent have had more or less serious dealings with the police. But money can open any door, even the door that leads into the Kremlin's offices...'

The oligarchy is well interlinked to international finance capital and together they are also interlinked with powerful mafias within the country who, in their own ways linked to roughly half of the Russian banks, control more than 40% of Russia's economy. About 80 per cent of the stock market shares issued in the Russian Federation are said to be in control of these mafia gangs, and billions of dollars obtained from criminal activities are regularly laundered in the west by the Russian mafia. Generally named after the cities or regions they operate from (such as Moscow mafia, St. Petersburg mafia, or Russian, Chechen, Azerbaijani, Armenian, Georgian mafias etc.), often with their 'dons' in Moscow who could well be the top government officials or officers in the armed forces, these mafias not only have links among themselves but also with mafias abroad. Russian mafias are now operating in about 50 countries, including the US. According to panicky reports in the American press, about 1000 big bosses with Soviet or Russian origins are said to be living and operating criminal gangs from Los Angeles and San Francisco. Ostensibly, the oligarchs and their visible billion dollar assets are legal entities; those of the Russian mafia are not. There can however be no clear differentiation between these different sections of 'the Russian bourgeoisie' and their leading segment, the Oligarchs. The mafia and the foreign and domestic bourgeoisie intersect at all points of the economy. Together they have built up Russia, in the words of Boris Nemtsov, a reformer and another beneficiary of privatisation, as 'a freakish, oligarchic capitalist state', 'bandit capitalism' according to others, in which corruption and criminalisation have become an integral part of the Russian economy and society.

Corruption is rampant. As *The Financial Times* recently reported, much of the state has been 'virtually privatised by big business'. They know no laws, pay few taxes and indulge in every kind of corruption. According to the 1998 Corruption Perceptions Index of Transparency International, when corruption perceptions of internationally operating firms are measured on a scale 10 (no corruption) to 1 (complete corruption), Russia scored only 2.4, a long way behind Poland (4.6), and even behind China (3.5) or India (2.9). Russia did have the satisfaction of scoring better than Indonesia (2.0) and Nigeria (1.9). Corruption apart, quite a few of Russia's men of big business are involved in crimes like embezzlement of public and private funds, killing of rivals, trafficking of drugs and smuggling of arms abroad. Contributing more directly to the criminalisation of economy and society is the fact that, as with the rough and violent ways of 'shadow economy' and underworld anywhere, bandit capitalism in Russia has its own rules of business and financial competition. The 'clans' bind 'their' workers and residents of 'their cities' tightly to the clan structures using ties not merely of patronage but even more of fear. And they enter into fierce struggles over the division of property rights and economic power. (So-called 'popular' privatisation, which took the form of distributing vouchers to the population at large, witnessed bloody gangland warfare to 'buy' them by force from the people for the investment funds of the clan oligarchies). Rivalries in the market are settled by ruthless methods. Murdering one's rival is a well known form of 'competition' and, in the absence of an effective legal system, debt collection relies heavily on 'Judge Kalashnikov'. It is quicker to kill than to intimidate or bribe, and killing of bankers, small businessmen, traders, is routine. Russia, which was once regarded as a country with a poor criminal record where people were killed with knives, has taken a qualitative leap forward into sophisticated crime. Scores are now settled not only with fire arms of all calibres but, as reported in the Russian press, even with bazookas and surface-to-surface missiles. The English word 'killer' is now popularly used in the Russian language for contract killers, and estimated at 1000 per year, the number of contract killings now runs into thousands. A majority of banks and business houses have to pay 'protection money' to their *Krysha* (literally 'roof' but actually 'protector', that is the mafia gangs) and in most cases it amounts to an average of 10 to 20 per cent of their profits. As crime grows, one in five Russians is now reported to be carrying arms on a daily basis and Moscow and St. Petersburg already figure amongst the most violent cities in the world. Even the initially tolerant west now recognises the 'threat posed by the Russian mafia', and the accompanying overall lack of security is an important reason keeping foreign investors away from Russia, though they have not hesitated to come in for the 'kill' where easy and quick profits are to be made. The predations of gangsters and corrupt officials are a serious barrier to the growth of small business in Russia. Big firms, however, even as they pay protection money, have their own private armies – known as 'security services'. Permitted by a law authorising the formation of 'agencies to protect people and their property', these have come up like mushrooms after a shower of rain and are reported to be over twenty-six thousand in Russia, with many more thousands armed recruits. In fact one industry which is flourishing in Russia is the hiring of security guards. Practically all business executives, bank managers and so on have security guards, often through regular agreements with mafia gangs. The omnibus presence of the mafia, in the economic life of Russia and otherwise, is apparent even to the casual visitor to Moscow – the taxies at the airport are mostly owned by the mafia. The *nouveaux riches* of Russia, of course, go about in their own armoured cars, accompanied by their own armed guards. Such is the atmosphere of fear and tension in the paradise of the new big bourgeoisie in Russia that one of them, Vladimir Gussinsky – who became a billionaire in the space of three years through speculative property deals and murky banking operations and has argued that dynamic businessmen like himself, five per cent of the population, must be put in command if the remaining ninety-five per cent is to work efficiently – finds it necessary to seek shelter with his family in London or employ fifteen armed guards to patrol the courts when playing tennis in Moscow!

The criminal sector has now become an inalienable part of the national economy in Russia. No one can guess as to the true extent of its scope but there is a general consensus that it is a very major part. According to estimates by criminologists and various organisations fighting organised crime in Russia, there are now about 6,500 well-organised gangs, owning allegiance to about 3000 gang leaders and 279 'godfathers', and employing roughly 6 lakh armed gangsters. 'Submerged Part of Criminal Iceberg: 7 Million Crimes a Year' was the headline of a recent article in the newspaper *Slovo* which, quoting from the statements of the deputy minister of Internal Affairs, Valery Feodorov, reported that about 10 million crimes were committed in Russia every year. According to official statistics and police records, economic and other crimes have been increasing every year since 1991, including crimes relating to taxation and in the sphere of banks and financial credit activity where the volume of money involved in crimes has been steadily rising. The administration, afraid of or in collusion with the mafia is obviously 'helpless' in the matter. Having helped spawn it all, the government finds itself powerless against the criminals who are running the economy, protected as these are by politicians, bigwigs in the government itself and the oligarchs, and even the orthodox church, who are often themselves actively involved in committing the crimes. Any one, including journalists, bold enough to question or put up resistance or show too much curiosity and try to discover the murky secrets of the business mafia gets simply bumped off. Crime has thus become a part of life in today's Russia. As minister Feodorov has summed up: 'The moral degradation of the Russians is gradually leading to total criminalisation of the society.'

XVIII

The oligarchy and the criminalisation of Russian economy and society have gone hand in hand. There are those who have compared Russia's Oligarchs with the legendary Robber Barons of America – the Vanderbilts, the Harrimans, the Carnegies, the Morgans and the Rockefellers – at the turn of the nineteenth century. But the comparison is fallacious. Exploiters and union-busters that they were, the latter at least contributed to the build-up of the productive infrastructure of US capitalism in its earlier golden age, 1865-1914. In contrast the Oligarchs of Russia have little to do with genuine productive activity in Russia and are almost entirely active in the sphere of circulation (in banking, export-import, or wholesale internal trade) and are notorious for investing or stashing away their billions abroad. (As noted by Robert V. Daniels, 'capital accumulated from speculation or from natural resource exports was squirreled away in Swiss bank accounts and London real estate to the tune of perhaps $100 billion a year'). The Oligarchs are racketeers par excellence, indeed a 'barefoot kleptocracy' which has come up on the basis of degradation of their own economy and fattened on what one of their critics has called the 'years of obscene profit'. Comprador in their relation to western capitalism, concerned primarily with their luxurious living and with investing or stashing capital abroad, the Russian oligarchs are a prely parasitical xcrescence on te Russian econoy. (They are wel connected to all the western embassies in Moscow, and, amenable to foreign pressure, were among the means whereby western powers exercised control over the Yeltsin administration. That Yeltsin-installed Putin is now in power, some feeble, often politics-governed gestures apart, has made little change in their character, place and role in Russia's economy and politics).

A parasitical excrescence, the place and role of Oligarchs in the Russian economy is a good pointer to the overall character of the new bourgeoisie in Russia and of capitalism that is being builtthere.

Based on a brutal 'grabification' of public property – a version of classical capitalist primitive accumulation wherein, as Marx said, 'conquest, enslavement, robbery, briefly force' played the key role – the new Russian bourgeoisie is not exactly what the ideologues of capitalism at home or their patrons abroad had anticipated even if they found it politically prudent to countenance, even welcome it, in any case to never oppose it. The latter's disappointment so to speak found an early expression in the observation of a US Treasury official when he told the well known journalist Seymour Hersh (in 1994) that the American experts had failed 'to anticipate fully the viciousness and rapaciousness' of Russia's new mafia capitalists: 'Much worse than the American robber barons. These guys take the fillings out of teeth after murder. It's a nightmare.' Another patron from the same tribe complained: 'We had a belief that the first generation of Russian capitalists would be nice guys, but they are ruthless motherfuckers.' Instead of investments rationalising the economy along proper capitalist lines, these capitalists, Russia's new bourgeoisie, for the most part, just socked their loot away in secret western bank accounts or squandered it on yachts and villas on the French Riviera. By the mid-nineties, this bourgeoisie had stashed more than 150 billion dollars in foreign bank accounts, investments, and properties – and this stashing has grown by leaps and bounds since then. At home they have preferred to 'invest' in furs, limousines, and high living. The overall consequence has been a capitalism whose anamolous character has led scholars to even argue that it is not really capitalism but some other formation. More to the point however is to note the specific criminal and parasitic character of the new Russian capitalism.

Let me here share economist Stanislav Menshikov's argument on this. Writing in mid-1999, Menshikov points out the strong presence in Russian capitalism of elements, or class of people, from Russia's preceding 'shadow economy' which, by the time Mikhail Gorbachev came to power, accounted for around 15 per cent of Soviet G.D.P. (Some of Russia's successful tycoons of today started their business careers inside the sphere of this kind of undercover activity.) 'Market reforms came as the logical reflection of the interests of this new class in search of an open and legalised capitalist identity'. This class, which now constitutes a substantial section of the new Russian bourgeoisie, because of its largely illegal past experience, is well versed in criminal and corrupt practices and does not feel any moral or legal constraints in the newly reformed system, which is immeasurably more liberal and favourable to the application of such practices. As Menshikov puts it: 'Corruption and crime are widespread in the Russian capitalist class not only because the legal infrastructure for observing contracts has not been set up, as is widely suggested by some liberal critics, but mainly because a large part of the class does not know any other means and sees criminal and corrupt ones as the most effective – at least in the short term, which is all that seems to concern them. While the criminal and corrupt part of the business establishment may well be a minority in the capitalist class, it is an extremely powerful one and sets the general tone.'

Again, the way 'privatisation' was carried out, most of the former state-owned assets were transferred to their new owners at a price that was a fraction of their actual value. Elsewhere the former so-called 'red directors' became the new *de facto* enterprise owners. In other words, an overwhelming part of country's productive assets came to be transferred to the new capitalist class practically scot-free. 'Multimillion – or multibillion – dollars fortunes were accumulated by the robber barons over decades in the United States; the same process took less than five years in Russia. The destructive nature of this large-scale rip-off is that physical capital acquired at minimal cost and through minimal effort is not considered by its owners to be worth putting to good use; it carries a strong psychological inducement towards parasitic behaviour and squandering.'

This apart, there is the strictly economic problem – what with the accumulation of society's surplus in a few hands and the plummeting average real incomes of the people – of finding a domestic market to sell the potential products. Low wages, constantly falling in real terms and not unoften unpaid, large scale unemployment, and mass property have the effect of narrowing the domestic market, making prospects for growth dim and incentives for productive investment meagre. Russia's new capitalists would rather use their capital assets 'for "financial investment" (buying into other firms), investing into government bonds (which, until August 1998, brought 60 or more percent annual interests) or moving capital abroad, where it is considered safer in banks, securities, and real estate than in the politically and economically unstable environment of Russia.' That almost all of today's Russian Oligarchs rose in banking, financial speculation, and special privileges granted by the state, makes such 'investment' the obviously preferable, almost 'normal' choice. Menshikov points out that 'not a single important new plant or factory has been built in Russia in the last eight years. The economy is operating exclusively by utilizing productive capacity created under socialism', and adds: 'It is clear that such an economic system cannot survive, because its physical capital is being depleted. Capital consumption allowances (depreciation) now exceed 30 percent of gross domestic product (GDP); net fixed capital investment has been negative for a number of years; and fixed capital stock is being reduced from year to year. It is difficult to find anything even remotely similar to macroeconomic suicide on such a scale in the modern world.' Menshikov concludes:

> ....Russian capitalism whatever its roots, is out of place in the modern world and does not have the internal economic mechanisms to grow. The most it can hope for is to stagnate and degrade if, of course, it remains in its current state of sterility.... In its present mode, it is also destined to plunge deeper into the morass of the poor and exploited periphery of global capitalism. The leaders of today's Russian capitalism are a unique species, sterile to the point of being uninterested in expanding its positions in the world or promoting its geopolitical interests, as any imperial

capitalist country normally does and should. One could claim that Russia is no different from what a growing number of other capitalist countries are becoming – clients of a unipolar US imperialism. Well, yes and no. Other countries are doing it without impoverishing their own populations and downgrading their own economic power and industrial potential. Russian capitalism is consciously selling its foundations down the river, never doubting that this is the only route to take. There is hardly any analogue of such suicidal behaviour in history.

XIX

Their professed preference for a 'normal and civilised' (that is only normally criminal) capitalism in Russia notwithstanding, Western powers have been happy enough with Russia's (till recently Yeltsin's) abnormally corrupt and criminal capitalist regime to sustain and bankroll it all along. IMF and World Bank have been regularly administering their neo-liberal 'economic medicine' to keep it going as it is, duly backed by the Clinton and Bush administrations in the United States. A friendly Clinton even travelled all the way to tell the hapless Russians that 'economic reform' is all and they must learn to accept their fate: 'as a friend I say I do not believe that you can defy the rules of the road in today's global economy, any more than I could defy the laws of gravity by stepping off the top floor of Spaso House' (the US ambassador's residence where he was speaking). Lack of security or of any genuine interest in economic revival of Russia has not prevented foreign capital from coming in to exploit the country's vast natural resources and now dirt cheap labour. For a crisis-ridden global capitalism Russia as a potential market has its own attraction too. And as global capital makes its plundering inroads into Russian economy, IMF and World Bank have continued to facilitate it all with their 'aid' that comes tied with their now standard 'conditionalities'. Thus, for example, IMF's offer of 10 billion dollars in loan to Russia in February 1996 had, among several others, the following conditions attached to it: (a) 'A major initiative toward the expeditious implementation of key structural reforms to enhance prospects for sustained growth and to make truly irreversible the move toward a market economy... continuing progress with privatisation, further trade liberalisation, including the elimination of remaining exports duties; and the initiation of a bolder agricultural reform strategy'; (b) 'The programme will be monitored very carefully – on a monthly basis, as under the standby arrangements during 1995'. Similar in form to the structural adjustment loans negotiated with indebted third world countries, the IMF loans to Russia are given, kept on hold and released, to make sure that Russia sticks to the path of market reform and submits or is accommodative to the west's, in effect America's requirements in foreign policy. As the debt mounts, the IMF's 'economic medicine' is not only devised to the enforce debt-servicing obligations, it is also intent on 'enlarging the debt'. By crippling the national economy, its reforms create a still greater dependence on external credits. Any departure from the Fund-Bank imposed policies, any suggestion or effort to bring back greater state control over the increasingly anarchic economy, to protect domestic industry, to clean up the mafia-controlled administration, to 'rethink some approaches and correct some steps' that, for example, Primakov, the somewhat nationalist prime minister proposed, is suspect, almost as the return of communism, and rejected, and the rejection is enforced with the leverage Fund-Bank has acquired in the economy. There is the perennial threat of loans simply drying up and a Primakov, despite his public commitment not to 'back track on the course of reforms', had to go, summarily dismissed by Yeltsin. A fully subservient and compliant Yeltsin, with his coterie, was seen as the best option and continued to be backed by Western powers, and by the Russian mafia as well.

All this well jells with the basic policy of US and its allies to reduce defeated and humiliated Russia to an eviscerated, backward country and maintain it as an economic and political appendage of the western world. Not only making a return to socialism impossible but keeping Russia down and out even as a capitalist country remains their primary objective. Behind the facade of partnership with the west in a globalised world, the reality is 'Russia's dilemma', as Piontkovsky has called it, 'that it poses as a partner but appears as a beggar'. Taking advantage of their recharged economic and political power, extorting concessions in exchange for financial aid, western powers in fact seek to push back the frontiers of Russia to those of sixteenth-century Muscovy, thus destroying any hope that it might again become a power on the world scene. I may add that the recent expansion of NATO needs to be seen in this light also. It is more than an extension of US hegemony to central-eastern Europe or within NATO. The deepened clientele relations of the new members – their re-satellising shift from the Warsaw Pact to NATO – also means not only acceleration of 'free market reforms' and therefore increased opportunities for western multinational corporation in these countries, but also their having to increase their military spending to be on the same footing with their western partners which will be a windfall for western arms manufacturers, those in the US being the principal beneficiaries. But most importantly, NATO expansion, bringing it as it does almost to the borders of Russia, also means increased US encirclement of Russia which also opens the door to the de facto extension of US influence in the Ukraine and Baltic Republics through the existing client regimes. This can only lead to the further subordination of Russia to the west.

XX

Russia's capitalist transition has continued the way it began, playing havoc with the country's economy and with the lives of the common people. The economy is in ruins, reduced, according to different estimates, to one-third or half of what it was when the transition began. Output in some branches of engineer and consumer industries is hardly 40 per cent of the level achieved in 1991. There is a sharp decline in agricultural production. Unemployment has increased drastically. Anything between 12 to 15, even 20 per cent of the able bodied population are reported to be out of work. At the end of 1998, the official unemployment rate was reported to be 11.8 percent with about another 10 percent either partially employed or considered employed but not paid. (Only 2.7 per cent bothered to register because actually receiving the meagre unemployment benefit was too difficult to be worth the effort.) Real incomes have plummeted 40 percent since 1991, 80 percent of Russians now have no savings while the country is saddled with more than 150 billion dollars in debt. A decade of 'economic reforms' has effectively demodernised the one-time superpower to turn it into a third world country, an exporter of energy products and raw materials and importer of finished goods.

For the people transition to 'market economy' remains an unmitigated disaster, polarising Russian society as never before and ravaging people in every aspect of their lives. The new rich at the top – a medley gang up of capitalist 'entrepreneurs' or Mafiosi bourgeoisie, banking, construction and media czars, managerial elite, bureaucrats and politicians – constituting about five to seven per cent of the population gobble up more than half of nation's assets. Russia is said to have more millionaires and billionaires than even the United States and its society is characterised by what the great American economist, Thorstein Veblen called 'conspicuous consumption of the rich'. The cost for one night at Maxim's, the Moscow night club that makes its Paris counterpart look a shabby cousin, amounts to one year's wages of a Russian worker. The vulgarly lavish life style of the rich is matched by the new rulers equally vulgar itch to indulge themselves beyond anything that Brezhnev and his coterie could dream of. The Kremlin is recently reported to have ordered a 6,000-piece silver dinner service to replace the 40 silver caviar dishes, 20 champagne buckets and 20 sauce boats now in use in four government guest houses around Moscow. (Significantly, in making the purchase Mr. Boris Yeltsin's Kremlin far surpassed the record of the most extensive buy held by Catherine the Great, the Tsarina who had bought the famous Orlov dinner service from France in the 18th century: it consisted of only 2,500 pieces.) This at a time when even by conservative estimates (of Russia's Academy of Sciences) over 40 percent of the population lives below the poverty line with fifteen million living at a level which is half of what is necessary for sheer physical survival, that is on the verge of starvation and reduced to beggary, when the middle class pushed into poverty, especially after the financial crash of 1998, is disappearing, when millions of the 'new poor' of Russia and one third of its children roam the streets of its cities.... (Since immediately after the Soviet collapse, the level of poverty in Russia was up 15 times in 1997; and after the August 1998 economic crisis, it soared higher, driving nearly 70 percent of the population to the brink of subsistence. 'Economic reform' has also brought the mass abandonment of children. By the end of 1998, at least two million Russian children were orphaned – more than at the end of the Second World War – and only about 650,000 live in orphanages. The rest are homeless. In what was once the second industrial power in the world, where schools turned out far more scientists and engineers per year than any capitalist country including the United States, ten million children currently do not attend school.)

The living standards of the people have steadily declined over these years of capitalist transition. Russia, the rump successor of a super power has slipped to an ignominious 67th position among the world's nations on the human development scale. Housing, education, basic health care, once universally available are a thing of the past, leaving life a nasty, brutish and short affair for millions. Poverty – which was unknown in the Soviet times – and the new magnitude of income disparities have their regional dimension which has sent the poor from outlying republics fleeing to large cities for survival, thus adding to the already intensified social problems of destitution, poverty, beggary, crime and a so-called 'sexual revolution'. Prostitution has grown into a 'screamingly obvious' flesh trade, 'the shameful phenomenon of export of girls as prostitutes', in the words of well-known Russian film director and Chairman of the Parliamentary Cultural Committee, Stanislav Govorukhin. The billions of dollars in Western currency that have come flooding into the country in the wake of liberalisation and market reform has led to a rapidly growing sex industry in Russia. According to Russian Interior Ministry, it has now become a $120 million-a-year business employing over 15,000 prostitutes and pimps. The explosive growth of the Russian sex industry, with its strip clubs, bars, sex shops and the 'night-time butterflies' (as the prostitutes are called locally) and the accompanying flood of pornography, has turned Russia into one of the 20 countries that lead the world in prostitution. Focussing particularly on the condition of the working class, this is how the American scholar Vladimir Bilenkin described the situation towards the end of 1996:

> Since his coup in October 1993, Yeltsin's regime has abolished virtually all fundamental economic, social, and legal achievements of the October Revolution. The privatisation of the means of production and the commodification of labor have logically led to the abolition of the constitutional guarantee of full employment. At present, at least 12 million people or 15 per cent of the labor force are unemployed with virtually no safety net in place. The guaranteed minimum wage and pension which under the Soviet regime roughly corresponded to the actual cost of living now come to only ten percent of it, i.e. far below what is needed to barely reproduce the worker's labor power. The real average income of working class families is now twenty five to thirty percent of that in 1990. These few facts alone clearly demonstrate that Russian capitalism has established a regime of super-exploitation of the laboring masses.
>
> Another hard blow against the working class has been the abolition of their rights to free and universal access to education and medical care, which started the process of rapid commodification of these services. Education at all levels has been stratified along class lines. Even a free full secondary education is no longer guaranteed by the constitution of the capitalist restoration. The vast state and enterprise owned Soviet network of crèches, kindergartens, summer camps, vacation homes, cultural centers for children and adults has been devastated by privatisation or otherwise become inaccessible to workers. The results have been a catastrophic decline in life expectancy, the sharp rise of infant mortality, the spread of social diseases like tuberculosis, child homelessness and prostitution.
>
> Restoration hit especially hard at working class women who have lost the rights which protected gender equality and included: paid pregnancy and maternity leaves, special measures for women's safety in the workplace, equal opportunities in education and vocational training, and equality with men in wages and job promotion. Child bearing is no longer considered a social function which the state and society as a whole have the duty to support. It has become a woman's private affair. Abandoned by the

bourgeois state, working class women have been exposed to the worst abuses of the market. First to be laid off, last to be hired, they make up about eighty percent of all unemployed and get the least skilled and lowest paying jobs. Sexual harassment in the workplace is rampant and goes unprosecuted. Many women are forced into prostitution as the only means to feed their children.

While the sons of the new privileged class easily escape service in the army, the youth of the working class has been used as canon fodder in the bloody civil war in Chechnya. Unable to find decent jobs or to receive higher education in the brave new world of Russian capitalism, they are being recruited into the mushrooming 'security services' and the private armies – now mustering 800 thousand men – created by all sorts of plutocratic cliques to defend their fiefdoms from one another and the impoverished masses. Another employer of choice for working class youth is the immense state apparatus of repression which is now more formidable than that of the Soviet period. Today, this apparatus is numerically superior to the Armed Forces, better paid and better equipped. The regime's real enemy is inside, after all.

Perhaps the most dangerous development for the working class in the long run stems from the politics of de-industrialisation of the country and its integration into the world capitalist economy as a source of raw materials and cheap labor, a market for inferior goods and obsolete technologies. Since the beginning of the 'reforms' there has been a steep decline in the number of highly skilled workers, as the most technologically advanced industries have been devastated and have reduced their output from sixty to eighty five percent. Today there remain only one million skilled workers employed, or but five percent of the industrial working class. At the same time, the number of bureaucrats per 100 thousand residents in Russia is now fifty percent greater than it was in the former Soviet Union. The de-skilling and massive unemployment transform ever larger sections of the Russian working class into déclassé paupers and threaten the class with its own disintegration.

Having abolished the constitutional guarantees of the Soviet period, Yeltsin's regime blatantly and daily violates its own constitution; above all, the fundamental norm of bourgeois right – the law of contract. According to trade union sources, by October 1996 the total bill for unpaid wages had reached 40 trillion roubles (almost $7.5 billion), close to a month of the total wage bill of the workers of Russia. Millions of workers do not get paid for three

> months. Often the workers are paid in kind, usually in whatever they produce. In one instance the administration paid its workers in coffins, in other by matches. There have been numerous reports of workers fainting at work because of malnutrition....

Faced with workers' opposition or fight back, the Russian authorities in recent years have turned from the speculative pursuit of the advised or imposed pro-western course to a somewhat chauvinist-paternalist path. But there has been no real improvement in the situation. As liberalisation has proceeded, price rise has persisted, real wages have kept on falling and the ranks of the jobless have been swelling, and nearly half of those employed routinely remain unpaid for months on end. Symbolic of the plight of the Russian people are the bizarre stories coming out of Russia in this regard, for example:

> 'MOSCOW: Teachers in central Russia will be receiving their monthly salaries in vodka because the government's coffers are empty, a news agency has reported. The 8,000 educators in the Altai Republic will get 15 bottles of vodka each.
>
> 'Officials in Altai, about 3,000 kms east of Moscow, had previously tried to pay part of the teachers' six-month wage arrears with toilet paper and funeral accessories. The payments were refused, Itar-Tass said.'
>
> 'MOSCOW: A Russian factory in the coal-mining region of Kemerovo found a creative way to pay two years' back wages to its workers: it offered them coffins. But for some reason, the seamstresses working for the Voskhod clothing plant in the township of Yaya are not happy about the deal. They are refusing to take the coffins in advance, explaining that "they want to live and not to die," it said'.
>
> 'AFTER not having been paid for more than a year, workers at a water purification plant in the Siberian city of Krasnoyarsk held a solemn funeral ceremony for their dear-departed salaries. The workers, according to *Izvestia*, erected a tombstone and placed a 500-rouble note (worth about three rupees) on it along with a brief epitaph: "Wages, we remember you. We love and mourn you. Date of death, October 1995".'

And then making the point directly and poignantly:

> 'Here is a desperate *cri de coeur* of Irina Grigoryevna, a paediatrician from the city of Kostroma who had not received her

> salary for months and who was rummaging through a pile of used clothes distributed in a local Red Cross bureau. "You can't imagine how humiliating all this is. I am not an alcoholic. I am not a drug addict. I am not a tramp. I worked for 20 years as a medical doctor. But I can't feed myself," Gazing into her meagre Red Cross food parcel she weeps, "I really don't know what we are going to eat this winter. I am afraid that we are going to starve".'

The unpaid wages are only a small part of the larger story of endemic poverty, hunger and starvation, of criminalisation of society and sharpened polarisation within it, indeed of economic, political and social ugliness that has accompanied the capitalist transition in Russia, which is being recognised even by those scholars in Russia who, in tune with changed times, regard and reject the Soviet past as a dangerously misconceived social experiment. Sociologist Yakov Gilinskiy is explicitly hostile to '1917' (the October Revolution) and what followed, and admires 'economic reform'- its 'progressive nature'. In his *Crime and Deviance* (St. Petersburg, 2000), even as he speaks up for 'economic reform', Gilinskiy notes the ugly facts of contemporary situation in Russia, of course, without recognising that they are more or less direct consequences of 'economic reform': 'The redistribution of property is being brought into effect by legal and illegal methods (bribery, murders, threats)'; 'a massive polarisation between a very rich minority and very poor (pauperised) majority'; 'Three levels of criminal organisations exist: (1) a criminal group, (2) a criminal organisation, (3) a criminal society. The business sphere of St. Petersburg and other regions of Russia is divided between mafia groups'; 'The contemporary Russian regime', the Presidential system, 'in its very essence it is undemocratic', 'a repressive state'; Political power is in the hands of the few known as nomenklatura, consisting 'partly of the old guard – former communists – and partly of new faces who are either criminals or oligarchs' controlling the largest economic monopolies in the country, such as gas, oil, the leading banks and media; 'delusions of democracy', people feel votes make no difference; 'as a result of the so-called democratic process, neo-fascist organisations... are gaining strength'; Unemployment – 'not accustomed to earlier' – is growing; 'Racketeering' all over, and mafiosi in police, state apparatus, boards of banks, everywhere.... and finally: 'we are left in a remarkable situation where there is no money for the health services, no money for education, no money for salaries, scientific research, culture or social work. The question is, where then does all the money go? Looking at the vast country houses, being built at enormous expense in the finest resorts surrounding the City, it would seem that there is only money enough for the highest government officials and the leaders of organised crime'. And so on.

What is happening in Russia has been well summed up as the 'endless collapse of everything essential to a decent existence'. In addition to what has been said above, to be particularly noted is the damage this 'endless collapse' is doing to sheer physical and socio-psychological survival of the Russian people. Here, as elsewhere, the gains made in 70 odd years of Soviet rule have been undone in a few years of capitalist restoration. With health care and social services gutted, T.B. and other diseases are ravaging the population and AIDS is looming large over its future. Health officials are quoted to be saying that the Russians are 'dying like flies'. In September 1997, the Russian State Duma reported that life expectancy had fallen far below the levels of other industrialised countries; per capita consumption of meat, milk and fish had fallen by about a third between 1990 and 1996, the rate of illness among schoolchildren had increase fivefold and only ten per cent of high-school graduates could be considered healthy, with forty per cent chronically ill. In terms of nourishment Russia now ranks 36th in the world. Infant mortality has reached third-world levels while the birth rate has plummeted. Life expectancy continues to go down at a rate of which there is no parallel in history. For men, in the six years since 1991, it has declined from 65 years to 57.5 years and half of Russian males below 16 years of age today may not live to qualify for pensions, that is live till 60 – a situation worse than 100 years ago. Population continues to shrink at a rate never seen before in peacetime. The Russian birth rate has fallen below zero and the death rate has soared – it is now 1.6 times higher than the birth rate... the highest ratio in the world.

With deaths so greatly exceeding births the Russian population is falling by about one million per year, as if a genocide is on. A third of those dying are within working age. The State Statistics Committee has in a recent report pointed out that Russia's population is likely to drop from 147.6 million in 1996 to 141 million by 2010. Other calculations suggest that if the present trends continue, in the next thirty years Russia's population may fall to 123 million – a demographic collapse not seen since the Second World War. Economist Sergei Glazyev is not alone in noticing (in his book *Genocide*) the consistent tendency of depopulation discernable in Russia, and concerned Russian doctors, recognising this demographic disaster as a direct result of the 'market reforms', have been meeting together in their conferences and congresses to ask the government to take urgent measures to save the prematurely dying Russian population.

Poverty and deprivation in Russia, coming as it does after an era of appreciable degree of economic certainty and social security, has led to an alarming deterioration in the psychological health of the people. Suicides doubled and deaths from alcohol abuse tripled in the mid-1990s. According to Russian psychiatrists, 25 million Russians are currently in need of psychological, psycho-therapeutic and psychiatric treatment, and the number of people suffering from depression in Russia is increasing 30 to 50 per cent annually. It is not surprising that mentally ill or psychologically disoriented Russians are drinking themselves to death at a rate unequal anywhere in modern time — often perishing from contaminated vodka (68 per cent of it substandard) now made in 'free private enterprises'. Others in desperation have been turning to religion for succour. Old churches in Russia are being reopened and new ones built, often with the understandable support of the 'new rich', the mafia and the state. There is growing attendance in the pews and a perceptible revival of rituals. This betokens no expression of any latent religious or spiritual curiosity. For the Church it is most often a trading in spirituality with the active support of the powers that be. Since its liberation during perestroika period, the Church in fact has rapidly turned into a vast commercial organisation which has been allowed to import alcohol, tobacco and other goods duty-free by courtesy of Yeltsin when he was in power and with a little assistance from the mafia. It has been accorded privileges which it did not enjoy even in Czarist times. Its conduct and commercial activities bear startling similarities to the ways of mafia groups. There is little spirituality in its behaviour, only political calculation and material greed. For the people their 'spirituality' is the social-psychological support they need to survive in the new, unkind and uncertain, 'elbow society' world of market reforms.

People's deepening desperation and despair in coping with this unkind and uncertain world has also led to a rekindling of interest in the occult, the rise of new sects, and the spread of spiritual quackery and all sorts of irrational forms of belief, such as astrology, fortune-telling and ESP. There is a proliferation of fortune-tellers, palmists, mind-readers, preachers and proselytisers. All sorts of horoscopes and occult literature are flourishing and bookshops are filled with books on astrology and black magic. Russian newspapers give weekly star columns, offering advice on what to do and when to do. Thousands of astrologers, black magicians, sorcerers and ESP specialists have appeared. According to press reports about 40 per cent of all people suffering from psychological problems in Russia turn to ESP practitioners, magicians and exorcists, the so-called 'alternative healers'. Concerned psychiatrists and mental health specialists had warned in the mid-1990s that if the situation was not changed in the near future, Russia would enter the 21st century as a psycho-pathological country. It has indeed done so.

XXI

As Yeltsin staged his first coup in 1991, and ousting Gorbachev took charge of the country, he promised people freedom, democracy and prosperity based on 'a normal civilised market economy'. Most Russians believed him and even outside Russia there was wide acceptance of the complacently ideological western view that after a period of more or less painful readjustment to market economics, Russia will move inexorably into the ranks of developed industrial countries. A decade or so later Russia presents a very different picture and appears headed for a very different possible future. Way back at the end of 1920s, referring to 'some of the lessons of history' and pointing out that 'the Soviet system with its nationalised industry and monopoly of foreign trade, in spite of all its contradictions and difficulties, is a protective system for the economic and cultural independence of the country', Trotsky had warned that a restored Russian capitalism 'would be a dependent, semi-colonial capitalism without any prospects', which would occupy a position somewhere between the third rate position of Tsarist Russia and the then position of India under the British. What is happening in Russia has reconfirmed – of course at a bitter price paid by the Russian people – the theoretical power of classical Marxism. In rejecting a planned for a 'free market' economy, in the current situation of economic and political domination of global capitalism, what has occurred in the come-late-to-capitalism Russia – formerly the super power Soviet Union – is a profound economic and social regression. While remaining a nuclear superpower, Russia has been rapidly sliding into the social, economic and cultural pattern of a third world country. In the economic sphere, there is the deindustrialistion, erosion of technological base, a mafia-led economy and the reorientation of the national economy towards a model largely based on the export of raw materials and import of manufactured products and food, and a growing dependence on foreign capital and its financial institutions. In the social and political sphere there is a thin stratum of rich, comprador economic and political elites at the top with the majority of the people below living in poverty, a small much-squeezed middle class, constantly increasing class differentials and increasingly sharp polarisation between rich and poor, unemployment and a shifting mass of underemployed, chronically impoverished workers, lack of social protection, lumpenisation and marginalisation of huge sections of population, absence of functioning democratic institutions and a pro-rich authoritarian government. All this has been almost inevitably accompanied by a pervasive moral decline and cultural degradation.

The obviously comprador nature of the new Russian ruling

elites, whose policies have led to the rapid decline of the country's economic and cultural wealth, not to mention its military might, is now widely recognised and not a few Russian economists and intellectuals (writing around 1996) are themselves advancing the idea that Russia should be considered a third world country, self-colonised or newly colonised by the West. Thus, for example, Ivan Boltovsky, writing of the 'Great Colonial Revolution in Russia' points out:

> What has Russia lost? By the beginning of last year 500 biggest enterprises worth not less than 200 billion dollars in real prices were sold out for approximately 7.2 billion dollars. All of these are now in the hands of foreign companies and the Russian companies allied to them. In this way 77 steel plants, 85 machine building plants, 66 enterprises of oil and gas, and 65 chemical enterprises were sold off for a pittance.

Says Boris Kagarlitsky:

> The capital flight is tremendous. In a certain sense it is better to be a colonial country where at least you know how much is taken away, what the rules of the game are, and who actually takes it away. Whereas here this kind of self-colonisation with the capital flight being mostly encouraged by Russia's own elite is much more dangerous. Russian firms and companies and individuals have by now in Western banks, according to one estimate, more than 180 billion dollars. And that's not the most recent estimate. By now the figure is probably more than 200 billion dollars. As far as its magnitude is concerned, the capital removed from the country legally and illegally is much higher than the debt we have incurred to the West. So in a way we can easily exchange the two.

Kagarlitsky underlines:

> The problem is accentuated by the fact that it's not as if the Westerners are exploiting the Russians. It's actually Russians together with the Westerners exploiting the other Russians. It's Moscow exploiting the rest of the country and inviting foreigners to help it exploit the rest of the country. You should understand – it's not external colonialisation, it's internal colonialisation.
>
> Apropos this, the well known journalist Fred Weir adds: 'the biggest parasites are the Russians' and the 'elite here are pretty good at muscling out their foreign competition when it comes to gaining control over Russian raw materials'.

In his analysis of the 'reform process' in Russia, Academician Leonid Abalkin, Director of the Institute of Economics (Russian Academy of Sciences) writes:

> The future of the society is already visible as a spectrum of different variations and scenarios... The variety of possible scenarios of Russia's development is now broad enough. If one is to take note of the extreme variations then these are limited to two. The first, which might be called optimistic, will lead to the regeneration of the greatness and pride of the country, to the creation of an effective and flexible economy, which will be oriented to the use of the highest achievements of science and technology and which will ensure high living standards for the whole population. This path is difficult and long. But it will guarantee that Russia occupies a proper place among the leaders of the world economy and pursues an independent internal and external policy.
>
> The second of these two extreme scenarios presupposes that Russia will convert itself into a raw material appendage of the highly developed countries with an extremely inelastic economic structure, exceedingly low level of per capita income and very high income differentiations, and as a consequence, with permanent social tensions. By this path the country will lose its national independence and probably also its national integrity....
>
> Both the scenarios as well as some intermediary variations are equally possible. But such a situation cannot continue endlessly. The magnitude and tempo of destruction of the Russian economy and society are such that one has to come to the conclusion that if these processes are not terminated in two to three years they would become irreversible. The opportunity for the regeneration of Russia will be lost forever.

This is how a review of the Indo-Russian Joint Seminar held in Calcutta at the end of 1998, published in *Economic and Political Weekly*, reported the views of two participating Russian scholars:

> Igor Bratischev's (MP and chairman, Parliamentary Sub-committee for Regional Socio-economic Development, the State Duma of the Federal Assembly of the Russian Federation) paper, 'Russia: Economic Foundations for a National Anti-Crisis Programme', explained the man-made systemic socio-economic crisis in Russia. The situation this early autumn can only be described in terms of the 'theory of catastrophes'. The main cause of the national catastrophe that Russia experiences now is an

> anti-national orientation of the economic and political course being implemented by the comprador, mafia-type, corrupted rulers of Russia;... The reforms during 1991-98, implemented by force and under control of foreign experts, have led to a disintegration of the economy, degradation of the science, culture, industries and agriculture, pauperisation of 80 per cent of Russia's population, and a sharp lowering of Russian citizen's longevity. The country is quickly transforming into a raw material appendage of the West; Oleg Maliarov's (Institute of Oriental Studies, Moscow) paper ... reiterates: 'Speaking about development policy and administration in any country we cannot escape characterising socio-economic system thereof'. The dismantling of the system of state regulation of the economy and the total rejection of planning in Russia make any development effort devoid of general sense of direction, of overall development strategy, of proper co-ordination in using various regulating tools, of effective control over the state sector and over its impact upon the economy as a whole. The socio-economic course of 'reform', since 1992, has made the Russian economy a transitional one; the destructive transition to a semi-colonial backward economy.

This, it may be added, is how Western capitalism wants it to be. The last thing it wants is rivals in the limited and shrinking global capitalist market; it would rather have new semi-colonial, third-worldised territories to exploit. We have earlier, in different contexts, already pointed it out. This is how Istvan Meszaroz put it way back in early 1990 as 'actually existing socialism' collapsed in East Europe:

> Western capital is not in the least interested in giving away its own markets, supplying at the same time also a generous 'Marshall aid' to the societies of 'actual socialism' (in accordance with the fantasies of former 'market socialists') in order to acquire for itself in exchange some forcefully revitalized competitors. What it needs and is determined to get are new markets and super-profits for itself, together with the economic and political domination of Eastern Europe (as well as of the Soviet Union and China in due course). Western capital needs such new outlets and areas of domination in order to help remedy the structural defects and contradictions of its own system, including the literally *astronomical* internal and external deficits of the US – counted in *trillions* of dollars – which represent the real debt problem today (and even more so tomorrow).

> In the pecking order of global capital the place assigned to the East is in no way better than the one into which the 'Third World' had been forced....

As an opinion poll towards the end of 1999 indicates, as against the 'fantasies' of their comprador rulers, the Russian people have a better sense of what Western capitalism is after. They see the West as an unfriendly force out to harm their country. The Romir Polling Agency's survey of 1500 people in 40 regions of Russia showed that while some 37.5 per cent believed Western nations want to split Russia and destroy it altogether, 41.1 per cent said they believed the West was attempting to turn Russia into a third world country.

Unless a major reversal of policies takes place and that too soon enough, third worldisation indeed appears to be the destined future of Russia. It may be added that the situation (of foreign domination, large-scale unemployment, gross income inequalities and paltry and costly social services, etc.) does not rule out a certain economic recovery. With greater political stability and as the Russian economy finally bottoms out and third world wage levels and consumption come to predominate, more foreign investment may come in and raw material exports surge. But this will be no much-promised 'take-off'. It will only confirm Russia's status as a third world country.

XXII

If the 'transition to market' failed to deliver on its economic promise and the initial euphoria over it was soon over, its promise of 'freedom and democracy' fared no better. Staging his counter coup of 1991, a compliant Gorbachev in tow, Yeltsin surely succeeded in banning the 'totalitarian' CPSU and various republican communist parties, but the much touted 'democratic revolution' turned out to be a myth, and remains a myth so far.

'The greatest myth the West has sold itself is that of the democratic revolution' says Prof. Nodari Simoniya, deputy director of the Institute of the World Economy. 'No such thing happened. There was merely a change-over from one Nomenklatura to another'. Indeed the nomenklatura has remained in the saddle through all the upsets of the recent past;

those now inheriting political power were, again, largely recruited from the ranks of the same nomenklatura, or apparatchiks, as they had replaced. In other words there has been only a reorganisation within the ruling class. 'We have merely moved from absolutism or totalitarianism to authoritarianism' says the analyst Myriam Salganik, adding: 'In the bad old days, the people never saw "them", those in power, as related to themselves. Today the same term "them" is used for the (new) rulers; the situation is identical'. And 'them', an oligarchy as Solzhenitsyn has described them, have been thinking of, even threatening, a more dictoratorial rule.

Boris Yeltsin staged another coup of his own (September-October 1993) which almost ended Russia's democratic experiment – he dissolved and forcibly disbanded the elected parliament, shelled and laid siege of its building, arrested the protesting members and finally promulgated a new ultra-presidential constitution which combined in the hands of the executive, the president and his government, the rights and prerogatives enjoyed by the ruling authorities in both parliamentary and presidential systems, (far exceeding those enjoyed by the CPSU general secretary once upon a time). The rights of the Duma – the lower house – were curtailed, not only compared to the parliamentary system of rule, but even compared to presidential ones. Restricted even in its legislative functions, the Duma today is a weak, almost powerless institution, whose debates and trials of strength are largely of a ritual character. A refusal to fall in line with the President's wishes is taken care of by favours to individual Duma members, paid out of the public purse and ultimately by the threat of early dissolution of the house by the President. The constitutional machinery and higher judiciary have little autonomy. In the new political set up, with all authority vested in the Kremlin, the president is a virtual dictator. No wonder, with the promulgation of the new constitution, Yeltsin was soon being spoken of as 'Tsar Boris'.

And Yeltsin went on ruling as a 'Tsar', of course with the full support and blessings of the 'democratic west'. A mostly unaccountable personal administration came to be built up alongside his ever increasing almost absolute powers as president. He surrounded himself with a much larger staff than that of the Central Committee of the defunct CPSU. The President's administration, staffed by persons who were bound together by no party discipline or service solidarity, employed 40,000 people, duly supported by a huge budget and essentially accountable only to him. A National Security Council, originally modelled on the American NSC, was set up but was soon not a consultative body that advised the President but a sort of super-government made up of a handful of very influential ministers who decided the fate of the country. This small committee was often compared to the old Politburo and, as in the Brezhnev period, it met behind closed doors and was accountable to no one. The President had a security service of his own, which did not report to any ministry – a Pretorian Guard as it were, needed by Yeltsin because, as he indicates in his memoirs, his relationships with the Minster for National Defence and with the Security Services were not always idyllic. More than half of Yeltsin's most eminent collaborators were former apparatchiks from Sverdlovsk where he was himself the leading communist party apparatchik once. In other words, much of the old nomenklatura was still there, though the rules that once governed recruitment and internal promotion no longer existed; they vanished the day the CPSU was dissolved, and nothing had been put in their place. But the Soviet tradition was continued in another manner. It was normal practice for a Secretary General of the CPSU to staff the Kremlin with his own men, who were known, outside the walls of the Kremlin, as his 'mafia'. So it was now with Yeltsin, the President. Yeltsin did not share power or see any one get too close to his chair. That was the main reason why Yeltsin's was a system of permanent shake-ups of ministers, prime ministers, etc. Almost inevitably as it were, there was Yeltsin's innermost circle, known as 'the Family', which effectively held and wielded power in Russia. (The 'Family' included not only his daughter Tatyana Dyachenko and her husband but in addition close associates like Anatoly Chubais and a few oligarchs such as Boris Berezovsky, etc. Its members reportedly controlled about 30 per cent of Russia's economy, indulged in all sorts of illegal and corrupt, even criminal activities to accumulate wealth, laundered money on a large scale and, including Yeltsin, held billions of dollars in foreign accounts. No wonder these people were most concerned about their survival if and when power changed and Yeltsin himself had an obsessive interest in managing a pliant successor. It is widely believed that Yeltsin's later decision to resign before the expiry of his term was as much the Family's as his own, in order to protect themselves and secure their interests in future through installation in power of Putin, a relatively new entrant to the 'Family'.)

Russia was democratic only in appearance. Behind the facade of democracy, it was not merely a super-presidential but a personal authoritarian system. Access to 'Tsar Boris' counted for much more than an individual's place in the hierarchy. Those who got to the 'Tsar' first won their case. Better still, they could have a dacha if they needed it, or a luxury flat in Moscow. They could travel in planes belonging to the presidential flight and enjoy other privileges, some of them paid in coin of the realm. (In 1994 Yeltsin rewarded the Duma for its 'good behaviour' by giving every deputy a holiday bonus of two million roubles; very few of them refused the tip.) Typical of Yeltsin was the rule by presidential decrees – thousands and thousands of them. In the first three years of his presidency alone Yeltsin signed about five and half-thousand legislative decrees and issued approximately eight hundred orders, coming up in close succession every year. In its own way illustrative of the dictatorial nature of the Yeltsin regime was the invasion of Chechnya, and a little later of Dagestan – going to war without consultation within government or clearance from the parliament and in complete oblivion of the roots of the crisis. Like an 'all powerful' Tsar, Yeltsin believed one could solve these problems by brute force. (North Caucasus is today a most volatile and socially restless region in Russia, because it is also the poorest and among the worst hit by the collapse of Soviet Union. In Dagestan alone nearly three quarters of its 2.2 million people live below the official poverty line and unemployment is estimated at 80 per cent, and as Alexander Iskandaryan of the Centre for Caucasian Studies at Moscow has put it: 'All over the Moslem world young men become radicalised when there is no land, no money, no jobs and no prospects'.) Coming up in close association with Russia's 'wild capitalism', it is no surprise that the Yeltsin regime was singularly favourable to the rise of criminality throughout Russia, and itself most amenable to penetration by corrupt and criminal elements. The new Russian state was no democratic replacement of the Party-State of the Soviet period. No less arbitrary and authoritarian it was a far more criminalised state. It was what the liberal Yavlinsky, in a rather infelicitous expression, had early fore warned of: an 'oligarchic, super-monopolised state with a criminal power structure.' Or, in the words of academician Illarionov: 'a state where law prevails but where mafia is ruling the roost'.

Though not based on a Party-State – and that is an improvement – the Yeltsin regime showed no interest in stimulating political life or giving it a new basis. The Polish sociologist Wlodzimierz had once spoken of 'the unvoiced assumption' among the new, post-1989 elites in Poland 'that people had to be demobilised in order to open the way for economic reforms (and that) the business of politics should be left to politicians'. The Yeltsin regime more than shared in this hostility to democratic will formation. It openly preached people's depoliticisation, arguing that this was essential if society is to be stabilised – a view which had also much in common with that of the CPSU in its later years when it relied almost entirely upon the apathy of the population to keep it in power. As a matter of fact the new elites in Russia (or Eastern Europe), for all their liberalism and love for democracy, never saw or espoused democracy in the classical sense of popular participation and control. Instead, they appreciated democracy as it had come to be redefined and viewed in the currently fashionable western theory of 'pluralist' or 'elite democracy', and therefore as a means of smoothening the process of leadership change and policy adjustment by the competing ruling elites. In this view any serious attempt to exercise influence or control from below becomes inherently 'undemocratic', 'a challenge to democracy' rather than a development of it. If at all, only such an essentially undemocratic democracy could be countenanced by the devotees of 'free market', those in search of freedom under capitalism. That is why, pointing out that 'economic reform', not democracy was the issue in the on-going transition, *The Economist* in Britain openly stated that 'reform proceeds despite democracy, not because of it', adding: 'it is sometimes necessary to insulate policy from the chaos of politics'. In other words, 'reform' best proceeds under authoritarian rule. And, its specificities of corruption and criminality apart, Yeltsin regime was the necessary authoritarian rule in Russia.

As people were sought to depoliticised and kept at a distance from political power, the emerging class of big capitalists, Oligarchs, Mafiosi and the rest, were busy penetrating and establishing their class power in Russia's 'democratic' politics. We have earlier noticed the formation of corporate structures as 'clans' in the Russian economy and their fierce struggles over the division of property rights and economic power. In this struggle it was obviously important for the clans to make the breakthrough to political power. As a result, each of the clans was placing its stakes on one or several competing political forces, parties or blocs, some of them even reaching out to the communists to ensure support or lobbying for the clan interests. Divergent political preferences of different sections of the emerging Russian bourgeoisie notwithstanding, their general class or particular economic interests demanded and therefore also determined their continued support to Yeltsin's authoritarian regime, where, in any case, in a rare symbiosis of government and big business interests, officialdom was almost totally identified with the rising capitalist class.

It is worth noticing the way 'democratic process of this period stood reduced to being 'all about Yeltsin fighting, winning and staying'. For this has its obviously negative implications for the present and future of democracy in Russia. It was not merely that the 'court of Kremlin' would not survive Boris Yeltsin's defeat – and it was not a body that was designed to hand over power should it be defeated – or that, mired in corruption and linked with Russian oligarchy and mafia, a good part of the concerned elite was likely to find itself in Lefortovo prison, so flagrant indeed was its abuse of power and accumulation of illicit wealth. It was also one of the symptoms of the overall crisis of right-wing politics of these years in Russia that much as it was deemed necessary, it could not find an obvious favourite to replace Yeltsin. In the meantime, as they waited for one, country's ruling elite and big business, together with their foreign backers, remained perfectly conscious of the value of having Yeltsin in power. This, for example, became abundantly clear in the 1996 presidential election when Yeltsin's chances for re-election – with his popularity rating in the range of 6 to 10 per cent – seemed hopeless. Of course, 'democracy' or 'no democracy', Yeltsin himself, along with the 'family' was determined to stay in power. Abusing his near-total, direct or indirect, control of the media (radio, television, newspapers and magazines), mobilising the entire government machinery and exerting all sorts of illegal administrative pressures, proscribing any form of political organising within the factories, spending massively to buy and bribe people, using many other dirty tricks besides, Yeltsin literally rigged the election, compelling a Polish diplomat to observe 'If this is free elections then the term has no meaning. It is a caricature to talk of elections under the conditions that we are seeing here'. But equally, if not more significant – and decisive for Yeltsin's victory – was the way Russian big business and financial tycoons, uniting their money, media and muscle power, came to Yeltsin's assistance. The Group of 7 Oligarchs pumped in millions of dollars into Yeltsin's coffers and undertook a publicity blitzkrieg in his favour (for which they were soon rewarded with tax favours and cheap state bonds to be resold at a handsome profit). They fed into and massively funded Yeltsin's harsh and deceitful negative advertising, especially against the Communist Party and its leader Gennady Zyuganov. Fearful of any change or reversal of policies, the threat that a change of government could pose to their power and plundered wealth, 13 of Russia's top bankers and business tycoons, in an open letter, warned: 'Those who are banking on ideological revanche and social confrontation must understand that Russian businessmen have the necessary resources to deal with excessively unprincipled and uncompromising politicians.' (Their money power apart, private security companies and new Russian business conglomerates are estimated to have some 600,000 men under arms.) Among Yeltsin's key 'democratic' supporters were Russia's five huge privatised oil companies and the state-backed private gas monopoly, Gazprom. Vagit Alekperov, head of the giant LUK oil company well expressed the big business interest in ensuring the re-election of Boris Yeltsin for a second term: 'Yeltsin is the only candidate who stands above politics. I'm always alarmed when I hear talk of possible nationalisation of our company.' (Yeltsin's campaign had an official budget of 3 million dollars, but estimates put the total expenditure at over 100 million dollars. The Oligarchs paid for at least most of this, of course to be soon compensated at the government's expense. Berezovski even claimed that the oligarchs had 'bought' the Kremlin).

The 'democratic west' had an equally strong interest in Yeltsin staying in power. He had of course created a market with a high crime rate, and that is not what serious Western investors wanted. He was also politically unpredictable and the west would have liked to have a more reputable and effective 'their man' in the Kremlin. Nevertheless Yeltsin had remained their best bet in Russia. He was all along forgiven a great deal because, as he himself put it when he was in Washington, he had 'killed the communist monster' and he was going to bring the lost Russian sheep back into the capitalist fold. The overriding concern of the capitalist west and its international financial institutions had been to ensure the irreversibility of 'market reform' in Russia. And Yeltsin, so far, had been the only immediately available force in the Russian political spectrum with a clear interest and commitment in this regard. The west was willing to countenance Yeltsin's violations of constitutional proprieties and making a mockery of democracy, for they saw him as the saviour of their 'free market' project for Russia. The essence of Yeltsinism was the restoration of capitalism in Russia under the aegis of transnational capital with support from its domestic and foreign political mobsters, it had nothing at all to do with the restoration of any kind of democracy. *The Economist* even rationalised it all saying, 'Russia being Russia', 'a free market democracy' was not something meant for the Russians.

Yeltsin was 'their man', the West's most pliant accomplice in its plans for Russia. He had to stay in power and not be thrown out as threatened by the presidential elections of 1996. Like the Russian oligarchs and big business, the west backed Yeltsin to the hilt. In order to facilitate Yeltsin's victory, France and Germany lent Russia 480 million and 2.7 billion dollars respectively and the IMF granted Russia a massive 10.3 billion dollar loan given for discretionary spending by the government rather than being linked to any 'conditionalities' or specific goals – an almost unprecedented deal in IMF history. Noted the economist Sergei Glazyev: 'And the speed with which it is coming into the country indicates that it will be available for Yeltsin to temporarily increase social spending before the election.' The US embassy and its various intelligence gathering agencies orchestrated and bankrolled Yeltsin's election. In a US corporate style exercise in 'free elections', a public relations team from the US, paid for by 'private' American investment banks, was engaged to manage Yeltsin's election campaign – his 'anti-communist war' – under the supervision of his daughter. An American president had once said of the Central American banana dictator Somoza: 'He may be a son of a bitch but he is *ourson of a bitch*'. His occasional 'nationalist' rhetoric notwithstanding, much the same could be said of Yeltsin as he went on to win the 'democratic' election of 1996 and stayed in power in the Kremlin.

XXIII

Yeltsin did the hatchet job for global capitalism – as best as he could – to secure the present and future of his country as a 'market economy', in the process leaving Russia's state and economy in thrall to mafia-run monopolies and its people reduced from adequacy to destitution. But unpredictabilities of the situation being what they were, his own and 'his family's' future remained uncertain, a matter of serious concern. Yeltsin's second and last term as president was coming to an end and there was far too much wealth accumulated through far too many shady and criminal deeds, many of them involving his daughter, universally reckoned as the centre of the ruling criminal gang that was 'the Family'. The future obviously looked worrisome. There was the need to safeguard his own and the 'Family's' financial interests, retain a necessary foothold in the power structure and, above all, ensure protection against prosecution for decade long misdeeds. The search for a pliant successor intensified. The man for the job was ultimately found in Vladimir Vladimirovich Putin, an obscure former K.G.B. colonel who was already a part of the presidential administration and 'the family'. In August 1999, Yeltsin dismissed the prime minister Stepashin whom he considered to be weak and not upto what was required of him, to push the virtually unknown Putin forward as the new prime minister and his putative successor. And then, in a clever New Year's eve manoeuvre that caught the Opposition flat-footed and short-circuited the normal democratic process, Yeltsin resigned full six months before the end of his term putting Putin into the job of Acting President and ensuring his election as the next president a few months later. Come to power as Acting President and (in May 2000) as President, Putin has kept the promises made in the deal between him and Yeltsin. Yeltsin and his family have been given full immunity against prosecution and 'the Family' and 'Family'-linked oligarchs have, on the whole, not only remained safe but increased their hold on Russia's state and economy.

XXIV

With Putin, while there is an appearance of stability at the top, the situation below remains much as it was under Yeltsin. So far at least, nothing really new or different can be said of the new regime. The brief five-week election campaign which ended with Putin's victory was almost devoid of choice. Putin spoke against the oligarchs and went chauvinistically patriotic over Chechnya but gave no indication of what he actually planned to do. While Russia's two state-owned national TV networks adopted an all-Putin-all-the-time news agenda and the oligarchs-controlled media campaigned for him just as they used to for Yeltsin earlier, Putin refused from the outset to elaborate a programme or debate his rivals. He grandly turned down the 80 minutes of free TV advertising time each candidate was entitled to, in favour of 'strictly carrying out state duties'. 'Putin is an enigma as far as his basic beliefs and intentions go,' said Sergei Markov, Director of the Association of Political Consultants in Moscow. 'He won the election by sounding notes that Russians want to hear, but actually saying nothing.' Perhaps 'an enigma' was *politically* the best thing to be for Yeltsin's protégé. But Putin is not an enigma any longer. While he does give the impression of wanting to move away from Yeltsin's legacy, publicly courts the support of people as diverse as Gorbachev and Solzhenitsyn, makes 'nationalist' noises at home and plays the global leader abroad, there are no significant departures from the way things were under Yeltsin, at best there are occasional conflicting signals.

Putin's inner circle is said to include, along with his old associates from the intelligence services, a handful of back-room power brokers, including some oligarchs. Putin may be making noises against them – 'the oligarchs will cease to exist as a class', 'No clan or oligarch should be given special access to a local authority, a governor, the president, the prime minister or a minister', etc. – or even move selectively or symbolically against some of them – often when they turn 'disloyal' or his political interests so demand – but he has, so far, shown no willingness or ability to cut down, much less eliminate, their clout in Russian economy or politics, to say nothing of charting out a different course of development for Russia. Putin in fact remains committed to Russia's 'economic reform' or capitalist restoration, though with an occasional plea for some state control over 'market players'. Privatisation remains a priority with him; he has pledged that there will be no overturning of post-Soviet privatisation – 'the authorities will not redistribute property and revise the results of privatisation'. And he is pushing ahead with privatisation in the agricultural sector. Through his Farm Land Bill of 2002, he is supposed to have taken a great step to carry Russia forward on the path of reforms towards a market economy. Putin hopes to achieve what his predecessor Boris Yeltsin could not.

In 1992-93, Yeltsin had passed laws on 'Land Reform' and 'Peasant Farming' providing for the right of private property in land. About 27000 state and collective farms were converted into joint stock companies with land and land shares nominally given to all the members of these farms including those managing them. Otherwise, so far as privatisation of land proper is concerned, the results were quite disappointing. As several studies have shown, in 1998, out of 91.7 million hectares of land under crops in the whole of Russia, only 5.9 million hectares were cultivated by new peasant farmers. In the value of total agricultural output, the share of farmers stagnated at a paltry 2 per cent during 1994-98. The de-collectivisation, except as joint stock companies, had not made much headway despite official and foreign patronage. What happens under Putin remains to be seen, though one can be reasonably sceptical about it. The outcome may well be the agricultural version of what has happened with 'privatisation' in the industrial sector.

Privatisation of land in the sense of creating a class of peasant farmers is an unfinished agenda of economic reform in Russia and is likely to remain so. It is not merely that important political forces, like the Communist and Agrarian Parties, are opposed to the privatisation of farm land, the Russian people and peasantry in particular have shown no enthusiasm for it. As reported by the well-known journalist, Fred Weir, in the *Christian Science Monitor* in early 2002, according to an opinion poll on this issue, about 50 per cent of Russians opposed private ownership of agricultural land and 12 million people belonging to the former collective and state farms were totally against the idea of privatisation. Similarly, according to the opinion poll conducted by *Sovetskaya Rossia* (July 13, 2002), 90 per cent of the peasants were against farm land sale. The peasants have not been willing, much less keen, to abandon the economic security, assured income, institutionalised social security and related benefits – in education, health care, cultural facilities, etc. – of collective farming for the insecurity and vagaries of privatised market economy. Many farmers who had left collective or state farms and started private farming, taking their share of a few hectares of land for cultivation, are reported to have surrendered the land and joined back in their collective or state farms.

Putin's Land legislation not only confronts this situation, loopholes in the new Land Code and corruption rampant in Russian society pose their own problems for its implementation. It can well happen that just as oligarchs grabbed industries in early 1990s, land may be grabbed by influential elements in the society. The land mafias can easily join in this grabbing, adding and giving free play to criminal and lumpen elements already plaguing the countryside. The former chairmen or heads of collective and state farms now managing them as joint stock companies may, much in the manner of many 'Red Directors' in the industrial sector, establish their de facto ownership over these enterprises. The 'land shares' of farmers, like 'voucher privatisation' of industries, may end up concentrating ownership in the hands of a few. A former governor of Krasnodar, one of the richest agricultural regions in the country, has expressed the fear that Putin's law on the land will open the door to speculators and leave Russian peasants as poor slaves. The possibility is real that it could well end up creating not peasant farmers but new classes of landlords and landless agricultural workers in the Russian countryside.

Putin's economics, it is obvious, does not hold any hope of better days for the Russian people. Much the same could be said of Putin's politics; it holds no promise of a democratic future for Russia. Even as Putin won the presidency without a defined programme for future action, there were enough indications for Fred Weir to write: '....whatever direction is chosen, the primary engine of change is almost certain to be a reinvented version of Russia's traditional curse: arrogant and authoritarian state power, backed by the security forces.' It was his ruthless conduct of the war in Chechnya as prime minister and the accompanying display of 'patriotic militarism' that earned him broad popularity among Russians and helped win the presidential election. 'Putin paved his way to power over the bodies of thousands of Russian soldiers and Chechen civilians,' said Andrei Piontkovsky, Director of the independent Centre for Strategic Studies. 'Why does anyone think he will stop using indiscriminate force now?' Putin certainly gave the impression that this is how he intended to tackle other problems. The recurrent theme of his election campaign was that Russia must have 'a strong state' capable of 'consolidating society' and restoring the 'national will'.

Putin sees a weak Kremlin as the main reason for Russia's post-Soviet decline and is a regular with rhetoric about Russia's great-power status. He is given to musing that Russians are 'genetically disposed' to want a strong leader. As an old KGB hand he admires and is enthusiastic about his loyalty to the intelligence services. He has been actively hostile to independent or dissident media, approved (KGB's successor) FSB's attempts to eavesdrop on e-mail and the internet, deployed the 'administrative resource' of the state, openly and massively, to back pro-Kremlin parties in the elections, and remains ruthless in dealing with Chechan and such other problems. There has been a large-scale induction of people from the military, the former Soviet KGB and other security forces – *siloviki* as they are called (derived from Russian word meaning 'force') – into the government. 'This has never happened in the past; the KGB has literally come to power', says Olga Kryshtanovskaya, who heads the Elite Studies Unit of Russia's Institute of Sociology. 'Whereas in the past people from security background generally did jobs connected with state security functions, you now find them holding high office in just about every ministry and government agencies.' (Kryshtanovskaya calculates that about 60 per cent of the inner-Kremlin circle around Putin, himself a former KGB intelligence officer, are now ex-military and security people. About a third of government functionaries are *siloviki*, as are 70 per cent of the staff members working for the Kremlin's seven regional viceroy-like emissaries.) In short, both thought and action-wise, the authoritarian streak in Putin is unmistakable; indeed it is so strong that a former US national security adviser Zbigniew Brzezinski has, even if somewhat rhetorically, asked whether Putin is Russia's Pinochet or its Milosevic.

Putin may or may not be Russia's Pinochet, now or in future, but the question underlines the dangerously authoritarian possibilities inhering in the Putin regime. Brzezinski's rhetorical question in fact goes beyond Putin to point to an aspect of the

Russian situation where, since the Gorbachev days, the worrisome contradiction between 'market economy' and democracy has regularly let the 'economic reformers' and their ideologues to argue for a direct, Pinochet-style authoritarian rule in Russia.

XXV

Struggle for power at the top notwithstanding, the elite in Russia, in power or in opposition, are all committed to the restoration of capitalism, the conflicts within only relate to the pace and the manner, or the form of this restoration, including, for the more hopeful, some form of western-style democracy, the more innocent among them even seeing it as a necessary accompaniment of a 'free market' economy. But while the will for capitalist restoration and integration into the world capitalist economy is there and is strengthened by the pressure of Western governments, the International Monetary Fund and the World Bank, the international 'business community' and a host of eager academic apostles of neo-classical economics, this restoration confronts far too many unresolved problems. And one thing is becoming increasingly clear: many of these problems are incapable of being resolved in terms recognisable to contemporary liberal democracy. While the inherited socio-economic structures, however much dismantled, the memory of social benefits now lost, or the egalitarian ethos and aspirations of even a deformed socialist past, all pose their own problems, more basic is the contradictory nature of the simultaneous process of 'marketisation' and 'democratisation' which has, as anticipated, surfaced sharply during the past few years. Russia's 'economic reform' and 'political democracy' are simply incompatible. For the ruling elite democracy is hardly the best means of preventing elements of existing civil society, notably workers and left out segments of the bureaucracy, old communists and the budding socialist opposition, from political protest and obstruction in response to bankruptcies of enterprises, unemployment accompanied by inflation, polarisation of rich and poor, which are already there and certain of acceleration as the inevitable accompaniment to the kind of economic structuring that a transition to capitalism demands, whether it is sought as a 'von Hayek's free market economy' or a more 'national' state-supported capitalism.

People's interest, their opposition to the new capitalist dispensation, immediately and in the long run, in fact puts a question mark over the future of democracy in Russia. While never denying the progressive attributes of bourgeois democracy, Marxism has always been sceptical about its claims to freedom, particularly as it relates to the working classes or the common people. This sceptism is finding substantial confirmation again in Russia. Democracy or ritual affirmations of the magic of democracy, like that of the market, did for the moment obscure class issues and bind the people together in opposition to the old regime on the basis of what they rejected. But the ideology and reality remained as far apart as ever, with the apparatchiks of the state, managers of the enterprises and mafias of the 'shadow economy' having the freedom to assume private ownership of public property or the nomenklatura to turn itself into a new class of comprador rulers. Democracy has certainly afforded a convenient 'legal' route to such transformations of the class and property relations at the top, as it has also secured a certain legitimacy for the powers that be. Nevertheless, even as a formal democracy it remains a threat to the emerging capitalist system. In fact there is an inherent tension between capitalism and democracy, the marriage between the two, even under the best of circumstances, has always been an uneasy one. It is not only that bourgeois democracy does not give rise to a thriving capitalism; on the contrary, even this democracy requires as its precondition an expanding capitalist economy. As Gramsci argued long ago, capitalist democracy is only stable if it can engineer real material concessions to its constituency. The emerging capitalism in Russia, mafiosi capitalism or the hoped-for 'civilised' capitalism, holds little promise or possibility of such concessions for the common people. In the meantime, democracy may well manifest what Marx, in his *Class struggles in France*, referred to as its 'incomparably higher merit'. He had written: 'But if universal suffrage was not the miraculous wand for which the republican duffers had taken it, it possessed the incomparably higher merit of unchaining class struggle, of letting the various middle sections of the petty-bourgeois society rapidly live through their illusions and disappointments, of tossing all the fractions of the exploiting class at one throw to the head of the state, and thus tearing from them their treacherous mask'. But then we must also not forget that in France it ended with the *coupd'etat* of Louis Bonaparte. So in Russia, as the disillusionment with market economy sets in giving rise to popular resentment and resistance, as 'the treacherous mask' is torn off the face of the new rulers and class forces collide on the terrain of democracy, the rulers may, as often in the past, dissolve the uneasy marriage in favour of capitalism. They may well decide that the imposition and maintenance of capitalist property relations upon an increasingly recalcitrant population requires 'political stability', which only a fully authoritarian rule can provide. This is not just a theoretical possibility.

The wild capitalism being established in the post-Soviet Russia inherently carries within it the need to be backed by a regime able to carry it through, which involves containing and repressing the discontent the process generates. Hence Yeltsin's and now Putin's authoritarianism behind the rather weak democratic forms, which however need to be maintained for the purpose of legitimacy they provide and for international public relations. But subjected to greater pressure from below, the full authoritarian option in the future is not to be discounted. This kind of authoritarian turn is not something unknown in the history of liberal democracy or capitalist societies when faced with difficult economic and social problems. Twentieth century is replete with such examples and scholars have drawn pointed attention to the parallel between the economic devastation in Russia and what happened in Germany after the First World War, culminating in the rise of the Weimar Republic, followed by a slide into a fascist regime through a democratic process under an unscrupulous and demagogic leader. It is not surprising that models of economic reforms in Latin America, specially Pinochetist Chile, have been popular with some Russian reformers from the very beginning. And, given the ingrained *dirigiste* reflexes of the ruling elite that has come up since then, one option revived from the early years, and now canvassed with encouragement from the Western experts, is precisely for Russia adopting a Pinochet model of dictatorship, which is economically liberal, that is, market-oriented, but ruthlessly authoritarian politically – 'a Pinochet type dictatorship, decorated with a few pseudo-democratic ornaments' that socialist Buzgalin has warned against.

This may not have happened so far. But the argument for it is there and the possibility is not to be ruled out. As noted above, such authoritarianism was advocated at the very beginning of capitalist restoration and the argument for it has persisted all along. Towards the end of Yeltsin's second term, the deepening crisis and nervousness about the future had the men in the Kremlin talking of 'plans' for 'emerging situations'. 'There is an air of desperation around Yeltsin now', noted an observer, Makarenko. 'It's the kind of air that breeds dangerous adventures.' Migranyan, a long-time member of the Advisory Council of President Boris Yeltsin, had always favoured an authoritarian political course for the country, arguing that a liberal democracy is unworkable in Russia. He was hopeful of roping in the Orthodox Church to strengthen his call for the establishment of an autocratic social order of the Tsarist type. So was his co-ideologue Tsypko. The leading liberal daily *Izvestia* wrote of the country being 'in need of tough men who can take bold decisions', as others of that ilk looked for 'a strong man' for a time of 'extraordinary measures'. Along came a Labed – a portrait of Pinochet, 'my teacher' as he fondly called this butcher of the Chilean people, adorning his office – with his promise *a la* Pinochet-Thatcher-Reagan of 'breaking the backbone of labour trouble-makers'. And the famous eye surgeon Svyatoslav Fyodorov, now a leader of the left-radical sounding Party of Workers' Self-Management – a party without a programme or ideology nevertheless – declared that Russia would be saved by 'Christ in the uniform of Pinochet'. And now, post-Yeltsin, President Putin is being assessed as Russia's Pinochet.

It is not necessary that Russia's possible authoritarianism should be exactly Pinochet-like. It is also possible that despairing sections of the population may themselves succumb to a populist authoritarianism. And, it has not arrived so far – Russia is at least nominally democratic. None of this however should obscure the continuing ruling class interest in a directly dictatorial regime to push through their capitalist agenda or subvert the outcome of a democratic election not to their taste. They may well go in for it in the name of defence of democracy against a conjured up threat of 'return of communism'. Needless to add that if and when Russian democracy, such as it is, gives way to an openly authoritarian regime in Russia, the west would be only too happy to provide it with material and moral support. Remember the notorious declaration of Henry Kissinger that rejected the overwhelming victory of Allende in Chile and prepared the ground work for the mass US-Pinochet butchery that followed: 'I don't see why we need to stand by and watch a country go communist because of the irresponsibility of its own people'. The historical record too is quite clear in this regard. Chile apart, Panama, Nicaragua, Haiti, Taiwan, South Korea, Indonesia, Nigeria, Zaire, and Philippines – to mention a few – offer examples of west-supported right-wing authoritarian governments whose claims to democratic fame have rested upon their ability to provide a stable and 'free' political environment for multinational corporations to do business on their own terms.

It can be legitimately argued that it may be impossible to create capitalism in Russia by democratic means. The capitalist restoration so far has been anything but a democratic process. That people have not been able to effectively oppose it, or that sections of it have themselves succumbed to it, does not make it democratic, only underlines its essentially authoritarian character. As it is, Russia has not been much of a democracy all these years, and is not one today. And it cannot be, not even western-style bourgeois democracy, in conjunction with the mafiosi or third-worldist capitalism it is building. Democracy in Russia will either be socialist or it will not exist. One implication of it all is that resistance to capitalist restoration and struggle for socialism have to go hand in hand. The other is that the struggle for democracy, 'to win the battle of democracy' as the *Communist Manifesto* puts it, should seek not only to defend, strengthen and expand whatever democracy is presently there in Russia, but also to so alter the present course as to keep open the option of a genuinely socialist future for Russia.

XXVI

Russia's chaotic capitalist transition has thrown up all sorts of political forces, parties and blocs, ranging from one extreme to the other. The right remains visibly dominant, pre-eminently represented by the present regime. The liberal or left-centrist opposition which had once profitably harvested a certain popular mobilisation of the perestroika period, is now not only fragmented but virtually insignificant in terms of public support. More significant is the fact that the differences between its real policies and the policies of the present authorities amount only to nuances within a shared pro-capitalism strategy. As with the similarly weak right-centrists, it has all sorts of links with the Putin-Yeltsin establishment and its leaders only hopeful of being more viable alternatives to Putin. There are the crypto-fascist Russian national chauvinists at the extreme right, a declining but potentially dangerous presence on the political scene, most vociferous supporters of a full-fledged authoritarian regime. A significant ideological-political current, with adherents over the entire political spectrum including the left, is moderate nationalists who see the west-led globalisation as creating a new world order in which Russia and the other republics of the former Soviet Union are assigned a place at the bottom of the global pyramid, their natural and human resources exploited for the benefit of the core capitalist countries and transnational corporations – and don't like it. They search for an alternative 'national' option for Russia – something like what Samir Amin calls 'the option for a realignment around the statist technocracy-national capitalism couplet'. In other words they hope for a 'national capitalism' while maintaining a strong role for the central state. The social basis of this nationalist current has been described as including 'the "red directors" of the industrial managerial class, whose power depends on the very survival of the industrial base; the agro bosses, who control the agricultural lobby; the controlling interest (often undisguisedly criminal) of the new private cartels; and the large number of middlemen, speculators, small entrepreneurs, and in general buy-sell-run types thriving in the waters of "privatisation" (that is, looting), who see the bigger sharks moving in. It also includes large sections of the Soviet professional class that are disenchanted by the failure of the neoliberal reforms: the formerly privileged scientific and technical intelligentsia whose social status has been threatened by the deindustrialisation of the country and the almost complete termination of state financing for scientific research and higher education'. This looks formidable. But the way economy and politics have crumbled in the post-Soviet period and come to be subjected to local comprador and global capitalist pressures in the wake of 'economic reform', this current has not been able to find an effective political expression so far and its hopes remain very much an unwarranted optimism. (Moving away from Yeltsin in search of credentials of his own, to be a leader in his own right, it is primarily among these and other nationalists that Putin is trying to find a constituency for himself.)

The point to note is that, their differences granted, including those between the comprador and nationalist sections of the new bourgeoisie, these currents or trends represent complementary rather than antagonistic, mutually exclusive ideologies or politics. Even those wanting a 'national capitalism' or even a Rooseveltian 'New Deal', are committed to the on-going 'economic reforms', that is, construction of capitalism in Russia, and are a part of the competing elite who even as they struggle for power in the political arena, stand together in the common cause of preserving their domination over the rest of society. In other words, whatever be their long term hopes, immediately the real issue for them, as for others, is one of choosing between economic tactics for market reforms and not one of choosing a different socio-economic strategy. But recent political developments, including electoral behaviour, also clearly indicate that a very significant part of the population is certain that the present regime is taking Russia in the wrong direction, that mere adjustments of the reform process are not enough, that a different strategic goal is called for. Not that a genuine alternative strategic goal is emerging. But there is a better organised expression of popular discontent, of people's participation in the political process, and of alternative policies.

Most significant development here is the emergence of communists organised as the Communist Party of Russian Federation (CPRF), which has risen phoenix-like from the ashes to become the largest political party in Russia. Despite the disbanding of the CPSU – consequent upon the August 1991 coup and counter coup of Yeltsin – communists as such were not put out of power. It was largely a case of one part of the former ruling *nomenklatura* usurping political power under Yeltsin to carry out the transition to capitalism. The rest of the party splintered into big or small political formations, unable to offer any kind of resistance or viable alternative to the new regime. But when they were again able to operate openly, they quickly established themselves as the largest party in Russia (as in Ukraine and Belarus as well). A plethora of other communist organisations also emerged out of the old CPSU. Several new non-communist leftist organisations too have come up since then – among them 'socialist' parties set up by wealthy businessmen, with extremely dubious ideas to match which make a mockery of the very notion of socialism. But the hegemony of the CPRF on the left is now universally recognised, albeit very reluctantly by the more Stalinist or neo-Stalinist organisations. Since its refoundation in February 1993 – with Gennady Zyuganov as the General secretary – the party has gone from strength to strength. With a membership of more than half a million (in a country with a population of 150 million), it is almost twice as large as any rival organisation warranting the label of a recognized political party. It has 20,000 primary organisations, 2,000 district and city organisations, and is fully represented in 88 out of the 89 constituent parts of the Federation – the one exception being Chechnya. The experienced and tested cadres from the old CPSU providing the middle level leadership, its members are recruited mainly from medium sized towns and rural areas – it has a rather limited presence in the metropolitan areas (like Moscow and St. Petersburg) which, in the eyes of the world, are the very incarnation of Russia – and the average age of members, significantly, is around 40 years. It has fairly good financial resources at its disposal thanks to a number of close links with lucrative business organisations and business people, indeed a whole range of powerful social and economic elites, who have found it politically convenient or useful to also support the re-formed and reformed communists.

That the CPRF has grown and won mass support over the years, and done so despite the unconstitutional banning of communist activity and in the face of enormous adversity, persistent official hostility and explicit media bias is not difficult to understand. The Party has had available to it, from the pre-collapse CPSU, a nation-wide network of organisational and administrative structures and experienced cadres to run a party machine. Support has also been available from many of the old Party functionaries who continued as local administrators under the new regime, but did not necessarily change their allegiances. The Party could not only appeal to a sense of tradition natural in such matters and rely on the ingrained sense of loyalty and attachment to the communist cause, but also benefit from the overwhelming sense of nostalgia for the old times that has quickly emerged in the popular consciousness. Again, the swelling numbers of those disaffected and disillusioned with the capitalist transition have found a viable political structure to give expression to their discontent, a 'natural' political home as it were, in this best organised and most articulate party of the left. As the largest party, to a degree it has benefited even at the expense of other leftist formations. It has also been suggested that programme-wise CPRF has also benefited from the deep-seated structural factors in Russian society which add up as an 'intrinsically strong role of the state in a whole range of key areas, which no amount of "liberalisation" or even "capitalisation" would be able to impinge on for a considerable amount of time.' This is how, noticing the 'positive fact that the CPRF is now the main political force of the country', it has been asserted that 'for the "Left" (however we define that term) there is one, and only one, organisational forum through which its cause can be advanced – and that forum is the Communist Party of the Russian Federation'.

XXVII

This however is a questionable proposition if our notion of 'the Left' has anything to do with socialism. For, as presently led, theory and programme-wise CPRF is not socialist in any traditional sense of the term. Most noticeable about this theory and programme is its strong 'nationalist' dimension which, even as it is a major factor in CPRF's rejuvenation, pushes it away from any commitment to socialism. Recognising that 'the real success of the CPRF's rejuvenation has undoubtedly been grounded in its encapsulation and embodiment of the nationalist cause in Russia', Jeremy Lester has most perceptively observed: 'Such a blend of communism and nationalism is nothing new, of course, in Russia. For all the internationalist rhetoric of Soviet communists, few observers have ever really questioned the predominance of prioritising a nationalist agenda. Nevertheless, the essence and nature of the current blend of these two forces seems to me to give off a different aroma altogether. This aroma is anything but socialist.'

The CPRF does not reject the on-going transition to market economy. It is conciliationist towards the neo-liberal policies and presents itself as a reform-oriented but a socially conscious opponent of 'shock therapy' kind of economic reform. It favours a rational and orderly, better managed transition to capitalism, one oriented to national needs, with a strong state sector, 'socially oriented market' and reconstituted minimum social services and security. Its economic programme calls for taking the commanding heights of the economy, especially 'income-generating enterprises', back into state hands, the state monopoly of foreign trade in the strategic sector, and similar other measures but without excluding a role for private 'national capital' and small private businesses. What it visualises has been described as 'a mixed economy with elements of capitalism and socialism'. The emphasis is on 'setting a balance of private and pubic interests that corresponds to our national needs and level of development'. To be sure, the entire process of 'privatisation' is to be reviewed and the tax system would be used in stronger ways to ensure some degree of greater redistribution, but as Zyuganov has been making abundantly clear, no real attack on the forms of private property that have emerged in recent years is contemplated. In tone and essence the economic programme of CPRF is thus not very different from that of the post-'shock therapy' reformers, particularly those with a nationalist orientation. The party's political programme seeks sweeping constitutional reform centred first on reversing what Zyuganov calls Yeltsin's 'state coup' of 1993, that is, on returning power from the Presidential executive to parliament. Parliamentary system and pluralism is accepted though the party also champions the ultimate aim of reconstructing Soviets, expressive of 'unity of action among power structures' as against the liberal conception of the division of powers. The party also stands for a 'voluntary' reintegration of the former Soviet Republics into a new Union. CPRF's programme is variously claimed to be 'left-social democratic', 'something between socialism and social democracy', or a programme of 'socialist orientation' which, according to the ideologue G.G. Kotovsky, recognising 'parliamentary democracy' and 'mixed economy', is distinct from the 'communist orientation' of the past. For Kotovsky, taking the best from 'our old bureaucratic socialism with communist ideology' and 'the capitalist way', it is even 'a new type of way out for humankind'. But 'way out' or not, it has obviously nothing to do with socialism as the classical tradition understands it. It is at best, and as in case of ex-communists in East Europe, social democracy's capitalism with a human face, but now with strong statist and, as we shall see, nationalist overtones.

Almost universally seen as a successor to the old CPSU, CPRF's lack of concern with the issue of socialism in Russia is evident in its attitude to the past. While the echoes of this past – whatever kind of socialism or Marxism it had – can be heard in the theory and practice of CPRF, the most striking fact here is its failure to come to terms with it, to be self-critical about it, to understand this past in Marxist terms and overcome it as socialists. This failure leaves the party carrying all the ugly inheritance of this past and thus vulnerable to the attacks of the enemies on this account. The problem here is that while an overwhelming majority of the population is against the present state of affairs and a sense of nostalgia for the recent past does exist and has lately become more pronounced, the society as a whole is not inclined to go back to this communist past. Associating the CPRF with this past and raising the spectre of a communist revival and return of the old authoritarian and repressive regime, Yeltsin and his ilk earlier and their successors now have been successful in depriving the party of the support of significant sections of the people, including the wavering intelligentsia even when it is now materially much worse off.

In failing to come to terms with their past as socialists, CPRF has almost inevitably carried quite a bit of this past within itself, and thus providing some justification at least for opponents' criticism. Unreformed in their dogmatism, unrepentant in their attitudes, the leadership's confused ideological postures do at times hark back to a dead and the least attractive part of the communist past. There is periodic admission of sympathy for Stalin, refusal tocondemn Stalinism, obvious antagonism to Khrushchev's 'thaw' and Gorbachev's *'perestroika'*, all feeding into the conservative-conformist moods of rank and file members of the party. The political dogmatism and organisational bureaucratism of the party has manifested itself in the forcing out of the 'dissident forces' opposed to the leadership of Zyuganov and an arrogant hegemonic attitude towards smaller parties of the Left. It has also led to rather weak or ineffective functioning of members in the conditions of a multi-party system marked by struggle between various ideologies and interests, and to the experienced cadres, with experienceonly of bureaucratic kow-towing, failing to provide proper leadership to the ranks and the people.

One cannot possibly assess the current state of the CPRF, under the leadership of Gennady Zyuganov, without taking note of the pivotal importance nationalism has in its ideology and politics, governing its definition of Russia's predicament and of its own tasks. Its nationalist political stance takes the CPRF very far from any concern with socialism. In its turn to nationalism, the currently dominant element in the leadership promotes ideas which have nothing in common with any tradition of the socialist left, including that of Lenin's Bolsheviks, and Zyuganov himself seems attached to some of the very worst aspects of the intellectual heritage of the Stalin years and marks an ideological regression in comparison even with Brezhnev and Gorbachev.

For Zyuganov, almost as a Hegelian, the ethnos or nation is the main 'agent of history' and his nationalism suggests not only some sort of inner organic unity of the Russian nation but also a Russian spiritual superiority over other nations. And the Russian ethnos is integrally connected to Russian communism; the 'Russian Idea', that phenomenon which is 'so mysterious and incomprehensible to the West', is a profoundly socialist idea. There is an inseparable linkage between the notion of communism and the Russian term *obshchina* (community), where priority has always been given to common, collectivist and community-driven interests, as distinct from private, egoistic and individualist ones. That is how Zyuganov correlates, as it were, *post*-communism with *pre*-communism of Russia. Russian orthodox Christian tradition too is integrally connected to Russian communism. Zyuganov constructs a symbiotic connection between communism and religion, more particularly, that most dominant of all of Russia's religions, Orthodox Christianity, drawing attention to parallel notions of communist collectivism and orthodox conciliarism (*sobornost*). Communism is also seen to be two thousand years old – 'because of its compatibility with the teachings of Christ'. Zyuganov's theoretical discourse is sermon-like, so rich with explicit religious themes, symbols and imagery as to transform ideology into *theology* and his practice here ranges from regular 'Bible readings', particularly from Zyuganov's favourite Book of Revelations, to kneeling down before the patriarch of the orthodox church. All this goes into Zyuganov's nationalism and he carries it in his person somewhat eclectically mixed with his acceptance of pluralism and parliamentary democracy, rejection of market and advocacy of socialism, sympathies for Stalin or the Tsarist empire building, implicit or explicit anti-semitism, a definition of his ideology as 'national socialism', hopes for Russia's great future and much else besides, using each of these elements in his ideology according to the needs of the hour. But, as Jeremy Lester has well summed up:

> Stripped of its many superfluities, Zyuganov's argument has been based on the overriding premise that in the aftermath of the 'overthrow' of the old order, the Russian communist faith can only be defended through the mechanism of nationalism and patriotism. To sustain this approach, he has consistently tried over the last few years to bridge what, in some cases at least, were nearly always considered to be unbridgeable divides.

Lester adds:

> as always in politics, it is a question of means and ends. For Zyuganov, on the very limited occasions he gives vent to socialist causes, it is absolutely clear that this is nothing more than a tactical ploy to help boost the ultimate ends he is striving for, the re-emergence of Russia as a *derzhava* – a Great Power defined in nationalist, messianic terms. Zyuganov is first and last a nationalist, and everything else is oriented around this. In any clash between his socialism and nationalism, the pretences of the former would very quickly be sacrificed on the altar of the convictions of the latter.

It is this radical, often chauvinistic and xenophobic nationalist stance that underlies CPRF's understanding of the current predicament of Russia. While reference is duly made to past 'ideological deviations', the collapse of Soviet Union and the allied countries is seen as caused, not by the corruption and demoralisation of the ex-CPSU *nomenklatura*, but by enemy agents, CIA conspiracies and, of course, traitor Gorbachev, together with the culture and ideology of a 'Judaic Diaspora' over a long period; whitewashing the mistakes and excesses of Stalin, the blame is put on the 'alien elements' around him in the guise of (note the names) Kaganovich, Yagoda, Beria, Mekhlis, etc.

The catastrophe that has overcome the post-collapse Russia is not understood as caused essentially by the capitalist transition it is undergoing. It is presented as if Russia has been the victim of something akin to a Western imperialist invasion and colonisation. As Zyuganov explained in his speech to the CRPF Congress in April 1997, the restoration of 'rampant capitalism' is resulting, in practice 'in the progressive colonisation of Russia. Or rather, it is a qualitatively new form of waging war against our country. The dirty money, lies and provocations with which the fifth column arms itself have proved no less devastating to Russia than the incursions of Batu, Napoleon and Hitler put together. In essence the Third Patriotic War is already raging in the wide territories of our country.' It is this nationalist orientation which determines the party's whole attitude to the capitalist transformation affecting the country. Dabbling in semi-mystical nationalist rhetoric, Zyuganov leadership makes the distinction between patriotic and traitor elements within Russia the governing division in the country, more central than the division between capitalism and socialism. The essence of the party's antagonism to the emergence of a capitalist system in Russia is not an attack on capitalism as such, but an attack almost exclusively directed at 'comprador' capitalists, and the moral perversity of the *nouveaux riches*, all of them traitors who, according to Zyuganov, refer to Russia in the most impersonal way as 'this country' and not 'my country'. Zyuganov prefers capitalists who have an affinity with the ancient traditions of 'Holy Rus' rather than the excessively modern Russia. Typical again is the response to the fundamental problem of non-payment of wages. Rather than being viewed as a class-related problem generated by transition to capitalism and therefore also as an issue for class-based mobilisation of the workers against this transition, it is seen primarily as a 'national disgrace' which the state must get rid of, using whatever funds it has. With the predatory power of IMF seen as the main enemy facing Russia and its own support for patriotic capital, what Zyuganov leadership seems to want is a 'national capitalism' which is properly paternal, that is, protective towards the masses. Prioritising of nation over class has involved not only a failure to see the basic social contradictions and antagonisms as essentially a product of the on-going capitalist transition, it has also meant a non-recognition of their positive potential as generating the necessary conditions and forces for a *socialist politics*. Hence also the fact that the CPRF's perspective on the future is one of a national struggle against foreign domination and not a class struggle for socialism which, of course, does not deny but subsumes the former. (It is noteworthy that while the CPRF has been able to retain a social democratic faction within it, so many other, more left-wing tendencies have been forced to leave).

Given the CPRF's nationalist perspective, its programmatic task is defined as a kind of national liberation struggle by all patriotic forces in all classes against imperialist capitalism and its anti-patriotic and largely criminal Russian stooges, a struggle which draws in not only workers and intellectuals but also patriotic capitalists. It is in pursuit of this strategic task that the CPRF led in the creation of the Popular Patriotic Union of Russia, with Zyuganov at its head, based on a very broad consensual understanding, 'patriotism with a human face' is how it has been described. This is seen as the only cement to unite people for Russia's 'salvation'. 'Salvation' is indeed seen as the primary or strategic requirement of Russia today.

A national or national-patriotic strategy may have its advantages for CPRF's electoral politics but it has 'inner' strategic dangers too. For one, the whole nationalist terrain of Russian politics is already overcrowded with everyone, from President Putin downwards, claiming to be a patriotic saviour of Russia. And competitive nationalism or patriotism has never helped the Left. Zyuganov may seem to have out-trumped Zhirinovsky, and Labed is no more, but far more dangerous claimants to populist paternalist nationalism with their Labed-like alternatives are waiting in the wings for the crisis to deepen and take over. For another, and most importantly, this national patriotic strategy, by turning the CPRF into a rather amorphously broad movement will push backstage any remaining vestiges of socialist ideology; even rhetoric of socialism may disappear. And this when the situation demands a foregrounding, indeed renewal of socialist ideology, and a communist party with an explicitly socialist strategy – a party that takes advantage of the enormous new opportunities to deepen class consciousness and conduct class-based struggles in different social and economic domains, that articulates nationalism with these class struggles and brings people together in a broad front for socialism on the premise that the future of Russia, now more than ever before, is tied to the future of socialism in Russia.

This is indeed what the Russian situation demands and such a strategic shift for the CPRF in future cannot be entirely ruled out. Immediately however, under the Zyuganov's leadership, a somewhat spiritual national-patriotism continues to underpin the political orientation of the CPRF and its new found national-patriotic allies. How far away from the socialist tradition this orientation takes you is again evident in the way the CPRF focuses on the issue of Russia's 'statehood'. At a mundane level this is a justifiable search for a state that puts an end to the 'humiliation' within Russia and Russia's playing second fiddle to the US and the West abroad. A great power statism is also not difficult to understand for the successors of the ex-CPSU. But the messianic understanding of nationalism also postulates the search for, and the need of, a saviour. Only this explains the growing positive appraisal of Stalin emanating from many sections of the CPRF, not least Zyuganov himself, who sees Stalin not as a Bolshevik or revolutionary, or socialist, but brackets Stalin with the likes of Ivan the Terrible and Peter the Great for his redoubtable state-strengthening and state-conquering achievements. Addressing a gathering of party workers recently, Zyuganov confessed that a decade back his party had failed to live up to Stalin's legacy but he defined it as a failure to 'preserve Soviet power'. If there is to be any vilification of the actions of past political figures in Russian history, the greatest vilification must be reserved for the likes of Trotsky and other old Bolsheviks for their 'perverse' anti-nationalist 'betrayal' of Russia. Given the nationalist privileging of the state, individual saviours like Stalin are seemingly worth more than all the grassroots democratic traditions of the (early) Soviets in Bolshevik history. Zyuganov's vision of the Soviets as expressing the supposed 'unity of action among power structures', and as being superior to a supposedly destructive division of powers, is very far removed from the conceptions of socialist democracy advanced by Lenin. It is not surprising that the slogan 'Proletarians of all countries, unite!' was excluded from the party's programme – without a vote and despite opposition – at the Third Congress in January 1995. Such indeed is the CPRF's departure from 'Soviet communist principles' as Viktor Tyul'kin of the Russian Communist Workers Party described them, that he told Zyuganov that his and the CPRF's actions are a dishonour to the 'communist' label and they should effect a change of name of their party!

The legitimacy of this reaction from the far Left notwithstanding, the fact remains that CPRF is today the major oppositional force in Russian politics. It is recognised as a party of legality and has been, despite being averse to 'confrontation' with it, a bastion of constitutionalism against the regime's unconstitutional or anti-democratic practices. It has pushed the quasi-fascist Zhirinovsky and his so-called Liberal Democratic Party to the margins of the Russian political system, fought the authoritarian demagogy of the likes of Labed and proved tactically astute and sophisticated in building a broad based coalition against the regime. It has been critical of the Yeltsin-Putin militarist policy on Chechnya and holds that the recreation of the Union should be on a voluntary basis. Notwithstanding the leadership's statist ambitions and preference for their own kind of paternalistic authoritarian system, the economic programme of the CPRF does address a great strategic choice as to the future of Russia. By emphasising national economic development, a strong industrial sector and a nationalised banking sector, the CPRF offers a progressive alternative strategy for the country against its current slide into impoverishment and peripheralisation. All this is to CPRF's credit. Nevertheless one cannot but share Jeremy Lester's regret and disappointment that 'out of the collapse of the old Soviet order, no better, no more principled left-wing alternative and vision was able to sustain itself on the political arena'. For all its concern for the interests of Russia, which cannot be separated from the interests of the Russian people, the CPRF does not question the restoration of capitalism in Russia. If in the political field the CPRF has combated the fascist Right, in the field of ideas and symbols, the Zyuganov leadership has made concessions to a Russian obscurantist mysticism and a chauvinist nationalism which have nothing to do with any kind of left-wing politics. It has signally failed to make a critical assessment of the Soviet past and remains innocent of class struggle and any authentic vision of socialism. Most grievous of its failures as a communist party is the abandonment of Marxism as the potential practical answer to both Russia's contemporary catastrophic social reality and the ideologies such a reality generates and is reproduced by.

This however is not all that has to be said of the Communist Party of Russian Federation. Its rejuvenated presence, the mass support electorally or otherwise the Party has acquired, signals that, even if passively, the working people who make up the majority of the Russian population are becoming an important factor in the political struggle. Not yet capable of joining forces independently in order to defend their own interests, it is through the CPRF that they have registered their rejection of the ongoing capitalist transition. It also suggests that with the lapse of time and the new situation in the country, the people now have a more lively fear of the present's 'economic reform' than they do of a return to the Soviet past. There may be good reasons to doubt the capacity of the present CPRF leadership to be self-critical enough to shift away from the nationalist to a socialist strategy, but the party itself is not yet a homogeneously nationalist party. Although dominant since the party's founding, the Zyuganov group, which is most closely associated with nationalist themes, is probably an ideological minority within the party. There are strong other currents much closer to socialism of some sort – be it neo-Stalinism, social democracy or authentic Marxism. The 'Leninist Platform' within the CPRF has openly challenged Zyuganov for his 'nationalist deviation'. And the mass membership is certainly propelled by ideas which are far more radical and to the left than those of the leadership.

Beyond the party and its membership is the fact that a decade after the Soviet collapse, the social and economic situation in Russia remains in flux and dangerously volatile. It is not likely to improve in the near future, given the current crisis and restructuring of world capitalism and the subordinate place the Russian economy is almost inevitably coming to occupy in it. As the crisis within grows more acute, the realism of the CPRF's programme, in every one of its dimensions, will be in serious doubt, you simply cannot accept capitalist restoration but reject its consequences. If the altered dynamics of the socio-economic process could mean a new threat of authoritarianism, it could also further underline the need for a clear workers' alternative to capitalist restoration. It is to be hoped that those opposed to Zyuganov's nationalism will grow in influence within the party and help it opt for this socialist alternative.

Hope expressed, it needs to be added that the CPRF, now or in future, does not exhaust the forces making for a renewed struggle for socialism in Russia.

XXVIII

Borrowing the sentiments of Robert Rozhdestvensky's poem 'Before a New Jump!', in a poignant passage, Jeremy Lester has thus written of Russia of our times:

> .... once again we have all been in a state of frozen anticipation over the last few years, residing in a perpetual waiting room, looking out with a heightened sense of both expectation and dread at where Russia was about to jump to next. Indeed, what other country has provided us with so many paradoxes this century? Here is a country which has stirred the political imagination of the Left far more than any other over these decades. Here is a country which has done more than any other to resist the onslaught of world capitalist hegemony. Here is a country which is still the key potential terrain of resistance to the capitalist globalisation. And here is a country which may well determine the nature of developments in Europe and beyond long into the next century. Yet notwithstanding all of this, what other country has so consistently shattered the dreams of the international Left? It seems it is the country's destiny to touch the extremes of left-wing optimism and pessimism. Perhaps the most uncanny thing of all is that it does so almost simultaneously.

As we ponder this simultaneity, *the* question arises: what then of the future of socialism in Russia? The question is surely worth some speculation.

Apropos this question, soon after the capitalist restoration under Yeltsin got underway in Russia, I had shared the following argument with an audience: As the capitalist transition proceeds, in place of the earlier political power-generated polarisation of society, it is engendering another more automatic economic and social polarisation of power and privileges, income and status, not only between classes but genders, ethnic groups and regions in which a minority floats to the surface while the majority sinks even further below the surface. The integrated material structures established over the decades are being dismantled and the economy 'restructured' to the benefit of the foreign capital and a small minority of local wielders of economic and political power, willing to accept comprador status. This minority will certainly benefit from the restoration of capitalism, but in light of the inadequate levels of development and international competitiveness, this minority can never attain the Western standard of living that fuels its aspirations without grinding down the mass of the people. This is how for the ordinary working people the transition is already turning out to be a calamity. Subjected to the crippling prescriptions of the IMF and WB, they are paying for it by a drastic cut in their standard of living, widespread unemployment and cuts in social services. An easy pace of work, guaranteed jobs, and a low but strong safety net were among the benefits of the Soviet system. Now as part of 'free market' prescriptions, the workers are being coerced to work harder, deprived of social benefits and pushed out of jobs. The acceptance of chronic mass unemployment as a constituent element of a restructured economy is serving to fragment society into a poorer version of an economically polarised 'two-thirds society' of western neo-liberal capitalism. All this is not a 'brief transitional period', as the new rulers would have the people believe, but once and for ever. But then all this is also a rude education in the reality of capitalism as well as the western priorities in the 'economic reformed' Russia. As jobs disappear, along with subsidised social security covering child and health care, education, food, housing and transport as well as art and culture, to give way to unemployment and inflation, mafiosi economics and politics and the vulgarity of

Big Mac-Coca Cola culture of late capitalism, the experience will sink into the popular consciousness, wearing out the early romanticism of the honeymoon with the West, waking people up to the reality of a polarised class society, in every way at odds with the dream world they had been led to visualise. The popular image of the American suburban shopping centre as epitomizing 'normal society' will fade away amidst the price rises, injustices and corruption of an actual transition to capitalism, which is also turning out to be a mafiosi capitalism. The people, meeting with real live capitalism everyday, will lose the early naiveté about it, a naiveté which is also showing up in the trauma of émigrés from the former 'socialist' Russia who are discovering the hard way that America is after all in many basic ways much like the party propaganda said.

The experience with capitalist transition, pursued with the advice and support of western experts and governments and strewn with broken promises and false expectations has given rise to discontent which has made the entire country one of social unrest and instability. Given the long depoliticisation of the people, this has certainly provided an initial advantage to reactionary or conservative-populist politics even as it has also exacerbated ethnic or national tensions and conflicts within and among the states, and fed all sorts of xenophobias, ultra-nationalism, irredentism and racial hatreds, including anti-semitism, and so on. But as this discontent is traced to its basic source in the emergent capitalism; as the customary social security, long taken for granted, is lost, the standard of living continues to be eroded, unemployment increases, inequalities intensify, the already yawning gap between the rich and poor further widens and it is clearly seen how market economy really works; as it comes to be recognised that the transition embarked upon is leading not to some idealised vision or realisable goal of a healthy and stable social democratic welfarism, but from a bad socialism to a bad capitalism, somewhere along the way an altogether different dynamics may be unleashed, making for a politics that opens up possibilities other than the attempted capitalist restoration. This fear has already persuaded the Russian rulers to go slow and placate the working classes in various ways; though this policy is impossible to sustain for long if the capitalist transition is to be carried through.

May be long-depoliticised, and demoralised and disoriented at the moment, the masses themselves remain passive longer than we think, suffering the hunger and deprivation of the new order. It is certainly true that since Stalinism had succeeded in eliminating any genuine revolutionary understanding among the Russian working class, it was either politically apathetic or the vacuum had now come to be filled by western bourgeois ideology, and it was completely unprepared for what was to come when the dominant fraction of its leadership sold out to western capitalism. It was left in a highly vulnerable position of having lost its confidence in socialism and lacking an organised political representation to confront an economic system which, though not yet fully formed, is surely uncongenial to working class interests. An immediate effective socialist challenge to the present regime is therefore not easy to visualise. It can even be that capitalism may not prosper but moral and ideological bankruptcy carried over from the old regime makes it highly unlikely that socialism will be revived here in our lifetime. Nevertheless it is reasonably predictable that given the nature of capitalism that is being built and the historical past of its victims, class struggle will erupt and escalate in the not too distant future. The crucial questions therefore are how and in what manner, how led and to what immediate and ultimate purpose, the temporarily deradicalised working class of Russia sheds its illusions about born-again capitalism, and to what extent the Stalinist disempowerment of the working class will delay its effective political assertion. The question is being asked: is there indeed a future for socialism in the former Soviet Union? At one level the response can be in terms of the one attributed to Zhou Enlai when asked if he thought the French Revolution had succeeded. He had replied, 'It's too soon to tell.' At another level, in more down to earth Marxist terms, one can hold that as the Russian working people come to share the fate of victims of capitalism, winning 'the theoretical awareness of their loss' as Marx had postulated, they may in their own way also share, as direct heirs of 1917 perhaps sooner than others, in the necessary worldwide recovery of socialism.

That is how I had argued in early 1995. A few months later, thinking along the same lines, I wrote in these notes:

The development of capitalism in Russia can only be at the expense of the working class. And, if it is going to be of the peripheral, third world variety, operating in harness with an openly authoritarian political regime, as it is turning out to be, it will be particularly savage and punishing for the vast masses of the Russian people. As the results of this peripheralisation become evident, as the workers realise that the drastic cuts in their employment and living standards are not momentary sacrifices imposed by the necessities of transition, but a permanent feature of the new economic dispensation, they will resist it ever more effectively. Already the rulers are finding it difficult to thrust the 'market economy' down the throats of the recalcitrant people. The economists and technocrats incharge of the capitalist transition, who sound like Harvard Business School graduates, bitterly complain about their worst handicap – the egalitarianism and thirst for social justice of their populations. They are discovering to their dismay that workers display considerable hostility to capitalist-style work norms which tend to destroy the relative control over the labour process which the proletariat enjoyed under the old regime. Hence the urgent and persistent calls to introduce a reserve army of labour to discipline 'lazy' and 'indifferent' workers. In this situation the rising discontent is likely to find initial expression in different nationalist and sectarian movements, though the more genuine of the nationalists may soon discover that no longer tied to the fate of the party, Russia's future is still tied to the future of socialism. But the bitter experience may also not only help the working class to realise that the Marxism once hastily discarded still provides a key to understanding the structures of pre- and post-1991 oppressions, but compel it to look beyond the alternatives of Stalinism and capitalism to, once again, socialism, but of a different, democratic kind. What this democratic socialism might look like is unclear but it is certainly likely to be more attractive than the peripheral, clientelistic, booty capitalism which is taking over Russia today. In other words, there is the possibility that the retreat from socialism may be temporary, that life and experience will guide the Russian working class back to socialism, a socialism, however, which will involve a reassertion of some of the long-forgotten humanistic and democratic principles of Marxism. In doing so, the Russian working class may also pose a challenge to the ideological constraints of late capitalist societies and stir the political imagination of their working classes by offering what Habermas in the 'Red Year' of 1968 called 'a competitive model that makes the limits of state regulated capitalism ... visible to the consciousness of the currently well-integrated masses.'

It is obvious that this possibility can be realised only if the Russian working class becomes conscious of its interests as a class – becomes 'a class for itself' as Marx said – and proceeds to organise itself and act to make its potential power real in terms of effective economic and political intervention. This of course is a very big 'if' and there are no inevitabilities or guarantees of victory in history which is instead, as Engels said, 'about the most cruel of all goddesses'. Immediately some hopeful beginnings are there but barely enough to sustain a minimal optimism. There is as yet no organised mass movement of workers and other oppressed layers, seeking to take power in their hands or capable of doing so, from the hands of the powerful clan-corporative structures that have already arisen in Russia in comprador relationship with global capitalism. A great deal of patient, stubborn work remains to be done before a genuinely democratic, strong and constructive socialist opposition movement of the oppressed comes into being in Russia, putting a radical, socialist, alternative before the people. It can never be too emphasised that this is going to be a long haul for the Russian working class. Even so, given the popular resentments against the emergent capitalism and nostalgia for the lost social security and cultural gains, the persistence of socialist ideas and the associated egalitarian sentiment among the people, the Left's growing recovery of the authentic socialist tradition, including the early Bolshevik, and the available evidence of polls indicative of a large base of potential support for the socialist alternative, it is legitimate to postulate the perspective of a struggle in Russia between those favouring a gradual transition to capitalism and those favouring democratic socialism, with the outcome not determined for some time to come. The objective conditions for socialism are largely present in Russia in the form of a highly developed economy – something not available to Lenin or his Bolsheviks – though 'entrepreneurs' of a mafiosi-capitalism together with the carpet-baggers from the west are busy plundering and destroying it, and reducing it to a comprador economy. But the subjective conditions are, as yet, largely absent. Herein lie the key tasks of the emergent socialist left as well as its opportunities to grow. It needs to equip itself theoretically, organisationally and practically, to be able to help educate, organise and develop a militant working class movement, one capable of forming alliances with the peasants and intellectuals in the tradition of revolutionary Marxism, as also of articulating its class struggle with the new social movements around issues of gender, ecology and peace etc., as they are coming up in Russia. This involves not only learning from Lenin on the subject of revolutionary consciousness and organisation but also rescuing the essential principles of Marxism from the ritual formulae used for gaining and keeping privileges into which they had degenerated under the deformed 'actually existing socialism' of the past.

At a fundamental level, the argument still holds.

XXIX

Russia, it may be suggested, remains a rather infertile soil for capitalism. There was after all a revolution in Russia – the Bolshevik Revolution, and the following years saw the creation of a new socio-economic system, generally recognised as socialism, which was despite all odds tremendously productive and transformed the lives of the people, providing them with a standard of living that was adequate, if not prosperous. The Soviet society, whatever its evils, was one that attempted to distribute resources and social services universally. Extremes of wealth and poverty, taken for granted in many other countries, were unknown and utterly unexpected. The old system had its disparities, to be sure, but in general these were neither as great nor as entrenched as they tend to be in market economies. Aware of the unpopularity of privilege in Russian ethos the Soviet regime throughout found it necessary to make elaborate efforts to rationalise or conceal the perks that it doled out to the elite. Hence, unlike the poor and marginalised masses of the third world countries, average Russians remain unaccustomed to and unprepared to accept sharp contrasts of wealth and poverty. Despite their famous patience, they are unlikely to endure quietly if the present trend towards mass impoverishment takes on a permanent cast.

Proclaimed ideology, even as indoctrination, together with its material realisation, however partial or deformed, also meant that something of the socialist ideal did manage to penetrate to deeper levels of consciousness and become internalised, even if thought of as elementary human rights or as a pattern of everyday morality which enjoins that society should be 'just', that the purpose of a society or a state should be to provide a better life for all its citizens, and not just to improve the opportunities for individuals to succeed. This morality survives especially as it conforms to the interests of the working people. In however vague a manner, the idea of socialism remains associated with the notion of a good society and the working class committed to some of its key concerns: job security, egalitarianism in opportunities and incomes, right to basic social services like education, health care, housing, etc. Observers have reported that egalitarian and collectivist attitudes run deep in Russia, that 'the idea that socialism is dead' is not popular among workers and intelligentsia of the provinces unlike sections of the middle class and elite intelligentsia of the capital, who have clearly opted for the capitalist road. Socialism is still alive in social relations and culture of the common people, they still value solidarities of former collectivism, its comradeship and readiness for mutual aid, dislike the cult of money, hate speculation and privilege, seek dignity of labour and want to do respected work. (Gorbachev, it may be noted, found some of the prevalent values or attitudes – egalitarianism, contempt or distaste for 'doing business' or 'making money', etc. – an obstacle in the way of his 'market reform'). The question indeed is whether the quite understandable resentment against the old system will prove stronger and more lasting than the surviving socialist ideal and the socialist subconscious.

Seventy odd years of experiment in socialism, this historical past, makes the social and ideological terrain for trying to establish a capitalist system in Russia fundamentally different from that in other parts of the world where capitalism has consolidated itself. The restoration of capitalism in Russia is not to be confused with the privatisation in England or France, or India, which is a process within an existing capitalist system. It is an unprecedented venture in history, unprecedented for being a venture in a society that has experienced socialism, however deformed this socialism may have been. This has its implications for the future of both capitalism and socialism in Russia. Obviously, these implications are negative for capitalism (its such basic norms as private property, profit motive, possessive individualism, etc.) and favourable for the socialist option in the future.

XXX

Swept up in the early enthusiasm for a transition to capitalism, the Russian people had switched their support to the parties of the free market right. But as the transition has proceeded it has brought only impoverishment and humiliation to people. 'Economic reform' has been accompanied by the imposition of capitalist criteria on nearly all aspects of social and economic life, boosting inequality, blighting cultural life and putting barbarism in sight for a once highly cultured and civilised population. But this experience of what Michael Ellman and others have aptly called *Katastroika,* has also been a forced education in elementary social concepts never successfully taught in the Soviet era – and these include capitalism, or shall we say 'actually existing capitalism'. The Russian people have learnt the hard way that life under capitalism is not as dazzling as promised by the neo-liberal ideologues or suggested by the American serials. Of course, there was the much crude anti-capitalist propaganda in the Soviet Union. 'Lies', the neo-liberal ideologues at home and abroad had called them, fed about capitalism by the censored Soviet media. The lies have now turned out to be true. In any case the future the Russians are being offered is neither Swedish nor even British but Bolivian. If there is no going back for them, there is nothing here for them to look forward to. Hence a widespread disillusionment with the market economy, the present state of affairs. As the liberal historian Yuri Afanasyev elaborates it: 'After all, the people speaking out against a market economy today are not simply extremist conservatives, but make up almost a majority of all our citizens. For them the prospect of a market economy resembles a Stalinist exercise in logic: "I'll force you to be happy, you bastard!" This time, people say, it is the market economy that is going to force happiness on us.'

Accompanying this disillusionment is a nostalgia for the vanished USSR. If an American survey sometime back reported that 'an overwhelming majority of Russians distrust their government and are deeply unhappy about the country's current political and economic state,' and want 'to reverse market reforms', a recent Russian survey reveals that a majority of Russians 'very much regret' the demise of the Soviet Union. Feeling humiliated and degraded, Russians miss being citizens of a great global power and an increasing number look back fondly at their economic security and living standards under the old system. The regime and its foreign backers are much disturbed by the growing popular support for the Communist Party reflected in the latter's electoral successes. The reason was thus summed up in a despatch to the *New York Times* sometime back: 'The angry, impoverished Russians who speak mistily of the days of subsidized meat, free rent, and a guaranteed income say they are voting for pensions and a strong social security net and not for the Communist repression of the Soviet state.' In other words, the people have been expressing their rejection of the status quo and a desire for the return of their lost welfare state. Typically enough, the Russians now have a joke about a signal achievement of Yeltsin: in three years he managed to do something which the Communist Party failed to do within 70 years, he made communism look good.

A decade or so of capitalist restoration has made even the much-reviled Stalin look good. There is a significant emergence of nostalgia for Stalin. A late 1990s survey reported a growing number of Russians regretting the absence of a leader like Josef Stalin – 'One can imagine what would have happened if Stalin were alive at the time of the next presidential elections scheduled for the year 2000', wrote the popular Russian weekly *Argumenti-i-Fakty*. And presently we have even leading non-communist members of the Russian Duma assessing Stalin as a great leader and a statesman. Opinion polls conducted on the eve of Stalin's 50th death anniversary have shown a surprisingly large number of Russians appreciative of Stalin. As a report has it: 'According to one such poll, one-third of Russians welcome the return of a leader like Stalin. The All Russia Centre for the Study of Public Opinion (VTsIOM) carried out a poll in 100 cities and towns over 40 regions of the country. According to Yurii Levada, director of the Centre, 53 per cent of respondents approved of Stalin overall, 33 per cent disapproved of him and 14 per cent did not state their position. The Public Opinion Foundation conducted a national survey... covering 1,500 adults throughout the country. According to the survey, '36 per cent of the respondents said "the Soviet dictator Stalin did more benefit to Russia than harm", 29 per cent said the opposite and 34 per cent did not commit themselves.'

Of course, this nostalgia for Stalin reflects Russian people's deep and growing disaffection with the current state of affairs and is primarily, as hinted above, the response of a people who only the other day were citizens of a great power and are now fed up with their country's decline and disintegration, and humiliation at home and abroad. Stalin is appreciated as a leader who, in the words of Duma member Gennady Raikov, 'despite all his defects, made Russia great'. Even so, this nostalgia cannot be entirely dissociated from a positive assessment of the country's communist past and the continuing loyalty of large sections of Russian people to old socialist values and to the political movements of the Left. It certainly indicates the distance Russian people have travelled since the days of Gorbachev's glasnost and it cannot be discounted that along this road they may one day also discover something of Stalin as a Bolshevik and revolutionary, as a socialist.

The nostalgia for the Soviet past, with or without Stalin, must not be seen as a passive phenomenon. Carrying the powerful wallop of contemporary discontent, it could well become politically explosive. The anti-communist syndrome is fast ceasing to be, and mention of socialism, despite government propaganda, no longer provokes negative reactions. No doubt, impressions of the past continue to haunt the people and *this* past remains a serious handicap for the renewal of socialist politics in Russia. The socialist left needs to come up with a viable explanation of what went wrong in the past, an explanation which Marxism alone can help provide. Nevertheless, it is time for alternatives in Russia. New openings to the left is the perspective in which Russian people's growing opposition to the market economy needs to be viewed.

The nostalgia about the past apart, there is plenty of evidence that, however much enthusiasm the market economy may have generated among the new power holders and their advisers, the enthusiasm is not shared by the population at large.

It needs to be remembered that even initially the initiative for actually dismantling the established communist regime in Russia, as also East Europe, mostly came from within their leaderships, in other words, from above. Even when popular movements from below against communist rule played some part (notably in Bohemia and the GDR) their role has been greatly exaggerated for obviously ideological reasons. People were surely opposed to the authoritarian political systems of single-party rule, but the widespread idea in the west and elsewhere that communism as such had no significant popular support at the time of its collapse was simply the result of western ideological preconceptions or the new fangled theories of 'totalitarianism' which had little grasp on the reality of Soviet type societies. Opinion surveys conducted around that time clearly demonstrated that substantial numbers held socialist values, particularly a commitment to egalitarianism and nationalised property. The way the former communists reemerged as significant political formations soon after the collapse, clearly showed that significant and in many cases large sections of the people retained perceptions of the former 'single parties' which were much more sympathetic to their record than 'totalitarian' theory could allow for. In the Soviet Union, 'the more democracy – the more socialism!' was the enthusiastic slogan at the beginning of Gorbachev's perestroika. Even as it denied that workers' two goals were compatible, *Moscow News* at the time acknowledged with some frustration: 'What do the workers want? First, they want socialism. Second, they want the dismantling of the command system'. Studies and polls over these years of capitalist restoration have only confirmed this preference – large parts of population in Russia have remained attached to socialist values and large minorities have remained loyal to the political movements of the Left that emerged from the former ruling Communist Party, the CPSU. In Russia public opinion's continued support for collectivist economic and social values and for social egalitarianism and social security is in fact reported to be far more extensive than its support for the CPRF. In 1996, opinion polls in Russia continued to show, for example, an absolute majority of the population preferring big industrial enterprises to be state owned rather than privatised. Other polls or surveys show that about half the population still identifies, however passively, with the concept of socialism. Only a minority supports establishing an unfettered capitalist system. When asked in a recent poll (reported in the *Economist* in December 1999), 'What economic system would you prefer?' 48 percent of Russians polled said they would prefer 'state planning and distribution,' while just 35 percent preferred 'private property and the market.' To the statement 'It would have been better if the country had stayed as it was before 1985,' 58 percent answered 'yes;' only 27 percent said 'no.' In other words, while capitalism is indeed the option of a privileged minority or those hoping to join it, the popular masses remain attached to the socialist achievements of the old regime and want, along with national independence and democratisation of the political system, socialised health care, education and housing, and they continue to believe that everyone has the right to a job. Moreover, they favour public ownership and control of key economic sectors and a planned economy. (This is the case not only in Russia. In 1995, five years after abandoning their old state with joy and enthusiasm, two thirds of the East Germans thought that life and conditions in the old GDR were better than the 'negative descriptions and reports' in the day's German media, and 70 per cent thought 'the idea of socialism was good, but we had incompetent politicians'. More recently, a decade after the fall of the Berlin Wall, *The Guardian* has reported 'a wave of nostalgia ('Ostalgia') for the communist way of life' in East Germany when, in the words of film director Leander Haussmann, 'we did not suffer everyday of the year'. He added: 'The happiest years of my life were spent in East Germany'.)

The issue of private property is still bitterly contested and far from settled in Russia. It is not only that the workers have no hope or possibility of becoming capitalist proprietors, vast majority of them have evinced no great desire to join the privatising cooperatives or share holding, nor for that matter the peasants to become small holders. The Yeltsin regime failed to overcome the resistance of collective farmers to denationalisation of land and restoration of capitalist relations in the countryside, and Putin has little to show for his privatising land legislation so far. It is indeed significant that, contrary to common misconception or expectations, and regardless of the controversy over the earlier forced collectivisation of agriculture, popular support for measures which would break up collective agriculture has turned out to be very limited. In places there has been active resistance to dissolution of collective farms. Far from surprising, this is a rational reflection of their overall favourable performance and manifest superiority to any available alternatives today. Especially so if it is remembered that notwithstanding its production or managerial problems – which were and are certainly amenable to democratically planned solutions – collective agriculture, besides assuring urban-style income stability, paid vacations and social security, was the basis of a full array of social support programmes ranging from local schools, housing, transportation services to daycare, after-school care, maternity leave, health insurance, retirement and 'disability' benefits, cultural activities and continuing educational opportunities etc. which enhanced the quality of daily existence, making for a new rural culture, a coherent and secure, collective way of life. Returning to small scale family farming, linked to the vicissitudes and uncertainties of a market economy, is not a prospect welcome to any significant fraction of the rural population. (The situation here parallels that faced by privatisation and the initial proletarianisation drive in the industrial sector where the enterprises were typically not only economic organisations but also housing departments, health centres, food shops, childcare institutions, food producers and restaurants, pubs and entertainment centres. To shed these roles in order to turn labour's relation to the enterprise into principally a wage relation has not been politically easy for most enterprise managements, and partly explains the compulsion of quite a few of them to form alliances with their own employees in defence of the old system).

XXXI

Decisive for any effective left-ward shift in Russian politics is how the working class acts, not so much in the current situation of political confusion and instability, but as it continues to undergo the experience of Russia's belated capitalist development. It needs to be remembered that given the industrial development that had taken place in the former Soviet Union, it had a relatively large and well-developed working class – 127 million strong – concentrated in huge work places (73 per cent of industrial workers were employed in enterprises of a thousand or more workers, 37 percent in enterprises of five thousand or more). Even on a conservative estimate, well over half of the economically active population in Russia belonged to the working class. Objectively speaking this working class, as it survives today, constitutes a pivotal social and economic force. Socialism in Russia has obviously no future without its positive intervention in what is happening.

This intervention, however, faces monumental problems. Most important here is the fact that this working class, indeed the Russian Left as a whole, cannot easily transcend the nature of the society from which it has emerged – sixty odd years of Stalinism which left in its wake an atomised and depoliticised society lacking experience of independent self-organisation or collective activity (with the exception, one may add, under Brezhnev, of bureaucratic-mafia gang up). If no independent working class organisation, imbued with an independent class consciousness, could develop under the past regime of bureaucratic absolutism, its benevolent paternalism only further depoliticised the working people – 'leaders' (rather patrons) acting on behalf of the people became a deeply ingrained tendency among them. Depoliticisation was the dominant feature of the working class in the former Soviet Union, particularly during the entire post-war era, growing much worse in the Brezhnev period when the gap between the official ideology and the realities of life within the Soviet Union and outside its borders produced an ideological vacuum soon filled up with consumerist longings among the people, including the working class. As a consequence, a class in itself, but not for itself, the working class had come to lack a collective identity and any organised means of expressing let alone acting, to realise its common interests. It is not surprising therefore that during the fateful years of perestroika, the entrenched bureaucracy at all levels was able to effectively defend and advance its corporate interests against the atomised and politically inexperienced workers, and even to manipulate their protests as in the case of the miner strikes of 1989-91. Even when the crisis of perestroika stirred sections of working class out of its passivity, the emergent workers' movement, totally alienated from the Communist Party, generally accepted the political leadership of the reforming liberals. When the crisis turned terminal, the working class simply failed to defend its interests and the ruling elites were able to seize the moment and define the terms of the transition to the new order, that is, carry out a nomenklatura and bureaucracy-led counter-revolution. It watched helplessly while the nomenklatura cliques, the criminal bourgeoisie and foreign capitalists went on to loot or destroy the productive forces of the country created by generations of Soviet workers.

With 'socialism' discredited, another negative factor in this period was the widespread illusion that privatisation would give workers a share in ownership of assets and more control over production, and make administration more accountable to the labour collective. Betrayed by the Party – which only the other day was telling them that they were the 'leading force of the Soviet Society', the creators and owners of the national wealth – the disoriented and demoralised workers even supported the early Yeltsin regime, promising economic reforms and democratisation, and later, much of the labour movement even sympathised with its free market project. The illusions have since evaporated as has the sympathy and support for economic reform, but large sections of the working class still remain atomised, with little capacity for independent self-organisation or collective action, and often enslaved by clan paternalism. As they retreat into the private struggle for survival, so many still cling to the hope that somehow management and/or state will defend or look after their interests – a legacy of the past when repression was also accompanied by a more or less benevolent paternalism.

Also, as is well known, it is hardest for workers to organise in periods of economic decline, and what we have in Russia is an unprecedented peacetime economic crisis. The Russian workers find themselves in an entirely new situation of economic insecurity and unemployment that is fast coming to resemble that of workers in Third World countries. This has inevitably had major negative consequences for workers self-confidence and for the possibilities of organisation and resistance. Enterprises going bankrupt and threatening more unemployment, or working at five to ten per cent of their capacity – while the bosses eagerly wait to shut them down completely, sell them, and get their kickback – or the need, in order to physically survive, to work at two or three jobs for twelve to fourteen hours per day, etc. – all this only strengthens tendencies to conformism and passivity. Workers' self-organisation and resistance also faces an enemy in the State's repressive laws, many of them aimed specifically against the working class. Added to this is the fact that privatisation has given owners and firm managements new, powerful means of repression against workers: the threat of unemployment, the ban on political activity in the workplace, and, increasingly, direct physical terror against worker activists by the so-called security services, or more simply armed thugs hired by owners and administration. While this psychological and physical intimidation is regularly enhanced by 'black legs' and informers within the ranks of blue and white collar workers, all sorts of former Soviet experts on the national and international labour movements now advise the regime on how best to divide workers and prevent their self-organisation, well-assisted by Western pro-capitalist unions led by the AFL-CIO international department with its Moscow based operation, the Free Trade Union Institute (FTUI).

Problems confronting working class organisation and resistance to the present system are indeed formidable. Even so, the workers of Russia have been protesting and struggling, not passively always, against the new economic policies and against the new ruling authorities. Entering the historical stage for the first time since the early days of the October revolution, sections of the Soviet proletariat have also demonstrated its capacity for independent action in defence of its interests; for example, in the great miners' strikes of July-August 1989 and March-April 1991 – the former at its peak involved around 400,000 workers, sent tremors through the Kremlin, and delayed the implementation of all-out marketisation – or in the emergence of an organised self-management movement over the issue of power in the enterprises. Such action and resistance or their threat was virtually a warning by the working class which along with the internecine conflicts of the new ruling class, led to the reformers' shift from 'shock therapy' to a slow and pragmatic programme of marketisation together with measures to placate the workers – slower offloading of jobs, wage increases to offset inflation, better share-holding in ongoing privatisation, etc. The logic of a market economy, an effective transition to capitalism, makes such pragmatism difficult to sustain, it only contributed to a further sharpening of the contradictions of the transition and led to a new wave of countrywise resistance which has continued since then as if an internal class struggle is already underway, even if in an expectedly silent or confused manner. The forms of struggle have ranged from spontaneous street actions, wild cat strikes and even individual acts of violence, to organised strikes of miners and workers of the oil industry, of agricultural workers, teachers, doctors and scientists and hunger marches by pensioners and their families. In 1997, alone there were seventeen thousand strikes officially registered throughout the year. Issues have ranged from regular payment of wages and payment of wage arrears to political demonstrations and marches including those in memory of October Revolution. More militant actions have included rail and road traffic blockades, seizure of enterprises, and locking out of administration. Strikes and rallies in major cities across Russia draw huge crowds of workers angry over chronically unpaid salaries and distress that capitalist transition has entailed, with a significant degree of support coming from the countryside, from various agrarian political groups and parties. There is the rise of independent trade union activism, and 50-million member Federation of Independent Trade Unions has been organising protest days to dramatise the plight of the working people. If workers resistance had once sought labour-management alliances to defend the country's industrial assets and the labour forces attached to them and then mostly lost out to privatisation, arguing (as for example at Moscow's famous ZIL plant) that 'privatisation solved nothing for us, it only changed the signboard over our tragedy', they are now asking the government 'to re-nationalise us'.

The workers are indeed resisting the implantation of capitalism in Russia. Of course, the number of those actively involved is, relative to the total strength of the working class, still small; but it will only grow. More important to note is an overall theoretical-ideological inadequacy: the resistance has been characterised by a basically, though not exclusive, trade union orientation. While the Russian workers' hostility towards the market economy remains clear, this hostility is manifested not through a struggle for an alternative, socialism, but largely through a narrow corporatist defence of their social rights, which may have well weakened or slowed down the capitalist transition but cannot block it, much less reverse the process for a socialist transition. The workers remain, to again use Marx's expression, a class-in-itself. Nevertheless, though essentially economistic in nature, the potential significance of such working class action or resistance is enormous for the future evolution of socialist politics in Russia. Only the Russian working class has to relearn Lenin's teaching (in *What Is To Be Done*?) that 'the spontaneous working class movement is by itself able to create (and inevitably does create) only trade unionism,' when what it needs to acquire in order to play its historical role is revolutionary *socialist* ideology and organisation.

It is not that socialist ideology or organisation is altogether absent in the current situation. On the contrary, socialist idea is more than just alive in Russia. In the chaos of Russian politics a democratic socialist tendency continues to have a significant presence. Between the two poles of a social democratic accommodation to neo-liberalism and nationalist populist accommodation to xenophobia lies a socialist left of many millions in search of socialist solutions to Russia's problems. Stalinist and other successors of the former CPSU apart, left of the political spectrum is burgeoning with a number of small noncapitalist post-party political groups – that even choose to call themselves parties – with broadly socialist programmes and platforms and struggling to establish their bases and working out mobilisation strategies. Significant among the tendencies represented is classical socialist politics which is not without its support within the CPRF. Together, each in its own way, they are questioning and resisting the ongoing capitalist transition and are doing so with a socialist perspective on the future of Russia.

The resistance itself, as hinted above, is not always exclusively trade-unionistic or corporatist. There is an aspect to it which is suggestive, indeed holds the promise of a socialist future for Russia. Workers' independent initiatives from below, even as they are throwing up a new breed of militant leaders, are imparting it a sharper, distinctly socialist character. And with the growing number of strikes, we are also witnessing the emergence of a Russian working *class* in contrast to their fragmented reproduction as 'workers' under the later Stalinist regimes. As it moves beyond the earlier corporatist struggles, this class is now signalling, in opposition to the comprador rulers, its presence as the only class absolutely committed to the defence, promotion and development of Russia's industrial base. The emerging organisational pattern – the adhoc strike committee, the permanent strike committee, the factory committee or the workers' council, the city workers' council or the Soviet – is suggestively reminiscent of its historical, that is Bolshevik, ancestry. Thousands of strike and factory committees operate in the country, as the workers learn their class politics the hard way. Particularly noticeable about this aspect of resistance, about these emerging forms of organisation and struggle is the eschewal of *economism*, very much in line with the revolutionary tradition of the Russian proletariat. Even on the level of the strike committee purely local demands are combined with political slogans and a workers' council has no problem combining its economic demands with a demand for the resignation of the president and the government or condemnation of the war in Chechnya. In some cases there are even attempts to establish workers' control over administration. Reporting on the workers' City Council of the mining city of Vorkuta, the American scholar Vladimir Bilenkin has this to say by way of conclusion:

> What we have in Vorkuta then is the early stage in the development of a dual power situation. The council has its representatives in the administration and the local government. It has its own workers' militia. Above all, the council is a genuine grassroots organisation of the working class, democratically elected by the local factory committees and closely controlled by them. Should a revolutionary situation arise the council has positioned itself to become a militant staff for taking power in the city and the province, and afterwards – the ruling legislative and executive organ of the proletarian dictatorship: the soviet.

Of course the Vorkuta Workers' Council is far from being a representative of the majority of working class organisations today. But, as the report says, it does 'give us a picture of what Russian labour will achieve tomorrow.'

XXXII

However weak or marginal at the moment, socialist working class politics *has* emerged in Russia. Its emergence has been accompanied, indeed sustained by the corresponding ideological ferment of the last few years. In this rather chaotic ferment, while Stalinism has continued to find varied expressions, and there is a revival of 'vernacular Marxism' at the grassroots level – a nationwide proliferation of a small-press workers' literature which is by no means ideologically homogeneous or, so to speak, politically correct – there has been an astonishing renaissance of radical ideas destroyed or lost after 1929. A whole range of both pre-revolutionary and early revolutionary ideas have been recovered, along with ideals and dreams of a different, older liberationary socialism, including those of Lenin and the first ten years of Communist International. Walter Benjamin had once warned that 'even the dead will not be safe from the enemy if he wins'. Over these years the victorious enemy has plundered not only the material possessions of the Soviet working class but also the historical memory of its revolutionary ancestors and their quest for emancipation. This latter plundering was indeed *the* distinguishing feature of Gorbachev's *glasnost* and there has been no respite since then. What we are witnessing today are the beginnings of a recovery of this historical memory, which includes not only a remembering but also a critical evaluation of the Soviet past, a Marxist coming to terms with it, something still absent or evaded by the Stalinists or the CPRF, presently dominated by the former junior party nomenklatura and middle class intellectuals. Once again it is the advanced workers seeking to act theoretically and think practically, who want to know exactly what went wrong after 1917 in order to avoid the tragic mistakes of the past. And in their quest they are rediscovering the fundamental ideas of classical Marxism. Says Vasily Shishkarev, an organiser from a Moscow car plant:

> What, in my opinion, was the main mistake of the communist leaders? In the *Communist Manifesto* Marx and Engels wrote that 'The immediate aim of the communists is the same as that of all other proletarian parties: formation of the proletariat into a class, overthrow of the bourgeois supremacy, conquest of political power by the proletariat.' As you can see the *Manifesto* speaks of the conquest of political power for the proletariat, not for the party. This is what Lenin meant when he insisted that every kitchen maid should be able to administer state affairs. But the general secretaries, the successors of the leader of the proletariat, had distorted the ideas of Marx and Lenin and established the power of the party. As the result the party that used to be the vanguard of the working class had become a bureaucratic clique.

Pointing out the present disproportion between the objective conditions in which the working class finds itself and its level of consciousness and organisation – 'all the objective factors are here. It is the subjective factor that is lacking. The majority does not have an understanding of what kind of workers' power is possible today and exactl what concrete forms it could take under the existing condtions.' – a worker intellectual from the Union of Tatarstan Workers writes:

> Workers are looking for the solutions to those problems that were not solved during the seventy years of the Soviet regime (e.g., the problem of bureaucratisation)... let us say the revolution has taken place and worker leaders have occupied the positions of power. Their first problem that wil have to be solved the next day will be the formation of new legislative and executive organs. It is obvious that in this situation the 'gentlemen' and the bureaucrats will quickly grow red again, will prove their revolutionary past, and will again become the heads of all offices because in the heads of the workers there remains the same old understanding of how workers' power is organised. Yet, by itself revolution does not solve all the problems that come after it. Do workers have sufficient knowledge of, or any experience in, self-organizing needed in order to prevent such outcomes? After all, workers will have to realize in practice not some absolute idea but how to use accumulated experience.

Characteristically sophisticated and realist, these are the voices of an emerging political vanguard of the Russian working class, marking the beginnings of its awakening to revolutionary socialist politics as it faces once again the possibility of mounting the stage of history. This working class and its new vanguard know that what lies ahead is a long and hard struggle. But they are also saying: 'This time it will be different.'

This hopefulness about Russia's socialist future is not to be lightly dismissed. Friends of Russia's 'economic reforms' have not failed to see them deepening the 'class antagonisms' and provoking 'the emergence of class consciousness', and feared a 'second edition of the socialist revolution'. We have *The Sunday Times* speculating: 'In the bad old days when the Soviet Russians were red – which may yet be remembered as the good old days – -they used to preach that capitalism contained the seeds of its own destruction. Nobody predicted that the best way to bring about the downfall of the capitalist system might be for Russia to embrace it.' From the other end, a critic, the Russian economist Igor Bratischev, in Calcutta for a seminar, has promised a 'new Soviet Russia' as the site for the next seminar!

XXXIII

There are reasons enough in Russia's present to be pessimistic. In the situation brought about by the failure of the Soviet project to offer a sustainable and credible alternative civilisational model to advanced capitalism, it is hardly to be expected that the Left in Russia could quickly turn forward to the task of offering a new perspective of advance towards social progress and emancipation. But, as suggested above, optimism in the matter is not to be ruled out. No doubt an entire period of awakening or disillusion will be required before the people cast aside the hackneyed beliefs which have been paraded as the latest wisdom and finally realise that capitalism is not the answer to their problems and a renovated Left is strong enough to lead them in a renewed struggle for socialism. But the period may not necessarily be a very long one.

The intelligentsia, a crucial factor in any radical transformation, is already disillusioned. In any case too numerous to be wholly bribed into a mafiosi capitalism, it may not be long before it recovers its revolutionary inheritance and role. The Russian workers, as they go through the hard school of life under capitalism, are learning their lessons and learning them faster because of its historical specificity as, at best, a late-coming *secondary* version amidst a crisis of global capitalism. Summing up the experience of the October Revolution, Trotsky wrote:

> The masses go into a revolution not with a prepared plan of social reconstruction, but with a sharp feeling that they cannot endure the old regime.. The fundamental political process of the revolution thus consists in the gradual comprehension by a class of the problems arising from the social crisis – the active orientation of the masses by a method of successive approximations.

The same 'method of successive approximations' will take the Russian working class towards another, more successful version of the revolution their predecessors made in 1917. The need is for a new leadership that can be trusted to carry forward this renewed struggle for socialism, leadership with a programme, a strategy and tactics which allow it to provide alternatives to the current recapitalising policies of the ruling elite and make for an effective presentation of the socialist option before the Russian people. If the political left in Russia is able to develop effective organisation and leadership and can mobilize the large potential working class base of support for socialism, it can become a real contender for power in the not too distant future.

The process which began with the dramatic collapse in Eastern Europe in 1989 and then disintegration of the Soviet Union and the turn to capitalism remains unconcluded. A 'revolution' or 'counter-revolution', it is still an unfinished one. The final act of this evolving political drama has yet to be – and may not be till we are well into the twenty-first century. Part of the worldwide struggle between capitalism and socialism, it is both the beginning and the continuation of a long conflict and the next major confrontation may yet again take place in the birth place of the first socialist revolution of our time. Building a successful capitalism in Russia is not going to be easy. The conditions, which include the immediate historical past and the interests of the powers dominant in global capitalism, itself in a long term crisis, are simply not conducive for capitalism to solidify there as a modern, relatively well functioning economic system answering, even in a limited or partial manner, to the needs of the people. The struggle for power in Russian economy which is on, will only sharpen as the transition proceeds, and whatever other dismal possibilities be there, class struggle by the working class, moved by a socialist vision and purpose, enriched by the incorporation of issues of peace, ecology and gender equality, will also be there among many other struggles over the future of Russia. This class struggle could still advance towards a renewed socialism in Russia – a socialism to which, as classically visualised, democracy is integral.

At the very least, it is indeed too early to settle the often raised question: Was 1917 the beginning of a heroic yet tragic diversion ending in capitalism or was the revolution, for all the questioning it has been subjected to by foes and friends, a positive step on humanity's road towards mastery over its own fate? The lethal legacy of a deformed socialism, in time may fade, especially if, as looks likely, the emergent capitalism is of the predatory third world variety. Having lost whatever even a deformed socialism had given them, the Russian workers once again possess nothing but their power to work. They still have a world to win and 'nothing to lose but their chains'. To borrow an oft quoted metaphor used by Rosa Luxemburg, who after the defeat of the revolutionary tide in central Europe in 1919, described the order reigning in Warsaw and elsewhere as 'built upon sand' – capitalism being built by Yeltsins and Putins may turnout to be a sand castle that historical tides of a renewed workers' movement will wash back into the sea. The emancipatory promise of 1917 may still be redeemed by the Russian working class.

3

China—Road to Capitalism

Optimistic speculation about the future of socialism in Russia, does not in any way change the overall situation. 1989 remains a dark turning point in the history of our times and the consequent period one of deepest ever 'crisis of socialism', which has engulfed not only former Soviet Union and Eastern Europe but the worldwide socialist movement as well as the still surviving countries of erstwhile 'socialist world', such as China, Vietnam, North Korea, Cuba, etc., all of which have once again entered an uncharted territory as Russia did in 1917, and the rest of them later at one time or the other. One noticeable difference between these countries and those of Eastern Europe is that the former, like Russia, experienced indigenous revolutions from below and not simply a 'revolution from above' carried out by the Red Army. While this gives the ruling regimes of the latter a somewhat greater legitimacy and resilience, it has neither saved them from the problems inherent in 'actual existing socialism', nor insulated them from the veritable gales of change sweeping through the now collapsed 'socialist' world, pushing its members back into capitalism. China is obviously the most important of these countries. It will not be out of place, therefore, to make a slightly extended comment on the situation in China, more particularly the reform process initiated under Deng Xiaoping's leadership, which is a subject of much controversy on the left and has significant implications for the contemporary crisis of socialism.

The economic reform in China and the consequent developments remain an immensely complex, and in many respects, opaque process. But one thing is abundantly clear: revolution in China is no longer on; instead China is now undergoing its own specific form of transition to capitalism. The process in fact took a definitive shape soon after the death of Mao, long before Gorbachev, the events of 1989 and the Soviet collapse, all of which only imparted it a new impetus. Though confronting similar problems and taking the same road, the Chinese leadership, however, has been careful, so far, to avoid some at least of Gorbachev's mistakes. Unlike Gorbachev, they have had no intention of loosening their monopoly of power even as they most certainly are engaged in an authoritarian transition to capitalism, and are well along that road. The massacre at Tiananmen Square made this very clear. Mao's socialist legacy has been repudiated and what is happening has very little to do with any Marxism or Leninism, though a socialist signboard may still continue to be flaunted. It is becoming daily more clear that, unless the process comes to be reversed, whatever China of tomorrow will be like, it will have little to do with Lenin or Mao and even less with Marx, it will not be socialism as the classical tradition understands it.

II

The Chinese Revolution, in many ways an extension of the October Revolution of 1917, was 'the greatest social upheaval of all times, at least in terms of numbers', with the Chinese Communist Party uniting all the progressive forces – workers and peasants in vast numbers, as well as national bourgeoisie (capitalists not linked or beholden to the bureaucrats and compradors who dominated the Kuomintang) and most intellectuals, even those whose orientation was heavily bourgeois – to drive the imperialists out of China, abolish feudalism in the countryside and set before the country the task of building a just and egalitarian, a socialist society. But with the setting of this new task, the old consensus, the New Democratic coalition, built up out of truly diverse class elements, which had made the revolution victorious broke down. Even otherwise, containing within itself as it did factions that reflected the multifaceted society out of which it was formed, the Communist Party of China had never been monolithic, the inner-party struggle was always there. But now differences and struggle surfaced within it on the question of building socialism in China, which is what Mao stood for. As long as Mao lived, he kept socialist transformation at the centre of the agenda and defended it against all attacks, mobilising the people through mass movements to transform society and in that process to educate themselves, educate the party, enlarge the consciousness of both leaders and led, and find new ways forward towards further transformation. However at every step of the way, Mao's line met opposition and resistance, primarily from a more 'orthodox' group at the centre who, rather than rely on the masses and put 'politics in command' to build socialism in their backward country, relied instead on planners at the top, stressed technology and expertise, hierarchy and one-man management, laid one-sided emphasis on material incentives and so on. In other words, they put 'economics in command' which could not but lead away from any socialist construction in China. Mao soon recognised them as 'capitalist roaders' entrenched inside the higher echelons of the party, an insurmountable stumbling block to the development of the socialist project. The differences only sharpened with the passage of years; patient persuasion, educational campaigns, party rectification as practiced hitherto, all proved ineffective in resolving the problem. As a last desperate effort to save the socialist project, Mao launched the cultural revolution asking the people and party cadre to 'bombard the headquarters' which however ended in a chaotic failure.

This prolonged inner party struggle over China's future was obviously a vastly complex process. Abstracting from its details and complexities, here is William Hinton's lucid account of what happened:

> As things turned out, although almost all Communists gave lip service to this concept (of building socialism), a large group of senior leaders, centered on Liu Shaochi and Deng Xiaoping, never really agreed with it. This group advocated a long period of mixed

'new democratic' economy, during which everything would be done to encourage the vigorous growth of private capitalism alongside state, cooperative, and mixed (state-private) ventures. Meanwhile the peasants on their newly acquired private plots, would settle down with their hoes as individual tillers, each responsible for his or her own profit or loss.

'When every peasant has a mule, a cart, and a plow, it will be time to talk about socialism,' said Liu Shaochi.

Thus the party split into two groups, each with its own agenda, and a long struggle broke out to determine which group and which agenda would eventually win out. The capitalist forces, confronted with socialist transformations on every front, opposed, dragged their feet, distorted policy, and diverted efforts to slow things down. When this didn't work, they pushed collective forms and mass movements to frenzied extremes, so discrediting and weakening them that they were threatened with disintegration from within. A regular pattern of right-wing obstruction alternating with ultra-left wrecking made it very hard for those building socialism to consolidate any new set of production relations, any new social structure, or any new ideology. For thirty years after 1949, those who were trying to create, develop and consolidate socialism faced fierce opposition from those who wanted to block, undermine, and cripple it in order to pursue a capitalist alternative.

Throughout these years, of course, the builders also made many mistakes which the opposition was able to seize upon to embarrass and confound them. What should be stressed in any realistic analysis, however, is that at no time did Mao and his supporters have a free hand to take initiatives, deepen and consolidate them, learn from mistakes, and move forward. Every step had to overcome not only the inertia of custom and tradition but also the determined opposition of a large, powerful, and cleverly led faction of the party itself. 'Never forget class struggle' was no ideal Maoist slogan. Intense struggle between social classes over basic policy permeated the whole period....

As long as Mao lived, however, the socialist forces and the socialist effort predominated – most of the time. After Mao's death came the deluge, the balance of forces tipped in favor of the opposition. Deng pulled off a military coup that toppled Hua Guofeng, Mao's successor, then presided over a great reversal....

In a poignant passage recalling Jinggang Mountain's association with the Chinese Revolution, this is what William Hinton wrote a few years back:

> In the last decade, Jinggang Mountain suffered considerable neglect, due in part to its remoteness, but primarily as a result of a political shift away from revolution towards technical modernisation, particularly the modernisation of the east coast.
>
> Carved into a great stone monolith at Huangyangjie, the all but impregnable pass guarding the northern flank of Jinggang Mountain is a metaphor Mao borrowed from Lenin: A single spark can start a prairie fire. And so it came to pass. The young men and women who raised the red flag here ignited a prairie fire that carried all before it, bringing more change to China in a few decades than two millennia had previously brought forth. But now, it seems clear, the fire has burned itself out, and, as the flames die down, it becomes apparent that change has not been deep. Fire burned the foliage off, but the roots of the old civilisation survived and are now sending up vigorous sprouts that push aside and overwhelm, in one sphere after another, all revolutionary innovations.

III

There is a view, promoted by the current Chinese leadership for their own tactical reasons and by scholars abroad for their neo-liberal ideological predilections, which claims that China's modern development really began only with the introduction of Dengist 'market reform'. The so-called 'snail's pace' of the earlier years is contrasted with the 'phenomenal growth' of the Chinese economy during the 25 odd years of 'reform'. On the occasion of the 50th anniversary of the Chinese revolution, we were even told that 'China should be celebrating 25 years of reforms rather than 50 years of Communism'. This view does not merely underplay the remarkable achievements of the previous three decades (at times casting doubt even on the need for land reform) but dismisses them as 'thirty wasted years', years of bungling, bureaucratism, excesses, arbitrary experiments, destabilising mass campaigns, and one terrible famine, etc., etc., necessarily associated with the Maoist effort to build socialism – and therefore a lesson for others still suffering from residual ideological hang-ups in this regard, in

China and elsewhere. This view however is both factually incorrect and ideologically flawed and serves to obscure two important facts: that the Mao-era achievements provided the basis for the success, such as it is, of even the Deogist reform, and that this 'success' of the post-reform period, for all its 'economic growth' and 'prosperity' represents a regression compared to the earlier Maoist years.

Under Mao's leadership China 'stood up', and uprooting the old feudal-comprador economy and politics, set out on the road of self-reliant socialist development. Once again, as in Russia earlier, history had confronted a people with the task of building socialism in a backward country, even more backward than Russia – something entirely unanticipated by classical Marxism. Mao responded, very much as Lenin had with his project of socialism in Russia during the few years that he survived the October revolution. We have noticed how Lenin's project got derailed, especially after his departure, and Russia under Stalin's leadership increasingly took a different path. Mao had his own criticism of socialist construction in the Soviet Union. While China's early post-revolutionary development carried the unavoidable imprint of Soviet experience and help, Mao rejected the Soviet development strategy and opted for a path significantly different from the one pursued by the Soviet Union. At a basic theoretical level he recognised the dialectical nature of the relationship between the 'base' and the 'superstructure' and therefore the important role of the latter in facilitating the transformation of the former, and laid a decisive emphasis on putting 'politics in command' in the construction of socialism, as against the Soviet practice, where there was a mechanistic understanding of the relationship between the 'base' and the 'superstructure' and, if anything, it was 'economics in command'. At a more practical, economic level, Mao's critique noticed in the Soviet practice 'measures which squeeze the peasant very hard' – a 'method of capital accumulation' which he disapproved and rejected – and 'lop-sided stress on heavy industry to the neglect of agriculture and light industry (which) resulted in a shortage of goods in the market and an unstable currency'. In China, Mao wrote:

'Our policies towards the peasant differ from those of the Soviet Union and take into account the interests of both the state and the peasant'; 'we ... attach more importance to agriculture and light industry'. 'The heavy industry', Mao said, 'still claims the emphasis in our investment', but, 'if you want to develop heavy industry you must pay attention to developing agriculture and light industry'. Mao argued for the economic principle of 'walking on two legs', for taking 'agriculture as the base and industry as the leading factor'.

The thorough and universal land reform, followed by collectivisation, liberated the long-constrained productive forces, primarily the surplus labour power of the Chinese peasants; collectively constructed and owned infrastructure – such as water management systems – was built; technology was sought to be taken to the peasantry; 'leave agriculture, don't leave village' policy was pursued through collectively owned township and village enterprises in fulfillment of Mao's cherished dream of industrialising villages rather than building factories in big urban centres – all of which not only ensured China's food security and gainful employment for the rural masses, but increased incomes for the people and therefore a high enough rate of savings and investment to enable China's socialist planning to establish a diversified industrial base in the country.

Maximisation of economic growth as measured in the percentile indices is of course not the goal of socialism. Yet even in terms of these indices, conventionally used by economic analysts and institutions like the World Bank, during the period 1953-78 Chinese industry grew at a rate of over 10 per cent, agriculture by 4 per cent, grain output by 3.7 per cent, the GNP at an average rate of almost 8 per cent and the economy as a whole grew from 7 per cent to 8 per cent a year (even when factoring in the declines suffered during the hardship years, 1959-1961). This was one of the fastest rates of growth in the world. Rooted in the land reforms of 1946-53, Maoist era was indeed an extraordinary achievement, creating from a near void the foundations of a robust modern economy in China. Recognising the Mao era economic progress, already achieved prior to the 'success' of the Dengist reform, the conservative mouthpiece of international capital, *The Economist* was compelled to ask: 'Does economic policy make any difference in China?' This apart, at the end of the Mao era, the country was debt-free, long sought oil resources had been discovered and exploited, the nuclear programme had proceeded apace, the UN seat had been acquired, and its long international isolation ended, China was not only a self reliant economy but also; an established world power.

The socialist nature of Mao era economic progress had also enabled China to feed, clothe and house, educate and provide adequate health care to its vast masses, nearly a quarter of world's population, in its first fifteen years. The basis for the achievement was precisely the socialisation of property which made it possible to adopt the necessary measures for the purpose, such as setting up a collective welfare fund, putting in place a universal public distribution system which gave every citizen a certain minimum of food and other essential commodities. The lowering of both the death rate for the general population and of infant mortality rate was accompanied by an unusually high level of literacy, especially at the primary and secondary levels of education. China overcame poverty (as defined in Third World countries such as India) and ensured relatively low levels of income inequality. Typical of the complex of rights and guarantees won by the common people during the Mao era was the 'iron rice bowl', a term often eagerly seized and disparaged in western analysis. This of course guaranteed jobs to the working people and made it impossible to fire without providing alternative employment. But this 'iron' security against joblessness only just captured the complex of social relations which being employed by the State represented in China. With it came employer-provided housing at minimal maintenance cost, free health care and maternity payments, worker compensation and other forms of insurance, pension and often other resources such as schools and recreational facilities – a full set of social benefits in an enveloping community setting which, together with job security, even at the relatively low level of the Chinese economy, made for conditions of life and work completely unfamiliar, in fact impossible, for workers in the vastly more wealthy capitalist societies. These conditions involved not merely relations of quantitative security. This security was accompanied by a relative egalitarianism in class relations including a healthy respect for the working class and its power (which however was exercised primarily through party structures). As a consequence of the social gains of the Mao era, there was essentially no unemployment in China, no begging or homelessness, virtually no crime, no shanty town slums and even among the relatively poor, no 'underclass' of social outcasts living in conditions of desperate and degrading poverty. Even the critics of Mao's policies admit that the Maoist period saw China's people, even its poor, emerge significantly better off than their counterparts in the other so-called 'developing' countries of the third world, a fact which, interestingly enough, the World Bank itself recognised way back in 1979. It only needs to be added that the Maoist period was one which had kept the market in check and was one of imposed or self-chosen delinking from global capitalism. While the Soviet aid in the 1950s was by no means a negligible factor in the first installment of industrial, technological, or military capability, the almost total embargo on foreign trade imposed by the imperialist powers in the 1950s and 1960s was used extensively by the Chinese to encourage self-reliance and embark on gigantic progressive social and economic changes remote from the constraints of external pressures. It may be noted that, contrary to the fashionable critics of Maoism, economic growth in the successive Maoist periods was stronger and better balanced in the long term, thanks to a constant effort at collective investment in different areas of the economy as well as social welfare.

Thus, when Deng took charge of China's destiny and embarked on his 'market reform', he did not do so in a vacuum. The international context of globalizing capitalism apart, a concrete domestic socio-economic and political base was available from which the Dengist reform could take off. Under Mao's leadership the Chinese people had created a proud and independent country out of the 'sick man of Asia' and then proceeded to develop its industrial economy at a rate comparable only to the greatest surges of growth in history. The rapid growth of the Deng era has rested on this prior achievement. The new regime was erected on the shoulders of the old one, not after wholly dismantling or destroying the latter, but using all its advantages. The success, such as it is, of post-reform growth has been made possible by the achievements of the pre-reorm economic regime, and often by the continuation, however temporarily or transformed, of several advantageous features of that regime.

Briefly put, there have been the advantages, for example, of planned economy, centralisation and effective state intervention, state sector and rural industrialisation, radical land reforms and the old collectivist management of the irrigation systems, and so on. Township and Village Enterprises, TVEs (*xiangzhen qiye*), which are recognised to have played a most important role in the contemporary economic growth, originated in the commune brigade enterprises (*shedui qiye*) as part of Mao's mass mobilisation development strategy to push forward rural industrialisation, their technological base significantly strengthened by the policy of 'intellectuals going to the countryside' during the cultural revolution which brought a large number of technicians and similarly qualified people to the rural areas. (An extension or continuation of the communal and village enterprises of the Mao period, the TVEs, of course, now stand transformed and indeed came to be known and noticed as such when the market reform policies in 1984 recognised ther *de facto* profit-making activities and encouraged the pursuit of profit and unrestrained accumulation.) If the earlier achievement of near-universal literacy and the improvement in the educational and health status of the work-force continues to make it a valuable asset for new economic purposes, the vast liberating social equalisation of the Mao era has in its own way helped by providing a huge and relatively compliant reserve army of labour for the development of a capitalist economy. Furthermore, as privatisation and market relations gain dominance and contradictions and tensions brought on by social polarisation escalate, the relatively egalitarian social base inherited from the earlier regime has made for a certain degree of social and political stability and, so far at least, prevented the situation becoming seriously unstable or explosive. Most importantly, there is the enormous stock of political and moral authority of the Chinese Communist Party built under and long associated with the name of Mao. The fact that power in China is still exercised by Communist Party at the head of a comparatively strong state, and not directly or exclusively by a bourgeoisie, has not only lent a necessary legitimacy to market-based growth, but also imparted to this growth, however temporarily, a certain non-comprador or self-reliant 'national' character, just as the surviving continuity with the old regime has had a certain limiting effect on the damaging impact of the growing internal and external *capitalist* environment. (China, for example, was able to limit the worst ravages of the 1997-98 Asian crisis because it still retained some elements of economic planning).

China's economic growth in the recent period, such as it has been, is, therefore, no exemplar of the so-called 'virtues of the market', a 'model' of neo-liberal success for other third world countries to follow. More to the point however is to note the irony involved. For based on the *socialist* achievements of the Maoist period, it has been *capitalist* growth, a growth *away* from socialism, a regression as compared to that earlier period.

This growth has certainly been remarkable, though not as remarkable as the ideological hype over it makes it out to be. But the question of socialism apart, it is doubtful if China can sustain even this kind or rate of growth for long. Advantages flowing from the Maoist era are fast getting destroyed or atrophied with the on-going privatisation and marketisation of the reform process. The down turn in the world economy makes export-led growth increasingly problematic for third world countries. Contradictions of whatever capitalism is growing in China are daily becoming sharper, posing their own problems in economic, political and cultural domains. The forces released by a crisis-ridden world capitalism, conflicting and common interests of its advanced countries, the power that global finance has come to acquire, pose different threats of their own.

Globalisation, even as it has facilitated the market-based growth in China, could as well, ultimately, push this growth along a comprador third worldist path. Unless, in a radical reversal of current policies, China returns to the socialist path.

(Some Chinese scholars have even argued that 'underlying many of the "miracles" in today's China' is 'a Chinese working class that has no right to unions or to labour negotiations', that 'as China has no comparative advantages in either resources or technology in today's world, and cannot advance either to a real socialism or a real capitalism, its competitive edge can only come from its unique system of dependent labour'. And one of them, Qin Hui, professor at Qinghua University, in his own way sympathetic to and critical of economic reform, privatisation etc., even asks: 'But even if economic magic of this sort, that does not treat people as human beings, did take China to the top of the world, what would be its value? Such a development would first of all threaten the existence of the Chinese people themselves.')

IV

The Maoist period in China is not to be noticed only in relation to the Dengist reform which followed – latter's 'success', retrogression, future or anything else. Representing an attempt at building socialism in a backward country, it has an importance that goes far beyond what happened or is now happening in China. Far too many countries in backward parts of the world – more or less 'underdeveloped' or 'developing' countries where the overwhelming majority of world's population lives – are today seeking a development that secures both economic growth and decent, humane conditions of living for their common people. This is something that five hundred years of capitalism including particularly the fifty odd post-colonial years of its much hyped modernisation and development strategies – 'development economics' and promises of 'trickle down' – have failed to deliver; even when the economy has done 'fine', the people have not, as a former President of Brazil once reported it in Washington. And this is precisely what less than thirty years of Mao's socialism delivered to the Chinese people. I would therefore like to underline the historical importance of the Mao period by emphasising a few points – supplementing, even repeating what I have said earlier as part of this differently focused argument – before turning to the Dengist abandonment of the Maoist path, the new 'reform' policies which, in effect, mean establishment or restoration of capitalism in China.

It is common with critics within China and outside to view the Mao period as a series of failed policies which only hindered China's economic development. Attention is focused on 'recklessness' of the Great Leap Forward or 'excesses' of the Cultural Revolution, on their negative aspects or consequences only. The 'cult of Mao' is condemned along with the 'authoritarian' politics and bureaucratic central planning of the period. Even when gains in the spheres of education and health-care are recognised, they are not seen as integral parts of the larger, and for its time exceptionally successful, socialist project, which remains dismissed as 'little more than a story of impractical, utopian dreams born from conditions of backwardness'. It was at best 'socialism in poverty' and that is supposed to clinch the issue against it. One does not have to deny the validity of such or, for that matter, more discerning criticism to insist upon the greater validity, and decisive relevance, of the point made by the eminent historian, E.H. Carr, in relation to the Soviet experiment in socialism. He had warned: 'The danger is not that we shall draw a veil over the enormous blots on the record of the revolution, over the cost in human suffering, over the crimes committed in its name. The danger is that we shall be tempted to forget altogether, and to pass over in silence, its immense achievements'. In other words, whatever be its negative aspects, it is the 'immense achievements' of Mao's socialism that need to be recognised, particularly by the people in the third world.

It has to be noted that these achievements were made against very heavy internal and external odds. Before the Communists swept to power in 1949, China was among the most destitute of the underdeveloped countries. Its conditions had steadily deteriorated during the previous two centuries. In the 19th century it was universally referred to as Asia's 'sick man', open to all sorts of imperialist interventions and plunder. China, in

1949, exhibited what have been described as 'the classic symptoms of economic backwardness': 'political corruption, social debility and class exploitation, economic stagnation, negligible technical change, and heavy demographic pressure.' Externally there was, throughout, the unremitting hostility of the capitalist world led by the United States – the economic embargoes, diplomatic isolation, threat of military intervention, and so on. These are the conditions in which the Chinese people, under Mao's leadership, set out on the socialist path. It has been suggested that if China had not opted for the Maoist strategy, it would have been just another Bangladesh. Years later Rene Dumont is supposed to have observed: 'How beautiful China is, when viewed from Bangladesh'. It can well be added: when viewed from any other third world country.

Central to the Maoist strategy was the principle of self-reliance, not autarky but a 'delinking' that postulated the primacy of planned, internally-generated independent development at national but also at provincial and local levels, bringing together the available resources and the needs of the people at every level, backed by the creativity and self-activity of the people, the politics of mass mobilisation. It was a *socialist* response not just to the internal constraints of socio-economic backwardness, but even more necessarily to the external pressure of globally dominant capitalism which inevitably makes for relations of subordination and dependency in the third world. Since the emergence of capitalism as a world system, the expansion of capital 'has projected itself beyond national borders to shape a world economy suited to its needs', and it 'has been shaping or blocking the development process almost everywhere in the third world during the second half of the 20th century' – this is how Selden and Lippit have described this external pressure. Mao's deliberate choice of self-reliance and self-sufficiency helped fend the distorting pressure of global capitalism off the Chinese economy. This choice was only reinforced by the break with Khrushchev's Soviet Union in 1960 (when the latter abruptly withdrew its technicians etc. from China and left a huge number of projects uncompleted).

Self-reliance, reliance on people's creativity and self-activity and mass mobilisation was a distinguishing feature of the Mao period. Advanced technologies in agricultural, industrial and military fields were developed and innovative structural arrangements like *danwei* (units), for example, came up. As one description has it: 'In a unit, multiple functions of party leadership, production, medical service and resource supplier form an integrity. Self-reliance under such a social structure in which politics, economics, service and supply existed together at the unit level created a sustainable society based on their own resources and needs and under the overall political guidance of the state.' (Emphasis on workers' technological inventiveness and fight against the hierarchical management techniques of the west were important issues in the Cultural Revolution). At the end of it all the kind of long term growth achieved was virtually without historical precedent. In less than three decades China transformed itself from a backward agrarian society into an industrial power – the only third world country in which the national exigencies of expanded production – in all sectors and at all technical levels – could be satisfied without extensive recourse to the external market.

Bourgeois economists' scepticism over them notwithstanding, the available statistics (from diverse sources) testify to the extraordinary growth performance of the Mao period in China. According to Samir Amin, China recorded GDP growth rate of 5.3 per cent in the period 1957-75; the growth rate in light industry was 11.2 per cent and in heavy industry 8.3 per cent. China's GNP increased at an average annual rate of 6.2 per cent between 1952-78. Along with it 'the Chinese Communists succeeded in reestablishing that elusive equilibrium (between agriculture and industry). With the massive assistance of modern inputs from the industrial sector (fertilisers, select seeds, insecticides, machinery), production of foodstuffs more than doubled in three decades (the annual rate of growth averaged an exceptional 3-3.5 per cent)'. According to Thomas Rawski, the GNP (in 1957 *yuan*) grew from 70 billion in 1952 to 105 billion in 1957, to 151 billion in 1965, and then to 266 billion in 1974 and 339 billion in 1978. This corresponded to successive annual growth rates of 8.2 per cent (1952-57), 4.7 per cent (1957-65),

6.6 per cent (1965-94), and 6.1 per cent (1974-78). The average annual growth rate in 1952-78 of gross domestic product (or its equivalent) was 6.2 per cent. The early *World Development Reports* (1981, 1982, 1983, 1984) indicated average annual growth of GNP per capita from 1960 to 1980 to be between 5.0 and 6.0 per cent. According to World Bank statistics China's growth rates were among the most impressive in the world between 1950 and 1975. Reporting that China's exports during 1952-73 rose at an average annual rate of 6 per cent, Luo Deming says: 'Although China was still considered a closed economy in this period, 6 per cent is a higher rate than what some open economies achieved in this period.' W. Deckers has written: '(China's) self-reliant planned economy was successful into the 1970s as a method for building an industrial as well as general infrastructure, providing for basic human needs, as well as military security and independence.'

Speaking of 'industrial achievements' of Chinese socialism – where 'through resource concentration and mass mobilisation China was able to develop a very comprehensive and sustainable self-sufficient industrial structure' – Li Xing says: 'Within two decades after the communists came to power, Chinese industry was transformed from a large backward one with low volume of capitalisation and poor techniques into one capable of production of aircrafts, ships, electric generators, locomotives, cargo ships, etc. Most remarkable was the successful development of a number of modern industrial sectors and advanced technologies – the successful launching of satellite communication, the explosion of atomic and hydrogen bombs – leading China into the frontier of world's major military powers.'

The industrial achievement, it may be mentioned, was accompanied and facilitated by an egalitarian income structure, underpinned by a narrow range in the wage scales, which secured a desirable 'equilibrium' in distribution between regions, between intellectual and manual work, between skilled and unskilled labour – the established social structures guaranteed a much better (that is less unequal) income distribution than anywhere else in the world.

Equally comprehensive, and in many ways more noteworthy were the achievements in the agrarian sector – in a country with the world's lowest arable land to population ratio, and despite what went wrong with the Great Leap Forward or the Cultural Revolution and despite the bureaucratic nature of central planning. Radical land reforms and collectivisation lifted China's agriculture from its age old stagnation and its vast peasantry from its equally old poverty. With China 'walking on two legs', agricultural development went hand in hand with industrial development, in the process ensuring food security for the country as a whole. Not only was the principle of 'equal exchange between the city and the countryside' implemented, but, with the interests of the overwhelming majority of the population in mind, the agrarian sector was privileged, as for example in the use or redistribution of the centralised social surplus. As part of the 'leave agriculture, don't leave village' policy, commune and brigade factories (*shedui qiye*) were set up which provided gainful employment in the countryside and reduced the urban-rural divide. Maoist China's innovative policies and initiatives not only preserved the worker-peasant alliance but created what was undoubtedly the most egalitarian society in the world.

Socialist China's economic achievement was indeed unprecedented. And while central planning was important, crucial to this achievement was the creativity, self-activity and participation of China's workers and peasants inspired by the revolution they had made and by the leadership of Mao. But economic achievement or growth is not what defines socialism, it is no criterion, much less the only or main criterion of socialism. Socialism is defined by the transformed relations between human beings, in production and consequently in social life. It is the promise of a qualitatively superior life to that under capitalism. And it is this promise that Mao's socialism had kept. Socialist China, despite initial and continuing backwardness and the pressures of global capitalism, had provided its working people with a life that was in many ways already superior to what even advanced capitalist countries offer their common people. And this superiority could only grow with further progress along the socialist road.

Taking note of the fact that 'the Chinese revolution and Maoist socialism were a great leap forward in transforming China from a semi-feudal and semi-colonial society into a modern world power within a very short period.' Li Xing, basing himself on and referring to the work of several scholars in the field, has written:

> Chinese economic performance cannot simply and primarily be assessed in terms of economic measurement. Such an approach is too narrow and inadequate to view the development of a socialist economy that attached great importance to welfare and equality. If the measure of success includes other elements, such as maximum number of people in the process of socialist construction, egalitarian income distribution, balanced development, reducing gaps and differences, technology developed to meet the actual needs of the people, China's socialist achievements are respectable.
>
> The most striking achievement of Chinese socialism lies in the importance it gave to social welfare and especially human development. Chinese socialist welfare systems covered all structural arrangements: full employment, income equalisation, controlled pricing, social security, occupational benefits, medical service, housing, and all sorts of subsidies. It aimed at providing welfare and security to the entire population and meeting the need of their material and spiritual well-being. Though China was one of the poorest countries in the world, its working class enjoyed comprehensive welfare service although at a low level. Some scholars argue that 'the workbased welfare system provides a level of coverage that would be considered comprehensive and generous in comparison with the most advanced welfare states in the west.'

He goes on:

> China's health care system during the period of socialism was internationally recognised as a model for the rest of the developing world during the 1960s and 1970s. Such a system contained many noteworthy and innovative features: (a) it strongly emphasised preventive health service over curative; (b) it mobilised people to carry out preventive health campaigns; (c) health care services were even delivered to remote rural areas; and (d) it commanded a relatively large proportion of national resources. Recent studies indicate that while the number of doctors practising western

> medicine per 1,00,000 population in China was 2.5 times that in India, the number of village-level health care workers was 4.5 times that in India (UNDP 1990). By the end of the 1970s, China had established a very effective rural health service; and about 85 per cent of villages had a health clinic (station) staffed by one or more trained health-care workers known as 'barefoot doctors', who ensured that the majority of the rural population received basic and necessary medical treatment, and helped and advised them on disease prevention.
>
> Social development especially human development indicators such as life expectancy are often considered as the most reliable showing the real extent of development and poverty. As the *World Development Report* (1981) points out, 'China's economic structure and national income per person, are similar to other low-income countries, but the physical quality of life of the bulk of the Chinese people is strikingly better than in most other low-income countries.' Chinese life expectancy increased from 36 years in 1950 to 64 years in 1979 which was considered by the World Bank as outstandingly high for a country at China's per capita income level.
>
> The system of iron rice bowl and other social welfare rights that the working class enjoyed in the years of revolutionary China not only gave material benefits, but had an important impact on relations of production. These social rights represent a significant degree of workers' control of the process of production, a right of much greater importance than the legally formal 'civil rights' claimed by the west.

Li Xing concludes:

> In order to grasp a balanced picture of China's development during the period of socialism it is necessary to bear in mind that the assessment of Chinese socialism must not depart from two important criteria: The first is whether the essence of socialism is ultimately control by working people in the development process of industry or agriculture, or in carrying out intellectual, service or other socially useful tasks and over their own productive activity; the second is whether the development strategy as well as development policies serve the interests of the working people. Such a consideration is important because the socialist model of economic development as manifested by Maoist socialism differs fundamentally from the capitalist model as revealed by the post-Mao restoration of capitalism not only in terms of the ownership of the means of production but also essentially in terms of to whose interest economic development should be oriented.

Li Xing is not alone in testifying to the socialist achievements of the Mao period. Pointing out that Mao's policies, among other things, prevented 'the emergence of a class of impoverished landless labourers', Luo Deming says:

> the state guarantees a minimum food supply; primary school enrolment is high; and basic medical care and family planning services are available to most people. As a result, hunger, disease, high birth and infant death rates, general illiteracy, and constant fear of destitution and starvation that haunt very poor people in other countries have been more or less banished. Life expectancy, whose dependence on many other economic and social variables makes it probably the best single indicator of the extent of real poverty, has increased rapidly. In 1950, China's life expectancy was 36 years, it was almost the same as the average level of the low-income countries (35 years). In 1978, it has risen to 64 years, and it not only far surpasses that of the average level of low-income countries (50 years), but also surpasses that of the average level of middle income countries (61 years). Furthermore, even in the poorest province, life expectancy is not far below the average for middle income countries.

Reporting the findings of a study on the subject T. Bergmann has written:

> We should not judge the Chinese model in terms of growth alone, because economic growth is a very unsatisfactory index of the rate of economic development, because it ignores the question of distribution of income and wealth, unemployment problems and economic infrastructure. China has gone straight to the roots of the problems that have been plaguing poor countries for many years – the lack of food and low levels of nutrition, gross inequalities of income and consumption, unemployment and a sense of social uselessness, and the blind expansion of the cities. She has been uniquely successful in the development of the people's economic life for the benefit of all instead of for the benefit of the few, and in placing the needs of man before those of machines.
>
> This study indicates better relative performance by China on all fronts. It has eradicated the worst forms of poverty; it has full employment, universal literacy and adequate health facilities. Not only has China been able to solve its unemployment problem, but it has been able to do so without any foreign aid during the

> last fourteen years. China also stands out as the only developing country without any internal or external debts outstanding and a uniquely stable currency.

China's socialism was not without its flaws or failures of policy. A pioneering enterprise of its size and scope was bound to have them. But these were the result not of any 'utopianism' as alleged by the critics, but of a revolutionary over-optimism and bad planning. There were also choices compelled by the external environment which Mao would rather have avoided. Economic isolation and embargoes, hostility of the United States, break with the Soviet Union which apart from its immediate economic damage, left China confronting Soviet Union as well – all this made for emphasis on heavy industry and large scale diversion of human and material resources into non-development domains like defence in order to ensure national security and survival of the socialist project. The subversion from abroad and the ever present threat of military intervention made for tight political control, a most significant absence of democracy within the country.

In a long term perspective, the most important flaw or failure of socialism in China indeed lay here, in the sphere of its politics. While appeals were made for mass initiative and people were successfully mobilised for a time and for specific purposes, no institutionalised avenues were made available for them to acquire knowledge of things and act or intervene effectively on a regular basis. The Party continued to know, speak and act on their behalf. Guaranteed employment, universal social security and welfare, an egalitarian income distribution, equality between city and countryside and self-reliant economic development were among the major achievements of socialist China. But effective mastery of social organism by the masses, a properly institutionalised socialist democracy was missing. Mao's last desperate effort, the Cultural Revolution, simply failed to produce one. This one promise of socialism Mao failed to keep.

Nevertheless, its flaws and failures notwithstanding, China's socialism retains its relevance for peoples in the third world. As Li Xing has rightly pointed out:

> In most developing countries, to guarantee a minimum standard of living and to eventually reduce inequalities in income distribution are the development objectives. But very few countries have given these objectives such a high priority as China did. Not only had China stated these objectives in words but had also worked to achieve them.

This is how Samir Amin summed it all up in the early 1980s, before the Dengist reform finally and effectively got underway:

> Socialism can claim no more impressive a victory in our epoch than China's developmental experience these past thirty years. When put in context, its achievement is all the more remarkable. From the 1920s onwards, China was wracked by civil war and warlordism; in the midst of this devastation the Japanese imperialists invaded China and wreaked still more havoc. On the morrow of the Chinese Communist victory, the country's level of development stood visibly below that of even India. Between 1950 and today, China's population has grown from 450 million to almost a billion. And yet it has managed to achieve considerable agricultural growth in unfavourable natural conditions, and to lay the foundations of a comprehensive and autonomous industrial system which despite its backwardness and shortcomings in certain respects, can feed, clothe, and house the people and meet the challenges of national defense and industrial and agricultural modernisation. China can now 'rise to the occasion' of development while other, more affluent and developed Third World Countries are being caught in an impasse. However backward it may appear by Western standards, China still disposes of a technological base that will enable it to reap the benefits of that revolution in science and technology on which it has embarked and, ultimately, to master the whole of its productive apparatus.

This however was not to be. Decisive here, perhaps, has been the promise Mao failed to keep. As Deng turned to 'the market', in effect, capitalism, for China's future development and lined up a bureaucratised Communist Party behind his turn, there was no serious questioning or opposition by the Chinese people who were soon going to bear the costs of this turn. Mao era simply passed into history to be condemned for its 'socialism in poverty'.

Even so, Mao's socialist project remains an exemplar. It is not Deng's but Mao's 'miracle', the revolution he made and the socialism he built, that the struggling people and their leaders in the third world need to take note of.

V

The inner-party struggle over China's path of development had been going on for a long time. The point of definitive departure from the Maoist path can be located in the Third Plenary session of the Eleventh Central Committee of the Chinese Communist Party in December 1978. Mao had passed away and Deng Xiaoping had consolidated his leadership of the Party. Mao's warnings and struggle against the 'capitalist roaders' in the Party were vindicated as Deng launched his 'economic reform' which amounted to a total reversal of the earlier policies, in effect, a decisive shift from the socialist to the capitalist road. From that time on the new leadership set in motion the process of dismantling both the socialist economic base and the socialist superstructure that the Chinese people had built with such effort over the past thirty odd years.

'Four Modernisations', a programme formulated by Chou En Lai as part of a socialist transition in China was transmuted into one of transition to capitalism in the name of 'using capitalism to develop socialism'. Deng continued to avow his adherence to 'Four Cardinal Principles': (1) Keep to the Socialist Road, (2) Uphold the Dictatorship of the Proletariat, (3) Uphold the Leadership of the Communist Party and (4) Uphold Marxism-Leninism-Mao Zedong Thought. But his 'economic reform' was a departure from the basic First and Fourth principles. It entailed privatising changes in the ownership structures – heralded by the 'individual household responsibility system' in agriculture – Open Door for foreign private investment and a shift to market principles as the overall guide in the economy. Henceforth, the 'central focus' (*zhongdian*) of all activity of the party and the state was to be on 'economic construction'.

Initially Deng rejected the so-called 'shock therapy', that is excessive privatisation, free market with no controls, unrestrained opening to foreign capital or exposure to the global capitalist economy. But 'market' has its own logic and Deng himself was soon (especially after his 1992 trip to Shenzen in the South) calling for an all out drive for what has been euphemistically described as 'market-led modernisation of the PRC economy'. There was to be a rapid generalisation of market relations in the economy, with planning – which among other things had shielded people from the ravages of 'the market' – taking a back seat. Deng Xioping declared that exploitation would be tolerated, especially in the Special Economic Zones and 'open cities' which would act as 'windows' on the global economy, by attracting foreign capital to a disciplined and 'competitive' labour force. China was well set on the road to capitalism. Deng's elementary pragmatic responses, as China travelled this road, were soon elevated into theory (*lilun*), 'Deng Xiaoping Theory', and socialism itself stood re defined as 'Socialist Market Economy', or the better advertised 'Socialism with Chinese Characteristics'.

VI

The immediate historical context of the Dengist 'economic reform' was the failure of the 'Great Proletarian Cultural Revolution', Mao's last desperate effort to save socialism in China by calling on the people to attack the 'capitalist roaders' entrenched in the hierarchical and bureaucratic state and party strctures. Initially full of promise and manifestive of the confidence and creativity of the workers and peasants, Mao eventually lost control of the movement and the cultural revolution got bogged down in unprincipled power struggles and ended up in conditions of anarchy and large scale persecution. Far from creating a new, more democratic form of government reflecting and responsive to people's commitment to socialism, the cultural revolution, in its failure, only laid the ground work for a reversal of Maoist policies in all fields. Its anarchic and exhausting denouement not only left behind a popular constituency for Deng's pragmatism, but the failure of its democratic thrust, the continuing neglect or absence of institutionalised democracy, made it all the easier for Deng to impose his deideological, pragmatic shift to capitalism on the people. To effect this shift, it was still necessary for Deng to come to terms with Mao and his cultural revolution. The first direct reflection of the post-Mao shift was evident by early 1978 with the launching of a nationwide campaign to 'seek truth from facts'. Once Mao's principle in his search for viable non-dogmatic revolutionary theory, it now epitomised Deng Xiaoping's strategy of downplaying theory in favour of a 'more flexible and utilitarian standard' to evaluate a new set of priorities and policies. The decisive shift away from Mao occurred, as already noted, at the Third Plenum of December 1978 when Deng carried the Party with him to repudiate the Cultural Revolution *in toto* and affirm the centrality of 'economic construction' – that is putting 'economics in command' – in place of 'continuing class struggle' – that is putting 'politics in command' – which was the focus during the Cultural Revolution. Collaterally Deng emphasised the need for socio-political stability and therefore the centrality of state's, and by implication the Communist Party's authority in the Chinese political system, as against the political campaigns and mass politics of the Cultural Revolution. This shift away from Mao and his policies found a more explicit expression in June 1981, when the Sixth Plenum of the Eleventh CC adopted a 35,000-word 'Resolution on Certain Questions in the History of Our Party since the Founding of the People's Republic'. The break with the Maoist period was sought to be documented and enshrined as the official party position. The notable aspects of the resolution were the verdicts that were passed on the 'Great Proletarian Cultural Revolution' and the overall contribution and role of Mao and, of course, the link between the two: the former was seen as having 'caused the most devastating setback and heavy losses to the party, the state, and the people in the history of the People's Republic, and this "Great Cultural Revolution" was initiated and led by Comrade Mao Zedong'. Mao was given credit for his role in the Chinese revolution, but the resolution also focused on Mao's 'shortcomings and mistakes', with the obviously tactical concession that Mao's achievements were 'primary and his mistakes secondary'. The 'mistakes' are seen to have chiefly occurred in his later years when 'he separated himself from the collective leadership of party, often rejecting or even suppressing the correct views of others. Mistakes thus became inevitable. A long period of comprehensive, serious mistakes led to the outbreak of the "Great Cultural Revolution" which brought the most severe misfortune to the party and the people'. Here, a clear departure was sought to be established from the post-revolution Mao era, a definite and determined discarding of not only class struggle and renunciation of revolutionary mass mobilisation strategies but also of the Maoist principle of putting 'politics in command' in the construction of socialism. This is not to suggest that the Party was altogether unanimous on the question of economic reform, the new line advocated by Deng. There was and continues to be considerable debate on the 'how far and fast' of it. But the differences, then or later, have been contained within the reform paradigm. Leadership's criticism of Mao's policies in terms of 'individual opportunism and adventurism' has been rejected as neither convincing nor Marxist. But 'Left' opposition to the reforms has never been, so far, effective or strong enough to pose a serious challenge to the dominant paradigm. On the anniversary day of October 1, 1984, Deng even declared his paradigm shift away from the Maoist path as China's 'second revolution'.

There were problems indeed with the economy, with the bureaucratised economic planning and the Maoist path of development. But instead of turning to the people and innovative Marxism, the new leadership turned to the market and global capitalism in a manner as to surrender the very project of socialism. This surrender, that is Dengist 'economic reform' has indeed led to remarkable 'economic growth' of the Chinese economy. But insofar as this economic growth is a capitalist development with its own exploitative logic, 'economic reform' in China has meant effective abandonment of socialism as Marxism understands it, notwithstanding ritualistic invocation of socialism, or the flimsy rationalisation of 'market socialism' rapidly fading into 'the socialist market economy' or 'social market', where in turn, it has been pointed out, 'the socialist' or 'social', 'like the smile on the Cheshire cat's face gets pretty faded in the sweat shops of Guangdong'.

VII

The shift from a socialist to a capitalist project has been accompanied and facilitated by an amazing indifference to matters of Marxism or socialist theory among the new leadership of China. The tone for the entire reform process or period was set by Deng Xiaoping's long notorious proposition: 'it does not matter if the cat is black or white as long as it catches the mouse.' The catching now to be done by the communist cat was of the 'mouse' of economic growth. Consistent with this view Jiang Zemin, as the Communist Party general secretary, proclaimed his determination 'not (to) get bogged down in an abstract debate over what is socialist and what is capitalist'. Such esoteric preoccupation is now remote from the more practical concerns of the Chinese leadership. The journal *Xinhua Ribao* has thus rationalised the entire issue: 'A tangerine growing in southern Anhui is called a tangerine, but the same fruit is called an orange if it grows in northern Anhui.' It goes on: 'The same object may have different characteristics in different social milieus. Security and stocks are capitalist in a capitalist society and are used by capitalists to exploit workers. But they can, however, be "socialist" in a predominantly socialist milieu.' And it is the Party which decrees whether a 'milieu', or a 'society' for that matter, is socialist or not. Guided by Deng, in a gross departure from the classical Marxist theory, the party in fact soon decreed that China was 'currently in the primary stage of socialism' which may run for a 'long period of time'! An overall ideological slithering has occurred which suggests that provided China becomes a strong economic power, the socialist phraseology can be adjusted as the situation unfolds. In effect, not socialism any more but, as Bettleheim has pointed out, 'the legitimacy of the regime is now based upon modernisation as a national goal'. This modernisation essentially means the restoration of capitalism in China.

However, the indifference to theory has not been absolute. It never can be for a communist party, however much it may have degenerated politically. So, over the years, Deng Xiaoping's pragmatic turn to the market was elaborated and given the status of a theory, 'Deng Xiaoping theory', which was not lacking in reassurance for the emergent capitalism in China, its private enterprise and foreign investors. The theory was officially paralleled to Marx-Lenin-Maoism and in due course written into the Party Constitution as the guideline for party policies (Later, Jiang Zemin was to claim and get the same status for his pragmatism). After the death of Deng, the 15th Congress held in September 1997 proclaimed Deng's theory as the new 'ideological banner' of the Chinese Communist Party. From then on China's ideological lodestar was no longer to be just 'Marxism, Leninism and Mao Zedong Thought' but 'Marxism, Leninism, Mao Zedong Thought *and* Deng Xiaoping Theory' – that is till recently, when Jiang Zemin too has immortalised himself as a theoretician and a guide by adding his 'Important Thought of Three Represents'.

Unlike in the erstwhile Soviet Union, leadership in China has not sought to expressly break off or dissociate from Mao or the Maoist past. Even otherwise the changes dictated by the new course have been generally cautiously worded and hedged in by reference to socialist commitment, suggesting the party leadership's continuing need to retain legitimacy and to placate those insisting upon socialist orthodoxy. There has been the customary reiteration of 'Four Cardinal Principles': keeping to the socialist road, upholding the dictatorship of the proletariat, the leadership of the Communist Party, and Marxism-Leninism-Mao Zedong Thought. But the theoretical break that the additional 'Deng Xioping Theory' involved was already clear in the four modernisations of agriculture, industry, national defence, and science and technology which were made the official goal of national development by the post-Mao government in the late 1970s. Socialist construction did not find any place in the reforms initiated by Deng in the name of this so-called 'socialist modernisation'. Instead what followed was a reinstatement of private ownership and enterprise, drastic restructuring of production relations and opening up of China for massive inflow of foreign capital. Typical of this 'modernisation' was a denial of socialist relations in the workplace in favour of a hierarchical pattern of management in the Chinese economy. This is how Deng put it in a speech in 1978: 'Enterprises should institute the system in which the factory director or manager assumes overall responsibility under the leadership of the Party committee, and they should set up effective systems for directing production. The trade unions should teach their members to support the administrative leadership in their enterprises and to help maintain the full authority of those who direct production.' Consequently, not socialist ideology but the development of management education got priority in China in the 1980s. As the management expert Peter Drucker reported it, with the purpose of developing 'newer and different types of managerial skills' required for 'socialist modernisation,' China sought 'assistance and co-operation, in the field of management education, mainly from the US, Canada, the UK, other western European countries, Japan and some other south-east Asian countries.' Deng's socialism postulated its management the capitalist way.

When Deng's Four Modernisation programme was launched in 1978, it was announced that rapid development and growth would be achieved by 'using capitalism to develop socialism'. 'To develop the market economy under socialist conditions, so that the market will play a fundamental role in the allocation of resources under the state's macro regulation' – this is how the crux of Deng's theory has been described. A rather ambiguous formulation, in practice it has meant not a necessary and legitimate *use* of market in a socialist transition, that is, as part of a fundamentally *socialist* planning, but a state-supported market-based economic development. Deng's theorisation of his economic reforms assumed, *á la* Gorbachev, an automaticity and neutrality of the market which does away with any sense that socialism – in which politics, not market, commands economy – and market-led economic development are mutually exclusive.

A pragmatic response to China's backwardness, Deng's theory was not what it is often made out to be – a 'seeking truth from facts' or working from practical consideration as the

Chinese leadership emphasises or a triumph of 'realism' over theory or ideology as others have averred. It was a decisive turning away from the socialist path in China in favour of a market-led economic growth which in effect meant a capitalist development. The quintessence of Deng's theory was early articulated in his fabled cryptograms, at least two of which have since become classic – 'To get rich is glorious' and the already noted still more notorious, 'it does not matter whether the cat is white or black, as long as it catches the mice, it is a good cat'. Consequently it simply does not matter whether the cat is 'socialism with Chinese characteristics' or 'capitalism with Confucian colours' as it has been called, or anything else for that matter. As long as it works for China's development, it is to be regarded as a 'good-ism' – *hao zhuyi*. This is how Deng later put it during his famous 1992 trip to the south, the special economic zones based on the premise 'let some areas develop first,' counterpart of Deng's policy to let some people become rich first: 'The sole factor to be considered in determining the usefulness of a policy was whether it expedited economic growth, promoted productivity and boosted the comprehensive strength of the nation.' In Deng's theory socialism was reconceptualised, really conceptualised away, as an ideology of modernisation and economic development of China. It is significant but hardly surprising that the slogans released by the central committee of the Chinese Communist Party on the occasion of the 50th anniversary of the founding of the People's Republic of China had little socialism about them, but everything about the nature, aims and objectives of China as a modernising nation-state.

'Deng Xiaping Theory' had little to say on the subject but Deng's reforms had carried the promise of democracy to the Chinese people. The goal Deng forcefully proclaimed in his speech of August 18, 1980 to an enlarged session of the politbureau was 'to reform and perfect in a practical way the party and state systems and to ensure on the basis of those systems, the democratisation of the political life of the party and the state, the democratisation of economic management and the democratisation of the life of society as a whole.' The goal remains very distant. In the meantime Mao era's 'four big freedoms' to the people including the right to strike work have been dispensed with. Following Deng and then with Jiang Zemin and others at its head, Chinese leadership has ensured that, while socialism has been given the go-by, the state did not wither away as Gorbachev's Soviet Union did.

China's shift away from socialism has been accompanied by a covering rhetoric which seeks to assure the Chinese people that moves towards a market-oriented capitalist economy are a way to better achieve socialism, that what is being built is indeed socialism, albeit with so-called Chinese characteristics. The enemies are however clear-eyed about what is happening. There is the reflexive daily fare of American press where every Chinese move towards capitalism, every 'opening' so-called, is praised and Deng himself was *Time's* 'man of the year' twice. Maybe the Chinese people, however disoriented or helpless at the moment, are also beginning to see through it all. A foreign correspondent has reported this joke doing the rounds in Beijing:

> Three presidents – Bill Clinton of the United States, Boris Yeltsin of Russia and Jiang Zemin of China are each driving down a road, the story goes, and their three cars approach an intersection. Mr. Clinton turns right as does Mr. Yeltsin. But when Mr. Jiang reaches the crossroads he hesitates and asks his passenger, China's former leader Deng Xiaoping, which way to go. 'Signal left and turn right,' Mr. Deng replies bluntly.

Such indeed is the Dengist theory which, in the name of 'building socialism with Chinese characteristics' is guiding China on the road of capitalism. But as the correspondent reporting the joke has commented: 'But woe to anyone who thinks that China will make a seamless transition to a capitalist economy any time soon. Mr. Jiang may have turned right in the popular joke but his car is still far behind the others and his road is full of potholes.'

VIII

Dengist theorisation apart, the post-Mao leadership had still to contend with compulsions of its Marxist or socialist legacy, and its particular expression in Maoist theory for building socialism in China. The theory the Chinese leadership here opted for was an evasion of real issues. Central to these issues was the most important consequence of the already noticed 'trick' that history has played on the doctrine of Karl Marx: instead of socialism being built on a base provided by the economic, political and cultural achievements of capitalism, one backward country after another has been called upon to build it. In this context, classical Marxism had viewed the development of forces of production as the signal, indeed the historical task of capitalism, creating the necessary economic-material conditions for the construction of a now necessary and possible higher form of society, socialism, a society based on *socialist* relations of production. Faced with this historically unanticipated task, the post-revolutionary backward countries were confronted, so to speak, with the task of simultaneously developing the forces of production and building socialist relations of production, that is developing the forces of production in a socialist manner as part of the process of building a socialist society. Aberrations apart, this is how Lenin had visualised *his* socialist project for backward Russia during the brief period he survived the Russian revolution, and this is what Mao, better theorizing it, attempted in another still more backward Asian country, China. The post-Mao leadership did not merely evade the real issues here but did so by so using their Marxism as to theoretically rationalise and defend their essentially pragmatic turn to market and capitalism.

Instead of confronting the specific issues of socio-economic development in a backward country from the standpoint of a *socialist* transition, as Mao had done and which issues were a distinctive feature of the debates of the Maoist period within the Party and Chinese society – wherein Maoists recognized the legitimate need to develop the productive forces – the post-Mao leadership evaded them with recourse to a mechanistic, economistic interpretation of Marxist teaching on the subject of forces and relations of production. In the process they ignored that historical materialism is essentially a theory of epochal social change, it is not and cannot be, a tool of analysis and prescription for day-to-day policies. It simply does not have the resources for the purpose. For a society engaged in constructing socialism, together with a recognition of the objective economic situation, these policies are primarily a matter, not so much of economics as of socialist politics and ethical principles. As Mao, moving away from the Soviet model of development, had insisted, it is politics which commands in a transition to socialism. This insistence had found eloquent expression in Mao's various slogans during the Cultural Revolution. The call to '*Grasp revolution, promote production*' dialectically handled the relationship between socialist goal and economic development, between superstructure and the economic base. By the slogans '*keeping politics in command*' and '*never forget class struggle*', Mao sought to maintain a proper balance between the growth of the productive forces and the development of socialist production relations. His call to '*fight self, repudiate revisionism*', combined as it was with mass politics and campaign for struggle-criticism-transformation, was an attempt to foster revolutionary consciousness, go ever deeper and eradicate the bourgeois outlook from its very roots, to be able to develop both productive forces and socialist relations of production and build a socialist society. The new Chinese leadership instead chose to put economics in command, the ideal standpoint for a capitalist restoration. In their economistic interpretation of historical materialism, they turned to a theory which, though not original, lay within their easy reach. It was the good old 'theory of productive forces', whose authoritarian practices under Stalin had proved disastrous for the socialist project in the Soviet Union. Now the Chinese opted for it with the additional disadvantage of 'economic reform' which, going far beyond the introduction of a carefully controlled 'market', opened the Chinese economy wide to the forces of internal and global capitalism.

As the differences on the all-important question of socialist construction sharpened within the party, the Liu Shaochi-Deng faction saw the relation between the advanced production relations and backward productive forces as the principal contradiction in Chinese society, needing, in the first instance, to be resolved in favour of the latter if any progress along the road to socialism was to be sustained. Against the Maoist approach and much influenced by the Soviet model of industrialisation, they put primary, almost exclusive, emphasis on the development of productive forces, an emphasis which came into full play under Deng Xiaoping's leadership in post-Mao China. Policy debates of 1986-87 are quite instructive in this regard, particularly Zhao Ziyang's Report to the 13th National Congress in 1987 (an analysis or argument which is still regarded as correct, despite the fall from grace of its proponent). Zhao presented his analysis in terms of classical historical materialism. Put briefly his argumently was that the productive forces in China were fettered by the relations of production (structure of ownership, etc.) and therefore these relations (characterised by state ownership in industry, the Commune system in agriculture, central planning of national economy, and so on) need to be changed, that is, replaced by new relations of production (and devices like 'the market') more conducive to rapid economic development. Zhao's argument provided a supposedly Marxist rationale for the dismantling of one sector after another of China's socialist economic base. Reminiscent of Deng's 'cat and mouse' aphorism and his advocacy of 'using capitalism to develop socialism', it was consistent with the basic line adopted during the entire period of reform and has been supported by leading Chinese academics and theorists.

The argument was well premised on a recognition of both the backwardness of China where socialist revolution had occurred and therefore the legitimacy of the need to develop the forces of production for building up a successful socialist society. But it proceeded to postulate 'a very long primary stage of socialism', during which as Zhao, arguing for market-determined reform of relations of production, put it, 'the growth of the productive forces is the immediate and decisive criterion' in judging policy, so that the reforms can be considered socialist if they are a means to the development of the productive forces, which, it was insisted, is a precondition for the successful establishment of socialism. The errors of the past, beginning in the late 1950s, were located in 'mistaken left thinking', or commitment to 'the higher the level of social ownership the better', etc., which had 'relegated the task of expanding the productive forces to a position of secondary importance'. The need now was to recognise the growth of the productive forces as the sole criterion in judging the desirability of particular policies of reforms. It is this which settles the question of their desirability for the construction of socialism as well. In other words, whatever is conducive to this growth (of the productive forces) is in keeping with the fundamental interests of the people and is therefore needed by socialism and allowed to exist. Conversely, whatever is detrimental to this growth goes against scientific socialism and is therefore not allowed to exist.

This point of view earned its adherents the apt label of the 'whateverists' – whatever develops the productive forces is good for socialism. (This incidentally, compares and contrasts with another 'whateverist' position adopted by the Maoist Hua Guofeng – whatever Mao said was right).

It should be obvious that this 'whateverist' position – the only criterion for appropriateness of a policy is whether or not it will develop the forces of production – is nihilistic towards any kind of socialist considerations. For there is then no criterion independent of that to indicate whether or not any policy or suggested reform of the production relations might be considered non-socialist. At times this position has been argued for as a matter of trial and error, of 'feeling out the stepping stones in order to cross the river', but without saying anything about what river was being crossed. Most of the time the criterion has been spoken of as 'good economic results', but it has been so interpreted as to evaluate and include or approve everything, from the operation of casinos on Hainan Island to the 'open door' policy in the Chinese economy. On this view, regardless of the fact that it is precisely their abolition as relations of exploitation which is the *raison d'etre* of the socialist project, even the capitalist relations of production which do develop the productive forces, often faster, could be regarded as directly promoting socialism! And they indeed have come to be so regarded. It is significant that any discussion of whether China was moving towards socialism or capitalism was banned by a decree issued in 1992 – controversies of this kind are viewed as attempts by the anti-reform lobby to distract attention from the country's achievements and put obstacles in the way of increasing productivity.

Scholars have noticed that discussion of 'socialist values' has been conspicuously absent in the speeches or debates of the reforming Chinese leaders. Economist Rozman has pointed out that as early as 1979 the 'consensus of developing the productive forces at almost any cost had relegated themes like the "socialist spiritual civilisation" to a secondary level and allowed Deng to lead with an ideology that gives China wide scope for flexibility in economic reforms.' The 'ideological flexibility' has included a campaign to demonstrate that 'socialism is not egalitarianism', and egalitarian social relations have been seen as incompatible with the development of the forces of production. Given the monopoly on Marxism and production of official knowledge exercised by the Party elite and their entourage of officially sanctioned intellectuals, such departures from socialist values are defended in the name of Marxism itself. This is epitomised by a Lui Guoguang's pronouncement about the incompatibility of socialism and egalitarianism: 'Socialism promotes the development of the productive forces, whereas egalitarianism hinders them. Therefore socialism and egalitarianism are not compatible. This is not a new form in theory; but merely a reversal of the reversed Marxist truth.' 'Whether or not this statement makes sense is less important', Greenfield and Leong have commented, 'than the power with which the proposal to abandon all state policies directed at ensuring social equality achieves immunity from criticism by claiming to embody a "Marxist truth"'. Even when the moral ravage wrought by the logic of market reform is recognised and the leadership gets worried about 'spiritual pollution', Marxist analysis of this logic and reiteration of socialist values are taboo. There is nothing surprising in the leadership's reaction to Wang Ruoshui's famous essay, 'In defence of humanism', written in 1983. Drawing upon *Communist Manifesto's* critique, Wang had written of market 'transforming the dignity of human beings into exchange value' and 'leaving no bond between human beings other than naked interest and unfeeling cash transactions', and concluded: 'Marx all along connected proletarian revolution and communism with questions of human values, dignity, emancipation, and freedom.' The official response was not a debate on these issues, but Wang's dismissal as deputy editor of the *People's Daily*, in a campaign against 'spiritual pollution'. (Suppression has been the regime's typical response when faced with inconvenient theoretical issues or questioning of Party's official position. A journal, *Zhen Li De Zhuiqui* (The Pursuit of Truth) was recently ordered to be shut down for being critical of Jiang's so-called theory of 'Three Represents'). Indifference to or abandonment of socialist values apart, in the name of developing the forces of production, planning has continued to increasingly give way to the market forces. There is no recognition at all that in any socialist construction, it is politics which commands the economy and not the other way around, and that socialist planning is not merely a form of economic organisation but an instrument of class power over society, the imposition of *democratic* decisions upon the economy so that it could be shaped to achieve the interests of the common people, which is after all what socialism is about. Without such planning a socialist project is simply impossible. To return to Deng's aphorism: that the cat is achieving its goal is unquestionable, it still remains to be asked what will be the deeper nature of the animal as it richly transforms itself on what it feeds?

In the meantime, while socialist ideology or values are pushed out of sight, except for occasional ritualistic purposes, capitalist ideology or values are taking over. Individual pursuit of prosperity is encouraged, the people are exhorted to 'enrich themselves', 'to be rich is glorious' asserts a Deng Xiaoping. In Shenzen, the town chosen by him as a major showcase of his economic pragmatism, a million Chinese from the interior invade it in a mad scramble for shares at the country's second authorised stock exchange after Shanghai, and even the best of the disillusioned youth are left with no aspirational model other than the supposedly liberal democratic advanced capitalism. The 'breathtaking' economic progress of China is iridescent with the values and ideology of a transition to capitalism. What was once referred to as 'undeveloped socialism', is now being spoken of as 'primary stage of socialism', a stage which will last a long time before socialism is attained. But the way the capitalist development and ideology have taken over, this already makes little sense. And if this 'primary stage is supposed to last a long time, at least 100 years on Zhao's reckoning, one wonders what indeed of socialism, of its vision, promise or motive force will be left at the end of this 'primary stage of socialism'!

Construction of socialism anywhere demands, as Marxism always postulated and Mao had insisted, that politics should be in command, that socialist politics and morality and not economics or the market should govern the organisation and development of the economy. As against this, the 'theory of productive forces' adopted by the post-Mao Chinese leadership in confronting the problems of socialist transition in a backward country, once again, as in the ex-Soviet Union, puts economics in command, a theoretical choice most favourable for capitalistic development – and a choice which has decisively contributed to the defeat of socialism in our times. In the intellectual climate resulting from this choice, the very meaning of socialism has been effectively lost in China. As a socialist economist, examining the policy debates of 1986-87, has observed: 'the idea of socialism had become so diluted that it would have been hard to identify an anti-socialist proposal unless its author labeled it as such... among the economic reformers, even proposals for privatisation and marketisation of the economy were cast as versions of socialism.' The authoritative labelling in fact was and is still being done by the Chinese Communist Party, self-identified as the builder and defender of socialism. In other words, if the reform process or the policies pursued remain strictly under the control of the Party or the Party guarantees that they *are* socialist, and not a restoration of capitalism, they stand certified as socialist. This is how the Chinese leadership has been certifying the construction of 'socialism with Chinese characteristics', even as, with the authority provided by the coercive organs of state power, it also identifies itself as Marxist, with additional claims to Leninism and Mao Zedong Thought as well. But neither logic nor historical experience can justify this political position, especially after what happened in the ex-Soviet Union. There was a party that self-identified itself as communist, Marxist and Leninist, which it was not, that self-identified the system it presided over as socialism, which it was not in any meaningful Marxist sense, and it is largely a section of the leadership that once self-identified as communist, which got and remains busy restoring capitalism in Russia. There are remarkable parallels in the situation of China today and the ex-Soviet Union including the communist leaderships' turn to market-oriented reforms which have already led to the universally accepted restoration of capitalism in Russia. Merely because a party defining itself as communist is in power does not make China a socialist country, any more than it did in the Soviet Union with Gorbachev or before him. We may well be witnessing in China the historical irony of a Communist Party in power (for how long remains uncertain) supervising a transition to capitalism!

IX

This transition, as 'economic reform', began and proceeded with dismantling the Mao era socialism-oriented structures and policies, establishing new private forms of ownership and control in the economy including changed production relations and increasing replacement of planning with reliance on the market. Described variously as 'modernisation' or 'market socialism', initially the 'reform' was supposed to be carried out within strict limits set on private exploitation, especially as to the hiring of labour, etc. But the logic of a market-led growth, its reliance on individual entrepreneurship or initiative to stimulate production cannot be kept within such limits and the 'reformers' typically turned, along with accelerated privatisation and marketisation, to foreign capital and the development of special economic zones. The limits placed on exploitative class relations in the economy simply broke down to give way to an effective transition to capitalism. As this transition has gathered momentum, apart from benefitting the elites, it has also led to the growth of a broadly based 'middle class' among both peasants and urban entrepreneurs which, limited though their proportion of the population may be – estimates vary – has provided a certain popular backing for a new order, which new order has also been sought to be better secured through changes in China's constitution. Thus, for example, 'state economy' soon stood changed to 'state-owned economy' so that the state sector too was now subject to the market and 'open to the outside world', 'the private sector of the economy (was allowed) to exist and develop within limits prescribed by law', and 'privately owned economies' (of individuals or foreign capital) were declared to be 'important constituent sections of China's socialist market economy' – and a recent amendment has made private property 'inviolable'. 'The State practices a planned economy on the basis of socialist public ownership' gave place to the now familiar term 'socialist market economy' and the expression 'socialism with Chinese characteristics,' a favourite of Deng Xiaoping that has come to mean capitalism through the back door, was enshrined in the preamble of the Chinese constitution.

China's 'economic reform' took off as being made up of two interrelated but separate parts, the rural 'reform' and urban 'reform'. It is no accident that the reformers' early efforts focused on the former, involving as it did the peasantry, the potential petty bourgeoisie par excellence, the segment of the Chinese population most susceptible to their appeal, especially the better off elements among them with their historically inherited class enthusiasm for individual ownership and production, and for sales in the private market. For this very reason the rural 'reform' initially appeared to be rather popular among sections of peasantry and provided the reforming rulers an important political-social base in the early eighties (which partly explains why the peasants took a rather indifferent or neutral position at a critical time in 1989). The rural 'reform' basically involved the dismantling of the Commune system and its replacement by the 'individual household responsibility system'. And the changes were enforced across the board by forcibly breaking up even those communes which were succeeding and had wide mass support. In late 1970s, comprehensive studies carried out by Central Committee's Research Group on Agrarian Policy had concluded: 30 per cent of collective villages were doing well, 40 per cent had problems but remained viable, and 30 per cent were doing poorly – that is, 240 million peasants were truly prosperous under collectives, another 320 million were holding their own, and only 240 million were faring badly. This clearly showed that starting from a scratch, history and economy wise, the rural cooperative movement was growing successfully in China and that, contrary to conventional wisdom, cooperation between equal small holders is not only natural but necessary for their economic, social and cultural advancement. China's reforming rulers however interpreted this growing success as a failure, and, as William Hinton has reported:

> Stressing the fact that many villages were still stagnating, which was true, and reiterating the theory that cooperation and agriculture were by nature mismatched, which was not true (but served the interests of those who opposed the socialist transformation to begin with) the Deng 'reformers' began dissolving collectives wholesale, beginning at places where communes, brigades, and teams were least successful. Using every means of pressure and persuasion, especially credit, farm supply, and tax policies that discriminated against collectives, they kept this drive going until they had almost entirely privatized agricultural production in China and dismantled a system that had taken almost thirty years to build.

This dismantling of the collectives was accompanied by changes in the agrarian law to make it possible for long-term leasing of land, thereby opening up the possibility of 'individual households' leasing out land to the upwardly mobile, 'get rich quick' peasants among them – the classic process whereby rich peasants and capitalist farmers emerge. The 'reformers' indeed saw the rich farmer as the agent of agricultural development in China. As for the rest of Chinese peasantry, the 'reformers' rediscovery of petty peasant economy as the panacea for all the ills of the agrarian sector meant being dispossessed of their land and thrown on the mercy of the market. Official propaganda celebrates that thanks to reform, the peasants are now liberated from their traditional dependence on land. Millions of peasants find, however, that they are liberated simply to be unemployed.

This draws our attention to what is perhaps the final significance of the rural 'reform' which lies not in the undoubted initial impetus it gave to agricultural production, but in its relation to the 'reform' in the urban sector. After 1984, the initial agricultural 'miracle' almost disappeared and the peasants' living standard virtually stagnated, even declined. But China's new urban capitalist economy grew at the highest rate in the world. This growth, it needs to be noted, has been all along based on the 'surplus' labour in the countryside, that is, peasantry released to be free labour by the agricultural reform. In the early 1980s China already had a 'surplus' labour force of over 100 million in the countryside. It is this large reserve army of labour which allowed China to develop capitalism, by developing 'rural enterprises' (TVEs, that is Township and Village Enterprises) and private enterprises, and by bringing in foreign capital. Without this 'surplus' labour, the Chinese rulers would have had to wage an immediate struggle against the working class – by no means an easy task – before proceeding down the road of capitalist development. Instead they had this new proletariat available to them – millions of hardworking migrant workers, men and women from the poor rural areas and known as *mingong* (literally peasant work) which is an abbreviation of the category 'worker with peasant status', that is, an employee without an urban residence permit. Working in big cities and Special Economic Zones (SEZs), they are there solely on the understanding that they sell their labour power and otherwise count for nothing. This new proletariat is much less self-conscious, much less militant, than the old proletariat of the state-owned enterprises. For them, even the most elementary civil rights, so beloved of 'reforming' intellectuals, do not exist, not to mention socialist rights – the iron rice bowl (job security, health care, pension or social security, etc.), initially available to the old proletariat. This large reserve army of labour plays a crucial role in keeping the labour force cheap, docile and vulnerable which is the cornerstone of Chinese capitalist prosperity.

When the 'reforms' were in turn introduced in the urban areas, they again began with the promotion of small scale entrepreneurship. But over the years private entrepreneurs have reappeared in a big way in China's industrial sector (there were hardly any a couple of decades back). The urban and industrial sectors of the economy have come to be placed under the control of the market forces and profit put in command of production in every sphere. Public sector has been getting a raw deal. The policy is to progressively unload the bulk of China's state-owned enterprises (SOEs). They are being leased or sold out. There is a significant willingness to allow enterprises to shed workers or go bankrupt and pass into private hands – bankruptcy has been even considered 'glorious' and the Chinese government's eagerness to enter the WTO has been viewed by scholars as partly propelled by 'the hope that competitive pressures from foreign capital will weed out state industries without having itself to take responsibility for their fate'. Privatisation is not merely a part of public policy, it is exalted as the way forward. There is a continuous enlargement of the capitalist sector in the economy under the patronage of the Chinese Communist Party, a capitalist sector which is making full use of the infrastructure and the industrial base created by the previous socialist development. Special Economic Zones (SEZs) in South China and Township and Village Enterprises (TVEs) in the countryside have been the catalysts of China's progress along the capitalist road. In 1980 four southern coastal cities (Shanton, Shenzhen, Zianmen, Zhuhai) were designated Special Economic Zones. These zones are a category in themselves, which are essentially exempt from any central planning and where the government has taken every care to attract foreign capital by providing cheap land and other infrastructure, all sorts of economic concessions along with cheap labour with minimum obstacles in the form of strict labour laws. Township and Village Enterprises (*Xiangzhen qiye*), which originated in the commune brigade enterprises (*shedui qiye*) of the 1950s but are now set-ups engaged in profit making and unrestrained accumulation, have proliferated as part of the explosive growth of private and semi-private enterprises in China mid-eighties onward. Symbolic, as it were, of the new ethos of the changed times, the People's Liberation Army which only two decades back joined the workers and peasants in their productive activities in various ways, itself went into the business of money-making and transformed itself into another business empire, equivalent to a multinational corporation, with interests in almost every lucrative sector of the economy (from pharmaceuticals to transportation, mining and real estate) and ownership of thousands of factories, not only manufacturing drugs, or cars, trucks, motor cycles and passenger aircraft, or refrigerators, television and pianos but opening five star hotels and running hundreds of motels and assorted entertainment joints as well. That is, till President Jiang Zemin's political compulsions led him to order the army to divest themselves of (that is privatise) their civilian holdings.

With the governing maxim of not bothering oneself about the colour of the cat so long as it catches mice, 'economic reform' has meant the adoption of an open door policy for the entry of foreign capital in China. 'Opening to the outside world', often in the name of acquiring new scientific and technical knowledge, is now a cardinal principle of China's economic policies, leading to a massive influx of foreign capital in the Chinese economy. China's interaction with and participation in the global economy has taken the form of its production, including the industrial, becoming increasingly and substantially export-oriented. The gradual relaxation of the terms for foreign investment, which, having started out reserving majority control for Chinese capital, have ended up welcoming enterprises that are wholly foreign-owned on almost any terms and almost anywhere they want to settle. The incentives provided to foreign investment and exemption from regulation or control that domestic state enterprises are still subject to, only enhances the advantageous position of the foreign capitalists. Significant in accelerating the capitalist transformation of China has been the dynamic of the diaspora, that is, the contribution of the non-resident Chinese. The bulk of the massive foreign capital for investment in the Free Export Zones of South China has come from Chinese expatriates based abroad. Hong Kong has played a vital role in the expansion of foreign inward investment and Chinese exports. Even more importantly, with some three million people in Guangdong province working for orders from Hong Kong, it is now being lauded as a successful demonstration of the benefits of the market-place. Once described as an earthly hell where the poor lived in 'deep fire and icy water', nowadays Hong Kong is being held up as an economic role model for Chinese cities. China's use of direct foreign investment and the related international borrowing as well as commodity trade, its overall shift to export-led economic development, are indicative of a degree and type of participation in the world economy entirely different from the Maoist period.

According to the government, the state-owned sector still plays a central and indispensable role in the Chinese economy. This, together with China's Township and Village Enterprises, representing another form of 'collective ownership', are often viewed as evidence of China's continuing adherence to socialism. The latter have even been assessed or lauded by sympathetic scholars abroad, including the well-known market-socialist Roemer, as providing a possible model for the future of socialism. In this regard two brief observation are in order. In the first place, two odd decades of 'reform' have witnessed a continuous dwindling of the importance of state-owned sector in China's economy. Forced to compete in the global market for which they were never organised, facing worker's resistance to the de-institutionalisation of their rights and increasingly denied the governmental support on which they had previously depended, the state-owned enterprises have been suffering losses or lagging behind and therefore subject to 'reform' by bankruptcies, forced mergers, factory closures, leasing or selling out, private shareholding in them or a new shareholding structure called *gufenhua* (a limited form of privatisation by which state-owned enterprises are supposed to sell shares to their workers). The end result of this 'reform' has been a continuous process of state-owned enterprises passing into private hands. Even otherwise, while workers in state-owned enterprises have continued to resist privatisation, they have been unable to resist *de facto* privatisations which have been carried out through sub-contracting, out-sourcing or the formation of partnerships with local and foreign capital. The state-owned enterprises have been, thus, steadily losing their once predominant status in the economy. As for the Township and Village Enterprises, spoken of as 'collective enterprises', the vast majority of them are now known to be privately owned, and even otherwise they are, as a scholar, Richard Smith, has argued, effectively capitalist enterprises. The local officials who are assumed to exercise the property rights of TVEs are often closely aligned to, and sometimes even appointed by local capitalists, and the desire to attract foreign capital has led to their being directly linked with foreign capital through joint ventures and subcontracting as well as restructuring of the state to facilitate the influx and expansion of foreign capital. In this fusion of local and foreign capital interests, most joint ventures between TVEs and foreign capital (mostly Hong Kong based capital) have boards of directors in which foreign partners are dominant or there are agreements in which strategic control of the enterprise is held by foreign capital. Needless to add that with both SOEs and TVE 'collective enterprises', the prime concern is maximisation of profit in their enterprises.

In the second place, and more importantly, state-ownership does not necessarily mean socialist ownership. A state-sector is not only compatible with a capitalist system, it is often found necessary for its more effective functioning. The absence of declared private ownership or its articulation in legal institutional arrangements does not rule out the possibility of effective private possession and control of production. As I have argued in an earlier chapter, we need to make, with Marx, a distinction between nominal, legal-institutional or *de jure* ownership and *real* ownership. The issue with any form of state or supposedly 'collective' ownership is one of effective possession and control of production, more specifically, control over production and use of societal surplus on the one hand and the conditions of production on the other. In China's state-owned enterprises, workers, that is the direct producers have no control over the production and use of their surplus, there is no democracy about whatever central planning China still retains. Similar is the case with the TVEs where it is the managers who exercise effective private control over the accumulation and distribution of surplus as profit. As regards the conditions of production, the nature of the labour process or the structure of power and authority at the point of production, once again, both in the SOEs and TVEs, the workers have no control over the conditions under which they labour – there is no democracy on the shop floor or, for that matter, in the local political setting or at the national level.

Using Steve Smith's rather infelicitous expression 'technicist Bolshevism' – a version of Taylorism which underpins the regime of labour control in what is often described as the Stalinist model of industrialisation – Gerard Greenfield and Apo Leong have written:

> Technicist-Bolshevism demanded greater control over the organisation of production and the labour process by a managerial and technical elite presiding over a 'backward' and 'undisciplined' proletariat which had yet to achieve a higher stage of class consciousness. The bargaining process which developed at the point of production involved a mixture of coercion and consent – with a decisive shift to coercion in the pursuit of Taylorist productivity. Combined with the bureaucratic intervention of the Party-state and trade union apparatus to enforce discipline, this regime of production alienated workers and generated quotidian forms of resistance which found expression in laziness, indiscipline, theft, absenteeism – 'irrational' acts interpreted as proof of the need to give managers absolute power to break workers' resistance to the ever-increasing pace and intensity of work. It is precisely the consolidation of this managerial-technicism and the reassertion of control over labour that underlies market reforms.

Beginning with the early 'director responsibility system', what we have in China is a continuing consolidation of the power of managers and their exclusionary control over production, exercised in close alignment with Party officials, and official trade unions. Ban on workers' right to strike has been supplemented by the freedom of managers to hire and fire workers (making for 'flexibility of the market' as the IMF-WB have it). While material incentives (such as piece-rates, bonuses, contract work, etc.) have been reintroduced to secure factory discipline and intensified exploitation of workers, the unconditional drive for maximising labour productivity has given a centrality to new systems of discipline and direct repression in controlling workers, which are most visible in the factory regimes involving foreign investment, their hyper exploitation of women and displaced migrant workers. As Greenfield and Leong have described it:

> In foreign-invested factories and joint ventures a strict regime of discipline is encoded in workers' contracts and notices are posted in factories listing fines and physical punishments for speaking or drinking water during working hours, being late, wearing name tags incorrectly, sitting or resting, going to the toilet too often, and so on. In a factory where there is a complex system of 46 rules and regulations, 80 per cent of the workers are fined monthly. This system is policed by private security guards and officers of the Public Security Bureau and local militias with a wider system of surveillance that relies on 'bird-cage management systems' (where workers are locked in factories and dormitories) and other forms of physical control and isolation both during and after working hours.

(In view of the claims made for them by 'market socialists', it may be specifically mentioned that the TVEs, particularly the joint-venture TVEs, share these deteriorated 'relations of production in the workplace', just as they have not been immune to such related phenomena as child labour, exploding factories, forced overtime, the 'freedom' to fire workers, and so on).

While the Special Economic Zones had the early benefit of a fully 'liberalised' system of labour employment, China's reformers had a specific 'problem' in securing the responsiveness of labour to free market forces in the state-owned enterprises, namely, the systems of job security (the iron rice bowl) and egalitarian wages ('eating from the same big pot') inherited from the Mao era. These were obviously seen as hindering productivity and undermining incentive to work, that is restricting the reformers' ability to extract maximum surplus value. A major barrier to China's capitalist development, the iron rice bowl, had to be broken and egalitarianism in wages discarded. Given the workers' resistance, the struggle over this 'problem' remained at the centre of the so-called 'economic reform' for a long time. It was only in 1996 that the institutionalised rights of workers were finally abolished with a final shift towards the privatisation or liquidation of state and collective enterprises. The 15th Congress of the Chinese Communist Party formally decided to push ahead with wholesale dismantling of the state sector and promotion of private enterprise. Jiang Zemin argued that socialism in China was in its very primary stage which would continue 'for a very long time' and it was officially stated that from now on the private sector would be 'an important' part of (China's) market economy.' As the *Economist* later put it: 'The 15th Congress in the autumn of 1997, was a watershed. It marked the start of this new phase with the suggestion that tens of thousands of small and medium-sized state enterprises would be cast loose upon private waters, to float or sink. In the spring of 1999, guarantees that acknowledge the private sector for the first time were written into the Constitution.'

The predominance of local and foreign private capital in shaping the labour process in China has seen unemployment reaching tens of millions and egalitarianism knocked out of its wage structure. As President Jiang saw the future: 'Inevitably there will be temporary lay offs and interim difficulties for the workers'. But as unemployment has surged and not only temporarily, official theorists have not been wanting in hailing workers' 'liberation' from bureaucratic controls and lauding virtues of 'free labour market' which guarantees workers their 'freedom' to work for individual rewards. Overcoming received 'theoretical obstacles', socialist theory has been 'rethought', that is, turned upside down, to argue in defence of commodification of labour power under socialism. As for the system of egalitarian wages, on the ground that 'socialism is not egalitarianism', the legitimate principle of distribution during the period of socialist transition – 'to each according to his work' – has been so interpreted as to justify the dismantling of the egalitarian wage policies and legitimise the ever growing income disparities in society. Lin Zili, one of the leading theorists of China's economic reforms, has even sought to justify such dismantling and the creation of a free labour market by doing away with the very notion of exploitation – and this in the name of Marx and Lenin!

If not much socialism is now left in China's economy (its state-owned and collective enterprises, the conditions of work and living conditions of its workers and peasants), with the market imperatives driving the Chinese economy on, there is even less socialism left in China's 'central planning'. Indeed, what the government does mean by socialism today seems to be mainly what it calls 'macro-economic' control and regulations of the emerging market. But insofar as China is already a market economy, so powerful is its market drive that it seems often to be outside the control of government. As in other market-led economies, the state stands reduced to being essentially reactive to changes generated elsewhere. What passes for 'macro-economic control' is at times little more than imposing some limits on private profiteering, manipulation and corruption, similar to the restrictions introduced in most of the leading capitalist countries after their earlier 'Robber Baron' stages. In fact, the way China's necessarily uneven development of market economy is taking place, it is leading to a peculiar economic and political decentralisation and a noticeable decline of national authority. In what has been called a 'centrifugal spin', provinces and townships have tended to become largely autonomous economic units, giving tax concessions to attract investment in competition with others, retaining their taxes and revenues, that is, building their own economies. There is a recognisable growth of regional 'overlordism', uniting party and state officials, business interests and the local military leadership and threatening national disintegration – the recurring nightmare of Chinese history which is posing its own problems for the authorities in Beijing.

X

At the moment China's market reforms and opening to the world economy do seem to have worked 'miracles'. Conventional economic indices – relating to rate of growth, direct foreign investment, foreign exchange reserves, trade surpluses, etc. – mark China out as the world's fastest growing large economy, (now the third largest economy in the world); its growth is claimed to be comparable to the industrial revolution in England. The accompanying rise in net per capita income reflects the higher living standards this growth has brought to large sections of the Chinese people, part of Asia's post-colonial middle class which according to the *Economist* is creating 'some of the biggest business and financial opportunities in history' for 'far-sighted Western firms'. Bearing witness to China's phenomenal economic success is the 'giddy euphoria' over it of western ideologues of free market, economic individualism and mass consumerism. *The New York Times* has gushed: 'There is not an adjective that soars high enough or detonates with enough force to describe China's economic explosion or the promise of its future. One-fifth of humanity, for decades locked in the dungeon of Mao Zedong's proletarian revolution, where they were whipped and exhausted by meaningless mass movements, are now fully unleashed in an epic pursuit of material wealth...The Chinese are buying, building and consuming as if there were no tomorrow.' That Chinese reformers prefer to speak of it as 'socialism with Chinese characteristics', or that Mao-era inheritance, including the Communist Party led-state, has not only contributed to the 'explosion' being celebrated but also enabled the Chinese reformers, so far, to exercise a degree of control over the reform process as well as avoid 'explosion' of another kind, does not take much away from the 'miracle' that 'the market' has worked in China.

It is not my concern to deny or eulogise China's 'miracle' which is there, freely available to anyone who wants to look for it. It has in fact so seized hold of the imagination of everyone on the right, and even on the Left, that anyone who does not buy in is looked upon with astonishment, pity, even ill-disguised contempt as an old-fashioned socialist. Nor am I concerned here with the future of this 'miracle', that is, China's ability to sustain its present pattern and rate of growth for long, except to say that it remains highly problematic. The economic contradictions and political strain generated within by the new dispensation are already compelling the Chinese rulers to go slow, think anew of social security system and development of the poor non-coastal western regions, and so on – without however giving up the more than two-decade old reform programme. In many ways, more important in making the present course problematic are, perhaps, the problems posed from without. China has finally joined the world economy after decades of trying to do something else (form a 'socialist world market' with Moscow, pursue Maoist self-reliance) but done so essentially as another 'Asian tiger', modeled particularly on Singapore under Lee Kwan Yew or South Korea under Park Chung Hee; once upon a time there was even talk of Guangdong catching up with the 'four dragons' (Hong Kong, Taiwan, South Korea and Singapore). To put it more specifically, China's swift growth has been largely propelled, like its South and East Asian predecessors, by exports. The recent experience – the financial turmoil in South and East Asia and the consequent crises racking the national economies in the region – surely raises crucial queries about the future of the Chinese 'miracle'. Having joined the global economy, China, by the very nature of its 'economic reforms', will face the consequences of its up and down swings, cyclic downturns and crises. Even if it is able to weather the storm upto a point, it cannot escape its 'recessions' and 'heating ups', its cyclical logic of booms and bursts. Increasingly dependent as its growth has been on foreign capital, the essential unreliability of international capitalism's drive to maximise profit has its own problems for China. Information technology having made it possible to move capital swiftly between production sites in search of cheaper labour and raw materials, there is no guarantee that the massive production of labour intensive goods in China will remain unchanged. China has every reason to worry about competition from potentially cheaper and more profitable production sites. There are already reports of foreign investors intending to move production from South China, where the booming economy is already pushing labour costs up, to Vietnam. Again, given the power of established economies, China's hope to penetrate and challenge them is no better than a dream. Instead, the overall situation China faces is one of ever-sharpening competition in the world's ever shrinking markets. This apart, the established economic powers, particularly United States and Japan are already torn between the attempt to capture the still-spreading markets of China on the one hand and to prevent it from emerging as a major competitor on the other. They would like to both exploit and contain the Chinese economy at the same time. This compels attention to the fact that integrated into the world capitalist economic system, China still lies at its periphery. However swift or 'miraculous' China's economic growth, its overall character, duly reinforced by its ideological-cultural fall out, has far from changing only confirmed China's peripheral location. This puts a question mark over China's ability to stand up to such 'containment', that is, retain whatever economic initiative, autonomy or independence of decision-making it still has.

Be that as it may, the impressiveness of economic growth does not by itself legitimise it as socialist, even if it is presided over by a communist party paying obeisance to Marx, Engels, Lenin (and Mao Zedong Thought). As we have argued above, economic growth in the sense of development of productive forces was seen by classical Marxism as the historical role and achievement of capitalism, providing the necessary economic conditions for transition to a higher stage of society where socialist relations of production are the basis of a exploitation-free, egalitarian and humane society – which capitalist society is not and cannot be. Backwardness of China confronted the Chinese communists with the task of developing the production forces along with the development of socialist production relations as part of building a socialist society. This is precisely what is *not* happening in China's economic growth. Instead, dismantling whatever socialism they had previously built in the Mao era, the Chinese communists have taken the capitalist road to first overcome their country's backwardness. 'Socialism with Chinese charactristics'is turning out to be 'capitalism with Chinese characteristics'. This point is important to make and repeat because in the current climate of 'free market delirium', enthusiasm for China's market reforms extends even to many on the Left. Rather than recognise what is really happening in China, and the evasion of the real problem it involves, they are either wishfully giving the benefit of doubt to the Chinese communists, or, forgetting what socialism is about, have taken to discoursing about such things as entrepreneurship, market efficiency and economic rationality. Some are even applauding China's market-oriented township and village industries (TVEs) as models of 'egalitarian' 'market socialism' – when, away from their origins in the Mao era, they are now not only market-governed, profit-oriented, most often *de facto* or otherwise privatised enterprises, but are also increasingly being sold-off or merged with bigger enterprises, or otherwise losing out to the bigger players in the market place. Yet others are dogmatically asserting: 'China is not simply a case of successful state-led development, it is an example of successful socialist state-led development.'

China, for the present at least, has taken the capitalist road; the policies pursued as 'market reform' have been leading to development of capitalism in China. Being led by the Communist Party does not by itself make the reform process socialist. State or public ownership in or of itself is not socialist ownership. It is wrong to identify state ownership (or nationalisation) with socialism, a degree of public control of the means of production is by no means incompatible with their capitalistic exploitation. Even with formal state or other forms of public ownership, effective management and control of enterprises can pass on to private individuals, as has indeed been happening in China, giving rise, as it were, to a state-based bourgeoisie existing alongside domestic and foreign capitalists. The state-owned enterprises in China are now run in ways which are not easily distinguishable from those of capitalism, and the surplus produced by the direct producers in these enterprises is appropriated and disposed of by those who, by virtue of their possession of political power, manage and control these enterprises. Borrowing Deng's aphorism, one can today well ask of the Chinese situation: does it really matter if a regime calls itself red or white so long as it exploits the working class? The still high percentage of state-ownership in the economy and the continuing direct investment by the government, the use of the state for regional and sectoral redistribution and a degree of macro-economic control together with sundry other such activities of the state, far from reflecting any socialist concerns suggest a disturbing resemblance to the 'guided capitalism' of more than one country in South and East Asia. And the way this capitalism is coming up – what with the use of state as a base for personal profiteering, the wielding of official power to accumulate private wealth, rent-seeking and plundering privatisation of public assets, the all pervasive corruption and nepotism – it has not only its analogues of 'primitive accumulation', it is also rapidly acquirin a grey economy of its own.

XI

The growth of capitalism in China, initiated by the Communist Party leadership, and fostered by foreign investment led by the non-resident Chinese has already produced its inevitable consequences, above all an unequal and uneven economic development, which is the structural logic of a capitalist economy. The privatisation in agriculture has produced apparently remarkable results but, as already evident, with doubtful future, since it is to the detriment of the bases for long term growth in so populous a country as China. Rural poor have been recreated, even a degree of feudalism is back, and in a process of accelerated urbanisation, tens of millions of peasants have migrated to the cities, adding to the ever-increasing number of unemployed resulting from the privatisation and reforms of the state-owned enterprises in the industrial sector. The market economy has been relentless in its revenge on Mao's much pampered peasantry, just as it has given short shrift to the vast labour force in the industrial sector. There is the emergence of regional economic imbalances and increasing poverty in the backward hinterland provinces. The acceleration of industrial growth has been focused on the coastal areas (Special Economic Zones) for their greater economic potential, widening the income differences between coastal regions and inland regions (There is considerable resentment at the higher standards of living observed among the beneficiaries of economic reform in the SEZs, which have been isolated from the rest of China, most obviously by barbed wire fences.) This is only an aspect of the unevenness of economic development in the country as a whole which, accompanied by the decentralisation of economic decision-making, has created powerful provincial interests, even comprador fiefdoms, raising doubts about Beijing's capacity to impose, even if it wanted, any new direction upon the economy. This unevenness of development has its disturbing implications for the 'nationalities question' in China, particularly in view of the break-up of the Soviet Union. These considerations apart, capitalist development has meant, along with widespread unemployment mentioned above, intensified income disparities, enforced underconsumption as the counterpart of the export surge, consumerism among the privileged that sharpens the social divisions in society, the ethics of making money fast and loose, and extraordinary corruption (reminiscent of Kuomintang before 1949) that a combination of free market and bureaucratic state control (of prices, quotas etc.) inevitably generates, with the *nomenklatura* graduating to nomenkleptocracy and a half of the country's money supply bought and sold underground, etc. etc. Added to all this are the ecological costs that market economy necessarily entails, with the multinationals coming in for toxic dumps and location of polluting industries.

The beneficiaries of the capitalist advance are the party-state bureaucracy, communist leaders turned 'bureaucratic capitalists' and their relatives, sons and daughters, along with foreign investors and private Chinese entrepreneurs, the latter two groups supplying the capital necessary for economic success in general, and for bureaucratic enrichment in particular. The losers are the people, above all the workers and peasants, who are paying the heavy economic and social costs of this restoration of capitalism. Among the costs is the growing loss of the gains of the past. Enumerated by Mark Selden some years back these gains included: the elimination of all major property-based inequalities and substantial reductions in intra-village and intra-urban inequality; elimination of foreign control of core elements of modern industry, trade and finance; gains in agricultural output outpacing China's growing population; gains for the industrial working class, including lifetime job security, generous pension and welfare benefits, heightened social status as well as modest gains in per capita household incomes; significant national gains in nutrition and life expectancy and rising basic levels of education and health care.

Most of these gains have already been lost or seriously undermined as a consequence of market-based reforms and turn to capitalism. For example, the communal health services in rural areas have been virtually decimated. This is directly linked to the big push towards market-based allocations in the Chinese rural economy, leading, among other things, to a dramatic fall in organisational support and financial security for public health services and communal medical insurance for rural population – which only brings out the inherent limitations of 'the market' when it comes to providing for 'public goods' or social welfare. Just when agricultural output has boomed and GNP growth rate stimulated in the years following the reforms in 1978, mortality rates in China have also gone up and life expectancy at birth has declined. Deterioration of health services has been accompanied by deterioration in the areas of socialised education; job security gone, unemployment has reappeared in a society which seemed to have decisively moved away from it; inequalities and income disparities have worsened in the city and countryside and between them; new property-based inequalities have emerged and gender-related discrimination in the provision of public and private goods has grown – all of which has cut deep into the earlier solidarities of daily social life. Unequal and uneven economic development has also given rise to new urban enclaves of private wealth and consumerism, and 'open door' has brought in not only profiteering foreign capital but also the entire baggage of the decadent culture of late capitalism in the West.

XII

China's progress along the capitalist road in the name of building 'socialism with Chinese characteristics' has consequences and aspects which, though already mentioned, need to be particularly noticed. The most obvious of these is the emergence of an increasingly polarised society. Three decades ago China was the most equal nation in the world. Now it is on the road to become one of the most unequal. Deng Xiaoping had opined that if some people got rich owing to their skills and enterprise, over time others too would benefit from the expanding economy. But this – the so-called 'trickle down' – has not happened. The material benefits, to which the apologists of the 'market reforms' regularly draw our attention, are by no means equally distributed. Instead, they are accompanied by increasing economic and social inequalities, a most skewed distribution of income and assets. According to a 1997 survey of urban household incomes, 45 per cent of respondents experienced a decline in income. In mid-1997 the top 1.3 per cent of urban households owned assets exceeding 2,00,000 yuan each, and cornered 31.5 per cent of the total, while the bottom 44 per cent of households owned 3 per cent of all assets. Countrywide, the situation is much worse. Party dissident He Qinglian has written of 'acute social polarisation' resulting from the reforms, 'a pyramidal social structure, akin to that in Latin America or Southeast Asian countries like Thailand and the Philippines. A small minority is perched on top of a huge mass of depressed or marginalised strata, comprising more than 80 per cent of the population, with a quantitatively under-developed middle class in between.' A whole new class of neo-rich has come up along with an ever expanding number of neo-poor in rural and urban areas. The number of *yuan* millionaires was estimated to have reached one million by the end of 1992 and has been since on the rise – their fortunes mostly built through 'primitive accumulation', that is, theft, violence, nepotism and corruption. At the other end more than a hundred million unemployed and underemployed Chinese – some estimates put the figure at 150 to 300 million - are reported to be 'wandering the countryside' in tandem with hundreds of thousands of 'laid off' workers in the urban centres. In a sharp contrast to it, the older socialist system with its relative egalitarianism – Mao's 'poor but equal' socialism – is being replaced by a society of massive economic and social inequality, of vast ill-gotten wealth alongside deepening poverty.

The opulent life-style of the new-rich Chinese is now comparable to their counterparts in the capitalist west. The skylines of cities like Beijing, Shanghai, Guangzhou are beginning to resemble the avenues in Paris, Frankfurt or Manhattan – their high rise buildings often owned by corporate houses from countries that were once denounced as hegemonic, imperialist or national enemies. (A sensitive visiting scholar has noticed 'the run-down premises of the Institute of Marxism-Leninism in Beijing, dwarfed by neighbouring skyscrapers erected by Taiwanese property developers'.) Impressive modern shopping malls, meeting 'the standards of top global shopping centres', have come up in major Chinese cities to cater to the consumerist appetites of China's new rich. There is glitter and gaiety even at midnight and unceasing traffic on the streets replete with KFCs and McDonalds. If new 'schools for the aristocracy' (*quizu xuexiao*) have arrived to cater for children of wealthy parents, costly entertainment sites such as karaoke houses and disco-ballrooms are cropping up in cities, catering for both China's own economic elites and businessmen from abroad, especially its wealthier neighbours – Hong Kong, Taiwan, Singapore, Japan and South Korea. The display of ostentation and extravagance at China's proliferating deluxe hotels, packed full with China's new rich, now matches that at any such locations anywhere in the world. China's emergent bourgeoisie, very much like the bourgeoisie and elites elsewhere in the Third World is beginning to enjoy life in the midst of mass poverty and deprivation that surrounds it.

This is how Robert Weil reported it towards the end of 1994:

> Of all the ideological announcements by Deng Xiaoping in advocating 'market socialism', the idea that 'some must get rich before others' has met with the most unqualified success. The 'new wealth' enjoyed by many leading party and state functionaries, military officers, public enterprise managers, and especially business people, both private entrepreneurs and those in semi-privatised ventures, is increasingly apparent. Many of these people can be found in the top hotels and Pierre Cardin stores, flaunting their cellular phones and beepers, fancy Western-style clothes, and air of self-important indulgence so reminiscent of the Chinese elite of the Guomindang period. It is they who can afford to join the new Jingnan Yongle golf facility in Beijing with dues of $12,000 and the Country Horse Racing Club, where membership

> in 1993 cost 80,000 yuan, or almost $14,000, with an advertisement bragging that 200 had already been sold to foreigners, and another 300 to 'Chinese managers and senior officials in joint ventures'....
>
> It is these people too, together with overseas Chinese and multinational corporations, who are buying into luxury apartment buildings like the French-designed Sunshine Plaza in the capital, advertised as 'The Most Splendid Contribution of China for Centuries', and the suburban Beijing Dragon Villas, in 'pure American-Canadian style' with broad lawns, starting from 'only' $360,000. Some have even begun buying plots in Florida. The measures of this new wealth are found in smaller things also, like private phones, installation of which 'will cost roughly a year's salary for an ordinary Chinese worker', yet with the demand already in the hundreds of thousands.... Others can spend the equivalent of thousands of dollars on imported liquors, or buy the single little abalone-stuffed mooncakes sold for the 1993 Lunar Festival at the Lufthansa Shopping Centre in Beijing for 1,000 yuan each, a city where the average resident earned just 197 yuan or $34 a month in 1992.

Weil additionally observed:

> It is these class elements as well, no doubt, who were the purchasers of the limited-edition jewel-encrusted gold watches issued for the hundredth anniversary of the birth of Mao Zedong on December 26, 1993. The most valuable were those with seals offered by the daughter and son-in-law of Mao costing as much as $19,388 each, and coming with $17,000 life and $20,000 property insurance policies. Mao would no doubt be flattered that even the *nouveaux riches* of China find his memory so valuable. But such timepieces are indeed the perfect hedge in more ways than one, in these days of growing uncertainty in China, sure to rise in value if marketisation continues, but 'politically correct' if things once again take a leftist turn.

Pointing out that popular misery and impoverishment is inseparable from marketisation, Weil had written: 'those who announced the "some must get rich first" policy failed to add the inevitable corollary: "many must get poor second"'. The number of *yuan* millionaires has thus grown in tandem with the number of people living under official poverty line. If such private wealth in contemporary China is a new phenomenon so is the reappearance of poverty in China which until the late 1970s had little poverty in the sense in which vast masses of third world people experience. The renewed poverty has come accompanied by millions of homeless peasant worker families as well as children begging in the streets once again or labouring in the sweat shops of the market economy. The 'success' of market reforms has left more than 150 million people jobless in the cities and villages, their situation made truly precarious with the reversal of the welfare gains of the three decades of Maoist egalitarianism. The dismantling of the communes not only broke up the production units in agriculture, it also ended the collectively organised social security and welfare system. The 'iron rice bowl' with its right to employment, minimum wage and basic necessities of life, is a thing of the past. The medical cooperative system, begun in the 1950s and greatly expanded by 'barefoot doctors' in the 1960s-1970s having gone extinct, health care, like so much else now privatised and commercialised is beyond the reach of the poor people. The poor are in fact no longer a part of any compact (implied or otherwise) with the Chinese ruling elite. Theirs is only the promise of the mythical 'trickle down' from the economic growth as and when it accrues. In the meantime, as they somehow eke out a living, the new unemployment benefits or the so-called 'lump sum parachutes', when available, are not enough even for beggars to live on. Given the rising inflation, the poor, even when in employment, can hardly make ends meet, unless they take a second job or look for other sources of income. The government has recently placed the number of the 'new poor' at 50 million but an estimate closer to reality would multiply the government figures at least three to four fold. Epitomising the desperate poverty and the accompanying malnutrition, illness and total degradation is the situation of the 'new poor' in Guangzhou, with the homeless peasant worker families camped around the railroad station and the children grabbing leftovers off tables in restaurants nearby, their ranks – made up mostly of migrants from the rural areas – swelling in rough proportion to the degree of 'new wealth' being generated in this centre of foreign investment and economic reform.

The inequalities between the rich and poor have been

accompanied by disparities between the centre and the regions, the Han and the ethnic minorities, the coastal areas and the hinterland, the 'First World China' of the south-east coast and the 'Third World China' of the central and western parts of the country. Overlapping these disparities is the rural-urban divide where, even as the urban workers too are bearing the brunt of market reforms, it is the ruination of the vast masses of China's peasantry which stands out as their most damaging outcome.

Workers in the state sector, with their institutionalised rights and benefits still in place, had it relatively easy initially. There was even a rise in urban workers wages in the 1980s. But since then wage cuts, inflation and lay offs have been creating an underclass of desperately poor urban workers – their conditions worsening all the more because they now have to pay for goods and services like housing, schooling, medical care, transportation, etc., that were formerly free or heavily subsidised. The shift to profit-maximisation in the state-owned sector has made for their even more ruthless exploitation. Adding to their woes is the rapidly rising unemployment resulting from the 'restructuring' of state enterprises, which has included, along with 'collective contract' 'the elimination of redundant labour' to raise productivity levels. As the Communist Party plunges ahead with its policy of privatising the state sector, with its inevitable consequence of bankruptcies, closures, and downsizing of existing industrial enterprises, the number of urban unemployed will only grow adding to the overall unemployment in the country which is already estimated to be anything between 150 to 250 million people. The expression 'awaiting a job' ('*daiye*') has long given way to the more realistic 'laid off' ('*xia gang*'). (It is obviously uncomfortable for a regime calling itself 'communist' to be seen putting its core constituency, in whose name it claims to be ruling, out of work. In an effort to cover up or avoid admitting the existence of unemployment the regime has invented such terms as 'off-post' or 'awaiting a job' (*daiye*), all too expressive of what are often referred to as 'Chinese characteristics'). The majority of workers who are able to find new jobs, particularly women workers, end up earning less than half the minimum wage. Workers elsewhere, in the

TVEs and the big or small private enterprises that have come up, as much or still worse victims of 'the market economy', share in this growing plight of workers in state or state-owned sector.

China's urban areas are reeling under the impact of workers' intensified exploitation and the newly generated unemployment and inequalities. The pain and trauma of China's turn to capitalism, however, is nowhere more evident than at the rural end of the rural-urban divide. Nowhere is the widening gulf between the masses and the elites more glaring than in the gap between the rural masses, that still account for over 70 per cent of China's population, and the new rich of the urban areas.

After the initial post-reform 'prosperity' in the countryside, mid-1980s onwards, farm incomes have failed to keep pace with rising prices, especially for agricultural inputs, and have actually declined in recent years. As a consequence of privatisation, the earlier collective agricultural technology support system has decayed. At the same time illegal fees, charges, fines, demands for 'contributions' and even outright extortion and labour duties reminiscent of feudal times have come to be levied on farmers. The farming regions are being made to pay for the high-flying profiteering and rising consumption levels in the cities. While the peasantry can be said to be suffering as a whole, almost as a class, privatisation and logic of the market has sharply polarised it and forced vast sections of it off the land. Their ever-worsening conditions, reflected in the massive unemployment ('surplus labour') in the countryside, are driving ever more farmers to flee for the cities. State expropriation of peasant lands, now a widespread phenomenon in China, has only added to this flight. Even with the market-led economic growth estimated at 10 per cent or more, there have been well-confirmed reports of a floating population of 100 million or more rural unemployed (growing at the yearly rate of 10-15 million), most of them young people, roaming the streets of urban centres of China in search of work. (Some reports even speak of a 'floating population' of 200-300 million peasants, and a Ministry of Agriculture estimate has projected a figure of 400 millions in the near future). Laws to check or restrict this migration to the cities have been simply impossible to enforce. It may be pointed out that central to the policies developed by Mao in the earlier revolutionary period was a determination to avoid just this kind of mass movement of peasants into the cities and the consequent growth of an urban underclass of impoverished, semi-migratory workers – hordes of unemployed, slum-dwelling or homeless ex-peasants. The market reform has made sure of this very outcome. Among the consequences is the emergence of a large, ruthlessly exploited servant class, mostly low-paid maids from the countryside. Often illegal entrants into the city or lacking proper resident permits, the migrant workers have no legal rights or any other benefits that the residents enjoy. Says Professor Cao Jinqing, a sociologist who studies migrant workers: 'Mao eliminated class differences. But with all the changes in China, class differences are coming back'. Many more Chinese are now saying what William Hinton had already reported in the 1980s: 'After all, the old man was right!' Richard Smith has written:

> China's economic miracle is less than brilliant for the millions of China's unemployed camped in train stations, public parks, and shanty-towns that have sprung up around China's cities. For the same market forces that are generating China's 'zooming growth' are also producing the largest pool of unemployed workers in human history. Of the 440 million rural farm workers in China, some 120 million rural peasants – equivalent to the combined total population of Britain and France – are unemployed. Many of these comprise a vast 'floating population' (*liudong renkou*) of migrant drifters who sweep back and forth across the country in search of work. These drifters – impoverished farmers, environmental refugees from desiccated farms, workers laid off from bankrupt rural collective enterprises – scrounge a living from temporary work, begging, prostitution, and crime. Their children are sometimes turned out onto the streets to fend for themselves. In 1994, UNICEF estimated that there were at least 200,000 homeless street-urchins between the ages of four and eleven roaming the streets of China's cities, sleeping in alleys, under bridges, in cardboard boxes, surviving by begging and stealing.

In official discourse this migration of displaced peasants and rural workers in search of work is testimony to the effectiveness of labour market reforms. This migration has surely provided China's market-reformers with a reserve army of labour which capitalist development invariably needs and welcomes. This migration is all the more welcome to China's capitalist-roaders in that, creating two distinct urban classes – those who are recognised residents and those who, as migrants, are not, it enables them to use these competing 'country cousins' to squeeze still more surplus out of the 'resident' urban workers, undermine latter's resistance to market reforms and, one may add, use the growing competition for jobs to practice their discrimination against women workers still more effectively. The floating workforce of 100 to 150 million 'blind' migrant workers, it should be remembered, are without contracts or welfare rights and without much trade union protection. The undocumented among them are paid less and are under constant threat of being turned over to the officials by employers. Even those who are working 'legally' are forced to hand over their ID cards, residency documents and entry permits to their employers, which prevents them from being able to leave of their own accord. Subject to rigorous institutionalised control from above, the migrant workers are essentially powerless and without any social standing and thus vulnerable to all kinds of economic and extra-economic coercion by the employers.

'Deng Xiaoping Theory' had early decreed that the construction of socialism in China demanded toleration of exploitation of workers, especially in the Special Economic Zones and 'open cities' which would act as 'windows' on the global economy, by attracting foreign capital to a disciplined and 'competitive' labour force. This tolerance, characteristic component of market reforms is, naturally, nowhere more visible than in these zones and 'open' cities with their over 80 million workers – men, women and children – subjected to systematic repression of labour rights and unrestrained capitalist accumulation. Women, constituting a major part of this 'new' workforce, are, among its most unprotected and unorganised elements. Isolated a thousand miles from their homes, in unfamiliar urban settings, generally uneducated and lacking even the basic knowledge of what few social services, benefits and protections are still available to them, they are the worst victims of the new capitalist exploitation. This is how Richard

Smith has summed up this particular aspect of China's market reforms:

> China's miracle is fading fast even for many of those in work. While market enthusiasts trumpet the dynamism, competitiveness and efficiency of Asian capitalism, the brave new world of China's 'socialist market economy' holds a grim future for many Chinese workers. In the most 'advanced' sector of China's economy, the fully capitalist joint venture factories in the Special Economic Zones (SEZs), workers are, to be sure, no longer 'whipped and exhausted by the mindless political campaigns'. Instead, many are physically beaten with cattle prods, and exhausted by fourteen-hour working days in sweatshops where child labour, forced overtime, curses, beatings, searches, needless industrial accidents, and the military repression of workers, especially trade unionists, are routine. In the Zones, 80 per cent of the workers are young women, most between the ages of sixteen and twenty-five – some are just children. Most live in crowded dormitories above their factories, housed in the notorious 'three-in-one' system that combines workshop, warehouse and dormitory all in the same building. At night in most of these dormitories, doorkeepers lock the women in behind barred windows and doors 'to prevent pilfering'. Outside such 'cages' in filthy canteens, meals are often ladled from troughs. Safety equipment, even basic fire-prevention sprinkler systems, are almost non-existent. By one estimate, three-quarters of SEZ workers suffer from occupational diseases and disabilities of one sort or another. By the age of twenty-five, women are usually refused work and required to return to their province of origin. Tens of thousands of young workers, many of them women, have lost their lives in the epidemic of factory fires, explosions, and accidents that has swept the coastal zones in recent years.
>
> Nearly a century and a half after Charles Dickens published *Hard Times*, even the *Wall Street Journal* seems shocked by conditions in the showcase of Chinese market reform, Shenzhen SEZ: 'Working conditions in some areas resemble those once described in nineteenth-century Britain, where Marx proclaimed the inevitability of social revolution.'

It is not only critics from abroad who have spoken of China 'reproducing the work houses of Dicken's England'. Scholars within China have noticed the current trends as a 'ruthless form of Social Darwinism'. He Qinglian has written:

> ...regression in capital-labour relations is a stark phenomenon in China today. What we are witnessing is a return to conditions common during the Industrial Revolution of the nineteenth century, of which Marx wrote the classic critique in his monumental work *Capital*. In the PRC today, workers employed in firms financed by Asian capital are typically forced to toil continuously for ten or twelve hours everyday, with a three or four minute trip to the toilet at specified times, and no weekend off. Workers in such firms earn very low wages, in poor and dangerous conditions. Accidents occur frequently. Fires due to the absence of safety measures regularly cause dozens of casualties. Many firms producing toxicants take no protective steps of any kind, a phenomenon widely reported in the media. Particularly in firms set up by Taiwanese or South Korean capital, struggles between workers and owners frequently erupt. Along the south-east coast, in cities like Shenzhen, Dongguan or Nanhai, the incidence of labour-capital conflict is very high. Though Guangdong Province has issued Labour Protection Acts, the 'East Asian dragons' seldom take them seriously.

Accompanying the misery and suffering 'the market' has brought to the vast masses of China's peasants and workers are a variety of regressive phenomena: revival of old practices – kidnapping and sale of children, young brides being sold to old farmers by their families, concubinage, etc.; rise of underground 'black society' gangs – 'Xinjiang Gang' in Shanghai, the 'Beijing' and 'White Shark' Gangs in Guangdong, the 'Ganzhou Gang' in Jiangxi, or the 'Wolf Gang' in Shanxi, etc.; growing number of drug addicts in urban and rural areas; reversion to an older division of labour resulting from loss of employment and independence by women, along with an overall lowering of women's social position and reinforcement of gender inequalities and oppression; and so on. A significant regressive development is the spread of prostitution once again, which has become a major tax resource for local governments, who give no protection to the women whose earnings they exploit. In cities like Guangzhou, as we have already noticed, there are large number of young female workers in factories, paid miserable wages, without any form of trade union protection or public oversight.

To be particularly noticed is the havoc 'market' is playing in the realm of morals, culture and ideology, the entire superstructure of Chinese society. Along with large other segments of this society, party leaders and cadres too have come to be afflicted by typically capitalist vices like acquisitiveness, consumerism, corruption, and so on. Money is working its values-confounding magic in a society which not too long ago held equality as its ultimate socialist goal. Makers of money, the gloriously rich, are the new model citizens of China; and in a process disturbingly similar to that in many countries of Latin-America, Africa and Asia, even the Red Army, once the last bastion of socialist ideas and rigour, has been losing these to the lure of profit. Indeed no area of Chinese life and society has remained untouched by the new morality and culture of the market. As the economist Yang Fan has pointed out:

> Utilitarian standards replace rational standards as the basis for judging things... and the standard of morality and conscience is replaced by the standard of money... Stimulated by a small minority getting rich quickly, people's desire to pursue wealth has become unprecedentedly strong, and the principles of the commodity economy have eroded everything... The activity of the whole society revolves around the word 'money'... It can be said that the secularisation of China's society is complete and that it is developing in an unhealthy direction.

In the era of 'getting rich is glorious', an atmosphere of 'money by any means' has become all pervasive. This is no mere aberration but the very way the market system works. Few question the means by which the first generation of China's capitalists – especially the communists-turned-plutocrats – are coming up. As a scholar has put it:

> They are doing so, in the main, by wholesale plunder of state and social property: embezzlement of state monies and foreign exchange, bribery, kickbacks, graft, profiteering on resale of state goods, currency manipulations, influence peddling, illegal privatisation of government-owned firms and properties, expropriation of workers' and peasants' housing and land – for lease to Western hotel builders, joint ventures, and so forth – and similar means other than the sweat of their brows.

Cashing in on bureaucratic power is common and one consequence is massive corruption in China's economy and society, which even the ruling elite have come to see as a threat to the system they are presiding over.

Corruption in China is not to be seen as just another malversion, a morally reprehensible behaviour that needs to be avoided or condemned. It is a more complex phenomenon. When, in 1978, Deng abandoned Mao's 'socialism in poverty' and called on China's masses to 'get rich!' he was careful to bar Communist officials from going into business – Mao's legacy had still to be coped with, it was still unseemly for actual cardcarrying Communists to become practicing capitalists. But the logic of 'getting rich', of the economic reform, ordained otherwise. By the mid-1980s, Deng gave the Communist caders the go-ahead to get into business in a big way. But these cadres, like Russia's once, lacked the personal capital to set up private businesses, and they did not own the state enterprises they ran. So without a 'legal' way to 'get rich' and go bourgeois, they began to build their fortunes through corruption. While some 'borrowed' state funds to plunge into the market, most others first enriched themselves by trading on their positions and then graduated to siphoning off state funds to set up private businesses. Soon, with Deng's mounting love for the market inspiring it, and his children joining in, it was a veritable orgy of corruption. The elite cadres accumulated wealth as capital in every possible way, beginning the process of recomposing themselves as China's red bourgeoisie.

The process continues. The mentality behind this 'power-generated capitalisation' is well expressed in the adage: 'Power must be utilised before its expiry date'. Acting on the principle, 'to each according to his power', the ruling elite are using the power they wield in the state to accumulate personal wealth and become a property-holding class. Relatives too are among the beneficiaries. Often it is a case of 'parents in government, children doing business' – 'one family, two systems' as it has been sarcastically described. Kin connections of this kind are ideal for 'rent-seeking' activities which are an important part of China's market economy.

Looking at corruption in China in terms of its changing forms, He Qinglian has pointed out that in the eighties and early nineties, it was mainly an individual affair; by 1995 it had developed from an individual to an organisational stage; and by 1998 it had developed further, from an organisational to an institutional or systemic stage. Corruption is now so integral a part of the system which is coming up in China that many advocates of economic reform have begun to rationalise and accept it as necessary. A well-known economist is reported to have said: 'Attacks on corruption are an attack on the market – we have to tolerate the one to develop the other'. Corruption in China can well be seen as one characteristic among similar others of what is being built as 'socialism with Chinese characteristics'.

Be that as it may, corruption is today rampant in China's economic and socio-political life, so rampant indeed that even the ruling elite have come to see it as a threat to their system. They have declared 'fight against corruption' as 'vital to the very existence of the Party and the State'. (Each year now hundreds of officials are prosecuted and punished for so-called 'economic crimes', a few even executed. But in a system in which political and economic power is still largely merged and there is no independent judiciary, the line between personal power and 'criminality' is necessarily vague. Prosecution or punishment for these 'crimes', thus, depends more upon one's 'connections' (*quanxi*) than the law, and, especially at higher levels, it is often selective or politically motivated, reflecting the power equations or struggles at the top).

Corruption, however, is only an aspect of the moral, cultural and ideological crisis gripping China in the wake of 'market reforms'. Its 'opening to the world' has meant not merely a wider and freer cultural exchange which is always desirable but an inundating flood of western capitalist culture. In an early reaction, describing it as a 'surrender on the cultural front', William Hinton had written:

> Once the party accepted Deng's aphorism 'It doesn't matter whether a cat is black or white as long as it can catch mice' and put 'enrich yourselves' forward as the key slogan, a huge wave of naive and avaricious Babbitry flooded China, submerging

everything in its path. Just as a large segment of officialdom and a large slice of the intelligentsia felt themselves affronted and frustrated by the frugality of socialist development and rushed to wallow in commodities and luxuries as soon as the bars were down, so they have longed for and now welcome with open arms Western bourgeois culture, including all its most Philistine and venal forms. They view as simple-minded and deserving of pity anyone who doesn't share their enthusiasm.

Free-market economics, rampant Friedmanism, dominates economic thinking. Soap operas, sitcoms, quiz programs, dancing girls, and fashion shows dominate prime-time television along with, of course, a goodly dose of competitive sports. Cops-and-robbers crime films, featuring heroic, incorruptible law enforcement officers, and boy-meets-girl romances of upwardly mobile entrepreneurial types account for a goodly share of new films. Rock-and-roll, disco dancing, and karaoke sing-alongs dominate the music scene. Pornographic videos and erotic magazines pass from hand to eager hand, all the more in demand for being banned.

The neocolonial implications of such massive cultural inundations should alarm anyone concerned with the health and autonomy of China's values, mores, and national ethos. The minds of young successor generations are being warped, seduced, and possessed by the market-oriented mass culture of the monopoly bourgeoisie of America, Europe, and Japan.

Such has been the progress of China's social and cultural degeneration that even the ruling elite, (headed by Jiang Zemin himself) have felt compelled to speak out against the 'Three evils' – money worship, hedonism and individualism – and the threat from 'extravagance and decadence'. People, including the armed forces are lectured on the need for 'spiritual civilisation' and its 'Three Virtues' – socialism and collectivism tagged on to patriotism. Appeals are made to promote ideological and moral education among young people – the strata who have been most vulnerable to westernisation and capitalist values. There are warnings and exhortations, even campaigns against 'bourgeois liberalism', 'spiritual pollution' and 'culture of consumerism', which however reflect not even elementary Marxist understanding that all these come indissolubly linked with market, that you cannot have market and yet escape the morality and culture of the market.

XIII

One consequence of the growing dominance of the morality and culture of the market is a crisis of ideas and ideals which has added to the party's concern about the unity of China's now deeply divided society and the declining legitimacy of the regime iself. The party leadership, of course, continues to invoke 'Marxism-Leninism and Mao Zedong Thought'. Even when described as 'socialism with Chinese characteristics' or simply 'market socialism', it is socialism that Party claims to be building. Whatever be the nature and quality of subjective commitment of different factions in the leadership, even for the committed capitalist roaders in the party abandoning the regime's fundamental ideological principles in this period of transition could be too risky – the party cannot move openly to capitalism without a wholesale loss of its ideological legitimacy. However phoney party's Marxism now, it remains useful as unifying and legitimising ideology for the system. As with ruling elites elsewhere in our times, word games are an essential skill for China's ruling elites. They continue to play these games to revise and interpret Marxism to suit the requirements of their transition to capitalism. A Jiang, for example, has justified his plea for greater privatisation with the argument: 'We would get nowhere if we study Marxism statically in isolation and separate it from its vigorous development in actual life'. However, even this utility is being questioned from within the party. 'Realistic Resources and Strategic Choices for China After the Soviet Upheaval' has called for renouncing the Marxist-Leninist legacy altogether as a liability for the party after the collapse of 'communism' in Eastern Europe and the Soviet Union. Reflecting the dialectics of the situation, sticking to Marxism is also viewed as dangerous. Even as he makes the customary gesture of disapproval against 'Rightist tendencies', Jiang warns: 'We should maintain vigilance... primarily against "the Left"'. Both responses are suggestive of the need to look for ideological support elsewhere.

With the rapid deterioration of the situation, the official ideology in any case is failing to provide even such legitimacy to the regime as it once di. In a significant move away from

Marxism, it is to nationalism that the Chinese Communist Party is now turning to unite the badly divided people and forge a new legitimacy for itself. Exemplifying this ideological shift is the 1991 'Realistic Responses...' document we have referred to above, which postulates nationalism as the new ideology to unite the people and rally them behind the regime. More recently we have Jiang Zemin's 'Important Thought of Three Represents' where the Communist Party becomes a supra-class, virtually 'national' organisation, representing not just workers and peasants but China's capitalists as well. Appeals are made to the 'lofty and noble traditional culture of the Chinese people', and 'Neo-Confucianism' is promoted in the search for 'self' and 'cultural identity'. 'Education in patriotism' is advocated, backed by strident slogans of 'nation in danger' and 'unification of motherland' (vis-à-vis Taiwan), etc. Deng's 'one nation – two systems' which never had any socialism about it is now even more a *national* proposition than ever before – (which may well come to be realised as 'one nation – one bourgeois system' in future). A 'rich country and strong nation' is how China of the future is visualised. The deepening social and cultural crisis together with the periodic protests and upsurges both in the rural and urban areas, is leading to a further tightening of the regime's control over society. It is not merely that the neo-liberal expectations that economic reforms would in due course lead to political reforms are not materialising. It is that not a socialist China, but a strong Chinese nation state, another great power on the world scene is now emerging as the goal of the Chinese Communist Party.

Among the people below, as the moral-cultural crisis caused by the growth of market forces and western influences takes its toll in the loss of ideals or higher purposes in society, other consequences are manifest. Most noticeable is the extending hold of religion and the emergence of phenomenon like the Falungong, giving expression to the misery and protest of the dispossessed and alienated victims of China's 'economic reforms'. The fact that the Falungong sect is sprinkled with high ranking, retired army officers and ordinary party members, lends credibility to more specific explanations: 'Many people, especially older cadres, are bothered by the moral vacuum in China today'; again: 'With its Chinese roots and its emphasis on clean living, Falun Gong has provided a convenient way to express opposition to the direction the party is taking – toward patronage, corruption and sleaze.'

What more than anything else seems to have immediately filled the void left by the bankruptcy of China's official ideology in a situation of growing moral-cultural disarray and ideological disenchantment, is consumerism, a characteristic para-belief system of the era of late capitalism. Following in the wake of China's turn to privatisation and profit-making in the free market, a wave of rampant consumerism has swept through China – with the 'gloriously rich' above naturally influenced by the 'window effect' of the example of their more affluent neighbours in Hong Kong, Taiwan, and to a lesser extent, Singapore, and their own example fuelling the consumerist appetites of those below. Mao's sober socialist response to China's underdevelopment, his pioneering effort to build socialism in a backward country amidst global capitalist domination now a thing of the past, hard work, simple living, and saving to so build up the country as to secure a better life for all its people, have given way to 'flash, dash, and extravagance unlimited'. The prominence of sign value over use and exchange value is a well-recognised feature of consumerism in late capitalism. Conjuring up and marketing of the rather indefinable 'highest grade' – *jipin* – is how this feature is finding expression in the conspicuous consumption of China's new economic elites. Conjured up for these elites, primarily the *nouveaux riches* caught up in the frenzy of ostentatious display of their wealth and those who, by virtue of political power, hold the strings of the public purse, 'the highest grade' is obviously beyond the reach of the majority, which however does not prevent it from exercising its consumerist pull on the society as a whole. It only needs to be added that the Dengist slogan 'To get rich is glorious' both invites and legitimises consumerism now rampant in China. And when all is said and done, and exhortations against it notwithstanding, consumerism is not without its usefulness for the Chinese leadership. It has been suggested that, since the

Tiananmen uprising of 1989, China's rulers have been pushing consumerism to distract China's mutinous youth and masses from political issues.

XIV

Consumerism immediately draws our attention to another aspect of capitalist development anywhere – its destructive impact on environment. And China is no exception. Scholars have pointed out the predominance of men in the leadership committees at all administrative levels of the government and the party in China, and the consolidation of these patriarchal power structures by the increasing feminisation of factory labour – driven by a low-wage strategy of national accumulation – and the new and old gender ideologies which undervalue the labour-power of women. To this we can now add another equally, and in some ways more significant aspect of the contemporary Chinese situation: the damage being done to environment by China's turn to the market. In other words, along with other capitalist practices, including the patriarchal systems of power and domination, China's economic development is today importantly marked by environmental destruction, a feature that is now more than ever integral to the capitalist system. In a long term perspective, perhaps nowhere is the impact of China's transition to capitalism, its market-led mode of production and consumption, having a more devastating effect than upon China's environment. And given the huge scale of China's transition to capitalism, this has ominous implications, and not only for the Chinese.

Here are some details of this devastating effect as reported by Richard Smith and other scholars. China's single-minded pursuit of market-led economic growth has turned big tracts of the country into environmental wasteland. The country has lost a third of its cropland to degradation from over-farming (soil erosion, desertification), energy projects (hydro stations, coal mining) and to industrial and housing construction. The area of desertification on average expanded by about 2,100 square kilometers annually during 1980s. Rural industrialisation since 1980s has polluted some 10 million hectares of farmland.

Presently over 400 million people are affected by soil degradation and the economic losses caused by soil degradation are about 16-25 billion *yuan* annually. One consequence of loss or degradation of arable land is China turning from an exporter to a net importer of grain. China has also come to face an 'unprecedented' water crisis largely resulting 'from enterprises neglecting environmental protection in the pursuit of profits.' Water supplies are drying up under the heavy demands of new industries, population and agriculture. Vast lakes have dried up entirely. Of China's 600 cities, 300 are short of water and 108, including Beijing, are said to be 'acutely short.' In 1995, increasing demand for water for irrigation and industrial use caused a 622 km stretch of the Yellow River, China's second largest, to completely dry up for 122 days. Many of those in China's hundred million or so 'floating population' of migrants are 'environmental refugees', fleeing from drought-stricken farms.

China's industries are reported to be among the 'dirtiest' in the world (and these include the TVEs which are notorious as the country's worst polluters and wasters of energy. Their small-scale operations and primitive technology mean that proportionally they waste more energy (coal) and more inputs than large urban industries). In absolute terms China is already the third largest contributor to global climate changes, after the US and Russia. Powered largely by huge reserves of coal, its rapid industrialisation is fast propelling China towards the dubious distinction of the world's number one polluter, pouring out hundreds of millions of tons carbon dioxide, sulphur dioxide, methane and soot into the atmosphere, blocking out the sun over many Chinese cities, and spreading acid rain as far as Japan. Of the world's 10 worst polluted cities, five are Chinese. Out of the 600 cities of China, in less than 1 per cent does the air quality meet the first class standard of national air quality. Globalisation-dictated, export-led economic growth has meant that Asia today has the world's most polluted air and it contributes between a fifth and a quarter of the world's emissions of greenhouse gases. China alone does half the damage. Some of its cities are so blackened by the air pollution that, as just mentioned, they cannot be seen by satellite. Air pollution is probably China's worst immediate problem. China's industrial emissions of greenhouse gases, particulates and heavy metals are growing at staggering rates, threatening to make China the world's largest producer of acid rain and the world's largest emitter of greenhouse gases. Asia is often lauded as the fastest growing economic region of the world. But this frenzied development is destroying Asia's environment and thereby also eroding its people's health faster than anywhere else on the planet. China is no exception to this erosion. As reported by China's National Environmental Agency, polluted air and respiratory diseases, including increasing lung cancer, are now the leading cause of death in urban and even rural areas of China.

Each year China's factories discharge some 36 billion tons of untreated industrial waste water and raw sewage into the country's rivers, lakes and coastal seas, so that four-fifths of China's rivers and lakes are 'seriously polluted', their waters unfit for drinking, their fish unfit to eat. Four of China's seven large rivers – the Huaihe, the Haihe, the Liaohe and the Songhuajiang – are among the worst affected. The colour of the water of 80 per cent of the 170 tributaries in the Huaihe river system has changed to black and green, and more than a half of these tributaries have lost their usage value. China also now faces a solid waste crisis. Whereas up until the early 1980s China did not really have garbage dumps because nearly everything was recycled, following the mass promotion of consumer culture with its excess packaging, disposable containers, and so on, China's cities now face a glut of garbage. China produces some 3000 tons of plastic wastes everyday and solid wastes piled outside cities are leaking toxins into the ground water. To add to these problems, China's for-profit market reformers have opened up Guangdong province to the establishment of toxic waste dumps for foreign capitalists whose waste is unacceptable in their own countries. (To all this environmental devastation may be added the damage done to China's fauna and flora. Of the 640 endangered species of animals and plants listed by the International Trade Convention on Endangered

Species of Wild Animals and Plants, 156, almost one-fourth, are in China).

As China's market-led economic growth has gone on destroying the environment – degrading the land and poisoning China's own waterways and atmosphere – consumerism now rampant in China has been making its own contribution to this destruction. Particularly noteworthy in this connection is the conspicuous consumption of China's *nouveaux riches* as they go about flaunting their wealth and seek to distinguish themselves from their poor and not so poor brethren. A good example here is what has been described as 'the latest product of the Communist Party's deliberate promotion of bourgeois individualism, entrepreneur worship consumerism, and the American lifestyle', namely, 'the car craze', with the communists-turned-capitalists trading in their antiquated Party-issue Red Flag limos for new Mercedes and Lexuses, and the companion class of new private entrepreneurs importing whole fleets of Mercedes Benz limousines, making China the largest foreign market for Mercedes Benz and soon for Rolls-Royce too. This car craze, reminiscent of the one in America in 1950s, has no basis in any rational assessment of transportation needs and is without any concern for its harmful ecological consequences. In fact a serious concern for environment remains a missing dimension in China's policies of economic growth even when environmental losses are now known to be undermining this growth itself. The Chinese have the resources for it but protection of environment is not among their priorities.

Environmental havoc in China is part of the havoc that capitalism is now wreaking upon environment all over the world, threatening the very future of humankind on this earth. It has become quite fashionable to make noises over it, especially in the advanced capitalist countries. Chinese rulers may not be, like their counterparts elsewhere, making these loud noises, but like them they too do not seem to be much bothered about the future of their country or the world. But warnings are not wanting. This is what Vaclav Smil, a leading authority on China's environment, said some years back – and the relevance of what he said is not confined to China: 'Tomorrow's China, behaving as if there were no limits to its prosperity, would inflict irreparable damage to its environment, and it would be the largest contributor to potentially destabilizing global climatic change. Continuation of China's runaway economic growth would then be a prelude to inevitable economic decline – and to more human suffering during the next century.'

This, however, is nothing accidental or the result of some 'mistaken' policies, it is the inevitable outcome of what is being built in China, of the chaos that is the free market, the profit-seeking system that is capitalism. And, as Richard Smith has written, China's 'capitalist development holds out the prospect of ever more devastating environmental disasters, if not global catastrophe'.

XV

Notwithstanding the changing official definitions of China's economic system – initially 'the planned economy leads, the market economy supports', then 'a planned commodity economy', followed by 'a socialist market economy', 'a socialist market economic system' or 'market socialism', and all along 'socialism with Chinese characteristics' – there is ample evidence now that what has been happening in China in the post-Mao period is a transition to capitalism. The Dengist 'economic reform' has certainly led to a remarkable economic upsurge in China but equally certainly this economic upsurge has a predominantly capitalist character. More important in many ways, it has also meant a reversal of the progress towards socialism in the previous period – a reversal of the Maoist effort to build socialism in an economically backward country, an effort which had, and retains, its pioneering relevance for the peoples of the post-colonial Third World. There were indeed serious problems with the Chinese economy towards the end of the 1970s, many of them, quite understandably, born of the Maoist strategy itself, others arising from the abrupt withdrawal of the Soviet Union's assistance in 1960 and the continuing pressure of global capitalism, and still others compounded by the economic damage caused by the Cultural Revolution going out of control. Unwilling or unable to find *socialist* answers to these problems, the new Chinese leadership, putting 'economics in command', sought answers in market economy and 'open door' to global capitalism. Such is the essential meaning of the 'reforms' carried out under Deng Xiaoping's leadership and continued after him. The 'reforms' have not been a legitimate use of market in a transitional socialist economy, but, much in the manner of capitalist economies, a primary reliance on the market to overcome China's economic backwardness.

To the extent these reforms have achieved their economic aims, far from restoring the legitimacy of the earlier socialist project, they have set in train basic socio-economic and political changes which have almost entirely undermined it. The Chinese leadership persists in calling what they are building 'socialism with Chinese characteristics'; but it is no socialism at all, only capitalism with Chinese characteristics, legitimised by an increasingly strident and xenophobic nationalism.

China remains a country ruled by a Communist Party, which continues to proclaim its commitment to 'socialism'. Though disturbed by this post-Mao development, many on the Left, within China and outside, still prefer to believe that Communist Party in control of state-power, with its macro-regulation and control over the economy, remains a guarantee of China's socialist future, at the very least a bulwark against China's proceeding towards full-fledged capitalism. But this belief misses out on the facts that the Communist regime itself has now become enmeshed in the accumulation of 'non-labour income' and the state has become the source of an emerging class of 'possessors of other people's labour'. The capitalist transition has indeed proceeded too far and fast in China for any illusions on the subject.

Far from being the revolutionary organisation it was, committed to socialism and its egalitarian values, close to the people and practicing mass mobilisation, the Communist Party has been presiding over China's frantic drive to build a 'market economy' and, affirming the values the formula embodies, it has been so interpreting and establishing the operational content of Chinese socialism that the very distinction between capitalism and socialism is blurred beyond recognition. 'White cat, black cat', Deng had said, 'if it catches mice it is a good cat'. A strong authoritarian party-state was virtually a functional necessity for ensuring stability and order in the transition process. This is precisely what the Chinese Communist Party has provided, along with, so far, a non-militant workforce that meets the imperatives of capital in this capitalist transition. It is the Party which has wielded the club to break the workers' 'iron rice bowl', depriving millions of Chinese of the one indelible gain from the social revolution they had made – the right to eat, to a job, to housing, and to a rough social security. Far from defending workers' interests in the workplace – where direct modes of labour repression and control are already underpinned by the freedom of managers to hire and fire workers – the Party cadre are using their power to help enforce new systems of discipline and punishment to extract the maximum surplus value. As a worker wrote in a letter to the underground workers' newspaper, *Zhongguo Laogong Tongxun*, recently:

> All this concentration of power and responsibility in the hands of party members means that a long arm of party influence stretches even further into the lives of workers at the plant. The 'three visits, one chat' system is a way of ensuring that absolutely nothing interferes with production at the factory. A party representative will visit the home of an employee when: 1. He or she is ill (to check that they are really ill); 2. If they show signs of not being 'satisfied' at work (to make sure that any dissatisfaction doesn't spill over into a collective dispute); and 3. if there are domestic problems at home (thus removing any vestiges of privacy). The 'one chat' is simple and covers all three visits: any problems or contradictions that may affect productivity must be discussed with management.

In the Communist-ruled China the native bourgeoisie (including the emerging bureaucratic capitalist class), the foreign as well as diaspora capitalists are surely getting what they could have ever wanted.

It is under a communist dispensation that China has turned to capitalism. Decisive in this turn, as in the ex-Soviet Union, is the role of the Communist Party leadership, often seen as the elites who have usurped power and come to rule in the name of the party and the people. There are differences and rivalries among them, but these are largely over specifics such as the pace, scale or timing or even particular beneficiaries of privatisation, etc. Barring a presently ineffective minority, they are *all* capitalist roaders as Mao called them, now developed beyond that to the point of being bureaucratic capitalists themselves. But the leadership's role does not exhaust the situation or its explanation. Obviously, it is not possible to snatch capitalism – even as 'market socialism' or 'socialism with Chinese characteristics' – out of the heavens *ex nihilo* and plant it on the ground. It must be born from the old society, shaped by the womb from which it emerges. It postulates the existence in society of class forces sufficiently strong to push for a transition to capitalism. In China it is the party-state apparatus which has provided the social power base from within which these forces, the new capitalist class and partners of global capital are emerging. Persons in positions of power in the party and the state have begun to love the market and learnt to use their power to accumulate private wealth and go into business. Among them are political leaders, mayors of cities, city and provincial officials, military and police officers, managers of state-owned and town and village enterprises, cadres in joint ventures with foreign investors and local entrepreneurs in regions or industrial sectors in which they exercise political authority. The communist cadres not only divert the profits generated by the state-owned enterprises into a wide range of essentially private perks but also use their party cards to 'borrow' or steal state assets to set themselves up as capitalists. In the name of privatisation, virtually a continent-wide expropriation of social property has been on – 'grabification' (*prikhvatizatasiya*) is what they have called it in Russia. Involved in this plunder of national assets and the accompanying corrupt practices are the sons and daughters of the party bosses who are simultaneously engaged in diversifying into various commercial and trading activities, tying up with companies in Hong Kong, the United States and other countries, or taking up positions with the biggest American and European banks and multinational corporations and representing them in China.

Known as 'princelings' in the west, they are a visible symbol of the 'comprador' dimension of China's economic progress. Such are the class forces pushing for China's transition to capitalism. The Party leadership is the most effective force among them. The *apparatchiks* at the top, a self-perpetuating elite, almost a ruling class, they were already, in Mao's time, 'capitalist roaders'. (Hence the justification for Mao's Cultural Revolution and the slogan: 'Bombard the headquarters!'). The market-oriented reforms have been an opportunity for them to not only capitalise on their official power and turn their bureaucratic privileges into personal wealth, but to transform themselves into a capitalist class, a part of the burgeoning bourgeoisie of China.

XVI

The distance Chinese Communist Party has travelled on the road to capitalism, and the degeneration of theory that has accompanied it, is well-illustrated by Jiang Zemin's Political Report to the 16th Party Congress (November, 2002) wherein he gave a call to 'free our minds from the shackles of outdated notions, practices and systems, from the erroneous and dogmatic interpretations of Marxism' and offered his own correct and up-to-date interpretation, the so-called theory of 'Three Represents'. Jiang of course had a problem finding a fully proper name for it, one that would put him on par with his predecessors Mao and Deng. In China they distinguish between *Zhuyi* (ism) *sixiang* (thought) and *lilun* (theory). The first term was already reserved for Marx and Lenin, the second for Mao, and the third for his mentor Deng. Claimed to be a 'theory', Jiang's contribution yet had to have a different, new name. He settled for *zhuyao sixiang* (important thought) – it was to be 'Important Thought of Three Represents'. Jiang's 'Thought' is surely important in its own way, but not in the way a theoretical contribution is normally assessed. 'Deng Xiaoping Theory' is banal enough. As its 'continuation and development' Jiang's 'Important Thought' marks a new low in the degeneration of Marxism in the Chinese Communist Party. As a critic, no Marxist himself, has observed: 'It is touted as his contribution to the creative development of Marxist ideology. Only in China can such nonsense as Three Represents be regarded as creative theoretical contribution to any kind of ideology. In any other respectable country it will be laughed off as wacky stuff. But in China it is serious stuff, likely to elevate its proponent, Jiang Zemin, to "sainthood".'

'Important Thought of Three Represents' is claimed to be a 'continuation and development of Marxism-Leninism, Mao Zedong Thought and Deng Xiaoping Theory', and now stands added to them in the revised Party constitution as the 'guiding ideology that the Party must uphold for a long time to come.' It calls for and offers 'a deeper understanding of what socialism is, how to build it, and what kind of Party to build and how to build it.' But reference to Marx, Lenin and Mao, or to socialism, is only a part of the ideological deception that the Party needs to indulge in. Jiang's 'Important Thought', if anything, continues and develops only Deng's 'Theory' and, in effect, confirms that China is now committed to capitalism in all but name.

According to Jiang's 'Important Thought', now incorporated in the Party constitution, the party represents '(1) the development trend of China's advanced productive forces, (2) the orientation of China's advanced culture, and (3) the fundamental interests of the overwhelming majority of the Chinese people'. Jiang's third 'Represent' is the usual, necessary, rhetoric, though even here it points to building not socialism but, in Jiang's words, a 'well-off society in an all-round way', which can well be interpreted as social-democratic 'capitalism with a human face'. The second 'Represent' has an obvious ambiguity about it. It surely does not mean the egalitarian culture of Mao's socialism. Again, what of the 'lofty and noble traditional culture' (along with its Confucianism) that Party's nationalist turn upholds? And, complaints about 'spiritual pollution' notwithstanding, it could well mean the culture of the country with the most 'advanced productive forces', the United States. On Jiang's premises, the US can surely claim to have the most advanced culture because it has the 'most advanced productive forces'! It is the first 'Represent' which is really important for its unambiguous statement and the implication that has been clearly spelled out, namely, the acceptance of businessmen and entrepreneurs into the Communist Party as part of China's 'advanced productive forces'.

The 16th Congress, writing Jiang's 'Important Thought of Three Represents' into the Party constitution, decided to open the doors of the Chinese Communist Party to entrepreneurs and capitalists of China. This however was nothing new or unanticipated. The influx had begun years ago and the Congress merely rubber-stamped an existing reality. According to a 1996 document, more than 5,400 private entrepreneurs were selected or recommended as members of the People's Congress above county level, more than 8,500 as members of the PCC, and close to 1,400 as committee members in the Youth League, not to speak of eight members in the National People's Congress itself. And by the time of the 80th anniversary of the Chinese Communist Party in 2001, 113,000 entrepreneurs – whose firms contributed more than 20 per cent of the country's GDP – had already joined the party. Behind this influx lay the hard fact of China's changed class structure under the impact of the Dengist reforms. As He Qinglian noted it some years back:

> The class structure of Chinese society has undergone a profound transformation since the beginnings of the reform-policy period in 1978. The elite, previously selected on a political basis, is now also being recruited on the basis of 'wealth' and 'merit' – profoundly affecting the underlying social structure. These new sections of the elite are now beginning to form their own interest groups, social organisations and lobbying channels, beyond the already established political ones. The working class, hitherto the constitutionally decreed 'leading class', and the peasantry, the 'semi-leading' class, have both been marginalised; intermediate social organisations are developing apace. All these processes have led to thorough-going changes in the relations between the state, society and the individual.

As Jiang saw and understood or interpreted these processes (in his 80th anniversary speech in July 2001), new social strata had emerged who are making significant contribution to China's economic progress. They were a part of China's 'advanced productive forces' who, therefore, deserved to be members of the party. Laying exclusive emphasis on ownership of property and evading the real issues of capitalism or class which are a matter of more than property-ownership, this is how Jiang argued for capitalists' entry into the party: 'It is not advisable to judge a person's political orientation simply by whether he or she owns property, and how much property he or she owns. But rather, we should judge him or her mainly by his or her political awareness, moral integrity and performance...' The argument was accepted. In 2001 itself, at the time of the 80th anniversary, a statement was issued by the Party welcoming businessmen into its ranks. The 16th Congress only provided the constitutional sanctions for their entry.

Jiang's rather innovative 'continuation and development' of the Dengist 'theory of productive forces' does not fully explain Party's easy acceptance of capitalists into its ranks. More than such theorising - which confirmed that the leadership had travelled far on the road to capitalism – there was a plain pragmatic reason for it. It was an answer to a serious problem confronting the Communist Party. The problem persists and the adequacy of the answer remains in doubt. The issue is nevertheless well worth taking note of.

China's post-1978 capitalist development has released new social forces in Chinese society. New classes have come up both in the city and the countryside with the growth of market economy. With the private sector accounting for almost 50 per cent of China's GDP, among these classes is a sizeable 'new entrepreneurial class', big and small capitalists of China. They are not only representatives of the 'advanced productive forces of society', as Jiang's theory has it, but, along with their material interests, they also have political aspirations. They need and want a share in political power, an assured place in the decision-making bodies. They are not only in search of political fora but idealise western-style democracy. It is not only difficult but dangerous to keep them out of power. With their increasing clout within the country and links with foreign capital, they can become a threat to the one-party system that Chinese Communist Party is presiding over. Hence the problem: Should they be allowed to develop their own political organisations and compete with the Communist Party? Or was it preferable to make an opening in the party for them? Led by Jiang the party opted for the second alternative. In other words, the Communist Party decided to preserve its rule – for the time being at least – by coopting the business elite that increasingly drives the country's economy.

Jiang's 'Important Thought' is vulgarisation of Marxism at its worst. The standard Marxist usage 'advanced class' stands replaced with 'advanced productive forces', which preeminently includes the capitalist class. The Dengist 'theory of productive forces' was bad Marxism. In 'continuing and developing' it Jiang goes one step ahead of Deng. With Deng it was only the precedence of productive forces over class struggle. Jiang gives precedence to the bourgeoisie over all other classes, including the proletariat, in the name of 'advanced productive forces'. Now that 'Important Thought' is 'the guiding ideology' of the Chinese Communist Party, henceforth, as 'advanced productive forces' and members of the party, China's capitalists too will be building what the party describes as 'socialism'. And since the words capitalism and imperialism find no mention in Jiang's theory and 'productive forces' is all that matters, foreign investors in China and the managers working in their concerns too are partners in building 'socialism with Chinese characteristics'!

(It has been suggested that with 'Three Represents', Chinese Communist Party is now a party of the whole people – 'Party will now have within its fold everybody, from (a) millionaires and entrepreneurs, (b) intellectuals, technological and creative elite, to (c) peasants and workers' – and that this is not without historical precedents – Liu Shaochi, for example, saw the Communist Party of China as 'a proletarian party of an entirely new type', 'which fully represents the interests of the Chinese nation and people', has 'waged an irreconcilable struggle against all the enemies of the Chinese nation and people' or those who 'betray the interests of the Chinese nation and people'. I will only add that this supra-class view of the party – which, incidentally, was not Mao's understanding – now reiterated by the 16th Congress, well jells with Chinese leadership's ideological shift from Marxism to nationalism that we have noticed earlier).

XVII

On present trends – with the private sector burgeoning in the rural and urban areas and the capitalist roaders in power – it may seem that China's present course is now irreversible. Even so, the road to capitalism in China remains very arduous and uncertain. Numerous obstacles – including popular opposition that I will take note of later – stand in the way. But even if these obstacles are somehow overcome, the capitalism that finally comes to be built under the present leadership is not likely to be an autonomous, self-generating 'national' economy, capable of providing a reasonable level of prosperity for the Chinese people. The long-standing weaknesses of the economy, the nature of political power, the outcome of the reforms so far, and the domination of global capitalism, all militate against such an outcome. The reckless turn to free market regulation of the economy together with the 'cancer', as it has been called, of largely foreign-funded capitalist development intentionally introduced by the government, has unleashed forces – and they will only grow with the passage of time – which are beginning to defy government control; it is doubtful if the current leadership even wants to control them. As noticed earlier, there is endemic corruption, made worse by inflation and, driven by the imperatives of the market economy, everybody is out to make quick money, to prosper at the neighbour's expense. With the Dengist exhortation to 'enrich themselves', the tendency has been strong to do so as fast as possible, with those in power leading the way. All this does not exactly hold the promise of a strong, self-reliant capitalist economy. Already we have the rich and the powerful seeking to be more rich and more powerful, cutting the corners and using every means at their disposal, while the vast majority of peasants as well as workers, having lost all equity in the means of production, are moving into the market as unemployed with nothing to sell but their labour power. It is a polarisation characteristic of a third world economy.

The reckless squeeze of the peasantry has weakened Beijing's command over the rural administration, now dominated by local satraps. The private deregulated financial and industrial system, lubricated with funds from abroad, has acquired an autonomous momentum of its own. The specific character of Chinese uneven development, even as it has created enclaves of wealth and prosperity on the coast while vast stretches of the interior stagnate, has produced provincial power centres, even fiefdoms, which have, again, greatly reduced Beijing's room for manoeuvre in the economy. In other words, the Dengist reform in China has had a tendency not only to compradorise the economy but also undermine the overall ability of the Chinese state to impose a national character on the development of capitalism in China.

In this situation the role of integration into global economy, postulated by the economic reforms, becomes crucial. Here, as noted in a section above, we need to look deeper into and beyond China's economic upsurge of recent years. For considerations already noticed in relation to the future economic development of Russia, global capitalism in crisis and the interests of the powers currently dominant in it are and will remain averse to the rise of China as a rival in the world markets. While China's opening to foreign investment, closer ties with the world economy have the long term possibility of accumulating heavy international debt, leading to debt peonage similar to Nigeria or Brazil, it will have real problems in gaining and maintaining a market share for exports to the West and Japan, or elsewhere, as competition stiffens, recession deepens, depression engulfs one country after another, and world rivalries sharpen. The opportunities once provided by the United State's Cold War politics (including Asian wars and an arms-driven US market) are no longer wide open the way they were to developing Asian economies, and China in any case is much too big to be another Asian tiger parlaying exports to the west into a prime source of development funds. But it is certainly not too big to be a happy hunting ground for multinational capital in search of quick or easy profits, or to import globalised cultural regression and moral decline as western capitalist culture penetrates and dominates one sphere after another – public media first, then literature, the arts, education, and science. China, like other third world countries needs to reduce dependence rather than seek integration into the world capitalist economy. Its integration into the global capitalist system and dependence on foreign capital is likely to push it into a new semi-colonial status. It will be an economy at the mercy of its creditors and of every adverse trend in the world market, plagued, as most third world economies have been, by 'short-term growth punctured by long-term stagnation'.

XVIII

China is not yet a properly capitalist economy and its structural integration into the world capitalist economy is still far from crossing the critical point of no return. While its accelerated movement towards capitalism, officially described as 'socialist market economy', has been widely applauded in the west, its lack of democratic political reform is deplored, and it is argued that the latter is necessary for the success of the economic reforms. It has even been suggested that a successful transition to capitalism will have to await the kind of political change – the overthrow of authoritarian power structures – that took place in ex-Soviet Union and Eastern Europe. Such argumentation, however, misses the real point. By retaining tight political control the communist bureaucrats may be personally benefitting from the capitalist economic system they are creating, but it is precisely the absence of democracy that has made the radical recapitalisation of the Chinese economy easy to enforce and contain the chaotic forces it has unleashed or the protest its cruel macro-economic consequences have evoked. Market-oriented reforms may have temporarily solved certain difficulties created by bureaucratic centralised planning, they have in the short run certainly secured spectacular economic growth in certain areas. But they have also generated new and more serious problems: unemployment, rural exodus, corruption, inflation, growing social inequalities, decline in social services, growth of criminality, subordination of the economy to the multinational banks and so on. The opening of the door to internal and external capitalism has provoked contradictions of all kinds, leading to any number of open and concealed conflicts in the Chinese economy and society. One much noticed reaction has been the so-called 'democracy movement' which most remarkably recruited forces both from the well-off classes who openly sought faster restoration of capitalism, and from the majority (some claiming to be Maoists) who had been harmed by capitalist developments of the Deng era. Orderly economic development demands a containment of such opposition or protest. Hence the utility of authoritarian political rule. The Tiananmen Square demonstration was ruthlessly repressed and it certainly led to a further hardening of the regime. But this was no *return* to Maoism mixed with 'Stalinism' as the Western media proclaimed at the time. It was an expression of the determination of the Deng regime to secure a more orderly transition to capitalism, if necessary to the total detriment of democracy. Democratic political reform, far from being necessary for the purpose of this transition could imperil the whole reformist scheme of things. In the event this situation has been quite welcome to the western media, who went on to rechristen Deng as an enlightened free-market reformer barely a couple of years after he was almost universally condemned as the butcher of Beijing. The Western governments too, hypocritically noisy about human rights from time to time to further pressurise it, continue to be appreciative and helpful towards China's authoritarian regime.

There is the dogma, current in the West and now in the ex-'socialist' East as well that there is a direct and logical link between market oriented economic reforms and political democracy, between economic 'freedom' and political freedom. It is certainly comforting for some to believe that a capitalist market economy is likely to yield political democracy. But there is, in fact, little modern historical evidence to support this belief. Deng Xiaoping's model is a good counter example, as are the many third world countries which combine neo-liberal economies with extremely authoritarian forms of state power. Even after Deng, China's recapitalisation has been proceeding in combination with a repressive political dictatorship, and seems likely to so proceed at least for the foreseeable future, unless, of course, this process comes to be reversed.

China is indeed no historical oddity in this respect. As already noticed in another context, Meiji Japan and Bismarckian Germany in the late 19th century are the most notable examples of capitalist industrialisation that proceeded under the guidance of highly authoritarian states. More recent historical examples are the much-celebrated 'little dragons' of East Asia, especially Taiwan, South Korea and Singapore, where, notwithstanding some trappings of democracy, capitalist development has been presided over by repressive one-party dictatorships. Then there is the notorious case of Chile where in the early 1970s, the democratically elected socialist government of the Marxist Salvador Allende was overthrown in favour of Gen. Augusto Pinochet, whose fascist-like regime then proceeded to impose a 'free market' economy. Capitalism in the modern world has proved compatible with a great variety of political regimes, not excluding fascism – and, if the case of present-day China is to be taken into account, apparently not excluding some form of Stalinism either. China's transformation from a dictatorship with strong Stalinist features to anything resembling democracy, bourgeois or socialist, is still a long way off.

It may be noted that liberals in the west have not been wanting in lauding the experience of the East Asian 'Newly Industrialising Countries' (NICs) – 'rapid industrialisation overseen by authoritarian political regimes, and the exercise of state power to repress and displace working class struggle, creating conditions for the expansion of state capital and large agglomerations of domestic and foreign capital in partnership with the state', as one description has it – and advocating it as a model for economic growth and development for the so called developing countries. Within China itself neo-liberal and 'market socialist' economists alike have been attracted to the East Asian NIC model because it legitimises the systematic state repression and coercion required to impose their agenda. Even dissident Chinese intellectuals in exile have begun to speak of the need for a 'new authoritarianism' to maintain stability, to break down the entrenched power of workers and overcome their indiscipline or resistance. The liberal teleology which charts an inevitable trajectory from economic development to political pluralism has no problems with justifying political authoritarianism in the so-called interim period of rapid economic growth and development. In any case, liberalism's primary concern is not political pluralism or democracy but 'free market', the capitalist character of this economic growth and development. It, therefore, has no problems with China's authoritarian road to capitalism. Problems here lie only for the Chinese people who, as victims, are suffering the consequences of both authoritarianism and capitalism.

China, which has gone in for a spreading market economy while still maintaining its authoritarian political structure has been aptly described as a case of 'market-Stalinism'. Sharing the disadvantages of both, China is full of explosive possibilities which do not exclude the country turning away from both market and Stalinism and returning to socialism of Mao Zedong and Karl Marx, which alone, I may add, now holds the promise of any genuine democracy for the Chinese people.

XIX

China's road to capitalism, as mentioned earlier, is not going to be easy or smooth. Numerous obstacles stand in the way, some of them extensions of long-standing historical phenomena, others arising from the legacy of a revolution only 50 years old and the achievements of the recent revolutionary past. The transition began and has continued amidst much confusion and ambiguity, and deception of the people. The capitalist roaders, though fast losing prestige still speak the language of socialism, a sign at once of their strength as well as weakness. The Communist Party leadership still finds it necessary to retain in the Constitution the jargons of 'persisting in socialism', 'persisting in Marxism-Leninism', and maintaining the primary role played by the state-owned economies and public ownership system. Scholars writing of the 'intellectual assessment' that followed the death of Mao, have pointed out that, for all their critiques of ultra-leftism, Mao's successors never really succeeded in marginalising his concerns regarding the emergence of oppressive, exploitative groups in post-revolutionary society. Mao's fear of capitalist restoration has continued to find expression even at the highest political levels. The experience with economic reform – massive dislocation of peasantry, unemployment and rising levels of inequality, declining social mores, the scale and intensity of corruption and speculation within the system, and so on – has among its consequences also a revival of radical Maoist ideas that have been sought to be marginalised in the past decades. Surveys have shown that the popular image of the new rich is not positive, their means to riches are widely regarded as questionable and even illegitimate. For the better educated the new rich have neither culture nor taste, and are thought to have a negative impact on the society as a whole which is still alive to the egalitarian ethos of the earlier post-revolutionary Mao era.

Insofar as they have been at it, the reformers have proved more able at undermining the existing doctrine than at furnishing a new persuasively and coherently articulated ideological framework. There is dissidence and opposition within the party, not solidarity but tensions and struggle for power at the top, which has only intensified after the passing away of Deng Xiaoping. There are so-called hardliners who still exist even at the highest levels of the party and state, along with significant numbers of lower level officials and professionals who, even as they carry out the reform, express their ambiguity towards its consequences and mourn the loss of older values. Deng's successors have been having their way, but their policies and plans to reduce the role of the state in the economy, have faced criticism from within the party leadership. The veteran communist leader, Deng Liqun, for example, has argued – in a document entitled *Certain Theories and Policies on Upholding the Primary Status of the Public Ownership System* –that market reforms introduced since the late 1970s would ultimately lead to privatisation of Chinese economy and with it to the demise of Marxism and Communist Party in China. The Dengist concept 'socialism with Chinese characteristics' itself has been questioned on ideological grounds. Criticism from within the party (He Qinglian and others) has been accompanied by criticism from outside. An incipient New Left has come up with its connotations of egalitarianism and planned economy and scepticism about the market. Dismissed by the regime as 'idealists', they are demanding opening up of 'the policy debate'. The argument is spreading beyond elite universities, think tanks and state-controlled newspapers. Radically-inclined economists are questioning the older economists, dubbed 'the New Right', for touting market reforms without regard for their social costs. Workers are producing and writing in underground newspapers. Complaints that China's leaders have forsaken the poor and sold out to foreigners echo cardinal themes of Mao's revolution. Marx remains a disturbing presence. Notable among the writings circulating in China is the book *Looking at China Through a Third Eye,* which is receiving continuing attention. Published in 1994, the book notes the adverse destabilising consequences of unbridled reform, the erosion and loss of central ideological and political control and the alarming decline of public morality. It points to the growing polarisation in Chinese society and the reemergence of class conflict, and advocates a return to revolutionary ideals and Mao Zedong Thought as the way out of the current crisis and its dilemmas. The significance of this dissidence and opposition is reflected in the orders Jiang was compelled to issue against 'stirring up controversies' and his warnings to Party cadres for vigilance against radical leftism. Together with growing popular resistance to reform, it also explains the leadership's exhortations to party cadres to obey the post-Deng leadership – exhortations that the Chinese media has been full of in recent years. It is demanded of party members – they add up to 58 million now – to carry out 'democratic centralism' and show solidarity in 'defending the Party's authority, maintaining unanimity with the Party Centre ideologically and politically, and assuring that the Party's line and the Centre's policies can be smoothly implemented and executed.'

The development of China during the three post-revolutionary decades has been described as making life available to people in three kinds of bowls, the 'golden', 'iron' and 'clay' 'rice bowls'. The internal barriers or sites of resistance to development of capitalism can be viewed in terms of what it has done or is doing to each of these bowls and the opposition this is provoking and likely to provoke in future.

The 'golden rice bowl', very much in the old Chinese tradition, refers to the powers and prerogatives of bureaucracy – substantial salaries, fringe benefits and illicit windfall profits – and its dominance over the economy, which led to the Chinese system being described as a 'position-power economy'. Some of these powerholders in the party and the state, whose corruption and capitalist-roading immobilism was a major target of Mao's Cultural Revolution, are already benefitting as technocrats and entrepreneurial upstarts or as 'bureaucratic capitalists', but the rest are losing out in the emerging market economy and are therefore a possible source of opposition to the capitalist transition underway. This opposition of course is not necessarily socialist in nature. Though, in this connection we must not overlook the still surviving Maoist elements and tradition within the party, as in the country as a whole, which the new Chinese rulers have not been able as yet to exorcise.

The 'iron rice bowl', as we have already noticed, refers to the social benefits, including life-time job security, that revolution provided to the Chinese workers, benefits far exceeding those found in most western capitalist democracies. As in the ex-Soviet Union, the Chinese reformers saw the guaranteed jobs and social security as a major stumbling block to raising labour productivity and modernising the economy. (They failed to see that stagnation or slow down on the plant floor was not the result of the 'iron rice bowl' but a response to the 'golden rice bowl', to the class exploitative nature of bureaucratic control and dominance over the economy). Hence the reformers' persistent efforts to break the 'iron rice bowl'. The workers have fought to defend their hardwon economic and social rights, though rather unsuccessfully so far. But this fight will continue and sharpen as they realise that their lost rights can be regained only along the road to socialism.

The 'clay rice bowl' refers to use-rights to the land which the peasants won through land reforms, a most important legacy of the revolution. Building a successful capitalism in China demands more than foreign and private or privatised domestic capital; it involves, by choice or otherwise, 'primitive accumulation' which first and foremost separates large masses of peasants from the land and turns their labour power into a commodity for sale in the market. This is already happening though without the corresponding industrial development adequate enough to absorb this uprooted peasantry; more than a hundred million are roaming the countryside and those absorbed are working in Special Economic Zones and elsewhere in conditions which are as barbaric as they can be under a peripheral capitalism. The result is an unprecedented social turmoil in rural and urban areas which is not without the possibility of creating conditions for a new worker-peasant alliance for a return to socialism.

This is how China's transition to capitalism is meeting with considerable resistance from below. The much-lauded 'gradualism' of this transition is itself a product of this resistance, forcing the political elite and the emerging capitalist class to moderate their policies. As part of this resistance, peasant protests, riots, even uprisings are emerging as a new reality in the Chinese countryside, involving hundreds of thousands of peasants across the country. Peasants are rising up against their steadily deteriorating living conditions as well as specific oppressions of corruption, excessive taxes and illegal levies, and the continued abuse of privilege and power by the party-state bureaucracy. 'A Study of Mass Incidents', a book circulated internally by the Chinese police in 2002, warns that large-scale public disturbances are increasing annually, particularly in the countryside, one reason being the growing gap between rich and poor. Uneven development accompanied by national oppression (or Han chauvinism) has whole regions -- Tibet, Xinijiang, etc. –in a continuous state of revolt or near-revolt. As a foreign observer, Ian Buruma, has commented: 'China today is a country of many small rebellions.' Qin Hui, writing of 'the brazen injustice being perpetrated today', even fears that 'if democratisation comes... there will be... great popular anger and determination to reverse the injustice... the outcome could be like Russia all over again... a new Bolshevik revolution...'

As against the rather scattered and amorphous resistance of the peasants, that of the workers in urban, industrial areas is more focused and visible. Throughout the state and collective sectors, in TVEs, private enterprises and foreign joint ventures growing resistance to new modes of coercion and exploitation has emerged to challenge the very logic of capitalist regime of production. The workers have been expressing their discontent over soaring inflation, non-payment of back wages, threat of layoffs in the collapsing state sector, hazardous working conditions, bureaucratic corruption and violations of workers' rights, including forced overtime, beatings, and physical and sexual harassment. Their fight back, increasingly militant and better organised, has ranged from petitions, sit-ins, blocking highways and slow downs to clashes with police, mass demonstrations with families, laying siege to party and government offices and above all strikes. (According to All China Federation of Trade Unions (ACFTU), there were 25,000 strikes involving 450,000 workers in 1995). It may be noted that, legally, the workers' right to protest is not allowed; any protest action without the local Security Bureau's permission is illegal in China. And the 1982 constitution had removed the right to strike. Also, the party-controlled ACFTU does not countenance workers' protest-actions or strikes. Workers have been bypassing the ACFTU and self-organising themselves into autonomous unions and genuine workers' associations to carry out their struggles.

These struggles have markedly increased in recent years. In 1994 there were 135,000 reported labour disputes. In 1995 they numbered more than 2 lakhs. The Chinese Labour Bureau admits this drastic rise in labour disputes and notes the significant fact that of the hundreds of thousands of cases in 1995 and 1996, over half were cases related to state-owned enterprises. The rise is really a trend which reflects workers' growing discontent and militancy. An official estimate, likely to be conservative, indicated that in 1995 some 1.1 million workers in more than 50 cities in China participated in protest demonstrations against the state-owned, private and foreign enterprises. The same figure (according to *Eastern Express*,

Hong Kong) leaped to 3.6 million by 1998. Typical of the emerging situation is this account relating to the year 1995: 'Newspapers reported that strikes "surged" in cities throughout the country in that year. In Liaoning and Sichuan, workers "again and again took to the streets and staged demonstrations to express their resentment" at unpaid back wages. In Shenyang, workers marched, shouting "We want to eat!" In Chongqing, protests erupted after a laid-off factory worker and his family committed suicide because they could not afford to buy food. A Communist Party internal circular reported that more than 12,000 strikes, protests and public petitions occurred in the first ten months of 1995 – in a country where strikes are illegal and labour activists severely punished.' The growing militancy of workers' struggle is typified by the strike of mine-workers of Liaoning in 2000 when thousands of workers, angry over the bankruptcy of their mine, were involved in a stand-off with the army that lasted several days.

These strikes and demonstrations, reflecting workers' growing collective resistance to their oppression and exploitation by the party-state and emergent capitalism, have evoked a two-fold response from the regime. There is a party-led counter mobilisation wherein official trade unions, while continuing to carry out some of their former functions – mobilising workers to raise productivity and output, consolidating managerial control over labour, maintaining labour discipline and industrial peace for the sake of 'national economic growth', etc. – are being deployed to enforce better capitalist discipline and otherwise consolidate the power of capitalist entrepreneurs (especially those aligned with or emerging from within the party-state). As an officially laid down policy, trade unions' defence of workers' rights must not conflict with the 'legitimate rights of investors'. This counter-mobilisation is well supplemented by violent state repression including mass arrests and imprisonment, and 'reeducation through labour' of so-called 'subversives', especially those who are Marxists or socialists, or seek to build autonomous unions and genuine workers associations. The resistance, however, continues. (It is significant that while liberal human rights campaigners in the west have organised public campaigns around a few victims of their choice, labour activists and organisers who remain committed to Marxism and socialism are not among them).

XX

Of course, the on-going popular opposition to the regime of capitalist restoration is not always or even mostly socialist. Nevertheless it is a challenge to the neo-liberal agenda and the privilege and power of the party-state, the two driving forces behind this restoration, and socialism is not entirely absent. It has been suggested that China today is a pressure-cooker society but without an outlet for the steam that inevitably builds up, thus presaging a blowout sooner or later. China does seem to be on way to times of troubles rivalling anything in its long and checkered history. But this does not necessarily rule out a return to socialism. I will conclude with two very brief observations.

The Chinese regime today faces opposition from above and opposition from below. The opposition from above includes the liberal intellectuals who, duly supported by the west, regard themselves as the only political alternative to the 'communist regime'. I am not here concerned with the clichés of their bourgeois ideology. I would only like to state that if the failure of the democratic movement in 1989 proved anything, it was that the Chinese liberal intellectuals are unqualified to provide any kind of leadership or alternative to the Chinese people. Evasive of more basic issues, their panacea remains western-style democratisation and representative institutions, and even here they have shown no stomach for any political mobilisation of the people. Again, when the Chinese working people are now faced with a desperate fight for the preservation of what is left of their revolutionary heritage, China's liberal intellectuals have pronounced 'corruption' as the biggest problem in China, thereby marginalising the issues of socio-economic equality, class and hierarchy, which remain the key concerns for the Chinese people. By following these liberals Chinese people can achieve only their own ultimate expropriation. Surely, they are not going to opt for this 'alternative'. There is no future for them along this path.

China's working people have a future only with socialism. And however confusing or bleak the present situation may appear to be, this future is not to be discounted. The opposition from below, people's own opposition to capitalist transition, apparently local, limited or sporadic, is still not without its undercurrent of the sentiment expressed in a worker's letter to the students in Tiananmen Square: that 'the wealth created by the sweat and blood of hundreds of millions of compatriots is squandered by the bureaucrats, China's biggest capitalists.' China's present history is not exhausted by a few decades of Dengist reform. It also contains Mao's socialism. Socialist values are still alive for many citizens and inform their ideas of democracy and freedom much more than liberal doctrines. The embattled workers have the defiant 'Down with the New-born Bourgeoisie', 'Yes to Socialism, No to Capitalism', 'Down with the New Nobility', 'Factories Belong to All the Workers', on their banners. Mao Zedong had once said: '*A single spark can light a praire fire*' and rarely has Chinese society been so inflammable. As the capitalist transition proceeds and the tendency towards economic and social polarisation comes to embed itself as a structural feature of Chinese society, not only will the popular resistance grow, it will also help the Chinese working people to free themselves from the ideological domination of both the ruling elites and the liberal intelligentsia and make of themselves a really independent political force, that is, a socialist revolutionary force. This polarisation has emerged as the 'obvious Achilles' heel' of the capitalist transition, making it the object of the most powerful attack on the liberal market reforms from the old Maoist Left. It is entirely possible that a new political left may emerge to provide political leadership to the growing but dispersed and sporadic struggles of the people in defence of their interests. The popular opposition may yet, eventually, come to seek a return to the socialist road.

It is indeed hard to imagine a rapid reversal of the present course in China. But the Chinese are an energetic and creative people with large reserves of revolutionary consciousness and motivation. Chinese peasants have for centuries produced leaders, often from their own ranks, to organise revolts, and Chinese proletariat has as revolutionary a history as any in the world. Docility has never been a permanent feature of the Chinese working people. China's increasingly restless and combative workers and peasants may yet throw a large spanner into the capitalist roaders' plans for a smooth transition to capitalism. No country has been more full of surprises in the recent past. China may once again surprise the world. The question posed by Mao, 'who will win, socialism or capitalism', not only remains on the agenda of the Chinese people, it may still come to be resolved the way Mao struggled to resolve it.

4

Cuba—The Hopeful Legacy

China went in for market-reform and was on its way to capitalist restoration much before the crisis matured in the Soviet Union and then erupted with Eastern Europe taking the road to capitalism even before the Soviet Union. But the rest of 'the socialist world' and the associated communist movement felt the full impact of this backward turn in history only after the Soviet collapse. The smaller, underdeveloped 'socialist' states or states of 'socialist tendency' from Vietnam to Angola, having undergone indigenous anti-capitalist revolutions, were, under Soviet inspiration, pursuing their own socialistic paths of development. Starting from much lower socio-economic levels, they were also reproducing contradictions and problems of bureaucratic deformation with that much greater force. None of these countries – 'small places where great revolutions had occurred' – had the space, the time, the material resources, the assistance, or the conditions of peace to make possible the correction of the distortions or deformations which inevitably arose in the course of collective human projects of such magnitude, undertaken in conditions so very punishing. Isolated to a degree from the capitalist world, that was partly of their own choosing and partly imposed by imperialism, they received significant material and political support, often guidance, from the Soviet Union. With the Soviet collapse that era was over and they were exposed to the full blast of the offensive of capitalist imperialism which had never given up hope of breaking the national will of these countries and forcing or sucking them back into global capitalism. They have resisted, each in its own way, yet for the most part succumbed, and the future, for the present, appears rather bleak.

II

Facing a crisis of its Soviet-style socialism, Vietnam was, already in the mid-1980s, struggling to rectify and chart out a different, revived, Vietnamese (as against the orthodox, Stalinist) path to socialism. Severely critical of what it described as 'bureaucratically centralised management of the command economy based on state subsidy...', Vietnamese Communist Party had proclaimed the need for 'renovation of our philosophy, our work methods and our organisational modalities, in accordance with the fundamentals of Marxism-Leninism and with the demands of our era', and found the answer in a new concept *'Doi Moi'* (renovation). This renovation strategy, for which 'economic growth' remained the governing purpose, included such privatising and market-oriented policies as decollectivisation of agriculture and the return to family-based farming, price liberalisation, the devaluation and unification of exchange rates, restructuring of the public sector including state-owned enterprises, a significant reduction in subsidies and the state budget deficit, and opening the economy to foreign investment. In other words, instead of moving leftward to innovate a *socialist* reform of the old economic and political practices, very much in the manner of Gorbachev's *perestroika, Doi Moi* too turned rightward to seek salvation in 'the market'. The collapse of Soviet Union and the 'socialist world', together with the offensive of a recharged global capitalism has pushed Vietnam further and faster along the road to a market economy – from its 'non-market socialism' towards a 'market economy with a socialist orientation' or 'market socialism' – signalling a retreat from any kind of socialism.

'The course of economic development places man in the central position, combining economic development with social justice and progress', declares the Communist Party. But such declarations of good intentions are belied by the reality on the ground where *Doi Moi's* adjustment and reform programmes have meant a steady transition to a market economy in Vietnam. In the name of 'liberation of the productive forces' control over trade and industry has been loosened to a degree inconsistent with any socialist orientation. Talk of opening to the market, participation in world economy, combining market with central planning, or of 'adjustment policies', etc., continues to miss the real issue which is not the desirability of all this but the degree and type of opening or participation, or the nature of combination and adjustment. Market-oriented practices in Vietnam have meant opening the door wide to foreign trade and investment, wooing foreign capital with the most liberal law and concessions, seeking loans and development assistance granted to client third world governments by IMF etc., devaluation of the dong, lifting of price controls and subsidies on consumer necessities, the reduction of public sector and creation of private enterprises in industry and agriculture, and integration into south-east Asia's cheap labour export economy. Global financial institutions (IMF, WB etc.) have come in with their consultants to formulate and help execute the reform programmes, and financial support has been made available only after Vietnam's compliance by way of satisfactory pursuit of economic reform and amendments to its foreign policy. Foreign capital has been successfully forcing the party leadership to pick up the pace of reform, particularly with regard to workers wages and social subsidies. The leadership itself has been steadily more accommodative to the reformers in the party. Mandated by *Doi Moi* a new constitution has been adopted, 'approving' all the economic laws that are in conflict with the declared socialist principles of the party.

Doi Moi has surely made for economic growth in Vietnam, recording remarkably high growth rates, significant initial gains in agricultural production and rise of per capita income. But this growth has an unmistakable capitalist character. 'Market economy with a socialist orientation' or 'market socialism' are only euphemisms for disguising the transition to capitalism that is on in Vietnam. That despite the promise 'to democratise social life', party's monopoly of political power and authoritarian practices remain (*a la* Chinese and perhaps to avoid what is seen to be Gorbachev's mistake) only makes Vietnam another case of development of capitalism under a single-party or otherwise authoritarian regime, the capitalist economy model we are familiar with in south-east Asia. The role of state sector continues to be emphasised, but state owned enterprises have lost whatever 'socialist orientation' they ever had. Managerial control has been strengthened in the factory and business criteria govern the practices on the shop floor. Theft of state assets is taking place, a large scale private appropriation of public resources in which political power (in the party or state) acts as the instrument of such appropriation. The socialist project abandoned, a new bourgeoisie is emerging from within the ranks of incumbent state enterprise managers and the more powerful segments of the party-state bureaucracy, even as there is a continuing debate within the party over party cadres holding private property or pursuing business.

At the other end labour stands commodified. There are 'open-air labour markets', facilitating Vietnamese export-led growth based on exploitation of passive and cheap labour. Salaries and wages, typically insufficient, are eroded by inflation. As the state enterprises are restructured, often altogether dismantled, there is growing unemployment and few of those retrenched can find new jobs. Worst affected are unskilled and women workers. The women are in fact the first to be laid off in the restructuring of the state enterprises and their position made still worse by the loss of associated benefits such as child care, maternity leave, etc. Decollectivisation has brought its own consequences with it – renewed class divisions, unemployment and mass impoverishment in the countryside. Erosion of social safety nets and welfare services has been a major consequence of Vietnamese transition to a market economy, often explained away as its negative side effect, not recognised as an element of its essential logic. With disappearing government support and privatisation of social welfare, the quality of education and health care for the people has taken a nose dive.

The growing inequalities, gaps between rich and poor and rural-urban divide that inevitably accompany capitalist development, are spawning their own social problems that go beyond the usual increase in such phenomena as child labour and prostitution. As part of the culture that market economy breeds, the young are discovering that more than anything else it is money that really matters. An internal brain drain is on, bleeding talent from the country's universities, hospitals and government ministries into business and private enterprise. Those in professions that once commanded stable government wages, subsidised housing and lifetime security – teaching, engineering, medicine, etc. – finding that real opportunities for getting rich are in tourism, real estate and trade, or with foreign companies, are moving into these lucrative pastures. There is more money to be made even as hotel receptionists, taxi drivers or doormen in upscale hotels. Even otherwise, with the jobs being cut, these are emerging as new options for the educated unemployeds of Vietnam to fight over. Looming large over it all is corruption that is now rampant in Vietnamese economy and politics. Involving the leadership and cadres of the Communist Party itself, corruption has affected the moral fibre of the party and badly dented its past 'poor but pure' image. As former secretary-general Nguyen Van Linh, the architect of economic reforms, has admitted: 'A number of party cadres have resorted to corruption and they are protected by high authorities...' Corruption in the party has been a cause for deep anguish and moral anger with the older revolutionaries and veterans of war against French and American imperialism. As one of them has put it: 'Most of us have at least 10 wounds, but none of them is as deep as the inner wound we feel now'.

The Communist Party continues to insist: 'We are socialist first and then only market-friendly policy-makers. We do not wish to be guided by the market in our policy-making'. But 'the market' has its own logic that defies whatever other 'wishes' the party may have and as Nguyen Van Linh has complained: 'We have not just created differences in society but allowed it to become a norm' even as, according to him, 'the party has (also) allowed itself to be ruled by the foreign investors'. The party has been running 'social evils campaigns' against prostitution, drugs, gambling, pornography, violent crime, massage parlours and karaoke bars, and other 'toxic cultural imports', but without recognising that this 'spiritual pollution', as they like their Chinese counterparts call it, comes in tandem with the material consequences of 'market friendly policies'. The logic of the market is also manifest in the increasing value put on money and personal gratification and the growth of a consumerist culture which have undermined the 'traditional values'. A nationwide preoccupation with getting ahead has led to the gradual disappearance of a sense of solidarity that was once a defining feature of Vietnamese life. The Party has itself recognised that the loss of 'a very egalitarian society' they once had – when 'at least in the difficult times, no one was alone' – has left the people 'disoriented'. It is this collective disorientation indeed which has sparked a return to religious practices, to pagodas and churches in Vietnam, which also draws our attention to the massive erosion of Marxist-Leninist ideology that has occurred in Vietnam in recent years. The communist leadership regularly invokes Ho Chi Minh and occasionally even asserts that socialism is not negotiable. But Ho, the communist revolutionary is being reinterpreted as a nationalist and socialism, except for rhetorical purposes, has become peripheral to the leadership's politics.

There is growing concern within the Party, especially among veterans from the pre-1975 period, about the adverse social consequences of the reform process. Hardline dissidence still exists even at its highest levels and the leadership still has problems with cadres at the lower levels carrying out its reform policies. The dissidents see 'social evils' as a direct result of the reformers' deviant political line and the campaign against them has been interpreted by observers as a result of the conflict between reformists and hardliners in the Party. Fears have been expressed within the Party that the present course could mean an end to socialism and the Party in Vietnam. Nevertheless the dominant leadership, pressurised and tempted by international financial institutions of capitalism, is continuing with its *Doi Moi* mandated 'market reform', undermining what still remains of the country's post-revolutionary socialist project. The opposition has been only able to slow down this process and force the leadership to be more cautious and restrained in pursuit of its reform agenda (especially in surrendering party-state domination to the market). It has no alternative *socialist* reform agenda of its own to offer. In other words, Vietnam's post-Soviet collapse retreat from socialism is very real, making Vietnam a showcase not of socialism but, as the enemies would say, of the impossibility of building socialism. Lack of room for manoeuvre, internally as well as externally, may explain but does not justify Vietnamese Communist Party thus retreating and negotiating socialism away to global capitalism. It has not been at all innovative in seeking a path of socialist survival. Instead of turning to the people, in its bureaucratic degeneration and corruption, it has been alienating the people and systematically squandering away the legacy of popular loyalty that it forged during its decades long struggle for national liberation and social transformation. Vietnam today is at a crossroads but its uncertain future is likely to be a return to an imperialism-dominated semi-colonial status. This will mean a loss of all the gains of the Vietnamese revolution, a betrayal of the heroic Vietnamese people who only the other day had thrown imperialism out of Vietnam in one of the most glorious chapters of the struggle for human liberation.

III

Of other small 'socialist' countries, North Korea continues to survive but more as a grim reminder of how extreme a caricature of socialism a supposedly socialist regime can be. This however is not to be dismissive about North Korea as just another backward authoritarian state, some kind of Albania or Cambodia of Northeast Asia as it is often made out to be. North Korea today is an industrialised economy in an urban setting – only about 4 million out of its 22 million people still work on land. And for all its failings as a socialist country, it is not without its achievements which are attested to even by critics (including some with impeccable CIA credentials): genuinely free housing; preventive medicine to a fairly high standard; infant mortality rates comparable to most advanced countries; self-sufficient neighbourhood practices that have generally averted the long lines for goods that characterised Soviet Union's later years; compassionate care for war orphans in particular and children in general; radical change in the position of women, and so on. Besides, what North Korea has achieved, it has done with next to no help from outside. There are good reasons for North Koreans' loyalty to the regime and reverence for Kim Il Sung, a fact that even the defectors from the system concede. An additional consideration here is that North Korea was born as a 'guerrilla state', anti-colonial and anti-Japanese to the core. A revolutionary nationalism underpins its existence. It is this revolutionary nationalism that underlay North Korea's unyielding recalcitrant postures that successfully kept other powers, including Soviet Union and China, at arms length and underlies its current defiance of the United States, a defiance which recognises that the US imperial hegemony cannot now rely, if it ever could, on economic superiority alone, it depends on periodic displays of sheer force, even wholesale invasion of countries which refuse to fall into line.

Even as it continues to face the hostility of the capitalist world, especially its chieftain, the US, the Soviet collapse has left North Korea with increasingly less room to manoeuvre for survival. The crisis of its Soviet-style socialism combined with the pressure of a recharged global capitalism has made its autarkic economy near-impossible to sustain. Unable or unwilling to look for answers to its problems from 'within socialism', North Korea is finding itself compelled to open up to the global capitalist economy. Foreign investment is sought, even Chinese-style foreign investment windows on the coast – Rajin Sonbong Free Economic Trade Zone, for example – are being experimented with, but it has remained a trickle. A chaotic economy, lack of infrastructure and uncertainty about the future has made the potential investors wary. Under constant pressure from American imperialism, it also confronts a southern-half, rather ambivalent about unification with it, which, if and when it occurs, is likely to be on capitalist lines, certainly a more realistic possibility than any other kind of end of North Korea that the global capitalist system hopes for. Led by the US, the system remains unappeased in its search for absolute domination of the world. Not particularly kind to South Korea either in recent years, it lies in wait to suck North Korea back into the capitalist fold one way or another. In the meantime question remains how long North Korea can survive as it is, in its fortress like isolation, defending whatever kind of socialism it has built.

Elsewhere, Albania has collapsed into obscurity once again but at the mercy of local and foreign free booters. In Cambodia, former communists' rejection of 'socialism' coordinated with the rather hiccupy presence of former royals has led to coalition governments with no pretensions to pursuing an anti-capitalist programme of development. In the western hemisphere, Grenada after the murder of Bishop and the American invasion has already been an offshore haven for shady banking capital; and the Sandinistas in Nicaragua, squeezed from office with the help and connivance of Gorbachev's Soviet Union are still trying to recover from the blow thus dealt them. Erstwhile 'Marxist-Leninist' regimes in Southern Africa – Angola, Mozambique, etc. – their anti-capitalist national projects defeated, have long since renounced the label. With varying kinds of resistance or acceptance, through direct pressure from the IMF and the WB or from the internal bureaucracies and bourgeoisies themselves, the former radical ruling elites have been pushed out or into a corner in the dozen odd underdeveloped 'socialist tendency' states that came up in the post-colonial period. Everywhere, instead of the working people, the axis of power now is the body of state officials and local bourgeoisies in partnership with transnational bourgeoisies, and comprador relations of production and domination are getting established with a new kind of colonial authority or supranational state embodied in the IMF-like international financial institutions of global capitalism. Cuba apart, all the more or less advanced small countries of the ex-socialist world have lost or seem destined to lose the economic and social war after winning the war of the battlefield.

As already noticed in other contexts, the collapse of Soviet Union has caused complete disarray in the world communist movement, though the official communist parties had by and large already lost their revolutionary élan and commitment as well as influence among the people and were in a state of stagnation, partly because of their subservient Soviet connection. Many in the west have now discarded the 'communist' label and gone completely social-democratic in order to facilitate their entry into the existing bourgeois political framework. The rest, mostly in the third world, their label notwithstanding, have got only more firmly confirmed in their reformist practices, without losing any of their inherited dogmatism or sectarianism. The need was a renewal, through a critical reflection over what has happened, over the chequered experience of the Second and Third Internationals, especially in the light of the new problematic posed by the significant emergence of mass social movements (around issues of ecology, gender equality, peace, human rights, etc). What has happened instead is a return and uncritical adherence to what can only be described as one or the other variant of the practical politics of the Second International, without however its commitment, once and at least in theory, to socialism as a replacement of capitalism. Occasional rhetoric of socialism only serves to conceal the fact that these parties no longer see or seek an alternative to capitalism. Soviet collapse has left them 'realists' with a vengeance. Even if deemed necessary or desirable, socialism is no longer a possibility to be presently fought for.

IV

In the midst of the worldwide 'crisis of socialism', with the former Communist regimes and parties succumbing one after another to the lure or power of the market, Cuba has stood almost alone and defiant, so far, against the global offensive of capitalism. Cuba remains the one society which has retained a revolutionary commitment although having to make concessions to global capitalism. Even as it retreats in some spheres of life, it has come to lead the world in others – for example, in the vision of an ecological society and the development of socialist democracy. Fidel Castro has continued to affirm his country's rejection of capitalism and total adherence to socialism. As he has put it:

> The collapse of socialism in certain countries does not at all mean it has failed. Due to several factors – treason included – socialism lost one battle. But I reject the notion that the future of humankind might depend on a system like capitalism that is based on inequality, selfishness, a ferocious competition among men, the most absolute irrationality and the most criminal waste of limited resources. In these respects capitalism as a system has not proven its efficiency anywhere in the world, least of all in the developing nations.

Cuba remains committed to socialism despite the fact that Cuba's economic as well as external political situation remains perhaps the most desperate of what still survives of the former 'socialist world'. Cuban economy, its impressive growth notwithstanding, never got out of its deep dependency on the Soviet Union and cannot now avoid paying the price of the final collapse of its former ally; though, it is well to remember, Gorbachev's perestroikan 'new thinking' had already abandoned Cuba. Politically, located at the very doorstep of the chieftain of global capitalism, the United States – a mere 90 miles from Florida – Cuba is now more vulnerable than ever before to any new imperialist offensive. The worldwide ascendancy of recharged capitalism and right-wing politics has dried up almost all other sources of economic or political support. In the disintegrated 'socialist' second world, each country is now busy fending for itself as best as it can. With the American victory in the Cold War, whatever ability to resist, manoeuvre or hold together the Third World ever had has been grievously undermined. And as 'the night of neo-liberal conservatism settles across Europe', with even the Left succumbing to it, the era when Cuba could look for some support from social-democrats in or out of power in some West-European countries is over. Nevertheless, with the odds so heavily stacked against it, Cuba has so far firmly rejected the idea of any retreat from socialism or a marketising and privatising dilution of the class content of its economy, politics or political leadership. The Cuban leadership has, instead, asserted that 'Cuba's major contribution to Marxism today lies in safeguarding its revolutionary project'.

This defiance is obviously most odious to an empire that regards Cuba as part of its zone of influence and domination in terms of both geography and economic system. For more than a hundred years Cuba was a 'virtual colony of the United States' – as Harvard historians Ernest May and Philip Zelikow have described it – until Cuban revolution occurred and Fidel Castro took over in January 1959. The United States has not just refused to accept the new regime but seen it as a threat to its imperial hegemony, and planned and plotted against it throughout. Within a few months the Eisenhower administration decided secretly to overthrow the Castro government, and equally secretly, took a formal decision to do so in March 1960. Terror attacks from Florida began in 1959 itself and continuing since then ave included uncountable number of attempts to murder Castro. The Kennedy administration which came in soon afterwards broke off diplomatic relations and imposed a far reaching embargo on Cuba in 1961, when Havana took over three hundred foreign, including American, firms or plantations. It maybe noted that the expropriations were carried through by a gvernment recognised by Washington, under powers enshrined in the Cuban Constitution of 1940 that authorised the state to take over properties in private hands if it was in the public interest. (Also, the agrarian reforms of the reolutionary regime did not single out US or foreign companies but applied to all large estates and the Cuban government was and has been willing to offer compensation to former owners). In a report written for President Kennedy at the time, historian Arthur Schlesinger identified the Cuban threat as 'the spread of the Castro idea of taking matters into one's own hands', which was indeed a serious problem because, as he added a little later, throughout Latin America 'the distribution of land and other forms of national wealth greatly favours the propertied classes, (and) the poor and underprivileged, stimulated by the example of the Cuban revolution, are now demanding opportunities for a decent living'. The original embargo, regularly intensified by the administtions which followed, continues, as does the hope entertained by its advocates. As one of them, Juan J. Lopez has recently explained, it 'increases the economic pressures that foment discontent among regime cadres and in the general population'; he adds: 'the maintenance of the embargo is conducive to an internal coup.'

The hoped-for coup has not materialised and Cuba remains defiant in defence of its revolutionary project, a source of inspiration to the poor and oppressed everywhere, immediately and most importantly in Latin America. It is thus that Cuba under Fidel Castro has become a major, if not the prinipal, target of the American imperialist offensive. Aided by a triumphant capitalist Europe, the United States is tightening the economic and political screws as much as it can, waiting for Cuba, bereft of Soviet trade or aid, to drop back into its imperialist lap in a Big Fall. Or as a Cuban minister has put it: 'They are not debating whether or not to cut off our heads, but how they will do it: knife or razor'. The corporate media is full of prognostications of the coming collapse. Cuba, we are told is 'living on borrowed time', 'Senor Castro is doomed and everybody knows it'. The only issue they insist is, 'how he will fall'. Frustrated in their hopes and CIA's countless attempts to physically eliminate Castro, even supposedly liberal commentators go impotently derisive in their attitude towards him – he is 'a sclerotic windbag', 'the last remaining member of the chamber of horrors', and so on. They simply fail or refuse to understand the man and the nature of his close relationship with the Cuban people. Of course what the enemies really hate are the ideas that Castro represents, and what they hope and call for is not merely the exit of Fidel Castro, but the liquidation of Cuba's socialist revolutionary project.

V

Cuba, however, continues to struggle and survive. It is not without its assets for the purpose. The Cuban Revolution (1959-60) is relatively young; however dented with the passage of time, revolutionary leadership and idealism are still very much alive in Cuba. The people have the self-pride instilled by a revolution defiantly made and sustained in America's own backyard. The nationalist hegemony, unlike Eastern Europe, is with the Castro regime in Havana and not with the

American-backed opposition in Miami. And this regime has now behind it four decades of revolutionary achievement which Cuban people continue to refuse to surrender to the recharged offensive of global capitalism.

Essential to the Cubans' ability to face the post-Soviet collapse difficulties in a way consistent with their goal of building socialism lies precisely in what they achieved from 1959 to 1989, and have continued to defend during the last decade. On the one hand, contrary to general impression fed by propaganda against socialism or Cuba, there was the impressive economic growth; Cuba produced a wide range of commodities for domestic consumption and for export, and even developed a capital goods industry, the silver lining of the devastating thirty-one year US embargo. Cuba's economic growth from 1960 to 1985 was the second highest in Latin America, behind only Brazil. Planned nature of this economic growth made for a sweeping economic transformation of Cuba. Land reforms apart, typical of Cuba's planned response to its previous underdevelopment and unequal development was the decision to prioritise housing in the countryside over housing in Havana, and to prioritise social projects and new factories over housing. On the other hand the egalitarian ethos governing its planning approach and apparatus enabled Cuba to record unparalleled achievements in matters of social welfare for the people. These achievements based on planned (not market-driven) economic development, though under severe strain now, remain a distinguishing feature of Cuban society today. Its inadequacies notwithstanding, Cuba's homebred Third-World socialism has significantly improved the lot of ordinary Cubans. Long exploited and oppressed, they have been elevated and empowered. Particularly noteworthy are the gains of the black people (who make up a majority of the population) and of women (who make up half) in matters of education, jobs, racial and gender equality. Now, with other Cubans, they share in all the fruits of their labour. The sharp racial, gender-based or poverty-generated discriminations and injustices of the pre-revolution era have given way to a remarkably equitable and harmonious social order.

Revolutionary Cuba is a just and humane society, though it still remains an economically poor and backward country. Along with elimination of poverty and dramatic advances in equality of wealth, the regime has enormous social advances to its credit in such areas as health care and education, making its health-care and educational systems by far the best in the Americas. They have a truly national health service, one that is fostered and funded by the government. All medical care is free at the point of access to every citizen; it is equitably allocated, not rationed. Treatment is given according to need, as judged by the best clinical standards. Infant mortality improved from 60 per 1000 in 1960 to 97 per 1000 in 1991. Life expectancy rose from 55 in 1958 to 70 in 1975 to 75 in 1991. Polio, smallpox, malaria, tetanus, tuberculosis, measles, whooping cough, typhoid, and diphtheria have all been wiped out by a public health programme using vaccination and clean water. Resources are allocated to training and employing vast numbers of health personnel. There are 31 thousand doctors and 40 thousand nurses. The doctor-patient ration is 1:300, better than in Britain. Before the revolution it was 1:2000. Underpinning Cuba's remarkable health care services is its world-class pharmaceutical and biotechnology industry owned and controlled by the Cubans themselves. Cuba's achievement here has won recognition worldwide. As *The Economist* acknowledged in 1996, 'Cuban medicine is disciplined and innovative... Cuban research establishments have made breakthroughs in vaccines, immunology and biotechnology.' Along with doctors, the numbers of scientists and teachers (including art and sports instructors) in Cuba in ratio to the population is the highest in the world. There are schools, nurseries and clinics everywhere. As the government proudly claims, 'in Latin America, more than three million children sleep every night on the streets. Not one of them is Cuban'.

Illiteracy is a thing of the past in Cuba and there is a minimum of social security for all. Cities are clean, free from crime or drugs, and life in general is rich in its quality of culture and social solidarity. Everyone has a guaranteed stake in the economy. The revolution ensured full employment for the working class, even if the wages are low. But it is the rural population, once landless and dependent on seasonal work on large sugar plantations and other farms, which has benefited the most from the revolution. The Cuban revolution was largely an agrarian one, land reform and literacy for all were among its first objectives. Along with the realisation of these objectives came improved education, medical care and working conditions, rural electrification, the construction of houses, schools, medical clinics and hospitals, and rising living standards. The benefits revolution brought to the peasantry are tangible all over Cuba. Now, the children of this class have education, medicine, farmland or jobs – as basic rights. And, along with fellow Cubans, they are armed and trained to fight in defence of the gains and ideals of their revolution. Obviously, the Cubans do not have any enthusiasm for restoration of the old order, which can only turn their country once again into a semi-colonial appendage of American capitalism. On the contrary, they have a strong interest in fighting against any such reimposition. Observers have pointed out that, aware of what is happening around them, not a few young Cubans see themselves as the last idealists in a world that cares only about money or profits in the market place.

The Cuban people have not yet lost their memories of United Fruit Company and the rest, of colonial exploitation by American capitalism – Cuba was one of the closest and most profitable of the United States' neo-colonies. With the advantage of neighbourhood, they are not ignorant either of what market economy means, even if it is an advanced capitalism. They are well aware of US' unemployment, homelessness, runaway debt, its culture of gun and drugs and other chronic ailments or shortcomings. They also know that the Third World is hopelessly in debt of the First-World banks and that living conditions are far worse in other Third World countries in the periphery or semi-periphery of global capitalism. These include their other neighbours in Central and South America, where, as one observer has it, 'the greater the influence of the United States the more kids were out in the street banging on your car windows to sell you Chicklets and shoelaces.' Few, if any, Cubans favour either opting for the 'magic of the market' or going back to US dependence. As a young Cuban said in a recent interview: 'We see socialism is difficult to achieve but capitalism is not the answer either.'

The Cuban people now also have the benefit of knowing the havoc that 'market reforms' in Eastern Europe and ex-Soviet Union have played with the economic and social life of these countries, the unprecedented misery and suffering they have brought to the common people. They continue to learn from this ruinous denouement by what the Chinese in their revolutionary days used to call 'negative example'. They do not want to follow the same path: where all gains of the revolution have been lost, unemployment has re-emerged and soared as have the prices, inequalities have intensified, and poverty and destitution have reappeared along with every vice of a Third-Worldised capitalist development. This prospect is infinitely worse than any current hardships in Cuba. At the very least, education, jobs and medical services more than compensate for the shortages, rationing and long queues. The experience of its former allies with the West-sponsored structural adjustment, its catastrophic legacy, has had a cleansing effect on Cuba's theory and practice in recent years. Few Cubans possess the masochistic impulses to endure the Sachs' 'shock therapy' which kills the patient to cure the illness!

No less relevant is the fact that, unlike East Europeans or Russians, for whom the model aspired after was represented by the advanced liberal capitalist regimes of Western Europe, Cuba's primary capitalist reference is and has been, not the 'successful' centres of global capitalism, but its 'failed' peripheries, particularly in Latin America. They realise that if they lose out to capitalism, their fate in a United States dominated Caribbean would be more like that of Panama, Grenada, Nicaragua or El Salvador. It is not surprising therefore that most Cubans should be convinced that their best chance for a better life lies with their present beleaguered regime.

Furthermore, there is a particular aspect to the Cuban experiment that makes it stand out from all other experiments in building socialism: the degree of *continued* popular support for the government and its policies. Political leadership has remained close to the people, responsive to their needs and sharing Cuban life's trials and tribulations with them. Given that the lack of connection between the leadership and the people was central to the final collapse of the experiments in Eastern Europe and former Soviet Union, this is a major asset for successful defence of the socialist experiment in Cuba.

Cubans have good reasons indeed to struggle in defence of their socialist project and they are not entirely lacking in resources for this struggle. And this is also the reason to hope for Cuba's survival and for socialism in our time.

VI

This is not to suggest even remotely that Cuba's struggle for survival is easy, that the offensive of global capitalism is not telling upon its socio-economic life, that concessions are not being extracted by it, or that no structural adjustments to market or globalisation are being made. That would be simply impossible. Cuba is not just a country struggling to save its socialist project, it is still a poor and backward economy. Four centuries of colonial past left Cuba with very fragile economic foundations, as a largely mono-cultural, sugar-based plantation economy, most vulnerable to world recessionary trends. Despite revolution and the consequent economic progress, Cuba remained dependent on its primary commodity exports and hence battered, like most Third World countries, by adverse terms of trade. Errors and inefficiencies of its socialist project were indeed a part of its problems, but as the Soviet Union collapsed and capitalism's new global offensive began, the problems plaguing the Cuban economy still mainly flowed from its status as a Third World island in a straitened international climate. The linkage with the Soviet Union, becoming a part of the 'socialist world', had not fundamentally altered the lop-sided or dependent character of Cuba's economy.

After the revolution, facing a hostile capitalist world led by the United States, which has been blockading it since 1961, Cuba sought economic and political refuge with the Soviet Union and the bloc led by it. But it did not take advantage of the relative freedom this provided for making maximal use of Cuba's own resources and expertise to diversify its economy and move, as much as possible, in the direction of self-sufficiency, which is a necessary condition, as Paul Sweezy has pointed out, for any 'developing country' to be able to resist the pressures emanating from global capitalism (IMF, WB, GATT or WTO, etc.) and pursue policies that are in the interests of its own people. Cuba simply got more and more integrated into the Soviet bloc's international economic organisation (COMECON) for purposes of international trade and otherwise. This integration was at best a mixed blessing.

If it provided respite from imperialist pressure and much needed economic assistance and partnership – the terms offered by the Soviet side were on the whole generous – Cuba's even partial adoption of Soviet-style economic institutions and practices, from central planning to ways of local management, reproduced problems typical of the Brezhnev era stagnation in the Soviet Union, problems relating to efficiency of investment, labour discipline and productivity, forms of organisation and motivation, bureaucratically centralised planning, local or popular participation, etc. More significant in the immediate context is the fact that this integration involved deep dependency on the Soviet Union, so that COMECON's collapse left Cuba in a desperate situation from which it has been struggling to extricate itself for the last ten years and more.

Between 1989 and 1993 – the years of 'Armageddon', as the locals call it – Cuba lost 75 per cent of its exports and 80 per cent of its imports. GDP fell by over a third and the currency literally collapsed. Without Soviet aid or subsidies Cuba lost not only direct cash assistance but access to the means of earning the hard currency that made imports possible. It was hard for Cuba to purchase food and other basic consumer items that were in short supply. There were severe shortages of food, fuel, clothing, soap and other basic necessities, adversely affecting people's standard of living which had been rising till then – the caloric and protein intake of the population was nearly halved. Without Soviet oil and fertilizer imports production fell precipitously especially in the highly mechanised sugar sector, rendering tens of thousands of workers idle for lack of fuel.

Cuba had little access to foreign credit and it no longer had political friends to whom it could turn for substantial aid. And so on. The cumulative effect of the collapse in the East has continued to be disastrous for Cuba. When account is taken of the continuing recession in world economy, the cutting off of all credits from the West, and America's hardened blockading since 1992 along with its relentless political and diplomatic pressure, Cuba's economic situation since 1989 has been truly precarious. There are few countries in this century's history that have taken such a beating – considerably greater than the amplitude in the US Great Depression of 1929-33. The magnitude of the crisis Cuba has faced over the last decade or so would have surely undone many a society, but Cuba survives. There has been neither a political surrender or an economic collapse, as hoped for by the United States. To quote Fidel Castro:

> No other country in the world would have been able to endure what we have endured. No other socialist country has been able to endure the collapse of the socialist camp or the loss to its imports in the midst of a blockade. No other country would have been able to endure such a situation without a system similar to ours because it would not have been able to guarantee an equitable distribution of resources.

VII

Accepting the new challenges, the Cuban government and political leadership have responded with quick decisions and energetic but prudently planned measures to cope with the near-impossible situation. The government soon declared the 'Special Period in Peacetime' which basically put the country on a wartime economy style programme involving both short term measures such as the rationing of basic consumer items and the partial replacement of mechanised with animal transport, and a long term rationalisation and restructuring of the economy. Necessary concessions have been made to privatisation and market. A new 'open policy' has been adopted with regard to foreign investment. As Castro himself has put it: 'Cuba's open policy is aimed at finding solutions to our problems – the need for capital, technologies and markets. Any investment is possible that contributes one or more of these elements and complies with the new regulations set forth in our legislation. We are not excluding anyone, not even while the blockade stands.' The new policy initiatives have included a partial process of privatisation and a restoration of market relations in certain key areas of the economy. The government has permitted the dollar to circulate next to the peso, made large investments in tourism, expanded efforts to diversify production in the domestic and export economies, and legalised private activity in the service sector. As the Cuban leadership has gone in for a maximal use of the available resources, including the Caribbean climate and Cuban beaches, a disciplined and socially conscious labour force and the supply of highly educated scientists and well-prepared technicians made possible by Cuba's comparatively large past investment in research and development, it has also seized the opportunity to rectify the mistakes made in the period of Soviet influence without however abandoning either the principles of central planning or its more basic commitment to socialism. As Castro made it clear in a memorable speech in July 1993, socialist commitment remains the overall limiting condition of the new programme of action.

Steps have been taken to rationalise the sugar sector and reduce dependence on it for foreign exchange, promote tourism in a big way and diversify into biotechnology and pharmaceuticals whose exports, essentially non-existent in 1989, now help bring in additional foreign exchange. With new geological finds the petroleum and petrochemical industries are coming up to provide the base for further large scale industrial expansion with the potential for eclipsing both tourism and sugar as national income earners. Even as sugar, nickel and citric continue to be the mainstay of Cuban exports, and therefore subject to hostile terms of trade, a conscious effort is being made to move away from the typical Third World pattern of agricultural and mineral exports. In agriculture, the linchpin of the economy, the state is attempting to boost domestic food production as well as sugar exports by transforming state farms into cooperatives, decentralising the decision making process, promoting farmers' markets, and encouraging the use of new techniques. Even as diversification of agriculture is planned, a major objective is to attain self-sufficiency in food. A major reform or renewal in this area has been the Third Agrarian Reform (after the first two in 1960 and 1963) which seeks to divide the gigantic state agricultural enterprises into smaller cooperatively 'owned and administered' units, with the aim of raising economic efficiency, linking incomes rigorously with the work contributed and production achieved, strengthening ties between the population and the land, improving the conditions of life of the rural population and enhancing the autonomy of local decision-making without the intervention of central authorities. At a time when the market has been allowed to play an increasingly important role in the development of Cuban life, the socialism-spiced strengthening of self-managing cooperatives helps consolidate popular support as what, along with social ownership in the industrial sector, is among the key pillars of the socialist economy.

VIII

The United States has regarded Latin America and the Caribbean as its special preserve for the giant American corporations to do business on their own terms. It has regularly intervened there to secure or prop up pliant regimes. Guatemala in 1954, the Dominican Republic in 1963, El Salvador and Nicaragua, Chile and Grenada in more recent years are examples of what happens when attempts are made to overthrow oppressive US puppet regimes. Radical reforming governments or movements in the hemisphere have been subjected to political and economic destabilisation, murderous terrorism by US-armed and trained death squads, sabotage, embargoes and blockages, US-backed military coups and outright invasions. Cuba, whose history as a traditional US domain goes back to the 1820s is no exception. Only, its breaking away from American domination to take a successful road to socialism has made it a special target of American interventionist offensive. As a scholar has recently put it: 'The catalogue of real offences perpetrated against Cuba is endless. Distortions of fact, lies, and chicanery have been the commonplace accompaniments of the thirty-five year old vendetta against Castro and his country. In 1961 the Bay of Pigs invasion organised by the CIA was preceded by a clumsy provocation involving the mendacious claim that the Cuban air force has rebelled; CIA terrorism and sabotage against Cuba was routine in the 1960s and the numerous well-documented attempts to assassinate Castro sit uneasily with the US public opposition to terrorism; the so-called missile crisis of 1962 seems to have had its immediate origin in a secret planned invasion of the island that became known to the Cubans; the retention to the present day of provocative US base on Cuban soil at Guantanamo is in blatant violation of Cuba's sovereignty and against the expressed demand of the Cuban government for its removal. But worse of all, perhaps, is the thirty-four year old blockade of the country, which, until 1990 guaranteed Cuba's heavy dependence on the Soviet bloc...' The collapse of the Soviet bloc has been seen by the United States as a new opportunity to suck or force Cuba back into its imperialist domain. Right after the cold war ended, the US navy extended its attack against Cuba. Seeking to render Cuba virtually incapable of surviving economically, the US reinforced its blockade of Cuba with a new (Helms – Burton) law passed by its Congress. Making a mockery of the very notion of a free multilateral trading system which the US claims to be defending everywhere, and in a gross violation of international law upholding the sovereignty of nations, the US has sought to penalise third countries or individuals for investment in Cuba or having trade dealings with it. The US led capitalist offensive against Cuba has taken a heavy toll of Cuban economy. This needs to be specially taken note of in any assessment of Cuba's achievement in saving its socialist system so far.

Incidentally, having all along supported or at least tolerated dictatorial, even right-wing terrorist regimes of unspeakable barbarity all over the globe, the pretence for direct or indirect US intervention against radical or reformist governments and movements has been to 'restore democracy'. So it is now with Cuba, the demand is for Cuba 'returning to democracy'! Cuba never had any democracy before 1959. The 'restoration of democracy' can only mean the restoration of Cuba's *status quo ante* with the triumphant return of exiles (in Miami and elsewhere in the US), waiting eagerly to reclaim their plantations and their property and reduce the Cuban population to the same happy state enjoyed by the poor and destitute throughout the rest of Latin America and the Caribbean. This 'restored democracy' will surely mean the end of the education, health care, and social services that have now for nearly forty years set Cuba apart from all other Third World countries.

IX

As Cuba struggles to survive and build, the capitalist offensive, as mentioned earlier, is telling upon its social and economic life. Shortages of food, transport, fuel, water and electricity are accompanied by the reemergence of the threat of unemployment as the factories close down. At the same time, the worsening economic situation, together with the admitted imperative to enter the world market, is exacting its price and compelling major pro-market adjustments in the economy. Foreign investment is coming in attracted by favourable pre-conditions in the form of a highly educated and disciplined yet cheap labour force, political stability and a stable currency, but the codes put in place for the purpose have also had to be as generous as any in the Caribbean. Tourism, the first industry to be opened up extensively to foreign investment, has already witnessed phenomenal growth, but there is no escaping its necessarily negative impact on Cuban society. State subsidies and social benefits have been severely trimmed. Small scale private business, private activity in dozens of professions, has been legalised along with private markets with new small shops springing up in the business districts. (Alleviating some immediate problems – relieving unemployment, making life easier for consumers – such privatisation, remains problematic in a long term socialist perspective). In view of the growing illegal market in US dollars, their possession has been de-criminalised. 'What is not efficient is not socialist' is publicly proclaimed and bonus linked with increased productivity. Regardless of ideological considerations, joint research, teaching and exchange programmes have been worked out with institutions abroad, many of them funded by private foundations, and so on.

These 'adjustments', the openings to market and foreign capital, to global economy and the capitalist world outside, however necessary or compelled by the objective situation, cannot but have adverse implications for the future of socialism in Cuba. Some of these are already only too visible in the emerging socio-economic dualism in Cuban society with all its corrosive consequences. With the shortages, black or grey 'underground' markets have grown, much facilitated by the dollarisation of the economy. The expansion and prosperity of the tourist industry is bringing in much needed foreign exchange, but it has also contributed to the growth of a dual economy in Cuba: a peso economy with scarce goods and a dollar economy of plenty (rental cars, luxury resorts and accessible luxury goods and scarce food items purchasable on the free – higher priced – markets as well as selected dollar stores). There is a new social and economic divide between those who earn dollars and those who don't, those who work for foreign companies and those who don't; something like a 'labour aristocracy' has arisen – dollar-earning privileged service labour demarcated from the peso-dominated wage sectors, leading to a sectoral exodus from the ranks of highly skilled professions. With their base-wage lavishly supplemented by tips in dollars, hotel receptionists, ushers and sweepers are earning more than skilled professionals which is having a divisive and disruptive impact on society. As a by-product of foreign tourism, prostitution has reappeared for the first time since the revolution – like increased crime, as much generated by economic deprivation as sustained by the emerging morality of the market place. 'Many people will now do anything for money', the Cubans are saying. Opening to the market has had its inevitable consequence in beggars reappearing on the streets in Havana where there were virtually none ten years ago. Equally corrosive for Cuba's socialism are the ideological and cultural influences now coming in more easily from the capitalist world, especially those flowing from America's 'cultural hegemony', its consumerist culture.

Like their counterparts elsewhere, American Left-wing has, for its own reasons, long advocated normalisation of relations with Cuba. But it is significant that sections of the mainstream, even Right-wing opinion in America, are now arguing that the present Cuban regime can be best undone, not by embargoes or blockades, but by normalisation of relations and opening of the borders which would expose Cuba to things, people, investments and ideas from the US, to the full blast of American capitalism and its culture. In other words, the argument is for an alternative tack which would try and undermine the revolution in Cuba by a strategy of commercial and cultural penetration.

Cubans themselves are not oblivious of this danger – 'the open window lets in fresh breeze, but it also brings flies and mosquitoes', as a Vietnamese communist leader has metaphorically put it. They are also aware of the fact that American embargo has in its own way helped Cuba to retain its sovereignty along with certain key elements of its socialist system. Leading Cuban philosopher Juan Antonio Blanco has argued that 'for the first time in its history, Cuba is independent' – after centuries of colonial domination and more recent dependence on the Soviet Union – and that it now needs some years respite to consolidate and get on its feet economically to be able to withstand the onslaught of US economic, cultural and political power that would accompany any relaxation or 'normalisation' of relations between Cuba and the United States. There is no doubt that a rapid and wholesale opening to the United States will have traumatic consequences for Cuba's economy, politics and culture which together could possibly undermine and destroy its socialist project.

At the same time Havana has never ceased to call for a lifting of the embargo, and has made continual attempts to engage US opinion to this end. The economic advantages of a lifting of the embargo are obvious and the Cuban leadership sees itself as capable of handling its adverse consequences *as socialists*. A friendly critic has observed: 'Those who believe that a lifting of the blockage would doom the regime underestimate Fidel Castro, a consummate guerrilla politician who is never more skilful than when wrong-footing conventional expectations. What tangible benefits would an end to the embargo bring to Cuba? According to one estimate, even a partial lifting would double Cuban import capacity and generate a 25 per cent increase in national income. A critical gain too would be Cuban access to credits from the World Bank, or even the IMF, and unimpeded trade with third countries. The American talons have not stopped Cuba from selling sugar, coffee, citrus, cigars and biotechnical products in Europe and elsewhere. But they have raised costs and enabled enterprises doing business with Cuba to demand premium terms. Last but not least, if Cuba could freely sell its products – Havana Club rum, Partagas and Cojiba cigars, *Son* CDs, Havana Gold coffee – in US markets, it would finally be in a position to correct its trade balance. These would all be economic benefits. But socially and politically, too, Cuba is most likely to salvage what is best in the revolution if it can escape the brutal claws of the blockade...'

Be that as it may, Cuban leadership and people are aware of the complexities of their situation. Many of the reforms are controversial because they are seen to be producing results that contradict the accepted and established values of the revolution, such as social equality, solidarity, and willingness to sacrifice. But the controversy is accompanied by a general recognition of the need for vigilance and rectification.

X

Centuries of experience of imperialism provides little evidence of the beneficial effects of foreign investment in countries of the Third World so far as the common people are concerned. Rather than ensure an autonomous and equitable socio-economic development of Cuba, it is far more likely to generate a class exploitative society within the country, and push the country itself back to the status of a technologically and financially dependent semi-colony in the periphery of global capitalism. The Cuban leadership is aware of the danger. It is aware that questions of foreign investment or technology import, of privatisation or marketisation (or 'globalisation' as such) are, in the final analysis, not economic but political, that is, class questions, which in this day and age cannot bypass the basic choice of capitalism or socialism. And this leadership, in Fidel Castro's words, is no 'fan of capitalism'. That is how, though compelled, in its struggle for survival to yield ground and make concessions to market and globalisation, Cuba has not so far succumbed to free market or capitalism.

Survival is a struggle and Cuba's 'structural adjustment' is a part of this ongoing struggle in which confronting problems from 'the socialist standpoint' is still the significant feature of the Cuban leadership's response to the crisis facing their country. The regime has encouraged criticism from 'within the revolution' and the prime effort has been to find 'solutions inside socialism'. It is this which gives the Cuban response to the 'crisis of socialism', Cuba's 'special period' model, its historical specificity, making it qualitatively different from Gorbachev's perestroika, East-European 'liberalisation', Vietnam's *Doi Moi*, or from China's 'socialist market economy' which is really an euphemism for 'the capitalist road'. The Cuban leadership has insisted that 'market reforms' in Cuba are not to be compared with those in China or Vietnam. Introducing reform measures of the 'special period' Castro had categorically asserted: 'Our main objective is to preserve the revolution and the achievements of socialism. We have not renounced socialism as our common objective.' Hence Cuban leadership's search for 'solutions inside socialism'. This has been a feature of Cuba's efforts at 'rectification' all along. Aware of the 'negative example' of the ex-Soviet Union, the Cuban leadership has sought answers to its problems from 'a socialist standpoint'.

XI

Che Guevara, speaking on behalf of the Cuban revolution, was quite critical of Soviet economic and political practices, more particularly the gross economistic disorientation of the socialist project there, its overemphasis on investment in production, 'the material base', and neglect of the more important non-material, ethical dimension of socialism, the creation of 'a new man', as he metaphorically defined it. He repudiated those notions that purported to defeat capitalism by relying on its own fetishes: 'In pursuing the quixotic goal of building socialism by resorting to worn tools inherited from capitalism – merchandise as the cell of the economy, profitability, individual material interest as an incentive, etc. – we may find ourselves in a dead end.... To build Communism while strengthening society's material foundations we must create a new man.' Che advocated moral or collective incentives as alternative to coercion or individual acquisitiveness in building socialism. Refusing to copy the models imported from 'actually existing socialist' nations, Che sought instead new roads to socialism, roads that would be more radical, more egalitarian, more humane, and more consistent with Communist principles. He insisted: 'I am not interested in economic socialism without Communist principles. We fight against misery, but also against alienation.... If Communism overlooks the acts of consciousness it may well be a system of redistribution but hardly a revolutionary ethic.'

Che had argued for a more authentic socialist transition in Cuba. Castro shared Che's argument and has continued with it. Economic dependence on and solidarity with the Soviet Union notwithstanding, Castro too had, on several occasions, questioned the way socialism was practiced in Eastern Europe and the Soviet Union. Under his leadership the Cubans have specifically rejected *copismo* (copying) Soviet or any other model, and sought to pursue a somewhat different path in Cuba. In terms of their own policies, the record of the Cubans has been remarkably good for a small country, relatively isolated and subjected throughout to a vicious imperialist blockade. Now, facing their worst crisis ever, the Cubans have responded with characteristic audacity and innovations, using the reserves (in consensus, social solidarity, education, health care, etc.) built up during the thirty-odd years of independence and social revolution.

Already, since 1986, a 'Rectification Movement' was on in Cuba to discover and rectify errors and weaknesses in the management of the economy, to 'improve socialism from a socialist standpoint' as the Cubans described it. On the agenda were such issues as reduction of reliance on material incentives, broader worker participation in decision-making, increase of socialist discipline, deepening of political consciousness, and so on. The overriding need to ensure better productivity was linked to progress in these areas. Following the collapse of COMECON, this movement became all the more necessary and went into the making of a new programme we have already noticed, namely, 'special period in peacetime' with its associated package of survival measures to cope with the new situation.

The new programme of course involved increased attention to political work among the people and a continued focus on the goal of socialism. But a distincitive feature was the leadership staying close to the people and involving them in the struggle for economic survival. If there was no oil from the Soviet Union, people in their millions took to bicycles imported from China – Fidel himself learnt to ride the bike at the age of 65, setting the example for others. If the sugar or potato harvest was in danger because of imminent rain, Fidel kept vigil all night keeping direct contact with local people and officials. In a new initiative revolutionary armed forces (RAF) were deployed to boost farm output. When harvesting machines could not be used, thousands of workers came forward from universities, schools and factories to save the harvest. Engineers, technicians and scientists came up with thousands of proposals to help resolve various bottlenecks created due to shortage of fuel and spare parts. Health care has always been a priority of the regime and here state enterprises effectively sponsored new breakthroughs in medical research and bio-technology. This is how Castro summed it up in his speech at the 17th Cuban Trade Union Congress in 1996:

> What we defend is Socialism, the power of the people, the work of the revolution. We have already recovered morally, politically from the blow of six years ago. Over the past year issues of great importance have all been discussed. The entire island has been involved. A lot of ideas have come up, a lot of knowledge has been gained. At the same time a lot of work has been done – planting, greening. Seeking solutions of all kinds, we are doing three times what we used to do – despite the number of factories that have stopped operating, despite the fact that we can now

> make only 6 thousand bus trips a day where once we made 30 thousand. For transportation we had to get two million bikes and improvise bike factories. The concepts of efficiency and self-sufficiency, of accounting and control, of savings, the spirit of studying everything, have been instilled. The process of re-arranging the labor force, re-dimensioning the plants – we can speak of all these without shame, knowing that this has happened in no other place, at no other time in history, that it is contrary to what has been advised and done everywhere else.

Most noteworthy in the Cuban experience is indeed its rejection of 'what has been advised and done everywhere else,' namely, the structural adjustments advised or imposed by the IMF and World Bank in the rest of Latin America and elsewhere in the Third World. The latter, imperialism dictated 'free market' policies, simply disregard distributional consequences. 'In free market politics, there is no place for compassion or sympathy' – this is how a 'liberalising' executive director at the IMF, representing India, put it while speaking of such adjustments after the precipitous collapse of the Mexican economy some years ago, an economy that had been held up as an example for other 'developing' countries (including India) to follow. Cuba has refused to tread this path. It has refused to let its citizens face their problems individually in the dog-eat-dog world of the market place. Instead, it has sought to preserve the social gains of the revolution and maintain the quality of life for its common citizens. Cuba has been able to do so by extending central planning – in terms of not only reduced energy consumption, greater rationing, planned investment in food production, better labour mobilisation, etc., but preservation of people's hard won social gains as well.

Cuba has consciously rejected the reigning neo-liberal orthodoxy, its 'free market' panaceas or the globalisation-liberalisation-privatisation road to national reconstruction, and stuck to its socialist road. Even as Cuba has defended its independence against the US, the state within has retained control over decisive branches of the economy while going in for pro-market reforms. The state has remained massively interventionist, with the public sector and central planning continuing to play their pre-eminent role. The scope for the market has been extended but it functions within the framework of a comprehensive national plan. The issues of socialism, the goal of an egalitarian society have not been 'forgotten', or 'eliminated to attract foreign capital', as has been charged by some 'left critics' of Cuba. Indeed it is planning that has enabled Cuba not merely to cope with the economic consequences of the collapse of the Soviet bloc but also ensure a socially just distribution of the costs of the general demise of the centrally planned economies of its former allies. While shortages have become acute, the hardships generally have been equitably shared by most Cubans. Rationing has been extended and food and other basic necessities are made available to people at low prices through well-organised distribution outlets – the nutritional requirements of the people have been restored to the earlier level. Strong measures have been taken to make sure that no one is left unprotected against the vagaries of the market. People are not homeless or panhandling and 70 per cent of salary continues to be paid to workers rendered unemployed because of plant closures due to lack of inputs or energy.

Cuba's austerity policy has not countenanced the turning of labour into a commodity subjected or ready to be subjected to the laws of supply and demand of capital, domestic or foreign. The state is itself channelling thousands of workers into service industries and small-scale production enterprises as a means of employing those idled by the crisis. Although 'exceptional' cases are allowed, employers must hire workers through a state agency. (In any case only a very tiny fraction of all workers – less than 5 per cent in 1996 – work in jobs connected to foreign capital and only a small part of these are hired directly by the foreign enterprises). Crisis in the economy notwithstanding, Cuba has sustained the essential class basis of its accumulation and economic development, and the leadership is not lacking in concern about how property ownership and the accumulation of capital could be controlled. Despite a few, and some even dangerously wide cracks in the edifice, its governmental, political and societal organisation has remained intact. Though trimmed, the systems of education, health care, rationing and social solidarity are still functioning and people have managed to hang on to 'normal' social life to a surprising degree. Not a single worker has been laid off in health or education. Instead the number of doctors and teachers has gone up. Not a single hospital, school or child care centre has been closed. The budgets for public health service, education or social security – they represent 60 per cent of public spending – have been maintained or have actually increased. Typical of Cuba's response to the 'special period', while air-conditioning has disappeared from offices, the Cubans have maintained strict temperature and humidity controls in their libraries and archives, films critical of bureaucratic attitudes are shown as before, seven-year-olds continue with their free violin, swimming and dance lessons and older children can tell the curious visitors from abroad, 'We are playing (because) we are kids' – they are not 'at work' or begging in the streets in order to survive as elsewhere in Latin America...

All this, a question of priorities, is quite a contrast with what is happening elsewhere in the world (including the desperate two-fold struggle by workers in the West for jobs and to defend their gains in the 'welfare state' that is being dismantled). The contrast with the countries of the third world, especially with the neighbours in Latin America is indeed stark. Any number of recent visitors to the region have felt compelled to notice and underline it. A British scholar has observed: 'Other Latin American capitals combine glittering downtowns and reflector glass skyscrapers with swollen *villas misérias* or shanty towns. Havana has neither... In cities of Latin America, abandoned children are a common sight – in Rio or Mexico City thousands of them living by their wits, many destined for abuse, exploitation or an early death. In Cuba, all of Elian's age are safe and well-cared for.' The situation with the children in fact best illustrates this contrast. 'I am haunted by "the street children" of Cartagena de las Indias in Colombia. At the crack of dawn, dressed in their rags, having spent the night sleeping on the ground "protected" only by a piece of cardboard, they wake to begin their search for glue to sniff...they had no right to food, to decent clothing, to a roof over their heads, to health care, to education, to affection. These children, and thousands like them, had sunk to sniffing glue in order to quell the pangs of hunger that they felt day and night...their system was used to solvent fumes, not food. These fumes soothe and destroy them at the same time' – this is how a distinguished social scientist from Belgium has seen it. In contrast, as the report of a Jesuit social worker has it, Cuba is the only country he knew in the Americas, 'where children do not go barefoot, where they do not go hungry, where they do not sleep on streets, and where they were able to read and write.'

Behind Cuba's achievement lies, on the one hand its rejection of IMF-WB prescriptions, on the other the unity of the Cuban people and their commitment to socialism. In an interview with a former Director General of UNESCO (in June 2000), surveying Cuba's ordeal of the nineties, Castro said: 'There were times when we were swimming in a sea of circulating money. Our national currency experienced an extraordinary devaluation, and the budget deficit reached 35 per cent of our Gross Domestic Product. I could see intelligent visitors almost faint from shock. Our peso, the national currency, dropped to a value of 150 to the dollar in 1994. In spite of this we did not close down a single health-care centre, a single school or daycare centre, a single university, or a single sports facility...what little was available we distributed as equitably as possible.' Continuing with Cuba's achievement in confronting the crisis it faced, Castro added:

> During these critical years, the number of doctors doubled and the quality of education improved. The value of the Cuban peso increased sevenfold, between 1994 and 1998, and has since remained consistently stable. Not a single dollar fled the country. We acquired experience and efficiency on a par with the immense challenge facing us. Although we have still not reached the production and consumption levels we had before the demise of socialism in Europe, we have gradually recovered at a steady and visible pace...The great hero in this feat has been the people, who had contributed tremendous sacrifices and immense trust. It was the fruit of justice and of the ideas sowed over 30 years of revolution. This genuine miracle would have been impossible without unity and without socialism.

That Cuba has survived and achieved what it has in the midst of a continuing confrontation with the United States, facing the full blast of its economic blockage and politics of intervention, is a matter of historic national and international significance for our times.

This, again, is not to deny that US-led offensive of capitalism is taking a heavy toll of Cuba's socialism. Notwithstanding their socialist priorities and 'equitable distribution of resources', Cubans are living through a traumatic period of declining living standards and unparalleled demands for economic austerity. But the basic consensus has held, there is no significant social retrogression, and they have evinced no interest in a return to capitalism. Of course discontent and resentment on the part of the average Cuban is not to be denied and there are sections of population still unintegrated into the revolution. But impartial observers have continued to report wide ranging popular support for the regime. The new hardships or temptations of the market have not provoked the kind of political change wished for in Washington and Miami, that is, a catastrophic collapse and the return of the US-backed emigré propertied elite. During the nineties, foreign observers had indeed often predicted a 'melt down' of the Castro regime. Few think that is in prospect today. Even in circumstances of great hardship most Cubans still feel they have something to defend, socialism they have struggled so hard to build. (An independent poll in Cuba, commissioned by the *Miami Herald* and conducted by the Costa Rican firm CID-Gallup – associated with the Gallup Organisation – in November 1994, that is, near the height of the economic problems, found that roughly 69 per cent of Cubans considered themselves revolutionaries or socialists or communists, and 58 percent thought the revolution on balance had more achievements than failures).

XII

Compulsions of backwardness, the negative legacy of the Soviet connection, the capitalist offensive and the passage of time, all have taken their toll of the revolution in Cuba. But on the whole Cuba has managed to retain its revolutionary commitment and idealism which its East-European and Soviet allies had long come to lack. The leadership's exercise of power has generally involved the people and not alienated them. So it has been with the reforms or changes of the 'special period'. It is not only that these have been determined by the people's capacity to assimilate, the Cuban leadership has throughout made special efforts to get the people's approval for them, often through what has come to be referred to as 'parliament at the workplace.' Policy measures are discussed in the factories and farms, and among social and political groups so that people are persuaded to give their approval. It is Cuba's democratic practice that sets Cuba apart from the former Soviet Union and the Soviet bloc societies in East Europe where the leadership had become indifferent or hostile to politics of mass participation, to people's active involvement in public affairs. That Cuba's leaders have enabled and encouraged mass participation, particularly at critical junctures, is the single most important reason for the Cuban revolution's survival till today. Whatever the criticism of it, if the Cuban political system has been able to contain the ineluctable economic dualism and social tensions sprouted by the contradictory nature of the reform process, and withstand the crippling US blockade and the increased global isolation, it is because the system is representative of the people's wishes, indeed far more representative than formal democracies elsewhere.

Criticism is of course there and not only by Cuba's regular detractors – 'from the *Wall Street Journal* and *New York Times* to prominent Cubanologists who make their living bashing Cuba from the safety of tenured positions at universities and reactionary think tanks', as Hobart Spalding has put it. While there is a legitimate demand from socialist critics on the left for a radically improved practice of democracy, for more effective exercise of people's power in Cuba, including workers' power at the point of production, non-socialist critics, ranging from the hard right to right-wing social democrats, and including many on the left, have conventionally concentrated on the predominant role or 'monopoly' of power of the Communist Party, 'single-party rule', the lack of 'free' elections and political pluralism, etc. I will be touching upon the general question of democracy in a later chapter. Immediately I would like to make a couple of observations on this conventional criticism before dealing with the specific issue of democracy in Cuba.

In the first place, that political power pre-eminently lies with the Communist Party and the Party leads in decision-making must not be allowed to cloud the question of democracy in Cuba and lead to the simplistic conclusion about Cuba being a totalitarian regime as the American propaganda with its rhetoric over 'restoration of democracy' makes it out to be. The conclusion is simplistic because it ignores not only that it is the Communist Party which has brought revolution and its benefits to the Cuban people, but also the obviously important historical fact of Cuban Revolution itself, of Cuba having undergone *such* fundamental changes as we do not go back upon, and which therefore need, however transitionally, a certain kind of 'monopoly' and exercise of power in order to be consolidated and guaranteed effective defence against the threat of counter-revolution. One has only to look at the regimes that have followed a revolution – in England in the 17th century, in America and France in the 18th century, and in Russia and China in the 20th century – to understand the way it is, and has been, with the exercise of power by the Communist Party in Cuba, where US-backed counter-revolution has remained a threat from the very beginning. This apart, the so-called 'single-party rule' in Cuba, as in other post-revolutionary societies of our time, needs to be properly understood as a product of history and not any theory of socialism.

Secondly, I will, for the present, readily concede that there is great deal to be said for political pluralism or platform democracy, that it is a necessary and desirable constituent of any well-functioning democratic polity – though this has its problems for socialists to grapple with in their struggle for power in formally democratic systems or in institutionalising it as a part of democratic practices of a socialist society. Having said that it still has to be recognised that apart from the fact that democracy in our time has its problems and they have their roots in capitalism, that private ownership of means of production presents insurmountable obstacles to democratising relations of production, there are any number of unresolved issues about political pluralism or platform politics in any setting – for example, what is actually done *after* the elections, or what of issues that have not yet been posed at the time of elections etc. However, more important in the immediate context of Cuba is the fact that far from being exhaustive of democracy, political pluralism or platform politics is not even necessarily democratic. Democracy surely goes beyond voting freely for one of several candidates. It cannot be simply assumed that this necessarily yields performance in line with the wishes of the electorate. Experience with the working of democracy in capitalist societies (including the advanced ones) makes it clear that political pluralism is no guarantee that majority concerns will be reflected or addressed, or that it will even offer people genuine choices. For example, real differences between rival contenders for power in England have persistently eluded scholars, compelling A.L. Lowell once and R.T. McKenzie more recently to describe them as 'shams', only one is 'a transparent' and the other 'an opaque sham'!

Democracy in Cuba, necessarily different in a number of aspects from what exists as democracy in capitalist societies – for example, it includes the right to work, health, education, social security in general – is certainly not perfect, as the Cubans themselves constantly remark. It has been one of the constants of the official Cuban discourse that the political structures should be periodically renewed in order to improve their functioning. Improving democracy has been equally one of the most widely discussed topics in the academia and elsewhere in the Cuban society. History of revolutionary Cuba is also a history of attempts to build and improve democracy in various spheres over the course of last 40 years.

Cuba never had any democracy prior to the Revolution. Democracy indeed came to Cuba with the Revolution, but for obvious reasons, democratic structures remained rather weak or poorly sustained, till after 1970 when the country witnessed a major move in the democratic direction. This move is best understood as a product of the evolving relationship between leaders and led before 1970: leaders pursuing popular policies and thus extending and deepening their base of support, and citizens actively involving and sacrificing themselves in the revolutionary process and thus gaining the respect and confidence of leaders. In other words, Cuba moved towards democratisation after 1970 as a result of the mutual trust that had developed between the leaders and the led in Cuba during the first decade of post-revolutionary struggle for socialism. After 1970, channels for popular participation in decision making were institutionalised throughout society, including in production. The Organs of People's Power – first established in mid-seventies and formalised in the 1976 Constitution and later extended and strengthened in 1989 and institutionalised in the 1992 Constitution – in a way even resemble the Paris Commune in the merging of executive and legislative functions and the direct election of recallable delegates whose salaries are on a par with those of their worker constituency. Noticing this, Peter Roman, an American scholar with more than ten years of extensive field work among the Cubans on the issue of democracy, has suggested that the key to understanding the Cuban concept of democracy is the *mandat imperatif* (which he calls the 'instructed delegate model') as developed by Rousseau, the Paris Commune, and later incorporated into the Soviets of the early revolutionary period of Russia. The *mandat* varies in important ways from the Lockean traditions that underlie bourgeois democracy. The central idea here is that representatives should be truly accountable and responsive to their constituents. Thus, for example, it matters less what a delegate thinks than what his constituency thinks.

Of Cuba's three-tired democratic set up – institutionalised at local, provincial and national levels – it is the local, grassroots level organs of People's Power (the Municipal Assembly and the People's Councils) that are the driving forces behind the Cuban democracy. As Roman has reported, two to eight candidates must stand for election for each Municipal Assembly (MA) post, they are nominated in popular meetings at which 75 per cent or more of the eligible voters show up regularly, elections are by secret ballot and a majority is needed for election. Usually well over three of every four eligible voters exercise their option to choose their representatives, and over 90 per cent voted for ratification of the 1992 Constitution. Further, each MA delegate is directly responsible to his or her constituency. They must hold regular office hours, and they must respond to specific complaints lodged by residents of their particular districts. A recall vote is possible if 20 percent of the voters, or 20 percent of the delegates in the MA, ask for it. Almost all the MA delegates are known personally to their constituents and are constantly on call, even at early hours in the morning....

Organisational variations apart, the principles and procedures elsewhere, with regard to the People's Councils (formed in 1989 and institutionalised in the 1992 Constitution) and at provincial and national levels, parallel those of the Municipal Assembly. It may be specifically mentioned that the Communist Party has no input into the nomination process or election, and party membership is not that important in getting either nominated or elected. The candidates for office do not run on a platform (or as a member of the party) but rather on their personal record, on the basis of what they have done for society in the past, which rules out demagoguery and false promises, and the use of money power. There are multiple candidates who may not necessarily belong to the Communist Party, though, admittedly but for good political reasons, Communist Party members predominate at state and national levels of democratic representation.

A significant feature of the Cuban response to the current crisis has been a new phase of participatory democracy. Following Communist Party's call for a public debate to 'make possible a consensus based on a recognition of the diversity of views that exists within the population and strengthened by democratic discussions within the Party and the Revolution, above all in the search for solutions, the examination of the means of achieving our socio-economic objectives, and in general in the perfection of our society', a major revision of systems of popular participation in decision-making has been pioneered to provide better checks on bureaucracies in charge of production and services, carry issues to the people to find solutions to specific problems, and build consensus around painful but necessary measures. It is not that mass participation was absent or inadequate earlier. On the contrary, the 'rectification' process of the late 80s had increased mass participation as one of its central goals and it was having success in that direction. But now there is still greater involvement of workers in workplace decisions and more comprehensive and better structured public discussion at the level of mass organisations like the Central Organisation of Cuban Trade Unions (CTC) and the Federation of Cuban Women (FMC). Cuban congresses of any of the mass organisations have always been places where critics have stood up and disagreed with government policies, even 'confrontation between the base and the centre over issues' has taken place to secure changes in official policies or generate new measures. Now they are still more active in influencing what happens both in Cuban work sites and throughout Cuban society.

The term 'rectification' has come to mean discussion of all the problems resulting from the Soviet and East-European abandonment of both socialism and Cuba, the embargo imposed by the United States, and the ill effects of the measures taken to cope with the current crisis – and the possible solutions to these problems. The discussion has involved not only the intellectuals but also the common working people. Workers and their trade unions – trade union participation is near universal among workers in Cuba – have concerned themselves with such issues as stimulating labour discipline and morale, improving efficiency and productivity, rationalising personnel and subsidy policies. People have been called upon to help formulate policies on such matters as excess money in circulation, illegal or corrupt accumulations of wealth, control over social and individual consumption, budget deficits, role of prices, tax on salaries, etc.

Cubans have been freely, even fiercely, debating – in conference sessions and numerous other formal and informal meetings – not only the specific problems and their solutions but larger issues including the pros and the cons of the new development strategy, its concessions to market and global economy. 'Our own bureaucracy' has been denounced as an enemy along with the US imperialism, controversy is raised over such issues as 'excessive egalitarianism' and 'paternalism' and, in the renewed interest in works by socialist thinkers, even Trotsky is no longer under a taboo. And significantly enough, this ongoing debate recognises the emergence of a dual economy in Cuba. The people are posing the issue and asking whether the new market openings will erode socialist and nationalist values or will be mastered so that the socialist project survives. Concern with concepts like equality, justice and solidarity is not just something to trot out on May Day, but something encountered daily, not only in speeches by the political leadership but also in private discussions with 'average Cubans'.

Castro, like other leaders, has been mobile, travelling everywhere, meeting workers and addressing people's assemblies, drafting and sharing the new development strategy with his people. Noteworthy is the way this countrywide discussion has been carried to the people in hundreds and thousands of public meetings across the land. This is how a report on this massive democratisation process goes:

> The 80,000 meetings were our attempt to bring every Cuban – from youth to the elderly, from every part of the economy and from every part of Cuba – into the process of discussing our problems and shaping policy for the future. This was the Fourth Communist Party Conference Referendum and we have developed various methods of involving all the people. Over the years, the participation of the people at large was a process maturing as a method of governance and as a right. At every meeting, most of which were small meetings of peers from a given community or workplace, all questions raised were discussed and all criticisms of leaders or suggestions for future programmes were recorded and passed on to higher echelons of the structure of meetings....

The Cuban scholar Haroldo Dilla, sympathetically critical of Cuba's democracy has thus described the early response to the Party's call for a public debate: 'For several months, Cuba experienced the freest and most democratic public debate in its history. Millions of people in thousands of settings (schools, labour halls, community centres) exercised their right to criticise, to propose solutions or simply to offer opinions on questions ranging from daily life to public policy.' Non-Cubans have written of 'Workers' Parliaments' in Cuba and scholars like Linda Fuller have pointed out that Cuban workers feel that they have their input into decisions that affect their lives at the workplaces, neighbourhoods, and beyond. Typical of the situation is this report by an American academic, A.L. Campbell:

> In the year leading up to the 17th congress of the Central Organisation of Cuban Trade Unions (CTC) in April 1996, workers in (essentially) all work sites throughout Cuba discussed 168 theses on the road forward for Cuba. This was not some staged top-down charade: 70,000 proposals were made from the grass roots during the process, and a large number of these led to changes in the final form of the theses. At the congress itself, again there was broad participation: there were 600 commentaries (or speeches) from the 1,900 delegates.
>
> Contrary to the belief that such gatherings are orchestrated cheerleading sessions for government policies, the discussion was neither restricted to 'worker topics' nor were the interventions dominantly 'hurrah for us' presentations. The first thing one is struck with on reading the 168 theses is the breadth of the topics covered, something we who live in the United States and champion the struggles of working people for job security and better wages sometimes forget is central to visions of socialism: the people who produce the wherewithal for the society to survive and advance should have a voice in all social policies. As a weak substitute for reading the whole work, a listing of the 12 groups that the 168 theses were divided into will give some idea of the breadth of the issues addressed: The world, the workers, and the situation in Cuba; Our strategy does not lead to capitalism; Fighting for an efficient and competitive economy; The decisive effort to increase sugar production; The problem of unemployment and the reorganisation of the labor force; Workers' wages; Union action regarding collective contract agreements and labor legislation; Working for the consolidation and triumph of the UBPCs (the new co-ops created from old state farms); Unions are by and for the workers; Defending the revolution means guaranteeing our power; Maintaining unity in the ranks of the workers...

Such mass participation, working people's effective intervention in decision-making – providing inputs for meetings of the National Assembly, the highest elective body in Cuba – is a distinctive feature of Cuban public life today. One can well ask of critics who persist in speaking of a totalitarian regime in Cuba: Where else, in what other country claiming to be democratic, around a quarter of the population, and a majority of the working class at that, are directly involved in discussing and deciding the most complex and controversial problems of their daily existence and the long term future of their society? And the Cubans are doing this in a global environment which is, for them specially, least conducive for such freedom of discussion and decision-making!

Cuba's democratic experience is, in its own way, reminiscent of the efforts of Lenin (early Soviets or later Workers' and Peasants' Inspectorate) or Mao (Cultural Revolution) to somehow empower the people through direct democracy or mass participation. The Cuban exercise, however, also carries with it a reminder of the lesson born of the failure of those efforts: the successful building of socialism demands not sporadic or ill-sustained expression but a careful yet firm multiform institutionalisation of popular democratic participation. This is not to suggest that all is well and 'final' with Cuba's democratic institutions or functioning. Far from it. Castro himself has openly acknowledged this. Peter Roman, who has argued that Cuban democracy is alive and well and is optimistic about its future, has nevertheless, like many other friendly critics, pointed to the weaknesses or inadequacies that still mark it. For example, while the system is functioning reasonably well at the lower levels, it is still top-down in many aspects – national planning overshadows local demands and the Communist Party retains a dominant control at the top levels. He has also noted that the higher one goes in government the more bureaucratic the job and attitude. Haroldo Dilla has argued for 'a more democratic party, more open to debate and permitting internal tendencies within the framework of unity around strategic propositions'. The weaknesses or inadequacies of Cuban democracy are partly explained by the in-built constraints of what in many ways is still a backward economy and a besieged one at that, and the ever-present threat of a counter-revolution from the United States – but only partly. Cuba's democracy still needs to be more democratic. What has been achieved only ensures that further attempts to find new structures, institutions and practices suitable to build socialism under the present conditions do not have to start 'from scratch' as it were. Cuba has a long, very long way to go, not only in politics but in economy and culture as well, before one can begin to speak of anything approaching 'socialist democracy'. In the meantime, however, it needs to be noted that the transformation of people's 'consciousness' wrought by their democratic experience, as part of their living the revolution as it were, is very real. This is an important factor in Cuba's survival so far, and remains an important factor in determining its future as well.

XIII

Ideological setback apart, the material costs of the Soviet collapse have indeed been very substantial for Cuba, particularly in the short run. But this may well make for real strategic benefits in the long run. The gravity of the crisis at home and the crisis of socialism abroad are compelling the Cubans to search within for solutions, both in order to survive and to find a way forward that preserves the gains of its socialist revolution. In other words, Cuba has to find a new basis for survival as well as for building socialism, and the model for success has to be of Cuban provenance. This is a fact and a challenge that Cuba's leadership and people themselves have come to understand and accept. Not a cause for resignation or despair, the current crisis is, as it were, a source of redemption for them.

Accordingly, in no other country in the world are issues of development and their reverberations debated on such a scale and with such fervour as in Cuba today. Old dogmas are being junked and there is a no-holds-barred critique of institutions and individuals. Radical rethinking is on, concerning strategies of development in the new period including its globalising compulsions. Abroad, the Cubans are making a specially focused effort to establish mutually beneficial economic linkages with the countries of Latin America. At home, the economic crisis is forcing the Cubans to conserve on energy use, to diversify their industry and agriculture and seek self-sufficiency in food, to practice greater flexibility in reconverting industries towards production with a smaller input content and so on. In brief, the rupture with dependency on the Soviet bloc has compelled Cuba to discard the Soviet model and seek their own road to socialism, to rely on greater and better use of domestic resources, encourage and reward innovative thinking, and more than anything else put politics, that is revolutionary politics, and not economics in command and thus find their own road to socialism. Like 'the Mao years in China', Cuba's new strategy of development has important lessons for the countries of the Third World which would, instead of succumbing to global capitalism for the benefit of the rich and privileged few among them, seek a different path that secures a better life for the vast masses of their poor and long-oppressed people.

XIV

Particularly significant in this regard is the environment-friendly nature of Cuba's new strategy of development. It is not merely that with the decline in chemical imports, Cubans have come to rely on natural fertilisers and biological control of pests. The US embargo, collapse of Soviet-style socialism, and the unfolding realities of the worldwide ecological crisis have both forced and persuaded Cuba to turn, metaphorically and otherwise, to 'the bicycle, the ox and back to the land' – a direction of salvation which has today become imperative for human survival on our planet.

Following the collapse of trade with the Soviet bloc when there was a crisis in the import of food as well as fuel, machines, chemical inputs and all the other technological requirements of an advanced agriculture, the Cuban government launched a country-wide effort to shift the nation's agriculture away from high input, that is, capital intensive agricultural technology, to low input, self-reliant farming practices, replacing chemical inputs with locally produced, and in most cases biological, substitutes, that is, chemical pesticides with biopesticides, and chemical fertilisers with organic fertilisers. In place of tractors, for which fuel, tyres, and spare parts were largely unavailable, there was a sweeping return to animal traction, the use of oxen, for example, which in any case, are more compatible with intensive farming than heavy tractors, because they compact the soil less.

Large state farms were seen to be incompatible with alternative new technologies. Cuba, therefore, radically reorganised its production in order to create the small-scale management units that are essential for effective organic-style farming, even as they also make for a more firm linking of people with the land. The state farms were turned into Basic Units of Cooperative Production, a form of worker-owned enterprise or cooperative. Nearly 80 per cent of all farmland that was once held by the state, including sugarcane plantations, was thus essentially turned over to the workers, the descendents of generations of small farmers, with long family and community traditions of low-input production. They remembered the old techniques like inter-cropping and manuring that their parents and grand parents had used and simultaneously incorporated new biopesticides and biofertilisers into their production process, and by mid-1995, Cuba had overcome its food shortage, and the vast majority of the population no longer faced drastic reductions of their basic food supply. Cuba's new strategy, based on decentralised cooperative production of course has an important political dimension to it, but its overcoming of a food crisis through self-reliance, small farms and agro-ecological technology is also indicative of the enormous economic potential of pursuing environmentally sustainable, alternative agricultural policies.

Cuba is today the first modern society to adopt an agricultural policy capable of sustainability. The Cubans are also beginning to understand that unrestrained industrialism – whether under capitalism or Soviet-style socialism – inevitably leads to ecological degradation and that the consumerist dream, the market induced desires syndrome, is ultimately unsustainable even in its home countries of advanced capitalism. There is also the growing awareness that 'unrestrained industrialism' is the structural logic of capitalism as a quintessential market-friendly system. Its market-governed accumulative drive makes it impossible for capitalism to harmonise its demands on the natural environment with what the environment can provide. Ecological degradation is thus deeply embedded in the very nature of capitalism, whose continued existence, therefore, portends an ecological disaster for humankind. The solution, certainly the possibility of a solution, lies only in planned socialist development. As Danio Machado, a leading Cuban scholar and activist has put it:

> Socialist planning is the solution for the ecology, and for the possibility of achieving harmony with the environment, with nature, and development that will not harm the future of humanity. The capitalist market, the encouragement of profits, cannot be the salvation for society or for the natural environment.

The Cuban struggle and strategy has the potential of becoming a new and valuable experiment in democratic socialist development consistent with a healthy, liveable planet for the human race.

XV

If, as a country committed to socialist purposes, Cuba's survival is a major gain for the Left everywhere, its survival as a socialist country remains a continuing challenge and threat to capitalism, currently dominant in the world. Hence the United States' unrelenting harassment of Cuba, the sentence of death passed on it by this chieftain of global capitalism, 'world's gendarme of counter-revolution' as Isaac Deutscher once called it. Such indeed is the logic of the US blockage of Cuba. Robin Blackburn has written:

> To grasp the logic of the blockage, it is enough to consult the candid pronouncements of the highest authorities in the land. Two documents say everything: the Clinton Administration's Report to Congress of 28 January 1997, *Support for a Democratic Transition in Cuba* (complete with an ineffable preface by the President himself), and the blue-ribbon *Task Force Report on US-Cuban Relations in the 21st Century*, co-chaired by Nixon's Secretary of State William Rogers, released in January 1999 by the Council on Foreign Relations. The *Task Force Report* goes straight to the point. 'Too often, discussions of the US policy towards Cuba start from the position that the policy over the last four decades has been a failure', we read – whereas in fact, the Task Force reports with

satisfaction, 'US policy towards Cuba, including the embargo, has enjoyed real, though not total, success', since 'the dominant goal of US policy towards Cuba during the Cold War was to prevent the advance of Cuban supported communism in this hemisphere' at a time when 'many young people, academics and intellectuals looked to Cuba as a political and economic model'. But, thanks to firm US counter-measures that have 'frustrated Cuba's ambitions to extend its economic model and political influence', it can be said that today 'Cuban communism is dead as a potent political force'.

What next? 'With this success in hand, the United States can now turn to the second stage of its long-term policy on Cuba' – namely, securing the downfall of the Cuban regime itself. Here, the Report points out, important lessons are to be learnt from Eastern Europe. Indeed, this is an 'experience that allows the United States to approach Cuba today with more flexibility than in the past', since it 'has learned something' about how to manage transitions to democracy there. What has it learnt? The Task force does not beat about the bush. 'Some who formerly served the old regimes, whether through conviction, opportunism or necessity, have become credible and constructive members of the newly emerging democratic governments and societies. The Polish armed forces – which enforced martial law against Solidarity in the early 1980s – are now a trusted NATO partner.' Likewise, 'some who today serve the Cuban government as officials may well form part of a democratic transition tomorrow'. Should anyone miss the hint, Clinton's Report spells it out even more clearly. 'Today, freedom's reach is broader than ever', intones the President. 'Although the Cuban armed forces constitute one of the most important pillars of the present regime in Cuba, they could potentially play a positive role in Cuba's transition. The militaries in other former communist countries have acquiesced or actually assisted in democratic transitions.' Such an about-face would not go unrewarded. 'A professional military that is sized to Cuba's needs, supportive of a civilian democratic government, and respectful of human rights can expect to participate in the Inter-American Defense Board, be welcomed to participate in international peace-keeping efforts and benefit from an array of military-to-military cooperation arrangements, including with the United States' (*sic*). What officer could hope for more?

Blackburn adds:

> The centrality of the Cuban military to American game-planning of the overthrow of the revolutionary government is no doubt fed by hopeful reports from exiles and the internal opposition. It also, of course, speaks of the seriousness of Washington's determination to finish off its opponent in Havana, since so long as the Cuban armed forces are not suitable plywood for an 'Inter-American Defense Board', they represent a daunting obstacle to a US recovery of the island.

'The seriousness of Washington's determination' in the matter notwithstanding, socialist Cuba has refused to die or capitulate, to be overthrown or recovered by the United States, and thus already scored a moral victory over capitalism. But Cuba remains a small beleaguered country. It has weathered the storm so far but there is no guarantee yet that one way or the other the Cuban revolution will not be crushed. There is no international revolutionary movement of any significance to support it, and the active solidarity it continues to evoke is obviously far too inadequate for its defence. Despite its heroic struggle, the odds against Cuba may prove to be too heavy and in the end Cuba may not survive. It is possible that foreign investment and entry into capitalist world economy makes the maintenance of an internal socialist order impossible, that the dual economy gets out of control, produces its own brand of 'capitalist roaders', and Cuba succumbs to the forces of global capitalism to become yet another example of Third-Worldised 'dependent' development. Or, if the economic pressure and menacing gestures from Washington do not produce the Big Fall and the apocalyptic prophecies from Miami prove false, the United States, in its arrogance or desperation, may go in for a bloody dictatorial adventure to restore the old order in Cuba. After Iraq and then Yugoslavia, Afghanistan, and Iraq again, and with the long history of American imperialist interventions abroad, this too is possible. But whatever happens and however it goes ultimately, Cuba is, and will ever remain, an example and inspiration for struggling people everywhere, especially in the Third World, people struggling against capitalism in their pursuit of an egalitarian and humane social order.

XVI

In the meantime, however, Cuba survives. That Cuba has survived and remains defiant in defence of its socialist project, is a testimony to the strength of its people and the tenacity of its leadership. In its survival and defiance, even as it gives hope to socialists everywhere, Cuba is creating an alternative vision for Third World countries. The vision of a self-reliant socialist (or socialism-oriented) development projected by Fidel Castro is clearly an idea whose time has come for people all over the Third World, offering an alternative to the capitalist road of economic development being imposed by the globalising IMF-WB-WTO combine and the multinationals, which is today causing such impoverishment and immiseration in Asia, Africa and Latin America. That Cuba is the exemplar of an alternative socialist development does not however mean that Cuba is in any way a perfect model of building socialism, to be mechanically copied over onto other countries. Obviously each country has to find and travel its own road to socialism. In fact, even in Cuba an essentially Cuban socialist model is yet to emerge. Over the last 40 years Cuba has made not just errors in the process of constructing socialism, but serious errors. Even today Cuba has any number of negative features which need to be shed, features which have so greatly helped its enemies to obscure its achievements. 'Rectification' has been on, but it has to go much further and do so in every sphere of Cuban life. What is needed is a far more thorough-going renewal and reorientation, which ensures that revolutionary politics remains firmly in command so that bureaucratic distortions in the party and polity are better recognised and taken care of, socialist ideology and idealism are reinforced, popular participation is broadened and better institutionalised, a democratic socialist culture is constructed, and the necessary openings to market and globalisation are so mastered and used as to discover and put in effect a new and viable socialist model of economy. A near-impossible task, no doubt, but not impossible. And Cuba is not resourceless for the task. As Haroldo Dilla, even as he asks for 'a major renovation of the political system in the direction of genuine popular power', writes: 'Cuban society has ample reserves in this respect: a strong network of popular participation, a political culture permeated by a sense of solidarity and cooperation, a social subject both educated and committed to values that are essential to socialist objectives, and a political class important segments of which have a sense of responsibility and a high level of social sensitivity.' Cuba *has* the potential to rectify and renovate, to thus struggle and survive. And it is important that Cuba survives, for in its struggle against capitalism, it continues to represent the promise and possibility of a different, better future not only for the peoples in the Third World but for the entire humankind. As Sinan Koont put it some years back:

> Cuba, small but committed, appears to have been saddled with a historic burden well out of proportion to its size. It is one of the last surviving potential transmitters of a hopeful legacy from humanity's initial twentieth-century experimentation with socialism, beginning with the 1917 revolution in Russia. This situation may be a curse, it may be a challenge, but it is something Cuba cannot avoid ...

The Cuban struggle so far has certainly been permeated with a sense of this 'historic burden' and the heroism it calls for. Fidel keeps telling his people: 'what you are doing is socialism'. 'Our enemy hates us', he says, 'just because we have done what we consider to be more just and noble, because we want the very best not only for our people but for all the people in the world. That is why we are so proud and happy to call ourselves internationalists, socialists, communists.' And Fidel Castro has reiterated: 'We understand what it would mean for all the lovers of peace and justice if the US succeeds in crushing the Cuban revolution. And because of this we consider defending it even at the cost of death.'

5

Of the First World, 'Globalisation' and All That

I

The collapse of the Soviet Union has been a historic gain for global capitalism. The challenge that communist regimes and movements born of the October Revolution had posed to its hegemony over 70 odd years has been eliminated, making for its almost unquestioned sway over economy and politics of the contemporary world. The 'communist threat' has receded globally, at least for the time being. The radical change in the relationship of forces and geography of power in international politics resulting from the dissolution of a great power and its system of alliances has led to the near complete supremacy of a group of major capitalist powers, centred on the United States of America. Of the reinforced capitalist hegemony, at least two aspects need to be immediately noted. The conflict of interests among these capitalist powers notwithstanding, they are firmly united in their economic structure. Transnational integration among the capitalist classes has still to reckon with the fact of the national locus of the owners and the boards of directors of the leading transnational corporations. But the transnational corporations have managed to bring a 'new class consciousness' to the world, consolidating it around themselves. The differences and contradictions remain and can be really sharp and explosive at times, but as in any class project, the part is subordinate to the whole, the particular to the general. Therefore, if there is one class in the contemporary world which could be said to be 'class for itself' in the Marxian sense, it is the monopoly bourgeoisie, more particularly of the United States, Germany and Japan. They are enormously powerful, very well aware of their interests and have the means, economic, political and military, to defend and pursue them the world over. The 'new world order', being promulgated only heralds the demolition of the barriers to the global domination of this bourgeoisie, so that the much celebrated 'free world', now more 'free' than ever before, remains a freely exploitable area in which giant multinational corporations can do business on their own terms. This class, feeling more safe and powerful that at any time since at least the first decade of the twentieth century, if not since the Paris Commune, is today determined to rule the world by its own lights, using its economic and cultural supremacy, and if needs be by the exercise of brute military force. *And* presiding over this system of global capitalist domination and oppression is the United States, the world's only remaining superpower. It is the most important single fact of world politics in our times that since the world war two, the US has been at the centre of world reaction. It has used its enormous resources to crush, curb and contain democratic movements and progressive or left-wing regimes in all continents. In the post-Soviet 'new world order', the US has arrogated to itself the natural right of international policing, continuing even more freely with its role of 'world's gendarme of counter revolution', as Issac Deutscher once called it, even as it also uses its military power to secure American capitalism's economic interests and imperialist domination abroad.

The emerging reality of the 'new world order', the reborn unilateralism of global capitalism or *pax-Americana*, the military might, technological prowess and economic clout as well as moral self-righteousness and cultural arrogance of the triumphalist capitalist west was early and fully displayed in the mounting and conduct of the First Gulf War, when, even as the Soviet Union was collapsing, western powers played fast and loose with the provisions of the United Nations Charter and, in the words of Canada's former Ambassador to the United

Nations, Stephen Lewis, 'conscripted (the UN) into the role of providing cover for US foreign policy', in the process shredding to bits whatever remained of either 'non-alignment' or 'North-South dialogue', reducing the rest of the world to an impotent, mute witness to the orgy of mass destruction visited on Iraq that brought alive the nightmarish memories of Hiroshima and Nagasaki. Thus was unquestioned western hegemony established in the oil-rich Arab world and a warning issued that only severe punishment awaits the governments which for one reason or another ran counter to the wishes or interests of American or global capitalism – a warning later brutally reissued by America's equally unilateral and indiscriminatory bombing of Yugoslavia, and more recently, by war on Afghanistan and then again on Iraq.

A more or less peaceful counterpart of this armed assertion abroad have been the recent policies of the American, indeed of global capitalism, whereby all economic and political means have been used, more particularly through international institutions like the IMF, World Bank and WTO and so-called aid and structural adjustment programmes, to thrust the western agenda down the throats of the rest of the world – in the areas of international economic development and monetary management, cutting edge technology, informatics, audio-visual production and services, trade and intellectual property rights, sports and culture, and so on. Leave alone any radical or socialist change, even the search for a 'third way' as it is sometimes called – any kind of relatively autonomous or self-reliant development that does not slavishly seek to follow the western approved capitalist model – is denied to countries of the third or former second world. Needless to add, global capitalism's renewed assertion abroad is not without its counterpart at home. All sorts of old or new right-wing agendas have come alive in the domestic domain of the countries of advanced capitalism, including the US The key word here has been 'roll back' and the welfare state continues to be dismantled. As Chomsky has put it, 'now they feel they can move on to roll back and unravel the entire social contract which developed through large-scale popular struggle over a century and a half, which did sort of soften the edges of predatory private tyranny, and softened them a lot.' This roll back is accompanied by a new offensive against the working classes and a 'restructuring' of capitalist economy to allow for their intensified exploitation.

More important than its current economic, political or military power is the ideological hegemony that global capitalism, with US at its head, has come to acquire today. The collapse of the Soviet and East European communist regimes and their ignorantly accepted or cleverly imputed identification with socialism, has enabled the capitalist propaganda at its most triumphant to proclaim the failure or defeat of socialism itself and the success or inevitability of capitalism. With the means provided by the contemporary communications revolution, a veritable carpet bombing of public consciousness has occurred producing an ideological consensus on behalf of capitalism, from one country to another, and from liberals and conservatives to any number of ex-socialists. The left as a whole has succumbed, singularly failing to play its time-honoured role, precisely when it was most needed, as critics of capitalism, of combating the consensus of the right (which, incidentally, makes nonsense of the much-vaunted pluralism of bourgeois democracy, gaining for it a spurious credibility only by a bizarre blowing up of minor differences among competitors in the politics of 'actually existing capitalism'). Once again, as in the fifties and sixties, 'the end of ideology' is proclaimed. 'An intellectual celebration of apathy', 'a consensus of a few provincials about their own immediate and provincial position (that helped them) to acquiesce in and to justify the status quo', as C. Wright Mills had then put it, 'the end of ideology' today is an equally myopic and status quoist celebration of the consensus around 'the triumph of capitalism', the near-exclusive dominance of its ideological discourse. Now it is not only the end of socialism, but the 'end of history' itself, its culmination in an eternal and inevitable capitalism. Once, these very bourgeois ideologues, theorising about 'Soviet totalitarianism' had claimed that the 'empire of evil' and its satellites were immutable, that it was a hell from which there was no exit. With their persistent myopia about historical change, instead of self-criticism, they have only produced a transfer: it is now capitalism which is a system from which there is no exit. Margaret Thatcher's 'There is no alternative' (TINA) – duly echoed by all and sundry including a Gorbachev once – has become the new chorus in defence ot capitalism. What is more, in its omnipresence and newly acquired immunity to criticism, capitalism has become virtually invisible, its invisibility well secured by another of the proliferating buzz words of our time, 'globalisation', and the accompanying clutch of concepts like 'liberalisation', 'structural adjustment', 'economic reform', 'new economic policy', etc. etc.

I have touched upon this subject earlier. Another, more focussed look at it, particularly in relation to the First World of capitalism, will not be out of place.

II

'Globalisation' is far from being an unambiguous or conceptually-clear theoretical construct. Given the fuzziness of language over it, Peter Marcuse has even called it a 'non-concept': 'a simple catalogue of everything that seems different since, say, 1970, whether advances in information technology, widespread use of air freight, speculation in currencies, increased capital flows across borders, Disneyfication of culture, mass marketing, global warming, genetic engineering, multinational corporate power, new international division of labour, international mobility of labour, reduced power of nation-states, postmodernism, or post-Fordism'. But this is not all. As Peter Marcuse adds: 'The issue is more than one of careless use of words: intellectually, such muddy use of the term fogs any effort to separate cause from effect, to analyze what is being done, by whom, to whom, for what, and with what effect. Politically, leaving the term vague and ghostly permits its conversion to something with a life of its own, making it a force, fetishizing it as something that has an existence independent of the will of human beings, inevitable and irresistible.'

Thus, for its ardent ideologue Thomas Friedman – a big time columnist of the *New York Times* – globalisation is a new technological-economic system based in the microchip and ruled by an 'electronic herd' of financial investors and multinational corporations, sweeping away everything that came before – capitalism and socialism, the nation-state, imperialism, class struggle, everything. And we have even well-meaning mainstream scholars coming up with what can at best be described as deceptively confusing interpretations. For John Harriss, for example, 'globalisation' is a recent phenomena. He views the use of the term 'in the last 10 years or so' as 'an indication that something has been happening out there', and goes on to describe it in conventional fuzzy terms: '...the world is more inter-connected and supposedly more interdependent than it was formerly, as a result of changes in the global economy – notably rapid movements of large volumes of money and the increased volume of trade – as well as of changes in communications and in information technology. These trends are related in turn and more controversially, with a variety of political and cultural changes, including perhaps especially the ideas of 'deterritorialisation', of the decline of the nation state and of a shift to politics of presence'. For Amartya Sen globalistion is almost as old as civilisation itself: 'Over thousands of years, globalisation has progressed through travel, trade, migration, spread of cultural influences and dissemination of knowledge (including of science and technology)'. Sen recognises 'the dual presence of abject misery and unprecedented prosperity in the world in which we live' – 'incomparably richer than ever before, ours is also a world of extraordinary deprivation and staggering inequality' – to end up urging support for globalisation 'in the best sense of that idea', and pleading: 'what is needed is a fairer distribution of the fruits of globalisation'. Globalisation's historically specific reality today is evaded through an appeal to its so-called 'idea in the best sense', which only adds to the prevailing fuzziness and confusion in the use of this term or concept.

Be that as it may, there are many reasons to doubt that 'globalisation' represents an accurate account of the phenomena it purports to describe. On the other hand, there are good reasons to treat it, in its current usage, as an ideological mystification.

III

As a theoretical concept, globalisation came up in the late 1960s and early 1970s to account for a recent complex of developments in global economy, particularly the major expansion and conquest of markets by the multinationals, seeking to present this international capitalist expansion in a favourable light, an alternative to Marxist vocabulary with its concepts of imperialism, capitalism etc. In its current widely accepted usage, acquiring new credibility with the collapse of 'Soviet socialism', the concept is characterised by two distinct emphases. In the first place, linked to what has been called the third technological revolution, this internationalisation of capital has come to be viewed as a tide sweeping over borders in which technology and irresistible market forces transform the global system in ways beyond the power of everyone to do much to change. The view is often buttressed by a kind of technological determinism where the new electronic technologies make globalisation not only possible or necessary, but inevitable. Globalisation is viewed as an entity in itself, an inevitable, irreversible natural process, which independently of any human will or politics is now taking over and transforming the world. In its second distinctive emphasis, globalisation is seen as a historical rupture of a qualitative kind from the changes that have been occurring in capitalism since its inception. The changes now taking place represent a distinctive and unique kind of 'epochal shift' – a notion which these days runs as a kind of *leitmotif* through a wide spectrum of intellectual currents, where 'post' is the presiding buzzword. We are told that we are now, since early 1970s to be precise, living through an epochal shift, the birth of a new era, a major qualitative leap so different from the earlier changes in the process of capitalist development that the very logic of capitalism stands superseded. In the globalised world of today there is no capitalism with its exploitation and oppressions, its classes and class struggles, its structural defects and explosive antagonisms, its chronic problems or crises. Imperialism too is now a thing of the past.

Around this notion of a technology-driven 'globalisation' has grown a new orthodoxy – that of 'a dematerialised world', which yet again suggests supersession of capitalism as an economic system and therefore obsolescence of the associated categories of analysis. In a recent article, speaking of 'the Myth of Weightless Economy', Ursula Huws has written:

> 'The Death of Distance', 'Weightless World', the 'Connected Economy', the 'Digital Economy', the 'Knowledge-Based Economy', the 'Virtual Organisation'. All these phrases were culled from the titles of books published in the six months prior to writing this essay, in spring, 1998. They could have been multiplied many times: 'virtual', 'cyber', 'tele-', 'networked' or even just 'e-' can, it seems, be prefixed interchangeably to an almost infinite range of abstract nouns. Without even straying from the field of economics, you can try 'enterprise', 'work', 'banking', 'trade', 'commerce', or 'business' (although the device works equally well in other areas: for instance 'culture', 'politics', 'sex', 'democracy', 'relationship', 'drama', 'community', 'art', 'society', 'shopping' or 'crime').
>
> A consensus seems to be emerging – in economics as in other fields – that something entirely new is happening: that the world as we know it is becoming quite dematerialised (or, as Marx put it, 'all that is solid melts into air') and that this somehow throws into question all the conceptual models which have been developed to make sense of the old material world. We are offered a paradoxical universe: geography without distance, history without time, value without weight, transactions without cash. This is an economics which sits comfortably in a Baudrillardian philosophical framework, in which all reality has become a simulacrum and human agency, to the extent that it can be said to exist at all, is reduced to the manipulation of abstractions...

The ideological-political implications are obvious. As in the current conventional conception of 'globalisation', capitalism, the historically specific capitalist processes, the capitalist exploitation of human beings and natural resources, simply disappear. The frenetic and feverish manner in which the information revolution is hyped, makes it appear that the entire system of organised capitalism dating back to Industrial Revolution (and even earlier) is being displaced by a new age of 'the electronic republic' and 'digital futurologies' where information or 'knowledge' is the only source of value and work is something contingent and delocalisable if not dispensable, where the demand or need to produce material means of living, indeed any assertion of the physical claims of the human body in the here-and-now is an old-fashioned concern, where 'the computer', lord and master of it all, refashions economy and society, human beings themselves, in its own image...

As capitalism goes out of sight, 'globalisation' as a universal category of analysis displaces the critical socialist concepts of 'capitalism', or imperialism, and together with its technological determinism undercuts any notion of radical or systemic transformative politics. Any kind of anti-capitalist project is ruled out. A natural, inevitable process, any resistance to 'globalisation' is futile. There is no alternative but accept its dictates. 'Globalisation' thus disarms any opposition to almighty capital, becomes an ideological tool instilling a certain fatalism in the working people, nations and states to induce them to follow policies of adjustment to the demands of global capitalism, at home and abroad.

The conventional theorising over 'globalisation' – 'globaloney' it has been called – mystifies the reality of our world. Postulating an utterly fictitious world of superseded capitalism, it makes capitalism safe against criticism and opposition and using the argument of 'inevitability', it wants us to believe that in this globalised world there is no alternative to the meek acceptance of the conditions necessary for its trouble-free functioning, which in effect means trouble-free functioning of the global capitalist system.

It only needs to be added that today quite a few on the left, indeed a painfully large majority, too has succumbed to the infashion 'globloney' of the right. This left has presently joined the right in accepting that 'There Is No Alternative' – not just no alternative to capitalism but, as we shall see, to a more or less (the right goes for more, the left somewhat less) ruthlessly 'flexible' capitalism.

IV

Globalisation is argued for as an almost automatic solution to all the encountered problems and contradictions of our economy, if not our society as a whole – its promise of universal benevolence reminding us of the once similarly hailed and revered notion of 'invisible hand', Adam Smith's assurance that went so grievously sour as soon as the logic of *capitalist* market asserted itself. This solution, as noticed above, is presented as a complete novelty as if the issue of globalisation appeared on the historical horizon only in the last couple of decades, marking an entirely new, qualitatively different phase in the development of capitalism. This, however, is only so much 'globaloney'. Globalisation is nothing qualitatively new in the history of bourgeois society, it is a process that has been going on for a long time, in fact ever since capitalism came into the world as a viable form of society four or five centuries ago. An ever-changing system, capitalism was born and grew, and grew to maturity only as a world system. In other words capitalism has always been a global or globalising system, one moving inexorably towards 'globalisation' from its very inception. The most significant elements of what is called globalisation have always been part of capitalist development, even if the specific forms and features of this development including globalisation – that is, the global process of capital expansion and accumulation – have been different in different periods (including our own). That capitalism is in its innermost essence an expanding system both internally and externally was pointed out by Marx a long time ago. Once rooted, propelled by the law of accumulation of capital, it both grows and spreads. The classic analysis of this double movement is of course Marx's *Capital*. But the *globalising* nature of capitalism was diagnosed and emphasised by him more than 150 years ago in the *Communist Manifesto* itself. Marx has been proved uncannily right about many things but perhaps nowhere has he been vindicated more completely than in his account of capitalist expansion or globalisation. Here, for example, are a couple of passages from the *Manifesto*: 'The bourgeoisie has through its exploitation of the world market given a cosmopolitan character to production and consumption in every country ... All old-established national industries have been destroyed or are being destroyed. They are dislodged by new industries, whose introduction becomes a life and death question for all nations, by industries that no longer work up indigenous raw material, but raw material drawn from the remotest zones; industries whose products are consumed not only at home, but in every quarter of the globe. In place of the old wants, satisfied by the productions of the country, we find new wants, requiring for their satisfaction the products of distant lands and climes... in place of the old local and national seclusion and self-sufficiency, we have intercourse in every direction, universal interdependence of nations...'. Again: 'The need of a constantly expanding market for its productions chases the bourgeoisie over the whole surface of the globe. It must nestle everywhere, settle everywhere, establish connections everywhere...'. Yet again: the bourgeoisie 'batters down all Chinese walls' and 'compels all nations, on pain of extinction, to adopt the bourgeois mode of production; it compels them to introduce what it calls civilisation into their midst, i.e., to become bourgeois themselves. In one word, it creates a world after its own image.' Of course, these passages from the *Communist Manifesto* (1848) are not a simple description of contemporary reality. A statement of general and long-term processes that have been part of capitalist development from the beginning, they are more an anticipation of the future that is ours today. They represent an analysis which is much truer today than when the *Manifesto* was composed. It is true, as we have pointed out before, that Marx underestimated the durability of capitalism and how long it could keep on expanding. But for all today's fashionable talk about 'globalisation', it would be hard to find a more effective description of what is happening today than what he wrote 150 odd years ago.

It needs to be noted that what is involved here is not merely expansion of capitalism but also its *domination* abroad. In the *Manifesto* as elsewhere, Marx's treatment of the exploitation process, which is the backbone of capital accumulation, is mostly focussed on the relationship between labour and owners of capital in Western Europe. But he was not unaware of the fact that while capitalism by its very nature lives by accumulation and geographic expansion, it does so in a most unequal fashion. 'The historic task of bourgeois society'. Marx had said, 'is the establishment of the world market'. But inequality, for him, was already a feature of the relationship between the advanced nations and the rest in the world market. The language is obviously Eurocentric and is but poorly qualified by the phrase 'what it calls civilisation' in its reference to the western bourgeois world. Nevertheless, suggestive of the process of unequal relationship or colonisation immanent in capitalist expansion abroad, the *Manifesto* noted that the bourgeoisie 'has made barbarian and semi-barbarian countries dependent on the civilized ones, nations of peasants on nations of bourgeois, the East on the West.' As we have noticed on an earlier occasion, there are firmer statements of this colonising dimension in *Capital* and late Marx, and Marx has in more than one place written of the havoc wrought by capitalism in its 'progress' abroad – for example, in India – likening it, in a telling metaphor to 'the pagan god, who would not drink nectar except in skulls of the slain'. This dimension of capitalist globalisation was, however, never subjected to a comprehensive critical analysis by Marx, for the simple reason that it came to maturity much after him. This task was carried out by Marxists who followed, notably Lenin whose study of *Imperialism*, among other things noted the dominating presence of monopolies in every field of economy and society and traced the growth of capitalism into a world system of not just colonial oppression but also 'the financial strangulation of the overwhelming majority of the population of the world by a handful of "advanced" countries'. Lenin drew specific attention to such phenomena as 'the predominance of finance capital', 'the rise of an all-powerful financial oligarchy', of 'a small number of financially "powerful" states.' He wrote of the usurer state and usuary imperialism, of the division of the world into a handful of usurer states and creditor countries and 'the rest of the world (which) is more or less the debtor to and tributary of these international banker countries'. He pointed out 'that the development of capitalism has arrived at a stage when, although commodity production still "reigns" and continues to be regarded as the basis of economic life, it has in reality been undermined and the bulk of the profits go to the "geniuses" of financial manipulation.' Lenin located finance capital in a non-industrial or speculative setting, noticed the 'extraordinary growth of a class, or rather, of a stratum of rentiers, i.e., people who live by "clipping coupons", ... whose profession is idleness', and showed how 'the export of capital, one of most essential economic bases of imperialism, still more completely isolates the rentiers from production and sets the seal of parasitism on the whole country that lives by exploiting the labour of several overseas countries and colonies.' These are issues, it may be noted, which are at the centre of the current phase of globalisation.

V

Marx's is analytically the most sophisticated recognition of capitalism as a system that is uniquely expansionary and international, one tangentially 'global' since the very beginning, but a more than working recognition of this dimension of capitalism was common to classical thinkers such as Adam Smith, and later to most mainstream economists before the first world war. Multinational manufacturing firms appeared in the middle of the 19th century and were well established by the beginning of the 20th century to make internationalisation of capital a common preoccupation not only of Marxist theorists like Luxemburg, Lenin or Bukharin. Analysts have pointed out that foreign trade and overseas income was a greater percentage of GNP in Europe during the late 19th century than at the end of the 20th century, that world financial markets in the late 19th and early 20th centuries were more fully integrated than they were before or have been since. As a commentator for the *Financial Times* of London has recently put it, 'Before 1914 the world economy was in many respects as integrated as it is today and in certain respects more so'. This integration, with capital and commodities freely traversing the globe, had also made for internationalisation of social and economic life. This is how John Maynard Keynes saw it: 'The inhabitant of London could order by telephone, sipping his morning tea in bed, the various products of the whole earth, in such quantity as he might see fit, and reasonably expect their early delivery upon his doorstep; he could at the same moment and by the same means adventure his wealth in the natural resources and new enterprises in any quarter of the world, and share, without exertion or even trouble, in their prospective fruits and advantages; or he could decide to couple the security of his fortunes with the good faith of the townspeople of any substantial municipality in any continent that fancy or information might recommend. He could secure forthwith, if he wished it, cheap and comfortable means of transit to any country or climate without passport or other formality....But, most important of all, he regarded this state of affairs as normal, certain, and permanent, except in the direction of improvement... The internationalisation of (social and economic life) was nearly complete...' Thus, if 'globalisation' is no novelty in the history of capitalist development, the associated notion of 'a borderless world' too is no recent invention.

Writing of 'the short twentieth century' (1914 to the end of Soviet era) E.H. Hobsbawm has demarcated three distinct periods: an 'Age of Catastrophe' from 1914 to the aftermath of the Second World War, marked by two world wars, two waves of revolution, the crumbling of colonial empires, an unprecedented crisis of capitalism followed by a crisis of liberal democracy; a 'Golden Age' from 1950 until 1970, marked by extraordinary productive achievements of capitalism, the rise of welfare state and Keynesian economics, the promise of 'developmentalism' in the third world; and finally a period of 'Landslide', 1970 to 1991, marked by a global crisis, mass unemployment and growing inequality, severe cyclical swings of national economies, crisis of third world developmentalism, erosion of the welfare state, rise of economic liberalism, and ending up with the general chaos resulting from the collapse of 'Soviet socialism'. These roughly defined three periods, eventually reflecting three phases of development of capitalism in our time are indicative of the essential nature of capitalist development which, given the contradictions inherent in capitalism, has always been a crisis-ridden, bumpy and uneven affair. It is no different with globalisation as a capitalist process. Its progress too has been essentially bumpy and uneven, and shot through with local, regional and more than regional crises. There have been periods of 'high' globalisation and periods in which economic flows have, to a greater or lesser degree, turned inward in response to changed economic and political conditions. Thus, the second half of the nineteenth century witnessed an escalating thrust of 'globalisation' as a part of capitalism's normal existence. It continued in the twentieth century and globalisation was really intense until 1914. Two world wars, a great depression, revolution in Russia and working class struggles somewhat interrupted this trend, creating what Hobsbawn has described as an interlude of national economics between eras of international economics. This interlude saw the domestic economies turn in on themselves and there was a prolonged shift to a period of 'national development', of 'largely delinked, managed national economies', as one description has it – the so-called Keynesian era which was the unique product of a catastrophic period for capitalism in the first half of the twentieth century. Once a certain degree of economic and political recovery was achieved, there was an increasing and uneven effort from the 1950s onwards to return to active globalisation. The effort picked up with the onset of the crisis in the 1970s, when together with a return to its normal functioning at home, capitalism resumed its path towards internationalisation with a vengeance, to be soon provided a new specific thrust by the collapse in the East. The erosion and disintegration of Keynesianism (with its regulated capitalism and welfare state) and the onset of so-called 'globalisation' not only reflected the depth of the new crisis but also demonstrated capital's inherent, and now increasingly desperate, drive to create a world economy 'in its own image'. Such has been the changing trajectory of globalisation in our time.

Viewed in this perspective, the increasing integration of national economies and the globalisation of trade and investment are not new phenomena, only a new phase in the normal existence of capitalism as a global system. What has taken place, far from being some new departure, is rather a return, a turning back to trends that marked the 'high' globalisation of the 19th century, a resumption of the drive that had temporarily slowed down during the intervening period of 'low' globalisation. And with this resumed globalisation, given the depth of the current economic crisis, we are also back – with a new vengeance this time – to pre-Keynesian economics and ideological hegemony of *laissez faire*.

The talk about 'globalistion' as 'a new era' or 'an epochal shift' therefore represents more an ideological-political phenomenon than a serious analysis of the new situation. But the phenomenon nevertheless has a certain basis – in the lived memory of a happy Keynesian past and in the significant fact of the end of the post-war boom in the 1970s, which sharpened the contrast between the new present and *that* past. The state-regulated and welfare-statist monopoly capitalism of the Keynesian era (roughly 1945-1975), really an aberration in the history of capitalism, was assumed to be the normal and natural form of capitalism. The globalisation over the past 25 years, when capitalism has come to resemble that of the late 19th century more than it does that of the 1950s and 1960s, could therefore be seen or interpreted as a dramatic break, a rupture, in the history of capitalism, one that effectively constitutes an epochal shift. Capitalism's global ascendancy following the Soviet collapse has made for both a world wide acceptance of this shift and its positive interpretation. The resumed hegemony of bourgeois ideology has even persuaded people to see in it the promise of universal benevolence! That many on the left have succumbed to 'globalisation' and its TINA chorus only reflects the disarray in the political and intellectual life of the left and the pervasive power of bourgeois ideology.

VI

It is of course mistaken, a case of ahistorical thinking, to interpret the era of 'globalisation' of the past thirty years or so as an epochal rupture with the essential logic of capitalism. But to argue that it represents a reversion to form for capitalism after the anomaly of the so-called 'Keynesian era', is not to even remotely suggest that it is simply that, that no new phenomena are at work. Capitalism *is* undergoing unique and important transformations, as it has throughout its history. Major changes *have* occurred in the capitalist economy since the end of the post war boom, with global capitalism acquiring quite a few significantly new features. This phase of 'globalisation' has its own historical specificities, its own specific contradictions and dynamics, as has been the case with other specific phases in the history of ever-changing capitalism.

The specificities of context or conjuncture of the current phase of globalisation lie in a new crisis of capital accumulation, the long drawn-out downturn and stagnation which brought the post-war 'golden age' to an end – something different from, or at least more protracted than, the classic episodic crises of capitalism – and led to dismantling of the welfare state at home and capital's furious thrust abroad in search of a new world of profits. This search has of course been greatly facilitated by the technological revolution of our time but the new scope and scale of movement of capital and commodities across the globe has been less due to technological than to political changes or conjunctures. Most noticeable here is the extension of capitalism directly associated with the collapse of the Soviet Union and communist regimes of Eastern Europe, as well as with the turn to capitalism in China and Vietnam. The demise of 'socialism' in the former communist countries of Europe and Asia, together with the crisis or collapse of third-world developmentalism – though not without leaving behind such sections of society as 'the great Asian middle class' as *The Economist* has rather courteously called it – and the consequent subjection of national-populist third world regimes to the rule of unregulated capitalism, has opened up vast new markets for sales and investment and thus accumulation of profits. The political victories of capitalism are thus central to the advance of the contemporary process of globalisation as compared to the historical period immediately following the second world war or the mid-1970s and certainly in relation to the inter-war period.

Today the capitalist world system has for the first time in history become really global. The scale, scope and speed of the circulation of capital and commodities, particularly financial flows between deregulated economies, is something unprecedented. Technological changes are a distinctive feature of the current phase of globalisation and those in the sphere of information and communications (computer, fax, e-mail etc.) have lent a rare velocity to movements of capital and goods across the globe. All sorts of new supra national institutions promoting the needs of transnational finance, production and trade (NAFTA, EU, WTO, MAI, multilateral trade agreements, etc.) have come up, which, together with changes in technology and politics have greatly increased the ability of capital to do what it has always wanted to do – turn the world into one 'free market' for finance, production, and wage labour. The whole planet has been opened up to capitalist penetration, making it possible for capital to extract and realise *relative* surplus value on a global scale – if not exactly everywhere at least somewhere in many parts of every continent and subcontinent – in a way that earlier forms of globalisation had not achieved. Globalisation today thus marks a qualitatively new stage of capital accumulation on a world scale.

The increasing strategic importance of multinationals or transnationals in capitalist economy is a significant feature of the new stage of globalisation. It was not till after 1945 that the multinational corporations, developed in the inter-war years, became generalised. In this, it is the vigorous expansion of the US multinationals in the 1950s, part and parcel of United States' hegemonic role at the time, that led the way. They created an environment in which giant corporations of all nations, driven by motives of self-defence as well as by their eagerness for new accumulation opportunities, had to turn multinational and widen their international base. But it was not until the 1980s that, with the aid of computerisation, the multinational corporations realised their full potential for worldwide control of production and finance. Today some 40,000 multinational corporations – fifty of them now receiving more revenue than two-thirds of world's states, and, with their subsidiaries around the world, owning one-third of the world's productive capacity – determine trade, investment and employment patterns across the globe. No nation, poor or rich is immune to their globalising pressure.

Associated with the increased strategic importance of multinationals in the global economy is the rising tide of foreign direct investment (FDI). Another key measure of globalisation, the speeded-up flow of direct investment from one country to another is also a response to the post-boom stagnation mentioned above. Capital needs no extra-special stimulus to seek out project opportunities, and the export of capital has been a tool for economic growth over the ages. Foreign direct investment – that is, multinational business – has always existed and many of the world's largest firms have been transnational from birth. Capital, therefore, was bound to take advantage of the current opening up of the planet to capitalist penetration. Still, any slowing down of economic growth intensifies the competitive drive in foreign as well as domestic markets. It is not surprising therefore that we witnessed an unusually great leap in foreign investment in the 1980s and then onwards. It is equally important to notice the changing composition of this new phase of direct foreign investment. Global operations of the multinationals in manufacturing and marketing have now undergone vital changes in many ways. One of these is a growing shift of investment at home from the manufacturing to the services – finance and insurance, communications, advertising and sales, the media, etc. etc. About 60 per cent of the total employment in developed countries is now provided by the services sector. As for manufacturing capital, it has been migrating in search of low wages and taxes and compliant governments wherever it can find them around the globe. In 1990s almost one-half of the FDI stock of transnational corporations (TNCs) in the developed countries was in the services sector, while manufacturing accounted for the largest sector in the developing countries. In other words, cheap labour and natural resources, along with unconcern for environmental pollution in the developing countries have persuaded the TNCs to shift a large share of their investment allocation to the latter. The first wave of foreign investment after the Second World War concentrated on raw materials and other primary products. Apart from investments of this kind, capital flowed to the third world for manufacturing enterprises to profit from the exceptionally low wages and to take advantage of the demand generated by the local rich and middle classes. The capital absorption capacity of these enterprises was, however, always limited and capital surplus in search of outlets was growing all the time. The new opportunities and the shift in the investment policies of the TNCs has meant a radical change in the situation. In the 'new international division of labour' as it is called – and which, dating from about 1970, is another significant development in the history of on-going globalisation – no longer is the third world relegated to only production and export of primary products and importation of manufactured goods from the first world. With technology increasing the global reach of capitalist production processes and allowing easier, cheaper and faster communication and transportation as well as breaking up of production processes into segments that can be parcelled all over the globe, we now have a more truly global manufacturing system with multinational or transnational firms investing abroad and producing key components of fully manufactured goods in countries ranging from Mexico to Malaysia. It may be added that this has had negative consequences for the wages and working conditions of workers in the advanced capitalist countries. The 'social power' of western labour has declined and impoverishment – or the threat of it – has returned.

The internationalisation of finance capital is another notably distinguishing attribute of the current globalisation process. The dramatic developments in the system of international finance, in the concentration of capital on an international plane that we are witnessing today, are even seen by some to constitute, in some ways, the real *differentia specifica* of contemporary capitalism. Over the last two decades or so, the world has seen a phenomenal growth of financial capital, accompanied by unprecedented forms of international credit and currency flows, including the utterly new role of bank lending across national borders. On a national as well as on an international scale, the financial sectors of the advanced capitalist countries seem to have taken on a life of their own. The sheer volume and the tremendous speed with which financial transactions occur in today's digital markets is evident in the fact that everyday more than one trillion dollars turn over in foreign exchange markets, only about 15 per cent of which represents actual capital flows and trade in commodities. This ballooning of international finance, together with the new ability to transfer money worldwide instantaneously has spawned a host of new methods of financial speculation and manipulation. The significant autonomy that these financial flows have developed from the actions of governments and central banks has meant not only a heightened volatility in world financial markets but also that these flows are engaged largely in pure speculation: more than 80 per cent of the capital in national exchanges is speculative and the primary form of international finance capital today is 'hot money' flows in search of quick profits.

Finally, we need to take notice of the ideological and cultural sweep of capitalist ideas and values that, in its own way, defines the current phase of globalisation, its neo-liberalism whereby the bourgeoisie today 'makes the world in its own image' with an impunity almost unparalleled since Marx wrote these words 150 odd years ago. With capitalism become all but universal, it has also become ideologically hegemonic as never before. It is not only that capitalist laws of motion, the logic of capitalism has penetrated ever deeper into the societies of advanced capitalism and spatially throughout the world. Today every human practice, every social relationship, virtually everything under the sun including the natural environment is subject to the requirements of profit-maximisation. Capitalism's technological ingenuity has made it possible for its principles to find their way into social, institutional and cultural spaces that even a few decades ago were beyond their reach. Commodity relations and moralities of the market are penetrating into every aspect of our lives, producing profit of course, but also ravaging morals and culture everywhere. Michael Lowy has written:

> Indeed, never until this end of the 20th century has capital succeeded in exerting such a complete, absolute, undivided, universal, and unlimited sway over the whole world. Never in the past has it had its current ability to impose its rules, its policies, its dogmas, and its interests upon all the nations of the globe. Never have international finance capital and multinational

> corporations been so out of control by states and peoples. Never before now has their existed such a dense network of international institutions – International Monetary Fund, World Bank, World Trade Organisation – devoted to controlling, governing, and administering human life according to the strict rules of the capitalist free market and unrestricted pursuit of capitalist profitability. Finally, never in any preceding epoch have all spheres of human life – social relationships, culture, art, politics, sexuality, health, education, sports, recreation – been so completely dominated by capital, so deeply submerged in 'the icy water of egotistical calculation.'

VII

Capitalism with its globalising thrust is a constantly changing system. It is not the same capitalism as it was, say, in the mid-19th century when Karl Marx wrote his *Capital*. Its development has been marked by slow or rapid changes, qualitative shifts or 'discontinuities', throughout its centuries old history. We have noticed some of these changes or shifts, specific new features in the current phase of its development. But it is wrong and ahistorical to focus on these real or apparent changes or discontinuities to argue, as theories of 'globalisation' (or 'post-modernity') do, that we have now moved into a type of post-capitalist economic system which is basically different from what we have known. In recognising the discontinuities, we must not lose sight of the fact that, at the level of the system, continuities within capitalism are more significant than the discontinuities. We need to be clear not only about what has changed but even more about what has stayed the same: the unique systemic logic of capitalism, the specific 'laws of motion' or 'logic of process' common to capitalism in all its forms and phases – the logic which indeed generates or governs the constantly occurring changes in capitalism. Massive changes have indeed occurred in capitalism in recent decades, but this has been part of a process in capitalism since its inception – a process which is a manifestation of capitalism's logic of expansion and integration both vertically and horizontally. 'Globalisation' today represents only a new phase of this historical process, no departure, only capitalism's logic extended across a much greater horizon. It is the logic of capitalism universalising itself and reaching a level of maturity never realised before.

Thus viewed, 'globalisation' is not what it is often made out to be, itself a driving force of world economy. It remains what it has been throughout the history of capitalism: the always expansive and often explosive capital accumulation process. It is a myth that the market now has as its principal purpose the service of human needs. It remains subject to capitalist imperatives of accumulation and profit-maximisation, an arena of aggrandisement for capitalists and their corporations. That is why it makes sense to speak of 'the capitalist system' rather than 'the global market'. The issue here is not just this or that phase of capitalism or just globalisation, but of a world economy still subject to capitalism's laws of motion. The more globalised economy of today remains one driven by classic patterns of capitalist investment and accumulation – and thus characterised by tendencies towards over accumulation and crisis. It features its classical correlates too: capital-capital competition in the market, capital-labour contradiction at home and imperialist exploitation abroad.

The universalisation of capital does not mean the universalisation of capitalist prosperity, success, industrialisation or development, as promised by the globalisers. On the contrary, it can only mean the universalisation of capitalist polarisation, for such is the structural logic of capitalist development. And this is precisely what has been happening. Capitalism's tendency to generate wealth for the relatively few and poverty for the many is as much in evidence today in both the developed North and the developing South as it was in the 19th century England of 'dark satanic mills' that Marx and Engels so perceptively analysed. Now, as then, the poor grow poorer as the rich grow richer. Polarisation abroad has meant the marginalisation and increasing impoverishment of whole regions outside the advanced capitalist countries. The class polarisations of capitalism are as much evident in the North-South divide as in the growing impoverishment of so-called 'underclasses' within advanced capitalist countries.

We may here specifically notice a key feature of contemporary globalisation that it retains from its earlier phases: its driving forces are centred in the imperial states and the dominant classes within these states who own or control and run the multinational corporations and banks duly backed by the international financial institutions. Thus we have, as in the past, 'globalising' nations and classes and the 'globalised', a hierarchical system of power, exchange and benefits: there are wealthy creditors and bankrupt debtors, super-rich speculators and impoverished peasants and unemployed workers, imperial states that direct international financial institutions and subordinate states that submit to their dictates, andso on. There has been much 'globaloney' over 'interdependence of nations' and its 'globally shared benefits'. Surely 'imperialism' is a more useful concept to comprehend this aspect of the reality of our globalised world.

Skewed distribution of benefits is however only one issue. 'Globalisation' is really the globalisation of capitalism's basic dynamics, including the contradictions inherent in its relentless drive to maximise profit and accumulate. As a consequence we not only have a ravaging of humanity, mass unemployment and underemployment and active impoverishment of large populations at the centre and in the periphery of global capitalism and a destruction of natural environment all over the globe but also a global economy characterised by over accumulation, enormous excess capacity and crisis of profitability, an ever-growing structure of debt, speculative volatility and financial turmoils and, typically, by recurring economic crises and prolonged downturns like the current one. By virtue of its inherent contradictions, though globally dominant, capitalism yet remains fraught with instabilities, beset as it is by economic breakdowns even in its most dynamic centres of investment and trade and by a sucession of national and regional crises – in Mexico, East and South-East Asia, Russia, Brazil, Argentina, etc. – produced by the globalist restructuring of recent decades.

There is an unending hype, 'infobabble' really, over information technology which, together with globalisation it has so remarkably facilitated, is supposed to usher in the epochal shift that takes us into a world beyond and better than capitalism, indeed makes the very notion of capitalism historically irrelevant. Involving two closely linked technological departure points, the computer and instantaneous communication system, a fusion as it were of computing and communications (*networks*) that has developed in an explosive trajectory in recent years, this technological development has been not unjustifiably described as a revolution, 'information revolution', that is. The importance, however ambiguous, of this revolution for our economy and social life is not to be denied. For good or ill, it has enormously significant implications for the present and future of humankind – implications that socialists need to take serious note of. As Reg Whitaker, in a most perceptive essay on the subject, has insisted, 'this revolution cannot be ignored by those seeking real alternatives. Cyberspace is a new reality, a spectre haunting the world. As some of the old terrains of struggle shrink, cyberspace expands as a new terrain to be studied, and to be acted upon.' But this revolution itself does not either change the structural logic of capitalism or offer, or make for, any alternatives to the present social order.

New information technology, as with technological innovations in the past, certainly makes people better at doing things they have always done. But even here we don't need to be breathless about it. It is difficult to see how, as claimed, the nature of manufacturing has been 'fundamentally altered' by it. The evidence so far shows only very small impact on productivity from the large investment made in information technology in the United States or for that matter elsewhere. Production has indeed been globalised, but it remains doubtful if the telecommunications revolution has really had a major impact. It has been suggested that 'the invention of relatively simple things, like steamship transport, did more for world trade than digitalised data transmission through fiber optic cables.' In other words, its truly remarkable technological innovations and the hype over them notwithstanding, in the ultimate analysis, 'information revolution' is only another case of incremental change in the way we do things.

'Information revolution' is emphatically *not* itself an answer to the problems we face – problems primarily born of capitalism and its structural logic. These are problems we ourselves have to solve, with or without the aid of technology. 'Information is power', or the computer as 'empowerment' do have a certain, though ambiguous, validity. But 'infobabble' over such propositions has little to do with any notion of redistribution of wealth and power in our society. A computer in every office or home will not somehow solve the problem of unemployment or economic crisis or regional economic decline and imbalances. The poor cannot 'unload' from the NET food and shelter or equitable economic development they are denied by the capitalist market. Information technology does not and cannot in any way alter capital's drive to accumulate or its quest for higher profits and stock prices. Instead it has only served to make this quest more penetrating and effective. As with other technologies under capitalism, information technology too is today subservient to capitalist imperatives of accumulation and profit maximisation. Command over information and its transmission has already become the key to success in the capitalist market place. A wholesale commodification of information by capital is on and the much celebrated 'cyberspace' is taking on the appearance of a 'vast mysterious collections of data looming like mega-fortresses fiercely guarded by giant corporations – while the "real world" wallows in urban squalor, petty criminality, violence and tawdry escapism.' This is how Reg Whitaker has posed and answered the key question: 'Does the Information Revolution offer *an alternative*? Yes and no. It does offer an alternative capitalist future, but it is unlikely, under present circumstances, to offer an alternative *to* capitalism'.

It will not be out of place to quote some more from Reg Whitaker, 'some uncomfortable but unavoidable facts' which are not without their presence within advanced capitalist societies as well:

> Most of the people of the present real world not only lack computers but even lack access to telephones. To most of the world, the Information Revolution is not even a rumour. The IBM

> television ads that portray 'solutions for a small planet' with cute clips of people in traditional and exotic settings discussing (with subtitles) various arcana relating to the latest IBM technologies perhaps tell us more about the imperial delusions of corporate power, or about the penetration by new products of Third World elites, than about any reality of 'solutions' for a 'small' planet. The Information Highway may be opening out like a vast autobahn across North America and Europe and the hyper-developed parts of Asia, but when it reaches into Africa and Latin America and the less developed parts of Asia, it reaches as narrow fingers into privileged islands; for much of the Third World, it simply stops short altogether. Nor is there any rational reason to think that the information revolution offers a magical solution to the endemic problems of poverty and underdevelopment. It is rather the latest name given to the enduring and ever deepening domination of the many poor by the wealthy few. Access to the Internet is as much use to a Bangladeshi peasant as hitching a ride on the Challenger space shuttle; but it is very useful to the multinational corporations that rule the global economic system that maintains Bangladesh as a ghetto of misery.

Again, on the promised information:

> Cyberspace will be a treasure trove of information only for those who already have treasuries to spend. For the rest of us, beneath the false promise of the Internet lies an overstuffed, cluttered, anarchically disorganized jumble of infotrash, so worthless that it has been discarded to lie along the sidewalks of the information highway for the casual use of anyone who cares to pick the odd item up. As time goes by, even this litter will be cleaned up and replaced by small business ventures selling baubles and beads: North American television viewers have already seen the future in the Shopping Channels.

Finally, while recognising the role of information technology under private or corporate control in purveying the ideology and culture of late capitalism, we also need to take note of the 'surveillance society' which is already here:

> With Foucault, the Panopticon – Bentham's plan for a prison designed in such a way that each prisoner was under constant hidden surveillance, or what amounts to the same, would believe that he might be watched at all times – became the quintessential

metaphor for a modern technology of power. Others have elaborated Foucault's insights into a concept of the 'surveillance society'. This technology of power rests on the accumulation of coded information used to administer the activities of individuals about whom it is gathered. In contrast to earlier political forms, the modern state lays less stress on overt coercion to sustain its rule. Instead it favours pervasive, and penetrative administrative power, primarily through the collection, storage and retrieval of information within an administrative context of regulated definitions of tasks, functions and roles that situate individuals and groups in relation to other individuals and groups in an administrative or organisational framework. Under a surveillance regime, people disappear into abstract, bureaucratic categories: 'client', 'customer', 'taxpayer', 'functionary', 'law enforcement officer', 'supervisor', 'shop steward', 'teacher'. The routinized exercise of surveillance *implies* coercion, but overtly involves only the marshalling of information as a means of regulating behaviour.

The lineaments of the surveillance state have been apparent for a long time, but the explosive advances in computer and communication technologies provide a powerful and ever-expanding toolbox of surveillance. From the workplace to the streets to the home, people are being subjected to ever more sophisticated, ever more specific, ever more invasive, scrutiny. Although many of these technologies were initially developed through the military-industrial complexes, force-fed by the national security states during the eras of world war and cold war, they are now very much central elements of contemporary capitalism, in two main ways. First, corporations are enhancing their surveillance capacities to increase competitiveness, both in terms of the productive process and marketing/distribution. Second, surveillance is increasingly relied upon by capital in general to reduce risks and provide a more stable environment for doing business, both domestically and globally. Indeed, the privatisation of surveillance has proceeded to the extent that it is perhaps more appropriate to talk about the surveillance *society* rather than the surveillance *state*. In effect, many of the aspects traditionally associated with the state's political rule – authoritative allocation of roles and regulation of behaviour, for example – are being quietly transferred to the private sector.

VIII

'Globalisation', on since the 1970s, which is currently being referred to as something new, an epochal shift or a major discontinuity in capitalism is actually capitalism itself coming to maturity, with capitalist imperatives of accumulation and competition reaching into every corner of the world. Here we need to take note of a decisively significant aspect of this capitalism now come to maturity. Coming after the long interruption of state-interventionist and welfareist Keynesian era, capitalism's resumed march forward to globalisation is at the same time a return to pre-Keynesian capitalism. In the implementation of the globalisation project, all Keynesianism simply stands doomed. Its dismantling of the welfare state, so-called 'restructuring', policies of privatisation and deregulation really amount to the reemergence of trends which have been part of capitalism from its beginning, indeed its essential core. Capitalism become truly dominant globally is also capitalism reverting to its inherent competitive and inegalitarian logic. Thus it is also capitalism showing its real face which, incidentally, is the face Marx had foreseen. The world taken as a whole, our globalised world, has indeed now begun to resemble the world Marx had both analysed and forecast. It is ironic that at the very moment Marx is being pronounced 'obsolete', the world is behaving in its most 'Marxian' fashion since 1914.

Even as we notice this distinctive aspect of contemporary capitalism, I may here digress a little to point out that far from being 'obsolete', Marx is more relevant in this era of globalisation than ever before. Immediately, in the context of today's capitalist triumphalism, I would like to mention what is central to Marx's analysis of the capitalist mode of production: his portrayal of the deeply contradictory nature of capitalist expansion, its perennial tendency to generate what he termed 'commercial crises'. In a prophetic reference to capitalism in the *Communist Manifesto*, Marx had written: 'a society that has conjured up such gigantic means of production and of exchange is like the sorcerer who is no longer able to control the powers of the nether world whom he has called up by his spells...It is enough to mention the commercial crises that by their periodical return put the existence of the entire bourgeois society on trial...In these crises, there breaks out an epidemic that, in all earlier epochs, would have seemed an absurdity...the epidemic of over-production.' And, the *Manifesto* had pointed out that the very methods on which capital relies to overcome these crises – 'by the conquest of new markets, and by the more thorough exploitation of the old ones' – are the methods by which it paves the way for more extensive and more destructive crises and reduces the means of correcting and preventing them.

In Marx's day, the process of 'globalisation' was still in its early days. But the validity of his analysis is today more than evident in the worldwide excess capacity, profitability crises and their financial turmoils, and a generalised 'economic crisis' – the downturn since 1970s that has worsened through every recession since. Even the mainstream economists who usually like to use more benign terms like 'business cycles' or 'slumps' or 'recessions' are uttering the word 'crisis' with increasing frequency. With the more pessimistic, even fearful reference to 'Great Depression' or 'collapse' is not taboo. In his famous *New Yorker* article – 'The Next Great Thinker: The Return of Karl Marx' (October 1997) – John Cassidy, no Marxist himself, says: 'Marx's view of free enterprise is now being echoed by many businessmen who would rather be flogged than labelled Marxists'. Ellen Meiksins Wood has written:

> There is no question that capitalism has become more universal, more unchallenged, more pure and unadulterated, than ever before. But the universalisation of capitalism looks very different depending on the point of view from which you see it. The globalisation-as-epochal-shift model tends to see nothing but capitalist triumph. The globalisation-as-historical process sees what Marx saw: the system's fundamental contradictions, the contradictory logic of capitalist expansion. Seen from that perspective, globalisation confirms Marx's expectation that every effort to overcome capitalist crisis paves the way for more destructive crises and narrows the options for preventing future ones. The contradictions of capitalism are manifesting themselves in new and aggravated ways precisely because the old ways of pulling out of crisis are, as Marx said they would be, less and less

available, in other words, precisely *because* capitalism is so universal.

IX

'Globalisation is only another word for US domination', Henry Kissinger has arrogantly claimed. Posing the issue equally bluntly, Fredric Jameson has asked: '...when we talk about the spreading power and influence of globalisation, aren't we really referring to the spreading economic and military might of the US? And in speaking of the weakening of the nation-state, are we not actually describing the subordination of the other nation-states to American power, either through consent and collaboration, or by the use of brute force and economic threat?' He adds: 'Looming behind the anxieties expressed here is a new version of what used to be called imperialism, which we can now trace through a whole dynasty of forms. An earlier version was that of the pre-First World War colonialist order, practised by a number of European countries, the US and Japan; this was replaced after the Second World War and the subsequent wave of decolonisation by a Cold War form, less obvious but no less insidious in its use of economic pressure and blackmail ('advisers'; covert putsches such as those in Guatemala and Iran), now led predominantly by the US but still involving a few Western European powers. Now perhaps we have a third stage, in which the United States pursues what Samuel Huntington has defined as a three-pronged strategy: nuclear weapons for the US alone; human rights and American-style electoral democracy; and (less obviously) limits to immigration and the free flow of labour. One might add a fourth crucial policy here: the propagation of the free market across the globe....' Jameson sees 'the US (and such utterly subordinated satellites as the UK)' as playing 'the role of the world's policemen' and enforcing 'their rule through selected interventions (mostly bombings, from a great height) in various alleged danger zones.'

These two views from opposite ends draw our attention to a most important aspect of the current phase of globalisation – America's hegemony over the global economy and politics. Its victory in the cold war, just as it confirmed America's leadership of global capitalism, also settled the question of what kind of capitalism it was going to be. Scholars have written of different, indeed 'rival variants' of capitalism, notably the 'Anglo American' (now really 'American') deregulated, 'free market', Chicago School version and 'the Rhine model of capitalism', based on high level of state intervention, corporate bargaining and welfare spending – 'social market economy' as it has been sometimes called – predominant in continental Europe. It is the former, essentially American model today, which is being imposed worldwide in the name of globalisation. A mood of triumphalism, induced by the relatively better performance of American capitalism, when the continuing crisis of global capitalist economy has been manifesting itself in one crash after another in countries across the globe, has led even Alan Greenspan, the normally cautious chairman of the US Federal Reserve to pronounce 'market capitalism as practiced in the US' to be 'the superior model' that other countries have to follow. If this has been the message from IMF, WB and WTO to the third and the former second world countries, recent concern with 'safety nets' to stave off popular discontent notwithstanding, the message being sent to the European governments, and accepted, is no different: US is the example to be followed. What is being offered, it may be noted, is no 'magic vision of America', that staple of establishment ideology, 'the American dream'. It is the reality of America today, the US model of capitalism with its huge and growing gap between the haves and the have-nots, its ridiculous minimum wage, 'working poor' and 'labour flexibility', its millions without health insurance and its terribly deficient welfare services now under constant attack. Europe is told that in the world of deregulated, 'free market' capitalism, it can no longer afford a bearable minimum wage, some degree of security of tenure, fairly decent unemployment benefits or old age pensions, or for that matter, a national health scheme. Henceforth, it has to rely on private insurance and private schools, on two-tier health and two-tier education. To cut a long message short, Europe must dismantle its welfare state. And capitalists and their governments in Europe have been only too willing to come along.

(It may be noted that since this welfare state was social democracy's main claim to gratitude and success, this dismantling marks its deepest ever crisis. This crisis however must not be seen as the result of betrayal by ambitious politicians and union bosses. It is really a question of the scope for meeting popular demands within the existing capitalist society. During the thirty post-war years of unprecedented prosperity the climate was particularly propitious for social democracy to prosper. During the last thirty years, on the contrary, conditions have become more and more unfavourable. If the collapse of 'Soviet socialism' has left capitalism free to let fall its mask, and to abandon any pretense of wearing a 'human face', its renewed and continuing crisis leaves it unable to wear one any longer).

In pursuit of its hegemony over global economy, the US has led in imposing an unequal economic order on the world. It is using its enormous power and dominance over institutions like IMF and WB to thrust extraneous agendas on other countries and distort the global market relations in its own favour. A pioneer in practising protectionism while employing the shibbolethus of 'free market' and 'free trade' to systematically prise open foreign markets, the United States today pursues the same policy in the name of 'positive economic nationalism', as Robert Reich, Clinton's former Labour Secretary has phrased it. But above and beyond its hegemony over global economy or pursuit of particular 'national' interests, America has, more evidently than ever before, emerged and self-identified itself, as the country with the power and responsibility to police the world in defence of capitalism. A leading diplomatic historian, Gerald Haines (who is also the senior historian of the CIA) has observed that after World War II, the United State 'assumed, out of self-interest, responsibility for the welfare of the world capitalist system.' President Clinton and his Secretary of State Madeleine Albright saw the US as the world's only 'indispensable nation', and Anthony Lake, his National Security Advisor, in line with a former such Advisor Brezhenski's public defence of the 'necessity' of American leadership in the world, even announced a so-called 'Clinton Doctrine': 'Throughout the Cold War, we contined a global threat to market democracies', now we can 'consolidate the victory of democracy and open markets' – the formula however is redundant since the latter adequately captures what is really meant by 'democracy'. More recently (1999), in his much noticed 'Manifesto for the Fast World' in the *New York Times Magazine*, the well-known columnist Thomas Fiedman has argued that since the United States is the country that benefits most from globalisation, it is also the one that has to take the main responsibility for sustaining it. 'Sustaining globalisation is our overarching national interest ... Globalisaion-is-US.' This, he clarifies, is different from 'old-fashioned imperialism, hen one country physically occupies another.' Now, it's a matter of maintaining an abstract globalisation system.' And this 'requires a stable geopolitical power structure, which simply cannot be maintained without the active involvement of the United States'. Bush Junior has since, in his own way, made abundantly clear what this means.

An important aspect of this 'active involvement' has been the bullying of the United Nations into becoming a body which ratifies and legitimises American decisions taken in America's interest, including its naked and lawless exercise of economic, politicaland military power. A Kofi Annan is imposed as Secretary General and the UN is sought to be reduced to an extension of the US State Department. The United States bullies or manipulates the UN when it can and bypasses it when it cannot. It threatens to withdraw from agencies like WHO and UNESCO when they offer as much as a hint of disapproval towards US policies and makes the payment of even defaulted dues contingent upon the reform of the UN system according to its wishes. American policies inside the UN, as outside, are fraudulently claimed to be 'the will of the international community' and the UNsummits – ranging from Environment and Human Rights to Population, Social Development and Women – invariably fail to breach the parameters of the currently dominant discourse of globalisation and generally end up rationalising the America-led domination of global capitalism.

This domination has an interesting ideological dimension in that America has souht a 'noble' or 'saintly' guise for its policies abroad. It pursues them in the name of 'human rights' and 'democracy' which only reveals how cynical or hypocritical the sole superpower's global politics can be. Take the UN Declaration of Human Rights, Half of it concerns social and economic rights. The West largely rejects them, the US totally. They limit themselves primarily to what they call civil and political rights. This apart, if the record of the UN on human rights is painfully bad, it is understandably so because it has been, and still is, dominated by the United States: the country with innumerable violations of human rights all over the world, from the Philippines at the turn of the last century to installing Marcos there after the war; from the invasion of Guatemala, the Dominican Republic and Grenada to the Vietnam war; from installing Suharto in Indonesia (and more than one million murdered in the course of Suharto's US backed counter-revolution) to imposing and sustaining dictatorial regimes in Latin America (including Pinochet in Chile) and Africa; not to mention the authoritarian regimes in the Middle-East, the Colonel's Dictatorship in Greece and the death of one million children in Iraq as a result of sanctions continued to be imposed by the United States and rubber stamped by the UN, with the total subservience of its allies, before it again attacked Iraq in a blatant violation of international law. America's interpretation of human rights, replacing the common interests of humanity with the particular interests and arbitrary actions of the United States, violates any meaningful conception of human rights. Even otherwise America's extremely selective concern with human rights in pursuit of its interests abroad has been justifiably regarded as a new form of imperialism, 'Human Rights Imperialism'.

It is no different with America's concern for democracy. The essential criterion once again is what best serves American interests. American policy makers have had no hesitation in lining up on their side some of the most corrupt dictatorial regimes that there were, often hailing them as members of their 'free world'. These have included the apartheid regime of South Africa, Syngman Rhee and the military rulers of South Korea, Ferdinand Marcos of the Philippines, Lon Nol and other dictators of South Vietnam, Ayub Khan and Yahya Khan of Pakistan, the Shah of Iran, the Duvaliers of Haiti, Pinochet of Chile, Suharto of Indonesia and any number of other tyrants or authoritarian rulers in Africa, Central and South America and the Middle-East, including, once upon a time, Saddam Hussein in Iraq. It is to them that American aid and armaments have overwhelmingly gone. 'He may be a son of a bitch, but he is *our-son-of-a-bitch*'. This has been Washington's refreshingly honest view of the Somozas, Batistas and Duvaliers of the world. Obviously, the absence of democracy is alright so long as a country is supportive of the United States. 'Democracy' like 'human rights' is only an ideological cover for the pursuit of America's more mundane material, that is, imperialist interests abroad.

Now that, having conquered the country through an illegal war, the United States is on its mission to bring 'democracy' to Iraq, here is one comment on it (by Naomi Klein in *The Nation*):

> The streets of Baghdad are a swamp of crime and uncollected garbage. Battered local businesses are going bankrupt, unable to compete with cheap imports. Unemployment is soaring and thousands of laid-off state workers are protesting in the streets. In other words, Iraq looks like every other country that has undergone rapid-fire 'structural adjustments' prescribed by Washington, from Russia's infamous 'shock therapy' in the early 1990s to Argentina's disastrous 'surgery without anaesthetic.' Except that Iraq's 'reconstruction' makes those wrenching reforms look like spa treatments.
>
> Paul Bremer, the US-appointed governor of Iraq, has already proved something of a flop in the democracy department in the few weeks there, nixing plans for Iraqis to select their own interim government in favour of his own handpicked team of advisers. But Bremer has proved to have something of a gift when it comes to rolling out the red carpet for US multinationals. For a few weeks Bremer has been hacking away at Iraq's public sector....
>
> As the Bush Administration becomes increasingly open about its plan to privatise Iraq's state industries and parts of the government, Bremer's de-Baathification takes on new meaning. Is he working only to get rid of Baath Party members, or is he also working to shrink the public sector as a whole so that hospitals, schools and even the army are primed for privatisation by US

> firms? Just as reconstruction is the guise for privatisation, de-Baathification looks a lot like disguised downsizing....

Ideological deception has its uses, no doubt, but there is nothing like exercise of naked military power to secure and sustain particular imperialist interests and overall global hegemony. With the collapse of the Soviet Union, the United States has acquired a global dominance as the one remaining military super power, indeed the dominant imperialist power in the world. Contrary to the notion that globalisation and the establishment of the world market have made military power redundant, the US maintains, by a very wide margin, the world's largest military. Empires throughout human history have relied on foreign military bases to enforce their rule and protect their interests, and in this respect Pax Americana is no different from Pax Romana or Pax Britannica. The United States has military bases in sixty-nine countries, with this number on the increase with the wars against Afghanistan and Iraq. The United States totally dominates NATO – recently redefined as a self-legitimating aggressive force – as well as the far eastern military alliances, especially the 'US-Japan security treaty'. Despite the publicly proclaimed end of the Cold War, the US military budget remains very large, accounting for fully a third of world spending on arms. For the US ruling class, in view of what it sees as its responsibilities in the global capitalist order – which one scholar has summarised as: 'to keep the system functioning; to control the underlying populations; to safeguard the United States as the centre of the international financial system; to maintain the United States (and, specially, US capitalists/corporations) in the top perch in the imperialist pecking order; and to prevent countries from breaking away from the system of global controls' – it is not enough to have a military bigger than that of any other power; it must be bigger than that of any plausible combination of other powers, and this applies of course not only to immediate situation but to what might be the situation five or ten years from now, when the potential challenges of today might become real. It is pushing ahead with plans for a capability to fight two major regional conflicts at the same time.

The United States has the world's largest stockpile of weapons of mass destruction, chemical, biological and nuclear, and is the only state ever to have used the nuclear weapons. It is an arch votary of the unequal Nuclear Non-Proliferation Treaty and, even as it regularly arm-twists the minor nuclear nations, has refused to ratify the Comprehensive Nuclear Test Ban Treaty (CTBT). It has unilaterally withdrawn from the Anti-Ballistic Missile (ABM) Treaty and is busy developing weapons like the nuclear bunker-busting bombs. According to a classified Pentagon report the Bush administration has directed the military to prepare contingency plans to use nuclear weapons against countries it sees as America's immediate or potential enemies, and to build new smaller nuclear weapons for use in certain battlefield situations. Despite objections from its European allies that it is unnecessary and will most likely trigger a new arms race, despite opposition of Russia and China, despite a protest by as many as 50 Nobel Laureates headed by Hans A. Bethe, one of the architects of the atom bomb, who have called it a 'wasteful' and 'dangerous' system, National Missile Defence System remains a priority on the agenda of the United States. Its National Security Strategy, with its policy of military supremacy over the entire earth and the doctrine of pre-emption, is nothing less than the declaration of a new imperial order to be backed up not only by the threat but also the aggressive, pre-emptive employment of overwhelming power against any country not to its liking. Most recently, following upon its yesterday's 'Star Wars Project' or the current 'Missile Defence System' –argued for as 'defensive shields', though nothing of the kind – the United States has gone in for their heavily updated, blatantly offensive successor, codenamed 'Falcon' (Force Application and Launch from the Continental US), to be completed by mid-2006 – its unmanned delivery vehicles, carrying a payload of 12,000 pounds and flying at speeds of up to 10 times the speed of sound, will be able to strike targets 9,000 nautical miles distant in less than two hours. As John Pike, head of the Washington think tank, Global Security.Org. has commented: 'It is about blowing people up on the other side of the planet even if no country on earth will allow us to use their territory'. The purpose, obviously, is to enable the US to *go it alone* against whichever country they please to subdue or destroy in their design to achieve world domination.

The global expansion of military power on the part of the hegemonic state of world capitalism is an integral part of economic globalisation. (The other advanced capitalist countries, tied into the system, are also reliant on the US as the main enforcer of the rules of the game). The American ruling class knows that economics are ultimately a matter of politics, that it is relations of power, above all military power, that command the market, that there will be no 'global market' without an American military empire. 'The hidden hand of the market will never work without the hidden fist – McDonald's cannot flourish without McDonnell Douglas, the designer of the F-15. And the hidden fist that keeps the world safe for Silicon Valley's technologies is called the United States Army, Air Force, Navy and Marine Corps.' – this is how Thomas Friedman, who incidentally was also an adviser to Madeleine Albright, has put it in his article we have noticed earlier. Friedman goes on to quote approvingly from foreign policy historian Robert Kagan: 'Good ideas and technologies need a strong power that promotes those ideas by example and protects those ideas by winning on the battlefield. If a lesser power were promoting our ideas and technologies, they would not have the global currency that they have.'

Naturally, the hidden fist has to come out of hiding from time to time if it is going to make its point. And here the United has a long history. Monroe doctrine onwards it is a history of armed interventions or wars along with coercive diplomacy, bloody coups and covert actions against other sovereign states to make the world 'safe' for American business. In the half century since the World War II alone, on one pretext or another – 'containing communism' 'protecting American lives', 'punishing "rogue" states', 'war on terrorism' or even 'promoting democracy' etc. – America has thus aggressed against countries as far afield as Greece and Cuba, Chile and Vietnam, Brazil, Guatemala and Dominican Republic, Grenada, Nicaragua, EL Salvador and Panama, Angola and Mozambique, Iran, Iraq, Libya and Afghanistan. And the list is far from complete.

There has been a great deal of noise over the end of the Cold War. It surely ended for the Soviet Union when it threw in the towel in 1989-90. But it has continued for the United States. When the Soviet Union collapsed, there was much talk in the US of a large and growing 'peace dividend' that would be available for all kinds of good works. But this 'peace dividend' never materialised. Instead National Defence outlays have continued to grow. An independent research study in mid-1990s calculated US defence expenditures to have exceeded the combined total of 13 nations behind it on the list of big weapons spenders. (Incidentally, the United States is also the world's largest exporter of arms and about 75 per cent of these sales go to countries where the citizens have no right to choose their own governments).

America's growing military expenditure is not difficult to understand. The declared objective of the Cold War was to defeat an imaginary threat of Soviet expansionism. The real objective was to rid the world of 'communism', meaning any and all forms of society organised on any but 'free market', that is, capitalist lines. The imaginary threat is no longer there. But what about the real objectives ? Way back in 1989, a distinguished American scholar of history, Professor Edward Pessen in a letter to the *The New York Times*, under the heading 'Cold War Isn't Over While the US Can Help It', thus summed up the cold war policies of the US administration from Truman to Reagan: 'We have formed worldwide military alliances against the "Soviet threat"; we ringed the Soviets with bases; we initiated what may turn out to be an irreversible nuclear arms race; we've toppled governments the world over that we found insufficiently anti-communist or uncongenial; in Arnold Toynbee's phrase, we became the new Roman Empire, everywhere opposing revolutions of the poor against the rich; we've waged massive unconstitutional wars against distant nations that had not lifted a finger against us; and we've stigmatized as possible subversives domestic critics of these policies and actions.' Obviously the real objectives are still very much there. 'Communism' is not entirely finished off, capitalism continues to have its enemies, 'the new Roman Empire', now vastly expanded, has still to be made and kept safe for the American multinationals.

Many of the interests that generated the first Cold War have been reasserting themselves, as in the dismemberment of Yugoslavia and the expansion of NATO in Eastern Europe right upto the borders of Russia. Galbraith has written of the autonomous character of military power in the US which in itself and as part of 'military-industrial complex' has not only prevented any reduction in military expenditure even after the Soviet power collapsed but also pushed for continuance of the old foreign policies. There is the politics of 'national security' at home common to both Republican and Democratic parties which well serves the interests of the American ruling class. US capitalism, it seems, cannot do without a permanent war economy, or for that matter, without wars abroad. The Cold War may be over, but according to the US Commission on National Security, reporting in 1999, 'since the end of the Cold War, the United States has embarked upon nearly four dozen military interventions... as opposed to only 16 during the entire period of the Cold War'. As a corollary, we have regular generation of, often tacitly complicit, demonised 'necessary enemies' to justify the globally repressive apparatus of the American national security state. ('Terrorism', a product of America's foreign policies and the depredations of global capitalism it presides over, is another recent excuse.) In other words, there is an enormously powerful, and in the present circumstances quite possibly decisive, domestic and foreign dependence of US capitalism on the continuation of the Cold War.

Hence also NATO's ability to survive the collapse of the adversary that was its *raison d'etre*. NATO's rationale as a counterweight to Soviet military power implied that it should have been wound up after the Soviet capitulation in the Cold War (1989-90). But by the late 1990s its role had been extended to such tasks as military intervention in the Balkans, to be followed later by NATO's expansion eastwards to the border of the former Soviet Union which has served both to incorporate Moscow's former east European clients within the western bloc and to reassert US primacy within that bloc. Today, redefined as a 'self-legitimating aggressive force', NATO is the principal tool in the service of Washington's global strategy. Military expenditures by the US and other NATO countries are now more than 10 times the level of former Warsaw Pact nations. NATO speaks in the name of 'international community', thereby expressing its contempt for the democratic principle that is supposed to govern this community through the United Nations. In fact, with the decision makers in Washington establishing, through NATO or otherwise, 'force' as the supreme principle in international politics to the complete detriment of international law, the UN seems set to succumb to the fate of the League of Nations. NATO's claim to an odd 'right of intervention' is disturbingly reminiscent of the 'mission civilisatrice' of 19th century imperialism and well jells with its contemporary version, the Huntingtonian thesis of 'clash of civilisations' and its appeal to preserve and defend the higher aspects of western civilisation in the world!

As the world's sole super power over the past decade and more, the US has shown a growing disregard for international legal norms. Whether on economic or political issues, the US has increasingly talked the language of sanctions and coercion. It has not hesitated to act unilaterally – of course mostly with the consultation of its allies in tow – whenever and wherever it has deemed fit. A decade back Iraq was one early example, the war over Kosovo that followed was another; and between them, the two also showed the extent and nature of US' growing domination of the world. Perry Anderson has written: 'the Balkan War has rounded off the decade with the military-diplomatic demonstration of the ascendancy of this constellation. Comparison with the Gulf War suggests how much stronger the New World Order has become since the early nineties. Bush had to mobilise a vast army to reverse the Iraqi invasion in Kuwait, in the name of protecting Western oil supplies and a feudal dynasty; without succeeding in either overthrowing the regime in Baghdad, or drawing Russia – still unpredictable – into the alliance against it. Clinton has bombed Serbia into submission without so much as a soldier having to fire a shot, in the name of a moral imperative to stop ethnic cleansing...; and brigaded Russia effortlessly into the occupation force as a token auxiliary. Meanwhile China, after the destruction of its embassy – on the heels of a respectful visit by its Premier to the US – has cooperated meekly in setting up a UN screen for the NATO protectorate in Kosovo, and made clear that nothing will be allowed to disturb good relations with Washington. For its part, the European Union is basking in a new comradeship-in-arms with the United States, and joint purpose in generous reconstruction of the Balkans. Victory in Kosovo has in this sense not been just military and political. It is also an ideological triumph, that sets a new standard for interventions on behalf of human rights – as construed in Washington: Chechens or Palestinians need not apply – around the world. The society created by the capitalist free-for-all of the past twenty years was in need of a good conscience. Operation Allied Force has provided it.' As for 'human rights' and 'a good conscience', here is Bill Clinton who presided over it all: 'If we're going to have a strong economic relationship that includes our ability to sell around the world, Europe has got to be a key ... That's what this Kosovo thing is all about.'

Away from Europe, essentially, this is what the recent wars against Afghanistan and Iraq have been about. The terrorist attack on the World Trade Centre and the Pentagon was a new godsend for a Wall Street suffering from economic stagnation and growing uncertainties and for the hegemonic state of global capitalism presently on a course of imperial expansion in pursuit of its political and imperial interests. The war against 'terrorism', which is in many ways a direct or indirect product of the projection of US hegemonic power is now being used to justify the further projection of that power. A 'new imperialism' which is necessary to discipline and reorder the world, is how a subservient Tony Blair has seen it. From the other end, Chomsky has seen it as establishing that US, the hegemonic power of global capitalism, is the world's 'leading terrorist state'. That some allies – 'Old Europe', for example – have not always or fully gone along with it only indicates that inter-imperialist conflict of interests remains a reality in capital's globalised world.

Militarism has been integral to America's imperialist expansion abroad. Described as 'imperialist militarism', it has never been devoid of mundane materialist objectives. Even in the Vietnam war, as historians have pointed out, 'tin, rubber, rice, copra, iron ore, tungsten and oil were integral to American policy considerations from the inception.' Oil in the Middle-East was obviously a key consideration in the two Gulf wars and the war in Afghanistan. But apart from specific economic objectives or military gains, a most significant aspect of America's use of military force since the end of the Second World War – its important wars from Korea to the Balkans, the Gulf and Afghanistan – has been its political objectives: the 'containment' of external enemies or of internal opposition, diverting attention from tricky domestic problems or even the narrower political objectives of electoral advantage through displays of 'toughness' or tough 'nationalism'. That is how it needs to be noted that as a globalising power America's militarism does not generally have territorial ambitions, it does not seek direct physical control or hegemony over specific colonies. It is, typically, the use of massive displays of force to assert the dominance of global capital so that this capital, particularly the American segment of it, can freely navigate the global economy without hindrance. If at times it has the appearance of a naked display of imperial power for its own sake, without any specific or immediate objectives – and an outright military victory is neither an issue nor even a possible outcome – it is just to show who is boss, that is, to make a general point about US domination of the world, its hegemony over global economy. As one comment has it, 'such display of imperial power only shows that US imperial hegemony can't now rely, if it ever could, on economic superiority alone, and that it depends on periodic display of sheer force. It hardly matters where or for what ostensible purpose, though it helps if the target is non-European or non-white.'

X

Even as we recognise US' global domination – 'US global preeminence' in Strobe Talbot's more polite words – it needs to be emphasised that this domination is far from being absolute. Though powerful, US is not all powerful, its domination is dense with explosive antagonisms and unanticipated problems. Obviously the United States is now the only superpower, but equally obviously that does not make it omnipotent. In fact, in important ways, one super power has less control over its allies and clients than it had in the two-superpower situation. The US is unable to impose its own order in Europe or elsewhere in the world. Pax-Americana, a shaky edifice anyway is coming unstuck in many places as the world under US hegemony becomes an increasingly insecure and unsettled world. The much talked of 'New World Order' is turning out to be 'New World Disorder'. Large parts of Europe, including Russia have come to be badly destabilised, relapsing, as between the wars, into irredentist nationalist rivalries and worse, and away from Europe, the Middle-East is explosive as never before. Instead of the promised world of peace, stability and international harmony – Fukuyama's 'universal homogenous state of liberal democracy' – we have had the continuing tragedy of 'liberated' Russia, war in the Balkans and cluster bombing of Yugoslavia, genocides and civil wars in Africa, massacres in East Timor and ethnic turmoil in Indonesia, wars against Iraq and Afghanistan and the wreckage and violence they have left behind, the never-ending bloody strife in Sri Lanka and Palestine and 'terrorism' – born, ultimately, of capitalism's injustices and iniquities – stalking the world. According to a commentary in the *Guardian Weekly* at the end of 1999,at least 30 conflicts were then raging around the world 'most of them exceedingly barbarous civil wars... Wars have become qualitatively worse. In the First World War 90 per cent of the casualties were soldiers, but now 90 per cent of the casualties are civilian... in just ten years two million children have died in wars, with six million seriously injured, 20 million displaced as refugees, 800 a month killed by land mines....' And all this is only suggestive of the 'disorder' in the world today.

In the final analysis, the 'new world order' cannot but be a 'disorderly' affair because it is a capitalism dominated world order, run by corporate power and by governments acting, as far as circumstances permit, on its behalf. Equity and fair play for common working people, consideration for the needs and aspirations of the poorer countries, a world of justice and humanity for all – there is no room for such things in the much-fancied 'global market place.' In his *The Age of Extremes*, Eric Hobsbawm ends his account of the 20th century by pointing out that richer, more productive and dynamic in recent decades, the developed world had also become incalculably more unstable, that poverty and unemployment along with their insecurity and resentment had reemerged with a vengeance as capitalism 'began to shed labour at a spectacular rate', that there was a widening of 'the gap between rich and poor countries' and 'a growing barbarisation' in 'all three worlds'. This is how it was at the end of the old century and therefore *is* at the beginning of the new one. And it cannot be otherwise. By virtue of contradictions inherent in it, capitalism irreversibly makes for development which is unequal, uneven and essentially exploitative within and across countries, to say nothing of the ecological destruction it necessarily involves; and, as late capitalism in the grip of a prolonged economic crisis, its contradictions are indeed generating a new barbarism, which is emerging as a specific feature of 'disorder' in the world today.

Capitalism, with its contradictions and the crises generated by them, is central to the current instability and disorder in the world. Contrary to the laboriously cultivated mythology of the ruling order, these contradictions are *intrinsic* and not *external* to capitalism, they are a part of its systemic logic. Globalisation does not change this systemic logic of capitalism, it only universalises it, that is, universalises capitalism's structural deficiencies and potentially explosive contradictions. Its new forms of capitalist domination – via debt, or the financial system, for example – only make these contradiction explosive in additional new ways. That is how the defeat of the old 'external' enemy, the 'end of the cold war', has left the world not less but a much more unstable place, more so than ever before. For the same reason, contemporary crisis of capitalism has acquired overall a new severity and durability, and is regularly exploding in one part of the world after another. The recurring crashes and their aftermaths – in Mexico, East and South-east Asia, Russia, Brazil, Argentina etc. – are perfect illustrations of the deep-seated and irresolvable contradictions that have come with the universalisation of capitalism. Even otherwise the scale and scope of global capitalism seems to have reached a point where these contradictions exceed the capacity of *any* economic or political power to lend even some limited order to them. There is not a single capitalist power, not even the US for all its dominance in the global economy, that has the kind of hegemony today that would allow it to bring a degree of discipline to global capitalism as was possible in the earlier post-World War II era under the US leadership. Hence the 'disorder' that the 'New World Order' is turning out to be.

To be specifically noticed in this regard are the classical correlates of capitalism we have mentioned earlier which globalistion remains riddled with – the three basic contradictions that Marxists have traditionally emphasised: between the major capitalist-imperialist powers themselves, between the imperialist powers and countries of the periphery and semi-periphery of global capitalism and, lastly, between the capitalist classes and the working people within the advanced capitalist countries. Before we take another critical look at them, it may be pointed out that these contradictions, expressing themselves in different forms and varying degree of importance simultaneously define the essential exploitative character of the 'disorder' of our times and, if the past is any guide, its revolutionary possibilities as well.

XI

Whatever the problems with the Pax-Americana, the United States occupies a position of preeminence within the global capitalist system; its preponderance of power is an important factor in holding it together and defending its interests the world over, if necessary by force of arms. Despite the many weaknesses or vulnerabilities of its capitalism, America remains a substantial economic power with its continental size economy, key natural resources, a huge and captive domestic market, size and diversity of scientific personnel, leadership in many areas of technological research and innovation and America-centred transnational and international financial institutions, etc. etc. Moreover, the demise of Soviet Union has left it as the world's only truly global military power whom no other capitalist state can hope to rival for quite sometime to come, if at all. And even if America can do much less with this power than it once could or now wants to, it alone has the capacity to take on the responsibility to police the world on behalf of world capitalism. As part of its share of ups and downs in the global economy – rare economic dominance at the end of the Second World War, long-term economic decline relative to other capitalist states, particularly Germany and Japan, reaching a rather low point of competitiveness in the early 1980s, growing strongly after 1992, while continental Europe stagnated and Japan fell into a deep slump, a likely slow down in future, and so on – its better performance in recent years has lent new credibility to America's assertion of primacy in the capitalist world. Again, beyond the issues of economic boom or decline, or preponderance of military power, or the cultural ascendancy that US has come to acquire, more basic to the question of hegemony in a Gramscian sense is the fact that the principles of the world order on which the so-called Pax-Americana is based are broadly shared by all the more powerful capitalist countries. Within the now victorious capitalist or imperialist bloc, the various components all share a fundamental interest in preserving the on-going system of capitalist or imperialist domination in the world.

There are thus good reasons why even when the compulsions of the Cold War, capitalism's collective necessity to confront another systemic rival and its alliance bloc, is no longer there, the capitalist-imperialist bloc has not disintegrated, its components continue to cooperate to sustain their collective domination of the world. It has also been argued that even otherwise history does not repeat itself and analogical reasoning can be most misleading, that with the changed economic and political circumstances, while it is once again almost wholly a capitalist world, it is a post-Clauswitzean one where events and processes of either pre-1917 or the 1919-39 periods will not be repeated. Attention is particularly drawn to the unaffordably high costs of another great war. The history of Europe and the European powers is no doubt incredibly violent and for hundreds of years their major activity was massacring one another, but it is suggested that while wars can be conducted against the weak, and at a terrible cost to them, the powerful will not now war among themselves. In other words, actual inter-imperialist wars are now simply inconceivable.

This argument has a great deal of validity in what it says about history, analogical reasoning, past experience and changed situation or circumstances. Besides imperialism and bourgeoisie have generally learnt their lessons from historical experience, including revolutions, better than those whom they oppress or the revolutionaries who struggle against them. Nevertheless, history of global capitalism over the last two hundred years is more than replete with evidence about the strong centrifugal tendencies within it, tendencies which in times of economic crisis have often found expression in armed conflicts between capitalist nations or blocs. The evidence is there, for example, in the developments between the Great Depression of the 19th Century and the First World War, or between the Great Depression of 1920s and Second World War. The important point is that these centrifugal tendencies are not something extraneous or accidental to capitalist process; they are inherent it it, coexisting with the centripetal tendencies at the very core of the capitalist process. The expansion of capitalism has always presupposed, indeed required cooperation among its various national components but there has never been a time when these same national components ceased to struggle each for its own preferment and advantage. The pressure for expansion, coupled with the uneven development of capitalism, necessarily produces economic as well as political strains among capitalist states; their relatively altered economic strength inevitably makes for economic and political, and if necessary or possible, armed struggle to redefine the relations among them within the global capitalist system. Hence periods of cooperation, of relative peace and harmony among capitalist states alternate with periods of discord and violence. Uneven development generates a recurring struggle for hegemony within the global capitalist system.

Therefore, the current cooperation or harmony, whatever there is, between the major capitalist powers is only a part of the larger story of development of global capitalism. And it is not without its other part which is already unfolding itself in the competition and conflict between these powers in different parts of the world. Paradoxically, the immediate historical context for this part of the story has been provided by the victory that cooperation of these powers gave them in the cold war. The victorious alliance of western capitalist powers itself took a beating from the collapse of the 'socialist' economy. The antagonism between the east and west during the cold war years played an important role in reducing or subsuming contradictions of national interests within the western alliance. With the rationale for the old solidarity gone, the conflicts of interests earlier papered over are again out in the open. And the competition and conflict is now all the sharper because of the prolonged down turn in the global economy since the early 1970s, the developed world witnessing a secular decline in growth rates and European and Japanese economies facing daunting structural problems. The idea of a peaceful and internally harmonious global capitalism, or for that matter, of a globalised and centralised imperialism, makes no more sense today than it did a hundred years ago.

In this context it is important to avoid a misunderstanding. With the collapse of Soviet Union, capitalism has indeed become universal, globally dominant as never before. Under the ideological banners of neo-liberalism and globalisation, capitalism is plundering the former Soviet bloc, making every effort to integrate China into its world market, pushing the rest of the third world deeper into economic and social chaos, and within the advanced capitalist nations themselves, imposing cutbacks and austerity. It makes sense, therefore, to speak, as we must, of global capitalism and its domination of the world, even as we also recognise the important role played by new forms of international integration and organisation of capital and the new speed of financial transactions in the global spread and domination of capitalism. But this does not in any way imply the disappearance of the nation state – an illusion which the hype over 'globalisation' and 'information revolution', their abstracted images of 'world economy' or 'global village', of capital moving across frontiers without let or hindrance (via the electronic circuits of digital information systems), of eroded national borders and sovereignties, tend to create. It is not only that international organisations like the IMF and the World Bank and the global reach of giant corporations do not add upto any kind of supra-national capitalist international or that universalisation of capitalism has not given rise to a politically unified international capitalist class or a global capitalist state that is capable of taking responsibility for the stable functioning of the global system as a whole, the national borders and sovereignties have not disappeared, the nation states have stubbornly held on through the universalisation of capitalism. While multinationals have indeed emerged as the new power, often with incomes more than some Third World countries, it is wrong to assume that their power to make profits is unconnected to the nation state. As James Petras and Henry Veltmeyer have underlined:

> Probably the most widespread misconception circulated by globalisation ideologues is the notion that the nation-state is anachronistic (or 'weak') before the onslaught of globalising corporations and new international actors. The reality is otherwise: never has the nation-state played a more decisive role or intervened with more vigour and consequence in shaping economic exchanges and investment at the local, national and international levels. It is impossible to conceive of the expansion and deepening involvement of multinational banks and corporations without the prior political, military and economic intervention of the nation-state.... The major policies stimulating vast tax windfalls, massive subsidies and lower domestic labour costs have all been formulated by the nation-state. The scale and scope of nation-state activity has grown to such a point that one needs to refer to it as the 'New Statism' rather than the free market. Globalisation is in the first instance a product of the New Statism and continues to be accompanied and sustained by direct state intervention.

This is not too difficult to understand. It is true, as Marx said, that capitalists have no nation. But this is true only in the sense that they have no national loyalties and will move wherever the imperatives of profit maximisation take them. It certainly does not mean that they have no roots in or no need for the state, or their own nation-state in particular. The nation state has been historically the central instrumentality for the organisation of capitalist power, capital's most comprehensive political command structure. The capitalists have always needed it, and still need it, to maximise profits at home and abroad. That is how global capitalism is a global system of national states and the universalisation of capitalism is presided over by nation-states, especially one hegemonic super power.

It should be obvious that the principal economic actors and classes in the world of global capitalism are still organised above all on a national basis, and there is very little that can be said about the global economy without reference to its national constituent parts, or about global economic processes without reference to relations among national economies and states. To be sure, individual capitals need not have a strictly national identity. Particularly in the age of multinational corporations and global financial institutions, capital is in part – and it is a significant part – organised in and through multinational forms. There are the increasingly important global economic institutions – such as the International Monetary Fund (IMF), the World Bank (WB) and the World Trade Organisation (WTO) etc., and proliferating multilateral trade and investment agreements – such as the North American Free Trade Agreement (NAFTA), the European Economic Union (EU), the Asia Pacific Economic Cooperation (APEC), the South American trade bloc (Mercosur) and so on. But these multilateral trade and investment pacts are yet deals negotiated between nation-states, some among them more powerful than others, and the global institutions like the IMF and the World Bank are effectively dominated by a handful of the world's most powerful nation-states. That is how these multilateral pacts and global institutions help extend the reach of these powerful states while significantly constraining those outside the core regions of the system or even integrating them into the world economy in systematically subordinated position – and are thus among the more important means of organising and defining imperialism in the age of globalisation. The relations among advanced capitalist economies and among their national states are obviously very different from the relations between them and weaker national entities. The decline of national sovereignity so familiar to theorists of the nation-state today is in fact a highly differential and unequal process which inevitably tends to exacerbate global power imbalances.

The purpose of my argument here is not to just draw attention to the continuing importance of the nation-state in the world capitalist system where the very existence of the system, including its crises, is shaped by the specific national forms of its constituent parts, each with its own history and its own internal logic, and by the relations among these national entities. It is to point out that global capitalism does not exist as a unitary entity, it involves the complex and contradicting interaction of many capitals, each organised in relation to a nation-state, that relations between these capitals or states entail systemic inequalities and hierarchies of power which inevitably make for antagonisms and conflicts, that, even as there is integration and cooperation among major national constituents of global capitalism, there is competition and rivalry too and given their uneven development, recurring struggles for dominance as well. The world of global capitalism is anything but a world of peace and harmony.

Given the essentially capitalist nature of 'globalisation', the 'global' economy today, if anything, means less, not more capitalist unity. 'Globalisation' may mean new forms of capitalist integration and cooperation across national boundaries, but it also means that a growing number of national and regional capitalists are compelled to enter into active competition in the world market. It, therefore, means intensified competition among national or regional capitals. In other words, what has been 'globalised', if there is any truly international economic force at the end of it all, it is the market which in effect means an unprecedented internationalisation of *competition*. And competition, as the classical view – of Smith, Marx and later Schumpeter – has it, is not about market equilibrium and prices, but about the search for sources of market power and profit. With universalisation of capitalism, that is, more and more capitalist economies entering into global competition, this search is now an increasingly bitter search, all the more bitter among major capitalist powers for the economic and political clout they have.

Over time it has become abundantly clear that inter-capitalist competition or rivalries are not time or space bound, but are open ended and continuous. Contrary to the post-cold war expectations, competition and rivalries, and therefore tensions and antagonisms, among the dominant capitalist powers have now increased side by side with their growing interdependence, and these are bound to intensify in the foreseeable future. The US remains the hegemonic power but its power projections in pursuit of its interests – legal redefinitions of national sovereignty (Helms – Burton), diplomatic intervention aimed at influencing development agendas (Francophone Africa), use of global institutions as instruments of US power (the IMF, the WB, the WTO) or their subversion to the same end (the UN), military interventions in regional conflicts (Gulf, Somalia, Bosnia, Kosovo), NATO's expansion and eastward thrust, wars on Afghanistan and Iraq; etc. etc. – have not only generated their own tensions and antagonisms, but also evoked opposition and defiance, from other capitalist powers including Japan, Canada and countries of the European Union, which have refused to subordinate their global interests or goals to those of the dominant hegemon. The US' efforts to retain its predominance in the world, to increase the advantage it has, through such initiatives as National Missile Defence programme will almost certainly trigger a new arms race and further exacerbate contradictions in the world of global capitalism.

Even where there is a certain historically evolved or inherited harmony of political objectives, as between the United States and European Union, there are objective antagonisms and serious conflicts of econmic interests whih can be seen in the latter's far from compliant response to the envisaged 'positive economic nationalism' of the US, be it over specific economic policies or such issues as America's illegal blockades of Cuba and Iran. The rapid growth during the post-war boom of European Economic Community in general and West Germany in particular was a crucial factor in US' relative decline. And the intensification of international competition which followed played an essential role in destabilising the world economy at the end of the 1960s and the beginning of the 1970s. The conflict of interests here is bound to grow and intensify, even if the United States is able to continue to enforce its domination over Europe in the near future. In the meantime, the European Union itself remains a troubled affair. National antagonisms persist and there are contradictions centring upon intra-European relations, particularly, in a long term perspective, relations between France and Germany. Conflicts arising from differences of interests among members of the Union are becoming increasingly difficult to manage so that it is even seen as a union in name only. It is these conflicts which are making it nearly impossible for the European Union to pursue a coherent political strategy. A good example is the Gulf crisis in early 1998, when Britain, France and Germany and the rest of the European Union, adopted different positions in relation to American policy on Iraq, or the more recent American war on and occupation of Iraq where 'old Europe', as the Americans described it, stood apart from the rest, asserting its opposition to the accelerated American drive for absolute global hegemony. Over and above all this, leading countries of the European Union have their contradictions and clash of interests elsewhere in the world, notably with Japan, just as Japan has them with the United States and other rivals in the globalised world.

These contradictions and clashes of interest are today fully visible in the sphere of international trade where, major capitalist economies have become dependent on export to a suicidal degree and with more competitors producing for the same global market, trade wars are being fought with equal vigour on all fronts and between different enemies. The much touted principle of 'free trade' is appealed to or subverted according to convenience and unilateral and multilateral trade aggression has substantially replaced, though not eliminated, concerted action, even within the WTO system. It is basically a situation of each-one-for-itself in the global market. The trade wars of the late 20th and early 21st century, straining and disrupting alliances that had come to be taken for granted in the last half-century or more, are as good an indication as any of the growing contradictions between the major capitalist powers. America's bullying approach to trade, its go-it-alone ways, the efforts to plough its own trade agendas through the differing interests of even its friends or allies, only further sharpens these contradictions.

Globalisation, in its possibly most important aspect is a new phase of imperialist domination of the world. That it is now a 'unipolar' world does not, however, imply any kind of American 'ultra-imperialism'. On the contrary, the end of the cold war and the Soviet collapse have ushered in a new period of recolonisation of the world. Their competition released from the restraints of their common front against 'communism', when even otherwise all conflicts could ultimately be contained within the framework of the confrontation between the two superpower blocs, major capitalist powers have scrambled for a new division of the world where areas once under Moscow's suzerainty – including central Asia with its oil and gas reserves – are also now open to capitalist exploitation, and neo-liberal programmes are more effective ways of achieving the imperialist ends, though, as the wars on Afghanistan and Iraq have made it abundantly clear, reversion to more violent means is never ruled out. In this imperialist scramble, irrespective of the western consensus of 'free market' and 'democracy', there are serious rivalries and conflicts over which capitalist power's interest will be served by which variant of 'free market' and 'democracy', which multinationals, US, European or Japanese, will have privileged access where to cheap labour, mineral extraction rights or privatised public enterprises and of course to markets for their goods, who will control international set-ups of the capitalist world and how, who precisely will be the patron and client states in the new world order? And so on. It has been suggested that 1990, when the cold war ended was a turning-point year when the decades-old post war era came to an end and a new *pre-war* era began. One could look still farther and say that international politics at the beginning of the 21st century, now increasingly resembles that of the opening decades of the 20th.

While the collapse of Soviet Union has left large parts of the world, especially in Europe, Asia and Africa in a state of instability and ever more vulnerable to imperialist exploitation, in the heartlands of world capitalism, as a result of competition among major powers for privileged positions in the new order, the global capitalist economy is getting regrouped into three empires or spheres of influence – centred on the United States in the Western hemisphere, Germany in Europe, and Japan in Asia. The United Nations' reports speak of 'The Triad' emerging in matters of global trade, finance and investment and this 'triad' is getting increasingly congealed into blocs of unevenly developed and hierarchically organised national economies and nation-states, essentially clusters of weaker nations centred on one or more of the major powers: an American bloc centred around the US economy, an European bloc organised through the European Union, and one in East Asia centred around Japan. These blocs, each with a dominant power – the US, Germany and Japan – are not merely competing regional zones of capital accumulation, they also sub-serve the defensive and offensive strategies of the concerned dominant power, each bloc an asset in the struggle for a position at the top of the hierarchy of capitalist nations. Cooperation among them is as much accompanied by as yielding to bitter rivalry and contention, to economic warfare. They may have freer trade within the bloc but on a global scale free trade is definitely in retreat. In the emerging conflicts of economic interests, even the use of extra-economic means is not eschewed by those who can, like the US, afford them. In other words three new centres of imperialism are emerging in Europe, North America, and East Asia. And if history is any guide, their fight among themselves for wealth and power will only grow more bitter with the passage of years.

Like other contradictions in real life, inter-imperialist contradiction too has its ups and downs, highs and lows. The

US, to be sure, is today powerful enough to want to see the entire globe as its domain. Germany and Japan do not have the military might to stalk the world, though they are major players in the global arena of trade, finance and investment. The level of contradiction witnessed in the periods of the two world wars is therefore entirely not there. But things may change as firm trade and investment walls are erected around the different regions. Uneven development inherent in the process of capitalist growth among nations may see the rival blocs come up more strongly, mobilise their resources to redress the military balance and mount their challenge for hegemony in the world. Worsening economic prospects, a further major downturn in the global economy will have its own consequences. As Robert Brenner has recently pointed out, the decades-long struggle for hegemony between US, Japanese and German capital is driving the world economy into recession – the evidence is there in the current turmoil of plunging exchanges, crashing currencies, Asia in crisis, excess capacity in the industrial countries and 'an obscene debt still weighing on the poorest sections of humanity'. This can only further sharpen the inter-imperialist contradiction. The three powers at the core, and their zones of capital accumulation, have their peripheral dependencies. Ties with such dependencies are especially useful to core countries in times of stagnation, financial turbulence and potential major crises. But when the crises become a reality, domestic economies lose steam still further, and accumulating internal problems are not manageable through the usual means, the stronger nations, in sheer desperation, turn more energetically to external expansion for relief. Hence the possibility of the three imperialist blocs going predatory when the pressures built up by the growing crisis of world capitalism can no longer be managed through the institutions of the global capitalist economy.

The process of globalisation has produced much that is new in the world's economy and politics, but it has not changed the basic ways capitalism operates. Imperialism and inter-imperialist rivalry among the three major capitalist powers – the United States, Japan and Western Europe under German hegemony – is a necessary outcome of capitalism's basic ways of operating. With the disintegration of Soviet power and earlier deterrence and global power balance gone, these new imperialisms are all the more free to fight among themselves. The continuing crisis in the world economy will make the fight all the more sharp and bitter in future. The inter-imperialist rivalry thus remains a major fact of our times. The implications of the situation are most grievous. In modern times the source of war on a world scale has always been inter-imperialist rivalry. We have witnessed two devastating world wars as a result of this rivalry. As we face a classic *pre-war* situation wherein the imperialist powers jockey for position against each other before they end up slugging it out, we cannot be complacent about the dangers of another great war. Referring to the 30 odd wars that raged in the decade of the 1990s, Jonathan Steel has written: 'the "new wars" rumble on, and they are inherently less easy to bring to a managed end than the old ones. So, if no one predicted the belligerence of the '90s, it would be folly to say too much about the next decade, let alone the coming century.' Saying 'too much' will be that much more of a folly because of the dangers implicit in the way the United States, militarily the most powerful state of the day, views its real or potential rivals and enemies and seeks to impose itself as the 'globally preeminent' state over and against all other states. Averting a third world war, therefore, must remain a priority for the peoples of the world. Perhaps revolution in one major capitalist country or another in time alone can effectively avert it. This however must not exhaust our understanding of dangers implicit in imperialism or inter-imperialist rivalries. For, even if a global inter-imperialist war is deemed inconceivable for various reasons, with the limits on conventional war lifted, this cannot be said of small wars or proxy wars in pursuit of rival imperialist interests – nearly 23 million are said to have died in 143 such wars, overwhelmingly in the third world, between 1945 and 1992. It may be added that with the ending of the east-west conflict, such wars will be more and more a part of the inter-imperialist politics and of the renewed primacy of the conflict between the North and the South.

XII

The North-South conflict has been in fact central to capital's outward expansion throughout. Capitalism as a global system (and not as a narrowly conceived 'mode of production') necessarily generates polarisation on a world scale making the contradiction between imperialism and the third world basic to the historical processes of our time – the most outstanding evidence here is the distinct and ever-widening gap between a handful of rich nations and the rest of the world. The sharpness of the cold war between east and west certainly eclipsed this fact for a time, just as the inter-imperialist conflict occupied centre stage in the years leading upto 1914 and remained important during the period between the two world wars; though throughout the third world was yet the real battle ground. The cold war is now over and the inter-imperialist contradiction too has taken a back seat. This contradiction persists and will deepen in the years to come, and may or may not find violent expression as before. Much has been learnt from the past and the imperialist powers have far more to gain from supporting each other against the third world than from fighting each other aggressively. The third world, now incorporating a significant part of the post-Soviet second world as well, is the enemy which will not only help the imperialist powers stay united, as Soviet-led 'communism' once did, but also bear the full brunt of their hostility and exploitation.

This hostility or exploitation was somewhat subdued while the Soviet Union lasted. With the October Revolution, the Soviet Union had emerged as a pole of global opposition to imperialism, a source of inspiration to liberation struggles everywhere in the colonised world. The post-war decolonisation owed much to the presence and politics of Soviet Union as a powerful and prestigious global rival to the imperialist powers. For the newly liberated countries of the third world cold war was always about imperialism's attack on their right to pursue a different anti-capitalist or self-reliant path to development. The Soviet Union was an ally and a support in their resistance to this attack. Soviet aid, given for mixed-up reasons of ideology and self-interest, helped these countries to withstand imperialist pressures and Soviet opposition to global capitalism provided them space to manoeuvre in pursuit of their interests. The passing away of Soviet Union was therefore passing away of an ally and a support, the loss of what was in many ways a buffer protecting them from the unfettered western economic and cultural penetration and exploitation, which has now left them open to such penetration and exploitation and led to a renewed sharpening of the contradiction between North and South. All along central to the structuring of the world expansion of capital, this contradiction is today all the more visibly manifest because of the accelerating globalisation of our times. The internal stagnation of advanced capitalism – which threatens to become its permanent feature – does not so much diminish as sharpen this contradiction so that the conditions of the overwhelming majority of the world's population, who daily suffer the depredations of imperialism and allied exploiters within, far from being stabilised, much less improved as promised by the globalisers, have only deteriorated during the last ten odd years.

As globalisation has proceeded, the terrain of third world economic development, or North-South conflict, has been recast on patterns hugely favourable to the North which is now better equipped than ever before to cope with nationalist or communist threats in the third world, and to promote the latter as a 'complement' to the economies of the advanced industrial capitalism. With its victory in the Cold War, global capitalism may have lost interest in the third world for purposes of countervailing economic aid or support, but interest in them as areas of economic exploitation not only persists but is stronger and can now be pursued with renewed vigour as well as arrogance, through those great enforcers of third world 'free enterprise', the IMF and WB with their structural adjustment programmes, or if necessary, through war like the ones against Iraq. Its declared aim was 'to eliminate the widening gap between the developed and the developing countries and ensure steadily accelerating economic and social development and peace and justice for present and future generations', but as designed and run by the US and its close associates in G-7 group of countries (UK, Germany, France, Italy, Canada and Japan), the central purpose of the 'New International Economic Order' (NIEO) has been to secure a firmer control over the economic and strategic resources of the third world countries, so that the multinational capital has an easier time exploiting them. No wonder 'the gap between the developed and developing countries' has continued to widen and 'peace and justice for present and future generations' remains as far away as ever. The NIEO 'principles' (20 of them) to 'ensure steadily accelerating economic and social development' having given way to 'globalisation, marketisation, privatisation', under the new dispensation it is going to be a world run by the rich, for the rich. The renewed economic assault of the North on the South is already here accompanied by efforts to impose its one-sided policies on such matters as population control, migration control, nuclear weapons proliferation, or preventing third world development from imposing 'excessive' ecological obligations on the North. The ideological bent and value system of the 'new world order' is well reflected in the argument (once advanced by World Bank's Chief Economist Summers and later picked up by others) that the fact of its being under-polluted justifies the export of polluting industries or economic activities to the third world. Not only is this already happening, the international trade in toxic waste with the third world has grown alarmingly as advanced capitalist countries run out of room at home. Poor nations are becoming the 'waste baskets' of the rich as tough environmental laws at home result in the advanced capitalist countries of the first world shifting their waste – millions of tons of solvents, acetone, cobalt, cadmium, medical and pharmaceutical and even radio active waste – to the so-called developing countries in the third world.

The end of the Cold War in Europe certainly does not portend peace for the third world. Of course there are diverse regional conflicts in the third world which have an autonomous logic of their own, born of history and the economic and political interests of the ruling elites as well. The end of east-west contention has left the market economies under pressure to dump their now surplus weapons abroad. These are available for use in such regional conflicts and are already being so used. But it is important in this connection to recognise two inter-related facts. In the first place the armament industry is a most profitable one in the West. In the United States, which controls more than 50 percent of the global market (in competition with Britain, Russia, Germany, China and France in that order) arms production is central to the functioning of its capitalist economy as a whole; it has been openly argued that as long as the possibility of 'small wars' around the globe remained, there was little danger of the current recession gathering momentum to turn into another Great Depression. War is terrible, but it is also terribly profitable, Lenin had pointed out long ago. The arms manufacturers are therefore all the time looking for new 'markets' for their hardware. And it needs to be remembered that the market economy does not merely react to market signals; market signals can be specially engineered. And sadly enough, they are engineered from time to time, something the ideologues of capitalism usually prefer to forget. This has ominous implications for countries of the third world. They are not immune to first world's search for markets for its arms, nor their regional conflicts to imperialist politicking and manipulation. Nor are they immune to imperialism's direct military intervention in pursuit of its specific economic and political interests, or deployment of forces the world over to ensure, in Pentagon's language, 'a more open international economic system.' America's wars on Iraq and Afghanistan and its assumption of the role of a global policeman and the accompanying 'low intensity warfare' in several parts of the world, have already made that abundantly clear. Imperialism still means war, the continuation of imperialist politics by other means and it has never been lacking in ideological justification. Among the latest efforts to thus justify imperialist wars of the present and the future is Huntington's *Clash of Civilisations*.

As is to be expected, imperialism in the age of 'globalisation' has its own specificities, it is in many ways different from the earlier capitalist imperialism when the imperialist powers typically conquered colonial territories or used direct military force to control them and competed over those territories typically by military means. Imperialism thus was primarily a relation between a capitalist and an essentially non-capitalist or backward world. With the 'universalisation' of capitalism imperialism today is more, though not entirely, a matter of relations within a global capitalist system of controlling, not particular territories, but whole world economy and global markets everywhere and at all times, so that the forces of the capitalist market prevail in every corner of the world, which inevitably means marginalising and impoverishing larger parts of it. It is in this context that the most powerful capitalist economies, the US in particular, seek to manipulate these market forces to their advantage. And they do so not only through the direct exploitation of cheap labour of backward countries by transnationals based in advanced capitalist countries but also more indirectly through things like debt and currency manipulation.

Of course, no longer a matter of direct colonial domination or use of military means – which however is not entirely ruled out – imperialism, like the global economy, is still a relationship between national entities, new forms of imperial domination – by means of debt and financial manipulation or even trade and direct foreign investment – are means of penetrating national boundaries, and imperial power, no less than earlier forms, is exercised by nation-states, whether directly, via blocs or through international agencies. Therefore imperialist rivalries, however much changed in form are still there and the contradictory processes of capitalist competition here are no less explosive than before. But this only intensifies the more basic overall contradiction between imperialism and the peoples of the third world as it has come to be under 'globalisation'. 'Globalisation', it bears repeating, is not any kind of end of imperialism and, details apart, imperialism very much remains as Lenin analysed it, it still means rapacious loot and plunder of the weak nations. As Istvan Meszaros has put it: 'Globalisation' is 'in truth yet another name for the continued enforcement of the most iniquitous socio-economic power relations between the capitalistically advanced and the "underdeveloped" or "Third World" countries of the global capital system.' Sub-commandant

Marcos of the Zapatista rebellion in Mexico is not alone in seeing it as 'the third world war' – a war which is being waged by imperialism against the peoples of the third world with all the means at its disposal to establish its economic and political domination, to control, direct and manipulate all thought processes which could conflict with its purposes, to mould all cultural expressions to its late-capitalist contours, in short, to remake the world in its own imperialist image.

That imperialism means ruthless exploitation of the weak nations is generally understood. But it is important to specifically recognise that capitalism itself, national or globalised, has little to offer to peoples in the periphery and semi-periphery of global capitalism. Arriving so late on the scene and with a colonial past, the countries of the third world, even when politically free had already given hostages to fortune in that quite a few options were closed to them. One of these was the much aspired development akin to that of the 'advanced capitalist' countries of the North. The rapacious exploitation of the human and material resources of the planet for the benefit of a few capitalist countries, which underlay the latter's 'advanced capitalist' development, was simply impossible to replicate. Neither the advantages of an imperialist past, nor the immense profits derived on a continuing basis from keeping the colonial world in structural dependency were available to the old or newly independent countries of the third world. Though still euphemistically described as 'developing countries', their development into advanced capitalist countries is even less of an available option now in the world of 'free marketing' globalisation. Enthusiasm of neo-liberal ideologues notwithstanding, the belief that capitalist market economy can usher in an era of economic prosperity for all in the third world has hardly any theoretical or empirical basis to validate it. Even in the advanced industrial countries, despite their initial advantages and immense wealth – a very large part of it the result of a transfer of surplus-value from the third world – capitalism has failed to generalise capitalist prosperity. True, the first world poverty is not the same as poverty in the third world, but today, under globalist 'restructuring', its levels are rising, inequalities of income and wealth are sharper than ever before, living standards are declining as the welfare state is sought to be dismantled, and unemployment – at an all time high since the Great Depression of the 1930s – is fast becoming a structural feature of the capitalist economy. Capitalism in the third world can only be a more dismal affair. A small section at the top of society will certainly benefit and prosper but not so the common people. The hopefulness of the so-called 'trickle down' theory has been well described by Galbraith as feeding horses with oatmeal so that sparrows can feed on their dung. Not much of a success even in the advanced North – where working people had to fight every inch of the way to extract concessions from the capitalists – the theory is even less likely to work with the peripheral or semi-peripheral capitalisms of the third world. Capitalism, in short, has simply no answers to problems of poverty and unemployment, hunger, disease, malnutrition and illiteracy that today afflict most parts of the third world, and globalisation of their economies will mean only more exploitation and further impoverishment and in its ultimate outcome perpetual peripheralisation within the global capitalist system.

The experience of peripheral and semi-peripheral capitalisms and globalisation so far more than vindicates this argument. The peoples of the third world are learning the hard way. They may in time win the necessary 'theoretical awareness' of the issues involved, make the choice they need to make and seek to travel their own historically specific roads to socialism. A long haul, this is a task that, as I have argued earlier, history's trick on the doctrine of Karl Marx has imposed on them, that of simultaneously 'developing the economy' and building a just and humane society. Or, to put it in more specific Marxist terms, they have to simultaneously develop the forces of production – which was seen as the historical task of capitalism – and build socialist relations of production in the economy as the basis of a just and humane society that is socialism.

That is how the Soviet collapse notwithstanding, anti-capitalist struggles in the third world will not come to an end or phase out, they will continue to resurface periodically.

The socialist dream and the humanism that it embodies will continue to straddle the countries and continents of the third world. For three-fourths of humanity – that is as many as more than four billion people – who constitute the third world, who more than any other parts of the human population have borne the brunt of exploitation and oppression that is capitalism, global or native, there is no other way out or forward except socialism. Only socialism – where people's politics, not 'the market', commands the economy and there is rationally planned use of available resources for human welfare – holds the hope and promise of emancipation for the long-exploited and oppressed peoples of Asia, Africa and Latin America. The dream that is socialism may have been adjourned in the former Soviet Union and Eastern Europe, or dimmed elsewhere in the west, it remains the only relevant cause and determinant of historical processes in the third world. And it may well be that the struggle for it in the third world proves decisive for the future of socialism in the first world as well.

XIII

Capitalism is inherently a polarising system at home and abroad. No doubt the periphery always suffers greater polarisation within and between countries than does the centre, and globalisation has greatly intensified class polarisation within the countries of the periphery where the local bourgeoisies or elites, abandoning whatever allegiance they once had to bourgeois-nationalist development projects in their home countries, in a 'secession of the successful' as it were, are moving over to find whatever place they can find in the global capitalist order. The associated richer sections of society too have been busy 'seceding' from the common people. But polarlisation within countries of advanced capitalism is no less real, expressing as it does that most basic contradiction of capitalism, between the bourgeoisie and the working class, which is now pushing the latter towards a situation similar in some ways to that long familiar to peasants and workers in the periphery.

This contradiction was largely dormant for a long period after the Second World War, till about the end of the 1960's. The cold war and the clever use of 'anti-communism' by the ruling classes was an important factor in distracting attention away from the essentially exploitative character of capitalism and thus obscuring this contradiction. Far more important in obscuring, rather muting or suppressing, this contradiction however was the 'Keynesian compromise' and its social welfare policies, particularly the construction in Europe of the most advanced social welfare states in the world. Incidentally, Soviet Union was again an important factor here. It needs to be remembered that even as its ugly face in the Soviet Union made socialism unacceptable in the advanced capitalist west, Stalinist socialism and the communist movement allied with it, forced a certain humanisation of capitalism and significantly contributed to the development of welfare capitalism, thereby also lending power and influence to social democratic theory and practice. In a rather paradoxical historical process, as the west moved away from socialism, fear of socialism civilised capitalism into accepting the modern welfare state. Of course the workers had to struggle hard and long for it, but what made it possible and sustained the 'Keynesian compromise' was the long post-war boom that underlay the so-called 'golden age' of capitalism with its rapid economic growth, low unemployment, mild business cycles and rising mass living standards, especially for the white male sector of the working class. Much of the success of the 'golden age', it may be noted, was due to the development of large-scale state interventions in the market that aimed to ameliorate both the severity of business cycles and the worst disparities of wealth, income and opportunity that had inevitably characterised capitalism in the pre-war period. The end of the post-war boom also saw the end of the 'golden age', giving way to the so-called 'leaden age', running from the early 1970s into the present, distinguished by slow growth, high unemployment, more severe business cycles and stagnating or declining living standards for the majority. Capitalism in crisis found it difficult to sustain the welfare state and decreed its dismantling. Social democracy suffered set back in one European country after another, losing out to the rightwing economy and politics of Thatchers and Kohls, and Ronald Reagans as well. The state interventionist policies yielded to an agenda of unqualified support for big business and similarly unqualified opposition to any sort of downward redistribution initiatives. The polarising contradiction of capitalism was again out in the open after a long time.

The Soviet collapse and the fillip it has given to unrestrained capitalism has led to a further sharpening of this contradiction. With this collapse not only the Stalinist socialism, but along with the democratic socialist options even the old social democratic model has been defeated. Fear of socialism has disappeared, 'the spectre' of communism haunting Europe since 1848 is laid to rest, at least for the time being. Capitalism has gained a new level of superiority and self-confidence. Flush with the sense of having conquered the world, it has been acting out its wildest dreams, firing workers, slashing wages, smashing unions, merging monopolies to make even bigger monopolies, undermining and dismantling welfare states. From capital's point of view the results have been wonderful: profits and stock markets have boomed, the rich have gotten richer even faster than during the Reagan-Thatcher years. But for the rest of society the main fruits of this capitalist orgy have been massive and increasing unemployment and monumental insecurity, resurgence of poverty and hardship on an unprecedented scale, extending even to countries that had once served as models of 'mass prosperity'. Even as, scorning accommodation, capitalism has been unabashedly reasserting its polarising tendencies, its ideologues have been arguing for acceptance of deprivation and destitution among at least a third or so of the population as inevitable.

Capitalism's resumption of global domination has meant no change in its character as a system of exploitation or the tendency to recurring crisis endemic to it. It has not brought any relief in its current long term crisis, now more universal than ever before precisely because of the resumed global domination. But it has left it more free and powerful in trying to resolve this crisis in an unabashedly capitalist manner, that is, resolve it at the cost of the working people. Its attempts to renew economic growth and confront the heightened competition accompanying the unrelenting global stagnation have come packaged as 'restructuring', which has become as much of a buzzword as 'globalisation' and is really 'globalisation' programme for the domestic capitalist economies at the centre, a counterpart of its 'structural adjustment' abroad. Even as governments have gone in for neo-liberal policies – tax breaks for the rich, privatisation of public sector, extensive deregulation, etc. – corporate 'restructuring' essentially refers to a set of strategies intended to cut costs and raise profits once more by lowering wages, regaining control over labour – euphemistically treated as returning 'flexibility' to the labour market, 'downsizing' – the fashionable word for throwing people out of jobs at more or less short notice, and such devices as speed-up, contracting out, two-tiered wage structures, relocation, etc. It includes union busting and, of course, pressuring government to roll back 'expensive' social reforms, that is, dismantle the welfare state.

There is much hype over new technologies, their necessity and benevolent usefulness in restructuring the economy. But a capitalist economy – whose motivating principle is profit-making and wherein fruits of production are privately appropriated – cannot use technologies, new or old, in a socially beneficial manner. Like earler technological changes under capitalism, the new technologies certainly make for higher productivity that benefits the capitalists but for the workers they only facilitate new methods of exploitation, and the new work arrangements accompanying them --well described as 'management by stress' – push workers to even higher levels of self-exploitation. Intensified exploitation apart, new technologies have been used primarily to displace and control workers. As even World Economic Forum's managing director Claude Smadja recently admitted: 'Labour has been the biggest loser in the globalisation process. New technology and enhanced productivity are scything jobs without spawning commensurate hikes in wages.'

Decades back, the American mathematician Norbert Wiener, the inventor of 'cybernetics', had warned prophetically that the new technology would lead to 'an unemployment situation in comparison with which.... even the Depression of 1930s will seem a pleasant joke'. The situation has begun to emerge. Technological change today is indeed a major factor in the loss of manufacturing jobs. Thus, for example, domestic US manufacturing output today is five time what it was in 1950 even as fewer workers are needed by the manufacturing sector. This is overwhelmingly the result of labour-displacing technology. We are back in familiar Marxist territory with dead labour replacing living labour and creating reserve army of the unemployed in the process. It is not surprising that with the growing capital intensity of new industries, thanks above all to new technologies, most capitalist economies have settled into a pattern, really pathology, of 'jobless growth.' Work has indeed been 'vanishing' in advanced capitalist societies – one has only to look at reports from the International Labour Organisation (ILO). New technologies do benefit a small section of workers but translated into higher productivity, they have meant either bigger unemployment or additional growth in the number of so-called 'working poor'. Marx had once observed that 'the theft of somebody else's labour time' is a miserable foundation to calculate our wealth. This is even more true today than it was 150 years ago.

Technology replacing labour is however a small part of the overall negative consequences of the on-going 'restructuring' for the life and work-conditions of the working class in the west, the most privileged part of the global capitalist system. Most obvious here is the increase in unemployment and under-employment, as businesses 'downsize' and 'shed labour' to reduce production costs. The situation is made worse by another kind of 'worker displacement' ordained by the process of 'globalisation': multinational corporations relocating their industries or plants and thus shifting manufacturing jobs overseas. The creation of this 'global assembly line' has become a critical component of the corporate strategy to cut costs, for the workers here have to be paid only minimal wages. That is how millions of workers come to lose their jobs, adding to the already increasing number of unemployed at home. Till recently unemployment in the highly developed capitalist countries was largely confined to 'pockets of underdevelopment' in those countries. But now, making a mockery of the post-war liberal-conservative-labour consensus which proclaimed 'full employment in a free society', unemployment has retuned to these countries on a scale not seen since the Great Depression and seems set to become a permanent feature of their economies. It is no longer a question of boom and slump. At the end of each cycle the number of jobless is higher than it was at the same point in the preceding cycle. In recent years, the number has reached double figures even in the official data which are known to arbitrarily exclude many categories of actually unemployed people, under one pretext or another, from their unemployment statistics. It has mattered little which government – social democrat, monetarist or Keynesian – is in power. And the phenomenon is no longer limited to the blue collar workers. It affects the whole population, including the middle classes. If industrial restructuring has decimated the working class as a whole, 'downsizing' has been cutting swathes through the middle class employment – we have *The Sunday Times* recently raising alarm about the fact that 'Redundancies focus on the white-collar workers' and that 'Axe falls on 50,000 civil service jobs.' As it becomes a permanent feature of the economy, mass unemployment has a most significant inter-generational aspect. Istvan Meszaros has written:

> Millions of young people are denied the chance of a job in every major capitalist country, unceremoniously obliterating the not so old memory of courtship about 'youth culture', while continuing to squeeze every possible drop of profit out of the remnants of such culture. At the same time, millions of older people are also forced to join the dole queues, and millions more are under an immense pressure for 'early retirement'.... Thus the age-group of the 'useful generation' is shrinking to somewhere between 25 and 50, and it is *objectively* opposed to the 'unwanted generations' condemned by capital to enforced idleness and the loss of their humanness. And since now the middle generation is squeezed between the 'useless young' *and* the 'useless old' – until, that is, it becomes itself superfluous, when capital deems so – even the temporal planes of these contradictions become all-confounding.

Unemployment is not an aberration of the capitalist system; rather it is inherent in the very workings of capitalism, of its capital accumulation process. We have, with Marx, long known that capital creates and needs a reserve army of the unemployed to maintain flexibility in the labour market and as an aid to control the employed. But now that our technological genius has made this disturbingly obvious in the form of 'jobless growth', and mass unemployment has come to stay, bourgeois ideologues have come to see and argue *for* it as a structural problem, a necessity inherent in the economy. It is '*structural unemployment*', a necessary condition for the economy to be in equilibrium and functional. Milton Friedman has even coined a scientific sounding term for this new orthodoxy, 'a natural rate of unemployment', a rate that is built into the very structure of the economy. Obviously, if this is the case, then there is nothing that can be done about it. Unemployment is 'structural' and therefore it is here to stay to the end of time. (If you have the inclination, you could blame it all on 'technological progress', which however is inevitable and, barring some pessimistic utopians, no one can conceivably oppose).

This kind of theorising is only so much apologetics in defence of the existing economic arrangements of capitalism. It obscures the fact that mass unemployment is structural to capitalist production only and not to the advancement of the production process as such. The admission that unemployment is now 'structural' is far more legitimately a call for a change in the *structure* – that is the social order – in which it has become necessary or unavoidable than an argument to justify and maintain the selfsame structure intact, at whatever human cost, accepting 'structural unemployment' as the *permanent* feature of the one and only conceivable structure or social order. (Incidentally, mass unemployment has its obvious consequences for the purchasing power in society which is critical to the working of capitalism as a market-based, profit-motivated mode of production. That the worsened position of the mass of consumers is an important factor in the crisis of over production or excess capacity plaguing the capitalist economies today is something the apologist theorising seems to be entirely oblivious of).

There are other ideologists of the system, however, who would rather do without such sophistications of theory and even as they recognise the 'shamefully high unemployment', have a more honest and straightforward *capitalist* understanding of and answer to the worsening problem of unemployment in their society. This is how *The Economist* put it in a recent editorial:

> Europe's long history of shamefully high unemployment shows that its labour markets are broken, and need to be fixed. A chief cause – especially of the rising toll of long term unemployment – is welfare benefits that are too generous for too long, and which place too few demands on recipients to find a new job.... There is little doubt, for instance, that France's anomalously high rate of unemployment among the young is partly due to the national minimum wage – at nearly 50 percent of average earnings (covering roughly 12 percent of wage-earners), this is high by international standards, and must prise many young workers out of the market. In other ways, too, governments must avoid adding to the cost of hiring labour. At present they discourage recruitment by offering too much 'employment protection' to workers once hired.

This by itself is not new, at least on the far right, but there appears to be a new willingness to be explicit about the need to depress the condition of workers in the interest of 'flexible' labour markets and a new inclination to include among the enemies of flexibility even rights and protections that all but the most rabid neo-conservatives might once have left intact. 'Flexibility' is indeed *the* code word in the ongoing restructuring of the economy: deregulate the labour market, weaken the social 'safety net' and even lift restrictions on environmental pollution in order to compete with third-world capitalisms by allowing the terms and conditions of work to sink towards the level of their less-developed competitors. Not only welfare provisions but decent pay and working conditions or even environmental protection are, it seems, obstacles to competitiveness, profitability and growth.

An associated problem for the working class here is that in the era of globalisation, capital is able to move about the globe to invest wherever opportunities are optimal (and labour costs are cheapest), while workers are, for the most part, consigned to whatever jobs are available. Unlike capital, labour cannot move about the globe at will, much less do it in an organised fashion. That is how multinationals now have a new weapon against their own working people. They can not only threaten to move plants and transfer production to cheaper locations abroad but are actually so moving them – especially their 'smoke-stack industries' – to the third world countries, the supposedly lucky beneficiaries of the much hyped over 'transfer of technology' across borders in the age of globalisation.

Capital's search for flexibility of labour has led to a fundamental change in the composition of the working class in most industrially or technologically advanced countries. Mass unemployment, as we have noticed, has become a permanent phenomenon. The slogan, 'the main thing is to have a job' has served not only to support the intensification of exploitation but also lay the basis for the further destruction of jobs. Full-time jobs have come to be replaced with cheap flexible jobs. An increasing proportion of the labour force is contingent, that is workers who work part-time, temporarily or seasonally, on contract, or as self-employed subcontractors. There is a shift from manufacturing to services, both white collar and grey. With the relatively well paid jobs in manufacturing rapidly eroding, the unemployed in this sector have shifted *en masse* to precarious part-time employment in low wage service sectors. Overall, the global 'restructuring' has produced or accelerated such processes as: casualisation of labour – expansion of part-time, short-term contract or other sorts of casual labour, employers using casual labour to cut wage and benefit costs and reassert their control over the labour market; feminisation of labour – woman at the bottom of the ladder, among the first to be forced back into unemployment or into miserably remunerated part-time labour, deservingly described as 'the last colony' for capitalist exploitation; informalisation of labour – as corporations shed workers and outsource to the third world, people are compelled to resort to the informal economy to survive, but capital also resorts to the informal economy to cut costs of production; housewifisation of labour – the growth of low-status, low-paid and ostensibly low-skilled jobs in the economy; peripheralisation of labour – Latin-Americanisation or thirdworldisation of a section of the working class in the advanced capitalist countries; and finally 'degradation of labour' on a scale not witnessed before – a constant feature of capitalist production process, especially since the Industrial Revolution, much worse now than when Harry Braverman explored it in his classic *Labor and Monopoly Capital* three decades back, it has been described as 'a process whereby workers have been separated from control of their work and subjected to a deskilling that has, in the worst cases, made them little more than the automatons depicted so well by Charlie Chaplin in the film *Modern Times*. Workers in assembly-line mass production are often little more than cogs in the machine. They experience degrees of alienation that make the conventional economic term "factors of production" most appropriate.' With the employment-wise condition of the working class thus deteriorating, it is not surprising that working class wages have continued to tumble over the past few decades and, as the profits of the capitalists have soared, inequality in society has grown dramatically over these years and now stands at its highest level since records have been kept. Overshadowing it all, with the fear of plant closures and downsizing constantly hanging over their heads, the working class remains gripped with a sense of insecurity, more acute than at any time in the past since the days of Great Depression.

True for the advanced capitalist countries as a whole, all this is no less true for the United States, the leading country of the capitalist world. Traditionally deficient in matters of social protection and welfare and with the lowest levels of unionisation in the advanced capitalist world, cyclical upswings notwithstanding, the condition of its working people has steadily deteriorated during the recent 'globalising' decades. As the large corporations in the United States have continued to restructure their operations on a worldwide basis, their demand for flexible workforce has led to a dramatic expansion of temporary work and the growth of a large class of 'working poor' with lower-wage, degrading quality of jobs. Increasingly, temporary workers are hired under a system known as 'planned staffing' which simply means that more and more companies opt for a flexibility in which they maintain a 'core' of permanent workers with a ring of temporary workers who can be hired or laid off at will, depending on the business climate. The proportion of people losing regular or permanent jobs is at an all time high. Between 1992 and 1995, 15 per cent of people holding jobs for more than one year lost their jobs; their new jobs, if they found one, paid 14 per cent less on average. The rate of job loss in the 'boom' of 1990s has been higher than in the recession years of the early 1980s or of 1990-91. Almost 30 per cent workers in 1997 were stated to be employed in situations that were *not* regular or permanent full-time jobs, and majority of the new jobs created were part-time and/or temporary. Between one-quarter and one-third of all employees in the United States today are 'contingent' workers, quite apart from the large and growing numbers in low-paid full-time work. Here contingent work is synonymous with 'non-standard' work, an euphemism which ranges widely from labourers recruited by the day and those hired by or working for temporary agencies to independent contracting and part-time or irregular full-time jobs in activities such as security and custodial work, janitors, drivers, restaurant and other low-grade services. In their search for labour flexibility, employers in alliance with the state are known to have attempted to make nonworking alternatives to contingent jobs unbearable, to make workers desperate and anxious enough to take any job, regardless of pay or workplace conditions. It is these contingent workers who move about or 'float' regularly between irregular jobs and represent the huge pool of underemployed and subemployed workers that make the official unemployment statistics look so rosy. Studies have revealed that, as is to be expected, women comprise greater proportion of these floating contingent workers. They are three times as likely to hold regular and irregular part-time work as men and making about a fifth of the overall female workforce, earn, on average, 20 per cent less than equivalent women employed full-time and 20 per cent less than their male counterpart part-timers. Minority groups, needless to say, fare worse than their Anglo peers, and minority woman worst of all. On the whole, African-Americans tend to be twice as likely to be lower paid temporary workers, and much less likely to be self-employed. Hispanics, meanwhile, have a larger share of low-wage 'on call' work. Overall it is increasingly a situation which has been described as 'a world of part-time, temporary, "flexible", low paying, no benefit jobs' – a 'new American sweat shop' made up of 'disposable and throw away workers', as the owner of one agency that supplies temporary or part-time workers for business recently admitted in the *New York Times*.

The fast growth of temporary and part time workers has meant a growing job insecurity which has not spared even the fabled American middle classes who are being rapidly absorbed into an ever-expanding mass of 'working class' employment, or unemployment, their erstwhile badge of honour now reading 'position abolished'. As a recent *New York Times* special survey has reported, 'white-collar, middle class workers are coming to understand first hand the chronic insecurity on which the working class and the poor are experts.' 'Americans', Michael Mandel of the *Business Week* notes, 'are living with a combination of growth and uncertainty they've never seen before.' And this includes the middle-class, white-collar Americans. John Beatty has thus reported it in a recent issue of *The Atlantic*: '...compared to their peers 30 years ago, America's 80 million white-collar employees are working longer hours, for the same pay and fewer benefits, at jobs that are markedly less secure, and for corporations that regard firing whole ranks of employees as a way to post paper gains and so win Wall Street's favour. The long arm of the job has reached into employees' homes, their nights, their weekends, and their vacations, as technology designed to make work less onerous has made it more pervasive. America's insecure white-collar workers are victims not of poverty, but of progress.... Back at the office, the average employee must cope with 200 e-mails every day, being careful not to use "alert" words like "union" or "boss" in e-correspondence since "investigator" software may be watching. Overwork and job spill would perhaps be bearable if one were being well paid for it. But while-collar men earned an average of $ 19.24 an hour in 1997, just six cents more than their fathers made in 1973.' Beatty goes on: 'What is to blame? The short answer is price competition. Second answer: in his book,

Only the Paranoid Survive (1996), Andrew Grove, the CEO of Intel... brings the new corporate insecurity home. "When companies no longer have lifelong careers themselves, how can they provide one for their employees?" Most white-collar workers have accepted their fate, albeit bitterly, resenting the fact that they have to pay for bad business decisions made by executives whose pay has risen an average of 70 percent since 1990.'

Insecurity for the working people, however, has its advantages for the capitalists, it even purveys miracles for them as Alan Greenspan of the Federal Reserve Bank, who presided over the so-called '90s miracle' recently testified to the Banking Committee of the American Senate. He attributed the miracle to 'greater worker insecurity'. Workers are intimidated, they are afraid to ask for a living wage and benefits, and that is a good thing. A presidential report on the economy has attributed its 'boom' to 'significant wage restraint' that results from 'change in labour market institutions and practices' – which in effect means practices like the non-enforcement of laws on illegal strike-breaking or allowing permanent replacement of workers for which the United States has been rightly cited by the International Labour Organisation.

The problem, it is clear, is not only high disguised unemployment and the growth of part time work, but the reality that except for a small minority at the top, jobs do not pay enough to live on. In 1993 27 per cent of all US workers were in jobs that did not pay them enough to live above the poverty level. Even when jobs are plentiful, new jobs are mostly bad jobs. They pay less than old ones; as noticed earlier, on average workers who get laid off and find new jobs receive 14 per cent less pay in their new jobs. And with lower wages and fewer hours, workers need more than one job to make ends meet, or have to work longer hours. Most American workers make less today in inflation adjusted dollars, and work 160 hours longer per year than they did in 1973. And it always remains a struggle. Multiple job holding and longer hours directly reflect the trimming of hourly wage levels, even as it spells more work and intensified exploitation. Flexibility of workforce also means that businesses don't have to provide fringe benefits to the workers such as health insurance, vacations, pensions, and union contracts. Throughout the post-war period the United States had little social protection or welfare by European standards and even that limited protection or welfare is now being drastically reduced. Union busting and its corollary, the attack on the social safety net – which has included a heartless assault on impoverished single mothers in the name of 'ending welfare dependency' – have further reduced workers' choices and made them available for poorly paid contingent work. It is not without reason that 'working poor' has come to be described as 'the latest American invention'. Overall, the US today is a typical, even if somewhat extreme example of the nature and quality of employment under advanced capitalism: a two-tier labour force with a small layer of highly skilled and highly paid workers on top and underneath a large body of semi-skilled and unskilled workers merging into, and easily replaceable by, the growing number of unemployed at the bottom. Those at the lower end of employment ladder regularly slip downwards, further into the mire, while still more sink and ever deeper into the Lazarus-layers of pauperism.

This of course is part of the larger reality of the United States as a capitalist society where the gap between the privileged few at the top and the deprived many at the bottom of society is not only big, it has been growing fast in the last couple of decades, and is today greater than in any other capitalist country (with the possible exception of 'capitalist Russia'). The top 1 percent of American households have more wealth than the bottom 40 per cent. The average CEO, who in 1960 earned 40 times the income of the average US factory worker, in 1993 got 149 times the income of the average US factory worker. The wages of the low paid workers have declined to an extent that today about 36 million people in the US (around 13 per cent of the total population) live below that society's poverty line. In the absence of welfare benefits, judged and denied as 'too generous' and 'dependency prone', increasing number of people are seeking food stamps and joining the lengthening queues of soup-kitchens.

Marx had written of capitalism creating and needing a reserve army of labour – 'it offers capital an inexhaustible reservoir of disposable labour-power'. The swelling ranks of the unemployed and subemployed contingent workers – men and women 'sloughed into the ranks of the so-called non-participants in the labour force' in the words of Harry Braverman – represent precisely such a reservoir of highly exploitable and flexible labour power. Of the phenomenon, inherent in capitalism, its process of capital accumulation, Marx had written: The 'first word of this adaptation is the creation of relative surplus population.' 'Its last word', he had added, 'is the misery of constantly expanding strata of an active army of labour, and the dead weight of pauperism.' For Marx, this 'last word' was one expression of the structural logic of capitalism: 'accumulation of wealth at one pole... at the same time, accumulation of misery, the torment of labour, slavery, ignorance, brutalisation and moral degradation at the opposite pole'. It is this logic which is now working itself out with the 'relative surplus population' of America, of course modified in its working by the circumstances of contemporary American capitalism.

Of recent American efforts to cope with this problem, to seek an answer, as it were, from within capitalism, Staughton Lynd has said:

> I have just become possessed by the hypocrisy of the Clinton administration's jobs rhetoric. I believe we are in a period like the early 1960s. You have a Democratic President who makes idealistic and compassionate noises. This guy was elected to create jobs. But in reality, his program is to help corporations cut jobs. The profit-maximising companies today are downsizing. And the Clinton Administration is pushing 'training' – which means you and I learning each other's jobs, so next year one of us will be gone. The 'jointness' that Secretary of Labour Robert Reich is pushing means, the boss says: 'We are going to lay off 30 per cent of you, and the union can decide who'.... American capitalism no longer has any use for, let's say, 40 per cent of the population. These are the descendants of folks who were brought over here in one way or another during the period of capital accumulation. They are now superfluous human beings. They are nothing but a problem for the people who run the society... Politicians may run

> for office promising full employment, but they don't want full employment. They never wanted full employment – even in the period of primitive accumulation in England when Marx wrote, or in that same period in the United States seventy-five years later. Today, in the period of decaying imperialist capitalism, it is as if the reserve army of labour becomes the whole world.

That tens of millions of hard working (or potentially hard working) men and women have no real economic future is a problem inherent in the structural logic of capitalism and an answer is possible only by going beyond capitalism to a democratically planned socialism. That was Marx's argument. The argument remains valid today for capitalism anywhere, including capitalism in America.

XIV

Capitalism, as we have repeatedly noticed, is a constantly changing system, incomparably more so than anything that preceded it. But in noticing and taking account of its changes, which all the time require new analyses from us, we must not make the mistake – that according to Raymond Williams the younger New Left in Europe made – of underestimating everything that has *not* changed in the capitalist system. And this 'everything' above all includes its essential structural logic. This logic was in its own way early manifested in the capitalist reaction to the end of the post-war boom in the 1970s – as the Thatcher-Reagan-Kohl policies aimed at dismantling the welfare state, breaking the power of organised labour and expanding the scope for capital accumulation through privatisation and deregulation etc. With the Soviet collapse, this capitalist project could be, as 'globalisation', pursued even more ruthlessly so that capitalism even in its advanced centres has come to be specifically defined by things like mass levels of structural unemployment, 'flexible' labour markets and changing patterns of work in the form of casualisation and low-paid part-time jobs or overwork for the remaining few in 'downsized' enterprises, more and more drastically cut down public services and welfare programmes, growing poverty and homelessness, and inequality restored to more than nineteenth century levels.

This makes it clear that the 'golden age' of capitalist prosperity and plentiful jobs was an aberration and that normal capitalism is an entirely different affair. In other words, the real face of capitalism, its essentially exploitative structural logic is today visibly evident as it has not been for a long time, making it easier for people to recognise capitalism for what it really is. This, obviously, points to possibilities of a renewed struggle for socialism, which possibilities, it is important to note, are only enhanced by the collapse of socialist challenge in the form of 'actually existing socialism' of the Soviet Union and 'social democracy' in Europe, which marks the current 'triumph' or global domination of capitalism.

In the long and even medium run the collapse of 'socialism' in the East may well have the opposite effect from the one being currently celebrated in the West by the neo-liberal ideologues of capitalism. For a whole epoch now, working class resistance to the permanent injustices of capitalism has been deflected away from adopting a radical course by a number of factors which we have had the occasion to take note of earlier. Not the least important among them were the ideologically disabling models of the actually existing 'socialism' of the East. No doubt there was the consistently hostile capitalist propaganda against the Soviet Union, especially the totalitarian connotations spawned by the rhetoric of the Cold War. But there was much in the reality of 'Soviet socialism' to lend credibility to this ideological offensive. The repulsive mask which Stalinism had put on socialism (or communism) was one of the biggest subjective obstacles to the development of revolutionary consciousness among the western working classes. They continued to identify the Soviet Union with socialism. And the ugly face of this socialism weighed heavily on the working class struggles in the west. The example of Soviet Union did not attract workers in the advanced capitalist countries; rather they were repelled by this historically produced equation of socialism with the Soviet Union. Even the communist parties whose politics was often misled or subordinated to the foreign policy requirements of the Soviet State could not persuade them that it was going to be different in their own countries.

The ruling classes in the West look full advantage of this equation and the consequent repulsion to effectively argue that a socialist alternative to capitalism can only be 'concentrationary' or authoritarian, and thus not only cover up the ugly realities of capitalism itself but gain legitimacy for their supposedly life and death struggle against 'the communist menace' at home and abroad. Sovietology as demonology entered into the official legitimating ideology of capitalism. Any radical questioning of the capitalist system was blocked by projecting the inequalities and alienation generated by the capitalist system as the inevitable costs of political freedom, an 'open society' – the only alternative being a Soviet-type 'totalitarian' society. Criticism of capitalism was filtered through the thick sieve of anti-communism, and a 'their system is worse than ours' mentality was built up to persuade workers to suffer evils of capitalism as necessary sacrifies which they must make to avid something far worse. The ruling classes were able to disarm their working classes ideologically not only through the directly deterrent example of the 'societies of actually existing socialism', but also through winning, in the name of a holy crusade against 'communist world domination', the complicity of the western labour movements in their imperialist politics abroad. While the multinationals raked in massive profits from their exploitation of the rest of the world, the fringe benefits flowing to them, only furthered the ideological-political disarming of the working classes in the first world.

The Soviet collapse means a radical change in this situation. It is not only that there is no Soviet Union any more to mislead the revolutionary movements emerging and likely to emerge in the West or to subordinate them to its *raison d'etat*, no more parodies of Marxism or pseudo-internationalism. Nor will these movements carry the burden of a grossly deformed and degenerated socialism, or be answerable for its ugliness and cruelties; though the burden of a genuine Marxist explanation of how all this happened will still be theirs. Equally if not more important, the ultimate collapse of the Soviet model of socialism, even as it will over time help undermine the easy but absurd identification of socialism with dictatorial rule and political repression, it has immediately deprived western capitalism of a bogey that has well served it over the years to control and discipline its working classes, to undermine their resistance to capitalism's exploitative domination. In other words, it has removed capitalism's favourite self-justifying *alibi*. There will be no easy escape now from its own domestic problems which the existence of Soviet Union had for long obscured or alleviated. Capitalism can no longer conceal its own ugly features by turning the light on its allegedly communist rival. The problems arising from the internal antagonisms or contradictions will have to be faced everywhere at the place where they continue to arise. Forces struggling against capitalism cannot be so easily discredited and even outlawed in the future as they were in the past, in the name fighting 'the communist menace', nor the western radicals so easily accused of being foreign agents. The cold war red baiting has lost its old power to terrify, and people, more receptive to radical ideas and politics are already raising issues which were earlier forbidden because they implicitly or otherwise clashed with the logic or norms of the capitalist market. There is a vital truth in American political scientist David P. Calleo's observation that 'the Soviet Union has threatened the west more by dying than it ever did while living'.

Istvan Meszaros has pointed out that 'for a long time in the past the people in the West who were convinced that only the socialist alternative can provide a way out of the destructive antagonisms and inhumanities of the global capital system were greatly handicapped by the mystification of the ruling ideology which could successfully misrepresent the *internal challenge* of socialism as an *external confrontation*: a "subversion" directed from abroad by a "monolithic" enemy'. The Soviet collapse has done way with this mystification and restored the validity of socialism as, what it always was and is now, an essentially *internal* challenge to the capitalist order.

This is how the western labour movement, now compelled to face its real situation the way it has not done for a long time, will return to socialism as *the* answer to its problems. It is all the more likely to do so because as Calleo has put it: 'The demise of the Soviet Union has encouraged the resumption of capitalism's old internecine character'. With the fear of socialism receding, or disappearing as an immediate threat, and with the renewed intensity of international competition, western capitalism is today franker and more cynically vicious in waging class struggle against the working people. Its 'globalising', that is, new-style colonising thrust outward in search of profits, its investment in 'good business' in the erstwhile 'socialist' countries and elsewhere abroad, coupled with domestic 'restructuring', will only spell more polarisation at home. All this will only help the working classes in the west to recognise, in a more direct and natural way, the real face of capitalism in their own countries. The end of 'Soviet socialism' has not meant the end of the essential irrationality and inhumanity, the class exploitative character or structural contradictions of capitalism. Deprived of the self-justifying alibis made possible by the deformities and backwardness of 'actually existing socialism', all this is now only more open and manifest than it has been for a long time. In its global dominance, capitalism stands naked, making it easier for the working people in the west to connect their low wages and chronic unemployment, the poverty and gross inequality in their societies, and such things as environmental degradation around them, to the nature, the systemic logic of capitalism, and move into action against it in a renewed struggle for socialism.

Initially arising as a socialist alternative to capitalism – socialism to be achieved by non-revolutionary means – social democracy early ceased to be any kind of socialist threat to the capitalist order. But consummated as what came to be known as 'the welfare state' – which really flourished during the post-war boom – it did to an extent curb the predatory logic of capitalism to give it the so-called 'human face' and make it more or less acceptable to the working classes. Essentially a compromise between capital and labour in the advanced capitalist societies, it was forced upon the capitalists by long, often bitter struggles of the workers whose demands, however, it was possible for the capitalist system to accommodate because of the unprecedented expansion of material production in these societies on a continuing capitalist or capitalist-cum-imperialist basis. Somewhat paradoxically an important factor contributing to the success of this reformist compromise was Soviet Union, especially its power and prestige at the end of the second world war; the existence of what was perceived as an alternative in the form of 'actually existing socialism' made capitalist states pay more attention to the social dimension in their policies than would otherwise have been the case. Commenting on the later collapse of the Soviet Union, Eric Hobsbawm has observed: 'It is one of the ironies of this strange century that the most lasting results of the October Revolution, whose object was the global overthrow of capitalism, was to save its antagonist both in war and in peace' – in war by defeating fascism and in peace 'by providing it with the incentive to reform itself after the second world war, and by establishing the popularity of economic planning, furnishing it with some of its procedures for its reform.' Be that as it may the important point is that the 'welfare state' – the public services, the social welfare provisions and 'the safety nets' that working class movements had struggled long and hard to achieve and that capitalism was willing and able to afford – eventually helped save capitalism from its own destructive tendencies. Social democracy did not in any way undermine or destroy capitalism. But by a limited curbing of its predatory logic, it softened the internal antagonisms and class polarisations of capitalism and thus helped in securing credibility and prolonged survival for it.

Now not only Soviet Union and its 'socialism' have disappeared, social democratism as well has been mortally weakened by the neo-liberal offensive of the recent decades. Adjustment to so-called 'globalisation' demands a dismantling of the welfare state. Globally dominant and yet in crisis, capitalism is neither willing nor able to afford the 'luxury' of a significant minimum wage, of permanent jobs, of a health service for all, of a welfare state instead of charitable institutions. The fiction of 'capitalism with a human face' must now be abandoned and the basic principle henceforth is the survival of the 'fittest'. Anything, literally anything that can conceivably be run for capitalist profit – from prisons to postal services, to old age pensions and social services – has to be privatised. Not only public enterprises, not just the means of communication and transportation, but health care and education can be and now must be subjected to the logic of the capitalist market.

Capitalism today is not only what it has always been, but is more so now without the restraints imposed by however-flawed 'socialist' states or social democracy as it came to be. In its efforts to remain 'competitive' in the global market, it is destroying the very services and institutions that have often rescued it from self-destruction. In other words, 150 odd years after the publication of *Communist Manifesto,* capitalism stands in almost as pure a form as when Marx first analysed it, it stands naked, without decoration or refinement, in all its stark and unadorned reality. Its true character and destructive long term effects are once again becoming plain for all to see – in the shape of mass unemployment and chronic job insecurity, growing inequality, social tensions and welfare dependency, and the daily impositions of its inhumanities on the 'unfortunate' millions below. As, their cherished illusions deflated, working people come face to face with 'actually existing capitalism' the way they have not done for a long time, as they perceive the intensifying problems through which the reality of their lives contradicts the pretensions of their society, they will surely no longer automatically accept what is as what must be. They will resist, and their resistance is bound to grow even if it will be sometime before it grows into a renewed struggle for socialism.

XV

The working people in fact have been already refusing to accept 'what is' as 'what must be'. As part of the growing popular resistance elsewhere in the world against the fallouts of 'globalisation' – Zapatista insurgency in Mexico and the Chavez phenomenon in Venezuela, the student and worker struggles in Indonesia, mass agrarian protests in India, landless workers upsurge in Brazil, general strikes in South Korea, Columbia and Puerto Rico, 'IMF riots' throughout much of the Third World from Zimbabwe to Mexico, and so on – the labour movement in the west, after a long period of decline, has been showing signs of new life in its struggle against the 'globalisation' ordained 'economic restructuring'. Popular protest actions have been a distinctive feature of the last decade and half in Europe, with the workers responding to the neo-liberal offensive of capitalism with petitions and electoral protests as well as mass strikes, one-day stoppages, blockades, occupation of unemployment offices, and cross-national actions against plant closures and threats to social welfare. The three central states of the European Union – France, Italy and Germany – have witnessed particularly vigorous actions, often bringing together trade unions, social movements, church leaders and prominent intellectual and political figures. There have been similar strikes and protests in other West European countries, including Belgium and Luxembourg. And far away, another advanced capitalist country, Canada, witnessed the biggest strike and the largest demonstration ever in its history in October 1996 when Toronto, the largest Canadian city as well as the industrial and financial heartland of Canada, was paralysed by a labour and community-based coalition demanding the end of government's neo-liberal policies, focusing on cutbacks against social services, education and health, and massive retrenchments in the private and public sectors. The growing polarisation in society is leading to an increasing politicisation of trade unions – most significantly and symptomatically in Germany.

Exemplifying the volatile social and political climate emerging in Europe, and suggestive of future possibilities as well, has been the French workers strike in December 1995, which paralysed Paris and precipitated the biggest demonstrations ever in the French provinces when the Chirac-Juppé right wing government tried to carry out the 'restructuring' instructions of the French industrial and financial establishment. Preceded by the mass protests of previous years, their tone set by the students' slogan, *'On prefere descendre dans la rue qu'y finir'* ('We'd rather take to the streets than end up in them') and followed by several years of continuing confrontational struggles, the three week December strike of workers in the country's rail and public transport networks against the Juppé plan for 'reform' of the social welfare system, triggered a much broader strike and social movement against the rightwing government's economic and social policies and soon grew into a generalised revolt against the overall social and economic orientation of French government and business over the previous decade and a half. Several hundreds of thousands of post-secondary and high school students, unemployed and semi-employed youth, teachers, trade unionists and social movement activists were out on the streets and even the private sector workers who did not strike, joined in through *'une greve par procuration'* ('a strike by proxy'), that is, by attending the huge demonstrations organised across the country and otherwise supporting the action of the striking workers. Here is a contemporary account of this protest movement – the 'social explosion' as it came to be called:

> The protest movement brought out the rail workers, public transport drivers and maintenance teams, nurses and hospital staff, postal workers, government office workers, central bank workers, garbage collectors, teachers, autoworkers, telephone operators, airline staff and airport maintenance teams, electric company workers, staff from some daily newspapers, print shop workers, and numerous others. It became obvious that this working class is not solely made up of 'middle-aged, blue collar white men,' as the stereotyped image of trade union membership would have one think. There were young and old workers, black workers, women workers, white and 'grey' collar workers, university and college-educated workers, and so on. There they all were in the streets of every city, town and village of France, headed up by the rail workers, chanting *'tous ensemble, tous ensemble!'* ('everyone together, everyone together!').
>
> The workers marched behind the banners of their workplaces, often with the combined insignia of all the unions, or they marched under the colourful balloons of their unions. At the marches, there was a spontaneous unity between unionized and non-unionized workers, between different trade unions, between workers from entirely different sectors of the economy. Also present were contingents from groups of the unemployed and the homeless, as well as students and small groups of organized immigrant workers.
>
> Artists were there, some on stilts, some juggling, some handing out 'guerrilla art,' lending the protests a carnival-like atmosphere. Theatre and dance companies in the working class

> Paris suburbs, in Montpellier, Lille, Marseilles, and elsewhere held assemblies to discuss the movement.

An expression of people's desperation and anger against growing unemployment and social insecurity, and the phenomenal rise in poverty, homelessness and the accompanying crime and violence in the country, 'the first revolt against globalisation' is how the daily *Le Monde* recognised this protest movement.

The rising wave of popular and working class protest has not spared even the citadel of world capitalism, the United States, where labour militancy is making a reappearance and there are visible signs of the rebirth of a combative trade union movement. The sporadic but frequent militant actions in Chrysler and General Motors, the strike at the United Parcel Service – the biggest employee action of its kind in the United States for many years and which concluded with major concessions for workers – and the successful strike of the airline pilots after the brutal suppression of air-controllers strike by the Reagan regime provide ample indications of this new trend. Equally significant, each in its own way, is the student anti-sweatshop agitation on the United States campuses, with students protesting against university licensing agreements with corporations such as Nike, Reebok, The Gap and Disney, that rely on sweatshop labour located in the Third World to produce their products, and the anti-globalisation demonstrations against the WTO and its sister institutions, the IMF and the WB. November 1999 saw a massive protest involving seven hundred organisations and upward of forty thousand people – workers, environmentalists, students, religious groups, etc. – bringing the WTO meeting in Seattle to a halt, grabbing not only the nation's but the entire world's spotlight. The 'Seattle Shock' *Business Week* called it in an editorial that warned of a popular backlash against 'our very economy system'. The 'economic restructuring' that is on has a Warren Bennis observing in the *International Herald Tribune*: '...Unless some solution is found to the dilemma facing those losing their jobs – a population segment that now includes the middle class as well as the poor – America will see public expressions of rage and fear that make the recent strikes in France look like a stroll in the park.'

It may be here noted that the governments of the advanced capitalist countries – 'liberal democracies' as they are called – have had no qualms about unleashing repression on people protesting against globalisation, using all the material and ideological means at their disposal. In other words, despite the noisy 'anti-statism' of the neo-liberal ideologues, the state is and remains active, and active in defence of the established order. We are not so much seeing an 'impotence' or 'dismantling of the state' as a change in its role and make-up, but its activism and, more importantly, the old alignment between state and business continue. The state in fact remains the capitalist state it has always been under capitalism. During the post-war boom the state, without losing any of its essential class character, had of course come to incorporate, to a greater or lesser degree, many aspects of the contemporary notions of 'social peace' and 'consensus model', as they are called. But, as noticed earlier, this was actually an exceptional period in the history of capitalism. These aspects, within society and the state, were a result of specific social and political struggles of the working people and the willingness of ruling classes to compromise in a context of strong economic growth and cold war compulsions which included Soviet Union's *civilising* influence on capitalism. But with the economic crisis of 1970s and extended downturn since then, and the retreat of the socialist threat especially after the Soviet collapse, the situation is radically altered. Capitalism, as it stands, both triumphant and unrestrained as well as in deep crisis, is neither willing nor able to afford the old ways of 'consensus' or 'social peace'. It is now 'business as usual' for capitalism and therefore for the capitalist state, with repression and ideological manipulation acquiring a new salience. In one sense, however, the state in this age of globalisation is indeed stricken with 'impotence' or 'dismantling' – a part of change in its role today. A state that acts strictly according to the rules dictated by neo-liberal ideology (or International Monetary Fund) does in fact become 'impotent' or has to be 'dismantled'. But this is only in relation to social protection and people's welfare. In relation to those who protest or challenge the existing order, the state remains quite 'potent' and strong, and fully committed to defend that order. In other words, even as it has changed to carry out its new role in globalisation, the state is now all the more openly reverting back to its 'lean and mean' role, a tool to be wielded exclusively in the interests of big business, the banks and the wealthiest layers of the population.

XVI

Clarity about the role of the state, more specifically the nation state, is central to understanding of both 'globalisation' and the struggle against 'globalisation' today. We have earlier touched upon this subject in different contexts. It is worth our while however to take another look at it, in view of the 'anti-state' hoopla of the globalisers.

The basic assumption underlying this hoopla, the key idea of neo-liberalism in recent times, against a background of the downfall of other ideologies, is variously the 'retreat', 'death' or 'impotence of the state' under contemporary global capitalism. On this view governments are regarded as powerless in relation to transnational corporations, to international financial institutions, and finally to inter-state formations in different parts of the world. The power is supposed to have passed to a transnational capitalist class united in a variety of international organisations. The more 'global' capital is, the less the state can do. Even otherwise, because the process of globalisation has initially taken place on the basis of neo-classical economics, it has presented itself in terms of reducing the role of the state in relation to both domestic economy and international markets. With 'private-property' enthroned and a 'free-market fetishism' taking over, any and every kind of state control is frowned upon as a departure from the received economic wisdom. The state is best done away with. And this is precisely what is now supposed to have happened under 'globalisation'. More specifically, the nation state is perceived to have been replaced by a 'transnational global economy'. The conventional view of 'globalisation' suggests a submergence of the nation-state by contemporary internationalisation of capitalist development, even if the process is admittedly still far from over. In any case, the internationalisation of capital and the development of the nation-state stand in inverse relation to each other so that the more internationalisation, the less nation-state. In other words, 'globalisation' involves a shift of sovereignty away from the nation-state to international agencies of capital, it is making the nation-state increasingly irrelevant. All this, however, like much else about 'globalisation', is only so much ideological mythmaking, 'globaloney' as it has been called, which has nothing to do with the reality of global capitalism and the nation-state today.

Looked at historically, the emergence of capitalism was closely tied to the rise of the nation-state and this linkage has shaped the development and expansion of capitalism throughout its history. Though its origins can be traced back to centuries past, it was only towards the end of the eighteenth century that modern capitalism finally came up, rooted in the social structures of particular western countries. This 'national capitalism', like modern nations themselves, was of course not a precondition for but a product of the development of capitalism as a world system. There is vital truth in Wallerstein's argument that 'modern states are not the primordial frameworks within which historical development has occurred,' and that 'they may be more usefully conceived as one set of social institutions within the capitalist world-economy, this latter being the framework with which, and of which, we can analyse the structures, conjunctures, and events.' Certainly, the systemic weaknesses of capitalism, its contradictions and endemic crises, are not strictly national in origin. They are global, and they are inherent in the system, rooted in capitalism's basic laws of motion. In the final analysis, they are not caused by any specific national policy, nor are they answerable to resolution by any specific national strategy. Nevertheless, modern capitalism grew up and has remained a nationally organised global system, and throughout its history, capitalists have needed and used the state to advance the interests of capital, subject of course to the influence of changes in the economic conditions and the strength of pressures from below. States have maintained order in society guaranteeing the continued existence and expansion of capitalism. State's role has been central to capital's monopolistic growth at home and imperialist expansion abroad. As capitalism has developed across the world, the role of the state has only increased (which incidentally creates real empirical difficulties for the currently fashionable idea that state regulation or control is somehow non- or even anti-capitalist). The state has throughout accommodated and accelerated the process of global integration and, in war or peace, served as an important adjustment mechanism of global capitalism. It is no different with the current phase of capitalist globalisation.

That capitalism has now again become directly, and more universally, global does not put an end to national societies or states. To say that capitalism is now universal as never before is not to say that all, or even most capital is transnational. We still have national economies, national states, nationally based capital, even nationally based transnationals. The production still takes place in largely nationally based companies and the capitalists can still successfully invoke 'national interests' to justify measures dictated by their selfish class interests. As global economic changes combined with domestic challenges have compelled capitalists to seek freedom from the class compromises of the immediate post-war period, to be able to chart their new course, it is through the state that they have carried out their class agenda which has included the removal of fetters on international trade and investment, smashing domestic unions and lowering wages, rolling back environmental regulation, and dismantling welfare-state protections. The state remains as important as ever for the capitalist system, domesticating the system-threatening aspects of neo-liberal policies and facilitating their profit-enhancing aspects in all their fury. It is the direct interventions by the US government, for example, that have underpinned the national economy in recent decades. Despite all the talk about the 'death' of the state, it is state institutions, ranging from national ones like the US Treasury and the Federal Reserve to international ones like the World Bank and the IMF that have managed to prevent a replay of the 1920s collapse, despite the recurrent financial crises of recent decades. They have kept the Third World crisis or 'melodrama' from metasizing into a global implosion. Instead they have used the crisis to great advantage in forcing a variety of 'reforms' on the debtor countries for the benefit of the creditors in the advanced capitalist world. The neo-colonial thrust of 'globalisation' is impossible to conceive without the support given to national capitals of advanced capitalist countries by their own nation-states.

It has been pointed out that 'globalisation' with all its neo-liberal policies, has almost nowhere led to a reduction in the size of the government apparatus or state expenditure. Indeed so powerful are the pressures in advanced capitalism to maintain a high profile for the state that in the 1980s and 1990s – the decades of supposed privatisation and globalisation – average state expenditure as a percentage of output actually rose in leading West-European countries. It is not only that while some government services have shrunk, others have grown – the most obvious here is the case of cuts in spending on social needs being accompanied by increases in spending on the repressive apparatus of the state – it is far more because of the sheer range of functions that the state is now called on to perform in this 'new epoch' of globalisation. Even a cursory look will reveal that the importance of state action in enabling the global capitalist system to function has, if anything, increased, not reduced as that system has spread internationally as never before.

'Globalisation' theory postulates decline of the nation state and national capitalist classes, the transfer of sovereignty from the state to the organs of some kind of unified transnational capital. However nothing like this has happened and seems unlikely to ever happen. Instead the transnationalisation of capital has been throughout accompanied by the proliferation of modern capital's original political form, the nation state, and this state is more universal today than ever before. Again, as globaloney has it there is an inverse relation between the internationalisation of the economy and the power of the state: the more globalisation, the smaller the role of the state. Instead 'globalisation' *presupposes* the state and while state may have lost some of its traditional functions, it has gained many more new ones, especially as the main conduit through which national (or indeed multinational) capital is inserted into the global market. Far from being rendered irrelevant, state is today the main agent of 'globalisation', its penetration of the capitalist logic deeper into the societies of advanced capitalism and spatially throughout the world.

State plays a central role as capital's channel into the global market, as the creator of the right environment for capital's accumulation, and as capital's main line of defence against internal disorder. Globalisation is so much a phenomenon of national economies and national states that it is impossible to make sense of it without taking account of competition among national economies, and national states carrying out policies to promote international 'competitiveness'. This quest for competitiveness demands a state that will keep social costs to a minimum, while keeping in check the social conflict and disorder generated by the policies to ensure this. Each state is the main agent forcing on its citizens the austerities and hardships needed to maintain or restore profitability to domestic capital. State promotes the free movement of capital while confining labour within national boundaries and subjecting it to necessary disciplines in the interests of capital. In addition to the usual policing and repression of labour and protesting social movements, the state continues to establish the essential infrastructural and juridical conditions relating to markets, private property, and contract within its territorial domain. It is mainly through the instrumentality of the state that the necessary policy choices for globalisation are made and executed and each state, again, is the main instrument for containing the conflicts engendered by these policies. A 'hands off government' is alright as a back up ideology when social justice is at stake. But state is all over the place when protection or rescue of capitalist interets is involved.

As the main agent of globalisation, states are becoming more and more attuned to accommodating and fostering capital accumulation on a world scale. They do so by creating and sustaining global markets. It is they who are making the necessary changes in the rules governing capital movements, investment, currency exchange, trade and migration flows that permit a new stage of global accumulation to come about. It is through inter-state relations, as these are formalised in international agreements, treaties, and the rules governing international agencies, that the necessary international juridical and infrastructural conditions for global capital accumulation are established and maintained. The importance attached by the international business interests to the WTO, tariff agreements, the governmental enforcement of contractual rights and the protection of intellectual property interests attest to the continuing, and growing, importance of the state, which in effect means the nation state. Even as the nation state protects and promotes capitalist interests at home, it provides every possible material, diplomatic and military support for the country's capitalists as they go gallivanting through international markets. One may add that even when policies deliberately designed to forfeit national sovereignty for the sake of globalisation are made, they are the result of policy choices made by the national state itself.

The powers of the nation state at the centre have not been in any way weakened by the spiralling internationalisation of finance, or the growing importance of multinational institutions. As sponsors of globalisation, providing ever greater opportunities for foreign investment and markets for the multinationals, especially in the decolonised periphery and semi-periphery of global capitalism, international agencies of capital like the IMF and the World Bank have indeed acquired enormous influence. But they cannot pursue their policies except through the agency of the state. They are above all agents of specific national capitals and derive whatever powers of enforcement they have from nation-states, both the imperial states that command them and the subordinate states that carry out their orders. Commenting on the policy making process of multinational institutions like the IMF, WB and WTO, William K. Tabb has written: 'before any of these organisations meet, the United States makes proposals which are discussed within the QUAD – a group composed of the United States, the European Union (EU), Japan, and Canada – which convenes separately, and, in secrecy, makes key decisions without the participation of the other members of the world community. The QUAD is not recognized in any of their charters, but it acts as an executive committee that determines their direction. In Seattle, the vast majority of WTO members waited outside the exclusive Green Room meetings, as they were called, for the QUAD to reach decisions that would then be discussed by the body. It was clear to the other delegates that they were essentially excluded from real decision-making.' That is how the multinational institutions that have emerged or grown functionally important with 'globalisation', do not so much bypass or displace the nation state as restructure and give it new roles – and in case of major capitalist powers, provide them with new instruments and power to pursue the interests of their respective national capitals. That these major powers do not always have their way, as they want it, in these institutions does not affect the point being made.

'Globalisation', the on-going universalisation of capitalism, as we have noted, is taking place in a world of nation-states. In a way, the whole point of 'globalisation' is competition as much between individual multinationals or transnationals, as between whole national economies. Behind every multinational or transnational is a national base, which depends on its local state to sustain its viability and other states to give it access to other markets and other labour forces. As a consequence, the nation-state has acquired new functions as an instrument of competition in the global market. This apart, today transnational capital may be more effective than was the old-style military imperialism in penetrating every corner of the world, but this penetration is still taking place in a world of developed and less developed capitalist countries, and is often accomplished through the medium of local capitals as well as the national states of the latter which are required to maintain the conditions of economic stability and labour discipline that are the essential conditions of profitable investment. The less developed states serve as transmission belts for other, more powerful capitalist states. This is also a situation in which every new opportunity for transnational cooperation between major national capitals is matched by opportunities for new kinds of inter-imperilaist rivalry – in which the nation state is again the principal agent. The logic of this rivalry does not rule out state-supported military adventures. Beyond it all, there is the more likely use of the military power of a single nation-state, the last remaining 'superpower', to sustain 'the sovereignty of the market'. In other words, the effort, peaceful or otherwise, to establish sovereignty over global markets, no less than the sovereignty over specific colonial countries in the past, is today a project pursued by state powers, and by one state above all.

The state remains central to the existence and functioning of global capitalism. It is impossible to think of today's globalisation without the complex of national policies implemented by national states. Pointing out that globalisation implies, among other things, those ruthless state actions we associate with neo-liberalism, that is, policies designed to enhance 'competitiveness' and 'flexibility', not just for individual firms but for whole national economies in the global market, policies which are adopted not just because capital *wants* them but because it *needs* them to generate maximum profitability in an integrated and competitive global economy, Ellen M. Wood has written:

> Contrary to much conventional wisdom today, 'globalisation' has made the state not less but more important to capital. Capital needs the state to maintain the conditions of accumulation and 'competitiveness' in various ways, including direct subsidies at tax-payers' expense; to preserve labor discipline and social order in the face of austerity and 'flexibility'; to enhance the mobility of capital while blocking the mobility of labour; to administer huge rescue operations for capitalist economies in crisis... operations often organized by international agencies but always paid for by national taxes and enforced by national governments. Even the imperialism of the major capitalist states requires the collaboration of subordinate states to act as transmission belts and agents of enforcement. 'Neoliberalism' is not just a withdrawal of the state from social provision. It is a set of active policies, a new form of state intervention designed to enhance capitalist profitability in an integrated global market.

It is worth noticing that the globalisers are themselves, in different contexts, coming to recognise the important role of the state in globalisation. The fragility of the global financial system because of the speculation and extensive risk-taking that have accompanied financial transnationalisation, has inevitably led to calls for a *more* active, interventionist state to protect the banks and the money markets. In the face of recurring financial crises, globalising capitalists have been retreating to national bunkers and their ideologues discovering the virtues of capital controls. The growing contradictions of globalisation have compelled even the World Bank to argue in one of its recent reports that 'development without an effective state is impossible.' In an explicit departure from its former thesis about 'overloaded governments' and advocacy of a 'minimalist state', the World Bank, with its advocacy of 'safety nets', 'good governance' etc., now sees the state as a necessary 'partner, catalyst, facilitator' of globalisation. The Bank now insists on the importance of 'an effective state', which 'harnessing the energy of private business and individuals...acts as their partner and catalyst, instead of restricting their partnership.'

Of course, we know all too well what Bank's 'effective state' or 'partnership' means. The World Bank is primarily concerned with the development of those state capacities which facilitate more effective integration into globalisation. 'Good governance' it advocates is obviously important for this purpose. Its advocacy of state action for social protection or 'safety nets' – well described as 'social democratisation' of globalisation – is to secure both stability in society and legitimacy for state as the agent of globalisation. But the nature of World Bank's concerns does not take anything away from the substantive point being made, namely, the World Bank's recognition that 'the state' is not an outsider to globalisation but an integral part of it. The state involved is, of course, the nation-state and a state acting in the interests of the dominant classes. Globalisation's neo-liberal state remains a capitalist class state.

There is an aspect to the centrality of the state in the globalisation process which needs to be specifically noted. Capitalist globalisation and therefore its oppressions are everywhere being experienced by people locally, and are everywhere mediated by their national states. It is no accident that people's protests and demonstrations that we have been seeing in so many countries across the world are directed against the actions of their respective states in pursuit of 'globalisation'. This draws our attention to the important question of state and the struggle against globalisation. Immediately, I would like to make only two very brief points in this regard.

As a historically specific phase of capitalist expansion, globalisation is capitalist exploitation of human beings and natural resources, aided and abetted by a direct collaboration between the state and capital. With its policies of 'flexibility', 'competitiveness' and 'globalisation', state has been active in restructuring the economy and worldwide promotion of the interest of capitalists to the detriment of everyone else. In many ways, the collusion or symbiosis between capital and state is today closer and more apparent than ever. The state is seen to be more visibly implicated in class exploitation than it has been for a long time. It is not surprising, therefore, that it is the actions of the state that have driven people into the streets, in opposition to the policies of the 'globalising' state. This not only suggests the centrality of state in the struggle against globalisation but also the key task facing this struggle today: people's opposition, their experience of globalisation in general, needs to be critically interpreted and theorised, and people's consciousness deepened, to recover state as *the* target of struggle against globalisation. This is important because the question of state power, of people's power in the state, their 'political supremacy' in society, is central to the success of struggle against globalisation.

There is good reason for me to stress this point. It is the ideological need of capitalism today to disguise and mystify the increasingly direct and obvious collusion between capital and state. The concept of globalisation well serves this need. Its 'anti-state' hoopla, the argument that the integration of world capitalism, the existence of transnational corporations etc., somehow makes the nation-state irrelevant, that the state has ceased to be a major player in the economy as a result of globalisation, not only directly denies or obscures this collusion, but has many other allied implications. The most important implication is that the question of state power, of people's power in the state, is no longer relevant, least of all central to any alternative, presumably, radical politics. And, aided of course by the recent collapse of socialist-communist politics and the general disorientation on the Left, 'globalisation's' ideological obfuscation has not been entirely unsuccessful: state as the classic target for political struggle against capitalism has virtually disappeared from the scene, giving way to all kinds of fragmented politics – of social movements, 'civil society', voluntary organisations or NGOs, identities, etc. etc. The positive role or significance of much of this politics is not to be denied but no struggle for people's interest, including struggle against globalisation, can by-pass the struggle for political power and state as *the* terrain and target of this struggle and still hope to be effective or successful.

The state in advanced capitalist countries is today the principal agent of globalisation. By the same token, state alone can be the effective means of blocking globalisation. At the other end, the imperialist states cannot just penetrate all borders without working through other local states which are often in direct and deliberate collusion with imperial powers and transnational corporations. In both cases, it is the state which has to be the focus or target in the struggle against globalisation. This in effect means that the struggle against globalisation has to be a struggle for people's power in the state, for political power in the right hands, a truly *democratic* political power. It means a state which does not simply 'intervene' in the capitalist economy or provide a 'safety net' against the ravages of capitalism, or practice some other kind of paternalism, but is willing and capable of seeking an alternative to capitalism, of subjecting the economy – above all its allocation of resources and disposition of economic surpluses – to people's needs in accordance with a social logic different from the logic of capitalist competition and profitability, of capital accumulation and market imperatives. This logic today can only be the logic of socialism as visualised by classical Marxism.

The second point – already made in another context but important enough to be reiterated – is that since global capitalism is nationally organised and immediately dependent on national states, national economies and national states remain the primary terrain of anti-capitalist organisation and struggle. Of course an international perspective, working people's solidarity across national frontiers, remains vital to any socialist movement. And today there exists a focus for such solidarity as has, perhaps, never before existed in the history of capitalism. The universalisation of capitalism has not brought about the cessation but instead the universalisation of struggle against capitalism. When, with globalisation, just about every state is following the same destructive logic, domestic struggles against that common logic can be the basis – in fact the strongest possible basis – of a new internationalism. But looking for that internationalism must not be an excuse for giving up on local national struggles. The main arenas of struggle against global capitalism still remain local and national. 'Workers of all countries unite' remains the motto but this 'unity' obviously begins at home. There is a growing space for common transnational struggles, but the established order has still to be primarily fought on our own home pitch. As the *Manifesto* put it a long time ago: 'the proletariat of each country must, of course, first of all settle matters with its own bourgeoisie.'

Socialism, like capitalism, tends to be universal and internationalism is indeed the only genuine reply to globalisation. But this internationalism will come up mediated by local and national struggles. In fact, they will be the main channel into the ultimately necessary international struggles. 'The final confrontation,' it has been metaphorically suggested, 'will take place throughout the planet, from Paris to Peking and from Seoul to Seattle.' But this 'confrontation' will grow on the basis of mutual support among various local and national movements in their respective struggles against their own domestic capitalists and states.

The nation state is indeed the concrete terrain on which the struggle for the radical transformation of society must begin and may have to be carried forward. It may be added that to argue that a nation state – and this includes states of the size and resources of Britain, France or Italy, or for that matter, India,

China or Russia – cannot provide the ground on which the radical transformation of society can be attempted is to rule out such a transition for the forthcoming historical period. It is to abdicate the struggle for socialism in our time.

XVII

As elsewhere in the world, after an initial period of confusion, the last decade and a half has seen a spate of protests and demonstrations against globalisation in the advanced capitalist world as well. But however significant in their mass support – even in the US, majority of Americans (52 per cent in the Hariss Poll) were reported to be sympathetic to the concerns of the demonstrators at Seattle – lacking a programme which could provide a genuine alternative to the agenda of transnational corporations and capitalist governments, they have not been able to mount an effective challenge to globalisation. The biggest obstacle here is the ideological hegemony of capitalism, its 'theory of globalisation', so that the opposition, insofar as it takes an articulated form, is directed at corporate globalisation rather than global capitalism. The effort is to seek a modification or reversal of neo-liberal policies or transformation of particular institutional arrangements, make corporations and the key international economic institutions – the IMF, the WB, the WTO – more democratic and responsive to human rights. There is little recognition that it is capitalism – not the increasingly global character of modern economy or society but *capitalist* globalisation, that is, the subordination of humanity to the profit interests of a few hundred giant transnational corporations – which is the real enemy. Most importantly, the underlying structure of power remains unquestioned, the question of *political* struggle against globalisation at the level of the nation-state remains unraised itself.

Particularly significant in the growing opposition to globalisation is the rebirth, after years of fatalistic resignation, of a combative trade union movement in the West, and Europe has witnessed some of the most powerful protest actions against neo-liberalism. But while the workers have fought and even won individual battles in defence of their rights and forced governments to abandon crucial planks of their neo-liberal policies, lacking larger objectives, they have been unable to launch a generalised counter-offensive against globalisation. Particular struggles have not jelled into nation-wide movements with a broader alternative programme which could turn popular revulsion into a successful challenge to globalisation. There is little continent-wide coordination and not even the barest minimum of working class internationalism.

Crucially important questions of politics and political struggle, of working class power in the state have, as elsewhere , remained unraised. Rightwing regimes giving way to social democrats in power in several countries across the European Union has reflected people's desire for a change, a rejection of the future being offered by the ruling classes. But there has been no turn to effective political struggle by people for a future of their own. Only alternating rightwing regimes have followed. The working class has been making its presence felt more as a 'class in itself' and not as a 'class for itself.' A major shortcoming or source of failing in the situation as a whole has been the continuing crisis of reformism afflicting the leadership on the left. Nowhere have the forces of the left been prepared for the changing conjunctures marked simultaneously by popular discontent and anger over the neo-liberal policies of the state and the exhaustion and disarray of the right as it seeks to pursue these policies. Demoralised and in disarray themselves, having long deserted any kind of radical or revolutionary perspective, the socialist and communist parties have simply failed to provide the requisite *political* leadership to the popular protest movements against globalisation. Instead they have generally preferred to insist on the social (as opposed to political) nature of these movements.

These shortcomings or inadequacies however do not diminish the historic importance of the emergent working class actions and popular protest movements, reflecting as they do the growing conflict between underlying populations (mostly but by no means exclusively working people) on the one side and ruling class (that is, capitalist) governments on the other. For the most part capital has had its way in the early phase of the post-Cold War period. Since then in a stinging rebuttal to the pseudo-Hegelian pronouncements about the end of history, people all over the West, as elsewhere, are fighting back. The ideological distraction of ruling class governments' so-called 'war on terrorism' notwithstanding, millions of people are entering the arena of struggle in defence of their rights against globalisation. The liberal ideological hegemony is beginning to break up and there is an audience again for anti-capitalist thinking. Not that such thinking was entirely absent previously. But many more are now extending their criticism of corporate globalisation to a critique of global capitalism itself. After twenty odd years of capitalist ideological domination, every mass act of resistance, refusal or rejection is important as suggestive of other, radical possibilities. As long as the idea that 'there is no alternative' was accepted, explicitly or implicitly, the search for one was unthinkable. Now, the search for a radically different society can at least begin. Having rejected *their* future, the future proposed by the rulers, the people can now begin the search for a future of their own. 'Another world is possible' is in the air, even if it remains undefined in terms of capitalism or socialism. Marx is back and it will not be long before people learn to so define things. At a time when most of the traditional left, particularly that in social-democratic and Communist Party circles, is in full retreat (sometimes outrightly casting their lot with neo-liberalism), the emergence of mass movements of protest against globalisation is surely an important first step in the necessarily long road of renewal of struggle against capitalism.

Particularly important for any renewed struggle against capitalism in the advanced capitalist countries remains the role of the working class. It has been for long fashionable to question or deny the revolutionary potential of the working class in these countries. In recent years there has even been much ideological 'theorising' about how the working class in the industrialised countries has simply ceased to be. One important message from the recent protest movements, especially in Europe, is that the working class not only exists but a good many workers are also recognising that they are willy-nilly trapped in a class struggle and are once again blaming the economic system for their situation. Especially significant is the message from France. Events of November-December 1995 have signalled not only the existence of a classical working class – defined as those who must sell their labour power to survive – but also the fact that for the first time this working class occupies a clear majority position in French society. The protest movement underlined the basic unity and mass character of labour in the country and reinforced its identity and its determination, as a class, to fight back the neo-liberal offensive of the capitalist state. For the past several years political pundits and sociologists have been announcing that conflict had given way to consensus and the classes had dissolved in the grey mass of untrammelled individualism. The working class action and the consequent popular uprising in France has set the record right: class struggle continues and collective action is not a thing of the past.

Class struggle and collective action against globalisation are in fact going to be one of the defining characteristics of the historical period which is now opening in the West. The dynamics of neo-liberalism have a polarising logic which has underlain much of the mass protest of recent years: poverty and struggle for livelihood at one pole of society, wealth and ostentatious living at the other. It may be sometime before this polarisation is better recognised as a normal phenomenon of capitalism in the age of globalisation, but class relations are already apparent and more frankly on view than in the last fifteen or twenty years, bringing the question of class and class struggle centre-stage in the awareness of the people. As even the *Economist* has recently noted: 'Many commentators think that class is dying, but ordinary people are not convinced. In fact class antagonisms may even be worsening – the proportion of voters believing there is a "class struggle" in Britain rose from around 60% in the early 1960s to 81% in the mid-1990s, according to Gallup...'. In a recent opinion poll in France more than 90 per cent of respondents replied that they considered the nation to be a highly polarised class society. The increasing class polarisation is no less evident in Germany. In an opinion poll published towards the end of 1997 by the *Frankfurter Allgemeine*

Zeitung, a newspaper scarcely to be accused of sympathizing with Marxism, the response to the question, do they believe that 'today, the class struggle is outmoded, (that) employers and employees ought to relate to each other as partners,' or rather do they hold that 'it is right to speak of the class struggle, (that) basically, employers and employees have totally incompatible interests?', showed that while in 1980 some 58 per cent of West-German citizens chose the former answer against 25 per cent for the latter, by 1997 the balance had been reversed – some 41 per cent still considering the class struggle to be outmoded, but 44 per cent thinking it to be on the agenda. In the former GDR – that is, among the very people who overturned the Berlin Wall – the majority is strikingly clearer: 58 per cent of adherents to class struggle against 26 per cent. Recent surveys show rising class awareness even in the United States where working class self-identification has historically been very low. A *New York Times* poll in 1996 found that 55 per cent of Americans now defined themselves as working class, while only 36 per cent defined themselves as middle class, a major reversal of the traditional American pattern; and no less than 60 per cent of those who had experienced a layoff in their family thought that 'the government should step in to do something' and attributed 'a lot of the blame for the loss of jobs on the economic system in this country'. In recent years, more than one economist has noticed the emerging reality of sharper class division in the United States. Paul Krugman has pointed to the rapid 'disappearance of the middle class' in America. Michael Zweig has argued that the much touted notion of America as a 'middle class society' is a myth. All this surely has its implications for the anti-capitalist struggles of the future.

XVIII

The question of class and class struggle and therefore of alternative to capitalism will increasingly come to the fore because, as a most important aspect of the polarising logic of neo-liberalism, the capital-labour compromise or 'partnership' of recent past is no longer viable. As we have noticed in other contexts, the immediate post-war decades witnessed unprecedent capitalist growth and as profits were high a portion could be passed down making it a period of rapid rise in working class living standards, and big changes in the pattern of popular consumption. It was not that this in any way altered the exploitative class relations of the capitalist system. Also, despite all theoretical obfuscation over it, the deciding issue for socialists has always been the *structural subordination of labour to capital* and not the relatively higher standard of living of working people which can easily disappear in the midst of a major crisis and escalating unemployment, the sort we are experiencing today. And the French rising of May 1968 and the Italian Hot Autumn the year after were even during this period a reminder of the essential limits of a social welfarist capitalism. Still, in the immediate historical context, the social and material progress during this period was noticeably undeniable. It could be argued that it is possible to improve your fate within existing society. But this is no longer possible. In Istvan Meszaros' words: 'When Marx was saying in the *Communist Manifesto* that the working class only has chains to lose, that is certainly not true of the working class of the G7 countries today or even yesterday. They have been very successful in improving their standard of living throughout this historical period.... What happened in the last decade or decade and a half was the coming to an end of this process because capital can no longer afford to grant benefits and significant gains to the working classes. Capital never gave anything away. If it was in tune with its own internal logic of expansion, self-expansion, then those gains could be provided. In fact they became dynamic factors in this self-expansionary process. That is not the case now.' In the midst of a major crisis since the 1970s, the 'long decline' as it has been called, capitalism even in its most developed forms can no longer deliver both profit or 'growth' and improving conditions of labour and life. Capitalists themselves – in their increasingly desperate demands for 'flexibility' – are admitting and arguing that the imperatives of the capitalist market do not allow them to survive and prosper without depressing the conditions of workers. The very future of capitalism, it seems, has come to depend on lowering the standard of living and work of the working classes. This has already sharpened the class conflicts and presages still sharper class conflicts in future.

This sharpening is also presaged by the current disintegration of Social Democracy whose reformist management of capitalist society, via the welfare state, has been a major factor in softening the class contradictions and ensuring the continued survival of capitalism. The way in which capitalism is tackling its current structural crisis – with growing unemployment and open attack on the welfare state – the message to social democracy has been plain: It is no longer possible to squeeze significant concessions out of capital. There is to be no more fooling with 'capitalism with a human face.' There is now no room for reformist management. And social democracy has succumbed to land itself in what can only be described as its terminal crisis. The collapse of social democracy not only means a renewed sharpening of the class contradictions of capitalism but, somewhat paradoxically, also foregrounds the question of socialism as the only viable alternative to capitalism.

Abandoning the original socialist aspirations of the movement, social democracy had long ago turned into reformist managers of capitalist society. But decades of accommodation to the demands of capitalism taking its toll, it found itself clueless and in complete ideological and programmatic disarray in the face of the recent, neo-liberal and globalising offensive of capitalism. It is significant that at the very moment when the right, headed by Reagan and Thatcher embarked on their naked class war against the working class, social democrats, along with much of the communist left, dropped any reference to class or class struggle. And now when the right-wing ideologues of capitalism are themselves preaching its limitations, they have been busy finding new reasons for faith in its adaptability. Marx had laid bare the ruthless social logic of the capitalist market disguised by the classical political economy. It is a measure of the ideological disorientation of European socialism today that while this logic is now being nakedly revealed in the financial pages of the bourgeois press and by economists of 'flexibility', these socialists, and even some Marxists among them, have been converted to belief in the 'social market', a capitalist market with a human face!

Social democrats in Europe, redesigned socialist parties and communists reformed into social democrats, have today gone down the 'free' market road of neo-liberal globalisation. *The Economist* has gleefully noted how the British Labour Party has discovered 'social-Thatcherism' – 'Blatcherism' others have called it – and Italy's former Communists, the PDS, 'have found free-market economics.' *The Times*, on its part, has found Blair the man 'to blend' Thatcherism and social democracy, and gone on to back the Labour Party for election for the first time in the newspaper's history. With the social democratic left joining the right in adopting neo-liberal globalisation programmes – the abandonment of full employment and reduction of social security, and acceptance of the universality of neo-liberal doctrines of economic growth – the traditional contrast between Left and Right has virtually disappeared. The terms in the social democratic vocabulary – 'progressive competitiveness', 'modernisation', 'neo-liberalism with a human face,' etc. – amount to little more than keeping up with capitalist globalisation. The 'buzz word', of course, is *The Third Way*. Once upon a time, 'social democracy' itself was claimed to be a 'third way' between communism and capitalism. Now that it has finally ceased, rather failed to be one, it has begun to speak of a new 'third way'. Defined less by what it is than by what it is not, it only reveals how much social democracy has moved in the direction of accommodating capitalism. There is vague talk about finding a middle course, or 'way', between 'market capitalism' (as if there is any other kind) and old style socialism (that is, old-style social democracy), based on a 'free market economy' but with a dose of social justice. But in practice there is no real departure from the first way. What social democrats are now being asked is not to be reformist managers of capitalist society, not even to manage that society as it is without reforms, but to manage it in the modern capitalist way and do so as 'social democrats' for this still has its usefulness for capitalism. And whenever and wherever social democrats have come to power, they have duly obliged. The 'Third Way' is the best ideological shield for neo-liberalism.

Pointing out that European social democracy, when in power, 'has responded to continent-wide slow growth and high unemployment by across-the-board moves towards an American model – accelerating deregulation and privatisation not only of industries but also social services, often well beyond the limits of previous conservative regimes,' Perry Anderson has written:

> Ideologically, the neo-liberal consensus has found a new point of stabilisation in the 'Third Way' of the Clinton-Blair regimes. The winning formula to seal the victory of the market is not to attack, but to preserve, the placebo of a compassionate pubic authority, extolling the compatibility of competition with solidarity. The hard core of government policies remains further pursuit of the Reagan-Thatcher legacy, on occasion with measures their predecessors did not dare enact: welfare reform in the US, student fees in the UK. But it is now carefully surrounded with subsidiary concessions and soter rhetoric. The effect of this combination, currently being diffused throughout Europe, is to suppress the conflictual potential of the pioneering regimes of the radical right, and kill off opposition to neo-liberal hegemony more completely. One might say that, by definition, TINA only acquires full force once an alternative regime demonstrates that there are truly no alternative policies. For the quietus to European social-democracy or the memory of the New Deal to be consummated, governments of the Centre-Left were indispensable. In this sense, adapting Lenin's maxim that 'the democratic republic is the ideal political shell of capitalism', we could say that the Third Way is the best ideological shell of neo-liberalism today. It is scarcely an accident that the most ambitious and intransigent theorisation of ultra-capitalism as a global order, Thomas Friedman's *The Lexus and the Olive-Tree,* should at the same time be a brazen paean to US world hegemony, and an unconditional advocacy of Clintonism, under the slogan 'one dare not be a globalizer today without being a social democrat.'

Social democrats turned globalisers is quite a tragic denouement of social democracy's long slide away from socialism, and seemingly a loss to the cause of socialism. But, may be somewhat paradoxically as mentioned earlier, this denouement can have an exactly opposite consequence. For the real casualty here is not the socialist project but the social democratic one. It represents the ultimate failure or exhaustion of social reformism and amelioration within the existing society. It means that globalisation is polarising the options and eliminating much of the apparently easier middle ground between just giving in to the harshest forms of capitalism and confronting it head on. The vacation of this middle ground implies that the possibility a truly anti-capitalist, that is socialist option is growing, not diminishing. The ultimate repositioning of social democracy in the camp of globalisers leaves open acres of space for the left to forge a political project in opposition to capitalism. The mass actions against neo-liberalism and globalisation that we have noticed above may well be the beginnings of a renewed struggle for socialism in the advanced capitalist countries of the world.

XIX

There are reasons enough to be hopeful about the renewal of struggle for socialism in the advanced capitalist countries. Real opportunities exist for a radical response to the challenges of globalisation, for anti-capitalist thinking and action, for the left to persuade people once again that society, and therefore life, can be changed by collective political action. Of course, in the final analysis it is how people seize these opportunities and how they struggle that will decide the future of socialism in the west, as elsewhere in the world. In the meantime, however, we cannot and must not discount possibilities of another kind. Here it is not a question of the emerging struggles against globalisation failing to overcome the shortcomings or inadequacies that we have noticed above, or that popular awareness and protests remain channelled into limited, even misguided, forms of organisation and action (only defensive tactics, single issue movements, identity politics, etc.). What I have in mind are possibilities of a different, dangerous kind.

Whileneo-liberalism has produced a risis of its own, increasing the strains along the fault lines of class and creating new forms of insecurities and vulnerabilities all around, the demise of historical communism and the exhaustion of social democracy, the defection of traditional working class parties from socialist class politics, has left the society with a political void. And nature, as we know, abhors the void. Therefore if the left does not come forward with an effective alternative to neo-liberalism, the void is likely to be filled with other, reactionary alternatives. If the left does not provide rational solutions to the crisis, the extreme right may well provide irrational ones. The forces of unreason will exploit the rising disillusionment and discontent for their own purposes. In fact they are already doing so. With the social-democratic left mirroring the free-market right, the neo-fascist right has grown considerably in Europe during the 1990s. Populations disoriented by social and economic 'landslides' are known to be exceptionally vulnerable to the politics of hate. Xenophobia, racism and religious fanaticism feed on social disappointment and despair. And regressive ultra-nationalist or racist utopias evoked by the fascists have invariably gone hand in hand with political authoritarianism. This is already happening, and not in advanced capitalist countries alone.

This is the other, dangerous future for the advanced capitalist countries that cannot and must not be discounted, if the left fails to mount a successful challenge to capitalism's globalisation and offer an alternative of its own. Marx had, even as he hailed the creative achievements of capitalism, seen this future implicit in the destructive potential of capitalism surviving beyond its historical time. Rosa Luxemburg had well summed it up with the poser: 'socialism or barbarism'. This can well be visualised as a choice confronting the West today.

This, needless to add, makes the struggle for socialism all the more urgent and relevant.

XX

Urgent and relevant, the struggle for socialism in the west has also become more possible today than it has been or a long time. Of course one must not be sanguine about the difficulties that lie ahead of this struggle. But the important fact remains that, as in many ways we have seen to be the case with the Soviet collapse, globalisation is creating new economic and political conditions in the west which make anti-capitalist struggle not less but more possible and potentially effective. I have argued this point earlier. But the argument bears being recapitulated for, as against the recognition of the revolutionary potential of the growing resistance to globalisation in the third world, there is a tendency to exclude the first world from the debate on the prospects for socialism in the years to come.

Central to the argument, again, is capitalism in its present stage of development, when its *in-built historical tendency* towards over-accumulation, stagnation, and increasing destruction of its own social and material conditions of existence has culminated in a *structural* crisis which gives every sign of being irreversible, when as 'globally saturated monopoly capitalism', it does not have much of a creative or productive future left for it, when its renewed global domination also marks the end of its long period of ascendancy as a market-based mode of production. As pointed out by Marx, there is always a day of reckoning in capitalist market and the latest came in the 1970s when the world economy began a downturn that has worsened through every recession since. The gap between business cycles is getting smaller, barely does recovery begin, the growth falters. In sharp contrast with the preceding post-war period, we are now into the fourth decade of relative stagnation – slow growth, declining wages, persistent unemployment. We do not much hear the word 'depression' – it is not entirely missing either and the capitalist state is always there to bale out capitalism in trouble – but, except for what is still left of the welfare state, the economic stagnation of the last quarter century looks little different from that of the 1930s. The *structural* nature of the current crisis has greatly reduced capitalism's margin of manoeuvre in dealing with its inherently self-destructive contradictions.

Victory in the cold war and renewed global domination have not in any way resolved the basic structural contradictions of capitalism. A new crisis of overproduction or excess capacity is driving down prices, wages, and eventually profits in the market place. The universalisation of capitalism means more capitalist economies producing for the same world market and therefore ruthless global competition. The major capitalist economies coming to depend on export to almost suicidal degrees, creates its own vulnerabilities for the system as a whole. To make themselves 'competitive' capitalists restrict the purchasing power of the very consumers they are competing to reach. And purchasing power in the market is crucial for the profitability of capital. Apropos this contradiction, it is important to note that capitalism no longer seems able to sustain maximum profitability by means of commensurate economic growth and production of real use values for the consumers. For such profitability, it is now relying less and less on absolute growth or increased production of use-values and more and more on simply *redistributing* wealth in favour of the rich and on increasing inequalities, within and between national economies, with the help of the neo-liberal state. In advanced capitalist countries, the most visible sign of this redistribution is the decline of the welfare state. On a global scale, as part of this shift in capitalism's search for quick and maximum profitability, we have the spectacle of phoney wealth being shuffled around at heightening speed in stock-market booms completely detached from material reality.

The threat of chronic unemployment was only latent in the capitalist mode of production for long centuries of its historical development. The 'reserve army' of labour was in fact viewed as a necessary and welcome element in the dynamics of capitalist expansion and profitable capital accumulation. So long as the contradictions and inner antagonisms of the system could be managed through what Istvan Meszaros has called *'expansionary displacement'*, the periodically worsening levels of unemployment could be considered strictly temporary, to be left behind in due course. But the ability of capitalism to absorb today's growing reserve army of labour is, to say the least, open to question and the old pattern, the long-standing balance that has up to now repeatedly saved capitalism from itself – the balance in which the danger of social unrest and disorder had been met not only by direct coercion but also by social provision – has been upset by neo-liberalism, exposing capitalism to the actual threat of chronic unemployment and class struggle it is bound to give rise to.

Capitalism used to extricate itself from its recurring crisis mainly by moving outward, by imperialist expansion. Now that capitalism has become virtually universal, such escape routes are less available. Capitalism no longer has the same scope for external expansion which used to save it from its internal contradictions. This leaves capitalism subject to these contradictions in historically unprecedented ways. The new forms of imperialism are of course there – financial control, manipulation of markets, debt, and so on. But, as against the old forms of imperialism, colonial expansion by military force, these new forms are more deeply rooted in the logic of the capitalist market and therefore more subject to its systemic contradictions.

Imperialist expansion however was only one of the means used by capitalism to ease or overcome its crisis. During the ascending phase of capitalism, a whole range of other meaningful alternatives could be contemplated (and successfully implemented), consistent with the interest of profitable capital accumulation and expansion. Historically most significant of these alternatives ensuring the continued survival of the capitalist system has been the implementation of the Keynesian strategies of moderate macro-economic regulations and social expenditures which made capitalism more viable, economically, politically and socially, by resolving the problem of overproduction through the increase of internal demand and establishment of more or less effective social welfare systems. Speaking as a lifelong votary of Keynesian strategies, John Kenneth Galbraith has written: 'The survival of the modern market system was in large measure our accomplishment. It would not have so survived had it not been for the successful efforts of the social left... Let us not be reticent: we are the custodians of a political tradition that saved classical capitalism from itself.' In the current shift from national Keynesianism to a global neo-classical economics, the reforms from the 1930s onwards which stabilised capitalism have been all now under attack in the name of establishing a so-called 'free-market' economy. These have included social security, regulation of banking and the security markets, labour laws, anti-trust laws and other restrictions on capital which had been put in place in the crisis of the inter-war period – all of which served to protect capitalism from the self-destructive logic of the system itself.

This conscious attempt to reverse the course of normal capitalism, which paradoxically saved capitalism from its own self-destructive tendencies, made for unprecedented growth of capitalist economy while giving capitalism itself a human face, may appear an ironical evolution, but it is an evolution which makes every sense in terms of the essential logic of capitalism and its current structural crisis.

The shift from national Keynesianism to a global neo-liberal economics more than anything else shows that the compromise between capital and labour, under the auspices of the welfare state, was but a truce, a strictly temporary phenomenon which in the longer run is totally unviable for capitalism. Defensive gains by the working class were made possible by the relatively untroubled post-war expansionary period of capitalism, which was itself something of an aberration in the history of western capitalism. But with 'globalisation' signifying a return to a period of normal capitalism and one in the midst of a structural crisis, even the once partially favourable elements in the historical equation between capital and labour have been overturned in favour of capital. The gains could be conceded by capital so long as they could be *assimilated* and *integrated* by the system as a whole and turned to its productive advantage in the course of its self expression and expansion. This is no longer possible. The welfare state and labour regulation are now incompatible not only with the rationality of short-term profits but even with long-term competitiveness and growth. As we summed it up earlier, capitalism can no longer afford to wear a human face, and, with the threat of socialism having receded, it also does not now need to wear it.

Capitalism today is a system which is globally dominant yet lives ridden with contradictions and vulnerabilities, not only without effective rivals but also with no escape routes. 'Capitalism with a human face' having ceased to be a sustainable possibility, globalisation has responded to capitalism's structural crisis with neo-liberalism, indeed with a reversion to good old *laissezfaire* capitalism and war against the working class through dismantling the welfare state and through down-sizing, speed up, contracting out, two-tiered wage structures, union busting, relocation etc. – and chronic mass unemployment. With the logic of 'free market' asserting itself, the gross conditions which inspired Marx's 19th century critique of capitalism are seen to be flourishing again. The ever more inhuman, divisive and ecologically destructive logic of capitalism can no longer be hidden discreetly, not even behind the screen of 'civil society'. Dominant and without rivals, capitalism stands naked and alone with all the destructive consequences of its structural logic, enabling people to see the real face of 'actually existing capitalism' with a clarity not possible for a long time. The conditions that used to sustain western workers reformism stand increasingly undermined. Karl Polanyi, and more recently even George Soros among others have pointed out that *laissezfaire* capitalism means a degree of instability and insecurity which is intolerable to most people, and finally undermines the ability of the system to reproduce itself. This is indeed how it is turning out to be. Such being the situation with contemporary capitalism, it is surely not far fetched to postulate revival of struggle for socialism in the first world. Socialist politics there is indeed not less but more possible now than it has been for a long time.

XXI

Such being the situation with contemporary capitalism also means that there is little scope now for Keynesian intervention in the capitalist economy or for a moderate defence of the welfare state. Confronting even partial issues with any hope of success implies the necessity of challenging the capitalist system as such, of moving towards detaching economy from the logic of capitalism. Instead of defensive action, politics perforce needs to turn into an offensive, offering alternative solutions, solutions which provide answers to the basic questions: what kind of economic growth? for what purpose? in whose interest? Answered in the interests of the people, these solutions today cannot but be a *socialist* alternative to globalising capitalism. Let it be clearly understood that without a broad nationalisation of private capital, a real and not merely juridical or formal social ownership ('the expropriation of the expropriators'), and without overcoming the 'free market' (democratic planning), it is impossible to carry out any substantive reform of the health care system or to improve social welfare significantly, to say nothing of building a socially just and humane society where all human beings are fulfilled by equality and freedom and a truly rich human life. The traditional programme of the socialist left is not only a real alternative, it is quite simply the only alternative – and one people are bound to rediscover before long. The first world has the necessary objective conditions, the material and technological resources for a truly socialist and democratic organisation of material life, and the mass protests and strike actions in Europe have the potential to provide the necessary subjective conditions. The electoral swings in favour of social democracy signify less the successful reinvention of reformist politics than the rejection by the working classes and people of the present and the future being offered them by neo-liberalism. People have begun to think and talk, to organise and mobilise in increasingly anti-capitalist terms. Requisite ideological-political intervention by the left can well help the current resistance to globalisation grow into an effective social force for a socialist transition in the West. Perhaps it is this prospect which drives the ideologues of capitalism to insist so heavily on the absence of any alternative and on capitalism as the end of history itself.

Apropos this prospect, while the choice between socialism and capitalism – really American style capitalism – will have to be faced all over the West sooner or later, in the current conjuncture it is in Western Europe that the issue has come to be posed most sharply, because of its historical circumstances, its social democratic achievements and left-wing heritage, and more specifically because of the contrast between its traditions and the American pattern of capitalism now being imposed. It is there that the basic contradiction of capitalism, its technological achievements and absurd social organisation, stands most clearly exposed. This is how the issue has been posited by Daniel Singer: 'Will the Left in western Europe now follow its leaders down the American way, forsaking its heritage and committing political suicide? Or will it rebel, use its imagination – discarding Stalinist crimes and social democratic impotence and, in trying to protect its immediate interests, reinvent a socialist project for our times?'

Thus posited the issue again brings into focus the question of historical role of the working class in socialist transformation of society. We have in different contexts noticed the more important general factors responsible for the failure of the working class in the advanced capitalist countries of the West to give rise to an effective movement for socialism as hoped for by Marx. This failure however was not absolute and there are good reasons to be optimistic about a different outcome in future. Despite all its inadequacies, the labour movement in Western Europe has to its credit important democratic victories as well as achievements of social democracy. The working class-based economic and political organisations, built up through bitter struggles in the course of last century and a half, succeeded in imposing limits (including those collectively known as the welfare state) on capital's unending thirst for more profits. In the Russian revolution, the European revolutions and revolutionary upheaval at the end of the first world war, and on more than one occasion later, for example in the late 1960s and mid-1990s, working class has given ample evidence of its revolutionary potential. The conditions that had led Marx to his conclusions about the revolutionary role of the working class, however modified by capital's evolution are still, or again, present and the conclusions themselves have been enriched by the theory and practice and the achievements of revolutionary Marxism after him. The working class remains strategically situated at the heart of Western capitalism as the only social force with the capacity to transform it. The neo-liberal offensive of recent years has unified the working class in new and unprecedented ways. Even if somewhat dormant earlier, the reawakened working class has been able to bring people together on the streets in dramatic protests against 'neo-liberalism' and 'globalisation'. Class is back and so is class struggle in the thought and action of the working people. With the complicity between the state and 'globalised' capital becoming increasingly apparent there are reasons to expect the economic class struggles to move on to the political plane and the working class emerging as, what it was traditionally expected to be, the leading social force of a socialist transition in Europe. It was the failure of the working class in the advanced capitalist countries to carry out a radical transformation of society when it was expected to do so which led to the tragedy of socialism in Russia and Eastern Europe. It is reasonably justified to hope that now, at the end of that tragedy, this working class finally begins to carry out its historical task and recovers the seemingly lost cause of socialism, of socialism as the only humane and truly democratic alternative to capitalism in our times as classical Marxism visualised it.

Index of Names

Index of Subjects